WHEN GREEN GROWTH
IS NOT ENOUGH

WHEN GREEN

GROWTH

IS NOT ENOUGH

Climate Change, Ecological Modernization, and Sufficiency

ANDERS HAYDEN

McGill-Queen's University Press

Montreal & Kingston • London • Ithaca

© McGill-Queen's University Press 2014

ISBN 978-0-7735-4407-9 (cloth)
ISBN 978-0-7735-4408-6 (paper)
ISBN 978-0-7735-9633-7 (ePDF)
ISBN 978-0-7735-9634-4 (ePUB)

Legal deposit fourth quarter 2014
Bibliothèque nationale du Québec

Printed in Canada on acid-free paper that is 100% ancient forest free (100% post-consumer recycled), processed chlorine free

This book has been published with the help of a grant from the Canadian Federation for the Humanities and Social Sciences, through the Awards to Scholarly Publications Program, using funds provided by the Social Sciences and Humanities Research Council of Canada.

McGill-Queen's University Press acknowledges the support of the Canada Council for the Arts for our publishing program. We also acknowledge the financial support of the Government of Canada through the Canada Book Fund for our publishing activities.

Library and Archives Canada Cataloguing in Publication

Hayden, Anders, 1969–, author
    When green growth is not enough : climate change, ecological modernization, and sufficiency / Anders Hayden.

Includes bibliographical references and index.
Issued in print and electronic formats.
ISBN 978-0-7735-4407-9 (bound). – ISBN 978-0-7735-4408-6 (pbk.). –
ISBN 978-0-7735-9633-7 (ePDF). – ISBN 978-0-7735-9634-4 (ePUB)

   1. Economic development – Environmental aspects – Canada.
2. Economic development – Environmental aspects – Great Britain.
3. Economic development – Political aspects – Canada. 4. Economic development – Political aspects – Great Britain. 5. Climatic changes – Political aspects – Canada. 6. Climatic changes – Political aspects – Great Britain. 7. Greenhouse gas mitigation – Political aspects – Canada. 8. Greenhouse gas mitigation – Political aspects – Great Britain. I. Title.

HC120.E5H42 2014   333.70971   C2014-904534-4
                                             C2014-904535-2

Typeset by James Leahy in 10.5/13 ITC New Baskerville Std

For Fran

Contents

Acronyms

AEF	Aviation Environment Federation
AFL	Alberta Federation of Labour
BA	British Airways
BAA	British Airports Authority
BAU	Business as Usual
BERR	Department for Business, Enterprise, and Regulatory Reform
CAPP	Canadian Association of Petroleum Producers
CAN	Climate Action Network
CAW	Canadian Auto Workers
CBI	Confederation of British Industries
CCA	Climate Change Agreements
CCC	Committee on Climate Change
CCO	Conservation Council of Ontario
CCCE	Canadian Council of Chief Executives
CCRES	Canadian Coalition for Responsible Environmental Solutions
CCHP	Combined Cooling, Heating, and Power
CCL	Climate Change Levy
CCS	Carbon Capture and Storage
CEP	Communications, Energy, and Paperworkers Union of Canada
CHP	Combined Heating and Power
CIW	Canadian Index of Wellbeing
CLC	Canadian Labour Congress
CLG	Corporate Leaders Group on Climate Change
CRAG	Carbon Rationing Action Group
CRC	Carbon Reduction Commitment

DECC	Department of Energy and Climate Change
Defra	Department for Environment, Food and Rural Affairs
DETR	Department of the Environment, Transport and the Regions
DfT	Department for Transport
DTI	Department for Trade and Industry
EA	Environment Agency
ECI	Environmental Change Institute, Oxford University
EEA	European Environment Agency
EEF	formerly the Engineering Employers' Federation (UK manufacturers' organization)
EKC	Environmental Kuznets Curve
EIA	Energy Information Administration (US)
EM	Ecological Modernization
EMT	Ecological Modernization Theory
ENGO	Environmental Non-Governmental Organization
EST	Energy Saving Trust
EU ETS	European Union Emissions Trading System
FCRN	Food Climate Research Network
FoE	Friends of the Earth
FQD	Fuel Quality Directive (EU)
GHG	Greenhouse gas
GDP	Gross Domestic Product
GPI	Genuine Progress Indicator
HPI	Happy Planet Index
IPCC	Intergovernmental Panel on Climate Change
LCFS	Low Carbon Fuel Standard
LowCVP	Low Carbon Vehicles Partnership
LSE	London School of Economics and Political Science
mbd	million barrels per day
MEP	Member of European Parliament
MP	Member of Parliament
NDP	New Democratic Party
NEF	New Economics Foundation
OECD	Organisation for Economic Co-operation and Development
ONS	Office of National Statistics
OTC	One-Tonne Challenge
OTCC	One-Tonne Corporate Challenge

PCAS	Personal Carbon Allowances
ROCS	Renewables Obligation Certificates
RCEP	Royal Commission on Environmental Pollution
RMT	National Union of Rail, Maritime, and Transport Workers
RMWB	Regional Municipality of Wood Buffalo
RO	Renewables Obligation
RTFO	Renewable Transport Fuels Obligation
SDC	Sustainable Development Commission
SEP	Soft-Energy Path
ShrEc	Shrinking Economies in the Developed World
TUC	Trades Union Congress
UK ETS	United Kingdom Emissions Trading Scheme
UKIP	United Kingdom Independence Party
UNFCCC	United Nations Framework Convention on Climate Change
WCC	World Council of Churches
WRAP	Waste & Resources Action Programme
WWF	World Wide Fund for Nature (UK and International); World Wildlife Fund (Canada and US)

Acknowledgments

This book emerged over many years and phases, starting with my dissertation research at Boston College. I am deeply indebted to my supervisor Juliet Schor for her invaluable support and intellectual inspiration, starting many years ago when reading her work helped me to see beyond the walls of economic orthodoxy. Thanks also to the other members of my committee, Sarah Babb and Charlie Derber, and to reader Brian Gareau for their encouragement and insights. Leslie Salzinger and the other members of the dissertation seminar provided important support along the way.

I am grateful to Doug McDonald for some of the best advice I have ever received, and to the other members of the environmental policy discussion group at the University of Toronto, including Gabe Eidelman, David Gordon, David Houle, Erick Lachapelle, and Mark Purdon, for helping me to gain new perspectives and work through ideas as I was writing.

I am indebted to all the interviewees who spoke with me. In the UK, I gained some particularly valuable insights from Tim Jackson that have influenced my analysis. Wolfgang Sachs has long been a source of intellectual inspiration and he again generously found time to speak with me in London. Thanks also to John Ackers and Jessica Rayburn of the Islington Carbon Rationing Action Group (CRAG) and Duncan Law of Transition Town Brixton, whose activities I did not manage to adequately incorporate into this study, but who inspired me with their commitment to change their personal lifestyles, their communities, and public policy. In Canada, Kim Fry provided many useful contacts in the environmental movement. I also received very valuable assistance from Rick Hyndman of the Canadian Association of Petroleum Producers. He almost certainly would not have agreed with much of what I have written; nevertheless, he helped me to better understand the dilemmas faced in Canada, and the contacts he provided were very helpful in opening doors.

At the later stages of revising and updating the text, I benefited from the excellent work of research assistants Karen McCrae, Lars Boggild, and Kirin Brown and from other contributions from Jeff Wilson, Megan Leslie, Maurie Cohen, Bob Finbow, David Black, Stephen Cushing, Alice Bows, John Evarts, and "adamsmith." Thanks also to the two anonymous reviewers, to Joanna Reid for her skillful editing, and to Jacqueline Mason, Ryan Van Huijstee, and the rest of the team at McGill-Queen's University Press.

I am grateful to Danny Wong, Heather Posgate, Alanna Cavanagh, Bob Huish, and Ed Ng for helping me to get through the most challenging moments as I worked on this project.

Special thanks to Fran Farrell for meeting me at the courier office to send off the manuscript and for so much more.

WHEN GREEN GROWTH
IS NOT ENOUGH

1

Introduction:
A Battle of Three Paradigms

We're gearing up for the biggest struggle our party has faced since you entrusted me with the leadership. I'm talking about the "battle of Kyoto" – our campaign to block the job-killing, economy-destroying Kyoto Accord.

> Stephen Harper, leader of opposition Canadian Alliance, 2002

The UK has proved that economic growth does not have to lead to increased greenhouse-gas emissions.

> Margaret Beckett, UK Environment Secretary, and
> Patricia Hewitt, UK Trade and Industry Secretary, 2005

We are living in an unsustainable society, whose core rationale – the maximising of economic growth – is incompatible with its long-term survival. A great deal of new thinking, and practical action, is needed to break away from our current trajectory.

> Anthony Giddens, sociologist, former adviser to Tony Blair, 2009

What is to be done about climate change? It is a question with the potential to unsettle core cultural assumptions and ways of organizing socio-economic life. It leads to consideration of a challenging and inconvenient issue: whether the continued prioritization of economic growth is compatible with the deep emissions cuts that climate science suggests are urgently necessary.

This book is about the political battle among three competing paradigms over how to respond to climate change and other ecological challenges. One possible answer is to carry on with business-as-usual (BAU), pursuing endless economic expansion while downplaying or denying the severity of environmental problems. From a

BAU perspective, considerable conflict exists between environmental policy interventions by governments and the pursuit of GDP growth and international competitiveness – and it is axiomatic that such economic goals deserve priority. To the extent that it acknowledges environmental problems, a BAU perspective has faith that technological solutions will emerge as needed, mainly through the workings of free markets and the profit incentives they generate. Moreover, economic growth is portrayed not as the problem, but as the solution – providing resources that can ultimately be devoted to environmental problems. The Bush administration, for example, illustrated a BAU viewpoint when it rejected the Kyoto Protocol's emissions limits as damaging to the economy, while putting faith in the future emergence of climate-friendly "breakthrough" technologies. The Tea Party brand of Republicanism that followed similarly highlighted a jobs-versus-climate-action conflict, while showing even greater hostility to proposed political responses to climate change.

In many countries, BAU has given way to a second paradigm: ecological modernization (EM) or, as many call it, green growth. "Business as usual is dead – green growth is the answer to both our climate and economic problems," proclaimed Danish prime minister Anders Fogh Rasmussen (McGrath 2009). As a political project, EM aims to decouple economic growth from resource "throughput" (material and energy inputs and pollution outputs). It relies primarily on improved eco-efficiency and lower-impact technologies, most often backed by market-oriented policies. Rejecting a growth-versus-environment conflict, EM emphasizes "win-win" opportunity. It sees investment in low-carbon energy as a source of GDP growth, profits, and jobs through what UK prime minister Tony Blair (2004) termed a "new green industrial revolution." Strong climate action is also perceived as a source of competitive advantage, as those who move first to develop low-carbon technology can capture the expanding global market for emissions-reducing solutions. In the words of the German Ministry for the Environment (BMU 2006), "Climate protection pays." As the world faced its worst economic crisis since the 1930s and concern grew that climate tipping points were near, EM talk of a "Green New Deal" spread. "We need to make 'growing green' our mantra," proclaimed UN Secretary-General Ban Ki-moon and former US vice president Al Gore (2009). Or, as green business advocates Lovins and Cohen (2011, 6) proclaimed, "Solving the climate crisis

IS THE WAY OUT of the economic crisis." Meanwhile, "green growth" was the core concept behind the Rio+20 Conference on Sustainable Development in 2012.

Ecological modernization is a reform project that aims to reconcile ecological concern with faith in economic growth. Sociologist Daniel Bell (1976, 237–8) argued that growth had become "the secular religion of advancing industrial societies: the source of individual motivation, the basis of political solidarity, the ground for the mobilization of society for a common purpose," while also serving as a "political solvent" to ease distributional conflicts. Economist Benjamin Friedman (2005) exemplifies this belief in growth when he maintains that economic growth not only leads to rising material living standards, but also is the foundation of social, political, and, above all, moral progress. Given the centrality of growth to the worldview of modern societies,[1] not to mention the workings of capitalism (or at least any variation of capitalism known so far), it is no surprise that government, business, and other mainstream actors favour pro-growth, EM responses to climate change – at least once they move beyond a BAU perspective.

Others, however, have challenged that secular religion, bringing us to a third, competing perspective. Advocates of sufficiency ask how much is enough, and question continued growth of production and consumption in the already-affluent global North (e.g. Princen 2005; Sachs, Loske, and Linz 1998; Schor 2005, 2010). This perspective emphasizes that the erosion of cultural notions of moderation and the institutionalization of the limitless expansion of production and consumption are key obstacles to lasting environmental solutions. Those who argue for new sufficiency norms often point out that eco-efficiency gains, e.g. lower environmental impacts per dollar of GDP, are frequently overwhelmed by economic output growing at an even faster pace. Sachs (2001, 156–7), for example, argues that efficiency alone is not enough: ecological sustainability requires both "technical" and "civilizational" change, "an intelligent reinvention of means as well as a prudent moderation of ends." Although not necessarily anti-capitalist, a sufficiency perspective represents a more significant challenge to the current socio-economic order, including the consumerist culture that sustains it ideologically, than does an EM paradigm focused on technology- and efficiency-based solutions.

The idea of sufficiency with respect to the scale of the economy – that is, the question of the limits to growth (Meadows et al. 1972) – burst onto the scene in the 1970s in the context of oil price shocks and resource shortage fears, before notions of sustainable development and EM superseded it in the 1980s and 1990s.[2] For a time, it was widely assumed in mainstream political and academic circles that the limits-to-growth debate was over and that economic expansion and environmental impacts could be decoupled – presumably forever. Yet considerable evidence emerged that economic growth was undoing the benefits of carbon-intensity improvements (i.e. falling emissions per unit of output) in many nations. To give one example for now, a study by the International Energy Agency (IEA) and the Organisation for Economic Co-operation and Development (OECD), which showed rising emissions despite falling carbon intensity in affluent nations, concluded that "economic growth is the primary driver behind increases in energy-related CO_2 emissions" (Unander 2003, 11). If that was the case and, at the same time, there was a growing sense of urgency over climate change, was there any sign of a re-emergence of sufficiency as a prominent idea?

I began writing this book seeking to understand the opportunities and obstacles facing a sufficiency perspective in growth-oriented societies more favourable to BAU and EM. The pages that follow examine whether, how, and why ideas of sufficiency are emerging in the context of climate change, despite great obstacles. Key to understanding these issues is the role of ecological modernization: the importance of its battles to overcome a business-as-usual discourse and practice, its appeal to a wide range of political and economic actors, and the evidence of its limits which can open up space for more far-reaching alternatives. I examine these issues by comparing the United Kingdom and Canada – the former seemingly one of the most successful nations to date in reducing its greenhouse gas (GHG) emissions and the latter one of the worst performers in terms of emissions levels, emissions growth, and climate policy implementation.

At the core of this book are the following questions: Are sufficiency-based ideas making inroads into the debate over climate change solutions in societies with strong pro-growth orientations? If so, how and why are they emerging in the ways that they do? The book also examines a number of related, secondary questions. To what degree has an ecological modernization program consolidated its position as the only politically viable response to climate change? What key obstacles does sufficiency face? What forces are creating opportunities for sufficiency to move onto the public agenda? Has the sufficiency perspective moved beyond small circles of academics and radical environmentalists and into the mainstream? How does the prominence of sufficiency differ between the UK and Canada, and why?

To answer these questions, I draw on evidence from semi-structured interviews with actors involved in climate politics; attendance at public events and conferences debating climate change responses; and analysis of documents such as government climate strategies, policy statements, speeches, op-eds, and press releases, as well as media articles (see Appendix 1: Methods). Note that where no published source is given for quotations in the subsequent chapters, the statements are from interviews (see Appendices 2 and 3 for full lists of interviewees). In some cases, quotations from interviewees' published writing rather than the interviews themselves are used where the wording is more concise or effective. These sources are cited in the text.

THE UK AND CANADA: "DIFFERENT ENDS OF THE PERFORMANCE LEAGUE"

The UK and Canada share certain commonalities yet have some fundamental differences. Both have a common democratic tradition based on the Westminster parliamentary system. Regardless of the political party in power at the national level, in recent decades, both have pursued neo-liberal, market-oriented economic policies, and have "liberal" (i.e. limited) welfare states (Esping-Andersen 1990). Both are members of the Group of Eight (G8) leading economies and have significant domestic fossil fuel industries. Most of their populations speak English – although Canada has a large francophone minority. In the late 1980s, they were also early leaders on the global stage in acknowledging the need to limit GHG emissions – under Conservative governments in both cases. Another key similarity – one generally taken for granted – is that in both countries, the pursuit of economic growth is a dominant social priority.

The differences between the two countries will become more apparent in later chapters, but the most important difference for the purposes of this book deserves highlighting. The UK became widely recognized as a world leader in taking climate action, whereas Canada lagged far behind, verging on climate pariah status as it failed to bring down its high per capita emissions to meet its international targets. As the United Nations Development Programme (UNDP 2007, 119) put it, the UK and Canada were "two countries at different ends of the Kyoto Protocol performance league." In the UK, GHG emissions fell significantly according to standard measures, an EM discourse became widely shared across the political and business mainstream (albeit with some backsliding toward BAU), considerable EM-oriented innovation in policy occurred, and an advanced, wide-ranging debate took place over the necessary changes in practices across society (WWF-International and Allianz SE 2008, 7). While I do not suggest that the UK was yet doing enough, it was one of the most advanced cases of EM with respect to climate change – possibly a prototypical case, with lessons for other advanced capitalist nations as they begin to grapple with achieving deep emissions cuts while continuing to pursue economic growth. In contrast, in Canada, strong federal climate policy was continually delayed, BAU practice remained dominant, and BAU discourse was still prevalent – despite consistent efforts by some actors to promote an EM discourse and some emerging signs of EM practice.

Other important economic and political differences existed between the two countries. While both had atypically large domestic fossil fuel industries for OECD nations, the UK's heyday as a leading non-OPEC oil and gas producer was behind it and production was falling. In contrast, Canada saw itself as an up-and-coming "energy superpower," an ambition particularly important to the province of Alberta, whose lucrative tar sands were a major source of Canada's GHG emissions growth. (Canada had an estimated 173.6 billion barrels of proved crude oil reserves, with by far the lion's share in the oil sands, while remaining UK reserves were only 2.8 billion barrels, according to the US Energy Information Administration's 2012 data.) A related difference was that in Canada, conflict over energy and climate policy threatened to exacerbate regional conflicts and national-unity tensions in a way not seen in the UK. There were also notable differences in the key industries in the two countries' most populous regions. The auto industry, which was threatened by some climate policy proposals, was of vital importance to southern Ontario. In contrast, London's dominant financial sector was both vulnerable to climate-induced instability and well positioned to profit from being a centre of global carbon trading. While the UK was a member of the EU, where its main trading partners were also committed to Kyoto and post-Kyoto climate action, some 75 per cent of Canada's exports went to the United States, resulting in concerns among its industries that costs could rise and competitiveness fall as a result of climate policy not faced by US producers. Other notable differences were size and population: Canada's thirty-five million people spread across the world's second-largest land mass, while Britain's sixty-three million people occupied an area about one-third the size of Alberta.

These two cases, which are similar enough to be comparable, yet differ in their degree of progress with climate reform and in key aspects of political and economic structure relevant to climate change, provide opportunities for understanding sufficiency's status and prospects. The variation allows for insight to be gained into the ways that different political-economic and social contexts create varying political opportunities (McAdam 1996; Meyer 2004; Tarrow 1998) for sufficiency in relation to business-as-usual and ecological modernization.

The chapters that follow put considerable emphasis on the years 2007 and 2008, during which the initial round of research took place. This was a time of particularly intense debate in Canada and the UK about how to respond to climate change, following Al Gore's 2006 documentary *An Inconvenient Truth*, the Intergovernmental Panel on Climate Change's (IPCC) fourth assessment of climate science, the release of the *Stern Review on the Economics of Climate Change*, and incidents of extreme weather that affected elite and public opinion. To establish context, this book also provides earlier background on the evolution of political and social responses to climate change, as well as details on some key developments up to 2012–13. These later updates offer an opportunity to assess the evolution of policies and proposed climate responses that emerged during the intense debates of 2007–08 – and also provide a chance to consider some additional, surprising victories for a sufficiency perspective.

The point of departure for this book is the long-standing debate over the relationship between economic growth and environment. Business-as-usual, ecological modernization, and sufficiency represent basic positions in that wider debate. The following sections examine in more detail these three paradigms, their relationship to

theories in environmental politics and sociology, and the theoretical
concepts of importance to subsequent chapters.

BUSINESS-AS-USUAL AND ITS PROMETHEAN FOUNDATIONS

Table 1.1 (on pages 12–13) provides one way of categorizing the
spectrum of responses to climate change. At one pole is the idea that
the pursuit of economic growth can and should continue without
major environmental policy interventions or changes of social practices. This BAU approach has roots in Prometheanism, which Dryzek
(2013, 52) calls the "unlimited confidence in the ability of humans
and their technologies to overcome any problems – including environmental problems." Similarly, in their analysis of the "dominant
western worldview," environmental sociologists Catton and Dunlap
(1980, 34) identified core assumptions dating back to the period of
early modern expansionary optimism, such as the "world is vast, and
thus provides unlimited opportunities for humans," and the "history
of humanity is one of progress; for every problem there is a solution,
and thus progress need never cease." Such modern articles of faith
were largely taken for granted from the Industrial Revolution until
the new wave of environmentalism in the 1970s and the *Limits to
Growth* report (Meadows et al. 1972). This growth critique provoked
a response from analysts such as futurist Herman Kahn (1976), co-
founder of the Hudson Institute, who emphasized the cornucopia of
resources that humans could access – if need be, in outer space once
the earthly bounty is exhausted – through technology and capitalist
productivity. Julian Simon, another chief defender of this viewpoint,
argued that economic growth within free markets – which create an
optimal framework for human ingenuity to bear fruit – had delivered
dramatic gains in human well-being. Moreover, the positive trends
could continue practically indefinitely without major resource scarcity or environmental problems. In Simon's (1995) words, "We have
in our hands now ... the technology to feed, clothe, and supply energy
to an ever-growing population for the next 7 billion years." Promethean views have had particular resonance in the United States, notably during the Reagan and George W. Bush presidencies (Dryzek
2013) – with echoes in Canada under the Harper government.

On the issue of climate change, Bjørn Lomborg (2001, chap.
24) emerged as one of the most influential academic proponents of

Prometheanism and BAU with his book *The Skeptical Environmentalist*. Unlike many less sophisticated advocates of staying the course, he did not deny that climate change was a problem. Rather, he argued that the cost of taking action to reduce GHG emissions would exceed the benefits. Lomborg estimated that continuing with business-as-usual would generate climate-related costs of roughly US$5 trillion globally; however, limiting temperature increases to 2.5°C would cost even more, nearly $8 trillion, while keeping the mercury from rising more than one degree would cost some $38 trillion (2001, 310). The rational response in his view, therefore, was not to spend significant sums on "low-yielding greenhouse gas reductions" (312), but to continue investing in economic growth, particularly in the developing world, and in new energy technologies, thereby leaving future generations with far greater resources. Lomborg also advocated openness to geo-engineering schemes, such as putting sulphur particles into the atmosphere to reflect the sun's energy back into space, as an alternative to emissions cuts. Meanwhile, he rejected two ideas with a strong affinity to an EM project: the existence of "no regrets" options, i.e. actions to reduce GHGs that produce net economic benefits, and a "double dividend," by which the revenue raised from carbon taxes or emissions trading could be used to cut other taxes in an economically beneficial way. He also criticized what he alleged was political use of climate change by the environmental movement, and even the Intergovernmental Panel on Climate Change (IPCC), to advance a sufficiency perspective. In *Cool It*, Lomborg (2007) returned to similar themes, arguing that rather than setting targets for near-term emissions cuts that bring significant economic costs, nations should spend a relatively small sum, 0.05 per cent of GDP or US$25 billion annually, on researching non-carbon-emitting energy technologies and tax carbon at the minimal level of $2 per ton. Furthermore, he argued that available resources should be concentrated on more immediate concerns, such as fighting disease and malnutrition and providing safe water in poorer countries. Lomborg (2010, 396) did, however, shift his tone somewhat in a later book, calling for greater expenditure – $100 billion per year globally – to tackle climate change.

Business-as-usual ideas have most frequently been associated with politicians, think tanks, and individuals on the political right, for whom demands for strong climate measures represent a threat to

Table 1.1 A Spectrum of Responses to Climate Change

Business-As-Usual

Prometheanism: tendency to downplay or deny seriousness of environmental problems; belief that technologies will emerge as needed in the context of free markets

Conservative variations reject strong climate action as a threat to laissez-faire capitalism, or take on religious overtones

Left-wing variations celebrate the social possibilities resulting from the advance of the forces of production unfettered by environmentalism and carbon constraints

"Hard energy path" (old version): fossil fuel energy system supplemented by nuclear power

Geo-engineering to avoid need for emissions cuts, e.g. fertilize the oceans to accelerate carbon absorption or build mirrors in space to reflect sunlight away from earth*

Ecological Modernization / Green Growth

"Hard energy path" (new and improved vision): nuclear power revived as low-carbon energy source, continued fossil fuel use through carbon capture and storage, large-scale production of biofuels

Weak ecological modernization: reconciling growth and emissions cuts through technology, efficiency, market-friendly environmental policies

"Soft energy path": shift to diverse renewable energy sources backed by much greater energy efficiency

Other varieties of techno-optimism, including "natural capitalism" and "cradle-to-cradle" industrial design

Strong ecological modernization: reflexive questioning leading to ecological restructuring of key institutions and practices; challenges to urban sprawl, frequent air travel, long-distance food system, etc.; overlaps with micro-level sufficiency (below)

Sufficiency / Critical Perspectives on Growth

Sufficiency: questioning the pursuit of ever-growing volumes of production and consumption

    Micro-level calls to limit specific products, practices, sectors
    Macro-level critique of economic growth and quest for a steady state or de-growth economy

Anti-capitalist: struggle to achieve climate justice and create an eco-socialist society that transcends capitalism's basic dynamics, which are seen to drive the need for endless economic growth and ecological degradation

De-industrialist / "Un-civilization": goes beyond the critique of growth and capitalism to question the desirability and viability of industrial civilization

---

* As knowledge of the scale of the climate challenge has grown, advocacy of geo-engineering is no longer limited to BAU proponents seeking to avoid emissions reductions. Some advocates of deep GHG cuts have begun to consider geo-engineering as a complementary strategy to buy time and avoid tipping points into runaway climate change.

an ideology celebrating free-market capitalism and a broader expansionary worldview (in addition to threatening some powerful business interests). This association was most evident in the United States, where the conservative movement had considerable success in undermining public support for climate science and policy (McCright and Dunlap 2010). One of the largest sources of funding for climate "sceptic" groups was Koch Industries, a privately owned oil firm, whose billionaire owner David Koch ran to the right of Ronald Reagan as vice-presidential candidate for the Libertarian Party in 1980. Koch, together with his brother Charles, was also a key source of funds for the Tea Party movement (Greenpeace USA 2010; PBS 2012). Prominent non-American proponents of BAU ideas included Margaret Thatcher's former chancellor of the exchequer Nigel Lawson (2008a) and Czech president Václav Klaus (2008). The latter, a follower of Friedrich Hayek, argued that the greatest threat to freedom and prosperity was no longer communism, but "environmentalism and its currently strongest version, climate alarmism." Klaus expressed fear of "people who want to stop ... economic growth" in order to cut emissions, adding: "Human wants are unlimited and should stay so. Asceticism is a respectable individual attitude but should not be forcibly imposed upon the rest of us."

While often expressed in economic language, BAU ideas sometimes took on religious overtones. Some interpretations of Christian-
ity even welcomed climate change and other forms of ecological degradation as signs of what was to come. In an analysis of the coupling
of ideology and theology and their influence in Washington, journalist Bill Moyers (2004) noted that James Watt, Ronald Reagan's secretary of the interior, told Congress that protecting natural resources
was unimportant, since, "after the last tree is felled, Christ will come
back." Similarly, during the Kyoto Protocol negotiations, Ford Motor Company executive John Schiller told Greenpeace activist Jeremy
Leggett (2001, 174): "You know, the more I look, the more it is just
as it says in the Bible." Schiller cited the Book of Daniel's prophecy
of earthly devastation – and Antichrist-led efforts to establish a world
government – that would mark the End Time and Christ's return.
With such a worldview, "the wreck of the Earth can be seen as Good
News!" (Scherer 2003), and was certainly not something to try to
stop – especially not via UN agreements. In fact, Canadian climate
scientist and IPCC contributor Andrew Weaver told a conference in
Toronto in August 2010 of having to contend with protests outside
his Victoria office from a religious devotee convinced that Weaver
was an agent of forces seeking to prevent the Rapture.

While BAU ideas were more prevalent on the political right, they
were not exclusive to it. Some leftists saw environmentalism as a fetter
on the full advance of the productive forces under capitalism, which
they perceived as necessary to expand social possibilities and human
capacities. Variations on this theme, with an unusual libertarian twist,
were prevalent in the British online journal *spiked*, such as O'Neill's
(2009) denunciation of Britain's low-carbon strategy as "the opposite
of revolutionary" and a recipe for a "slow, meek and visionless nation."

Whatever form BAU ideas take, and whether they deny the existence of climate change or merely downplay its significance, they lead
to complacency in the face of a large body of evidence documenting
the severity of threats from climate instability and environmental
degradation. The work of the IPCC, research on the crossing of recently identified "planetary boundaries," including safe CO_2 thresholds (Rockström et al. 2009), the Millennium Ecosystem Assessment,
ecological footprint analyses showing the extent of ecological over-
shoot, and other such studies suggested urgency rather than complacency was the appropriate response. Nevertheless, BAU ideas played

an important role in climate debates in Canada and reasserted themselves in the UK, as later chapters will discuss.

ECOLOGICAL MODERNIZATION AND THE
GREENING OF CAPITALIST GROWTH

Those adhering to notions of ecological modernization take the need to combat climate change much more seriously, although they, like BAU advocates, continue to emphasize the possibility and importance of continued economic growth. EM can take on a variety of meanings (for reviews, see Buttel 2000; Christoff 1996; Dryzek 2013, chap. 8; Mol 2011; Mol and Jänicke 2009; J. Murphy 2000). An important distinction is between EM *theory* and EM as a political *discourse*, which is closely linked to an ecological-reform *program*. (In subsequent chapters, unless there is specific reference to EM theory, EM refers to a discourse and/or program.)

EM *Theory*

As a social theory, EM differs from the main environmental sociological perspectives of the 1970s and 1980s (Catton and Dunlap 1980; Schnaiberg 1980), which emphasized systemic ecological destruction and the limits to growth. In contrast, EM theory spotlights positive environmental improvement and seeks to account for the processes behind it (Mol 1995; Mol 2003, 2011; Mol, Sonnenfeld, and Spaargaren 2009; see also Christoff 1996). EM theory maintains that, alongside the economic rationality that has long dominated, ecological rationality is increasingly influencing modern societies and transforming key institutions, including the state, science, technology, and business and the market. One important transformation is that businesses, consumers, and other economic actors have joined the state and social movements as "social carriers of ecological restructuring" (Mol 2003, 61). As a result, market dynamics play an increasing role in advancing ecological reform. Another key development is the rise of an environmental state whose commitment to ecological protection can generate new dynamic growth sectors and export opportunities (e.g. Jänicke and Jacob 2004). EM theory is thus optimistic about reconciling economic growth and environmental sustainability, and rejects claims that capitalism's basic dynamics conflict with ecological limits.

EM theory also highlights changing discursive practices and new ideologies. Based on research in Europe, Mol (2003, 62) writes, "neither the fundamental counterpositioning of economic and environmental interests nor a total disregard for the importance of environmental considerations are accepted any longer as legitimate positions." In other words, both business-as-usual and ideas of limits to growth are seen to be withering away. Furthermore, EM theorists have argued that continued modernization and greening industrial development is the sole viable alternative: "The only possible way *out* of the ecological crisis is by going further *into* the process of modernization, toward ... hyper- or superindustrialization" (Mol 1995, 42; italics in original).

EM theory thus provides a theoretical lens that helps one to see processes of ecological transformation within modern societies and has value in interpreting the forces behind them. In particular, its view of business as a potential carrier of ecological reform ideas, and not simply an obstacle in all cases, is an important corrective to less nuanced analyses. Yet EM theory suffers from a weak empirical basis underlying its implicit – and occasionally explicit – normative claims that only a limited range of solutions need be pursued, as discussed in more detail below.

EM *Discourse and Reform Program*

A key concern of this book is the degree to which EM has become established as the dominant political discourse and reform program. Hajer (1995, 3) provides a social-constructivist analysis of the rise of EM as a policy discourse that "recognizes the ecological crisis as evidence of a fundamental omission in the workings of the institutions of modern society. Yet, unlike the radical environmental movements of the 1970s, it suggests that environmental problems can be solved in accordance with the workings of the main institutional arrangements of society. Environmental management is seen as a positive-sum game: pollution prevention pays."

Like mainstream interpretations of "sustainable development," EM discourse involves a "rhetoric of reassurance" (Dryzek 2013, 159). It implies that continued economic expansion and climate stability are compatible, and radical social change is unnecessary – allowing for possible common ground among policy-makers, economic elites, moderate environmentalists, and others, including much of the public, who are wary of calls to significantly challenge modern consumption patterns. In addition to the economic opportunities from climate action, the promise of maintaining existing lifestyles is also a key theme. For instance, a "route map to a low-carbon economy" from Friends of the Earth (FoE and Cooperative Bank 2006, 4) in the UK appealed to people by stating: "Daily life does not need to be radically different. In a low-carbon economy we will have warm houses, leisure, jobs, and be able to travel. What will change radically is how energy efficient our lives are, and where we get our energy from."

The reform program accompanying an EM discourse aims to restructure capitalism by channelling its powerful drives toward the decoupling of growth and environmental impacts. Jänicke (2008, 558) writes that the "urge to modernise is a compulsion inherent in capitalism"; EM reform thus aims "to change the direction of technological progress and to put the compulsion for innovation at the service of the environment." A precursor of EM reform emerged in Japan, where in 1974 the Ministry of International Trade and Industry (MITI) launched a drive for knowledge-intensive, resource-saving production following the first oil shock (Mol and Jänicke 2009, 17). Other leaders in embracing EM included Germany, the Netherlands, Finland, Norway, and Sweden (Dryzek 2013). These countries stood out, relative to other affluent nations, for their high energy efficiency, low per capita emissions of pollutants including CO_2, low per capita generation of wastes, and environmental policy innovations. A latecomer to EM was the UK, which embraced an EM discourse and program in its response to climate change (Paterson 2001). More recently, France, South Korea, China, US states including California, and some Canadian provinces – including British Columbia, Ontario, Quebec, and Nova Scotia – have been among those expressing EM-oriented ambitions to seize economic opportunities from lower-carbon energy technologies.

EM reform programs tend to share common themes, with some deviation from the ideal type. Among these themes are "win-win" ideas emphasizing the complementarity of environmental protection and economic growth, integration of environmental policy goals into all areas of government, innovative policy approaches, and promotion of clean technology (J. Murphy 2000; see also Revell

2005). Innovative policy usually refers to shifts from "command-and-control" regulations to market-based instruments – for example, ecological taxes or trading schemes, and co-operative or voluntary agreements between government and industry (Christoff 1996; Revell 2005) – although some EM analysts see a role for "smart" regulation combining strict eco-standards and flexible implementation (Jänicke 2008).[3] An EM program can take a more left-leaning, less market-oriented form, such as labour union demands for state-led industrial strategy to create green jobs (e.g. CLC 2008); however, this represents a move away from an original premise of early EM theorists such as Joseph Huber, who favoured limited government intervention (J. Murphy 2000). EM reform typically also includes a shift from reactive, "end-of-pipe" approaches to anticipatory, precautionary measures (Christoff 1996).

While the promotion of "clean technology" is central to all variations of an EM program, different technological emphases are possible. One debate pits those favouring a "soft energy path" (e.g. Lovins 1976; RMI 2007) – based on renewable energy and much greater energy efficiency – against advocates of a new-and-improved "hard energy path." The latter vision includes efforts to revive nuclear power as a low-carbon energy source as well as "sustainable fossil fuels" (Jaccard 2006), such as "clean coal" power plants with carbon capture and storage (CCS) – a technology that aims to prevent CO_2 from entering the atmosphere and to deposit it underground instead. Another debate, discussed in more detail in later chapters, centres on biofuels, which gained considerable policy and financial support from governments in Europe and North America despite warnings over their negative social and ecological impacts.

Although debate exists among EM advocates over technical options and the best policies to promote them, the dominant "weak" version of EM generally downplays or rules out the need for more radical forms of social change, whether that involves questioning economic growth and capitalism or even just scaling back environmentally problematic sectors. "Strong" EM, which goes further toward advocating extensive social change, but has been less influential in mainstream politics, is discussed in more detail below.

Both the importance and limits of EM reform are key themes in the chapters that follow. A win-win, job-creating, profit-producing project that does not require questioning of economic growth clearly has wide potential appeal, and can play a key role in enabling climate reform to begin. However, among the shortcomings of EM is that, in some cases, the discourse can obscure the lack of real reform. As discussed in the next chapter, Canadian federal governments have made use of an EM discourse since the early 1990s, albeit without a corresponding implementation of effective climate policy or success in reducing emissions. In their analysis of the province of Alberta's integrated resource management policy, Davidson and MacKendrick (2004, 48, 50) argue that "the symbolic features of EM may be employed while its substantive features are not." As a result, an EM discourse can mask a significant gap between what is said and what is done, allowing governments to maintain ecological credibility while pursuing BAU development: "EM has the potential to facilitate a form of symbolic political strategy described by Edelman (1964) as aiding in the concealment of tensions and contradictions regarding a given policy issue, while giving the impression of goal achievement. Such symbolic practices utilized in official policy discourse could become quite powerful, particularly if they are able to exclude ideas that economic development and environmental protection are in serious tension." Similar criticisms appeared in Britain. Despite EM reform being more advanced in the UK, it fell short of what many observers believed was needed, and critics interpreted the Blair government's "aspirational discourse" regarding climate policy as a "mass tranquilizer" while "business as usual for polluting production, distribution and consumption" continued (Harriss-White and Harriss 2006).

Going beyond EM rhetoric to change economic practices and seize win-win opportunities is more difficult in certain political-economic contexts – a problem that EM advocates do not always acknowledge. Developing nations often lack the technological and financial capacities to adopt clean technology and boost efficiency, while other obstacles are apparent in some wealthier nations. Australia, like Canada, is a major fossil energy exporter with many trade-exposed, energy-intensive industries. Despite severe vulnerability to climate change and the EM language of its Labor governments, Australia struggled to overcome opposition to climate policy initiatives from key sectors. In light of the Australian case, Curran (2009) concluded that EM is "not available to all states equally," as it requires a more politically challenging ecological restructuring in some national contexts (205; original quotation from Dryzek et al. 2002). Subsequent chapters will show that the difficulties of launching meaningful EM reform in Canada were particularly great.

Industrial Ecology, Natural Capitalism, and Other Forms of Techno-Optimism

Other perspectives have a strong affinity with EM, sharing a vision of economic growth decoupled from ecological impacts. Industrial ecology aims to redesign production processes and reduce the impacts of products over their life cycle, thereby harmonizing relations between industrial and natural systems (Graedel and Allenby 1995). Eco-technology advocates celebrate potential "factor-four," "factor-ten" (Schmidt-Bleek 2000), and even "factor 100" eco-efficiency gains, by which each dollar of economic output would generate 75, 90, and 99 per cent less resource throughput, respectively. In their call for "natural capitalism" and a new green industrial revolution, Hawken, Lovins, and Lovins (1999) similarly highlight the possibility of "radical resource productivity" improvements. The follow-up book, *Climate Capitalism*, maintains that the climate crisis could be solved at a profit, primarily through energy efficiency, renewable energy, and other technological solutions, and enlightened entrepreneurship (Lovins and Cohen 2011). Meanwhile, McDonough and Braungart (2002, 6–7) reject the "strident and depressing" environmental message that people should limit their consumption, make sacrifices, and share resources. Instead, they speak of going beyond "eco-efficiency" to "eco-effectiveness" so that every product, after its use, could be returned to the biosphere as a nutrient or perpetually recycled in the "technosphere" of the industrial economy. Such a "cradle-to-cradle" cycle could, in theory, continue without limit if powered by sustainable, renewable energy. McDonough and Braungart's vision is a long way from current practices, but it does stretch the EM vision of decoupling economic growth from environmental impacts to perhaps its outer limits.

Technological re-design and breakthroughs are undoubtedly needed to address climate change, but what if technological solutions simply do not exist for some key GHG sources on the timescale required or do not address anti-ecological features of expansionary modern societies?

"Strong" Ecological Modernization

The dominant "weak" form of EM reform focuses on technology and efficiency gains to deliver economic and ecological benefits, a process driven by elites in business, politics, and science. Critics argue that such a policy discourse may actually produce anti-ecological outcomes since it does not question systemic features of modern societies that are ecologically problematic, while its "narrow economism" works against "non-materialistic views of nature's 'worth.'" As such, weak EM may simply put a "green gloss on industrial development," serving, as noted above, as a rhetorical device to manage radical dissent and legitimate existing policy (Christoff 1996, 484, 486). A "strong" form of EM would go beyond an economistic, technological, and technocratic focus to embrace ecological values and priorities more fully. It would also involve citizens in broad democratic debate and reflexive questioning about the direction of modern societies and the ecological restructuring of key institutions and practices (Christoff 1996, 2005; Dryzek 2013).

The weak-strong EM distinction is evident with proposed responses to global warming. Gonzalez (2005) noted that as business groups such as the World Business Council on Sustainable Development and the International Chamber of Commerce moved beyond BAU and climate change denial, their preferred solutions remained limited. These involved weak EM strategies emphasizing eco-efficiency and technological innovation (e.g. new vehicle designs, improved fuels, and methods to sequester GHGs) and driven by "corporate social responsibility" and market-based policies such as emissions trading. However, these organizations failed to put their weight behind strong forms of EM that could enable less energy-intensive lifestyles – most notably curbing urban sprawl and building communities based on public transit, cycling, and walking.

A noteworthy set of climate change prescriptions, which can be categorized as strong EM, can be found in British journalist George Monbiot's (2006b) book *Heat: How to Stop the Planet from Burning*. His preferred solutions are technological, on the grounds that public acceptance will be greater the less the material sacrifice and disruption to modern life. He found that technologies already existing or on the horizon could cut emissions by 90 per cent in most sectors in

Britain, but not aviation, for which no technological or efficiency-based solution was foreseeable. He was forced to conclude that "the only possible answer is a massive reduction in flights" (xix). Monbiot also advocated a system of tradable carbon rations for individuals to ensure that efficiency gains actually reduce total emissions, rather than enable the purchase of more carbon-emitting goods and services. These proposals represent strong EM as they involve reflexive questioning of key aspects of modern life, going beyond improved technology and efficiency.

In subsequent chapters, the discussion of EM focuses on its weak form, which is most prevalent in public debate. A number of ideas that could be considered expressions of strong EM are examined under the banner of sufficiency, a perspective with which strong EM has conceptual overlap.

SUFFICIENCY: "WHAT ABOUT THE APPETITE ITSELF?"

In this book, the set of alternatives I explore with greatest interest are those that embody ideas of sufficiency, and which question the necessity and desirability of infinitely growing production and consumption (e.g. Barry 2012; De Graaf, Wann, and Naylor 2014; Hayden 1999; Princen, Maniates, and Conca 2002; Princen 2005, 2010; Sachs, Loske, and Linz 1998; Schor 2005, 2010). One early voice of sufficiency was economist John Kenneth Galbraith (1958, 92), who asked "How much should a country consume?": "If we are concerned about our great appetite for materials, it is plausible to decrease waste, to make better use of stocks available, and to develop substitutes. But what about the appetite itself? Surely this is the ultimate source of the problem. If it continues on its geometric course, will it not one day have to be restrained? Yet in the literature of the resource problem this is the forbidden question."

Precise definitions of sufficiency are hard to come by, but the idea is typically understood to involve limiting consumption and production volumes, and variations on the theme of "knowing how much is enough" (FoE Europe undated). As Princen (2005, 6) puts it, sufficiency is "the sense that, as one does more and more of an activity, there can be enough and there can be too much." For Germany's Wuppertal Institute for Climate, Environment and Energy (2008), sufficiency "refers to lifestyles and business conduct bringing to an

end the overuse of goods and thereby of resources and energy." Two
Wuppertal researchers, Sachs and Santarius (2007, 160), write that
the point of sufficiency "is not to fall victim to excess and overstretch,
but to take only as much as is beneficial for the well-being of individuals and the whole. Whereas ... efficiency requires us to do things
right, sufficiency calls for the right things to be done."

The sufficiency perspective draws on empirical findings, discussed
below, showing that steady production and consumption growth frequently overwhelms per-unit eco-efficiency gains. Sachs and Santarius (2007, 159) note that "the efficiency strategy has an Achilles
heel ... it does not prevent greater overall consumption. For the sum
of all savings may be eaten up and compensated by global growth in
demand for goods and services. In fact, that is what has been happening" (see also Santarius 2012). For example, the Energy Information Administration (EIA) reports that in the US, between 1990
and 2007 (before the economy went into recession), GHGs emitted
per dollar of output fell 28.0 per cent, yet total GHG emissions grew
16.7 per cent as economic growth outpaced eco-efficiency gains. A
similar situation was evident in many other industrialized nations
and with many other forms of environmental impact. In light of this
problem, Sachs and Santarius (2007, 158–65) argue that a comprehensive ecological strategy has three components: efficiency, consistency (i.e. technologies consistent with nature), and the often
neglected idea of sufficiency.

In terms of the I=PAT equation – used by many environmental researchers and advocates to depict environmental impacts as a product
of population, affluence (per capita consumption), and technology
(impact per unit of consumption) – EM focuses exclusively on "T."
However, sufficiency also sees a need to limit the "A" variable, at least
in already affluent nations. In other words, sufficiency-based policies
or proposals emphasize the need to limit, in one manner or another,
the volume of economic activity to meet environmental goals.

Sufficiency can target different levels of activity. At the macroeconomic level, ideas of sufficiency lead to a critique of GDP growth
as a dominant social goal – and to a quest for ways to manage without
growth in a steady state economy (e.g. Daly 1996; Jackson 2009; Victor 2008), or even de-growth (Alexander 2012; Kallis 2011; Latouche
2009). Rather than directly questioning the growth of the economy
as a whole, micro-level sufficiency seeks to limit specific practices,

sectors, and consumption of products that are considered excessive, such as meat consumption or air travel (Hayden 2014a) – or other manifestations of the modern emphasis on "faster," "further," and "more" (Sachs 2001). Micro-sufficiency can include sufficiency with respect to distance and speed, such as more local and regional sourcing to reduce the miles travelled by goods or deliberately designing cars and trains to have lower accelerating power and top speeds to achieve "sufficiency in performance levels" (Sachs 2001, 158). This macro/micro level distinction plays an important role in subsequent chapters.

A tendency exists in public debate to see sufficiency as merely a personal-level strategy to voluntarily reduce consumption; some theorists also narrowly define sufficiency in this way (Alcott 2008). However, Sachs, a leading sufficiency theorist, emphasized in an interview that it was a mistake to locate sufficiency at the personal level and ignore the institutional and even technological levels. A report for the European Parliament likewise stated that eco-sufficiency requires changes in infrastructures and social frameworks, "including measures such as environmental taxes, environmental planning and new concepts of labour" – the latter to provide alternatives to the "work-and-spend cycle" (SERI et al. 2006, 12–13). My interest in this book is not primarily with individual-level action but with efforts to advance sufficiency at the societal level.

Proponents of sufficiency typically argue that it is not only ecologically necessary, it could be also socially desirable, with a possible "double dividend" of living better while consuming fewer ecological resources (Jackson 2005). They draw on studies showing relatively little, if any, connection between rising per capita income and well-being or happiness in affluent nations (e.g. Donovan and Halpern 2002; Easterlin et al. 2010; 2012; Frey and Stutzer 2002; Kasser 2003; Knight and Rosa 2011; Layard 2005; for a counter-view, see B. Stevenson and Wolfers 2008). While EM seeks to decouple economic growth and environmental impacts, sufficiency advocates reframe the challenge as one of decoupling well-being from commodity consumption – or, in other words, improving consumption efficiency (Manno 2002). As discussed in subsequent chapters, this idea that "good lives don't have to cost the earth" (Simms and Smith 2008b, 21) has been central to efforts to gain greater traction for sufficiency in mainstream climate debates.

Advocates of sufficiency call for one further form of decoupling: that of global justice from a project of endless economic growth. For many writers, sufficiency is essential to "justice in an age of limits" (Sachs and Santarius 2007, 26). Sufficiency in the already affluent global North involves leaving ecological space for poverty reduction in the South (e.g. Schor 2001), while acknowledging the "ecological debt" stemming from the North's historic and ongoing appropriation of Southern resources (e.g. McLaren 2003; Salleh 2009; Simms 2005). There is an affinity between the sufficiency perspective and the broader climate justice movement, whose proposed solutions include reductions in excess consumption and large-scale wealth transfers to the South to compensate for the North's historic responsibility for the climate crisis and its disproportionate impacts on the poor (Climate Justice Now! 2007).

While sufficiency challenges core tenets of capitalism, its proponents often sidestep an explicit critique of capitalism – and, indeed, sufficiency could take politically conservative forms if consumption reduction were to be concentrated among less privileged people. However, Kovel (2008, 9–10) puts forward an eco-socialist formulation of sufficiency: "Socialist as well as bourgeois economists have scarcely begun to criticize consumption; indeed, from every corner, we continue to hear that the overproduction endemic to capitalism is also underconsumption, as though this latter were a disease to be remedied by more consumption of more commodities – when in truth, the level of consumption already imposed by capital is the immediate instigator of ecological crisis, and therefore, of the derangements of climate change." Kovel adds that "the only cure for the disease that is consumerism will be the universalization of freely associated labor, applied ecocentrically. It will require the fruition of human being, as a creative part of nature, to overcome the curse of 'having,' capital's induced possessiveness, that now rules the world" (14).

In a world in which a capitalist political economy and consumerist culture and self-conceptions appear to be firmly entrenched, one may be tempted to rule out sufficiency-oriented responses as unrealistic. Yet, as we will see, such ideas have not disappeared and, in fact, have gained renewed currency in light of the climate challenge and doubts about the adequacy of EM. Meanwhile, some proponents of climate action have drawn on ideas from both EM and the sufficiency approach, raising the possibility of a synthesis between the two perspectives.

CRITICAL POLITICAL ECONOMY PERSPECTIVES ON
GROWTH, CAPITALISM, AND ECOLOGY

Before turning to the struggle among business-as-usual, EM, and sufficiency in Canada and the UK, it is necessary to introduce additional
analytical perspectives. The main analytical challenge to EM theory
has come from some neo-Marxist political economy perspectives,
which argue that capitalism's systemic dynamics drive ecological degradation, undo the gains from eco-efficiency, fetter deployment of
green technology, and restrain state environmental policies. Such
analyses also highlight capitalism's bias toward efficiency-based and
possibly risky technological solutions at the expense of potentially
more effective measures, while showing that evidence of successful
EM in wealthy nations may be illusory when one widens the scope to
the global level.

"Treadmill of production" theory offers a metaphor of capitalist
societies running in place as they increasingly despoil the environment (Gould, Pellow, and Schnaiberg 2004, 2008; Schnaiberg 1980;
Schnaiberg and Gould 1994). The relentless drive for economic
growth is seen to be a product, in part, of firms' endless quest to accumulate capital and stay ahead of competitors by investing in new
techniques that allow more output with fewer workers. As a result, the
state, too, has a compelling interest in promoting limitless economic
growth to absorb each new round of displaced workers and provide
the revenues it needs for social spending to legitimate the social order (and the rule of particular leaders). Constant output expansion
is thus needed simply to maintain employment and social stability,
yet each cycle of expanded production is ecologically problematic,
according to the theory, as it requires increasing withdrawals of the
earth's energy and resources while adding ever-more pollution.

While EM theory sees potential to break this link between ecological impacts and growth, eco-Marxist John Bellamy Foster (2002,
2009, 2012) casts doubt on such hopes. He explains why more efficient use of materials and energy does not necessarily produce net
environmental improvements. Efficiency gains lower production
costs and increase profits, which owners invest to expand output and
generate even more profit and reinvestment. Greater efficiency can
thus lead to more production and, counterintuitively, more resource
consumption or pollution. This "Jevons paradox" – also known as the

"backfire effect," an extreme form of the "rebound effect" (chapter 7) – was first noted by nineteenth-century economist William Stanley Jevons, who found that demand for British coal skyrocketed as coal use became more efficient.

Foster (2002) provides an additional reason to doubt that the "magic bullet" of technology can save capitalism from self-inflicted environmental crisis. He notes the role powerful corporate interests have played in blocking possible transitions to ecologically sound forms of energy, transport, and urban development. Most notable is the "automobile-petroleum" complex, which consists of many of the world's largest corporations – including the car, glass, rubber, steel, and petroleum industries, as well as trucking companies, highway builders, and suburban real estate interests – and represents the industrial cluster around which capital accumulation has centred since the Second World War. Incidentally, this complex includes Canada's two most important industries, oil extraction and automobile production, which at key moments resisted proposals for stronger climate policy.

Among capitalism's anti-ecological features for Foster (2002) are the short-term time horizons that guide capitalist investment decisions without concern for long-term sustainability. Similarly, O'Connor's (1994) "second contradiction of capitalism" concept emphasizes pressures leading firms to externalize production costs to maximize profit in the short term. By resisting paying the full cost of sustaining the "conditions of production," including the natural resource base and ecosystem services necessary for capital accumulation to continue, capital's own cost-cutting strategies eventually come back to haunt it through increasingly costly crises. In terms of climate change, an example of the second contradiction can be seen in the escalating costs of storm damage to the insurance industry – a vulnerable lynchpin in the global financial system – partly as a result of capital's earlier resistance to measures that would have limited GHG emissions.

Unlike EM theorists, critical political economists emphasize potential conflict and contradictions between ecological protection and the state's role in ensuring the conditions for continued capital accumulation. As we will see, there have been powerful examples of these contradictions in both the UK and Canada, such as proposals to expand British airports despite the Labour government's expressed climate concern and Canada's strategy of becoming an "energy superpower" regardless of the carbon consequences. Given the structural power of capital – based on the dependence of the state and political leaders on business investment to provide the tax revenues and employment creation necessary for legitimacy and re-election – neo-Marxists argue that business demands for new opportunities for profitable investment typically trump ecological concern when the two are in conflict (Newell and Paterson 1998).

That said, a range of capital accumulation strategies exist, including a potentially more ecologically benign EM program. It has been evident for some time that state officials in Europe were attempting to integrate climate policy and capital accumulation strategy, hoping to create new sites of accumulation, technological innovation, and export opportunities through the transition to a low-carbon energy system, with the UK a leading example (Paterson 2001). Some critical political economists highlight the emergence of a new "climate capitalism," which has engaged powerful business actors in the construction of new carbon markets, with the goal of "squar[ing] capitalism's need for continual economic growth with substantial shifts away from carbon-based industrial development" (Newell and Paterson 2010, 1). A range of business sectors – including finance, insurance, renewable energy, nuclear power, and industrial producers of green technology – can profit from strong climate action and, in many countries, have become part of the coalition calling for it. The jury is still out on whether such a strategy is capable of reconciling capitalism's drive for growth and accumulation with climate stability.

Even if capitalism does show itself capable of responding to climate change, the solutions it puts forward to enable its endless expansion may be deeply problematic and provide grounds to consider alternatives. One set of concerns relates to the "carbon colonialism" of global carbon markets, which critics argue are allowing the rich North to acquire land and resources in poor countries to serve as a sink for its emissions and allow its profligate consumption to continue. Meanwhile, Buck (2006, 66) argues that "capitalism may well accumulate itself out of, or through, an ecological crisis." Yet he warns of the "dark sides of new technologies" that capitalism may turn to, including new "pollutions we cannot yet imagine (or that are imagined in only the most dystopian science fictions)" (68). Even without calling upon a sci-fi imagination, grounds for concern already exist over a new "ecological-industrial" complex's promotion of risky climate solutions, including a nuclear power revival, carbon capture and storage, and industrial-scale biofuel production, which threatens to aggravate deforestation and hunger in the global South.

One can trace capitalism's bias toward such market-oriented, technology- and efficiency-based solutions – i.e. weak EM – back to the fact that other potentially effective alternatives have the drawback of limiting accumulation opportunities. Gonzalez (2005, 2009) maintains that this is the case for halting urban sprawl, which is resisted by capital since it would limit a central source of demand for automobiles and other consumer durables. With regard to biofuels, Magdoff (2008, 34, 48) locates their appeal in the promise of a "magic bullet" that allows capitalist societies to "continue along their wasteful growth and consumption patterns" and avoid "any questioning of an economic system that by its very nature must keep on growing."

One final, particularly important challenge to EM as a theory and political program comes from world-system theorists, who argue that evidence of EM success within wealthy core nations often indicates little more than a transfer of impacts to poorer peripheral nations in a process of unequal ecological exchange (Jorgenson 2012; Rice 2007; see also York and Rosa 2003). Such processes of emissions transfers via international trade (Peters et al. 2011) are particularly relevant to assessing the UK's apparent success in cutting carbon (chapter 7).

Critical political economists thus provide several insights into EM's limits, which turn out to be an important factor driving some people to consider more far-reaching alternatives.

CAN EM REFORM DELIVER A "CARBON REVOLUTION"?

EM theorists have provided case studies of environmentally driven reforms in specific sectors (e.g. Mol 1995; Sonnenfeld 1998, 2002), documented the expansion of environmental policy and management capacities across nations (Weidner 2002) and the spread of EM reform to Asia and other emerging economies (Mol, Sonnenfeld, and Spaargaren 2009), and explored the character of trend-setting nations (Jänicke 2005). Such accounts illustrate instances of ecological rationality making its mark on modern societies and identify driving factors behind EM-oriented reform. Although these are valuable contributions, EM theory has not managed to show that the reforms and best practices it highlights are representative of overall trends or that resulting eco-efficiency gains are adequate for ecological sustainability in a context of relentless production growth (Schnaiberg, Pellow, and Weinberg 2002; York and Rosa 2003). Quantitative studies by EM theorists have generated only scant support for the contention that modernizing societies are beginning to resolve core environmental problems (Sonnenfeld and Mol 2006). Indeed, scholars have criticized the scepticism that some EM theorists hold toward quantitative empirical analysis (York, Rosa, and Dietz 2011, 80).

Evidence of a successful EM program would require, at a minimum, a decoupling of economic growth from the most important environmental impacts. In graph form, with ecological deterioration on the y axis and per capita income on the x axis, this theoretical trend would appear as an inverted U-shaped curve; after a society reaches a certain point of wealth, environmental impacts would begin to decline. Such an "Environmental Kuznets Curve" (EKC) is based on the highly contested claim, popularized by the World Bank in 1992, that in the early stages of economic development environmental degradation increases, but as countries modernize, they move beyond a "dirty" industrialization stage and gain capacity to solve environmental problems.[4] Several cross-national studies have shown, contrary to EM theory and the EKC, and in line with critical political-economy perspectives, positive correlations between levels of affluence and ecological footprint – a relatively comprehensive measure of a population's demands on global natural resources (York, Rosa, and Dietz 2003b; Rosa, York, and Dietz 2004; Hayden and Shandra 2009). Similarly, positive associations exist between nations' ecological footprints and their standing in the world-system hierarchy (Jorgenson 2003; Jorgenson, Rice, and Crowe 2005; Jorgenson and Burns 2007). Analysis has shown that the most economically advanced nations consume fewer resources per unit of economic output than developing nations, but these advanced, eco-efficient nations still generate greater environmental burdens as their efficiency gains have generally been insufficient to counteract the effects of higher production (York, Rosa, and Dietz 2004). In other words, evidence may exist for *relative* decoupling of economic growth and per unit environmental impacts, but there is little sign yet of the *absolute* decoupling necessary to tread more lightly on the earth. Meanwhile, a study by Australian physicist Graham Turner (2008) found that in the thirty years since *The Limits to Growth*, the data was in line with the unsustainable trajectory of that report's standard run or business-as-usual scenario. As I discuss in later chapters, awareness of such evidence of the "myth of decoupling" (Jackson 2009) has been an important factor in driving a radical reflection on growth, sometimes from surprising sources within political circles.

As for GHGs specifically, evidence of decoupling has not been strong. Cross-national studies show strong positive, albeit non-linear, links between economic output and CO_2 emissions (Shi 2003; York, Rosa, and Dietz 2003a) as well as between economic output and methane emissions (Jorgenson 2006). Jorgenson and Clark (2012) found evidence of limited, *relative* decoupling over time of economic growth and CO_2 in developed countries from 1960 to 2005, but far too little to break the continued strong link between per capita GDP and total emissions levels – while the positive relationship between per capita emissions and economic development actually intensified over time in less developed countries. A strong relationship also exists across nations between per capita consumption expenditure and GHG emissions associated with the consumption of goods and services (Hertwich and Peters 2009). Aspects of *de-modernization*, notably de-urbanization and declining per capita GDP, played a key role in the most "successful" cases of CO_2 reduction to date: the former Soviet republics (York 2008). Similarly, large emission declines in many countries in the wake of the recession beginning in 2008 drove home the continued linkage between output and emissions, as did the emissions surge in 2010 as global growth recovered; however, cuts in emissions in years of negative growth are generally not as large as GHG increases in years of expanding output (York 2012). Meanwhile, Tapia Granados et al. (2012) showed that changes in world GDP have a significant effect on CO_2 concentrations, with years of above-trend GDP growth seeing a greater rise of CO_2 concentrations.

Such relationships are not necessarily fixed; indeed the acceleration of EM reform in response to climate change is about changing them. Some nations, including Britain, also appear to have achieved significant, absolute GHG emission reductions even as their economies have grown.[5] Such cases merit examination for lessons they may offer about EM's potential contribution and limits in the shift to a low-carbon society. If examples of EM reform such as the UK can provide models for decarbonizing economic growth at a pace adequate to the ecological need, and with reasonable prospects for emulation by others, then the case for considering more socially challenging ideas of sufficiency would be significantly undermined.

It is important to clarify one issue at this point: as we have learned more about climate change, the bar for an EM project has been raised. The challenge now is not merely to show that economic growth is possible without increasing emissions, but that growth can continue while emissions decline deeply and rapidly. The McKinsey Global Institute (MGI 2008), a wing of the international consulting firm, estimated that to keep atmospheric CO_2 concentrations from exceeding 500 parts per million (ppm) while preserving economic growth would require increasing carbon productivity (i.e. the dollar value of output per unit of CO_2 emitted) tenfold by 2050. Although 500 ppm is still a very risky CO_2 level, one which would likely still allow warming of more than 2°C, the carbon productivity improvements required would be "comparable to the magnitude of the labor productivity increases of the Industrial Revolution," and such a "carbon revolution" would have to take place in one-third of the time (7–8). MGI nevertheless put an upbeat spin on the possibility of bridging the imperative of stabilizing carbon and the world's "right to" and "need for economic growth" (11). *If* the lowest-cost abatement options were adopted, it estimated that little sacrifice of GDP would be needed, with a total cost of 0.6 to 1.4 per cent of global GDP by 2030 (15). However, others who crunched the numbers concluded that the carbon revolution would require just that: a revolution. Marxist economist Minqi Li (2008) calculated that, even with historically unprecedented improvements in emissions and energy intensity, to stabilize atmospheric GHG concentrations at a safer level of 445 ppm CO_2 equivalent[6] and avoid global temperature increases of more than 2°C would require, even in the most optimistic scenario, a considerable contraction of global economic output by 2050.[7] That, in turn, would require a break with a society organized around endless economic growth and capital accumulation. Some scientists maintain that the decarbonization challenge is much greater still, arguing that the safe threshold is no more than 350 ppm of CO_2 (Hansen, Sato, et al. 2008; Rockström et al. 2009) – which implies the need for rapid, near 100 per cent decarbonization given that atmospheric levels are already roughly 400 ppm. Whatever the ultimate targets and the potential to improve carbon productivity, the arithmetic is daunting. This inconvenient math of decarbonization, which cuts to the heart of whether a project of green growth goes far enough in addressing the climate challenge, is an important theme in later chapters.

An additional issue to consider in the battle among business-as-usual, ecological modernization, and sufficiency-based responses to climate change is their relationship to core political imperatives. Environmentalists and participants in other social movements "have a much better shot at achieving their goals when they can attach their agenda" to one of the state's core political imperatives, argue Hunold and Dryzek (2005, 77). Historically, these imperatives included ensuring survival in competition and conflict with other states, keeping domestic order, and extracting resources to carry out these functions. Over time, the state's need for revenue evolved into an economic imperative to ensure conditions conducive to capital accumulation and economic growth. Meanwhile, maintaining domestic order evolved into a legitimation imperative, i.e. ensuring that potentially unruly subordinate classes acquiesce to the political-economic order through, for example, welfare-state reforms (Dryzek 1996; Dryzek et al. 2003; see also Meadowcroft 2007, 14). In sum, one can think of the security, economic, and legitimation imperatives as the core concerns of contemporary states.

Linking environmental goals to the legitimation imperative has at times provided important opportunities for green ideas. For example, in the 1970s, the United States was an early environmental legislation leader. President Nixon, facing a powerful challenge from the anti-war, student, civil rights, and other movements, tried to restore political-economic legitimacy in part by embracing eco-reforms (Dryzek et al. 2003, 59). Since then, maintaining legitimacy has increasingly required governments in advanced capitalist countries to perform environmental protection functions (Meadowcroft 2007, 14) – or at least provide the appearance of performing such functions. However, cases can arise where the legitimacy imperative is in tension with environmental goals.

Some theorists focus on legitimacy as a need of the political-economic system as a whole – which state leaders must attend to, as noted above, to maintain internal order (Dryzek et al. 2003). Legitimacy can also refer to a core need of governments and other

political actors, including leaders or aspiring leaders, and parties –
not to mention businesses (Macdonald 2007). A lack of legitimacy
can undermine political actors' capacities to achieve core goals such
as maintaining power or achieving it in the first place. In subsequent
chapters, examples will emerge of all three perspectives – BAU, EM,
and sufficiency – connecting to political actors' legitimacy needs in
different contexts.

While the security imperative has been seen to run counter to environmental goals (Dryzek et al. 2003, 67), recent efforts have linked
the security and climate agendas. Although there are a variety of ways
to make this linkage, one element of security – energy security – is
of particular importance to climate politics. As we will see, energy
security concerns played an important role in pushing forward an
EM reform project and climate action in the UK, whereas in Canada
they played an opposite role, contributing to the political influence
of a BAU perspective and to keeping the country wedded to a carbon-
intensive growth path.

BAU and EM perspectives have a clear political advantage over sufficiency primarily due to their ability to connect to the economic imperative. Although proponents of BAU may very well be short-sighted
in their belief that conventional patterns of economic growth can
continue into the future, their perspective is often perceived to be
in line with the immediate economic interests of states and powerful business actors. Meanwhile, EM, at its core, is about the promise of reconciling environmental goals with the apparent need for
economic growth. In contrast, sufficiency – at least in the form of a
macro-level critique of the limits to GDP growth – involves an uphill
struggle to challenge that perceived imperative (Dryzek et al. 2003,
58).

CHAPTER OVERVIEW

With these theoretical concepts in mind, it is time to turn to the
competition among BAU, EM, and sufficiency in Canadian and British climate politics. Chapter 2 looks at the difficulties in moving beyond BAU to EM in Canada, where the political-economic context
was inhospitable to ideas of win-win climate action. That is followed
by analysis of individuals and groups struggling to put ideas of sufficiency onto the agenda in Canada and the major obstacles that they

faced (chapter 3), and some of the limited ways in which sufficiency nevertheless managed to make inroads in the Canadian climate debate (chapter 4). Chapter 5 examines the development of Alberta's oil sands – a main reason why Canada struggled to move beyond a BAU path. An EM solution was elusive in the oil sands, a site which some considered a prime candidate for sufficiency-based limits on expansion. Chapter 6 turns to Britain and its considerable success in creating a wide coalition around a "positive agenda" of ecological modernization, which enabled a move beyond BAU. On closer inspection, however, that EM project illustrated very significant limits given the need for deep and rapid emissions reduction (chapter 7). Awareness of those limits, combined with a critique of economic growth's faltering capacity to improve well-being, was one of the key forces driving ideas of sufficiency onto the agenda in the UK. Those forces, and the ways in which a macro-level critique of growth reappeared in the UK, are discussed in chapter 8. With a direct critique of the limits to economic growth facing great political difficulties, the idea of sufficiency made greater inroads when formulated in more limited ways in the UK, including calls for micro-level sufficiency with respect to specific products, practices, or sectors (chapter 9). Chapter 10 looks at a number of ways in which ideas of sufficiency encroached on the sphere of the British state, which remained committed to the perceived imperative of economic growth, but might inadvertently be opening up space for a greater role for sufficiency in the future. Finally, chapter 11 draws out some comparisons of the UK and Canada. It also highlights the appeal, importance, and limits of ecological modernization, while reflecting on sufficiency's inroads to date and its future prospects.

It is with Canada's difficulties in moving forward on EM that we begin.

PART ONE

The Laggard

2

Canada: Stuck between Business-as-Usual and Ecological Modernization

Before examining sufficiency's struggle to make inroads in Canada, it is important to understand the context created by another front in the battle of paradigms: business-as-usual versus ecological modernization. This contest garnered most of the attention in Canada, a country torn between – on the one hand – strong environmental values and an internationalist tradition of contributing to solving key global challenges, and – on the other – the fact that its privileged position in the world and its economic strategy were tied to carbon-intensive sectors threatened by climate policy. While EM promised green growth, a heading in the *Globe and Mail* – above an article about industry's worries over climate policy proposals (Stueck and McCarthy 2008) – was indicative of the way many Canadians saw the issue: "The New Climate: Green Versus Growth."

FROM EARLY LEADER TO BACK OF THE PACK

Canada once garnered praise as a global climate leader and a beacon of hope to environmentalists. Guy Dauncey (1988, 261, 263), a UK Green Party member, wrote that "during 1988, awareness has grown (at least in Canada) of just how serious a threat to the world the greenhouse effect presents," pointing to "many signs that Canada is about to emerge as the first nation in the world to take a clear stand on planetary, ecological and economic issues." Toronto hosted the first major global climate conference in 1988, with Environment Canada scientists – backed by the Mulroney Conservative government – playing a lead role in raising awareness of the issue (May 2006). Canada also gave crucial support to the World Commission on Environment and Development and the 1992 Rio Earth Summit – among the central players were Canadians Maurice Strong and Jim MacNeill. Canada was one of the first nations to ratify the UN Framework Convention on Climate Change, signed at Rio. David Hallman, World Council of Churches' Climate Change Programme coordinator, met Canadian officials prior to Rio. He was impressed by Canada's willingness to oppose the US and seek mandatory reduction targets and timetables. "Canada was prepared to take a very independent foreign policy position," said Hallman. "That was kind of the high-water mark." However, critics soon began to see Canada as something of a "rogue state" in global climate talks – as early as the first Conference of the Parties in 1995 in Berlin, under a Liberal government (Broadhead 2001).

In later years, Canada's climate record was among the world's worst. It was a top ten total global emitter, despite its modest population. In 2011, Canadians emitted some 20.4 tonnes of GHGs per person, roughly double the level in Britain and triple that in Sweden (OECD 2013) – placing Canada in the same high-carbon class as Australians, Americans, and residents of some Gulf states. Canada's emissions were not only high, but also grew at the fastest rate in the G8, up 28 per cent from 1990 to 2007. That left Canada 34 per cent above its Kyoto Protocol target, with no hope of meeting its commitment domestically. Although the economic slowdown and the impact of policy (mostly provincial) helped bring down GHGs in subsequent years, emissions still sat 19 per cent above 1990 levels in 2011. In that year, Canada announced that it would withdraw from Kyoto – the first ratifying nation to do so. Canada also lagged in adopting new renewable energy sources such as wind and solar (WWF-International and Allianz SE 2009).

International climate performance rankings reflected such results. Canada was long ranked second to last on WWF's G8 Climate Scorecards – until the end of the climate-unfriendly Bush era in the US pushed Canada into last place. Even less flattering was Canada's annual ranking near the bottom of the Climate Change Performance Index produced by two European NGOs, Germanwatch and Climate Action Network Europe, which placed Canada fifty-ninth out of sixty countries, ahead only of Saudi Arabia, in 2010. At international climate conferences, Canada regularly received "fossil of the day" and "colossal fossil" awards, given by NGOs to the nation doing the most to obstruct progress. The United Nations Development Programme (UNDP 2007, 10, 43) singled out Canada as "an extreme case" of failure to curb emissions. Yale University academics, who produced a yearly Environmental Performance Index, ranked Canada 102 out of 132 countries on climate change in 2012. Even the Conference Board of Canada, a business-oriented research organization, repeatedly gave Canada a "D" for its GHG record.

A curious gap existed between Canada's high rankings on international surveys of ecological values and its record on several environmental performance indicators (Boyd 2003). Pollsters Michael Adams and Keith Neuman (2006) went as far as saying the "environment is Canadians' secular religion" as it returned temporarily to top spot among public concerns, where it had been in the late 1980s. While climate concern ebbed and flowed, some polls showed that Canadians (72 per cent) were more likely than the world average (65 per cent) to say it was "necessary to take major steps very soon" to address the problem (BBC World Service, PIPA, and GlobeScan 2007; see also CanWest 2007). Surveys in 2009 showed that Canadians were also more likely than the global average – 76 versus 67 per cent – to agree that the environment should be protected even if it slows growth and costs jobs. Canadians were also more willing than the average – 54 versus 48 per cent – to pay higher prices to address climate change, demonstrating views similar to citizens of Germany and Britain, two recognized climate leaders (Brechin and Bhandari 2011, 874, 876). However, significant regional differences existed, with Quebecers more likely than prairie residents to see climate as a top priority (Nanos 2010). Widespread climate concern also coexisted with a sizable minority current of climate scepticism. In a Gallup (2011) poll covering 111 countries, Canada had the seventeenth highest percentage of people saying that rising temperatures were "a result of human activities" (54 per cent). But it was also near the top – in twelfth place, with the United States number one – in the percentage attributing rising temperatures to natural causes (24 per cent). Surveys also suggested that despite wide climate concern, this concern did not run deeply. Canadians were less likely than the global average – 47 versus 56 per cent – to agree that global warming was a "very serious problem," with relatively large numbers of Canadians (37 per cent) saying it was merely "somewhat serious" (Brechin and Bhandari 2011, 875).

Federal politicians long acted as if they believed the appearance of climate action was essential, but actual action was not required – and was best avoided if it entailed sacrifices by the public or key industries. Eddie Goldenberg, trusted adviser to Prime Minister Jean Chrétien, revealed that the Liberal government doubted that Canadians were ready to accept the policies needed to meet the country's Kyoto targets, despite the polls showing strong support for the treaty (Whittington 2007; see also K. Harrison 2010; J. Simpson, Jaccard, and Rivers 2007, 78–9).

Outside observers caught on to Canada's contradictions. "You think of yourselves as a liberal and enlightened people, and my experience confirms that. But you could scarcely do more to destroy the biosphere if you tried," wrote British journalist George Monbiot (2006b, ix, x) in the Canadian edition of his book *Heat*. Australian scientist Tim Flannery (2008) concurred: "Almost every Canadian I've met has professed deep concern about this issue. Yet ... Canada as a whole has been spectacularly – almost proudly – cavalier in its attitude to the warming of our planet."

Canada's record did have defenders, such as the Canadian Council of Chief Executives, which urged greater efforts "to get the facts out on the Canada 'story' ... and our responsible approach to environmental management" in order to promote "the Canada 'brand'" (CCCE 2010, 54). Defenders also frequently emphasized "national circumstances," which, they argued, made Canada's task more difficult than other OECD nations. These included rapid population growth due largely to immigration, cold temperatures and vast spaces requiring high energy use for heating and transportation, and a carbon-intensive economic structure with a growing role as a fossil fuel exporter. Canada's more rapid GDP growth was also a factor behind – or, for some, a justification excusing – higher emissions. While critical of Canada's inaction, Simpson, Jaccard, and Rivers (2007, 83) noted that if its population and economy had grown at the same rates as in Europe from 1990 to 2005, Canada's GHGs would only have increased 6 per cent.

Canada did in fact have a tougher task in achieving its Kyoto goals than others, including the UK. While Canada's target of a 6 per cent reduction below 1990 levels was similar to that of other major signatories, it represented a 29 per cent cut below projected BAU emissions in 2010, compared to 3 to 9 per cent below BAU estimated for the EU or 12 per cent for Japan (K. Harrison and McIntosh Sundstrom 2007, 5). If Canada were an EU member state, it would undoubtedly have had a much less onerous target under the EU's burden-sharing system, which allowed some states to increase emissions due to their national circumstances, balanced by deeper cuts by those facing an easier task, such as Germany and the UK. On the other hand, appeal to national circumstances could degenerate into excuses for inaction. ("Our industrial structure is very carbon intensive so we can't easily cut emissions." "Our electricity system is very low carbon already so there's not much more we can do." "We're too small to matter, so why bother?" "Our country's so big that we have to travel longer distances than others." Etc.) While acknowledging Canada's special challenges, the National Round Table on the Environment and the Economy (NRTEE 2007, 6) added a key point: "We are one of the wealthiest countries in the world, and are therefore better positioned to bear the costs and risks of GHG ... reduction policies."

Canada was not a climate laggard in all areas. It did have a low-carbon electricity system – less than half as carbon intensive as in the UK (WWF-International and Allianz SE 2008, 18, 30) – mostly due to abundant hydroelectricity, as well as nuclear power concentrated in Ontario. Some provinces and municipalities took significant action, discussed below. One could also argue that, while Canadian policy was far too weak to deliver the deep GHG reductions that climate scientists estimated were necessary, other nations' policies were often not that much more demanding in practice.[1] Meanwhile, in 2008, Canada's House of Commons became the world's first elected chamber to approve legislation with the goal of an 80 per cent emissions reduction below 1990 levels by 2050. Then again, the Harper minority government fiercely resisted this opposition-introduced measure, ultimately defeating a second version of the Climate Change Accountability Act in the Senate in 2010.

FEDERAL CLIMATE POLICY:
WIN-WIN RHETORIC MEETS POLICY AGONY

Canada's climate record certainly was not due to a lack of policy activity over the years. The federal government oversaw a series of initiatives, starting in 1990 with the Progressive Conservative government's "Green Plan" and the "National Action Strategy on Global Warming," which proclaimed that "the risks associated with inaction on greenhouse gas emissions are too great to wait upon the results of

further research before commencing first actions. The limitation of
emissions must begin now" (CCME 1990, 17). Canada's poor record
also developed in spite of the fact that the federal government consistently accepted the scientific consensus that climate change was
largely a product of human activity (at least until the Harper government sent more mixed signals on climate science). Also striking
were the presence of an EM discourse whenever political initiatives
occurred and the broader failure of EM to establish itself as the dominant discourse with respect to climate change, let alone the dominant practice. Indeed, rather than win-win benefits, one participant in
the process, speaking at the Climate 2050 conference in Montreal in
2007, referred to the "policy agony" that Canada had experienced.

The Liberal Era, 1993–2006: EM Talk, BAU Practice

The use of EM language in Canada actually began under the Mulroney Conservatives, whose 1990 Green Plan spoke of climate change
offering "opportunities" rather than sacrifice or serious lifestyle
change (Simpson, Jaccard, and Rivers 2007, 48). In this period, Jean
Chrétien's opposition Liberals absorbed the sustainable development zeitgeist and framed environmental policy and economic gains
as going hand in hand. The 1993 Liberal Red Book campaign document pointed to economic opportunities, noting that companies "are
discovering that 'green economics' is the economics of efficiency …
Innovative solutions to domestic environmental problems can be
marketed worldwide" (Simpson, Jaccard, and Rivers 2007, 52). This
EM language carried over to the Liberals' various climate initiatives.

The 1995 "National Action Program on Climate Change" focused
on voluntary and cost-effective actions to "enhance opportunities at
home and maintain or improve Canada's competitiveness abroad"
(Environment Canada 1995, 10). An example was the Voluntary
Challenge and Registry Program to encourage GHG cuts in the public
and private sectors. The "National Climate Change Process" of 1998
similarly emphasized the search for cost-effective policies leading to
economic benefits and business opportunities. So, too, did the resulting "National Implementation Strategy" of 2000, a major theme
of which was "promoting technological development and innovation" and related "commercial opportunities, at home and abroad"
(NCCP 2000, 9; see also Broadhead 2001).

In 2002, Canada experienced a divisive debate over Kyoto Protocol ratification, which largely boiled down to a battle between BAU and EM perspectives. Kyoto opponents included the right-wing Canadian Alliance, all provincial governments except Quebec and Manitoba, and business heavyweights – such as the Canadian Council of Chief Executives, Canadian Manufacturers and Exporters, Canadian Association of Petroleum Producers, and Canadian Chamber of Commerce – united under the banner of the Canadian Coalition for Responsible Environmental Solutions (CCRES 2002). These opponents warned of soaring energy prices, competitive disadvantage relative to the US, and hundreds of thousands of lost jobs.

Business did not reject the need for GHG-reduction policy per se, but proposed its own "made in Canada" approach (CCRES 2002). While business expressed support for policy that went a very limited degree beyond BAU, it strongly objected to the GHG-reduction targets under Kyoto and the costs involved.[2] This acceptance of some action, but not enough to meet strong GHG targets, foreshadowed later positions taken by dominant business voices.

One key BAU defender was Canadian Alliance leader Stephen Harper (2002), who wrote a fundraising letter urging party members to "block the job-killing, economy-destroying Kyoto Accord." He called Kyoto, which allowed carbon-credit purchases from poorer nations, "a socialist scheme to suck money out of wealth-producing nations." Harper criticized the accord for being "based on tentative and contradictory scientific evidence about climate trends" and for "focus[ing] on carbon dioxide, which is essential to life." He added, in distinctly un-EM language, "THERE ARE NO CANADIAN WINNERS UNDER THE KYOTO ACCORD" (capital letters in original).

On the other side, the Liberal government had its wavering resolve strengthened by support from environmental groups, most of the labour movement, and the bulk of public opinion. An EM perspective was central to the pro-Kyoto forces' claims. The David Suzuki Foundation and WWF commissioned a study showing that a policy package taking Canada more than halfway to its Kyoto targets would add 52,000 jobs and increase GDP by $2 billion relative to a BAU scenario (Tellus Institute 2002). An EM discourse was also central in enabling the Canadian Auto Workers (CAW) – unlike their US brethren – to take the not-so-obvious step of backing Kyoto. The CAW rejected auto firms' fear mongering, calling Kyoto an "Automobile Opportunity for Canada." "Why do we support something that the corporations say could destroy our jobs?" asked CAW president Buzz Hargrove (2002). "Striving to meet our Kyoto targets will inspire us to do more in our economy, and to do it better." The Communications, Energy and Paperworkers Union (CEP), which had many members at risk of displacement, also backed Kyoto, while calling for a "just transition" plan to assist those negatively affected (Martin 2002). In the end, Parliament ratified the protocol. An EM discourse was key to this symbolic victory for green and left-leaning forces, but BAU was the ultimate winner in terms of policy and practice. Kyoto ratification did not lead the Liberal government to implement any substantive policy constraining or penalizing emissions by businesses or households.

The Government of Canada (2002) did release a "Climate Change Plan for Canada" in the same year it ratified Kyoto. It included, for the first time, significant regulatory proposals going beyond voluntary measures. Reduction targets for large industrial emitters in the oil and gas, manufacturing, and electricity sectors were to be set through legally binding covenants negotiated with key industries. Emissions trading was to build on these covenants – amounting to a potentially innovative combination of negotiation, regulation, and markets. EM elements also included an overriding language of "opportunity" – a word appearing five times in a four-page executive summary – and a coordinated innovation strategy, reflecting the Liberals' emphasis on new technologies to cut emissions and boost the economy (VanNijnatten 2004). However, behind the scenes, the government worked to limit the impact of climate policy on business. Following negotiations with business, notably the oil and gas industry, the government made key concessions, including a pledge that emissions reduction costs would not exceed $15 per tonne of CO_2 – well below the carbon price necessary to meet the Kyoto target.[3] The government also accepted industry demands that emissions regulations be intensity based, i.e. calculated per unit of output (Macdonald 2008) – thereby removing any constraint on production growth and, conversely, allowing emissions to grow as production expanded.

By February 2005, when the Kyoto Protocol came into force, no legally binding covenants with industry had been signed and emissions trading had yet to begin, although a voluntary agreement with the auto industry to reduce vehicle emissions was in place. Later that year, the Paul Martin government released yet another plan: "Project

Green." It included two new funds to subsidize emissions reductions, on top of earlier spending commitments. Despite the growing "Kyoto gap" between actual emissions and Canada's target, Project Green scaled back the emissions reductions expected from industry – from 55 megatonnes (Mt) in the 2002 plan to 39 Mt (Macdonald and Van-Nijnatten 2005; D. Marshall 2006). Industrial emitters, source of almost 50 per cent of Canada's GHGs, were now called on to make only 13 per cent of the proposed reductions. Compared to earlier climate policy documents, the federal government's EM rhetoric seemed to grow thicker,[4] even as resistance from industry caused the government to look to other social sectors to take up the slack. Government also abandoned plans for legally binding covenants with industry, promising instead to regulate – but only after more consultation, which further delayed the break with BAU practice.

A general pattern was evident. While using an EM discourse, Liberal governments continually backed away from implementing measures that policy analysts considered most likely to reduce emissions – regulations and carbon pricing, either via a tax or emissions trading. Government also increased spending on the problem – some $10 billion budgeted through to 2012 – and exhorted voluntary action. Dale Marshall (2006) of the David Suzuki Foundation wrote in the left-wing *Canadian Dimension* magazine that "Instead of polluter pays, it was pay the polluter." Similarly, Jaccard et al. (2006), writing on behalf of the centre-right C.D. Howe Institute, said Canadian climate policy amounted to "burning our money to warm the planet." They added, "For 15 years Canadian governments have layered one GHG policy over another ... The names changed, but the policy approach did not: it consisted primarily of offering information and subsidies to encourage voluntary reductions in emissions" (26–7).

One group that, with hindsight, did express satisfaction with the Liberal climate record was the Canadian Association of Petroleum Producers (CAPP). In a presentation, CAPP president Pierre Alvarez (2007, 2–3) spoke of the fears that Kyoto ratification would undermine competitiveness and cause "major economic damage," and that "the federal government would discriminate against oil and gas because of its high growth rate." Alvarez then pointed out the "realities," including the fact that the "government never proposed industry GHG policy based on the Kyoto target." He added that proposed GHG targets for industry were based on "reasonable principles" and "designed to avoid undermining of competitive position." Meanwhile, former Liberal environment minister Sheila Copps (2004, 85) recalled that "environmental interests were often trumped by commercial interests." She wrote: "Whenever issues came to the table, the environment minister found himself or herself in a minority ... As long as the cost of doing nothing was more attractive to business than doing something, the corporate lobby, especially the oil and gas lobby, would always convince the government that waiting was better than acting."

The Conservative Era: BAU When Possible, EM Rhetoric When Necessary

Stephen Harper's minority Conservative government took office in 2006 with a commitment to turning Canada into an "energy superpower" and "an obvious inclination to do as little as possible" on climate change (Macdonald 2008). The Tories inherited the climate scepticism that predominated within the Canadian Alliance – and before it, the prairie populist, free-enterprise Reform Party – prior to its merger with the Progressive Conservative Party. The Conservative position prior to the 2006 election "was essentially that of the business community: scale way back on emissions reduction requirements to balance 'long-term economic growth,' spend money on research and alternative energy, do nothing whatsoever about fossil fuel emissions except favouring intensity reductions, and wait patiently for science to develop a clearer picture of the problem and possible solutions. It was as close to a business-as-usual position on GHG emissions as could be devised without using the actual words" (Simpson, Jaccard, and Rivers 2007, 97).

Among the government's first actions was the scrapping of almost the entire array of Liberal climate programs. Environment Minister Rona Ambrose soon announced that it was "impossible for Canada to reach its Kyoto target" (Sallot 2006), even though international carbon-credit purchases were an option to fill any gap between domestic emissions and the target. John Baird, her successor, later emphasized the threat of economic ruin from attempting to meet Canada's Kyoto obligations: "To achieve that kind of target through domestic reductions would require a rate-of-emissions decline unmatched by any modern nation in the history of the world – except those who have suffered economic collapse, such as Russia" (House of Commons 2007).

The Conservatives took a first shot at their "made-in-Canada" climate policy in October 2006. The Clean Air Act tried to shift environmental attention onto smog and air pollution while setting weak long-term GHG targets – 45 to 60 per cent below 2003 levels, but not until 2050 – along with emissions-intensity targets that would allow industrial GHGs to keep growing for some time before then. Widely panned by environmentalists and the media, the act did at least acknowledge the need to go beyond voluntary action to regulatory measures.

A sharp upturn in public climate concern in late 2006, along with opposition threats to defeat the Clean Air Act, forced the government to dig deeper. It reinstated many of the previous government's climate programs and restored much of its proposed regulatory agenda. The April 2007 "Turning the Corner" plan upped the Tories' GHG reduction targets to 20 per cent below 2006 levels by 2020 and 60–70 per cent by 2050. It promised new regulatory targets for industry, requiring cuts in emissions intensity and payments of a maximum $15 per tonne for excess emissions. In addition to buying emissions credits from other regulated firms or offset projects, compliance options included payment into a technology fund used to develop and deploy low-carbon technologies. The government also pledged to strengthen energy efficiency standards and translate a voluntary agreement with automakers into fuel efficiency regulations.

The plan met a harsh reception from environmental critics, including Al Gore, who saw in it a made-in-Houston strategy serving oil industry interests (Canadian Press 2007). A key concern was the use of intensity rather than absolute targets, mirroring the climate-policy choices of the Bush administration, the Alberta government, and also the previous Liberal government. Intensity targets were, in effect, a way to sidestep conflict between growth and emissions reduction as they allowed firms that grew more to emit more, a fact that made intensity targets particularly attractive for sectors such as the fast-growing Alberta oil sands. An Environment Canada executive explained, "One key reason why Canada has chosen an emissions-intensity approach over a cap approach is because certain sectors of the economy are growing so rapidly that to choose a cap that is not essentially an emissions-intensity cap – that is, to chose a real hard cap – is effectively choosing that level of economic growth that the country is prepared to see take place. And that's very difficult for any government." Although the political logic was clear, a possible, even likely, outcome was that emissions intensity would fall while total emissions still rose.[5]

Critics also drew attention to the government's masking of environmentally weak targets by changing the base year from 1990, the established UN standard, to 2006 – a switch it also pushed for in international negotiations. The move effectively grandfathered the emissions spike in the interim years, an adjustment that was, again, particularly beneficial for the oil industry. The promised 20 per cent reduction by 2020 amounted to only a 3 per cent reduction from 1990 levels. This fell far short of the IPCC's estimate that rich nations needed to reduce emissions 25 to 40 per cent below 1990 levels by 2020 to keep atmospheric GHG concentrations from exceeding 450 ppm CO_2e (Gupta et al. 2007, 776), the level widely seen as the threshold for avoiding a temperature increase of 2°C or more. Meanwhile policy analysts concluded that the package would not be enough to meet even the weak 2020 targets (Bramley 2007a; Simpson, Jaccard, and Rivers 2007, 194–6).

Turning the Corner, like the various Liberal plans before it, was later dropped without implementation of its core provisions. However, it was a political success for the Conservatives as it helped them to neutralize the climate issue at a key moment. When climate was near the top of public concerns, it allowed the government to claim it was acting, but without endangering the economy. At the same time, the Conservatives denounced at every opportunity the previous Liberal government's inaction – neglecting to mention that this inaction was due largely to resistance from a broad range of conservative forces.

A MADE-IN-CANADA HYBRID: BAU-EM DISCOURSE. Turning the Corner did not have strong targets to reduce emissions, but it did reuse the Liberals' EM rhetoric and recycle much of their policy. The press release accompanying the plan dropped talk of environment-economy conflict, saying it would "promote investment in technology and innovation in Canada, yielding long-term economic benefits from enhanced productivity, improved energy efficiency, greater competitiveness, more opportunity to sell Canadian environmental products and know-how abroad, and more jobs for Canadians" (Environment Canada 2007). The day after the plan's release, Environment Minister

John Baird proclaimed, "We are going to unleash the power of the environmental economy" (CBC Radio 2007). Only a week before, Baird had reiterated that meeting the Kyoto targets would be disastrous and "manufacture a recession" (CTV 2007) – drawing on a Government of Canada (2007) forecast of 275,000 lost jobs, sharply higher electricity and gasoline prices, and a 6.5 per cent fall in GDP – but presumably the Tories' own plan would bring win-win benefits. Once the Conservatiyes were forced into a new position, an EM language was a convenient, almost obligatory, way to justify their choices.

The Conservative's partial embrace of an EM language of opportunity paralleled a move by some environmentalists who had not abandoned a sufficiency-based critique of economic growth, but turned to EM when fighting to overcome resistance to climate action (chapter 3). Political pressure pushed both groups toward EM, but it was not entirely natural terrain for those on either side of the spectrum who continued to see a growth-environment conflict.

Indeed, the Tories were reluctant EM converts, frequently reverting to a BAU emphasis on the costs of climate action, the need to "balance" economic growth and environment (rather than the two going hand in hand) or having to choose between them. To illustrate the theme of "The Economy and Climate Change," Canada's embassy in Washington, DC, used an image of a balance scale with the Earth in one pan and a golden dollar sign in the other (Canada-US Monitor 2009). Stephen Harper (2008) told the Canada-UK Chamber of Commerce in London, "I know that in some circles it is not politically correct to suggest that environmental targets must be balanced with economic imperatives," before arguing for just such a balance. An uneasy mix of BAU and EM was also evident in an op-ed entitled "Saving the Planet, Without Killing Jobs" by James Rajotte (2008), an Edmonton-area Tory MP, who emphasized the need for "balance" and a "reasonable" approach, while simultaneously highlighting the "massive economic potential in developing, implementing and exporting environmental technology."

Canada's most powerful CEOs moved toward a similar combined message. The CCCE's (2007c) report, *Clean Growth: Building a Canadian Environmental Superpower*, recognized that climate change required "aggressive global action," called for appropriate price signals and technological investments, and identified "major economic opportunities" (1). At the same time, the report noted, "Tackling our environmental challenge will have costs for governments, businesses and individuals, and we should not pretend otherwise" (5). The CCCE called for "an overall policy framework that recognizes competitive realities" (6). In its *Clean Growth 2.0* update, the CCCE (2010) continued to mix calls to seize opportunities in the "huge" global clean energy market (8, 11) with pleas to avoid overly ambitious climate action. Reflecting the support from many firms and business associations for a carbon tax or cap and trade (Belfry Munroe 2010),[6] the CCCE called for carbon pricing, but starting "at relatively low levels" to avoid "unnecessary impacts on competiveness" (2010, 5). It urged a "high degree of policy alignment" with the US, including delaying regulations for trade-exposed sectors until the US acted so as not to put manufacturers at a competitive disadvantage (5, 36–7). The CCCE also defended tar sands development (23–4), backing only a minimalist, intensity-based "Alberta model of emissions pricing" for upstream oil and gas (5). This position, reflecting elements of BAU and EM thinking, was linked to the dual nature of Canada's energy resources. As the CCCE explained, Canada had abundant oil, coal, natural gas, uranium, and hydroelectricity, as well as significant potential in biofuels, wind, and tidal power – and it supported developing all of them (2, 38).

STILL WAITING TO TURN THE CORNER. Policy change lagged behind the partial rhetorical shift. More than six years after releasing the Turning the Corner plan, the government still had not produced policies that would enable the meeting of its modest carbon-reduction promises. In fact, it had further weakened its reduction targets. After the 2009 Copenhagen Accord, Canada matched the US pledge of a 17 per cent GHG cut below 2005 levels by 2020 – equivalent to a 2.5 per cent *increase* from 1990 levels. Environment Canada (2012, 4) estimated that existing federal and provincial initiatives would only reduce GHGs by one half of the amount needed to meet the 2020 target. The government turned this into a claim that Canada was already halfway to meeting its Copenhagen commitment. However, given the long lead time to develop and implement new policy, Canada's Commissioner of the Environment and Sustainable Development concluded that it was "unlikely – based on what is in place or proposed – that Canada will meet its 2020 target" (Vaughan, Leach, and Reinhart 2013). Indeed, the subsequent Environment

Canada (2013a) emissions trends report showed a growing gap between projected emissions and the country's 2020 target.

The measures that the Conservatives implemented revealed a great deal about the kind of climate policy that could make headway. From the government's early days, it included measures that could justify themselves purely in electoral terms, such as tax credits for the purchase of public transit passes. This was a costly way to cut carbon – as the subsidy mainly rewarded people who were already taking the subway or bus, rather than generating a shift to public transit (Simpson, Jaccard, and Rivers 2007, 186) – but was a visible campaign promise designed to appeal to the urban voters the Tories needed for a majority government. The April 2007 announcement of a phase-out of inefficient incandescent light bulbs was another visible signal of an intention to act – and establish environmental legitimacy – at a time of high public concern about climate.

Another core element of Conservative "climate" policy was support for biofuels, which became the single most expensive federal environmental program. In addition to up to $2.2 billion in subsidies over nine years, in May 2008, the House of Commons passed Bill C-33, resulting in a requirement of five per cent ethanol content in gasoline by 2010 and 2 per cent renewable content in diesel by 2011. This law was approved, with Liberal support, at the height of concern that biofuel policies were driving a devastating rise in global food prices – and despite warnings by government experts that the life-cycle environmental impacts of biofuels "were found more often to be unfavourable than favourable" (De Souza 2008). As in the UK, biofuels were tempting for Canadian politicians – a solution that appeared to fulfill EM's win-win promise. Government could claim to be cutting vehicle emissions while creating jobs, without inconveniencing key economic interests in the auto industry or making drivers change their lifestyles, all while scoring political points with farmers – not to mention pleasing the agro-fuels lobby that had close ties to the Harper government (CanWest 2008; S. McCarthy 2008). However, by 2013, enthusiasm for subsidizing biofuels appeared to be waning, as the government announced that it would no longer consider applications for its "ecoEnergy for Biofuels" subsidy program.

The government's significant financial support for new energy technology included a $1 billion "Clean Energy Fund" announced in May 2009. The bulk, $650 million, was for carbon capture and storage (ccs) demonstration projects. ccs was a high priority of Canadian business (CCCE 2007c, 5), especially the fossil fuel industry (ICO2N 2007), and a central element of modelling scenarios for how Canada could make deep GHG cuts (NRTEE 2006, 2007; Pembina Institute and Suzuki Foundation 2008, 2009). The National Round Table on the Environment and the Economy put the matter bluntly: "Canada's growing role as a major energy exporter is compatible with deep GHG emissions, but only if carbon capture and sequestration (ccs) is perfected" (NRTEE 2006, 1). According to David Lewin, a senior vice president at EPCOR, an Edmonton-based supplier of mostly coal-fired electricity, ccs was also a key low-carbon technology in which Canada could lead, based on expertise in power plant design and geology, as well as a large storage capacity in depleted oil fields. Alberta – rich in coal and high-carbon oil – was funnelling even more money into ccs than the federal government (chapter 5). With billions of dollars of ccs support, Canada was swinging for the fences, hoping for a technological home run to reconcile deep GHG cuts with energy superpower aspirations – and to take away that policy agony. In other words, ccs held the promise of bridging a BAU present and an EM future, without having to question fossil fuel–based growth.

After a changing of the guard in Washington, the government dropped its "made-in-Canada" rhetoric in favour of harmonizing climate policy with the US. In 2009, after the Obama administration strengthened vehicle fuel efficiency standards, the Harper government followed suit – showing that the US could drag Canada forward as well as hold it back. (Although the auto-sector regulations might have been a step forward, critics noted that they required little more than historical, business-as-usual improvements [Partington and Bramley 2010].) The abandonment of more extensive US climate legislation in 2010 gave the Harper government a further opportunity to delay comprehensive GHG limits, as it could claim Canadian business competiveness would decline if it acted without the US taking similar steps. However, renewed US interest in climate change after the 2012 election once again put pressure on Canada to do more.

On one issue, the Canadian government felt it could move ahead of its southern neighbour without excessive economic cost. In 2010, it announced plans to require new coal-fired power plants to achieve emissions similar to a natural gas plant, in effect ruling out new coal plants without ccs after 2015. In a manner typical for any Canadian climate policy announcement, Environment Minister Jim Prentice turned to an EM language, stating, "This will create new jobs in the clean energy sector, while helping Canada meet its commitment to greenhouse gas reductions" (Environment Canada 2010a). The government finalized the regulations, albeit after watering down the proposed performance standard, in 2012.

By 2013, a national carbon price was still lacking, the Conservatives having dropped their cap-and-trade plans. Although the government had applied sector-by-sector regulation to vehicles and coal-powered electricity, and had promised for years to regulate other key sectors, there were still no federal measures to constrain large industrial emitters, including the oil sands operations that were Canada's fastest growing GHG source. Environment Minister Peter Kent veered back to a BAU framing to justify such inaction: "Our focus for the next several years is going to continue to be on maintaining the economic recovery and we will do nothing in the short term which would unnecessarily compromise or threaten that recovery." He added, with respect to the tar sands, "It is not our intention to discourage development of one of our great natural resources" (Chase 2011).

While the government was in no rush to introduce oil sands regulations, the same could not be said of its overhaul of environmental legislation in 2012. The changes, including a complete rewriting of the Environmental Assessment Act, were delivered only months after a request from a grouping of oil industry associations for revisions to "outdated" environmental laws "focused on preventing bad things from happening rather than enabling responsible outcomes" (CBC 2013a). Briefing notes for the environment minister also revealed that "pipeline development," which had become urgent for a government and industry seeking new ways to get oil sands products to market, was "certainly among the major industrial sectors that are top-of-mind as we consider the modernization of our regulatory system" (De Souza 2012b; see also Scoffield 2013).

CHILLY RELATIONS WITH WARMING SCIENCE. Paralleling the lack of policy to stimulate an EM process was the lingering impression that the Conservative government was hostile to climate science, even though it did not directly question the science in official documents. Shortly after becoming prime minister, Stephen Harper denied ever having questioned the scientific evidence behind climate change – despite referring to "so-called greenhouse gases" only a week earlier (Delacourt 2006). Other observers saw things differently. "This particular government has been a government of skeptics," said IPCC Chairman Rajendra Pachauri, in light of Canada's efforts to weaken targets for rich nations during the Bali climate conference. "They do not want to do anything on climate change" (AFP 2007). The UK-based journal *Nature* (2008) singled out Canada in an editorial. It condemned the government's "manifest disregard for science," adding that since Harper took power, "his government has been sceptical of the science on climate change." Meanwhile, more than 120 Canadian climate scientists signed an unprecedented open letter criticizing the Tories' weak domestic policies and international obstruction, while encouraging strategic voting for the environment in the 2008 election (Canadian Press 2008).

One reason for these critical assessments was that the government had prohibited Environment Canada scientists from speaking to the media without prior authorization (Munro 2008). This tactic had an impact. An internal Environment Canada document stated, "Media coverage of climate change science, our most high-profile issue, has been reduced by over 80 per cent." It also noted that senior federal climate scientists felt frustrated by efforts to "muzzle" them (De Souza 2010).

The government also acted to deflect attention from its own studies of climate change impacts and illustrated a tendency to withhold other inconvenient information. The release of a major Natural Resources Canada study outlining threats to Canada, from prairie droughts to erosion of traditional subsistence lifestyles in Arctic Aboriginal communities, was expected in November 2007 – inconveniently just before global climate talks in Bali (De Souza 2007b). The 450-page report (Government of Canada 2008) was quietly posted on a website several months later, on a Friday after 5 p.m., but only after details had been leaked to the media. A 500-page Health Canada report warning of major health impacts from more droughts, violent storms, and heat waves was also several months late (Rennie 2008). It eventually emerged with a low-key press release highlighting the government's Turning the Corner plan, without a word about the findings (Health Canada 2008). Meanwhile, an Environment Canada presentation documenting a range of growing environmental impacts from tar sands operations, including "high-profile concern" over contamination of the Athabasca River and estimates that tar sands GHGs were on track to increase 900 per cent from 1990 to 2020, was marked "secret" and had to be obtained by journalists using access-to-information laws (De Souza 2011a).

Cutbacks also inhibited the ability of government scientists to produce policy-relevant work. For example, the government closed the Canadian Climate Impacts and Adaptation Research Network, saying it had completed its mandate, prompting vigorous criticism from Canada's IPCC scientists (De Souza 2007a). *Nature* (2008) was particularly alarmed by the government's decision to close the office of National Science Advisor. As the government moved into an austerity drive in 2011, critics alleged that Environment Canada climate scientists were targeted with a disproportionate share of the cuts. Forty-six climate scientists on limited contracts were told their services were no longer needed (Taber 2011). According to one junior climate researcher, "Over the past several months we have seen major cuts to Environment Canada that are leaving it without any real scientific or research power. We have seen many prominent scientific jobs cut, research funding slashed, and our ability to effectively do environmental assessment and management largely neutralized" (Birch 2011).

These developments and others led some critics to conclude that the government was engaged in a "war on science" (C. Turner 2013). If, as EM theorists argued, ecological rationality was emerging as a transformative force within modern societies, the Conservatives were doing their part to limit the production and awareness of the science upon which that rationality was based. Like their US counterparts (McCright and Dunlap 2010), Canada's Conservatives played a role as an "anti-reflexive" force, undermining the environmental-impact science that enabled reflexive, ecological modernization.

BAU VOICES: GROWTH VS. ENVIRONMENT, AND GROWTH (OBVIOUSLY) MUST PREVAIL

Some voices in the debate resisted any climate policy action, even the Tories' limited measures. Among them were climate science deniers, including Calgary-based Friends of Science – which later evolved into the Ottawa-based International Climate Science Coalition – and journalists, largely concentrated in the right-wing *National Post* and

Canwest newspaper chain, such as Terence Corcoran, Peter Foster, Lorne Gunter, and Lawrence Solomon. Others, such as the *Globe and Mail*'s Margaret Wente, claimed to take climate change seriously, but still found grounds to reject almost any proposed solution. Such voices not only worked against an EM project – their prominence was also a significant obstacle to a sufficiency perspective.

One notable BAU voice was Rex Murphy, newspaper columnist, commentator on *The National* news hour, and host of CBC Radio's cross-country call-in show. Murphy (2009) suggested that perpetual economic crisis was the logical outcome of acting on climate concern. He added that it was curious that "those who have been warning the rest of us for nearly two decades that we are in a 'planetary emergency'" did not speak up about the "upside" of economic downturn:

> Maybe because it's "an inconvenient truth," and the telling of it would make explicit what has always been the real equation of the global warming scare. Which is, that if people believe the planet is on the path to apocalyptic ruin because of the world's dependence on petroleum – and that, without exaggeration, is the message of the global warming advocates – then the world's economies must radically shrink. We must do and have less of everything. We must make less, travel less, buy less – and endure the deeper hardship of more people out of work.
>
> That is the inescapable message of a serious belief in global warming. No amount of chatter about a "green economy" or Twittering about all the "green jobs" about to materialize as soon as we "wean ourselves from our carbon dependency" – all rhetorical sugar-coating – will change it.

EM supporters would, of course, object to that vision of a green economy. Sufficiency supporters might be of two minds – accepting that a conflict existed between growth and climate stability while rejecting the idea that making and buying less necessarily implied misery and hardship. Indeed, many sufficiency advocates saw opportunities for better, more satisfying ways of living. But that argument – always difficult – was easier to make in a society with broad consensus on the need for deep GHG cuts than in one where it was still a mainstream idea to dismiss "the global warming scare."

Another example of the difficulties that BAU's continued strength represented for sufficiency was evident in the debate over the rebound effect, a.k.a. the "efficiency paradox." A report by two CIBC economists provided evidence that efficiency gains allow increased consumption and ultimately increased energy use (Rubin and Tal 2007). Their findings led them to argue that "energy efficiency is not the final objective – reducing total energy consumption must be the final objective to both the challenges of conventional oil depletion and to greenhouse gas emissions" (4). Evidence of the rebound effect's importance could, in principle, serve as a key argument for those calling for some degree of sufficiency (chapter 8). However, the argument could also be spun the other way, and it was in Canada's "national newspaper," where Wente (2007b) was quick to respond to Rubin and Tal's report. "The efficiency paradox means that Canada's greenhouse-gas reduction targets … are highly unlikely to be met," she argued, noting the government's focus on increasing energy efficiency. "Of course, there are other ways. We could shut down the oil sands, the auto industry and immigration. We could order people to live in smaller houses and take away their cars. Or we could have a really great recession. How would you like to run on that platform?" In other words, rather than having to dig deeper to limit increasing consumption, the efficiency paradox was another reason to put serious climate action in the realm of the impossible – at least until some future point when technology would ride to the rescue. "One day, we'll develop energy sources that can replace fossil fuels. Till then, it's all just talk," maintained Wente.

The way in which BAU voices used the prospect of slower growth to dismiss climate action indicated some of what sufficiency was up against – an issue returned to in the next chapter. First, though, it is worth considering the forces that rejected any such trade-off between growth and climate action.

ECOLOGICAL MODERNIZATION'S CONTINUED STRUGGLE TO TAKE OFF

It was the kind of Edmonton day to make one yearn for global warming. A visiting Russian hockey player complained in the local paper, "Here is like North Pole." Yet in an industrial park in the city's northwest end, in the heart of oil country, minutes away from what was for many years the world's largest shopping mall, I caught a glimpse of the green economy struggling to break through. Entering the offices of Conergy Sales Canada, I was greeted by an international assortment of photovoltaic panels – including some from head office in Germany, homegrown Canadian product from Day4 Energy, and others made in China by BP Solar. I was there to speak with Kyle Kasawski, the firm's president. In a province with a surprising amount of sun but minimal support for renewable energy, he helped build ETI Solar into Canada's second largest solar company, which Hamburg-based Conergy later bought. Kasawski saw great opportunities in a transition to decentralized renewable energy and was a strong advocate of the feed-in tariffs (premium rates paid to renewable electricity producers) that had spurred the growth of Germany's green energy sector. Canada was far behind in this process – symbolized by the fact that German interests had bought up Kasawski's firm – yet some progress was evident. As Kasawski and I talked, Guy, an installer of solar and wind energy systems, entered the room. He spoke enthusiastically about the ecological benefits of his job and the opportunities ahead in upgrading his skills. The environment and economy did not always go hand in hand, especially in Alberta, but here was a living example of EM's promise. "You may not think of it this way, but you're an interesting sociological phenomenon – an agent of ecological modernization," I told Kasawski as I was leaving. "The funny thing is, I'm such a capitalist," he replied. "I don't see a conflict between capitalism and the environment."

Many others in Canada were working toward an EM transition. Such ideas had a strong presence within four of the five main political parties, environmental groups, some major businesses, the labour movement, and at provincial and local levels.

Four Pro-EM Parties

The choice of former environment minister Stéphane Dion as Liberal leader in 2006 was largely a product of an upsurge in climate concern. Owner of a dog named Kyoto, Dion (2007) gave a first major speech as leader – before the Economic Club of Toronto and the Toronto Board of Trade – that was straight out of the EM textbook. "Old thinking is based on gloomy tradeoffs, pitting a cleaner environment against a weaker economy," he argued. "But those tradeoffs are not a law of nature. They simply represent a failure of ingenuity." Refusing such gloom, he stated that, "Yes, Canada will cut megatonnes of emissions, but we will also make megatonnes of money." Adapting his EM vision to the Canadian context, he added, "I want Canada to become the global centre of expertise for carbon sequestration ... If we can make Fort McMurray a centre for sustainable development, we will be able to do it everywhere in the world."

Grant Mitchell, an Alberta Liberal senator, provided a similar perspective in an interview. "If done properly, climate change policy would be an economic stimulus," said Mitchell. He added, with evident frustration, "Somehow there is this implicit acceptance of what I would call a right-wing, spin-doctored assumption that dealing with climate change is going to hurt the economy." Mitchell argued that business typically exaggerated the cost of environmental initiatives, "but once they undertake to do it – whether because they feel they should or because they're forced to do it – their engineers, technologists, scientists, and business people find the cheapest way to do it. Almost inevitably, these problems are solved much more quickly and with much less expense than ... even the most optimistic imagined." So, if acting to stop climate change could bring economic gains, why was there so much resistance? One key reason Mitchell identified was that "these types of Conservatives, particularly the very right-wing ones, hate government regulation ... To them, environmental policy means regulation."

That right-wing impulse was evident in the debate over Dion's proposed "Green Shift," which included a revenue-neutral carbon tax balanced by corporate and personal income tax cuts and social spending to compensate low-income earners. While the proposed tax rate was low,[7] it was still a bold proposal. A carbon tax had been a political taboo since 1994, when Prime Minister Chrétien reassured Alberta energy executives that it would not be on the table. Stephen Harper denounced Dion's proposal as "insane" and a measure that would "screw everybody across the country" (C. Clark 2008), backed by attack ads claiming that it would be a "tax on everything." Further to the market-fundamentalist right, Terence Corcoran (2008) of the *National Post* argued that Harper was in no position to criticize: "All government carbon plans – Liberal, Conservative, Republican, Democratic – could accurately be labeled crazy economics."[8]

The Green Shift's promise of creating a "richer, greener, fairer Canada" (Liberal Party 2008b) did not resonate strongly with voters. Dion eventually downplayed it during the 2008 campaign, as he led the Liberals to their lowest popular vote in more than a century. Whether it was the message or the messenger – Dion stood out as a leader with greater personal integrity, but lesser strategic and communication skills than most – or bad timing as fuel prices were skyrocketing and the economy slumping, it was a significant defeat for an EM vision. An additional factor in the defeat was vote splitting with other parties also putting forward left-of-centre, green-leaning ideas – not to mention attacks coming from some of those same quarters.

In the subsequent campaign, Liberal leader Michael Ignatieff dropped the carbon tax in favour of cap and trade. Ignatieff put less emphasis than Dion on green themes, but the Liberal Party (2011) platform continued to propose an EM climate response, pledging action to "remain competitive and keep high-paying jobs in Canada" as the world makes the "great transition ... to the low-carbon, high efficiency economy of tomorrow" (42). Despite the new leader and new policy, Liberal support fell further still in 2011, the party dropping to third place for the first time in the country's history.

The New Democratic Party had long backed a left-leaning, labour-oriented EM program. "Good jobs. Quality jobs. Sustainable jobs. Jobs that match the economy of tomorrow. I'm talking about Green-collar jobs. And lots of them," said NDP leader Jack Layton (2007). Yet in 2008, the NDP reasoned that it could best capture Liberal votes – federally and in BC – by criticizing a carbon tax as harmful to low-income and working people. Instead, it favoured an auction-based, cap-and-trade policy with revenues used to invest in public transit, renewable energy, home retrofit subsidies, and "just transition" for displaced workers (Layton 2008). The NDP (2011, 12–13) presented similar ideas in the subsequent election, along with a pledge to eliminate fossil fuel subsidies and redirect the funds to "encourage cleaner energy production."

Growing environmental concern and a prominent new leader, Elizabeth May, gave a boost – and, in 2011, a first-ever seat – to the Green Party. May and the Greens did on occasion put forward a more radical sufficiency message questioning the desirability of infinite economic growth and ever-rising consumption in a finite world. However, the overriding message in the Green Party of Canada's (2007b, 2011) "Vision Green" policy documents and in its election campaigns was an EM focus on efficiency, technology, and business opportunity, driven largely by a green tax shift – an idea they had proposed before the Dion Liberals embraced it.

The Bloc Québécois (2008), which until 2011 held a majority of seats in pro-Kyoto, hydro-powered Quebec, put forward its own sovereignist EM program designed to benefit the province. This included a "territorial approach" to emissions reductions – with Canada's 6 per cent reduction target under Kyoto divided among the provinces – that would allow Quebec to profit from its relatively low emissions by selling carbon credits to other provinces. The Bloc also backed the Montreal Climate Exchange as a centre for the potentially lucrative carbon trade.

In 2008, 61 per cent of voters backed parties proposing some version of an EM climate response – and yet the one major party still predominantly in the BAU camp formed a minority government. In 2011, the Conservatives won a majority of seats, but once again a large majority (59.4 per cent) of voters favoured pro-EM parties. Vote splitting was far from the only obstacle hindering EM in Canada, but until it was addressed – whether through electoral collaboration to present common candidates, a merger of parties, proportional representation, or voters concentrating their support on a single centre-left-green party – EM politics at the federal level would likely be held back.

Environmental Groups: Coalescing around Ecological Modernization

Presenting a more united appearance than the pro-EM political parties were Canada's major environmental organizations. Although some environmental groups' climate proposals included elements of sufficiency, including calls to stop tar sands growth, the environmental movement's dominant message was of EM opportunities made possible by greater efficiency, technology, and an effective policy framework.

This perspective was evident in a statement representing the consensus view of eleven of the country's leading environmental organizations (Tomorrow Today 2008).[9] The groups argued that "our economic well-being is not at odds with protecting our environment" (3),[10] adding, "Realistic pricing of GHG emissions will assist Canada in creating a clean and competitive economy" (5). The groups' vision for "how we can live in greater harmony with the Earth" and reduce "the human footprint of resource consumption" (3, 27) put a heavy emphasis on technology, with the side benefit of greater economic power: "The technology exists today to double, and even triple, the fuel efficiency of personal vehicles. Imagine the savings on gasoline if the average new car in Canada used four litres to cover 100 kilometres instead of eight. Imagine homes that used 60 per cent less energy for heating and cooling than today's homes and provided power to the grid from roof-mounted solar-energy systems. Imagine our industries leading the world in greenhouse gas pollution solutions ... In fact, Canada can become a 'Sustainable Energy Superpower'" (8).

An emphasis on efficiency and technology driven by appropriate policies – bringing ecological and economic gains – was also found in the Sierra Club of Canada's (2007) report, *Stopping Global Warming: Towards a Low-Carbon Canada.*[11] WWF-Canada's (2007) vision of "climate solutions" highlighted "dramatically improving energy efficiency" and technology (wind, solar, renewable energy storage, hydrogen fuel infrastructure, CCS), along with stopping forest loss. Meanwhile, the EM message was unmistakable in two reports co-sponsored by the Pembina Institute and the Suzuki Foundation (2008, 2009) on the prospects for a 25 per cent emissions cut by 2020, entitled *Deep Reductions, Strong Growth* and *Climate Leadership, Economic Prosperity*, discussed below.

Business and Labour as Carriers of EM Ideas

While Canadian business served, on the whole, as a fetter on the introduction of climate policies capable of driving deep GHG reductions, some businesses did call for strong government action while seeking profitable ways to cut carbon. These included emerging businesses whose core activities centred on a low-carbon transition. Among them were firms in renewable energy, the voluntary carbon offset market, and, for a time, the nascent carbon trade. Of greater weight were conventional firms aiming to green their practices, or at least their image, while taking advantage of emerging profit opportunities. Most of the eighteen CEOs who signed the Executive Forum on Climate Change's (2005) call for urgent action to stabilize the climate had a clear stake in the transition – in sectors such as hydroelectricity (BC Hydro), public transit vehicles (Bombardier), lightweight materials for transportation (Alcan), biofuels (Iogen Corporation), insurance (Institute for Catastrophic Loss Reduction), and forest products (Catalyst Paper and Tembec).[12] Members of the Forest Products Association of Canada, who cut their GHGs 44 per cent from 1990 to 2007 by improving efficiency and switching from fossil fuels to waste-wood biomass, were an early Canadian example of the trend – already common in Britain – of major businesses pledging to become carbon neutral (FPAC 2007a). Meanwhile, the nuclear sector, its suppliers, and employees in the Power Workers' Union saw an opportunity in climate action to revive their industry. EM ideas were also evident, as noted, in the CCCE's (2007c, 2010) calls for "clean growth," although they were mixed with a dose of BAU caution.

Whatever their motives – including shaping an eventual policy framework to suit their interests – some corporations functioned as carriers of EM ideas. Among them was General Electric Canada (GE), which had a stake in all varieties of electricity, including nuclear, hydro, and wind. "Being stewards of the environment and being competitive – as businesses and countries – does not have to be an either-or proposition. We can win in both areas," GE Canada president and CEO Elyse Allan (2007) told the Climate 2050 conference in Montreal. She added a further reason to act, echoing another EM theme: "We know enough today to act on climate change, and there's no reason to delay action. In fact, the longer we wait, the harder it will be to adjust – economically, environmentally and socially – to control emissions."

The labour movement was also a key supporter of an EM climate response, as shown during the Kyoto ratification debate. The Canadian Labour Congress (CLC 2008) put forward a left-leaning EM strategy in its *Climate Change and Green Jobs* paper, with a greater role for public investment, corporate regulation, state-led industrial policy, and protective carbon tariffs than most market-oriented EM formulations, but the same win-win, pro-growth language. According to the CLC (2008, 2), "The biggest challenge of our generation could also be the biggest opportunity of the century for economic growth and good job creation." Labour did not back every climate policy proposal, sometimes finding itself in an anguished position when jobs were threatened. For example, the CAW (2007) rejected fuel efficiency policies that favoured smaller, imported vehicles. Nevertheless, the autoworkers did reaffirm support for Kyoto and appeal to environmentalists to find common ground as part of an EM coalition. Indeed, some environmental groups and labour unions – including the Communications, Energy, and Paperworkers, which represented many oil sands workers – joined the Blue Green Canada (2012) alliance, which argued that Canada could create more jobs by eliminating fossil fuel subsidies and instead prioritizing a low-carbon energy transition.

Provincial and Local EM

While the federal government was unable to move much beyond BAU, some provinces launched EM projects to cut GHGs while boosting the economy. Quebec committed to meeting the Kyoto target of a 6 per cent GHG reduction by 2012. In 2007, it introduced North America's first carbon tax on energy producers, distributors, and refiners. Quebec's climate strategy included a push to export renewable electricity from its vast hydroelectric resources and emerging wind-power sector, while in 2013 it launched an effort to make the province a leader in electric-transport technology. In 2008, British Columbia introduced a broad-based carbon tax – and its Liberal government survived to tell the tale. The tax was one of BC's key tools to cut GHGs 33 per cent from 2007 to 2020, while "stimulating low-carbon economic development" based on its renewable energy and "world-class biomass resources" (BC 2008, 3, 10). After four years, per capita consumption of fuels subject to the carbon tax fell 19 per cent in BC compared to the rest of Canada, while the province's GDP kept pace with the country as a whole (Elgie and McClay 2013). Despite the initial success, doubts grew over BC's commitment to its climate targets as fossil fuel extraction and export – in the form of liquefied natural gas – became increasingly central to the province's economic strategy (Hoekstra 2013). Alberta also introduced a carbon price in 2007; however, its intensity-based measures and climate strategy were far too weak to avoid large emissions increases in the years ahead (chapter 5). For this reason, it does not merit classification as an EM reform.[13]

Ontario was once denounced by environmentalists as a provincial climate laggard for resisting stronger auto-industry regulation and delaying a coal-power phase-out (Sierra Club of Canada 2007, 4). However, it came to be home to one of North America's most noteworthy EM initiatives. Ontario (2009) passed its Green Energy Act with much fanfare, proclaiming its intention "to attract new investment, create new green economy jobs and better protect the environment." At its core was a feed-in tariff system to encourage green investment by providing guaranteed, premium prices for renewable energy – an approach inspired by EM leaders such as Germany and Denmark. These premium prices would lead to some increase in electricity bills, but in return they would generate, the government hoped, upwards of 50,000 green jobs. Another goal was to help the province close its remaining coal-fired power plants, which was scheduled to take place in 2014, and would be one of the world's most significant carbon-reduction achievements. The act's implementation generated numerous controversies and criticisms, including questions about financial incentives and preferential grid access given to Samsung of South Korea for a $7-billion plan to build four factories to make wind and solar equipment. The WTO also ruled against the act's domestic-content requirements, designed to ensure that, even as a latecomer to EM reform, Ontario could capture a share of the job-creation benefits. Although the level of job creation was less than initially hoped, the act did trigger manufacturing investments in the province by renewable-technology makers from countries including Germany, Spain, Italy, the US, and China, as well as from within Canada. In a country where a green counterweight to the dominant petroleum sector was lacking, one of the act's most significant potential impacts was on the balance of political forces. Over time, it promised to bring more businesses and employees in the growing green-industrial sector into an advocacy coalition favouring strong climate action, as occurred in Germany as a result of its renewable energy laws (Hey 2010).

Quebec, BC, Ontario, and Manitoba – provinces representing three quarters of Canada's population – also backed a cap-and-trade system with hard caps rather than intensity targets, and joined the Western Climate Initiative (WCI), an effort to establish a carbon-trading system among American states led by California. Although the WCI later faltered, Quebec and California moved forward and agreed to link their cap-and-trade systems by 2014, while BC reached a deal with California, Oregon, and Washington to harmonize GHG-reduction policies, including carbon pricing. It appeared to be no coincidence that the early leaders among provinces had low-carbon electricity systems based on hydro power (QC, MB, BC) or nuclear (ON), putting them in a better position than fossil fuel–powered provinces to see climate policy as an opportunity rather than a threat.

One predominantly coal-fired electricity province, Nova Scotia, did nevertheless turn to EM reform. Its Environmental Goals and Sustainable Prosperity Act, introduced by a Progressive Conservative government with all-party support in 2007, set a GHG-reduction goal of at least 10 per cent below 1990 levels by 2020. In 2010, the province's NDP government set ambitious targets for renewables to supply 25 per cent of electricity by 2015 and 40 per cent by 2020, through policies including a feed-in tariff system for community projects. The plan was driven not only by hopes of green jobs, but by concerns often downplayed in the rest of Canada: enhancing domestic energy security and reducing vulnerability to the rising cost of fossil fuel imports. Nova Scotia's (2010, 3–4) "Renewable Electricity Plan" explained to residents, "Every time you turn on a light switch, money flows from your pocket out of the country to places where the coal we burn originates. Not only does this drain wealth from the province, it puts Nova Scotians at the mercy of political turmoil and natural disasters in faraway lands."

Nova Scotia planned to meet its renewable targets through its own wind, solar, biomass, and (perhaps one day) vast tidal resources, as well as through hydroelectricity imports from Newfoundland and Labrador's Lower Churchill region, starting with the Muskrat Falls project. Lower Churchill was of such great economic and symbolic importance to Newfoundland that the Harper· government, struggling to restore legitimacy in the province after years of conflict with Premier Danny Williams, backed it with a multi-billion-dollar loan guarantee and win-win EM rhetoric. A campaigning Stephen Harper called the project an "essential opportunity for an entire region of the country – Atlantic Canada – to get off of fossil fuel electricity generation [and] to move to a clean energy source. This is part of fighting climate change" (Canada.com 2011).

Meanwhile, some Canadian cities had a strong record, with the pro-EM, UK-based Climate Group (2005) recognizing Toronto as an early top-five "low-carbon leader" among global cities, while also praising initiatives in Calgary, Regina, and Halifax. Toronto (2007) later unveiled an ambitious climate plan aiming for 80 per cent emissions cuts by 2050, building on past actions such as its "Better Buildings Partnership," a job-creating, energy retrofit policy that was a model for London and the global C40 Cities Climate Leadership Group. Another Toronto innovation was Lake Ontario deep-water cooling, which replaced conventional air conditioning in downtown office towers. Proudly listing a range of cost-cutting and environmental benefits from that system, Mayor David Miller (2007) proclaimed, "it's win-win-win-win-win!" For its part, Vancouver launched a not-so-modest plan to become the "World's Greenest City." Goals included creating 20,000 new green jobs while reducing GHGs, per capita ecological footprint, and the carbon footprint of food 33 per cent below 2007 levels by 2020. According to Vancouver's (2009, 11) action plan, "Becoming the greenest city is more than an environmental objective: it's also a savvy economic strategy, for it will offer a competitive advantage in attracting highly mobile investment dollars, businesses, entrepreneurs, and talented workers."

Other EM Voices

Among other sources of calls for an EM climate response were the Ottawa-based think tank Sustainable Prosperity, the publication *Corporate Knights*, Tyler Hamilton's "Clean Break" column in the *Toronto Star*, and the government's own advisory body, the National Round Table on the Environment and the Economy. Devoted to "bringing the environment and economy together," the NRTEE produced a series of reports on "climate prosperity." In addition to the standard EM celebration of economic opportunities, the NRTEE consistently backed a national carbon price.

The Conservatives tired of that message and, in 2012, announced the closure of the twenty-five-year-old body established by the Mulroney government. Before shutting its doors, the NRTEE highlighted the dangers of Canada's lack of a low-carbon growth strategy. "Canada is unprepared to compete in a carbon constrained world," wrote the NRTEE (2012, 16). It warned of "missed opportunities and growing economic risk" (18). Possible risks included penalization of billions of dollars of Canadian exports by trade measures targeting emissions-intensive goods and the erosion of Canada's international reputation, which could limit the marketability of Canadian goods and investment opportunities abroad (19). "Allowing an economy to centre its trade on high-carbon exports *in the absence of a long-term transition plan* can lead to long-term stagnation and economic malaise," the NRTEE added (61; italics in original).

Others issued similar warnings that Canada risked a fall off the "bitumen cliff" if the demand or prices for oil sands crude were to decline significantly, which could occur, for example, if the nations of

the world acted on their expressed commitment to limit warming to
no more than 2°C (Clarke et al. 2013).[14] The threat of falling behind
in the global "mega trend" toward low-carbon energy was also expressed within the government bureaucracy (De Souza 2012a). However, neither the opportunities from action nor the risks of inaction
had yet enabled EM to become the dominant climate response.

OBSTACLES TO ECOLOGICAL MODERNIZATION IN CANADA

Why was EM reform not the primary climate response in Canada despite support from many actors and the freqent, albeit not dominant,
use of EM discourse? As noted above, Canada faced particular national circumstances that complicated GHG reductions. Being a big,
cold country helped to some degree to explain why Canada's emissions were high to start, but since the country did not get any bigger
or colder after 1990 – and actually got a little warmer – these factors
did not explain why emissions grew as they did. More rapid population and economic growth than many other OECD nations did help
explain some of that increase, but not all of it – nor did they explain
the failure to construct a consensus among government, business,
moderate environmentalists, and others around an EM project of
low-carbon growth. Other political-economic factors provide a more
complete understanding.

Prioritization of Growth – In a Fossil Fuel Export Economy

Canada's overriding concern for economic growth and international
competitiveness certainly was a key constraint on climate action. As
Smith (2002) pointed out, under the Liberals, Canadian climate
policy focused on avoiding negative economic impacts and finding
the lowest-cost options, even at the cost of weakening environmental
objectives. A similar pattern was evident under the Conservatives.
Of course, Canada was far from unique in prioritizing growth and
competitiveness. However, its economic structure and position in the
global economy put particular constraints on its climate-response
options.

Unlike most other high-income nations, Canada was marked by
its historical role as a staples economy and remained heavily dependent on primary commodity exports to core capitalist nations. Political economist Harold Innis analyzed successive waves of constrained

development based on staples exports – such as fur, fish, wheat, wood, and minerals – to more powerful nations, notably Britain and later the US. Canada did experience a period of growth in manufacturing and more technologically advanced exports from the 1960s to 1990s, but after 2000, it regressed to the earlier pattern of staples dependence with the expansion of fossil fuel exports (Stanford 2008). Efforts to become an "energy superpower" via expanded tar sands exports were leaving the Canadian economy less diversified and deepening this dependence, further strengthening those political forces that resisted strong climate action. With increasing investments in, and institutional commitment to, an oil sands–based economic strategy, Canada was moving from a "staples trap to a carbon trap," finding itself ever more locked in to a high-carbon path at the expense of a green-energy future (Haley 2011; see also T. Clarke et al. 2013).

To the extent that Canada had moved beyond staples exports to manufacturing, it was largely through automobile production – with a heavy emphasis on big, gas-guzzling, and, for a time, very profitable automobiles. In 2004, Ontario surpassed Michigan to become the North American jurisdiction with the greatest vehicle output (although Michigan regained the title in 2013). Auto production was a key source of corporate Canada's profits, Ontario government revenues, and high-paying, unionized jobs. A powerful political bloc thus resisted vehicle GHG emissions reduction policies that threatened to limit the market for large, domestically built vehicles or antagonize the automakers and drive investment elsewhere. For example, in 2006, Ontario premier Dalton McGuinty and CAW leader Buzz Hargrove denounced the Harper government's proposals to regulate vehicle emissions. Sounding at the time like a BAU resister to climate policy, McGuinty stated, "One thing we will not abide is any effort on the part of the national government to unduly impose greenhouse-gas emission reductions on the province of Ontario at the expense of our auto sector" (Canadian Press 2006a).

Given Canada's heavy dependence on the "automobile-petroleum complex" (J.B. Foster 2002), EM's promise of reconciling economic growth with environmental objectives faced particularly strong obstacles. However, with time, the automobile side of this complex became a less prominent obstacle than the petroleum side. Once the Obama administration strengthened vehicle fuel efficiency standards, Canada felt able to quickly follow suit. The auto industry's crisis of 2008–09, which brought declining output and employment, also contributed to Ontario's turn toward green energy as a way to revitalize its manufacturing sector. At the same time, the country was becoming ever-more dependent on the tar sands for profits, tax revenue, and jobs.

Regional Disparities and a Federal-Provincial Minefield

Strong climate policy also threatened to impose greater costs on regions where fossil energy and GHGs were concentrated (figure 2.1). Alberta was the most vocal opponent of Kyoto and later calls for deep GHG cuts. However, the lack of a national climate action consensus was not only an Alberta issue. Saskatchewan was another significant oil-and-gas producer that, under Premier Brad Wall, scaled back its already limited carbon-reduction measures. These two provinces, along with Nova Scotia and New Brunswick, depended heavily on coal for electricity and resisted federal measures that could sharply drive up their power costs. Other provinces, such as Quebec, had much lower emissions per dollar of GDP or per capita. "In a way Canada is a microcosm of the global community," said an Environment Canada executive. "You've got the heavy emitters, you've got low emitters, and people in between."

The most high-profile political challenge nevertheless involved Alberta, where fears abounded that federal climate action would be comparable to a return of the National Energy Program of 1980, which was seen to have benefited central Canada at the province's expense, and which left profound resentment. The reluctance of the federal government, regardless of the party in power, to introduce strong carbon constraints reflected in part a desire to avoid rekindling western alienation and even separatist sentiment. Meanwhile, since provinces had jurisdiction over natural resources, including fossil fuels and electricity, the federal government did not have full control over climate-relevant policy. Potential existed for a constitutional clash and a national unity crisis if the federal government imposed GHG targets that limited the ability of recalcitrant provinces to develop their natural resources (Makin 2007). The choice of weak carbon-reduction targets was thus consistent with the need to maintain legitimacy of the Canadian confederation domestically (even if that same choice threatened to erode Canada's legitimacy in the global arena and, over time, might generate its own tensions domestically).

Figure 2.1 GHG emissions per capita, by jurisdiction (tonnes CO$_2$ equivalent)

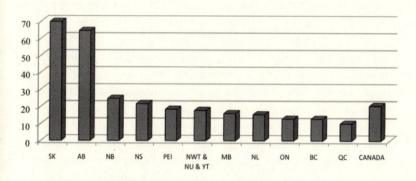

Data Source: Environment Canada (2013a, 35); data for 2011.

Canada's weak federal-provincial relations system was not successful in managing these regional disparities and in reaching a consensus on sharing the efforts of GHG reduction, a problem exacerbated by a lack of determined federal leadership or the emergence of a province able to play a climate leadership role (Macdonald 2008). (The European Union, which in 1997–98 and 2008 reached agreements among its disparate member states on allocating emissions reductions efforts, provided a notable contrast.) Instead, Canada saw the emergence of an incoherent patchwork of climate measures, as a few provinces introduced significant green policies while others remained committed to a high-carbon growth path.

Ideology

A number of observers identified the ideology and institutions of neoliberalism as another, related constraint on climate action. After the first decade of weak responses, Bernstein and Cashore (2002) noted that Canadian environmental policies were strongly influenced by a "liberal environmentalism" norm complex that embraces economic expansion, free trade, and market forces to address environmental issues. They argued that policy responses to climate change are "likely to be possible only to the degree that they are seen as consistent with Canada's competitive and trade goals" (225). Soron (2004) argued that Canada's contradictory approach – ratifying Kyoto, yet working to weaken its provisions in international talks and avoiding strong domestic measures – was a product of its "broader strategic commitment to an emergent neoliberal trade and investment regime which has in many ways deepened its dependency upon the US and created significant barriers to the pursuit of meaningful environmental reform at home and abroad" (44). CAW economist Jim Stanford (2002, 56) maintained that Canada's climate goals were compatible with economic growth, but only if the government abandoned its "laissez faire approach to economic and industrial policy."

The constraints of neo-liberalism, while significant, were not the full reason why Canada lagged far behind in EM reform. Other countries, such as the UK under New Labour and later the Conservative-led coalition, were also committed to neo-liberalism and yet achieved a better, if not spotless, climate record. However, breaking with neo-liberalism was particularly important in Canada. Unfettered markets pointed toward the most profitable short-term path: continued fossil fuel–centred growth, letting the carbon fall where it may. Shifting Canada off its carbon-intensive trajectory would require more determined political action than in countries with a lower-carbon economic structure. In addition, neo-liberalism took a particular form in North America that, as discussed below, had a more corrosive effect on national climate policy efforts than in the EU.

Although neo-liberalism was a constraint, government commitment to it was selective. Alberta ruled out intervention to slow down tar sands expansion as an unacceptable limitation on the market, yet it was willing to subsidize CCS to the tune of $2 billion (chapter 5) – and the federal approach was similar. Meanwhile, after attacking the Liberal's carbon-tax proposal and abandoning its own cap-and-trade plan, the Conservative government was in the curious position of favouring the least market-oriented response: sector-by-sector regulation.

Outside of government, ideological obstacles were particularly strong on the libertarian right – where objections existed even to the Harper government's minimal climate policies and to corporate support for a limited version of EM. For true believers in unfettered markets, calls for climate regulations or carbon pricing amounted to a "yellow brick road to green serfdom," which is how columnist Peter Foster (2010), channelling Friedrich Hayek, depicted the Canadian Council of Chief Executives (CCCE 2010) report on "clean growth."

So Close to the United States

Proximity to the US was an obstacle to a Canadian EM project in more ways than one. First, US climate inaction – exemplified by withdrawal from the Kyoto process – generated concerns among Canadian manufacturers and energy producers that they would lose out in the US market due to cost increases not faced by competitors (CCCE 2002, 2; Doern 2005). Since roughly 75 per cent of Canada's exports went to its southern neighbour, it had seemed unlikely that Canada would ratify Kyoto without the US. Canada did ratify, but continued competitiveness concerns vis-à-vis the US helped explain why policy measures with a fighting chance of achieving the Kyoto target were never introduced and, even after the Kyoto goals were replaced with much more modest ones, policy implementation continued to be delayed.

Second, as discussed in more detail in chapter 5, the US looked to Canada as a secure, friendly petroleum source – creating economic opportunity and vast GHG emissions from Alberta's tar sands. Meanwhile, economic integration with the US through NAFTA provided no impetus to stronger climate action, unlike the EU's impact on Britain. In fact, NAFTA's proportionality clause – which prohibited Canada from reducing the percentage of its total oil and gas output that it exported to the US – severely limited Canada's ability to reduce fossil fuel exports, were it to try to do so to cut GHGs or ensure its own energy security (Laxer and Dillon 2008). More speculatively, exposure to media and culture from the US, where climate scepticism was strong, particularly among conservatives, likely contributed to sowing uncertainty among some Canadians and strengthening homegrown climate contrarians' resolve.

The end of the Bush era did change matters to some degree, although less than many observers first expected. Replacement of a BAU president with one favourable to EM raised expectations of comprehensive US climate legislation and a cap-and-trade system that would force Canada to catch up. Such expectations were later dashed as climate issues became entangled in the culture wars polarizing US politics, but narrower action by the Obama administration during its first term, notably on vehicle fuel efficiency, did lead to new Canadian policy. Additional pressures on Canada to improve its climate record grew after the president's 2012 re-election and statements that he would only approve the Keystone XL pipeline, which would carry Canadian crude to the Gulf Coast, if it would not "significantly exacerbate the problem of carbon pollution" (Obama 2013). At the same time, US oil output was growing rapidly, raising the possibility that it would not always be as eager to import Canada's high-carbon oil.

Big Country, Frontier Mentality

Another obstacle to EM was the impact on mentalities of living in a country with the world's second largest land mass, but a population little more than half that of Britain. As sociologist and former MP Lynn McDonald put it, Canadians "are still living on the frontier ... Europeans have learnt to live with limits more, but there was always an escape in the Americas. But that escape is no longer available and our mentality hasn't caught up with that." Former environment minister Sheila Copps (2004, 91–2) similarly wrote:

> I remember hosting a G8 environment ministers meeting in my hometown of Hamilton where British minister John Gummer singled out Canada as one of the worst offenders in the growth of fossil-fuel emissions. Mr. Gummer was right. Our great size as a country had been a blessing and a curse – a blessing because, unlike the United Kingdom, we have huge tracts of uninhabited land and a sense that the country and its environmental potential is unblemished; a curse because the very vastness of Canada has led to a sense that we don't need to plan our urban living in the same sort of detail as the Europeans. We just keep building out, out, and out with the sprawl, congestion, and fossil-fuel emissions that go along with the North American mentality that the car is king. The Europeans don't have that luxury.

It is difficult to specify precisely how significant this factor is, but one way that the frontier mentality manifested itself was in a tendency to see climate change as not only a threat, but also an opportunity to open up new areas for resource extraction – in line with a Promethean or Cornucopian worldview that underlies BAU. According to one voice in the *Globe and Mail* (Zellen 2008):

As the polar ice melts, we'll witness the gradual emergence of a
brand new world, unlocking what just a few years ago would have
been unimaginable economic opportunities, as the long-closed
Arctic waterways open up to rising volumes of commercial shipping
and naval traffic, and as the thinning (and later disappearing) ice
makes it more cost effective, and technologically viable, to explore
the region's undersea natural resource potential, and to fully develop those new discoveries.

This new world is not unlike that discovered by early explorers
when they journeyed across the Atlantic, from the Old World to
the New, in search of undiscovered countries and riches. We, too,
are on a journey of discovery to a new and unknown world – a
world full of riches that are unknown, but not unimagined.

Understanding the prevalence and importance of such frontier
thinking would require further research; nevertheless, such ideas
undoubtedly undermined the case for carbon-reduction policies in
at least some Canadian minds. The sense of endless opportunities
and possibilities for escape inherent in frontier thinking may also
help to explain the contradictions between the fact that Canadians
expressed considerable climate concern in opinion polls, but did not
appear to feel that concern deeply enough to demand strong climate
action from their leaders.

Other factors noted above that also held back EM reform included
the strong presence of BAU and climate-sceptic views in the media
(and indeed within government), as well as the political divisions that
prevented an EM majority from forming governments in 2008 and
2011.

HARD CHOICES: THE NEED TO GO BEYOND "WIN-WIN"

One of the first scholarly editions following Kyoto ratification on the
implications of climate change for Canada, *Hard Choices* (Coward and
Weaver 2004), was notable for a distinctively un-EM title. Critics of
Canada's record and outdated frontier mentality might find the title
of another book, *Stupid to the Last Drop*, journalist William Marsden's
(2007) account of the drive to develop Alberta's oil sands despite
the ecological consequences, to be more relevant to understanding Canada's failures. Regardless of whether a difficult context or

short-sighted folly was more important, EM clearly faced considerable
challenges in establishing itself in Canada, given the factors identified above.

Some key sectors saw major costs right from the outset of climate-
related reform efforts. For example, David Lewin of EPCOR recalled
that during negotiations with Environment Canada under Minister
Stéphane Dion, his power company asked where the much vaunted
win-win opportunities were. "We never did get a good answer because
there isn't one," said Lewin. He acknowledged that some other industries could benefit and saw some potential for Canada to lead in
CCS technology, but added, "There will be huge pain, too, in some
sectors. So we shouldn't kid ourselves ... It's going to be extremely expensive. We are moving into a much higher cost electricity environment than we have ever been in before."

Similarly, when asked about obstacles to large GHG cuts in Canada,
Rick Hyndman of the Canadian Association of Petroleum Producers
stated, "The real obstacle is cost. And then right behind that, or related to it, is the lack of public support and political will to do things
that will have a cost fall on the public." He added, "There's a total dis-
connect in the public's mind between doing something and bearing
the cost of having to do it ... The failure to accept that by the public
and the failure of the politicians to actually tell them they have to do
that, I think, has kept us from doing anything serious."

Other factors, such as resistance from within the petroleum industry, also had something to do with it, but Hyndman raised an important challenge to EM. He acknowledged the existence of some win-
win options, and expressed frustration, for example, over the failure
to introduce win-win measures such as stronger building efficiency
standards. However, referring to analysis of carbon-cutting options
by the consultancy McKinsey & Company, he argued that to get large
emissions reductions, "pretty soon you get into significant cost." He
added, "The win-win argument, I think, in a way has a net negative
effect because it lulls the population [into thinking] they don't have
to incur any cost to deal with this thing, and that's not true."

One might take coal-power and oil industry representatives' comments on the costs of climate action with a grain of salt, but others
provided a similar perspective on the limits of an EM framing of the
issue. An Environment Canada executive with years of experience
with the climate file stated that one key change over time, in addition

to growing recognition of the climate problem, was "the recognition that action may impose costs on industry and society at large – that it's not necessarily a win-win situation."

Analysis from environmental organizations also showed that strong climate action would have economic costs, even if these groups highlighted other messages. Behind the titles of the *Deep Reductions, Strong Growth* and *Climate Leadership, Economic Prosperity* reports by the Pembina Institute and David Suzuki Foundation (2008, 2009) were findings that challenged an EM message. Economic modelling for these reports showed that a 25 per cent GHG cut below 1990 levels by 2020 would leave GDP 3.0 to 3.2 per cent lower than under a BAU scenario – i.e. $53 to $56 billion lower (MKJA 2009, 73), or roughly $1,600 less per Canadian. "Output reduction" relative to BAU would be a key emissions reduction source, representing 8.7 or 15.5 per cent of the needed cuts, depending on the scenario (MKJA 2009, 34–5). Absolute reductions in output in carbon-intensive sectors such as petroleum refining and natural gas extraction would result, and the slowing of GDP growth would be most significant in Alberta, with GDP 12 per cent below BAU projections by 2020. A carbon price far above the levels considered by governments to date – $50 per tonne, rising to $200 by 2020 – would also be needed.

That said, this economic analysis did find that GDP would still grow considerably, although more slowly – 2.1 per cent annually compared to 2.4 per cent in a BAU scenario (Pembina Institute and David Suzuki Foundation 2009, iii–iv; see also MKJA 2009, 11–12). Alberta would still have the country's fastest economic growth rate and employment growth would not be affected. The costs were certainly manageable in a rich country and compared favourably to estimated costs of climate inaction (Stern 2006). However, the study assumed widespread and rapid adoption of CCS – a technology with questionable prospects. The emissions target chosen, albeit deep by Canadian standards, was at the low end of the 25 to 40 per cent range many international environmental groups and climate scientists called for in rich nations by 2020, and others saw a need for much deeper cuts by rich nations (e.g. Athanasiou et al. 2009; Hansen, Sato, et al. 2008). In other words, the level of economic output Canada would have to give up to do its part to avoid climate catastrophe could be considerably greater than this study acknowledged. Even using the study's figures as a guide, it would require much greater public willingness to accept economic costs than had been evident so far, not to mention political conflict with the sectors and regions most affected.

Indeed, a hostile reaction followed. "There will be blood," wrote one *National Post* commentator on the implications of the Pembina Institute and Suzuki Foundation's proposed targets (Libin 2009). Environment Minister Jim Prentice called the conclusions "irresponsible," adding that Canadians would not accept GHG targets that would reduce GDP growth by such a degree, while ministers in Alberta and Saskatchewan rejected "divisive" curbs of their economies (Curry and Walton 2009). Whether the conclusions were "irresponsible" or the start of an "adult conversation about tackling climate change," as the Pembina Institute put it (Demerse 2009), this debate suggested that gaining support for deep GHG cuts in Canada would require dethroning economic growth as the top priority, contrary to win-win EM rhetoric.

With demands for climate action unlikely to go away, something had to give. To break through Canada's climate logjam, and create price signals that passed real costs onto consumers, Hyndman gave his personal support to a carbon tax – and other oil industry figures later followed (Belfry Munroe 2010; Van Loon and Mayeda 2013) – as long as its design did not create competitive disadvantage for industry or transfer wealth out of Alberta.[15] Others, as discussed in the following chapters, were willing to question the priority given to economic growth or at least certain forms of growth – notably that of the tar sands. Although very different in key ways, including regarding who would bear the cost, these perspectives shared the idea that the economic win-win sphere was not big enough in Canada to fully address the problem, and, therefore, there was a need to prepare people and build support for some economically costly action.

CONCLUSIONS

Whether an inherent conflict existed between economic growth and climate stability was a more complex question, but given existing technology, significant conflict existed between a growth strategy centred on fossil fuel exports and the deep emissions cuts required for Canada to be a responsible contributor to global climate solutions. This basic problem, which was complicated by other political-economic considerations, notably the concentration of high-carbon economic activity in certain provinces, hampered Canada's ability to live up to its seemingly strong environmental values and past leadership on green issues.

Canada's climate battles often pitted one side rejecting strong climate action as too costly against another emphasizing economic gains from carbon reduction. These tensions between BAU and EM reflected the dual nature of Canada's economy, as climate action offered opportunities to some firms and sectors, while threatening the dominant high-carbon sectors with major costs and limits on their expansion. Beyond questions of interests, ideology was also a factor, as Canada needed to move beyond neo-liberalism to make a low-carbon transition, while some on the libertarian right rejected any expanded government role to kick-start an EM process.

A form of synthesis between BAU and EM perspectives also emerged. When in power, the Liberals embraced an EM discourse of economic opportunity, but facing strong business, conservative, and regional resistance, never implemented policies capable of moving Canada substantially beyond BAU in practice. The Conservatives, on the other hand, came to power steeped in climate scepticism, but were pushed by public opinion toward announcing some limited action. Tory rhetoric also changed, with a degree of win-win language accompanying climate policy announcements, while still emphasizing the costs of climate action, which needed to be "balanced" with the perceived imperative of economic growth.

Whatever discourse they used, Liberal and Tory governments long limited themselves to policy instruments that would not impinge heavily on business or broader economic-growth objectives, i.e. voluntary measures, public spending, and intensity-based regulation (Macdonald 2008) – the latter repeatedly delayed and consisting of weak targets relative to the environmental need. The Conservatives did later introduce regulations on vehicle emissions and coal-fired power plants, but were in no hurry to put constraints on most large industrial emitters, including tar sands operations. Some other elements of Canada's climate policy playbook were also evident. Do a few visible things now (e.g. subsidize public transit passes, pledge to phase out incandescent light bulbs). Spend money in ways that promise immediate political gains (e.g. first-generation biofuels). Invest in technologies that will hopefully expand the win-win terrain in the future (e.g. second-generation biofuels and, especially, CCS). Until technology provides a way out of Canada's dilemmas, keep fighting at global talks – and in Washington and Brussels (chapter 5) – to ensure that carbon constraints and green energy policies elsewhere do not undermine a fossil fuel–based growth strategy. If US action changes the cost-benefit calculation by lessening competitiveness concerns from being ahead of the US, or threatening costs from falling behind, re-evaluate. Above all, do nothing that will prevent the rapid expansion of output from the increasingly dominant fossil fuel sector.

Many groups within Canada worked toward something different: a vision of green jobs, profits, and prosperity. However, despite pockets of opportunity and innovation, they were not yet able to overcome the forces of resistance and establish EM as the dominant perspective. It was also questionable how appropriate EM's win-win rhetoric was to Canada's political economy, given the challenges and costs key sectors and regions faced in moving off a carbon-intensive growth path.

The centrality of the BAU-EM conflict created a very difficult context for sufficiency to find a viable way into the political fray. Sufficiency shared the EM view that strong climate action was necessary and the BAU suspicion that this would conflict with the pursuit of endless economic growth. Yet raising the idea of curbing growth risked fuelling the BAU perspective, which warned precisely of a low-growth future if climate action went too far. But if there really was considerable conflict between endless GDP growth and deep emissions reductions, *and* those deep emissions reductions had to occur to avoid climate catastrophe, then the difficult task of challenging growth had to be confronted. It is to that perspective that we now turn.

3

"Excuse Me, Excuse Me": Struggles to Put Sufficiency on Canada's Agenda

Amid a sea of suits at the Climate 2050 conference in Montreal, I listened to GE Canada's president and CEO deliver a template ecological modernization speech, peppered with talk of "thinking green – and earning lots of green too." I noticed the fellow next to me, an employee of a global manufacturing firm with a strong environmental reputation, drawing in his notebook a human brain with various segments, dollar signs branded onto each of them. "That's all they can think about – money," he told me, referring to the typical business response to climate change. "There's no reflection on what they've done to this point to damage the planet." That led to a discussion of the limited range of ideas – a standard EM diet of technology, efficiency, and new profit opportunities, backed by market- and corporate-friendly policies and a new global climate deal – presented at the conference. Where was the discussion of the excesses of our consumerist, growth-oriented societies, he asked? Where do we start in achieving the deeper social and economic reorganization that is needed, or even creating a conversation about it?

A few days later: another city, another conference, a similar encounter. As the Business of Climate Change event in Ottawa drew to a close, I overheard a discussion behind me about the absence of "excessive consumerism" and "excessive capitalism" on the agenda. I turned around and struck up a conversation with Randal Goodfellow, who played senior roles in bio-products and renewable energy firms. "We're living by the wrong philosophy," he told me. "We have a flawed image of the good life," the "pinnacle" of which is Las Vegas. "The math doesn't work if everyone is trying to consume like us in the wealthy nations – we don't have three planets," he noted. Goodfellow advocated lifestyles of simplicity and less consumption, but

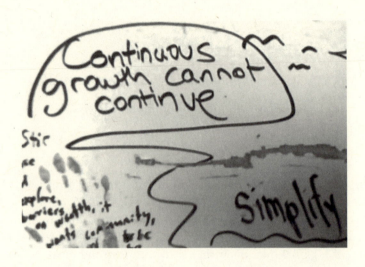

Figure 3.1 Message wall, Occupy Halifax, October 2011. Photo by author.

emphasized, "It's not capitalism but excessive capitalism that's the problem." Although he was not talking about revolution, no one wanted to discuss these issues in such forums, he added. Well, not exactly no one. Such perspectives were generally kept off the agenda at such elite business and government events, but there always seemed to be at least one dissident in the house.

Dissenting voices regarding contemporary excess also were evident at events open to a wider public audience. "The excessive consumption of a hyper-individualistic society is very dysfunctional," said one voice from the floor during a debate over carbon offsets in Toronto. "We're trying to sustain a lifestyle that cannot be sustained – that's the problem," said another during an event about green electricity. Such voices of sufficiency were audible if one was listening for them, but it was as if they had to continually edge their way into a discussion framed around some other aspect of the climate question.

The idea of sufficiency was typically absent from the climate solutions proposed by government, business, mainstream political parties, and, for the most part, even environmental groups, but it did make its way into the debate in various ways. This chapter looks at some of the individuals and groups struggling to find ways to put a transition beyond economic growth and excessive consumerism on the agenda as a core part of the solution to climate change, while it also considers the great obstacles facing a direct challenge to the growth paradigm.

PROPHETS OF A NEW ECONOMY: INDIVIDUAL CRITICS OF GROWTH

A critique of economic growth was not entirely absent from Canada's climate debate. However, without support from organizations with the capacity to put macro-level sufficiency on the mainstream agenda, such ideas came largely from relatively isolated, individual voices.

The Academics

Many of the most prominent voices critical of growth in Canada came from the academic world, where the space available to challenge economic growth without undermining one's career was somewhat larger than in other parts of the social world, including the political sphere and even the environmental movement. Although these academics spoke of great obstacles to their ideas and worked to find ways to expand discussion of alternatives to growth, there were also signs of emerging opportunities to be heard.

Peter Victor (2008), an ecological economist at Toronto's York University, presented a direct challenge to the growth paradigm in his book *Managing Without Growth: Slower By Design, Not Disaster*. He argued that further economic growth was not viable in the long term for environmental reasons, growth was failing to increase well-being in the already affluent nations, and growth was neither necessary nor sufficient to meet key social objectives. His LowGrow economic model showed that in Canada, opting for a period of slower economic growth, and then no growth, combined with a steep $200 per tonne carbon tax could cut GHG emissions significantly (181–3). With the right complementary measures – including work-time reduction, active labour market policies, redistributive social spending, reduction and redirection of investment, and population stabilization via lower immigration – low/no growth was compatible with full employment and reducing poverty. He also showed that global CO_2 emission cuts of 60 per cent over fifty years were possible if improvements in energy intensity and CO_2 per unit energy matched the high end of recent historical gains, but only assuming zero growth in high-income nations (111–20). In a later article, Victor's (2012) modelling of Canada's economy showed that a degrowth scenario – with large reductions in work time and income – would lead to much deeper GHG cuts by 2050 than business-as-usual, low/no growth, or selective growth scenarios, with higher-growth scenarios requiring much greater, historically unprecedented reductions in GHG intensity to reach an 80 per cent GHG reduction target.

Victor did not see low or zero growth as an objective in itself. Rather, he urged strong action on climate and other environmental problems without worrying so much about the impact on GDP. "We need to question the primacy of growth, which is used as an argument against doing what is right on the environment," he said on CBC Radio's (2008) *The Current* – on one of the occasions that his radical message broke through into mainstream media.

The conclusion that we could manage without growth was of great potential significance given the limits of decoupling growth from environmental impacts to date. Yet prior to his book's release, Victor had limited expectations about his findings' impact. "We have a society committed to growth. And I think it will take a long time before that commitment gets reflected upon in any thorough way," Victor told me. "We can conceive of an economy which doesn't rely on growth and yet still performs very well in other respects. The hardest part is getting from where we are now to such a configuration. And I am not very optimistic. I put my ideas out there because I think that if you don't even see the possibility, then it's going to be even harder to get there." He also acknowledged that much more work was needed to further develop such an analysis, but few resources were being channelled in that direction. "You've got an enormous amount of intellectual energy and resources going into the promotion of growth," he explained. "And what you've got questioning that is a handful of people – so few really that we are kind of like endangered species in that we have trouble finding each other, even with the Internet."

Nevertheless, his book did find a receptive audience, a fact that suggests that the obstacles to a sufficiency message coincided with significant unease over pursuit of endless growth. One indication of this was that some 150 people had to be turned away from the Toronto launch of Victor's book in November 2008, which coincided with the global economic slowdown's relatively late arrival in Canada. He was also inundated with requests to speak. "It's quite encouraging," Victor told the *Toronto Star* (Goar 2008a). "People come up to me at these events and say, 'I've been thinking these sorts of things for a long time.'" Victor told me in 2012 that he sensed a growing mainstream interest in his work, which he attributed in part to the impact of the financial crisis in encouraging a wider range of people to consider the possibility that we may need to learn – whether for ecological or other reasons – how to manage without growth.

Another Canadian academic engaged in questioning growth was William Rees, a professor at the University of British Columbia's School of Community and Regional Planning and originator of the "ecological footprint" concept. Like other sufficiency advocates, claims that eco-efficiency and technology provided adequate answers to climate change and other ecological problems did not impress Rees. Improved efficiency amounted to a "kind of mythic idol worshipped to sustain the status quo," he said, and which allowed us to "become more efficiently unsustainable – not a particularly productive advance."

Rees gave a mixed picture of the inroads made by the idea of sufficiency with respect to GDP growth. On the one hand, "Those of us playing the limits-to-growth card aren't getting a lot of currency," he said. "There are an increasing number of voices at the margin, but not in the mainstream." He added, "The idea of limits to growth is an anathema to any government in the world today, which is very much beholden to the corporate sector for its political support." The "privileged, moneyed elites" who have gained significant control over the political process in most countries "are threatened by any limit to growth because then the only viable option for relieving poverty is income redistribution. Indeed, any threat to the capitalist techno-industrial structure of our society threatens their well-being. I think the inherent hostility to material limits is exceedingly strong." He added that, although he had irregular contact with individual dissenters among senior government bureaucrats, "Clearly there is no department of any government in Canada that would argue against maintaining continual growth. In fact, government scientists today are effectively muzzled on any significant issue – prevented from openly discussing even their own research results."

Even so, he saw some evidence that "limits to growth is back on the table." As we spoke, an email arrived, with the headline "Power

Plant Rejected over Carbon Dioxide for First Time," about the blocking of a coal-fired plant in Kansas due to its climate impact. "That's a
limits-to-growth decision," said Rees. "If everyone felt there were excess capacity for carbon dioxide assimilation in the ecosphere, there
would be no question about that plant going forward." Meanwhile,
the ecological footprint method that Rees and one of his students
have developed (Wackernagel and Rees 1996) – which estimates the
amount of land area needed to support a population's consumption
and which he designed "precisely to reopen the whole question of human carrying capacity" – had been adopted for many uses around the
world by numerous organizations including the European Commission and WWF. The related concept of "one-planet living" had spread
in the UK and elsewhere. "To the extent that eco-footprinting is now
a global phenomenon and clearly rubs our noses into the limits issue,
I think it has had some success in reopening that limits-to-growth
question," said Rees. Indeed, eco-footprinting enabled organizations
to raise the matter of ecological constraints indirectly and to document the limits of EM strategies, although often without speaking specifically of "limits to growth."

Thomas Homer-Dixon, a professor of international affairs and
environment at the University of Waterloo, was another Canadian
raising such issues. In his assessment, findings from climate science
implied the need for 100 per cent emissions cuts before 2050, which
would likely constrain economic growth, as would the decline of
easily accessible fossil energy. "Global warming fundamentally challenges capitalism's growth imperative," wrote Homer-Dixon (2007,
264). However, he said in an interview that global warming was far
from the only problem. "Getting rid of carbon isn't enough. Every
single system is stressed," he said, referring to problems with nitro-
gen, sulphur, biodiversity, topsoil, and water use – "all independently
of climate." He offered this image of the problem: "We're like a fully
loaded freight train speeding down towards the end of a track and
the track ends. There is a cliff beyond the end of that track. We've got
an enormous amount of momentum. And we're having a party in the
cab. Nobody's looking out the window. Well, a few people look out
of the window and say, 'excuse me, excuse me.' But nobody is paying
attention."

Homer-Dixon predicted "sometime this century growth will end.
It could be voluntary or involuntary." In principle, it was possible to

decouple material throughput growth from GDP, but, like others, he noted that GDP growth was overwhelming eco-efficiency gains, which were unlikely to be sustained indefinitely in any case (Homer-Dixon 2007, 98–9). Referring to the *Limits to Growth* report's scenario of large-scale global collapse beginning around 2030 (Meadows et al. 1972), he stated, "I'm wondering if we're going to make it to 2030." Unlike some conventional Malthusians, he did not ignore the role of efficiency and technology, stimulated by the price mechanism and scarcity-induced incentives, to push back limits: "I have explored in real depth the contrary argument: the cornucopian argument ... We have science. We have markets. We have democracy and so we're historically exceptional or biologically exceptional because we've got this unbelievable problem-solving ability. I take that argument really, really seriously ... The problem is that we are creating challenges faster than we can solve them."

This "ingenuity gap" (Homer-Dixon 2001) can be addressed from two sides. While the dominant emphasis has been on trying to increase the supply of ingenuity, Homer-Dixon noted, "Another place to start is to slow down the rapidity with which the requirement curve is rising. That would involve things like reducing our material throughput, because to the extent that we're putting more and more load on the world environment and resource system, we are generating harder and harder problems for ourselves." However, he said, "if we are going to ramp down material throughput for the whole planet, it means that probably we are not going to be able to continue growth as we define it now." Homer-Dixon noted a paradoxical problem: "Slowing down the rapid rate of increase in our requirement for ingenuity itself imposes an ingenuity requirement. You have to be smart to figure out how you don't have to be so smart." Any move toward a steady state alternative would raise challenging questions, such as how, in the absence of growth, to maintain the technological innovation that is not sufficient but still necessary to address environmental challenges.

Homer-Dixon (2006; see also 2011) put forward a critique of growth in publications including the *New York Times* and *Foreign Policy*, writing that "we really need to start thinking hard about how our societies – especially those that are already very rich – can maintain their social and political stability, and satisfy the aspirations of their citizens, when we can no longer count on endless economic growth."

He also tried to put these questions to government, having been invited to make a presentation to the Department of Finance in Ottawa. He sent Finance officials a description of his talk, with a proposed title of "Beyond the Growth Imperative." It was sent back to him with a revised title: "Sustainable Growth." "I was blown away. That's really indicative, isn't it?" Homer-Dixon said. "It just didn't fit the mindset."

While political and economic leaders were for the most part "not even on the page," he noted that his *New York Times* piece on the new limits to growth "ruffled fewer feathers than I was expecting … It seemed like people reacted more as if that were much closer to a mainstream and acceptable argument than it was a number of years ago."

Homer-Dixon saw the possibility ahead of an intensifying climate crisis provoking authoritarian responses. One danger of such a "war mobilization scenario" was that an authoritarian government would suppress the freedoms, creativity, and innovation needed to develop both technological solutions and new ways of living. "The standard response in a world of crisis is clamp down on all the weird guys," he said. "Shut down people on the margins." Instead, he argued for "distributed problem solving," which means "lots of people trying different things and experimenting – and that involves maintaining freedom."

Creating space to explore radical political, social, and economic alternatives was also on the mind of Lynn McDonald, a sociology professor emerita at Guelph University, former MP and NDP environment critic, and co-founder of JustEarth: A Coalition for Environmental Justice. McDonald (2007, 2008) called for profound "social change to meet climate change," including moves away from consumerism and deep reforms to corporate structures and capitalism, amounting to a new "green Enlightenment." "We need to have a really substantial change," said McDonald. "There is this naïve idea that efficiency will do it." With respect to the idea that growth and environment could go hand in hand, McDonald stated, "it can only in certain respects – such as more growth in the windmill and solar panel industries. Obviously, the earth is finite and you cannot count on sustainable growth in an unlimited fashion. But it is not popular to say these things." She added that it was not just a matter of "getting the right things going," but "stopping the things that are wrong," and urged consideration of moratoria on high-carbon growth such as tar sands expansion, new airport runways, and highway construction (McDonald 2007). To create a forum to grapple with the necessary social change, including sufficiency-based ideas such as carbon rationing, proposed by Monbiot (2006b) in the UK, McDonald proposed a series of town hall meetings or "think-ins" across Canada. This, she argued, would give a platform to voices excluded from mainstream discussions focused on "technological fixes." It would allow people to say, "Look, we need to be more serious about this."

Despite their different focuses, all of these academics emphasized the limits of an EM project, particularly the fact that eco-efficiency gains were failing to keep up with economic growth and, in their assessment, were unlikely to be enough in the future. Similarly, they all struggled to find ways to open up public discussion about the fixation with growth and potential alternatives, as others outside the academic world were also trying to do.

The Politician

"I'm in a really foul mood," began Toronto City Councillor Gord Perks (2007a), prepping the audience for a blunt analysis of the state of the planet. This was not a typical outward image for an elected politician. However, for Perks, a former environmental activist, the implications of climate change were stark. He was one of the rare elected politicians to argue that climate change required a radical embrace of sufficiency. "The future we're going to live in cannot be like the present. That option is not available," he told a "climate justice" teach-in in Toronto organized by environmental, social justice, labour, and aboriginal activists. He believed that we probably could not avoid severe consequences from climate change, including rising oceans, declining food production, and "a dramatic increase in human migrations on a scale never seen before." The likelihood of such a future, he said, left a choice of two visions. "Fortress Earth" was an outcome feared by many observers, in which privileged parts of the world gate themselves off, restrict immigration, and fight resource wars abroad. Indeed, it was a scenario for which the Pentagon, among others, was preparing. Instead, Perks favoured a "Just Earth" based on a globally equitable distribution of resources, including the Earth's limited carbon sinks. "We can't live the lifestyles our parents lived. We need to surrender many of our privileges – of race, class, consumption – and live a lifestyle that doesn't consume at the expense of other places." At a previous public talk, he explained that sustainable globally equitable per capita carbon emissions were between half a tonne and one tonne per year, compared to Canada's 20-tonne average (Perks 2007b). The upshot: "we need to consume 95 per cent less." This, Perks added, would require "a non-consumer, non-military society."

When asked about reactions to his calls for radically reduced consumption, Perks described various forms of resistance depending on people's ideological predispositions and social position. His blunt message met a rough reception from an older Rotary Club crowd with a belief, as Perks described it, in the notion that "our current economic and political arrangement is one of perpetual growth and that's a good thing … It's only when regulators get in the way that we slow down the inevitable march of progress." But Perks said that kind of BAU reaction was no longer as common as in the late 1980s, when he worked for Greenpeace and would "get red-baited and laughed at." Instead, Perks increasingly encountered forms of "intellectual juggling" to "come up with new strategies that maintain existing structures and somehow respond to a more and more obvious imperative for change." These included the beliefs that "there is a technology fix coming around the corner, and that if we buy slightly better gizmos to replace the current gizmos we have, then everything will stay the same and the ecological crisis will be averted." This new perspective – that is, EM – led to a "green consumerism that is, unfortunately, very convenient to large manufacturers and retailers, and given the kinds of resources [they] can put on the table, it's fast becoming the dominant kind of response to climate change."

It was not only among conservative or centrist defenders of existing social structures that Perks encountered resistance. "There is an area where you get resistance even among really progressive people," he noted. "You can't solve the problem just by getting people on to public transit, using energy efficient light bulbs, and buying local. Even if you do all those things you still don't get there." Alongside structural change in the economy, he argued, "some lifestyle change in terms of the individual" was also necessary. As an example of the latter, he said: "I have decided I am not going to fly anymore. It's just too much carbon. And when I talk to folks about that, first they look at you like you're kind of an oddball. Then they say, 'Boy, do you ever have your principles' as if I have made some giant sacrifice they wish they could make, but they are not convinced, or [ask] why shouldn't they get to go visit art galleries in Paris … That's the part that I still haven't figured out how to teach very well. But it's the conversation we have to start having … In my view giving up certain unsustainable privileges … isn't having less, it's an argument about having different."

Yet resistance was not the only reaction. Perks told of a CBC radio interview in which he took issue with a spokesperson from a green trade show whose message amounted to "Go buy more stuff to save the planet." Perks said, "What amazed me is that I got emails from all over the country from people saying, 'Finally an elected official who is talking about how we need to buy less stuff.'"

To gain support for a vision of more justice and less stuff, Perks emphasized the potential for a better quality of life. On the one hand, he thought it was time to consider some consumption aspirations as "out of reach, as ridiculous." For example: "You don't get unlimited travel in this lifetime. The planet just can't provide that to ten billion people. You don't get several thousand square feet for each family. We just can't build that housing stock and heat it." On the other hand, a less consumptive society could emphasize benefits such as the ability to work less and enjoy increased leisure, universal access to high-quality education and healthcare, better air and water quality, real participation in workplace decisions, toxin-free food, fewer wars and less violence, and more equitable wealth distribution. "You start to realize that stepping out of the hyper-consumption economy for ecological reasons frees up political and economic space to address other deep problems that we have had for a very long time," said Perks. "We have a moment right now where we could find a common purpose of replacing the consumer economy with a just economy." Organizing around that common purpose, however, was in its infancy as mainstream environmental groups were reluctant to talk about justice, while labour and other social movements had yet to fully realize the implications of ecological limits. "I think the synthesis is there," he said. "What's missing are the voices talking about the synthesis."

Perks admitted that he did not always raise these broad issues: "I self-censor a bit, too. There's only so far I can take certain audiences." For example, he said, when he was working to build support for Toronto's ambitious climate plan:

I certainly didn't sell it to my colleagues on the basis of some of the deeper analysis of where we have to get – not publicly. With some of them, privately, I talk a bit about that, but if I want to get twenty-three votes on the city council floor, I am not going to find twenty-three votes for a broader discussion of global justice ... But I will be able to say, "Here's the efficiency argument for investing here," or "Here's the air quality improvements your constituents will experience if we don't truck food so far" ... So in certain circumstances, I am stuck with really instrumentalist ways of persuading people to take action, and I don't talk about how the city of Toronto has to make a better compact with solidarity work in the Third World or the trade union movement. It just doesn't serve any function ... [As] for that deeper conversation, you can hint at it, but you can't go at it directly in certain positions. Darn.

The Businessman

Another individual yearning for a deeper conversation about consumption excess was Randal Goodfellow, who, as noted above, held senior positions in bio-product and renewable energy firms. "The big gorilla is in the corner and we are not really talking about it," said Goodfellow. "Excessive consumption – that becomes the issue of concern to me because we have had an equation that says 'To be happy you need more goods.' And so you chase more and more goods. But does it ever make you happy? ... Now compound that with the fact that the world around you is giving you less satisfaction because it's been degraded environmentally."

Goodfellow, who worked on producing energy in less impactful ways, recognized technology's importance, but also saw its limits. For example, with bio-based energy, "I think we overestimate how much material, particularly from a biological base source, that we have available close by," he said, adding that transporting biomass long distances was economically and environmentally costly. "The question is: Do we have to use as much as we do? Do we have to go here, there, and everywhere all the time? Is there not something simpler we could do?" he asked. "We ultimately have to look at reduction in consumption, reduction in demand, which comes partially through the efficiencies of engines, efficiencies of buildings, or whatever, but it [also] has to come from consumers' desire to consume less. That's the tougher thing to do."

Like other sufficiency advocates, Goodfellow wrestled with how to raise the issue of consuming less in a way that could achieve mainstream buy-in. He welcomed, for example, action by corporations to cut costs and increase profits by reducing waste, but noted, "Even in that, we are still trying to produce the same number of units for somebody to consume – we are just trying to do it more efficiently ... But how do we take it to the next step?"

For Goodfellow, a key part of the answer was religion and spirituality, which could drive a different view on what mattered. So, too, could reaching the age when one had achieved one's material goals and started asking, "Isn't there something more?" Goodfellow urged redefining symbols of success, pointing, for example, to the "not-so-big-house" movement – "the symbol being not how big your house is, but how well built and energy efficient it is." Such ideas could be linked to another kind of "win-win [that] could be done without consuming more."

Challenging excessive and growing consumption was daunting, Goodfellow acknowledged, "because you are actually putting to question some of the tenets of the economy, business, and capitalism." Yet he held out the possibility of an economic vision based on "not more and more and more, but the right amount, the right stuff. There's got to be a way in which you can still have a business doing the right stuff versus more stuff. Other nations like China can do more stuff cheaper, but who can do the right stuff properly? Maybe that's the discussion."

The Malthusian Public Servant

Peter Salonius, a research scientist with the Canadian Wood Fibre Centre of Natural Resources Canada, had a particularly stark perspective on humanity's transgression of limits to growth: "We've been in overshoot since ten thousand years ago." That is, ever "since we developed agriculture and left hunter-gathering behind." After forty years as a soil microbiologist, he reluctantly concluded that the shift to agriculture began an unsustainable process of disrupting complex, nutrient-conserving ecosystems – and we have been sending precious nutrients on their way out to sea ever since. Other of his colleagues pinpointed the beginnings of ecological overshoot at the start of fossil fuel use, while ecological footprint analysis suggested that humanity began consuming beyond the means of the earth's limited bio-capacity in the late 1980s. In any case, Salonius emphasized that the important thing was not when the problem started, but in which direction humanity would go from now on. Turning things around would require halting further economic and population growth, he argued, and then gradually scaling back population.

While growth critics often called for limits on the growth of per capita consumption, Salonius maintained that, due to entrenched habitual behaviour, "It's a lot easier to change the number of people that have got footprints than to change the size of an individual's footprint." Whether population or per capita consumption was the appropriate target – and the political implications of the two positions were very different – both met similar forms of resistance. Salonius was particularly critical of Canada's immigration policy, which increased the population by roughly 300,000 people, or one per cent, annually: "In Canada, you can't live without producing carbon dioxide. You have to heat your house, you have to take public transport, or you have to drive … So if you have more people … you increase the amount of carbon dioxide you produce. So stop increasing the population if you really are serious about decreasing the amount of CO_2 you are putting into the atmosphere. That's fairly logical, it's almost straightforward … Oh, yeah, but we have to have economic growth."[1]

The reply he received within government circles that a growing population was needed to facilitate economic growth did not impress Salonius. "Shrinkage, depression, recession, economic contraction – call it what you will, it's going to be uncomfortable. But … either we plan for it or nature will impose it. And nature has nasty ways of imposing things." As for the prospects for decoupling growth and ecological impacts, an idea that Salonius heard much about in policy debates – it was, in his estimation, "magic phantasmagorical wishful thinking."

On the climate question, Salonius saw value in rationing carbon through a tradable credit system that "gives the poor guy on the street the same number of credits as Conrad Black," and would transfer wealth to low income earners with less carbon-intensive lifestyles who could sell credits to others. "It's a lot more fair, but it's just not happening. Successive ministers of the environment say, my god, any kind of strictures on the economy are just unacceptable." When I said that in Britain, then–environment secretary David Miliband gave initial support to tradable carbon rationing and some pilot projects had taken place, although the government had shelved the idea for now, Salonius replied, "It's definitely more serious than it is here."

The Activist

"Is it proper, now that our biggest problems result from our size, to have growth as our goal?" Environmental activist and author Mike Nickerson had worked for years to put that "question of direction" on Canada's public agenda. His efforts included distributing pocket-sized "sustainability cards," giving countless public talks, campaigning for a new Genuine Progress Indicator to replace GDP, and writing a book, *Life, Money & Illusion: Living on Earth as if We Want to Stay* (Nickerson 2009). Climate change was only one issue motivating him to promote sustainability rather than growth as society's dominant goal, but a central one that he believed had contributed to the public's doubts about the current path. "Everyone knows something is wrong," said Nickerson, speaking of reactions he received at public talks. "But a lot of them haven't really put together the fact that what served us so well for so long is now central to the problem." Helping people see that "growth-based economics are past their 'best-before' date in the developed world" was central to his work. Nickerson (2008) wrote: "One by one, people are realizing that human activity cannot grow forever on a finite planet. When enough people understand this, the conventional wisdom will shift. It will move from 'Our purpose is to expand production and consumption' [to] 'Our purpose is to enjoy living while managing the planet for generations to come.'"

Nickerson's work aimed to "increase the rate at which this realization takes place," encouraging consciousness change one person at a time. While issues of economic structure were involved, he defined the challenge as being primarily about change in the realm of ideas: "Capitalism is very much the fundamentalist state religion of our time and its deity is growth. All things are done in order to expand capital so that we can do more of this wonderful provision that has brought us out of dire need and into affluence. So as long as that ... is seen as the primary value of our society – to produce and consume more – then shifting and wholeheartedly aiming for sustainability will always be stifled."

In Nickerson's view, one should consider the emerging focus on EM responses to climate change in light of the fact that "most people take it as a given that we have to grow." Like other sufficiency advocates, he was sceptical about reconciling deep emissions cuts and continued pursuit of economic growth. "The math makes that look like a really far-fetched argument," he said, but added that EM may serve as an intermediate step toward questioning growth. "It does allow some people to think about [sustainability] who otherwise would not allow themselves to think about it at all, and if they think about it for a while they'll start to catch on," he said. A further step would be to realize the potential quality-of-life benefits of a new direction. "We had to be trained to spend all our time consuming things and working most of our time in order to have the money to be able to pay for them," said Nickerson, whereas before industrialization: "We got together and told stories, worshipped, appreciated the world, sang and danced, we played sports, we celebrated … And so much of that has been lost that we have been impoverished immensely in order to keep industry expanding to the extent that it's actually able to consume the planet and destroy ecosystems and so on. We have all that to reclaim. We could be having so much fun that there just isn't time to destroy the planet."

Until then, Nickerson said, there could be costs for those who stood up before others to question the current path. He put forward an analogy of the caterpillar and the butterfly: "The caterpillar spends its entire life collecting natural resources and growing – very similar to our industrial society. And then it comes to the point of enough. It goes into a cocoon and begins to transform into a butterfly. When it comes out the other side, it lives very lightly. It is beautiful, which is an expression of what life has to offer, and its purpose is to launch the next generation." He added, however, that, "Inside the cocoon, microbiologists have discovered that the first cells of the caterpillar that begin to turn into butterfly cells are actually attacked by the immune system of the caterpillar." The people who questioned "the established legitimacy of society" were like the butterfly cells and caught various forms of "flak," ranging from being shunned to even more serious sanctions.[2] But just as a core is created around which a butterfly can develop, and which becomes strong enough to resist the attacks of the caterpillar, Nickerson saw a parallel phenomenon emerging in human society, as growing numbers of people realize the impossibility of infinite growth on a finite planet, and come together to support each other to live by a new vision and begin constructing a new system: "We need to hang in there and continue to beat the drum and help other people recognize and make that shift. It's an individual mind-shift ... And each person that goes through that adds to the conventional wisdom that will ultimately tip the balance. Then, as when enough of the butterfly has formed from the caterpillar to show a viable alternative and all the rest of the caterpillar turns fluid and moves into the butterfly, we will be on our way, as a society, toward a viable future."

Media Voices

The occasional voice of sufficiency could also be found in Canada's mainstream media, which was otherwise dominated by BAU and EM perspectives on climate change. For example, the headline of one *Ottawa Citizen* article read, "Reality Check on Climate Change: Shift to Low-Carbon World May Be More Radical Than Stern Suggests"; the piece featured William Rees and Thomas Homer-Dixon casting doubt on Nicholas Stern's claims of continued growth with deep emissions reductions (Butler 2007). *Toronto Star* environment columnist Cameron Smith (2008), in an article entitled "Heresy: The Upside of Low Growth," welcomed demographer David Foot's estimates that Canada, with an aging population and low fertility rate, could experience rising per capita incomes with annual GDP growth as low as 1 per cent. "From an environmental viewpoint, that could be a godsend. It would prevent the environmental footprint of Canadians from expanding. Instead of more people producing more goods for more consumers, we would have fewer people producing sufficient goods for a more stable population," wrote Smith. *Toronto Star* columnist Carol Goar (2008b) acknowledged in a piece on "Curbing Conspicuous Consumption" that "Belatedly, it has begun to dawn on economists that unbridled consumption is not financially – or ecologically – sustainable. But no one knows how to re-engineer a system built to produce a ceaseless outpouring of aggressively marketed goods and services." In a subsequent column, "Contemplating Life Without Growth," Goar (2008a) perceived a growing interest in charting a new economic path: "Something's stirring. It's not a groundswell. But a conversation is beginning about what recovery really means." The *Globe and Mail*'s London-based European bureau chief, Doug Saunders (2008), in a piece entitled "Getting Ready for a No-Growth Future," acknowledged without enthusiasm that in light of the climate crisis, the "zero-growth movement ... is enjoying a significant renaissance today." He urged closer scrutiny of steady state economists' work: "Not only do their ideas make more sense today, but they're an eerie portent of the future." The *Toronto Star*'s Peter Gorrie (2010) likewise noted that "a small but growing band of economists argues for a zero-growth economy," a phenomenon to which he was clearly sympathetic in light of climate change, the over-shoot of nature's limits according to ecological footprint data, and the "ecological debt" of industrialized nations to developing ones.

In addition to such relatively rare incursions of sufficiency-oriented ideas into the work of Canadian journalists, a sufficiency perspective also edged its way into the press through letters to the editor from individual citizens. "You say that 'improved technology' is the way out of our climate change crisis. Please! We've had improved and improving technology up to our eyeballs for the last 150 years ... We need instead improved ways of living on planet Earth," said one letter to the *Globe and Mail* (D. Cohen 2007). Another letter objected to the same paper's use of the term "economic miracle" to characterize Alberta's oil sands: "An economic miracle might begin with a premier being elected on a promise of not growing their province's economy. An economic miracle would be the development of a population reaching a consensus that it is happy to make do with less 'stuff' if it means social justice for all, sustainable supplies of fresh air, clean water and healthy soil, and peaceful relations with its local and global neighbours" (Rowberry 2008).

What is the significance of these individual voices questioning economic growth? On the one hand, they were like voices in the wilderness or an "endangered species," as Peter Victor put it. Although many had their own networks, they had yet to coalesce into a united movement or find strong institutional support for their ideas, nor had they succeeded in making the question of growth a central item of public debate. Yet enough such voices appeared in varying contexts to suggest that concerns over endless economic growth were not too far below the surface. Comments such as "Everybody knows something is wrong" were backed by Canadian pollster Allan Gregg who, as climate change temporarily became the number one public concern before the economic downturn, concluded that "people know that the life of conspicuous consumption is out of control" (Laghi 2007). But where does one go with that concern in a society committed to, and seemingly dependent on, growth in order to function at all smoothly? In their own ways, advocates of sufficiency were working to open up space to advance the idea of an economy guided by aims other than growth, but they all confronted significant obstacles to the kind of "economic miracle" they had in mind.

FROM ADBUSTING TO MAKING AFFLUENCE HISTORY: ORGANIZATIONS QUESTIONING GROWTH

Canada was certainly not without organizations that took direct aim at contemporary capitalism's growth imperative and consumer culture. After all, living next to the world's leading consumer republic simultaneously gave Canadians a chance both to participate in and maintain a critical distance from their neighbours' excesses. Canada not only had among the planet's highest per capita ecological and carbon footprints, it was also home to one of the world's most prominent anti-consumerist groups: Adbusters, organizers of "Buy Nothing Day." With the climate crisis high among its concerns, Adbusters (2009) named ecological economist Herman Daly its "Man of the Year" for his promotion of a steady state economy, adding that, "thanks to the overwhelming evidence [... that] humanity must stop pumping CO_2 into the atmosphere, mainstream economists are grudgingly coming to accept that there are ecological limits to growth after all." Adbusters later played a central role in launching the Occupy Movement, in which one current of thought was that a "finite planet cannot have infinite growth" (e.g. Occupy Ottawa 2011).

Canadian organizations that emphasized rejection of the growth imperative as a core solution to climate change, and other environmental problems, were mostly small and operating off the mainstream radar. Post Carbon groups, inspired by the work of American Richard Heinberg, emerged in various towns and cities across the country, including in the heart of the oil patch ("Carbon Sanity in Wild Rose Country" was the aim of Post Carbon Red Deer, Alberta, for example). These groups worked toward an "energy descent" in response to concerns over peak oil as well as climate change, based on principles that included "transition to a steady state economy," "reduce consumption," and "produce locally" (Post Carbon Toronto 2008). Similar goals of improving community resilience and cutting

carbon emissions motivated the emerging Canadian movement of
Transition Towns, inspired by UK examples, in which a critical perspective on growth was present, if not always front and centre. The
need to move not just beyond growth, but beyond capitalism, was
a prominent theme on the Climate and Capitalism website, edited
by Canadian Ian Angus (2011). That site included, for example, debate over proposals for an "Ecosocialist Economy of Stasis" based on
"near-zero economic growth," which would require "drastically cutting back many lines of production, closing down others entirely, and
creating socially and environmentally useful jobs for workers made
redundant by this transition" (R. Smith 2007). (Similar ideas were
voiced by Canadian author Naomi Klein [2011] in a much discussed
article, "Capitalism vs. the Climate," that urged an end to the "cult of
shopping" and a "managed transition" beyond the growth imperative, which would require a contraction of the profit-driven corporate sector.) Meanwhile in Quebec, participants in the voluntary simplicity network and Friends of the Earth Quebec were among those
promoting "convivial degrowth" as a solution to the climate crisis and
other "*maladies*" resulting from "*l'american way of life*" (Mouvement
québécois pour une décroissance conviviale 2007). They played a
key role in bringing together like-minded thinkers and activists at the
International Conference on Degrowth in the Americas in Montreal
in 2012, while two other degrowth conferences took place in Vancouver in 2010 and 2011.

The de-growth theme was also taken up by the Make Affluence
History campaign, led by the Toronto-based group Global Aware –
and later by the Winnipeg-based, Christian activist magazine *Geez*,
whose campaigns included "De-Motorize Your Soul" and "Buy Nothing Christmas." The idea of Make Affluence History came to Kris
Orantes, a Guatemalan-born Canadian, when he was in London,
England at the time of the 2005 Live 8 concert. Orantes saw a need
to complement the international Make Poverty History campaign
by challenging the over-consumption of the affluent, which he saw
as the driving force behind many environmental problems and "the
central factor behind structural and systematic inequalities which
characterize today's global society" (MAH 2007). While Orantes saw
some role for technology – for example, with websites such as free-
cycle.org enabling people to find free goods, clothing swaps, and free
community events – he emphasized the need to "change that basic

structure of needing to consume." Like other sufficiency advocates in Canada, a main challenge facing the MAH campaign was simply to create space to put forward new ways of thinking and living. Orantes spoke of the importance of building communities of practice to push for and live in non-consumerist ways, as well as taking such ideas outward to friends, family members, co-workers, schools, and universities – where his group put much of its effort in conducting workshops to challenge prevailing discourses. To help people withdraw from the dominant consumerist model, MAH's website also presented a number of suggestions under headings such as: "Question your wants," "Fix stuff up," "Downsize your life," "Live simply," "Conserve," "Choose ethically," "Grow a garden / plant a tree," "Go Veggie," "Ride a bike," "Boycott corporate media," "Build community," "Ad bust," and "Think." Ultimately, the core message of the campaign was a very demanding call for personal and social change under the slogan of "Consume Less. Be Sustainable. Challenge Desire."

Others emphasized channelling desire in new directions, such as the Vancouver-based Work Less Party, founded by Conrad Schmidt. It captured considerable public attention, at least regionally, through its creative antics, including Work Less Party parties, in favour of a 32-hour work week. A shorter work week stood out as a way to channel labour-productivity gains toward the benefits of greater leisure time, while rejecting the "theology of growth" that party activists saw as a driving force behind climate change and other environmental ills (O'Hara 2005). An off-shoot of the Work Less Party, De-Growth Vancouver, presented candidates in that city's 2011 municipal elections. Meanwhile, other groups, such as Nova Scotia–based GPI Atlantic, led by Ron Colman, made a more indirect challenge to economic growth by focusing on developing new indicators of social progress to replace GDP. All these groups struggled in their own way to get a sufficiency message into popular consciousness, but the odds of success seemed greater to the extent that the critique of growth's devastation and injustices were balanced with a vision of alternative ways of living that could be equally or more satisfying.

Churches as Sufficiency Advocates

Canadian churches were among the organizations in which a critique of endless growth in light of climate change found expression.

Although sufficiency-oriented ideas were not necessarily dominant within the churches, these institutions had a tradition of moral
critique that could serve as a foundation to question the ethics of
limitless expansion of production and consumption. In some cases,
this critique involved challenging particular forms of growth. For example, Luc-André Bouchard (2009), Roman Catholic bishop for the
Diocese of Saint Paul, which includes the Athabasca oil sands, issued
an attention-getting pastoral letter questioning the "moral legitimacy" of rapid tar sands development and called for an end to further
expansion until solutions became available to its numerous environmental problems. Directing his criticism not toward the region's
workers, but to the "company executives in Calgary and Houston,
to government leaders in Edmonton and Ottawa, and to the general
public whose excessive consumerist lifestyle drives the demand for
oil," the bishop concluded that "the integrity of creation in the Athabasca Oil Sands is clearly being sacrificed for economic gain."

Kairos, a faith-based ecumenical organization committed to social
justice whose member churches represented eighteen million Canadians, launched a three-year Carbon Sabbath initiative in 2007, in
which themes of sufficiency were prominent. Its campaign literature
quoted Bartholomew, Ecumenical Patriarch of Constantinople, urging people to "make every effort possible, each from where God has
placed us, to rein in our reckless over-consumption," while adding
that "our thirst for oil is killing people and the planet." The campaign emphasized personal efforts to reduce one's carbon footprint
alongside community and political efforts, including questioning the
pace of tar sands expansion.

David Hallman, programme officer on energy and environment
for the United Church of Canada and coordinator of the Climate
Change Programme for the World Council of Churches (WCC), was
among those who sought to bring the idea of consumption sufficiency into the climate debate. In explaining the WCC's conclusion
that "an energy efficiency revolution must be accompanied by a sufficiency revolution," he said in an interview, "We are not convinced
that technological innovation is the panacea that some of its proponents claim it to be ... It's a kind of blind faith in technological innovation which we think is not historically justified." In addition to seeing
the need for deeper economic and lifestyle change to address climate
change, Hallman (2002) wrote: "We perceive a growing awareness

that an ever increasing level of material consumption is no longer adding to an improved quality of life. Indeed, there are indications that there is an inverse ratio as families need to work ever more strenuously to afford the material goods advertised to them as requirements for the good life. This treadmill leaves them with an ever-diminishing sense of emotional and spiritual satisfaction through the loss of time to nurture their relationships with God, their families, the community and the natural world around them."

Global justice was also a key concern for Hallman and the WCC, as it was for many other sufficiency advocates. Hallman framed these justice issues in both political-economic and faith-based terms: "Our analysis of the climate change issue is very much tied to an analysis of the economic systems in the world that continue to impoverish the majority and enrich a minority as a function of the economic power concentrated in the hands of the minority and bolstered by military powers." He noted that "the majority of that human activity that's contributing to greenhouse gases ... has come historically from the industrialized, the rich industrialized countries," while it "was becoming evident that the impacts of climate change would be disproportionately distributed, with the poor and marginalized being the most vulnerable." The implication was that "the rich have the primary responsibility to make the changes that reduce the causes of the problem." Or, as Hallman (2005) wrote, "God's justice demands that those responsible be held accountable and required to change their behaviours that are causing harm to the vulnerable." Justice implied movement toward sufficiency at both ends of the continuum: "On one end, there are millions of people without adequate food, water, and shelter to give them a good quality of life. They suffer from insufficiency. On the other end, there is a minority within the world's population whose consumption levels are so much greater than their needs that the consequences of their lifestyles are jeopardising the well-being of the whole planet. They live by gross over-sufficiency. For them (us), we need to ask what is enough to constitute a good quality of life and what is too much – endangering the planet and even diminishing their (our) own happiness and spiritual well-being."

These three issues highlighted by Hallman – the limits of an EM project relying on technology and efficiency, the critique of economic growth's failing capacity to deliver improved well-being, and global justice concerns – were key drivers of demands for sufficiency

in response to climate change. Whether framed in spiritual or secular terms, they amounted to a compelling intellectual argument for
sufficiency in response to climate change; of course, such arguments
were not in themselves enough for such ideas to carry the day.

OBSTACLES TO MACRO-SUFFICIENCY: FROM BUSINESS RESISTANCE TO ENVIRONMENTALIST RELUCTANCE

Calls for a sufficiency-based turn away from a growth economy ran
into several serious obstacles. These included business resistance, the
power of consumerist values and the ideology of growth, government
dependence on growth, labour's concerns over employment, a need
for more fully developed economic alternatives, and even resistance
among environmental groups.

Business: "We Are Not Going to Do It by Tightening Our Belts"

Advocates of sufficiency-based responses to climate change not surprisingly identified resistance from business as a key obstacle. For
example, David Hallman (2002) of the World Council of Churches
highlighted the role of "commercial interests that would be hurt by
a reduction in the use of fossil fuels" in stirring up fears that strong
climate action would wreak "havoc with the economy and lead to
significant job loss." (This was not only an obstacle to a sufficiency
response, but to EM as well.)

With the exception of rare individuals, discussed above, it did not
appear that turning away from growth was even on Canadian business's radar as an option to consider or, more to the point, contend
with. When asked if, within business, it ever came up for discussion
that pursuing economic growth as a dominant goal might be part of
the climate problem, John Dillon, vice president of policy and corporate counsel for the Canadian Council of Chief Executives (CCCE),
replied, "No, not put that way. I think clearly everyone accepts that
we have to do better on energy efficiency and reducing the energy
intensity of GDP ... But I don't think any business that I talked to accepts that it means absolute limits on economic growth."

Clearly, macro-sufficiency was not the preferred response of business, which was ever seeking to expand markets for its production in
order to realize profits. Although some specific sectors had concerns
that strong climate action would limit their sales opportunities, it was

not obvious that Canadian business was particularly concerned, at least not yet, that a more general anti-growth or anti-consumption message would take hold. As Rick Hyndman of the Canadian Association of Petroleum Producers put it: "I just don't see, in any significant way, people forgoing production and consumption to avoid CO_2 emissions ... You show me that somewhere and then I'll believe it ... If we're going to solve this problem, it's going to be through technology and having low-emission energy and low-emission production of the goods and services that people want to consume. We are not going to do by it by tightening our belts, I don't think."

In fact, corporate Canada actually showed signs of wanting to put more emphasis on the issue of excessive consumption – at least when framed as a matter of individual or household choices – thereby shifting attention from the regulation of industry. The conditions in which business could embrace a limited degree of sufficiency-based thinking, and the related opportunities and pitfalls for sufficiency-based approaches, are discussed in the following chapter.

The Public: Confronting the Junk in Our Heads

Before business would find a sufficiency response more threatening, and feel compelled to respond to it with more than casual dismissal, a larger breach would likely have to occur in the first line of defence around the growth model: the public's attachment to steadily growing consumption levels. Advocates of sufficiency were well aware of what they were up against. As Toronto councillor Gord Perks saw the challenge: "I think there is a deeply set emotional thing around buying stuff that is so normalized that our task isn't so much to get people to reason their way through to understanding the role that consumption plays in the destruction of ecosystems and the biosphere. Rather the task is to give people the emotional tools to confront that junk in their head. And that's a real struggle." Similarly, David Hallman of the WCC stated, "As modern or postmodern people in the wealthier countries, we have defined ourselves very much as, primarily, consumers – more so than as citizens, more so than as community participants ... We have vast economic systems from marketing and advertising to product development that are aimed at feeding that self perception. So for us as faith communities to start talking about sufficiency, we recognize that we have to focus the discussion at a very profound level of values that gets beneath those economic and consumption-oriented self perceptions."

In addition to consumerist consciousness, sufficiency advocates identified a powerful growth ideology confronting them. Mike Nickerson noted that "most people take it as a given that we have to grow," while he saw a need to challenge growth as the "religion of the day." Thomas Homer-Dixon added, "We have equated growth with peace and growth with freedom," a phenomenon that persisted even though "growth is now starting to generate the conditions for war and is starting to generate the conditions for authoritarianism." Or, as William Rees, put it: "People adhere to cultural myths and narratives despite contrary data. The growth myth has tremendous staying power despite dangerous global change. It's like a pseudo-intellectual armour that deflects the harsh barbs of reality."

Government: Stuck on the Treadmill

Powerful obstacles to sufficiency were also present in the government sphere. Former MP Lynn McDonald noted that in the early 1980s, the idea of "zero energy growth" (D. Brooks 1981), which she supported, was prominent in environmental circles. However, it "really didn't get very far in Parliament," which was "very much geared to business." Such ideas also met resistance in her pro-labour NDP, which feared that any deviation from growth would destroy jobs and alienate working-class supporters. McDonald noted that the NDP – through a motion introduced by a young Bob Rae – brought down Joe Clark's Conservative government in 1980 over its gasoline tax increase (foreshadowing NDP opposition to BC's carbon tax and the federal Liberal Green Shift in 2008). In McDonald's estimation, no change had occurred within parliament on such questions since then. Thomas Homer-Dixon concurred: "It astonishes me how much the issue of growth is not part of our public discourse and not part of our policy agenda."

In 2008, I asked an Environment Canada executive with many years of climate policy experience if the evidence of insufficient decoupling of GHG emissions from economic growth had led to any discussion within government of the idea that prioritizing economic growth might be part of the problem. He replied that "decoupling is the basis for a lot of what we do. It's the basis for our emissions-intensity approach that you can have growth without emissions growing in the same ratio. But having to go from that to saying we should actually be less interested in growth itself is a step that I haven't heard being put forward seriously or discussed seriously in the public debate." He added, "I think it would be very difficult for any government to indicate that it was prepared to put up with slower growth in order to achieve emission reductions, and I think governments are a long way from coming to that assessment." It was not surprising that governments would find an embrace of slower growth to be very difficult politically; however, given the stakes, it was noteworthy that – unlike in the UK (chapter 10) – in Canada, the idea was apparently not being discussed at all in federal government institutions and advisory bodies, not even being given some preliminary thought as a Plan B if decoupling were to prove inadequate.

As for why political leaders remained so committed to economic growth, several factors appeared to be at play. Among them: dependence on growth and continued capital accumulation to expand state revenues to pay for programs and pay down public debt, a broader expansionary ideology (which created obstacles to even thinking beyond either BAU or EM), reluctance to challenge consumerist aspirations and risk antagonizing voters, and, as noted, the pro-business orientation of government leaders. Homer-Dixon (2007, 193) proposed an additional explanation: "By its very nature, capitalism constantly displaces labor, which can erode the economic demand essential to maintaining capitalism's vigor. Economic growth – sustained in part by a culture of consumerism – absorbs displaced labor into new jobs and industries. The process both maintains demand and ensures that the unemployed and underemployed don't coalesce into an angry and destabilizing underclass." He added in an interview, "We've punted the distribution problem down the road by using growth as a way of lubricating friction between classes."

Labour: Threatened by the Prospect of Less

Organized labour was also attached to growth-friendly climate solutions, specifically to a left-leaning version of EM. I asked Nick DeCarlo of the Canadian Auto Workers (CAW), one of the labour movement's main proponents of a left-green economic transformation, whether, in light of climate change, growing production volumes and the priority given to economic growth were ever questioned with the labour movement. "It's where you get real friction. I mean people are worried about exactly that kind of thing," he replied. "You don't want to reduce the amount of sales ... People see their jobs at stake." One should understand such a response, he explained, as a product of economic insecurity, as workers felt intense pressure to make concessions on wages and working conditions so that they could sell more of their product just to hold onto their jobs. DeCarlo, who had been involved in various initiatives to green the auto industry, spoke of the obstacles to proposals aiming to limit the need for consumption. "One thing I just can't even approach at all is the idea that we will build cars that last longer. You can't make that part of the campaign because it's a non-starter and I won't get any support for that in the union," he said. However, openings existed to promote ideas such as extended producer responsibility, in which cars come back to the factory after use for disassembly and recycling, thereby creating more jobs. DeCarlo added, "You can't even talk about reusing a part in a new vehicle because a new vehicle has to have new parts ... There's not even a chance of getting any support for that one. And that's simply because that's the way that they see their livelihood. If you don't have a different way of seeing how to guarantee your livelihood, you can't get past that."

A key part of the problem, DeCarlo explained, was the lack of an organizational capacity to ensure that workers displaced by green initiatives benefit from a just transition to new jobs. "If you are going to reduce the number of suvs, you need a plan to replace that with something," he said. While wide agreement existed within Canada's labour and environmental movements on the need to deal with transition issues, he said, "the problem is nobody's really solved how to do it ... Unless you have some plan for transition, and that means control over the market, you don't have any guarantee of transition." Indeed, this was a problem not only for sufficiency-based approaches that aimed to produce and consume less; it was also an obstacle to an EM strategy that involved shifts to more efficient and less carbon intensive methods. DeCarlo gave the example of building a more efficient, lighter car made of composite materials: "If you make it of composites, that undermines the steel industry. Steelworkers lose their jobs." Similar challenges resulted from the closure of Ontario's coal-fired power plants: "It turns out that people we represent in Great Lakes shipping, 30 per cent of what they ship is coal. Close down the coal-generation plants and 30 per cent of their work is gone. Whenever you come up with any proposal, it has all these ripple effects. So the union movement remains paralyzed because it doesn't have a plan that gets everybody together ... So what tends to happen is people fall back on protecting their own industry and their own jobs, and then you never get to a solution. That's the big problem."

Although transition concerns are also relevant to an EM strategy, in a growing economy, displaced workers left to their own devices are likely to have a better chance of finding work elsewhere, all other things being equal. In any low- or no-growth scenario, a society's capacity to provide a just transition becomes increasingly essential.

Whatever the future possibilities, for the time being, labour's general predisposition was to address climate change by expanding economic activity, not scaling it back. CAW economist Jim Stanford (2002) outlined this perspective during the Kyoto Protocol ratification debate, arguing that there were "two roads to Kyoto: more or less." He wrote, "A strategy to meet the Kyoto commitments in a manner that enhances our economy, rather than undermines it, will seek out avenues in which GHG emissions can be cut back by doing more work and more spending, not less" (54). He rejected the green critique of economic growth and ideas of "consuming less, driving less and turning down the thermostat," equating them with post-communist Russia's emissions reductions through economic implosion. Instead, he argued, "Canadians can continue to do the things they like doing, including driving and staying warm in the winter, but do those things more efficiently. That will require us to spend more energy, attention and money on finding more efficient ways of doing things. And as long as the right rules and incentives are in place, that effort should boost the economy" (54). For Stanford, policies such as publicly funded energy efficiency retrofits of buildings and promotion of hybrid vehicles – which, having two different engines, required more investment and labour – represented the way forward. In later writing, Stanford (2008) appeared somewhat more open to a green critique targeting environmentally damaging growth within capitalism, arguing that forms of growth that consume more natural resources and emit more pollution need to be closed off or made unprofitable, "while simultaneously stimulating more beneficial and benign forms of growth" (184). Some common ground with advocates of sufficiency was also evident on the issue of work-time reduction. "Where consumption is actually reduced (in societies prosperous enough to do this), this could be attained through widespread and equitable reductions in working hours," wrote Stanford. Still, his core message remained that "We should protect the environment by doing *more*, not by doing *less*," as he called for a "peaceful 'world war' on climate change" involving large-scale investment in environmentally beneficial activity (186).

As discussed in the following chapters, questioning of the model of endless economic growth was not entirely absent within the labour movement. Meanwhile, the case of Alberta's tar sands illustrated that circumstances could arise in which Canadian labour unions, including the CAW, supported efforts to slow or stop specific forms of high-carbon growth.

What Is the Economic Alternative?

Lying beneath consumerist consciousness and the growth ideology, the business drive for ever-expanding profits, and adherence to the treadmill by both the state and labour was an economic system that depended – or at least was widely perceived to depend – on never-ending growth to function in a socially tolerable way. What a steady state alternative would entail, and whether it was possible within capitalism, were questions still needing answers and, more generally, a lot more people asking them. "I don't think we've got that worked out," said Homer-Dixon. "We aren't even investing resources in thinking about what the alternative would look like." Although he noted that ecological economist Herman Daly and others had provided some pieces of the answer, he added, "I think we really need some cognitive liberation here because the place we go is some kind of communistic or socialistic system, and that is obviously not where we want to go because we need – and here's the trick – we need to maintain the space for liberty and innovation. We need to have highly innovative societies that don't experience material growth. It almost seems oxymoronic. It seems like there's an internal contradiction stated like that: innovative steady state ... I don't know how we manage that."

Others, such as eco-socialists, argued that a break from a growth economy would require a fundamental transformation of capitalism (e.g. R. Smith 2007). Peter Victor's (2008) book, *Managing Without Growth*, took thinking on these issues forward considerably, outlining policies that could allow Canada to meet core social and climate goals in a macroeconomy without growth. Victor acknowledged that "every aspect of these issues requires a great deal of additional work ... getting from A to B is going to require many minds."

Environmental Group Hesitancy to Embrace Sufficiency

Even environmental groups were hesitant to confront questions of economic growth and consumerist excess. David Hallman of the World Council of Churches said, with regard to the concept of sufficiency, "This is an area where we part company with some of our usual partners in civil society groups. Environmental organizations, by and large, are very important partners for us, but they are anxious to get their message across in a way that will be appealing politically. And the concept of living with less, which goes beyond the concept of living more efficiently, is one that often makes them nervous because they think that it will be interpreted by the public as sacrifice and will be unattractive to garnering support for their broader environmental agenda. So, they are not always very happy when we raise these more foundational questions."

When asked for examples, Hallman spoke of his personal experience of collaboration with two large mainstream environmental groups in the United States that "are both very closely connected to working with business and industry to move them into the ecological sustainability stream, and they are doing wonderful work in that. But they are firmly lodged in that middle stream in your schema [i.e. in EM] and are not keen on us raising the questions which some of their business and industry partners would interpret as interference with the market. So one obstacle within, as we raise this issue, is the fact that our usual partners are not necessarily always happy to hear us."

This discussion reminded me of *Guardian* journalist George Monbiot's (2007d) comment: "When you warn people about the dangers of climate change, they call you a saint. When you explain what needs to be done to stop it, they call you a communist." When I asked Hallman if he had run into some version of that, he replied, "Absolutely. And that doesn't scare us particularly because we have a longer history of raising critical questions about the functioning of the global economic system in the context of global economic justice than in the ecological sphere." He cited, for example, the churches' critical perspective on trade deals, role in boycotting products from apartheid South Africa, and more general calls for "ways to function economically that meet the needs of everyone in a better way ... If that gets labelled as 'communist,' that is not a surprise."

In fact, the word "communist" was no longer the most likely derisive label, but the tension between belief in the need for radical change and struggling for public acceptability was still a concern for some environmentalists. Kim Fry of Greenpeace Canada explained that:

> An organization like Greenpeace has fought for a very long time to be credible. We're always fighting for credibility. It's so easy to be discredited for everything that we do even when I feel that we're being incredibly reasonable ... But you wouldn't believe what we get called ... We've been called "eco-terrorists," "economic terrorists," we're "unreasonable," we're "radical" – all of those things. So it's always a delicate battle to present ... your argument in a way that you continue to have credibility. Because Greenpeace depends so much on membership, donations, and public support, I think there's always this fear that we're going to be seen as not credible and that the space gets closed off to us completely. And that we won't be able to sit down with the CEO of a company who's going to pull the economic leverage that is going to change those logging companies, so it's a delicate balance.

Fry's personal view was that the environmental movement could no longer avoid taking on unfettered growth and consumption, or the broader systemic issues to which they were linked:

> We're saying, "We're serious. We're solutions based. We're credible and we can work with industry and help transform it, etc. etc." And I think there's value obviously to doing some of that work. But I don't think that Greenpeace and the broader NGO world has been clear enough that the Western lifestyle is unsustainable and the current capitalist model that drives pretty much every country in the world is not sustainable. And these are the reasons why. This is the kind of alternative future that we should be building, etc. I don't think that's ever explicitly said ... It can be extrapolated from things that we push. But it's very rarely clear. And I

understand why people haven't been clear about it. But I think that we don't have the luxury of being vague anymore and that we really have to move on to be more clear about what we're about and that it's not just tinkering with the system, which is sometimes very important, but really fundamentally shining the spotlight on the ways in which we can't continue to live.

A key limitation on the issues environmental groups chose to work on was the need to safeguard their funding, whether from corporations, foundations, and governments – or, for that matter, from individuals, often in high-income brackets, caught up in their own forms of consumer excess. William Rees, while noting that some environmental groups had begun to use his ecological footprint concept, added that they often shied away from the message he intended it to convey: "It's absolutely the case that a number of environmental organizations won't talk about limits to growth because they are beholden to corporate and government agencies for their funding. I think this is a real problem because the dependence of these organizations on the very system they are criticizing for their existence prevents them from being full-voiced critics. I don't think there is any question about this."

Similarly, Gord Perks, who worked in the environmental movement before becoming a Toronto councillor, noted that the "institutional weight" of Canada's large environmental groups "is predisposed against the [less] consumption argument. They tend to have lots of corporate donations or relationships with big companies, who are in the business of moving as much product as they can." He noted that, on the other hand, within these same groups, "the people working on the climate issue are by far the most radical ... [and] are injecting the deeper analysis ... So there's an interesting tension going on inside those organizations."

An additional challenge, identified by Kim Fry, was the pressure on environmentalists to focus on immediate concerns and strategy rather than big-picture issues. Asked if a critique of economic growth ever came up in discussions she had been a part of at Greenpeace, she replied:

Yeah, but it doesn't get talked about explicitly. I feel like one of the problems in the NGO world is that people are so overworked and there's so much work to do that ... as a campaigner, there's not a lot of time for reflection ... In terms of reflection on that bigger picture, there isn't a lot of it – and not as much political discussion. People also get wrapped up in the details of policy. And so a book comes along like *Heat* by Monbiot that really is a pretty deep challenge to our system. In terms of a mainstream piece, it is the most critical in suggesting that we really need to re-work our economy. And people are sort of like, "Ach, that's so radical and blue sky and that will never be socially acceptable and we've got to be realistic."

AUTHOR. People say that within Greenpeace?

FRY. Yeah, people within Greenpeace say, "Oh, Monbiot, with his numbers. And what he's saying is so out there." Even though if they took a few moments, I think they might agree with what he's saying. It's just that there's such a focus on strategically what we can say. It's all about strategy, strategy, strategy.

Greenpeace was, in fact, one environmental group that did take challenging positions on issues such as stopping tar sands growth, pushing further than many others. Still, Canada's large environmental groups largely shied away from challenging the prioritization of economic growth and from calling for a less consumption-oriented society in response to climate change.

How long this would be the case remained to be seen. Dale Marshall, a climate change policy analyst with the David Suzuki Foundation, said some within the environmental movement wanted to inject the growth question into the debate, while others feared becoming "completely marginalized as a movement because nobody is there." His organization – distinct from its founder's personal views – emphasized "a Nicholas Stern–type approach of addressing the climate problem within the mainstream economic view that growth has to continue." However, Marshall noted that within a few decades, GHG cuts of 80 to 95 per cent would be needed: "In the long term, if you want my opinion of how this plays out, I think we are going to have to challenge the growth paradigm." His personal view, which was not the consensus of the movement, was that, "We can do the first few steps, even quite a few steps, while continuing along this conventional economic theory of growth. But at some point, a little ways down the road, but not too far down the road, we are going to have to challenge that assumption as well."

SPECIFICALLY CANADIAN OBSTACLES TO SUFFICIENCY

The above-mentioned obstacles to ideas of macro-sufficiency were similar to those faced in the UK and elsewhere, but others were more specific to Canada. Some of these – such as a huge, sparsely populated land with a frontier mentality, economic dependence on particularly carbon-intensive sectors, and regional disparities in the sources of GHGs and costs of climate action – also held back a shift from BAU to EM. However, taking the issue onto the terrain of sufficiency faced yet more obstacles specific to Canada.

Kim Fry of Greenpeace, whose critique of "unfettered economic growth" was linked to a radical green-left political vision, expressed frustration, in 2008, that "particularly in Canada, the political space just doesn't exist" to discuss such ideas: "Unless I'm talking to International Socialists or a group of radical students, I don't dare use the word 'capitalism' anymore. I talk about it ... and say we need a different economic model. But there are different ways that I go about it that I think are not as jarring and that people don't immediately put up walls to. I feel that Canadians are just not particularly radical, we're not a very radical country and people aren't very open to certain kinds of ideas and visions."

Whether this phenomenon was a product of Canada's history and political culture, a different balance of political leanings and reporting in major media outlets, or cyclical ebbs and flows of radicalism, other interviewees similarly expressed frustration at the limited range of mainstream debate on social change to combat climate change. "Canada is just so backward," said former MP Lynn McDonald. She contrasted the coverage in the *Guardian* in the UK with Canada's media: "Here there's just nothing giving anything equivalent. Environmental stories are making it in, but they are not as challenging in terms of the ideas. They are not as critical." Although a content analysis would be needed to confirm this assessment, one could hypothesize, based on interviewees' impressions and my own, that significant differences in mainstream reporting on climate change existed between the two countries. (Or as a friend of mine suggested, Canada's equivalent of George Monbiot, a radical green voice, was Jeffrey Simpson, a centrist proponent of EM.)

The inability to achieve widespread consensus in Canada on the need for EM reform and the limited EM measures to date also held back efforts to bring more radical ideas of sufficiency into the debate. Supporters of strong climate action had to continually struggle against the forces of business-as-usual. One result, discussed in more detail in the next chapter, was that even those with a radical growth critique often held it back in favour of less controversial EM arguments when confronting conservative opponents of strong climate measures. In fact, some conservatives seemed more comfortable than greens in arguing in mainstream venues that "the biggest CO_2 emitter of them all is prosperity" (Wente 2007a), presumably betting that most Canadians would never question or seek to redefine "prosperity."

Given that EM had yet to be tried to any significant degree, it was also hard to make the case that much more politically challenging steps had to be taken. This point came across in an interview with Senator Grant Mitchell, a Liberal from Alberta. When asked if statistics, which showed that economic growth was outpacing reductions in emissions intensity in many wealthy countries, suggested a need to reconsider the priority given to economic growth, he replied: "Why would you jump to that conclusion before you've done everything you can to get the emissions output per unit of production down as low as you possibly can by using the technology that we know? Generally it's accepted that the technology exists today to solve this problem. Why would you go to that level – let's cut growth – before you've exhausted all of the other possibilities? And we haven't even begun to try ... By solving this problem, you might actually stimulate growth *and* solve the problem."

Meanwhile, Canadian advocates of sufficiency tended to be well aware of research showing the weak links, if any, between rising incomes and happiness in affluent nations, but spoke of obstacles to taking advantage of these findings due to the lack of public awareness and debate on them. "We need to reconsider what makes us happy. Research shows having more stuff isn't what makes us happy," said Homer-Dixon (2008), who added, "We don't have a place for that discussion." Similarly, Lynn McDonald noted in 2008 that Canadian researchers John Helliwell and Alex Michalos were among the key contributors to this well-being research. Yet, she added, "I don't think that this is particularly well known – it's known to academics." In contrast, in the UK, such research had gone well beyond academic and activist circles, and was seized on by political leaders and even prime-time TV shows, expanding the space available to question growth and consumption. Comparing the high-profile embrace by the UK government of new well-being indicators with the "below the radar" work on such issues in Canada, Helliwell told the UK's *Guardian*, "Canadian statisticians and researchers also poll subjective wellbeing across the country, but the data have thus far not attracted much policy attention" (Stratton 2010; see also Michaelson 2010). That said, the release in 2011 of a Canadian Index of Wellbeing by academic researchers and NGOs did provide a very limited opening to advance the idea that GDP growth and improved well-being did not go hand in hand (chapter 4).

It was no easy task to confront an economy geared toward growth to allow capital accumulation, overlaid with a culture of consumption and a "secular religion" of growth, in which business, government, and labour all had stakes in further accelerating the treadmill, while even environmentalists were reluctant to challenge matters. The idea of sufficiency, particularly when formulated as a macro-level economic-growth critique, was clearly at a serious disadvantage relative to EM and BAU approaches. Awareness of the vast array of obstacles to any shift away from the growth paradigm created a further hurdle. "It's unrealistic, we're doomed," was the most frequent criticism that Mike Nickerson heard in response to his efforts to shift society's direction from growth to sustainability. Yet he and others carried on undaunted.

CONCLUSIONS

One could depict calls to turn away from endless growth of output and consumption as "marginal" in Canada given their absence from the climate solutions proposed by government, business, mainstream environmental groups (with rare exception), and political parties (with the partial exception of the Green Party). However, I propose that a more appropriate characterization would be that such ideas were lying "under the surface," searching for opportunities to emerge. Sufficiency-based critiques of economic growth and consumerism frequently came forward at climate conferences and public events, even when other topics were the focus of the official agenda. A range of individual voices – from the worlds of academia, business, the public service, politics, activism, media, and the general public – called for efforts to go beyond growth in light of climate change and wider ecological concerns. So, too, did several small organizations that were largely off the mainstream radar. Churches, with their tradition of moral critique, were another source of critique of excessive consumption – and possibly among the best-positioned organizations to take such ideas beyond the usual green circles. Whatever the source of sufficiency-based ideas, a recurring theme was the struggle to find ways to open up a public discussion of the question of growth and the need for alternatives.

The array of Canadian voices calling for sufficiency in response to climate change was quite rich and complex. This was potentially a great strength, but also a great challenge if critics of growth were to try to coalesce into an effective social movement. This array included some on the reformist and revolutionary left, others who went out of their way to say they were not anti-capitalist, as well as Malthusians whose ideas could lead in conservative or authoritarian directions. Some sought to redefine affluence, others to make affluence history. Religious or spiritual foundations were important to some. Differences over the relative importance of population and consumption growth were a potential cleavage.

Sufficiency advocates also deployed a variety of strategies to try to put the idea on the agenda. These included changing consciousness one individual at a time, encouraging lifestyle change, preparing communities for an energy descent, celebrating the opportunities to work less, working to sow the seeds of a revolutionary movement, fighting in the trenches of electoral politics – many (though not all) of which were complementary. Much work lay ahead if this range of voices and approaches was to be articulated into a more influential political force, but the prospects seemed better to the extent that a positive political vision incorporating a new vision of quality of life was part of the message.

The forces driving a sufficiency-based critique included the belief that EM reform relying on technology and efficiency was not a full solution, evidence of economic growth's limited capacity to improve well-being in already affluent nations, and concerns for global justice in an ecologically constrained world. Yet powerful obstacles kept pushing the issue back into the shadows. Business resistance to suggestions of limits on output was one factor, while advocates of sufficiency perceived another, more immediate line of defence for the growth economy: the public's embrace of a consumerist vision of the good life, part of a wider growth ideology. Canadian governments showed no sign of even acknowledging that any option existed other than continued prioritization of growth, to which they looked for rising revenues and solutions to problems such as capitalism's continual displacement of workers and the need to moderate class conflict, not to mention the need to enable further capital accumulation. Labour also feared lost livelihoods with any slowdown of growth. Questions remained about how a low- or no-growth economy would ensure high levels of employment and cope with other key social challenges (although some important work had emerged in that area). A variety of constraints on environmentalists, such as a desire to work with business, maintain an image of respectability, and preserve funding, also made many of them reluctant to raise difficult questions about growth and alternatives to it.

Sufficiency advocates also expressed frustration with Canada's limited spectrum of acceptable discussion of social change to combat climate change. The fact that Canada had yet to seriously embark on the easier step of EM reform made it hard to see EM's limits, and contributed to environmentalists and climate activists continuing to focus their efforts on building support for an EM project in the face of conservative opposition. As we will see in the next chapter, even those with a radical critique of growth held it back at key times – the danger of highlighting a conflict between growth and GHG reduction was that it might drive people away from support for strong climate action and back toward business-as-usual. Meanwhile, the relatively limited public discussion of the determinants of well-being and happiness – despite the efforts of some organizations and individuals – also deprived Canadian sufficiency advocates of one key factor that created opportunities for their UK counterparts.

This litany of obstacles did not, however, prevent sufficiency from making some inroads in Canada when framed in more limited ways than a direct critique of economic growth.

4

Sufficiency's Small Steps Forward in Canada

Critical perspectives on economic growth and consumerism found inhospitable political terrain in Canada and remained largely beneath the surface in the mainstream climate debate. Ideas of sufficiency were, however, able to emerge in other, more limited ways. These included a type of double messaging by prominent environmentalists, who critiqued growth in certain contexts, but put forward elements of an ecological modernization message in others. Campaigns for sufficiency at the micro level sought to limit certain sectors, practices, or consumption of specific commodities. The idea of "less" made inroads with respect to some highly visible symbols of ecological excess and, paradoxically, as this chapter describes, in cases where it became linked to a broader economic growth agenda. Circumstances even emerged when it was in the interests of business to embrace a limited degree of sufficiency, including calls to conserve energy, which represented a borderland between efficiency and sufficiency. Campaigns for voluntary, individual lifestyle change represented a relatively uncontroversial outlet for ideas of sufficiency – and upon such campaigns some activists hoped to build something far more consequential: a wider movement for a less consumption-oriented society. Meanwhile, efforts to develop alternatives to GDP as an economic indicator resulted in some very limited gains for the critique of growth.

DOUBLE MESSAGES: GROWTH IS LIKE CANCER, CLIMATE ACTION BOOSTS GROWTH

"Economists think they're so smart that they think they can keep the economy growing forever. Not only do they believe the economy can grow forever, which it cannot, but they think it must," David Suzuki

(2007), Canada's most prominent environmentalist, told the prestigious Canadian Club of Toronto. "Steady growth forever when you live in a finite world is the creed of the cancer cell," he added. "When are we ever going to ask, then, how much is enough? Why do we need all this stuff?" To drill home the point that "our demand for steady growth is suicidal," Suzuki presented an analogy, often used by critics of exponential economic growth, of test-tube bacteria who double in number every minute and completely fill the tube after one hour, having consumed all available food. At fifty-five minutes, the tube is only 3 per cent full – no sign of trouble on the horizon. At fifty-nine minutes, the bacteria's growth prospects still look good as the tube is only half full. But Suzuki added a twist to the tale: imagine that in the last minute the bacteria develop technologies that give them three extra test tubes full of food. "So they're safe, right? They have quadrupled the amount of food and space. So what happens? Sixty minutes, the first test tube is full. Sixty-one minutes, the second is full. Sixty-two minutes, all four are full. By quadrupling the food and available space, you buy two extra minutes." Having seemingly demolished the idea that new technology can push back the limits to growth for long, Suzuki added: "Every biologist that I talk to agrees with me that we are long past the fifty-ninth minute. And here we are, one of the richest countries in the world, and we are still demanding more ... We think that in the name of progress, growth has got to be everything and we'll dig up and use every bit that should be the rightful legacy of our children and grandchildren. That's the insanity of what's going on today ... We've got to get on with finding ways of living within the productive capacity of the planet. And that's what the challenge of climate change is."

Ten days later and a few blocks away at the Toronto Stock Exchange, Suzuki shared the stage with one of those economists who maintained the economy could and must keep growing. Nicholas Stern, on a Canadian visit organized by the British High Commission to spread the word about his review of the economics of climate change, appeared before the press. "The growth strategy is to go onto a low-carbon economy as a world. The other strategy of ignoring this issue is eventually anti-growth," said Stern. "There are lots of opportunities for growth if we get it right" (David Suzuki Foundation 2007a). He added a key political consideration: "The idea that the environment and economic growth can go together is what has changed the debate in Europe." Suzuki looked on and listened before putting forward a complementary message. "It's a huge opportunity. And we can't predict what will come out of it. But you can be sure there will be unexpected results and technologies that will be huge plusses," he said, drawing a parallel between climate action and the space program's technological and economic spinoffs. In a press release on the event, the David Suzuki Foundation (2007b) went further in promoting an EM message, quoting Stern as saying, "Changes in energy technologies and in the structure of economies have created opportunities to decouple growth from greenhouse gas emissions."

So is growth the creed of the cancer cell? Or can it be decoupled from GHGs and other ecological impacts – in a sustained way, giving us more than the bacteria's two extra minutes? It was unrealistic to expect Suzuki to challenge Stern on this issue before the press, which would have distracted from Stern's useful arguments for critiquing the Harper government's climate policy. However, other examples existed of tension between pro- and anti-growth messages from Suzuki and the foundation that bore his name. "Economy needs a better goal than 'more,'" proclaimed one item on the David Suzuki Foundation (2006) website, which stated: "It's one of those questions that drifts in the shadows of our modern world, just waiting to be asked: 'How much is enough.' Yet few people do." Clearly, Suzuki, a long-time critic of growth, worked to bring that question out from the shadows. However, when he, his foundation, and their allies faced BAU proponents claiming that climate action would contract the economy, they tended to reach for EM-like arguments about economic "opportunities" (although not always "growth" per se), rather than calls to turn away from growth or consume less. For example, to challenge the claims of Kyoto Protocol opponents, the Suzuki Foundation and WWF commissioned and promoted a study concluding that GHG-reduction policies would increase Canada's GDP by $2 billion relative to a BAU scenario (Tellus Institute 2002). Later, in April 2007, Suzuki found himself battling Environment Minister John Baird, who claimed that meeting Canada's Kyoto commitments would cause a recession and destroy some two hundred thousand jobs. Suzuki responded on the CBC national news that the government's worst-case scenario failed to consider job creation opportunities from a clean energy transition and savings on health care costs from cleaner air. The Suzuki Foundation and Pembina Institute later promoted an EM message in reports entitled *Deep Reductions, Strong Growth* and *Climate Leadership, Economic Prosperity* (chapter 2).

I had a chance encounter with Suzuki at the Toronto launch of Peter Victor's book, *Managing Without Growth*. It was clear from our conversation – and from his speech to the Canadian Club, among other statements – that this book's title was more in tune with his personal views than the pro-growth message that the David Suzuki Foundation sometimes promoted. (Indeed, Suzuki's personal views were not necessarily those of the foundation.) But he said the argument of a conventional pro-growth economist such as Nicholas Stern that it would cost less to stop climate change than to not do so was "fine with me." Given the limited political space for ideas of sufficiency within Canada, it was understandable that leading environmentalists sometimes had to put the growth critique aside and piggyback on a pro-growth message.

A similar pattern of highlighting a growth critique in certain contexts but downplaying it in others was evident with the Green Party and its leader, Elizabeth May. Upon becoming leader, May, echoing Suzuki, said, "Unlimited economic growth is the ideology of the cancer cell" (CBC 2006). In 2007, May spoke at a Sierra Club event in Mississauga, Ontario. Wondering if a few months as leader had watered down her message, I asked her during the Q&A whether, given the fact that economic growth had outpaced carbon intensity reductions in many countries, it was time to confront endless economic growth. I prefaced the question by saying it might be a difficult one for someone in electoral politics to address. Without hesitation, May repeated her comments about growth and the cancer cell, adding, "I have no problem with your question." She argued that we must put economic growth on the agenda and "de-consumerize" our aspirations, adding that the drive for "more stuff" was increasing the stress in people's lives and alienating them from each other at the expense of well-being. During the discussion, she also called for sufficiency with respect to meat consumption and air travel, noting that the latter was a sector where no adequate technological solutions existed for its GHG emissions. ("I'll never go [by air] on a vacation again because I can't justify that flying," she stated.) A sufficiency message also came through that November when May invited "other political parties and all Canadians to join her in observing Buy Nothing Day, the day when citizens take a stand against rampant consumerism."

She said, "Many of the environmental problems we face come down to a single, inescapable truth – we must consume less" (CBC 2007a; Green Party of Canada 2007a).

Yet the message on growth was more ambiguous in the Green Party's Vision Green documents produced in 2007 and 2011. A critique of excess consumption was absent. A critique of economic growth was present, but it shared space – uneasily at times – with statements more in tune with EM. The 2007 document did refer to the need to work within "the scientifically verified limits to growth set by the carrying capacity of our planet" (Green Party of Canada 2007b, 4), said that "continued exponential growth is counter to the realities of a finite planet" (71), and pledged to rewrite NAFTA as "a fair trade agreement" based on principles including the recognition of "limits to growth and resources" (146).[1] A more indirect critique of growth was present in the call for alternative indicators of well-being to replace or complement GDP (13–14, 126). The Greens also advocated some forms of sufficiency at the micro level by pledging to reduce air travel and the number of cars on the road through improved rail service (26), end federal funding that encourages urban sprawl and vehicle use (66), and scale back transport needs by encouraging local food production (68). However, the main emphasis was on EM solutions to climate change: technology (especially renewable energy) and efficiency, stimulated by market-oriented policies (a green tax shift) backed by some new regulations. In addition to many references to "smart growth," the party characterized the shift to a low-carbon economy as "the single biggest business opportunity in human history," adding: "Improvements in labour productivity drove economic growth after the Second World War. We must now repeat the exercise as we improve the productivity of resource and energy use" (10). Above all, it emphasized that the "central driving principle of Green Economic Policy is *maximizing efficiency*" (10; italics added). Vision Green was actually less critical of the limits of efficiency in a context of relentless production growth than was the UK Conservative Party's Quality of Life Policy Group (2007) report issued around the same time (chapter 8).

With an unprecedented opportunity on the national stage during the 2008 election debate, May kept her heretical views on growth to herself, instead reiterating the EM idea that fighting climate change was "the greatest economic opportunity of our time." Facing a prime minister who emphasized climate action's costs, at a time of economic insecurity as the global financial crisis deepened, her choice was undoubtedly wise politically. While an overwhelming majority of Green Party supporters surveyed, as well as their leader, accepted the need for "limits to economic growth and consumption to achieve a healthy and sustainable environment" (Camcastle 2007), making a real priority out of attacking the "cancer" and finding a politically viable way to advance such ideas in front of a prime-time audience was no easy matter.

May's sympathies for the growth critique were again apparent at the International Conference on Degrowth in the Americas in Montreal in 2012, where she said the Greens were the only federal party to talk about "limits to growth." However, fraternizing with the degrowth crowd seemed to be in tension with the EM perspective May expressed in the *Canadian Business Journal*, in which she was quoted as saying, "there is no conflict between climate action and economic growth and sustainability" (Guy 2011). One might be able to reconcile these positions by arguing that there are ultimate limits to growth of the human economy, but solutions exist to the specific problem of climate change without sacrificing growth. Nevertheless, in light of such ambiguities, some party members presented a motion to clarify the Green stance on limits to growth. As the motion's initiator put it on the Green Party of Canada (2012) website, "Sustainability is central to our policy. However ... we do not expressly describe sustainability as inconsistent with exponential economic growth." The motion stated that exponential growth in a finite world would produce "catastrophic results" and called on the party to promote an "economy that evolves to be better not bigger."

The point of drawing attention to such inconsistencies and tensions is not to criticize any individual or organization, but rather to highlight the political difficulties in taking a sufficiency-based critique of economic growth into the mainstream, where there is great pressure to link one's ideas to the perceived imperative of economic growth. In addition, there is an evident challenge in more coherently synthesizing the critique of infinite growth with the idea that some economic opportunities could result from the transition to a low-carbon energy system.

The tension or, more positively, the dialogue between a critique of economic growth and calls for environmentally sound forms of economic expansion was also evident in statements by the Alberta Federation of Labour (AFL), whose leaders met David Suzuki to discuss climate change and which became the first provincial labour federation to develop a climate action plan (J. Foster 2007). The AFL was not the most obvious source of such ideas in light of the obstacles to a critique of growth within labour and the fact that Alberta's carbon-intensive, oil sands–fuelled growth had created beyond full-employment conditions that benefited many workers. Yet the AFL's (2007a) *Climate Change Policy Paper* had a very critical take on economic growth and "our structural dependence on a destructive path." While criticizing the dominance of the corporation and free-market ideology, the AFL noted, "Our economic model only continues to function with continuous growth – anything else produces economic crises typified by extreme social suffering, unrest and upheaval. But constant growth requires ever increasing production, consumption and population. All of these have negative environmental consequences" (4). The paper veered back toward an EM vision in its discussion of the tar sands, rejecting any environment-versus-economy trade off and arguing that, "We do not have to give up on development to achieve lower emissions. We need to clean up oil sands production to make sure it operates in a more sustainable fashion." It added, "action on climate change will create good jobs" and create "opportunities for labour" (6). Yet within this same policy paper, the AFL returned to sufficiency-based themes: "We are deeply immersed in a culture of consuming and convenience. Canadians happily sit in the middle of an economy that relies on growth, over-consumption and blindness to waste and consequences. Our individual choices help feed the system that heats the world … So it is not enough to blame governments and industry. We must all take a piece of the responsibility. For Albertans, that means changing our attitudes toward consumption – *choosing to buy less and to buy more consciously.* We need to reduce our personal reliance on cars and on wasteful devices and toys. We need to look at our own energy consumption and look at ways we can reduce our personal impact" (8; italics added).

The AFL advocated a range of other measures to address the climate crisis – both doing things "better" and "differently." Among them: "Adopt a new look at economic growth: we need to slow our pace of activity and become less reliant on growth." Proposed measures to reduce that dependence included "Just Transition programs for workers displaced by environmental change." Similarly, as discussed in more detail in the next chapter, the AFL called both for better technology and the slowing of the pace of development in the tar sands (10, 11). The AFL's document had some tensions within it, but it did make an initial contribution to synthesizing elements of EM and sufficiency into an economic strategy.

SUFFICIENCY: INROADS AT THE MICRO LEVEL

The idea of sufficiency could also appear at the micro level through calls to limit specific practices, production in specific sectors, or the consumption of certain goods – representing a less fundamental challenge to the social order than calls to limit macro-level GDP growth. In Canada, micro-sufficiency campaigns made important inroads, although their range was not as extensive as in the UK.

The idea of limiting meat and dairy consumption, for example, was long absent from Canada's climate debate. ("Eat less meat? It's a message we hardly ever hear," proclaimed one mainstream media report [Read 2008].) Major environmental groups were reluctant to highlight this issue despite some animal-rights and vegetarian activists' efforts to promote an "eat less meat" campaign.[2] Some mainstream environmental groups, however, did raise these issues in the safe, non-confrontational context of suggestions to those looking to make voluntary lifestyle changes, as discussed below. The volume of air travel – another GHG-intensive activity that triggered intense public debate in Britain – was not a major topic in Canada. Campaigners' reluctance to take on such issues could be understood, in part, by the fact that this would require not only confronting influential economic interests in the airlines and the agricultural sector, but also challenging strong public attachment to these forms of consumption. Meat consumption, for example, is closely tied to culture and family life, noted Dale Marshall, a climate policy analyst with the David Suzuki Foundation. "Saying that people need to become vegetarian is probably the most difficult," said Marshall. "Once you start attacking that, there is then possibility of a backlash becoming that much greater." Meanwhile, gas-powered patio heaters, which were driven off the floors of several leading UK retailers, escaped widespread critical scrutiny in Canada, although they raised the ire of a few (e.g. Jaccard 2007). Even SUVs – a very visible symbol of high-carbon consumption and, for the Canadian Autoworkers (CAW 2007), the recipient of disproportionate attention in the climate debate – did not, as in the UK, face sustained, organized campaigns aiming to turn them into a pariah vehicle.

Bags, Bottles, and Bulbs

Canadian campaigners nevertheless had some success with efforts to cut consumption of other items (Hayden 2014a). As in the UK, these included plastic bags and bottled water. Groups including the left-leaning Polaris Institute and Council of Canadians, faith-based organizations, labour unions, and environmentalists campaigned against bottled water, which they labelled an "unnecessary and wasteful product" (T. Clarke 2008). Their concerns included plastic-waste volumes, inadequate health protections, and the privatization and commodification of an essential element of life. Climate change was also a factor. Officials in London, Ontario estimated that producing bottled water generated 150 times more GHGs than tap water – one reason the city eliminated bottled water sales at all its facilities (Weeks 2008). The Federation of Canadian Municipalities called on other cities and towns to institute similar bans. Soon more than one hundred municipalities, colleges and universities, and school boards had done so, while Nova Scotia and Manitoba imposed similar restrictions on bottled water purchases by provincial departments (Straight Goods 2011).

In 2008, on the same day that it banned bottled water sales at its facilities, the nation's largest city, Toronto, approved a mandatory five-cent charge on disposable plastic shopping bags, following smaller communities such as Leaf Rapids, Manitoba, and Huntingdon, Quebec, which had banished such bags altogether. Anti-bag sentiment also led to plastic bag phase-outs at provincially owned liquor stores in Nova Scotia, Quebec, and Ontario. The latter province, along with British Columbia, Manitoba, and Alberta, reached agreements with retailers to reduce plastic bag distribution by 50 per cent. Such measures had an impact: Quebec, for example, reported a 52 per cent reduction in plastic bag use from 2007 to 2010, while Toronto saw a 53 per cent reduction from 2008 to early 2012 (Radio Canada 2012; Toronto 2012). (That, however, did not prevent Mayor Rob Ford from opposing Toronto's plastic bag charge, and, after many rounds of contentious council debate, he succeeded in eliminating it.)

Reducing landfill waste was often the main benefit that supporters of such measures highlighted, but the idea that less plastic bag use could help combat climate change was raised by some politicians and entered public consciousness.[3] The University of Toronto bookstore, for example, sold reusable bags with these words: "This Reusable Bag is part of our effort to reduce our environmental footprint. By using it, you are helping to fight climate change."

Plastic bags had many environmental downsides, but their contribution to climate change was small. Resource Conservation Manitoba (RCM 2008), an environmental NGO, calculated that *annual* plastic bag use in the province consumed the equivalent of 1.9 litres of gasoline per person, equal to driving a reasonably fuel-efficient mid-size car 23 km in the city. The danger thus existed that efforts to curb this form of consumption could serve as a symbolic substitute for more significant environmental measures. As if it intended to highlight that point, in December 2009, the city of Fort McMurray, at the centre of Alberta's oil sands, decided to ban plastic shopping bags (Shupac 2009). The local council's search for green legitimacy was a key reason why the high school student who spearheaded the measure found a receptive audience. Councillor John Vyboh explained, "Maybe this was one way to send a message to the rest of Canada or the province, or the world for that matter, that we do care about the environment and we're not afraid to show some leadership on some of these issues" (Brooymans 2009). The decision came at the very moment when Canada – committed to fully profiting from its tar sands inheritance – was earning the "Colossal Fossil" award from NGOs for its role in obstructing global climate talks in Copenhagen.

Although opposition to such measures certainly existed, as in the UK, plastic bags and bottled water were *relatively* easy targets for campaigns seeking to challenge over-consumption given their high visibility as symbols of ecological excess and the ready availability of alternatives. Extremely important was the fact that the businesses threatened by lower consumption of these items were of limited economic importance and political power. To a limited degree, other firms stood to gain from providing alternatives, such as the producers and retailers selling reusable bags. Whether in the long run such campaigns would serve as useful entry points to begin fashioning a consumption model appropriate for a low-carbon society, or amount to little more than symbolic action that distracted from the need for deeper social change, remained to be seen.

Another relatively easy target was the high-wattage incandescent light bulb. In 2007, the federal government announced a phase-out of the offending bulbs by 2012 – a deadline later extended until 2014 – although it justified this measure in terms of greater efficiency rather than sufficiency. Following Australia's John Howard, the Conservative Harper government found in banning incandescent bulbs a high visibility, low-cost measure to send the politically necessary signal that it was acting on then-intense public concern over climate. The measure's potential environmental benefits were not neglible; however, scepticism of the government's intentions in shoring up its green legitimacy was warranted as this small initiative was not accompanied by more significant measures to turn away from a carbon-intensive growth path.

Cutting Food Miles

Long-distance food transport came under scrutiny in Canada, as it did in the UK. Reducing food miles is a form of sufficiency with respect to distances travelled by food – a challenge to the modern trend of longer supply lines enabled by cheap fossil-fuelled transport (Sachs, Loske, and Linz 1998, 145). The idea of living with limits was clear in the title of *The 100-Mile Diet*, a bestselling book by two Vancouver writers (Smith and MacKinnon 2007), who sought alternatives to their GHG-intensive "SUV diet." Local food initiatives grew in visibility, such as Local Food Plus (LFP 2011), a Toronto-based non-profit that sought to foster "local sustainable food systems that reduce reliance on fossil fuels, create meaningful jobs, and foster the preservation of farmland – and farmers." In addition to certifying and labelling locally produced food, LFP built links among farmers and processors seeking predictable markets, large institutional buyers such as universities, and consumers seeking socially and ecologically responsible food.

The potential to build a coalition bridging the divides between rural and urban – and between environment and economy – also appealed to those with political power. Expanding local food production was a prominent theme in Toronto's (2007) climate action plan, leading in 2008 to approval of a Local Food Procurement Policy. Ontario's NDP called for similar "win-win local procurement policies" at the provincial level (ONDP 2011). For its part, the province's

Liberal government provided financial support for local food initiatives – some $116 million from 2003 to 2012. In 2013, with all-party support, Ontario passed a Local Food Act to increase awareness and set "aspirational" goals for public access to, and procurement of, local food (OMAFRA 2013). Although there was debate over whether the policies were strong enough, the government clearly saw benefits from "more sales of local Ontario foods" (OMAFRA 2008). "When we buy Ontario, everyone wins. It is good for our families, good for the economy and good for the environment," the province's agricultural minister stated. While campaigns to cut meat and dairy consumption faced opposition from many farmers, local food promotion could connect with the interests of the province's $34-billion agri-food sector. Other provinces – including Quebec, Nova Scotia, and Manitoba – saw similar potential in local-food initiatives.[4]

Controversy exists over whether local food is necessarily a lower-carbon option since transport is often a small component of food's total carbon and ecological footprint, and local methods could have greater impacts in other ways (chapter 9). Leaving aside that contentious debate for now, the key point here is the convergence between a sufficiency-based focus on living within local limits and the interest of the provincial government, local farmers, and agri-food businesses in agro-industrial expansion. This convergence expanded the space available for such ideas to grow. In other words, local food represented a special case in which the idea of sufficiency could be linked to the economic imperative that powerfully shapes state action.

Consuming Less Energy: A Borderland between Efficiency and Sufficiency

Energy consumption was one area where Canadian environmental groups were relatively vocal in demanding "less." (Transportation was another, at least that by private car, truck, and, to a lesser degree, airplane). Such thinking also made inroads into public policy and, eventually, statements by leading business groups. With energy consumption, not only were the GHG stakes high, the boundaries between efficiency and sufficiency were not always clear. Both concepts found a home in the notion of energy "conservation," which included all means of reducing energy demand, and which made important if still limited inroads.

A generation ago, "zero energy growth" was an influential idea in Canadian environmental circles and it left a lasting legacy (D. Brooks 1981). It drew on Amory Lovins's (1976) pioneering work in the US on a soft energy path (SEP), which aimed to limit energy demand to what renewable and ecologically benign sources could supply. Early Canadian formulations of a SEP not only emphasized the need for greater efficiency; they also identified the prioritization of economic growth as part of the problem. Brooks and Paehlke (1980, 452) wrote: "It is our view that a SEP will not be fully accepted as a viable possibility until the mystique of GNP as a measure of societal achievement is broken and/or until the lack of a necessary association between GNP and per capita energy use can be demonstrated more widely and clearly."[5]

Even as they continued to promote sufficiency with respect to energy use, over time SEP advocates downplayed questioning of economic growth and – at the macroeconomic level – turned to an EM approach focused on decoupling economic output and energy use. Ralph Torrie (2006, 1), a leading Canadian SEP advocate, described this paradigm shift: "In the old paradigm, the demand for energy commodities (fuels and electricity) was seen as being fundamentally tied to economic growth. Energy policy and commodity supply investment were built on the premise that commodity consumption must grow for economic output to grow. However, never-ending growth in the production and consumption of fuels and electricity is neither environmentally nor economically sustainable ... [In the new paradigm,] the connection between economic output and commodity production is broken to the extent that the [energy] service demand can often be met with less rather than more consumption of fuels and electricity."

A similar perspective became dominant within Canada's environmental movement. The Tomorrow Today (2008) coalition of the country's eleven leading environmental groups stated that to avoid catastrophic climate change, "we must use less energy to meet our needs" (7),[6] while it downplayed any conflict between strong climate action and economic growth (25). Even if these organizations did not directly question economic growth, by seeking to cap and even reduce energy consumption, environmentalists had taken on a challenge that appeared almost as daunting. Recessions aside, Canadian domestic primary energy consumption had risen steadily since data collection began in the 1920s (Torrie et al. 2013, 6), even though it had not grown as quickly as GDP since the 1970s. Government projections showed no end in sight to the upward trend in demand (NEB 2013, 25–32). The data left some policy analysts dismissive of the possibility of reducing energy use through efficiency and changes to material-intensive lifestyles (J. Simpson, Jaccard, and Rivers 2007, 116–17). The country's leading business lobby, the Canadian Council of Chief Executives (CCCE 2007a, 9), similarly dismissed talk of absolute reductions in energy use in the analysis behind its first "clean growth" report. It urged "recognition of the link between energy and development," stated that "energy demand will continue to grow," and emphasized that it "is unlikely that citizens, in either the developed or developing world, will accept a curtailment of their energy use" to solve climate change. For the CCCE, the key to addressing climate change was to increase supply of affordable low-carbon energy through new technology rather than cutting demand (although its position on this point would later evolve, as discussed below).

Despite scepticism in powerful places, the notion of using less energy made important if still limited inroads in public policy, at least in some provinces. In Ontario, for example, the Liberal government established the Ontario Conservation Bureau in 2005 and appointed Peter Love, former executive director of the Canadian Energy Efficiency Alliance, as the province's first chief energy conservation officer. Love was tasked with creating a "culture of conservation."[7] From 2005 to 2030, Ontario, a province with thirteen million residents, aimed to reduce projected peak electricity demand by 7,100 MW and overall demand by 28 terawatt hours (TWh) – a reduction equivalent to taking 2.4 million homes off the grid. It spent some $2 billion from 2006 to 2011 on electricity conservation programs (OPA 2012).

For the Ontario Conservation Bureau (2008), conservation comprised five different approaches, mostly based on efficiency and technology, but led by "conservation of use."[8] This was defined as "using less energy – pure and simple" through "changing our consuming behaviour" (e.g. turning off lights, unplugging electronics, adjusting thermostats, reducing use of powered appliances). The authorities stopped short of suggesting anything as rash as buying fewer electronics or appliances, but the idea that we should be "thinking about conservation in all our activities" did open up a space where sufficiency-based thinking could reside.

Ontario's effort to create a culture of conservation began to change some everyday practices. For example, a "right to dry" law overturned all bans imposed by housing developers on residents drying clothing outdoors. "There's a whole generation of kids growing up today who think a clothes line is a wrestling move," said Premier Dalton McGuinty (Usborne 2008). "We want parents to have the choice to use the wind and the sun to dry their clothes free." The fact that legislation was needed to permit people *not to consume* electricity illustrated the extent to which wasteful, climate-damaging practices had become embedded in modern society. The precise impact of this measure was hard to quantify, but, according to Chris Winter of the non-governmental Conservation Council of Ontario, it sent a high-profile signal that "conservation is good and we shouldn't have roadblocks to it." Meanwhile, the Office of the Premier of Ontario (2007) told government employees to leave jackets and ties at home during hot, humid summer months so thermostats could be set at 26°C, a climate-friendly measure pioneered in Japan. Four years later, an Ontario public servant reported that, despite some complaints from those who preferred a well-chilled office, these new norms had taken hold and, as summer approached, a memo reminded employees "to dress for the warmer office temperatures while maintaining a professional appearance."[9] The government also targeted Ontario residents' practice of keeping an old, inefficient fridge in the basement – and the "Great Refrigerator Round Up" removed some 230,000 old units from 2007 to 2010 (Ontario 2010, 38).

Conservation initiatives reduced *peak* electricity demand by an estimated 2,445 MW from 2005 to 2012 (ECO 2013), a significant amount, although increased efforts would be needed to meet targets for 2015. Ontario's *total* annual demand fell from a high of 157 TWh in 2005 to 152 in 2007 – even before the recession and manufacturing crisis scaled back demand further – and to 141.3 in 2012 (IESO 2013). Limiting demand and shifting it to non-peak periods – along with new natural gas and renewable supply – enabled the province to reduce coal burning 90 per cent from 2003 to 2011, on track for a complete phase-out by 2014. The Ontario government was thus able to claim that, "Conservation is now a cornerstone of long-term electricity planning" (Ontario 2010, 2, 6). Indeed, with figures showing that every dollar in conservation spending had saved $2 in avoided costs – some $4 billion overall – the province proclaimed a "Conservation First" energy vision (Ontario 2013; OPA 2012).

Ontario's conservation efforts contained much that was ecologically positive, but their limits were also significant. Critics repeatedly argued that much more could be done to promote a conserver culture. In addition to calls for more ambitious conservation targets, critics noted that conservation efforts focused on electricity, the source of a limited and, due to the coal phase-out, declining share of the province's GHGs. The government lacked a comprehensive conservation strategy covering all major energy sources, including transport fuels (ECO 2010, 18; G. Miller 2013) – not to mention other natural resources.

Environmentalists had originally sought a wider program of change. In fact, before scaling back its efforts, Ontario (2004) did launch a multi-issue "Ontario Conserves" initiative that went beyond electricity and energy to include a full range of threats to air, water, and land, based on the idea that "We are consuming our resources at an unsustainable rate." That broad initiative ultimately faded away and the central role in conservation was assumed by the Ontario Power Authority, the body responsible for ensuring reliability of the province's electricity supply.

Electricity system reliability and economic concerns, not climate change or broader environmental concerns, were in fact the main drivers of Ontario's conservation efforts and were key to understanding how an opening emerged for a degree of sufficiency-based policy in this case. The 14 August 2003 blackout that struck Ontario and the northeastern US focused attention on the fragility of the power system, upon which the rest of the economy depended. Chris Winter of the Conservation Council of Ontario noted that "two days after that blackout you heard every politician of every stripe say the word 'conservation' more times than they had in the past ten years." Beyond that particular incident, on the hottest summer days, demand threatened to surpass available supply, raising fears of future blackouts with coal-fired plants and nuclear reactors scheduled to come offline. "We are dangerously close to an unforgiving precipice, which threatens to undermine Ontario's continued prosperity," Energy Minister Dwight Duncan (2004) told Toronto's high-powered Empire Club. While announcing a range of measures to stabilize the electricity market and expand production, he added, "We will cut overall demand, and the government will cut its own consumption, so that we can lead by example. We're going to be a world leader in conservation." With business fearing power shortages, the Ontario Chamber of Commerce also urged "aggressive electricity conservation" (OCC 2007, 9). Other jurisdictions such as California had shown that conservation was a cheaper and faster way to avert a supply crisis than building new facilities – and Ontario (2010, 37) came to celebrate it as its most "cost-effective resource." As Minister Duncan (2004) put it, "A megawatt saved is every bit as good as a megawatt built."

Ontario's embrace of conservation illustrated that the idea of consuming less energy was able to carve out a significant niche for itself when there was a risk to electricity system stability, which the government had to ensure as a matter of high priority for the functioning of the entire economy and particularly its key electricity-intensive industries. However, sufficiency with respect to energy consumption, and a soft-energy path more generally, still had to contend with hard-energy path solutions, namely proposals to build new nuclear power plants, which promised considerable economic spin-off benefits for firms and workers in the province.

In such a context, to make further gains, soft-energy path advocates had to link their cause to the state's priority of stimulating new growth. The Ontario Green Energy Act Alliance (2008) argued that a strategy combining stronger conservation measures with new renewable sources would be cheaper and less risky than nuclear, while helping to revive a lagging manufacturing sector and would turn Ontario into a leading centre for North America's emerging clean energy industry. That argument made a significant breakthrough with the government's Green Energy and Green Economy Act – passed in May 2009 – which included a major boost to renewable energy through a German-inspired feed-in-tariff system and gave the government additional powers to promote energy conservation.

This was a case where the idea of sufficiency could hitch a ride on an EM project: through the concept of "conservation" where it overlapped with energy efficiency. But the idea of consuming less was primarily a means to the still-dominant end of economic expansion. As Energy Minister George Smitherman (2008) put it, "Using less energy doesn't just reduce the carbon. It doesn't just reduce the bill.

It also makes our province more productive so we have an economic advantage as well."

Less – Of Someone Else's Product

The idea that climate stability required scaling back some forms of consumption and production was sometimes even voiced within high-carbon sectors. However, economic actors in these sectors tended to focus not on their own products – whose legitimacy was challenged in a context of demands for climate action – but on the output of other sectors.

Take, for example, an initiative by Aeroplan, Air Canada's frequent flyer program, to encourage its employees to stop driving to work – for which they were rewarded with air miles that would allow them to fly more (Jang 2007). Meanwhile, the Canadian Auto Workers called for "powerful measures to slow down the oil sands boom" to limit GHG emissions (CAW 2007, 9). To complete the circle, employees at major firms involved in Alberta's tar sands were encouraged to commit to low-carbon lifestyle changes including flying less (Pembina Institute 2004, 2005). Put it all together – drive less, fly less, and stop oil sands growth – and emissions would really start to fall. However, it was a difficult step for business and labour to go beyond seeing someone else's product as a problem to participating in a wider social project of reining in all carbon-intensive practices and sectors.

SUFFICIENCY WITH A CORPORATE TWIST

Business support for endless macro-level economic expansion was solid, with the exception of rare individual business people who questioned the ecological viability of that path. However, the above examples of support for less consumption of somebody else's high-carbon goods or services illustrated that conditions existed in which corporate Canada could back narrowly defined versions of sufficiency that fell short of a direct critique of economic growth.

Yet it was still surprising to see the Canadian Council of Chief Executives (CCCE 2007a, 4) present this analysis of the limits of efficiency, which echoed the critiques of sufficiency theorists: "Even with more efficient appliances and better insulation in new homes, overall emissions of GHGs by Canadian households continue to rise. Population increases and other demographic changes are partly responsible for this increase, along with the fact that the average size of a new home has grown over time. Similarly, automobiles are becoming more fuel efficient but these gains are offset by increases in the overall number of miles traveled ... And as is the case in many other countries, air travel has risen considerably in the past decade, contributing to the overall growth in GHGs." Similarly, CCCE VP John Dillon noted, "The average television you can buy today probably uses energy more efficiently than one of similar size from five years ago, except that many households have two or three." Concern within Canadian business over consumption levels had also been evident in a statement by the Executive Forum on Climate Change (2005), which called for a climate regime that included "incentives to lower consumption and to change consumer behaviour."

This acknowledgment within business of the problems created by rising consumption could be understood in terms of personal, political, and economic factors. First, informed individuals within business, like others concerned about climate change, reached their own conclusions about contemporary excess. "This is more of a personal view," said one business community interviewee who preferred anonymity, "but I guess we all have our favourite example of the things that really are excessive. I wonder why so many people feel the need to drive SUVs ... I have my HDTV now and the picture is a lot better, but I don't really see the point of 50-, 60-inch screens." He added, "It's a little bit tricky when you get to something like carbon consumption because one person's excess is the next person's necessity. Some people drive minivans because they've got four kids they need to take places. Some people don't take public transit for a variety of reasons, some of which are noble, some of which are not ... But I think we do need a kind of social consensus around ... what kinds of things we need to be doing to change our behaviour." Similarly, Rick Hyndman of the Canadian Association of Petroleum Producers expressed personal frustration at the auto industry's production of oversized vehicles.

Beyond such personal views, Canadian business had a political interest in shining the spotlight on consumption to the extent that it broadened the focus of debate beyond regulatory policies targeting industry. Indeed, this was a consistent theme in corporate Canada's climate message over the years. According to Simpson, Jaccard, and Rivers (2007, 63), during the National Climate Change Process from 1998 to 2000, the CCCE's predecessor, the Business Council on National Issues, "blamed consumers more than producers for GHG emissions." Dillon saw the issue somewhat differently, stating that, for the CCCE and other business organizations, GHG reduction was a matter of "shared responsibility." He explained that the Liberal government's commitment to Kyoto "left a lot of people worried that business would end up carrying the burden for that target." He added, in reference to emissions reductions more generally, "The concern that's still out there and still very strong is that so much of the attention is focused on industry when this is a national objective." This concern helps to explain the CCCE's (2007b) calls for "all segments of Canadian society" to do their part in reducing GHGs and its willingness to raise questions of consumption and lifestyle: "Very little has been done to explain to Canadians their contribution and their responsibilities, and the impact that aggressive action to reduce emissions will have in terms of the cost of energy, and higher prices for consumer goods and services ... No government seems willing to suggest that *real progress requires sacrifices,* yet it is hard to imagine making a significant dent in consumer emissions without *serious attention to lifestyle,* energy use and transportation choices" (CCCE 2007a, 4; italics added).

The CCCE's (2011) subsequent report on "building a culture of energy conservation" furthered its analysis of rising consumption volumes overwhelming the gains from energy efficiency (see also CCCE 2010, 7, 27), and made clear additional economic factors that could lead business to embrace a limited formulation of sufficiency. The report noted that despite a 22 per cent reduction in energy consumed per unit of GDP from 1990 to 2008, total end-use energy consumption in Canada still grew by 25.7 per cent (CCCE 2011, 10). In addition to increases in average home size and passenger-kilometres travelled (3), the chief executives identified factors including significant growth in commercial floor space (17), rising use of air conditioning (15, 17), expansion of truck freight (11), and "the sheer increase in the number of energy-using appliances, computers and electronic equipment" (15) as causes of the growth in consumption. The CCCE reported that the number of computers, TVs, music systems, DVD players, espresso machines, and the like grew 55 per cent from 1990 to 2008, while the energy consumption attributed to them rose almost 150 per cent. The CCCE also acknowledged that the rebound effect – cost savings from greater energy efficiency enabling more consumption – was part of the reason why efficiency was failing to reduce energy consumption (12). It added that "the focus of energy and environmental policy has too often been on the questions of energy supply, whereas it is really on the demand side of the equation where the greatest potential for positive change exists" (7).

Yet in terms of solutions, the chief executives (not surprisingly) backed away from a direct critique of consumerism, stopping short of calling on consumers to limit purchases of large homes, vehicles, or energy-consuming gadgets. Instead, they urged "making conservation the new norm" by improving energy literacy and, above all, putting a price on carbon and letting energy prices rise (2011, 26–8). The CCCE's recommendations did, however, step beyond an EM framework by calling for action to "get more people out of their cars and using public transit, car-pooling, cycling and walking," a shift that, in the long run, would require urban densification rather than the "'sprawl' that seems to afflict so many of our largest urban centres" (23–4). Even for business, certain types of high-carbon, energy-intensive growth had become deeply problematic. Some eco-Marxists argued that leading business organizations did not question urban sprawl as a cause of climate change due to the demand for consumer durables and profit opportunities it created (Gonzalez 2005), but the CCCE's position showed that conditions could emerge to change business's perspective. The Council's emphasis on "reducing overall energy consumption" also reflected a change in tone from only a few years earlier when it expressed scepticism that the public would accept a curtailment of energy use (CCCE 2007a, 9).

The CCCE (2011, 2) explained its new emphasis on cutting energy consumption in EM rather than sufficiency terms, citing economic benefits: "The cheapest form of energy is the unit that is not used. Better conservation practices will help to insulate Canadians from volatile energy prices, reduce costs for public institutions such as schools and hospitals, and improve the international competitiveness of Canadian companies." The "prospect of continually rising energy bills" due to growing global energy demand was a key motivator behind the new message (6), as the "most energy efficient countries will have a great comparative advantage in a world of expensive energy" (CCCE 2010, 27–8). Getting people out of their cars would also reduce the traffic congestion that is costly to business and improve workplace productivity (CCCE 2011, 2). The chief executives concluded on this EM note: "It is time for Canadians to get serious about energy conservation, for the health of our economy as well as the environment" (31).

The CCCE, like some other mainstream actors with their eyes open to the data, acknowledged the problems with ever-rising volumes of consumption, even though it ultimately steered the discussion back to the safer language of EM. Yet the fact that business could be driven to identify consumption levels as a problem, even as it continued to depend on high and rising consumption for expanding markets, represented the emergence of a contradiction that might grow as pressure to cut emissions and energy use intensified in the years ahead.

While the chief executives emphasized longer-term economic concerns to justify their embrace of energy conservation, situations could emerge in which business backed less consumption or growth of specific kinds to ward off immediate threats to economic growth more generally. This was evident, for example, in the Ontario Chamber of Commerce's acknowledgment that conservation initiatives had become a "necessity" as concern grew over the reliability of Ontario's electricity system, even though the organization's primary focus was on ensuring expanded, affordable supply to enable future growth (OCC 2005; 2007, 9, 38). Similarly, as discussed in the following chapter, conditions emerged in which some oil companies actually called for a temporary slowdown of oil sands expansion (with the aim of blocking competitors' projects, thereby reducing their own costs for scarce inputs, notably labour). Such examples certainly did not represent any fundamental rethinking of growth as a top business priority, but were special cases of temporary alignment of business interests with calls to slow certain forms of growth or reduce demand for certain commodities. These examples indicated that sufficiency-oriented campaigners might find specific, limited instances when they could link their micro-level demands to business interests and, paradoxically, to the wider economic-growth imperative.

Two other reasons why some businesses could support calls for less consumption of high-carbon goods and services were the profit opportunities from providing alternative products as well as the PR benefits (including diverting attention from a firm's own emissions). These rationales were evident in campaigns encouraging individuals to change lifestyle and consumption practices.

Consuming less could be framed as a matter of voluntary individual action rather than a social project. An individualized focus led toward much less contentious political terrain, onto which some businesses and governments were prepared to move. However, other groups sought to take such lifestyle change efforts further by uniting individuals into a broader movement to question a consumerist vision of the good life and, indirectly, a growth-based economy.

The One-Tonne Challenge

An early example of a lifestyle change promotion was the "One-Tonne Challenge" (OTC), officially launched by the federal Liberal government in 2004. The OTC asked Canadians to reduce their annual GHG emissions by one tonne – an average 20 per cent cut in emissions directly linked to individuals and households. In addition to an online GHG calculator to allow people to determine their emissions and develop a personal action plan, as well as national marketing and outreach initiatives, the Government of Canada (2004) produced a guide with suggested lifestyle changes. The vast majority of these changes fell within the bounds of an EM framework, emphasizing more efficient energy use to meet given demands (e.g. check tire pressure, seal air leaks at home, maintain your pool more efficiently) or consuming differently (e.g. buy a fuel-efficient vehicle or Energy Star appliances). In fact, stimulating consumer demand for new, low-GHG products was a government objective (Environment Canada 2006). However, a few OTC suggestions urged people to actually consume less – that is, reduce demand for energy-based services and high-carbon commodities (e.g. drive less, give up your second vehicle, "don't buy more than you need" in terms of vehicle size, turn down the thermostat, limit the need for and use of air conditioning). In this way, government itself engaged in a limited promotion of sufficiency-oriented ideas.

While Canada under Liberal governments was a climate laggard in most policy areas compared to the UK and other leading European states, this was not the case with lifestyle and behaviour change. As in Britain (chapter 10), the emphasis on lifestyle change was driven in part by the political difficulties of introducing climate-related tax and regulatory policies. In Canada, such difficulties were encountered at a relatively early date. A carbon tax was long a political taboo due to fossil fuel sector and regional opposition, while, in the face of business resistance, the government struggled to develop regulatory measures and carbon trading for large industrial emitters. For example, from 2002 to 2005, the government weakened its target for industrial emissions reductions, from 55 to 39 Mt, even as total reductions needed to meet its Kyoto commitments had increased from 240 to 270 Mt (Macdonald and VanNijnatten 2005). At the same time, the government stepped up efforts to get Canadians to voluntarily cut their personal emissions, putting an additional $120 million into the OTC in 2005, on top of the $45 million previously budgeted for 2003 to 2006. However, the OTC ultimately had little chance to have an impact as the incoming Conservative government scrapped it in 2006.

Critics found many flaws in the OTC. The most common criticism was that relying on moral suasion and voluntarism was unlikely to produce significant GHG reductions without being part of an integrated package that included stronger regulations and financial incentives (e.g. Macdonald and VanNijnatten 2005; Stanford 2002). Also needed, critics argued, was a supportive social infrastructure, including, for example, convenient public transit, to enable lower-carbon lifestyle choices. Without strong complementary policies, the rebound effect was also likely to undo many if not all of the initial gains, as money saved on greater energy efficiency would then be spent on other energy-consuming goods and services. Meanwhile, commenting on initial plans for the OTC, CAW economist Jim Stanford (2002, 54) took exception precisely to the initiative's sufficiency elements, rejecting what he saw as its "underlying assumption that the key to meeting Kyoto lies mainly with getting Canadians to get by while doing less: less driving, less heating, less air conditioning." One could also question the target of a one-tonne reduction for all Canadians. Equitable at first glance, it ignored the fact that high-income earners had much larger carbon and ecological footprints on average (Mackenzie, Messinger, and Smith 2008) and produced more "luxury emissions." Hence they could have been asked to make greater reductions.

The focus on personal behaviour change also had the potential to be individualizing and depoliticizing, distracting attention from the need for government and corporate action and wider structural change. The "One Tonne Corporate Challenge" (OTCC), a pilot initiative of the Pembina Institute supported by Environment Canada in 2003–04, provided an example of such pitfalls. Hundreds of employees from four of Canada's largest oil and gas producers – Shell Canada, Petro-Canada, Suncor Energy, and ConocoPhillips – committed to actions that would reduce their annual personal GHG emissions by 4,601 tonnes. "And they've been pleasantly surprised to find out just how easy it can be," reported the Pembina Institute (2005). "The One Tonne Challenge is about taking personal responsibility for improving our energy use, and we are very proud of our employees' enthusiastic response to the program," added a Suncor spokesperson. The Canadian oil and gas industry's responsibility for some 162,000,000 tonnes of emissions per year at the time went unmentioned (Environment Canada 2013a, 15). Meanwhile, a central component of the OTCC was the Pembina Institute's (2004) One Less Tonne online tool, which included twenty actions individuals could take to meet the one-tonne target and calculated both the emissions and financial savings from each action. This tool remained online for public use, sponsored for a time by Suncor, Petro-Canada, Shell, and two firms who came to be key players in controversial tar sands pipeline proposals: Enbridge and TransCanada. There was certainly some value in engaging fossil fuel industry employees on the climate issue and in spreading the word about the benefits of actions such as washing clothes in cold water. However, one cannot help but conclude that fossil fuel corporations' interest in such programs was in shifting attention from their own vast emissions and the lack of strong public policy to reduce them – while simultaneously gaining PR points and shoring up their green legitimacy.

Although some scepticism about the motives behind such voluntary lifestyle change initiatives was warranted, the OTC did have the merits of promoting greater awareness of GHG sources in everyday activities. It could never be enough on its own, but the promotion of carbon literacy and new norms for responsible citizen behaviour was surely a piece of the larger climate action puzzle, as long as it did not obscure government and industry roles. The fact that the OTC suggested a need for less of some types of consumption also represented a limited opening for the questioning of material needs in a carbon-constrained age.

The Good Life

Environmental groups later launched similar programs that took the One-Tonne Challenge's approach further in key ways, albeit with a far lower profile and fewer resources behind them. One example was WWF-Canada's (2008) "Good Life," later rechristened the "Living Planet Community," an "online community for concerned Canadians who want to stop talking about climate change and start taking personal action to reduce their CO_2 emissions." The website suggested a range of actions to which people could commit, while providing overall tallies of emissions thereby avoided. Illustrating awareness of the pitfalls of an individual-level focus, WWF-Canada named a further goal: to "demonstrate the need for governments and business to take swifter action to reduce our greenhouse gas emissions." Most significant for a sufficiency perspective was the attempt to link individual change to a new vision of well-being: "In the past, living the Good Life meant lavish spending, excess waste and the trappings of material goods. But in today's climate-conscious society, WWF-Canada is redefining The Good Life to represent a life that is healthy for us, for the planet and for future generations." Although the initiative stopped short of critiquing a growth economy, it included questioning of the consumerism that sustains it.

Like the OTC, the Good Life's suggested actions included a mix of EM and sufficiency: efficiency improvements requiring new purchases and other actions to avoid consumption – with a richer mix of the latter, including "fly less" and "eat less meat." Also noteworthy was the backing of corporate and government sponsors for specific actions. Not surprisingly, ideas such as "buy green power" and "replace your window A/C" (with a more energy efficient unit) were more likely to find sponsors – Bullfrog Power and Natural Resources Canada, respectively – than actions where no new purchase was involved, such as "choose not to own a car." However, some sufficiency-oriented ideas did find corporate backers in cases where cutting GHG-intensive consumption opened up opportunities for alternative sales. While suggestions to "fly less" went sponsor-less, a related action, "teleconference with overseas colleagues," was supported by Bell Canada, provider of virtual meeting services, under the slogan of "Think more … Travel Less." Another sufficiency-based action – "eat local foods" – found a sponsor in Liberté, a Canadian dairy products supplier whose interests in increased local sales overlapped with the drive to reduce

food miles. (Coincidence or not, WWF made no mention on the site
of cutting dairy consumption, even though dairy cows were a major
GHG source.) These examples provided a further small-scale illustration of how the playing field was tilted against climate solutions that
did not simultaneously create sales opportunities, which was the case
for most but not all sufficiency-based ideas. The Good Life campaign
also represented a case of a large mainstream environmental group
finding a relatively safe, uncontentious way to step beyond an EM
framework and suggest not just a need to consume differently, but
also to consume less.

We Conserve

Another NGO campaign that built on voluntary lifestyle change was
the Conservation Council of Ontario's "We Conserve" initiative (CCO
2008b). For the CCO's executive director Chris Winter, "conservation" was a catch-all term for environmental commitment meaning
that "I'm doing my part to reduce my environmental impact." This
multi-meaning term also drew on the legacy of the Science Council of Canada's (1977) work, *Canada as a Conserver Society*, which, in
a previous era of resource-scarcity fears and early climate concern
(10), had outlined an agenda to move beyond a consumer society
through a mix of new technology, efficiency, and sufficiency.[10] The
CCO likewise had elements of sufficiency and EM in its message – indeed, it could be seen as working toward a synthesis between those
perspectives. It suggested that a conserver society would have a role
in "promoting new growth" (CCO 2008a) of a greener kind. Yet elsewhere Winter (2008, 6) wrote, "it is inevitable that the exponential
economic growth of the past century cannot be maintained" and,
hence, an "orderly and voluntary transition to a conserver society"
was needed.

To begin that transition, the CCO suggested personal actions incorporating a range of technological, efficiency, and sufficiency-based
ideas, including "drive less" and "live local" – "live, work, shop, and
play within a walkable mixed-use community" – which would, among
other benefits, cut the need for transport and vehicles. Winter also
revealed his family's lifestyle choices online, stating, "We have no
car, commute by bike, and are members of Autoshare. We plan local

vacations." He added in an interview, "By living a conserver lifestyle, we actually have a higher quality of life ... a conserver lifestyle does not mean sacrificing. It's a different way of life and in many cases, healthier, better, more affordable."

The campaign was also noteworthy for trying to link personal action ("I Conserve") to a wider movement ("We Conserve") with a social transition strategy, potentially making it more politically challenging than other voluntary lifestyle change initiatives. Winter's goal was to get every individual – as well as businesses, organizations, and municipalities – to commit to conservation. If large numbers were to do so, a "critical mass" would exist to demand supportive government policy and infrastructure while providing a base for mutual support. He emphasized in an interview that there was already a "small but widespread green economy and social infrastructure in place to help people live better and conserve at the same time," which could be further developed to enable deeper change. Winter (2007) set ambitious targets for this united conservation movement, including a 25 per cent reduction in residential electricity demand, a 30 per cent cut in gasoline consumption, and 50 per cent of Ontario's food being locally and sustainably grown within five to ten years. One could certainly question whether the cco's strategy could achieve these goals given existing trends, resistance from powerful vested interests, and continued popular appeal of consumerism. One could also ask whether the capacity was in place to provide a just transition for workers who would be displaced. Nevertheless, the We Conserve initiative did illustrate an effort to build on, and go beyond, individual lifestyle change to create a movement for a lower-impact society with a higher quality of life, incorporating a strong degree of both EM and sufficiency.

Yet at a time when Ontario was preparing to spend billions of dollars on nuclear power and automobile industry support, the cco struggled to find long-term funding for its minimally staffed conserver society campaign. As Winter put it, "we are not even at the starting point where government takes transition seriously." Meanwhile, Winter anticipated opposition from some of biggest players in the Ontario economy; the "losers in a conserver economy are the automakers and the urban sprawl home builders," he said. Despite the resistance, Winter later took the theme of a voluntary transition to a conserver society to the national level with the "Canada Conserves" initiative that aimed to "help Canadians to live better with less" and to restore Canada's status as a leader in conservation.

These initiatives to promote individual lifestyle and behaviour change were places where ideas of sufficiency could find a safe refuge and make initial inroads into the Canadian climate and sustainability debate. In its most limited formulation, encouragement of a purely individualized, depoliticized form of personal action risked becoming a distraction from the need for change at the government, corporate, and societal levels. But when linked to promotion of a less consumption-oriented vision of the good life and action to build a movement for social transition, efforts to promote individual change had greater potential to contribute to creation of a low-carbon society. To be successful on a large scale, though, they would eventually have to confront some of the same obstacles facing a more direct challenge to a growth economy.

NEW WELL-BEING INDICATORS

As noted in chapter 3, Canadian researchers and NGOs were important contributors to the emerging global effort to develop alternatives to GDP as the dominant economic indicator, alternatives such as a Genuine Progress Indicator (GPI). Important work on such measurements was done in Nova Scotia by GPI Atlantic, whose founder Ron Colman was also contributing to Bhutan's efforts to promote Gross National Happiness, and in Alberta by the Pembina Institute (2005) and ecological economist Mark Anielski. Many of the people promoting alternative well-being indicators saw their efforts as a challenge to the wider growth paradigm. However, others with a less radical agenda also took an interest in the issue, such as Liberal finance minister Paul Martin, whose 2000 budget gave the National Round Table on the Environment and the Economy $9 million to develop new sustainable development indicators (Wilson and Tyedmers 2013).

Much Canadian work on alternative well-being indicators came to centre on the Canadian Index of Wellbeing (CIW), produced by academics, backed by Atkinson Charitable Foundation funds, and championed by former NDP premier of Saskatchewan Roy Romanow. The first full version of the CIW, based on sixty-four indicators in eight domains, was released in 2011. From 1994 to 2010, Canada's GDP grew 28.9 per cent, but the CIW rose just 5.7 per cent – and in fact plummeted 24 per cent from 2008 to 2010, much more than the decline in GDP following the recession (CIW 2012). These figures were consistent with sufficiency advocates' argument that greater economic output was not strongly associated with well-being. The data also highlighted the importance of avoiding the economic turmoil of recessions, which was highly destructive of well-being. While Canada did well in some areas – e.g. community vitality and falling crime – the environment was the domain that deteriorated most since 1994, with large increases in GHGs and per capita ecological footprint. "The Environment domain speaks volumes about the tension between the relentless pursuit of economic growth and the finite reality of a planet experiencing massive climate change and dwindling natural resources," stated the CIW report (2012, 5). More Canadians also faced a "time crunch," as almost one in five working-age adults felt high levels of time pressure, prompting the authors to write, "Certainly economic growth is laudable. *But what does it mean to a society if it comes at the expense of less free time, fewer social connections, lower personal satisfaction, and a more stressful life?*" (9; italics in original).

The CIW's significance for critics of growth was limited in some important respects. First, unlike the UK (chapter 10), no government in Canada, federal or provincial, had adopted the CIW, or any other alternative well-being measure, as an official statistic. Those involved in developing the CIW were not optimistic about federal adoption any time soon – although hopes were higher for local and provincial adoption (Wilson and Tyedmers 2013). In addition, whereas the GPI's originators saw it as a replacement for GDP as a societal welfare indicator, the CIW was promoted as a measurement to complement GDP. Most significantly, the radical critique of growth that motivated many proponents of GPI was downplayed in the CIW. Wilson and Tyedmers (2013, 196) wrote, "The focus has changed from using alternative metrics to question failings of GDP and economic growth toward promoting a growth platform with fewer associated environmental and social costs."

That said, the existence of a measurement showing that well-being had not increased in line with economic growth, the environment had seen the greatest deterioration among any measured domain, and the material affluence of Canadians was accompanied by high levels of time poverty did offer opportunities for those seeking to promote alternatives to the growth paradigm. It remained to be seen to what degree the voices of sufficiency would be able to take advantage of this opportunity to change Canada's social and political priorities.

CONCLUSIONS

A key theme in the previous chapter was the struggle by sufficiency advocates to find ways to put the questioning of growth on the public agenda and open up discussion of the need for alternatives. Or, to paraphrase the David Suzuki Foundation (2006): How does one bring the question of "how much is enough" out from the shadows of the modern world? In this chapter, we have seen some ways in which that question did emerge from the shadows, albeit falling short of a head-on critique of GDP growth as a social priority.

Some prominent voices in the environmental movement – such as David Suzuki and Green Party leader Elizabeth May – did occasionally denounce the dogged pursuit of economic growth and consumerism, reflecting the views of many greens who doubted the wisdom of infinite growth on a finite planet. Yet even these high-profile figures picked their moments to depict growth as a "cancer" and tended to shy away from that line of argument when it came to a public showdown with opponents of strong climate action, reaching instead for less controversial EM-like arguments highlighting economic opportunities. There was almost certainly a way to synthesize a growth critique with recognition of the need and potential for certain forms of green economic expansion, but more work was needed to develop a coherent and consistent message.

Meanwhile, excess consumption and production could be targeted at the micro level. In some sectors, namely aviation and meat and dairy, the lack of adequate technological and efficiency-based solutions to high GHG emissions made lower consumption particularly important, but the relatively limited public discussion in Canada stood out in contrast to the UK. Taking on those issues through sustained campaigns would not only mean confronting the significant economic interests at stake; it would also require the willingness to challenge widespread public attachment to these forms of consumption.

However, concerns over excess consumption did find some politically viable outlets at the micro level, offering lessons about ways in which sufficiency-oriented ideas could make inroads in the contemporary political economy (Hayden 2014a). Successful campaigns to cut consumption of plastic bags and bottled water resulted in numerous provincial and municipal actions. These items were ubiquitous, visible symbols of ecologically profligate consumption, for which consumers had readily available alternatives, and whose producers were of limited economic and political importance. These factors helped explain why these commodities were targeted not only by environmentalists, but also by some politicians – even in Fort McMurray, Alberta – needing to demonstrate action on climate change and other environmental challenges. The Conservative federal government's ban on another relatively easy target, incandescent light bulbs, had some similarities as it was driven by the need to show ecological commitment, although it was justified in terms of greater efficiency rather than a sufficiency-based challenge to consumption excess.

In terms of core political imperatives, one can interpret politicians' interest in limiting such commodities as a linkage of environmental concern to the legitimation imperative – i.e. the need to show that their rule and the broader political economy are legitimate and able to address key social concerns. Legitimation was coming to require at least the appearance of action to combat key environmental challenges. However, plastic bags and bottled water were not large GHG sources, and the question remained whether measures to limit them would serve as an entry into wider action to change a high-carbon consumption model or as a symbolic substitute for it.

The carbon stakes were potentially higher with efforts to reduce food miles and conserve energy, and thus the inroads made by sufficiency in these realms were more noteworthy. Sufficiency usually faces a major disadvantage in running counter to key actors' economic interests. In the case of food miles and energy, however, micro-sufficiency found a connection to the interests of the state and business by expanding sales of local foods and ensuring that excessive demand did not overwhelm the capacities of the power system, upon which GDP growth depends. Paradoxically, sufficiency with respect to certain goods or practices appeared to face better prospects when it could be linked to increased economic output in some other form. In other words, these were instances where the idea of sufficiency, narrowly defined, attached itself to the economic growth imperative.

The cases of reducing food miles and energy conservation also illustrated the potential for the boundaries between sufficiency and ecological modernization to become blurred – creating opportunities for radical ecological ideas to benefit from the overlap with a more mainstream agenda. Some political actors may frame their support for such measures in terms of the need, in a finite world, to limit the quantities of energy consumed or food miles travelled. Yet they may find more powerful allies on these issues who celebrate local agro-expansion as a form of "green growth" or, like the Canadian Council of Chief Executives, embrace energy conservation as a way to increase business competitiveness and enhance long-term economic growth prospects by reducing vulnerability to rising fuel prices.

Although it seemed unlikely that business would ever back a societal vision in which sufficiency played a central role, these examples showed that, in special circumstances, business could support certain narrowly defined versions of sufficiency. These circumstances also included situations where calls to cut the consumption of some other firm's product provided businesses with economic opportunities to sell greener alternatives or enhance their own green legitimacy by providing positive PR opportunities. Meanwhile, there were political advantages to business in shining light on the problem of rising consumption to the extent that it shifted the focus of debate from the regulation of industry onto consumer behaviour.

Campaigns promoting voluntary lifestyle change were a relatively uncontroversial way for sufficiency-oriented ideas to appear. Initiatives such as the federal One-Tonne Challenge emphasized EM themes of more energy-efficient behaviour and consuming differently, but also opened some space for the idea of consuming less. The tendency of such initiatives to individualize responsibility could divert attention from the need for broader political, corporate, and societal action; however, some groups worked to avoid such pitfalls by linking individual change to a wider conserver vision of the good life and a movement for societal transition. These activist efforts had few resources behind them and struggled against the odds. However, in them one could discern the outlines of a social vision that included EM elements, yet went beyond them, combining some growth of green economic activity, the scaling back of other high-carbon, high-impact activity, and an emphasis on quality of life over quantity of material goods.

There was one sector in Canada for which the idea of sufficiency was arguably most relevant: Alberta's oil sands, a source of rapid, high-carbon growth. That issue, which cut to the heart of Canada's difficulties in shifting to a low-carbon society, is the focus of the next chapter.

5

Alberta's Oil/Tar Sands:
Time to Step on the Brake?

Almost everything about the tar sands was big, from the profits to the pollution to the political stakes. The total area in question in northern Alberta was about the size of Florida and larger than England. At the Oil Sands Discovery Centre, the gift shop sold T-shirts and giant beer glasses with the slogans "Size Matters" and "Bigger is Better," while postcards celebrated the 400-tonne trucks that were reportedly like driving a three-storey house ("The Toys in Our Sandbox!"). Advocates of sufficiency with respect to tar sands growth agreed that size mattered, but suggested that this operation had to be cut down to size to attain climate policy goals and regional environmental sustainability. Many others accepted – at least on the level of rhetoric – that business-as-usual could no longer continue in the oil sands. However, ecological modernization through technology and efficiency appeared to have limited prospects to resolve the full range of problems generated by rapid growth, strengthening the argument for limits on the scale of activity. Such ideas clearly faced an uphill struggle given the dollar values at stake, but anti–tar sands campaigners were nevertheless able to gain a wide range of allies and win partial victories that provided lessons for the politics of sufficiency.

WELCOME TO FORT MCMONEY

My first impression of Fort McMurray was quite positive. I went to the hotel ATM and walked away with $40 more than I had requested. At first, I thought had stumbled upon a magic money machine – undoubtedly I was not the first person in town to have had that feeling. Either that or the person who used the machine before me wasn't too concerned about picking up all his money. A couple of bills hardly make a difference when you are standing on something like $1.4

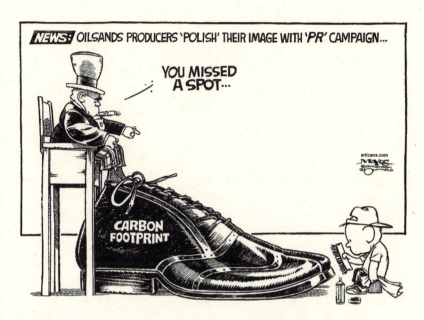

Figure 5.1 Malcolm Hayes, *Edmonton Journal*, 25 June 2008.

trillion, one estimate of the value of the oil sands – equal to 18 per cent of Canada's tangible wealth (Sharpe et al. 2008).

Whatever the explanation, it was an appropriate welcome to Fort McMoney. To others it was Fort-zilla, or ground zero of "the most destructive project on Earth," as Toronto-based Environmental Defence (2008) described it, and the "biggest environmental crime in history," according to the UK's *Independent* (C. Milmo 2007). The occasion for the hyperbolic, front-page British coverage was a decision by BP, the company that once claimed to have moved "Beyond Petroleum," to reverse its policy of staying out of the area. As oil prices neared $100 a barrel, BP could not resist jumping in. All the other oil majors were already involved, including Shell, which had raised eyebrows in the UK for simultaneously sponsoring events exploring "how to succeed in a low carbon economy" while expanding its tar sands involvement. Indeed, the UK's Advertising Standards Authority rebuked Shell for suggesting that such investments were "sustainable." Also involved were Statoil, the mostly state-owned energy company of soon-to-be "carbon neutral" Norway, not to mention other firms less concerned about presenting climate-friendly images, including ExxonMobil and China's Sinopec and China National Offshore Oil Corporation (CNOOC).

Although many multinational oil firms were recent arrivals, Suncor, established by US-based Sun Oil, began commercial extraction of bitumen from the oil sands in 1967, while Syncrude – a joint venture that came to involve Canadian Oil Sands Limited, Imperial Oil (controlled by ExxonMobil), Suncor, Sinopec, and others – began operating in 1978. During the 1970s, when oil prices were rising and so was US concern over energy "independence," oil industry and American interest in the tar sands was high. However, their interest later waned as oil prices fell and scarcity concerns receded. In 1993, the Alberta Chamber of Resources established the National Oil Sands Task Force, composed of oil industry and government representatives, to develop a strategy to make tar sands development economically attractive. Its 1995 report, *The Oil Sands: A New Energy Vision for Canada*, set out a twenty-five-year strategy to achieve output of one million barrels per day by 2020. To reach these goals, in 1997 Alberta introduced an industry-friendly royalty structure and the federal government gave new tax breaks for tar sands investments. However, the real gold rush only began in the new millennium.

In addition to the eagerness of Alberta's political and business classes to develop the resource, renewed American interest was a key factor behind the oil sands boom. Even before the events of 9-11, growing US desire for Canadian energy was evident in the May 2001 *National Energy Policy* report, released by Dick Cheney in Toronto, which stated that continued development of "Canada's recoverable heavy oil sands reserves" could "be a pillar of sustained North American energy and economic security" (National Energy Policy Development Group 2001, 8-8). (While north of the border, Cheney also fired a dismissive shot at the idea of consuming less energy, remarking that, "Conservation may be a sign of personal virtue, but it is not a sufficient basis all by itself for sound, comprehensive energy policy. We also have to produce more.") Interest in secure, friendly oil sources only grew after the terror attacks. "Since 9-11 there's a new factor in the oil and gas markets and that's the security of supply issue," explained Alberta's sustainable resource development minister Ted Morton (Bennett 2007a). "And that has thrust Alberta right to the top of the attention of not just the oil and gas sector but also the Western world, and that's what's contributed to the growth

TAR SANDS OR OIL SANDS?

Whether to use the term "tar sands" or "oil sands" is a matter of contention. Both terms have long been used, often interchangeably. Many environmental groups and other critics use the term "tar sands," while the oil industry and Alberta government prefer the cleaner-sounding "oil sands." According to the Alberta (2008a) government, "The hydrocarbon mixtures found in northern Alberta have historically been referred to as tar, pitch or asphalt. However, 'oil sands' is now used most often to describe the naturally occurring bitumen deposits ... Oil sands (or oilsands) is an accurate term because bitumen is a substance that contains oily sand. It makes sense to describe the resource as oil sands because oil is what is finally derived from the bitumen." Nikiforuk (2008, 12) countered that, by the same reasoning, people ought to call tomatoes "ketchup" and trees "lumber." In any case, more important than accuracy were matters of public relations. As the Pembina Institute explained, in 1995, the National Oil Sands Task Force sought to improve public perceptions of the resource as part of its strategy to greatly expand tar sands output. This industry and government grouping selected oil sands over the dirtier-sounding alternative as part of its rebranding of the resource as a "national prize" (Woynillowicz, Severson-Baker, and Raynolds 2005, 3). Since government and corporate directives on appropriate terminology strike me as slightly Orwellian, I choose to keep using the term "tar sands" and to alternate it with the term "oil sands." That is consistent with the language I was familiar with during my Alberta youth, when my father did occasional engineering work in Fort McMurray.

you've seen over the last five or six years." It was no coincidence that George W. Bush's 2006 proclamation that the US was "addicted to oil" and would reduce dependence on Middle Eastern imports came as government officials and oil executives from both countries met in Houston to plan a "fivefold expansion" in tar sands output in a "short time span" (CBC 2007b). With a confessed addict needing more reliable sources of a fix, the Albertan and Canadian governments were more than willing to seize the opportunity.

It was only in 2003, as oil prices rose, that the US Energy Information Administration (EIA) acknowledged the oil sands as "proved crude oil reserves." It suddenly increased the estimate of Canada's economically recoverable reserves from 5 billion to 180 billion barrels, putting Canada second in the world behind Saudi Arabia for a time, and later third behind Venezuela (after the EIA included that country's heavy-oil reserves). Under different economic conditions or new technology, 315 billion barrels of oil were "potentially recoverable" from the tar sands. Meanwhile, rapid economic growth in China and India drove a major increase in world demand. With most of the world's remaining oil reserves in the hands of state-owned oil companies such as Saudi Aramco, and/or in difficult countries in which to operate such as Venezuela, Iran, Iraq, and Russia, Alberta's oil sands became attractive not only for the US state, but for private sector oil firms as well. Indeed, according to one estimate, more than half of the world's oil reserves accessible to private companies were in Canada (Hussain 2012).

In light of these changed conditions, capital flooded in and output skyrocketed, as did exports. Annual capital expenditures in the tar sands increased from $1.5 billion in 1998 to $18.1 billion in 2008, before slowing with the broader economy in 2009 (CAPP 2011, Table 4.16b). The dramatic impact on the Canadian economy was illustrated by the fact that in 2008, for the first time, planned investment in the oil sands exceeded that of the entire Canadian manufacturing sector (Statistics Canada 2008). Meanwhile, tar sands output grew much more rapidly than proponents envisaged in the 1990s, reaching a million barrels per day long before 2020. Crude bitumen production increased from 0.65 million barrels per day in 1998 to 1.9 million in 2012, and was projected to reach 3.8 million barrels per day by 2022 (AER 2013) and 5.0 million barrels per day by 2035 (NEB 2013, 29). Meanwhile, Canada became the top exporter of petroleum to the United States in 2002. By 2012, it supplied 78 per cent more crude oil to the US than Saudi Arabia, according to the EIA.

The torrent of oil sands investment, coupled with rising oil prices, set off the most rapid period of economic growth ever recorded by a Canadian province. Statistics Canada (2006) reported that Alberta's nominal GDP grew 43 per cent from 2002 to 2005, an average annual rate of 12.7 per cent, comparable to China's 14.8 per cent – with real GDP in Alberta growing 4 per cent per year. At the peak of the boom, Alberta experienced a budget surplus of $4.6 billion in 2007–08, while its roughly 3.5 million residents enjoyed the lowest income taxes in Canada, no provincial sales tax, and no provincial debt – despite the fact that the royalty rates paid by the oil industry were low by international comparison. The boom left Alberta with the highest share of its population employed and the lowest unemployment rate of any North American province or state. A growing income gap among provinces also resulted. By 2007–08, Statistics Canada figures showed that Alberta's per capita GDP of $75,804 was 61 per cent higher than the Canadian average. According to Alberta premier Ed Stelmach (2007b), within Canada, "economic power is shifting ... In fact it's fair to say that Alberta is the engine that drives the Canadian economy and produces prosperity not just for Albertans but for all Canadians." Or, as Nikiforuk (2008, 56) put it, the tar sands had made Canada a "suburb of Fort McMurray." There was some hyperbole in these statements and, as discussed below, not all Canadians benefited equally, but a dramatic shift in economic power was occurring.

DREAMS, PROVINCIAL AND PROMETHEAN

Oil sands growth was the fulfilment of a dream, an Alberta dream – not only of riches, but of rising up to assume a place of power and influence within Canadian Confederation and the wider world. During my youth in Alberta, I absorbed a selective history/mythology of Western Canadian alienation that went something like this: My province was settled by hard-working farmers, many from central and Eastern Europe, recruited by a federal government aiming to open up the hinterlands for exploitation and needing toilers with the capacity to eke out a living in a brutally cold, empty yet beautiful landscape. These people and their descendants were at best ignored by the Ottawa-Montreal-Toronto triangle of power – which was focused on the dramas of Quebec and Ontario – when not being ripped off by the banks, railways, grain company cartel, and tariff-protected manufacturers from the east. Oil began to change all that. Led by our "blue-eyed sheik," Premier Peter Lougheed, we began to stand up, but they used their National Energy Program to push us back down. Our bumper stickers said, "Let the Eastern bastards freeze in the dark," but oil prices and our share fell. Boom turned to bust and our dream was delayed. But a quarter century later, Canada was, in Prime Minister Harper's oft-repeated words, an "energy superpower," and that meant Alberta was finally on top.

Tar sands development was also the fulfillment of a more universal, Promethean or Cornucopian dream. One early advocate of massive oil sands development was none other than Herman Kahn, co-founder of the Hudson Institute, who challenged the Club of Rome's limits-to-growth views in the 1970s with arguments about the boundless potential of capitalism and technology to overcome scarcity. Among Kahn's (1976, 4, 31) predictions was that humanity would likely soon colonize space to serve its needs for resources and living space. So far, that has turned out to be overly optimistic, but parts of northern Alberta could now be mistaken for the moon, in line with Kahn's prophetic vision. During the first oil shock in 1973, Kahn, acting as an informal US government envoy, proposed a crash program of tar sands development to Canada, involving billions of dollars in foreign investment and the labour of tens of thousands of temporary workers from Korea (Nikiforuk 2008; L. Pratt 1976). The Trudeau government declined, judging that such a massive export-oriented project would unbalance the Canadian economy and threaten the ability to meet future domestic energy needs. Although the plan was shelved, the scale of what later transpired actually exceeded Kahn's dreams in terms of investment and output. In a speech to the Canada-UK Chamber of Commerce in London, Prime Minister Harper (2006) later echoed some of Kahn's favourite themes of a resourceful Earth giving up its gifts through technological mastery: "An ocean of oil-soaked sand lies under the muskeg of northern Alberta – my home province ... Digging the bitumen out of the ground, squeezing out the oil and converting it into synthetic crude is a monumental challenge. It requires vast amounts of capital, Brobdingnagian technology, and an army of skilled workers. In short, it is an enterprise of epic proportions, akin to the building of the pyramids or China's Great Wall. Only bigger."

Some past proposals to carry out this epic enterprise were particularly outlandish, such as "Project Oil Sands," which revealed a great deal about modern Promethean thinking. In the late 1950s, Richfield Oil proposed detonating a nuclear warhead underground to melt the bitumen – a low-cost way to separate it from the sand and provide the United States with an abundant energy source. The Alberta government was interested, a bomb site was selected, and the US government agreed to supply the hydrogen bomb in the spirit of "atoms for peace." However, the project was shelved due to Canadian government concern over nuclear testing and proliferation, while Richfield Oil eventually turned its attention to cheaper conventional oil in Alaska (Marsden 2007, chapters 2 and 4; Nikiforuk 2008, 129–30; Payne 2007).

This Dr. Strangelove–like proposal was never implemented. Nevertheless, for some observers, contemporary practices in the region were a "dystopian fantasy," as the *Financial Times* described it. "The process of turning Canada into an energy superpower is an awe-inspiring, but disturbing, sight," noted the correspondent for the global capitalist elite's leading daily (Crooks 2007). That was also my impression upon visiting the area. My notes that day were a little more raw than usual. "Oh my God," I scribbled at first view of the massive tailings ponds. The sight of the sprawling, belching, production facilities provoked a "Jesus!" followed by a series of expletives and exclamation points, which was all I could articulate at first. Add the Philip Glass soundtrack, I later thought, and you've got another Koyaanisqatsi sequel. Maude Barlow, water adviser to the United Nations and chair of the left-leaning Council of Canadians, referred to the scene as "Mordor," the dark middle earth of *The Lord of the Rings*, and *Wired* magazine profiled the tar sands' "Apocalyptic Landscapes." Alberta's former Conservative premier, Peter Lougheed (2006), called it a "moonscape." Lindsay Telfer, director of the Sierra Club of Canada's Prairie Chapter, who flew over the site as part of Alberta's oil sands multi-stakeholder committee, said she spent much of the time watching others' shell-shocked reactions. She recalled the response of one Alberta Energy staff member: "I turned to him as we were getting off the plane and he was just shaking his head going, 'There's no way it's sustainable.'" And yet I could also understand the comments of a visitor from France whom I overheard saying, "C'est quand même impressionnant la puissance qu'il représente." ("Even so, the power that it represents is impressive.")

THE DARK SIDE OF THE BOOM:
ECOLOGICAL AND SOCIAL IMPACTS

The oil sands were one important factor behind Canada's GHG emissions growth and failure to meet its Kyoto commitments. Production of a barrel of oil from the tar sands – including the energy-intensive extraction and upgrading phases – generated roughly 3 to 4.5 times more GHG emissions than a barrel of conventional oil (Brandt 2011, 4; Huot and Grant 2012, 3). Oil sands defenders preferred to cite life-cycle "well-to-wheel" figures, which showed a narrower differential and were the basis of their claims that there was no significant GHG difference with conventional oil.[1] From 1990 to 2011, emissions from the tar sands grew 224 per cent, from 17 to 55 Mt, according to figures from Environment Canada (2013a, 25; see also Huot and Grant 2012, 4) – surpassing the total CO_2 emissions in Sweden and nearly equal to those in Bangladesh, a country of 150 million people (EIA 2013). Mech (2011, 18–20) estimated that with a more comprehensive accounting of emissions, including those linked to upgrading exported bitumen in the US, production and processing of natural gas used in the oil sands, production of other required inputs, and loss of carbon storage due to the disruption of boreal forest, total GHG emissions could be as much as double the federal government's figures. Other analysts suggested that the figures should also take into account the downstream burning of petroleum coke, a by-product of oil sands upgrading and refining that *Scientific American* described as "possibly the dirtiest fossil fuel available" (Biello 2013; OCI 2013). Whatever the actual total, the Alberta (2012) government and oil industry downplayed the numbers, stating that the tar sands accounted for 7.8 per cent of Canada's GHGs and only 0.14 per cent of global emissions (CAPP 2013c). Yet those numbers were significantly higher than only a few years earlier, when Alberta (2008b) said the oil sands caused just 4 per cent of Canadian emissions, and the percentage was destined to keep rising.

The tar sands were one factor – along with dependence on coal-fired electricity, emissions from conventional oil production, sprawling suburban developments and automobile dependence, and large homes and large vehicles made possible by high levels of affluence – that contributed to Albertans' extremely large carbon footprints. In 2011, per capita GHG emissions in Alberta were 64.5 tonnes of CO_2 equivalent, more than triple the Canadian average of 20.4 tonnes and six-and-a-half times more than Quebec's 10.0 tonnes (Environment Canada 2013a, 35). Alberta's per capita emissions also dwarfed the levels in other affluent nations, such as the United States (21.4 tonnes), fellow northern oil producer Norway (10.8 tonnes), the UK (9 tonnes), and Sweden (7 tonnes) (OECD 2013).

Rick Hyndman, senior policy adviser at the Canadian Association of Petroleum Producers (CAPP), did not deny the need to curb growing oil sands emissions, but felt that the sector received disproportionate attention. "If you looked at all the media, you would think oil sands production–related emissions were a huge part of Canada's inventory … It's just that people anticipate this huge growth in the oil sands so there is all of this focus on it, plus the environmental groups decided this was a cause they wanted to take on and blow out of proportion in our view," said Hyndman in 2008. There was an important kernel of truth in this perspective. Even if the tar sands vanished overnight, Canada would still be well above its Kyoto target and have emissions growth similar to the G8's second worst performer, the United States.[2] After 1990, Canada also saw large emissions increases from transportation, electricity generation (a trend that later began to reverse as some provinces reduced coal burning), and conventional oil production. Canada clearly also had other problems to resolve to move onto a low-carbon path.

However, the tar sands still had special significance. The political and economic power of those who would profit most from oil sands expansion and who consistently fought to protect such growth from tight carbon constraints was a significant factor undermining Canada's capacity to introduce strong climate policies capable of meeting deep GHG reduction targets. Meanwhile, even if the tar sands were a relatively small source of current total emissions, the rate of growth was astonishing and, short of a miraculous tech fix, destined to conflict with the need for emissions cuts. Federal government projections showed that, under a BAU scenario with existing policies, oil sands emissions would triple from 2005 to 2020, from 34 to 101 Mt – a 67 Mt increase. By 2020, the oil sands alone would account for some 14 per cent of Canada's projected emissions. Moreover, tar sands emissions growth would counteract other key emissions reductions efforts, dwarfing, for example, the projected 39 Mt reduction in Canada's electricity sector due to provincial efforts (Environment Canada 2013a, 21, 24, 25). These projected emissions figures, based on tar sands output of 3.3 million barrels per day (mbd) in 2020, would soar further skyward if output reaches the target of some 5 mbd by 2030. Indeed, if current emissions trends continued, the oil sands alone could soon emit more than Canada as a whole could justify based on estimates of globally equitable GHG reductions in wealthy nations to avoid more than 2°C of warming.[3]

Skyrocketing GHG emissions occurred despite the industry's much vaunted success in improving energy efficiency and cutting emissions intensity. In defence of petroleum producers' environmental record, CAPP's president stated that: "Oil sands emissions intensity – the average volume of carbon-dioxide waste generated per barrel of production – has fallen by 45 per cent since the province started keeping track in 1990" (Alvarez 2008). The more environmentally relevant, but unmentioned, point was the impotence of such improvements in preventing emissions growth as production rose at a far faster pace. Other observers, however, zeroed in on the basic problem. For example, David Hallman of the World Council of Churches argued that the tar sands were an area where the notion of sufficiency was particularly relevant in Canada: "It's probably a really good example of how the efficiency revolution will not be sufficient ... The companies are becoming increasingly efficient at extracting the fuel, but it is always going to be a very energy intensive type of development" (see also Nikiforuk 2008, 120–2).

Furthermore, it was far from clear that per barrel emissions reductions, as inadequate as they had been in preventing total emissions from rising, could be sustained in the future (Environment Canada 2013a, 23). One problem was that one-time gains from past measures, such as shifting from burning coke to natural gas, were already exhausted. While the Royal Society of Canada (2010, 89) concluded that "there is some promise for further reductions in GHG intensity," it added that a growing share of future output will come from "in situ" production, used to extract bitumen lying too far below the surface to be mined and which emits more GHGs. In fact, the previous downward trend in oil sands GHG intensity stalled from 2005 to 2011

(Partington 2013b), while the industry conceded that "there will be a slight increase in intensity over the near to medium term" (CAPP 2013b). Meanwhile, estimates of past intensity improvements were revised downwards. Environment Canada (2013b, 9) reported a 26 per cent intensity reduction in the oil sands from 1990 to 2011 – much less than the 39 per cent estimate only three years earlier (Royal Society 2010, 93).

CO_2 was far from the only environmental problem. Upstream production facilities generated problems such as vast quantities of natural gas consumption; major disruptions to boreal forest from surface mining operations; declining caribou populations; a thirst for large volumes of water, resulting in concerns over disruption of the Athabasca River's flow; and the creation of huge, toxic tailings ponds. The death in 2008 of some 1,600 ducks unlucky enough to land in one of those ponds drew public attention to the unresolved environmental challenges. Significant concerns existed over downstream water quality and health problems, including a contentious debate over what appeared to be abnormally high rates of some cancers among Aboriginal people in Fort Chipewyan (Chen 2009). The Royal Society of Canada (2010) said there was no credible evidence yet for the "cancer cluster" claims, although many local people and others were far from assured – and catches of deformed fish in local waters did not help matters (see, for example, Mech 2011, 28). The Regional Aquatics Monitoring Program, funded by industry and directed by a multi-stakeholder committee, maintained that oil sands operations had not significantly increased contaminant levels in water. However, other researchers found evidence of elevated levels of toxins downstream from tar sands facilities, along with inadequacies in the official monitoring program (E. Kelly et al. 2010). These conclusions were backed by an independent scientific panel appointed by the Alberta government (Water Monitoring Data Review Committee 2011, iv–v), and later by Environment Canada and Queen's University scientists (Kurek et al. 2013). Other concerns included air pollution and acid rain in the Fort McMurray area. Pollution problems also emerged at distant processing facilities. These included elevated levels of airborne contaminants and cancers in the "industrial heartland" northeast of Edmonton; however, researchers were not yet able to confirm a causal link (Simpson et al. 2013). Health concerns were also growing near the refineries in the Great Lakes basin and elsewhere in

The Laggard

the US that were processing rapidly growing volumes of bitumen, including problems caused by dust from huge open-air piles of petroleum coke (Lefebvre and Kesling 2013). Meanwhile, a series of pipeline spills highlighted the risks of transporting Alberta's heavy crude (Crosby et al. 2013; Vanderklippe and Tait 2012).

In light of the vast range of ecological concerns, one anonymous oil executive quoted in an influential industry journal, the *Petroleum Economist*, confessed, "It's an environmental freak show" (Brower 2006). David Schindler, a renowned University of Alberta ecologist told reporters, "If there was a Guinness Book of Records for unsustainable development, this is it" (Schoof 2008). Meanwhile, a *National Geographic* feature summed up its unflattering 2009 portrayal of the tar sands in its title, "Scraping Bottom."

The federal and Alberta governments, and the oil industry, begged to differ. They mounted a series of campaigns, such as CAPP's attempt in 2008 to launch a "different conversation" about the oil sands. Alberta (2008b) spent $25 million on a PR campaign in 2008 to defend the province's deteriorating international image and its record in "proving that environmental protection and economic development can happen together." When that effort failed to blunt the criticism, Alberta launched a further PR offensive in 2010. Meanwhile, federal government documents showed that Canada considered hiring a professional PR firm in Europe (De Souza 2011b), where there was a struggle to "defend Canada's image as a responsible energy producer and steward of the environment including climate change issues," according to government documents (FoE Europe 2011, 7). As part of these efforts, Alberta's representative in Washington, Gary Mar, told the US House Energy and Commerce Committee that, "Alberta's oil sands industry is one of the most regulated in the world, with strict legislation and standards to protect our air, land, water, and wildlife and manage greenhouse gas (GHG) emissions." He added that, "Alberta is the only jurisdiction in North America with mandatory GHG reduction targets for large emitters across all sectors, including the oil sands."[4] Meanwhile, the evident failings of Alberta's monitoring of the cumulative impacts of tar sands production added to the image problem abroad, forcing the federal government to take a more active role in a new joint monitoring effort. Oil sands defenders – including Prime Minister Stephen Harper, Environment Minister Peter Kent, and Alberta premier Ed Stelmach – also tried to shift the focus to Canada's democratic credentials and human rights record, which compared favourably to most major oil exporters. For some observers, that made the tar sands a source of "ethical oil" (Levant 2010) – the petroleum equivalent of fair trade coffee.

Beyond the environmental questions, the social impacts of rapid tar sands development were double-edged. Doubtless, many Albertans benefited considerably from higher incomes and jobs for the taking during the years when the sector was booming, notably prior to the global economic downturn of 2008. However, boom-style development typically has many negative impacts on communities due to a range of pressures, including extreme housing shortages, price inflation, and inadequate public health and municipal services – and Fort McMurray was no exception (Royal Society of Canada 2010, exec. sum. 12, 231–4). The Regional Municipality of Wood Buffalo (RMWB), which includes Fort McMurray, saw its population grow 125 per cent from 2000 to 2012, from 51,850 to 116,407, including more than 39,000 people living in work camps. This growth put severe stresses on local infrastructure and public services. In 2006, the RMWB reported that it was deficient in seventy of seventy-two quality-of-life indicators established by the Federation of Canadian Municipalities – and that was before its population jumped a further 16 per cent in 2007 alone (Pembina Institute 2007b, 6; RMWB 2012). One particular irony was that, as local residents spent ever more time stuck in traffic, the municipality tried to get oil sands workers out of their cars by improving public transit and providing priority bus lanes (Agrell 2011). Meanwhile, the combination of a disproportionately male population, many of them a long way from wives and girl-friends, pocketing supersized paycheques, had predictable results. "There are 11 pages of escorts in the Yellow Pages (annotated, in my hotel room)," noted the *Guardian*'s correspondent (Edemariam 2007). Meanwhile, the *Economist* (2007a) noted that drug abuse in the Fort McMurray area was more than four times the provincial average, which created safety concerns for employers and lucrative opportunities for the Hells Angels, the Indian Posse, and other narco-entrepreneurs (Nikiforuk 2007; Tetley 2005).

The excessive pace of growth during the boom years also overwhelmed the rest of the province in many ways. The consequences of chronic labour shortages were not limited to the lengthy 24/7 queues for coffee at the Fort McMurray Tim Hortons, but included inadequate health care staffing and the fuelling of inflation across Alberta, which eroded much of the increase in workers' nominal wages (T. Clarke et al. 2013, 48–9). In line with Herman Kahn's vision, employers turned to widespread use of temporary foreign workers throughout the province; these workers were often housed in grim conditions and vulnerable to exploitation by employers and labour brokers (AFL 2007c). Housing costs shot through the roof, leading to growing numbers of homeless people across the province – many of whom were gainfully employed. A joke going around the Internet offered tips for people arriving to work in Alberta – number one was "Bring your own house." The extent of Alberta's housing crisis was evident when players on Edmonton's Canadian Football League team found themselves without a roof after making the squad, prompting media reports of "20 homeless Eskimos still looking for a place to stay" and fan offers of basement suites (T. Jones 2007). Finally, in a province that took pride in its consistently high rankings on national and international tests of educational achievement, the boom led many young people to forgo higher education and choose instead to take up work such as driving trucks in the tar sands for a higher income than, say, this assistant professor earns.

Albertans themselves were not completely at ease with the gold rush around them. As I sipped a cup of organic "Alberta Crude" from the fair trade, locally roasted coffee shop that had set up shop in my conservative, suburban hometown, I picked up a copy of the local paper, which editorialized that "Alberta's economic prosperity has yielded many benefits, but as [Premier Ed] Stelmach pointed out in an address to the St. Albert Chamber of Commerce, there is a 'dark side of the boom.' We're not sure if his words were actually a play on the Pink Floyd album *Dark Side of the Moon*, but in a strange way the words from the track *Money* sum up the mood in this province. 'Money, get away. Get a good job with good pay and you're okay. Money, it's a gas. Grab that cash with both hands and make a stash … Money, get back. I'm all right Jack keep your hands off my stack'" (St. Albert Gazette 2008).

A media report proclaiming "Albertans not happy campers" (Bennett 2007b) cited an online Canadian Press Harris/Decima opinion poll of 1,400 western Canadians in September 2007, which found the most "angst and unhappiness" and concern over decline of civility in Alberta, despite the province leading the nation in growth and per capita income. A Strategic Counsel (2008) poll of eight hundred Albertans in January 2008 found that only 26 per cent said their quality of life had improved in the previous five years, boom years, while 32 per cent said it had gone down (although a very large majority still said the oil sands were a "good thing"). That poll found that 62 per cent of Albertans believed that the pace of economic development had been "too fast," while other pre-recession polls similarly found that a majority of Albertans "support slower growth" (Henton 2008; Leger Marketing 2008), and a suspension of new tar sands project approvals until environmental and infrastructural issues had been resolved (Pembina Institute 2007a).

Ecological economists in Alberta attempted to measure whether the province's rapid economic growth was in fact delivering higher levels of well-being. The Alberta Genuine Progress Indicator, comprised of fifty-one environmental, social, and economic indicators, showed that while the province's GDP grew 483 per cent from 1961 to 2003, the GPI fell 19 per cent over the same period and was basically flat after the late 1980s (Taylor 2005). Although Alberta's GPI was not updated to take into account the oil sands boom years, more recent GPI figures were available for Edmonton. They showed that the capital city's real GDP per capita grew strongly, albeit irregularly, from 1981 to 2008, while the composite Edmonton Wellbeing Index fell steadily from 1983 to 1998, recovered some of the lost ground between 1998 and 2006, then remained flat during the peak boom years until 2008.[5] Overall, these estimates showed that although some increase in well-being was evident in Edmonton in recent years, it was still not back to 1981 levels and, more generally, GDP and GPI diverged considerably.

Despite the apparent unease and seeming divergence between rapid growth and levels of well-being, Albertans did not express in the ballot booth a strong desire for change, rewarding their pro-expansion Conservative government with another landslide victory in 2008 and a victory again, though narrower, in 2012. In fact, in 2008, only 41 per cent of eligible voters bothered to vote at all. Alberta had become the province with the lowest electoral participation, with Fort McMurray – at 21 per cent – having the lowest turnout within the province. It was only after the tar sands boom came to a halt in late 2008 that rumblings of discontent led to a serious political threat to the Conservative government. This threat arose from the Wildrose

Alliance, which was further to the right and even less inclined toward climate action that might limit energy sector expansion.

Even environmental groups were reticent, at first, in demanding an end to tar sands growth. In 2005, eleven major groups issued a "declaration by Canada's environmental community" that was critical of the rapid pace of oil sands expansion but did not actually call for that growth to stop (CPAWS et al. 2005). Instead, the consensus position set out "minimum conditions" for further oil sands development, including stronger vehicle fuel efficiency standards; fiscal reform (namely stopping tar sands subsidies, increasing royalty payments from the industry, and using resource wealth to fund energy efficiency and renewables); and regulatory and policy measures to ensure environmental integrity, with the goal of "carbon neutral" oil sands operations by 2020. The declaration also emphasized the "clear links between inefficient use of transportation fuels in North America and the growing demand for synthetic crude oil from the oil sands." Overall, the statement implied that greater energy efficiency, policy reform, and "innovation and strong leadership" could solve the tar sands' problems.

Demands for a moratorium began to emerge in 2006, first from the left-leaning Parkland Institute (and its director Gordon Laxer), the Canadian Centre for Policy Alternatives, and the Polaris Institute, which released a report, *Fueling Fortress America*, calling for a five-year pause in tar sands development (McCullum 2006). Some environmental groups also began to call for a moratorium, although they had different perspectives on how far to push. One can interpret a moratorium as a time-limited form of sufficiency – a judgment that enough of a given activity has taken place, at least until solutions to key problems emerge. In effect, it is a measure that responds to the "ingenuity gap" (Homer-Dixon 2001) by slowing down the rate at which demands for ingenuity are rising, thereby buying time to fill the gap.

The Pembina Institute (2007b) eventually backed a more limited version of a moratorium than some other environmental groups, setting out conditions for "responsible oil sands development." Pembina called on government to mandate real GHG reductions and was, at the time, the main source of demands that the tar sands become "carbon neutral" – through fuel switching, energy efficiency, CCS, and carbon offset purchases (McCulloch, Raynolds, and Wong 2006). The institute also sought other changes – including royalty reform, provision of adequate social services and infrastructure, reformed decision-making processes, and development of a strategy for more diversified and greener economic development – to maximize benefits to the province's people. Pembina (2007b, 8) emphasized that a "moratorium on new approvals is not a moratorium on economic growth," while Dan Woynillowicz, a senior policy analyst with the institute, added that once conditions for responsible development are met, "We don't fundamentally oppose oil sands production." He explained in 2008 that, as an Alberta-based group, Pembina recognized that "Alberta's economy is very dependent upon the oil and gas industry." He added that rather than a decades-long moratorium, as was placed on Canada's Atlantic cod fishery and on Mackenzie Valley natural gas pipeline development, "We're looking at it more as a pause that would allow the government to catch up ... So ultimately the economy is going to continue to benefit from current production and even new growth." In effect, Pembina's call for a moratorium was a plea for a brief period of sufficiency until the sector was in a position to move beyond BAU to EM. By 2013, although it had moved away from use of the word "moratorium," Pembina was still opposing the approval of new projects on the grounds that the pace and scale of development was far in excess of regulators' ability to manage the impacts.

The Sierra Club of Canada called in 2006 for a tar sands "time out." Like the Pembina Institute, its conditions for lifting a moratorium included establishing sustainability thresholds to "guide and impose limits on development," explained Lindsay Telfer of the Sierra Club's Prairie Chapter. She added, however, "I am absolutely positive that we've gone beyond those thresholds already." Telfer referred to the range of social and environmental excesses plaguing the Fort McMurray area, from overloaded classrooms to "massive toxic tailings lakes [that] we have no idea what to do with," and suggested that whatever sustainability indicator or threshold one chose, "almost all of them" had been exceeded. While the idea of a "time out" implied that, in principle, growth could resume later, Telfer was suggesting that enough was enough already. In later statements, the Sierra Club of Canada's (2011) Prairie Chapter reiterated its opposition to further oil sands development, calling on government to "cease new oil sands approvals and lease sales."

Greenpeace was most prominent among Canada's major green groups in campaigning to "stop the tar sands" outright. In 2007, it opened an Edmonton office with Mike Hudema, an Albertan who previously ran San Francisco–based Global Exchange's "Freedom from Oil" campaign, as its tar sands campaigner. Greenpeace's tactics ranged from direct action – blocking a pipe discharging toxins into Syncrude's tailings pond – to culture jamming the province's brand through a mock travellingalberta.com website that promised vacation adventures such as "tailing sailing" in "Canada's Rocky Mountain Playground – a carbon based energy power-house."

"At the end of the day ... are there any limits on growth?" asked Hudema, as he explained the reason for the campaign. "In the twenty-first century we can't be developing this project. We can't be developing the dirtiest source of oil on the face of the planet, the most energy-intensive source of oil on the face of the planet." He added, "We know what the scientific community is telling us. We know what people are already witnessing, whether it's people in Tuvalu who are already being evacuated from the islands, whether it's people in our own backyard that have either faced droughts or the mountain pine beetle coming in ... We already see these effects. And we know that they are going to get worse the more carbon that we are polluting into the air. We know things are going to get worse the more trees that we cut down. We know things are going to get worse if we pollute our water systems. This is going to do all of them on a massive scale that we haven't seen before on our planet. And this needs to be off limits."

As an organization, Greenpeace did not take a position against economic growth per se. In fact, its international office argued that a zero-carbon energy system was possible globally by the end of the century, without limiting economic growth, through aggressive promotion of decentralized renewable energy and energy efficiency. But for Greenpeace, oil sands expansion was clearly a type of high-carbon, high-impact growth that had to stop and be reversed.

One prominent voice backing moratorium demands was IPCC Chairman Rajendra Pachauri. While stating that Canada "should be doing much more" on climate change, Pachauri added that tar sands projects should be put on hold until technologies such as CCS are better developed (Beaudin 2009).

Environmental groups also found support among labour unions in opposing further oil sands expansion. One might expect labour to back further growth given the vast number of direct and indirect jobs created and the bargaining power that beyond-full-employment conditions gave Alberta workers during the boom years. Yet in a statement on "climate change and green jobs" approved at its 2008 convention, the Canadian Labour Congress (CLC 2008) denounced the oil sands as "the single most destructive development project anywhere on Earth" (9), and promised to "actively push for a drastic and dramatic slowdown in the tar sands" (10). According to the CLC, "to supply the United States with cheap oil we are racing in a Klondike-like gold rush, digging a hole the size of Florida, elevating our dollar and dislocating workers. Unfettered expansion of the tar sands hurts everyone and needs to be slowed down" (10). The stance was in line with the Canadian labour movement's past positions in favour of strong climate policy, such as Kyoto Protocol ratification, and its penchant for left-leaning critique of corporate Canada's direction. In addition to the CLC's expressed concerns over the oil sands' impacts on the environment and Aboriginal people, it concluded that expansion also threatened the interests of many workers in other sectors and regions. The oil export boom was a key factor behind the Canadian dollar's rise from an all-time low of US$0.62 in 2002 to US$1.10 in late 2007, before returning to a range roughly between US$0.90 and parity. The higher currency dealt a heavy blow to the competitiveness of Canadian manufacturing and contributed to the loss of nearly 250,000 manufacturing jobs from 2004 to 2007, even before the global economic downturn (Lin 2008). Over a longer time scale, almost 500,000 manufacturing jobs were lost in the ten years after the Canadian dollar began to rise (Porter 2012). Other sectors, including tourism and tradable services, were also negatively affected by the high dollar (Clarke et al. 2013, 2). For many in the labour movement, the oil sands resource boom – followed by a rising currency and negative impacts on other sectors and regions – was a textbook case of "Dutch disease." (Concerns about oil exports driving Dutch disease were echoed in 2012 by Ontario Premier Dalton McGuinty and federal NDP leader Thomas Mulcair, prompting an intense reaction from oil sands supporters and a contentious debate about the oil sands' net benefits to Canada.)

The Canadian Auto Workers (CAW 2007, 8–9), whose members were among those the rising dollar hit hardest, called for "powerful measures to slow down the oil sands boom." According to the CAW, "The Western oil boom is having many negative consequences for Canada: it is tying us ever closer to the U.S. economic orbit, it is distorting the economic federation, and it is producing inflation and higher interest rates. And the oil boom is the main reason we have busted through our Kyoto targets." In a later analysis of the difficult prospects facing the auto industry after the financial crisis, the CAW's president repeated concerns that the Canadian dollar was "still far too high (driven up by financial speculators and the tar sands boom out West)" (Lewenza 2010). While the CAW faced difficult dilemmas that led it to resist some climate policy proposals – choosing to defend its members' jobs rather than support policies to encourage the purchase of smaller vehicles most often produced by Japanese and other foreign firms (CAW 2007, 15) – there was an important lesson in its support for limits on oil sands growth. Ideas of sufficiency typically face serious obstacles as they inevitably challenge some group's economic interests, whichever sector or product they target; however, they may also be able to find supporters in other sectors who would benefit economically by scaling back a particular high-carbon sector.

Even in Alberta, where the boom drove unemployment downward and wages upward, organized labour proposed "rules to set the pace of growth at a rate that doesn't overwhelm our workforce, our infrastructure or our environment" (AFL 2007b, 9). At the peak of the boom, the Alberta Federation of Labour (AFL) even joined the call for "No New Approvals for Tar Sands Development" (2008). In a submission to the province's Multi-stakeholder Committee on Oil Sands, the AFL (2007b, 4) argued that by allowing a one-time burst of "super-heated" development, government was failing to ensure maximum job creation for Albertans over the long term, with the predictable result being a "construction boom, followed by a construction bust." The AFL also expressed concern over the "perverse" royalty structure that resulted in "literally billions of dollars in foregone public revenue," as well as the lost opportunities for value added activity in upgrading and refining bitumen in Alberta to result from the construction of new pipelines to export raw bitumen. Meanwhile, in its *Climate Change Policy Paper*, the AFL (2007a) stated that a "solid starting place is to require oilsands producers and developers to better use existing technology to reduce emissions ... But that is not enough. We need to face the oilsands dilemma head-on, which will mean *consciously deciding to slow its development*" (10, italics added). In calling for a "temporary moratorium," the AFL emphasized that "this is not about stopping development, but both managing the pace of the development and making the development carbon neutral" (11). Subsequent AFL position papers in 2008 and 2009 further developed these themes of developing the tar sands in a more orderly and environmentally responsible way, with a focus on high-value-added processing in Alberta, rather than racing to maximize the extraction and export of raw bitumen. Indeed, the AFL opposed both the Keystone XL and Northern Gateway pipeline proposals. The AFL position was clearly quite different from Greenpeace's call to shut the oil sands down, emphasizing hopes for a form of ecological modernization of the tar sands that would more fully benefit the province and its workers, but both organizations could agree that oil sands growth – at least prior to the 2008 downturn – was excessive, and a moratorium was needed.

Among political parties, the Green Party of Canada (2007b, 76; 2011, 48), not surprisingly, called for a tar sands moratorium. So, too, at least prior to the economic downturn, did the Alberta NDP (2006), which called for "a complete moratorium on tar sands projects until all aspects of development, including human health and cumulative environmental impacts are properly assessed." Its federal cousin likewise said during the 2008 election campaign that it would "halt any new tar sands development" (NDP 2008b; see also NDP 2008a), as it criticized the Conservative government's "fast tracking" of new tar sands projects without conditions to mitigate environmental and local health impacts. Citing a range of problems from carbon emissions to First Nations no longer being able to eat local fish, federal NDP leader Jack Layton asked, "Is no one going to say this is going to stop?" (Galloway 2008). Calling for limits to oil sands growth did, however, open up the labour-based party to attacks from Conservatives, who claimed to be defending unionized workers. "Why is Jack Layton threatening thousands of good union jobs right across Canada?" asked the Conservative Party of Canada (2008) as it identified seventeen different unions, from Boilermakers to Teamsters, that a moratorium would affect. Indeed, the NDP faced challenges in bridging its environmentally critical position on the tar sands with its drive for further electoral gains. Opposing oil sands expansion was particularly popular in Quebec – where Layton called for an end to fossil fuel subsidies and the redirection of those funds to renewable energy during the 2011 campaign – but less so in the west, where the party sought to defend and expand its traditional bases of support. After becoming the official opposition in 2011, with new pressures to present itself as a responsible alternative government in waiting, the NDP, in a perspective voiced by environment critic Megan Leslie, shifted from talk of a "moratorium" toward a gentler sounding "pause," which suggested that one could press the play button again soon once a plan was in place to "develop the tar sands sustainably" (S. Bell 2011). This struggle to find the right wording reflected the NDP's difficulties in reconciling the apparent environmental need for sufficiency with respect to tar sands growth and hopes of an EM solution that would not alienate those whose livelihoods depended on the sector. Indeed, Layton's successor as NDP leader, Thomas Mulcair, shifted further from talk of a moratorium. He called instead for carbon pricing to internalize environmental costs, more domestic refining to capture greater value added, an east-west pipeline to meet Canadian energy needs, and a more ecologically responsible pace and manner of development to balance Alberta's energy economy with the interests of other provinces (CBC 2012b; S. Pratt 2012).

As for the Liberal Party (2008a), under Stéphane Dion, it focused on an elusive EM response, rejecting both "unrestricted and rapid development of the oil sands" and calls for a moratorium, while promising "the necessary tax incentives to oil companies to invest in technologies that reduce their greenhouse gas emissions and make them more energy efficient." His successor, Michael Ignatieff, called the tar sands a matter of national unity and defended them after the critical portrayal in *National Geographic*, while expressing a commitment to environmental sustainability. In so doing, he revealed the contortions that even the sharpest of intellects could find themselves in when confronted with the dilemmas of high-profit, high-carbon oil sands growth. "My concern is that, at the moment, it's barely environmentally sustainable, and it's barely socially sustainable," said Ignatieff. "The Conservative government has done nothing about this. We need to move forward. But am I proud of this industry? You bet. It's a world leader. We just need to make it better" (O'Neill and Alberts 2009).

Even some conservatives expressed unease over the manic pace of expansion in the boom years. Most notable was Peter Lougheed, who championed tar sands development while Alberta's Tory premier from 1971–85. The much revered Lougheed called for a moratorium on project approvals to allow the citizenry to rethink overheated, unsustainable development and establish a proper planning process. Lougheed's intervention actually came before some environmental groups, including the Pembina Institute and WWF-Canada, made similar moratorium demands and was important in expanding the political space for such ideas. "What is the hurry?" asked Lougheed (2006). "Why not build one plant at a time, and I hope the new government in Alberta will reassess this and come to the conclusion that the mess, and I call it a mess, that is Fort McMurray and the tar sands will be revisited."[6] Lougheed was influenced by an aerial tour of the region. "When you actually see the magnitude of it by helicopter, it just gets you. I was appalled by what was happening there," the province's elder statesman told reporters (Tibbetts 2007).

Demands for a moratorium also came for a time from Fort McMurray itself. As early as June 2006, the council of the Regional Municipality of Wood Buffalo, led by Mayor Melissa Blake, voted unanimously to seek an end to future oil sands development until the area could catch up with infrastructure, housing, and public service needs (Liepens 2006; Walton 2007). Meanwhile, Alberta's Aboriginal leaders, the Assembly of Treaty Chiefs, unanimously approved a "No New Oil Sands Approvals" resolution in February 2008 (Keepers of the Athabasca 2008), joining a burgeoning list of organizations making similar demands (No New Approvals for Tar Sands Development 2008). In addition to a wide range of environmental groups and some left-leaning organizations mentioned above, other moratorium supporters included faith-based groups such as Kairos, as well as Albertans Demand Affordable Housing, and even the Northeast Sturgeon County Industrial Landowners who were concerned about excessive development in the proposed "upgrader alley" in the "industrial heartland" near Edmonton.

The tar sands boom was so excessive at its peak that, in 2008, even some oil companies backed a partial moratorium. Petro-Canada, Suncor, Husky Energy, Shell Canada, Imperial Oil, and others signed a letter asking the province to suspend land lease sales in three areas near Fort McMurray, ostensibly to protect potential conservation areas (Scott 2008). However, the oil companies undoubtedly had issues other than environmental protection on their minds. Sceptical observers noted that the firms needed to counter their serious environmental image problem, which threatened to generate support for much more restrictive policies, while the areas in question had lower-grade bitumen and were of less interest to them. Most importantly, blocking new projects in those areas for a time would keep out new upstarts and help contain the cost of inflation and labour shortages that threatened the profitability of their own projects (DeCloet 2008). In a situation as extreme as that during the tar sands boom, even some of the main players driving the development came to see the need for a degree of sufficiency with respect to growth – at least somebody else's growth.

The call by some oil firms for a partial moratorium was little more than a tactical move within the industry's broader strategy of long-term oil sands growth. A month before the call for a partial moratorium, I asked Rick Hyndman of CAPP about proposals for a full moratorium on tar sands expansion until technologies are available to address the GHG problem. He rejected the idea, arguing that the main problem was not with oil producers but consumers: "Even with oil sands, three quarters of the emissions come out of the tail pipe." He also emphasized the world's need for new sources of oil supply to support economic growth: "So whose gas tank isn't going to have the gas in it? That's one thing these guys who say [there should be a full moratorium] never focus on ... The development of the oil sands is increasing the supply of oil in the world, I think. It will probably increase less if we put a moratorium on that. So should there be the less production in the world, should there be less economic activity in Canada? No ... Our industry saying is no. We should put in the best technology and keep investing in the technological improvements ... but let's not cut off the supply of oil."

During Alberta's 2008 election campaign, Premier Ed Stelmach also rejected limits on tar sands growth – whether the call was for a shutdown of the oil sands, a full moratorium, or merely a partial one (D'Aliesio and Markusoff 2008). In one of his first statements as leader, he had put such ideas in the realm of fantasy, saying, "There's no such thing as touching the brake" (Canadian Press 2006b).

Stelmach's laissez-faire approach was not symmetrical, as his government had been stepping on the gas with a royalty structure that was
very generous to the industry – made somewhat less so in 2007 – and a
regulatory process designed to encourage development. In any case,
Stelmach (2007a) said, "My government does not believe in interfer-
ing in the free marketplace. You cannot just step in and lower the
boom on development and growth – in the oil sands or elsewhere. If
that were to happen, the economic consequences for Alberta, and
for the economy of Canada, would be devastating." His successor,
Alison Redford, showed no greater inclination to slow development;
indeed she championed a national energy strategy to gain support
from other provinces for further oil sands expansion and the pipelines to enable it.

ECOLOGICALLY MODERNIZING THE TAR SANDS?

Having rejected any measures to limit growth, but facing an increasingly pressing need to demonstrate environmental and climate concern, industry and government not surprisingly held out the promise
of a technology-heavy EM response. "The answer to all of this is technology, investments in technology," said federal environment minister Jim Prentice as he defended the oil sands from critics (O'Neill
and Alberts 2009). Speaking to the Canada-UK Chamber of Commerce in London, where he aimed to drum up oil-patch investment,
Stelmach (2008) also promised an EM response as he tried to soothe
British climate concerns. "Our goal is to reduce oil sands greenhouse
gas emissions to equivalent or less than those of conventional oil ...
using a combination of renewable energy, energy efficiency and
conservation and science and technology. Particularly carbon capture and storage," he stated. In its 2008 "Climate Change Strategy,"
Alberta (2008a, 24) put most of its emission reduction eggs in the
carbon capture basket, hoping that the technology could deliver 70
per cent of the 200 Mt in emissions cuts below BAU projections that
it pledged by 2050. In the same year, Alberta budgeted $2 billion to
support CCS, which Stelmach (2008) hailed as the "largest amount
dedicated to carbon capture and storage anywhere in the world."
Stelmach also highlighted CCS's "enormous potential for additional
value-added development," its revenue-generating use in enhanced
oil recovery, and "the development of technology we can market

world-wide ... all creating new jobs, opportunities and energy revenues for Albertans."

The large CCS subsidy from a government claiming not to intervene in the marketplace corresponded with the vision of a coalition of corporations active in Alberta's fossil fuel sector that proposed a public-private partnership to build the "Integrated CO_2 Network." The ICO_2N coalition saw opportunity for Canada to become not only an energy powerhouse, but also an "environmental superpower" by capturing CO_2 from upstream tar sands facilities, upgraders, and coal-fired power plants in northern and central Alberta, and transporting it via a 1,000 km pipeline network to underground storage sites, such as mature oil fields (ICO_2N 2007, 2008; Kaufman 2007).[7] Rick Hyndman of CAPP added that developing cost-effective forms of CCS was "critical" not only for Alberta and Canada, but also to get other nations on the path to deep GHG reductions: "The world is not going to stop using coal. So we need to get that [CCS] cost down so that the Chinese and Indians and Russians, as well as Americans ... will actually pick it up."

CCS might have been the best available hope to square oil sands expansion with GHG reduction and counter the problem, as former federal environment minister Charles Caccia described it, of "attempting to ride two horses galloping in opposite directions" (Kolbert 2007). However, it did not address any of the tar sands' other ecological impacts. Serious doubts about the technical limits of CCS in the oil sands also emerged. A briefing note, marked "secret" and revealed by the CBC, from the Canada-Alberta Carbon Capture and Storage Task Force (2008) to federal and Alberta ministers had this to say about the tar sands: "Only a small percentage of emitted CO_2 is 'capturable' since most emissions aren't pure enough. Only limited near-term opportunities exist in the oilsands and they largely relate to upgrader facilities."[8] For its part, the Royal Society of Canada (2010, 91, 93) concluded that, since the geology of northeastern Alberta is generally not suitable for storing CO_2, "the direct impact of CCS on reducing oil sands GHG emissions is not likely to be substantial." Even in the limited situations where CCS was technically possible for tar sands–related emissions, issues of cost arose. Briefing notes for Canada's EU ambassador – obtained by journalists – encouraged him to highlight Canada's CCS investments in defending the oil sands, but they privately conceded that CCS might be prohibitively expensive (S. McCarthy 2011; see also Huot and Grant 2012, 8–9; Royal Society of Canada 2010, 91). The oil industry itself conceded – at least in private, as it lobbied government not to strengthen GHG-reduction requirements – that the "challenge with the oil sands is that current technology is not yet available for deployment to a significant degree."[9] The Royal Society (2010, exec. sum. 4) reached a similar conclusion: "Technological solutions, such as carbon capture and storage (CCS), will not be sufficient to eliminate projected GHG increases from oil sands operations over the next decade."[10]

Alberta in fact had no plan or ambition to prevent rising emissions over that time: its 2008 climate policy aimed for further GHG *increases* of 15 per cent until 2020. A mere 14 per cent GHG reduction below 2005 levels by 2050 was to follow (Alberta 2008a). The province's 2020 target was far weaker than the federal pledge of 17 per cent emissions cut below 2005 levels; indeed, GHG increases from Alberta's oil sands posed a "major and growing challenge" to Canada's ability to meet its modest international commitment (Royal Society 2010, 292). Alberta later conceded that it did not have the policy in place to meet its own weak 2020 target in the face of rising oil sands emissions, prompting it to consider a significant tightening of its carbon-pricing regime.[11] Meanwhile, Alberta's goal for 2050, equal to a 16 per cent *increase above 1990 levels,*[12] was nowhere near UK and EU targets of 80 per cent below 1990 levels or the even deeper cuts some observers believed necessary.

To critics such as the *Globe and Mail*'s Jeffrey Simpson (2008), Alberta's Climate Strategy was full of Orwellian statements on action to "reduce" GHGs when the correct word was "increase," leading the normally restrained, centrist columnist to call the strategy "a study in political deception." Among the misleading statements was that Alberta's (2008a, 5) strategy would "deliver a 50 per cent reduction in emissions by 2050," which had a degree of "truthiness," but only relative to projected BAU emissions by that date, rather than current levels or the international benchmark of 1990 levels. However, one straight-talking passage in the strategy explained Alberta's (2008a, 4, 13) "practical and achievable" approach:

Governments around the world can choose from a variety of options to meet their obligations, including: carbon capture and storage and other transformational technologies, renewable energy, emissions offsets, energy efficiency programs, taxes, slowing down economic growth, or sweeping changes to the very structure of their economy. Alberta's strong and vibrant economy is founded on resource extraction and value added upgrading, so our strategy ensures we build on this strength – *we are not prepared to forgo the opportunities our strong and vibrant economy provides.* Our greenhouse gas emissions profile is strongly linked to the production and use of fossil fuels. Our policy approach to climate change is mindful of this reality and in fact helps strengthen our current economic structure. (italics added)

Alberta's explicit refusal to limit its drive for a particularly carbon-intensive form of growth left it, despite its occasional EM rhetoric and claims of responsible environmental stewardship, on a path that was far out of line with international expectations of the necessary emissions cuts in the affluent world. To what degree this would affect Alberta's and Canada's international legitimacy in the future remained to be seen.

OBSTACLES TO A MANAGED SLOWDOWN

Given the emissions data, some limitation of tar sands growth – even if only to delay further development until GHG emissions could be adequately addressed (Paehlke 2008) – was almost certainly needed if Canada was to make an equitable contribution to global GHG-reduction efforts.[13] The oil sands boom's excesses were so extreme that environmentalists, labour, some conservatives, and even some oil companies called, in their own ways, for some slowing of growth. However, efforts to construct a winning coalition on the issue faced several major obstacles.

One obstacle, as noted above, was ideological. According to Dan Woynillowicz of the Pembina Institute, the Alberta government was "dismissive" of calls for a tar sands moratorium "on the grounds that it's inconsistent with their view that market forces should ultimately dictate the rate and scale of development." Woynillowicz added that there was a similar "ideology of letting market forces decide" within the oil industry. However, other interests could trump ideology – as was evident in the ideological flexibility of the Alberta government, which intervened heavily in the market to promote oil sands development and to subsidize CCS.

Even more central than ideology were the economic interests of the oil industry, which had a powerful political influence. Greenpeace's Mike Hudema saw the challenge this way: "With the tar sands you are looking at battling against the world's largest industrial project that has every single major multi-billion dollar oil company involved in it. So you are looking at some of the biggest corporate players in the world, and you are really looking at taking on that corporate power directly when you are saying ... that we need to shut the project down ... It's definitely tough because in Alberta, you've had a government that's been in power for over forty years of one-party rule – a government that's very wed to the oil and gas industry. And you are looking at billions of dollars of investment going into keeping this running, and keeping business as usual going."

Lindsay Telfer of the Sierra Club added: "The oil lobby is so strong. It has so much money and creates so much money." She noted that, despite the fact that the royalties paid by oil companies were very low compared to other jurisdictions around the world, the province was "rolling in money from royalties" during the boom years. Given the vast revenues the industry created for the provincial, as well as the federal, government, Telfer asked, "Are you really going to bite the hand that feeds you?" Or as Stéphane Dion, then federal Liberal environment minister, told the *New York Times*, "There is no environmental minister on earth who can stop the oil from coming out of the sand, because the money is too big" (Krauss 2005).

Economic dependence on the oil industry for jobs, high average incomes, and low provincial taxes was also a key obstacle to popular uptake of the idea of sufficiency with respect to oil sands growth. While the excesses of the recent boom were widely acknowledged, there was undoubtedly considerable fear among Albertans, who had experience with the extremes of a boom-and-bust resource economy, that measures to limit tar sands expansion would lead to painful economic contraction rather than a more balanced prosperity. Environmental advocates of a moratorium were therefore very aware of the need for an alternative economic agenda for the province (while also warning that the excessively rapid boom itself would inevitably be followed by bust).[14] "In Alberta, we get asked over and over again, 'If not oil sands, then what?'" said Telfer. In fact, as other Canadian sectors such as manufacturing faced troubled times, the country as a whole became increasingly dependent on the tar sands – a point that oil sands supporters tried to use to their advantage.

Environmentalists had differences among themselves about how quickly a move could be made away from oil sands dependence; however, they agreed that Alberta badly needed to diversify its economy and that its large renewable energy potential had, despite some innovative initiatives, barely been tapped. The Pembina Institute (2007b, 8) highlighted the "almost unparalleled opportunity to think big and to diversify our economy beyond fossil fuels" given Alberta's "enviable position: no public debt, a culture of entrepreneurship and innovation, and world-class renewable energy potential." The Sierra Club's Telfer saw particular hope in decentralized renewable energy systems and micro-generation, which could coincide with a decentralization of economic and political power: "If we were successful at decentralizing energy economies in the world, I think the other decentralized processes would likely fall into place." In Alberta, where much of the population favoured a "hands-off" state, she saw potential to build links between conservative rural landowners and others with more left-wing leanings around an economic vision in which communities created their own energy. Meanwhile, Hudema asked, "Why aren't we building a different energy economy?" He added: "Alberta is a perfect place to do that. It's the sunniest province in all Canada. It's one of the windiest provinces in all of Canada, has huge geothermal potential, and we have the resources to be able to make that transition. It's simply a government that does not want to consider change and wants business as usual at all costs."

The power of the energy-security discourse, which, in Canada, emphasized US needs for reliable supplies of petroleum, also worked against calls to limit tar sands growth. This situation was significantly different from the UK and other EU countries, where energy security concerns related to dependence on Middle Eastern and Russian supplies provided a powerful motivator for investments in low-carbon energy and efficiency. In Canada, energy security was, as noted above, a main driver of the initial US interest in the oil sands. It also became a main selling point used by Canada, Alberta, and the industry when continued American support was in doubt. For example, Alberta bought a full-page ad in the *Washington Post* of 2 July 2010, headlined: "A good neighbour lends you a cup of sugar. A great neighbour supplies you with 1.4 million barrels of oil per day." In it, Premier Ed

Stelmach wrote, "Continuing to develop Alberta's oil sands has many tangible benefits to the U.S. The obvious benefit is that it provides the U.S. with access to a secure and reliable supply of energy."

An additional obstacle to shifting Alberta away from tar sands–driven business-as-usual was that the federal government, assuming it actually wanted to limit expansion, had to worry about re-igniting the fires of Western alienation. Such intervention was unlikely under the Conservative Harper government, but the potential for future conflict was real. Former premier Peter Lougheed warned of a coming constitutional clash over the federal government's right to protect the environment and the province's right to develop its natural resources, resulting in "significant stress to Canadian unity" (Makin 2007). The political imperative of preserving the legitimacy of the Canadian federation was thus a factor that any federal government – regardless of its political stripe – had to consider regarding oil sands policy.

THE BATTLE OVER OIL SANDS GROWTH GOES INTERNATIONAL

While Canada's internal political dynamics made it hard to imagine that domestic forces alone could stop rapid tar sands expansion, key battlegrounds emerged in Europe and the United States. These international battles provided important opportunities for advocates of sufficiency with respect to oil sands output, while proponents of expansion put considerable resources of their own into these skirmishes.

Canadian anti–tar sands activists built links with groups in Britain and elsewhere in Europe, connections that Hudema described as "very important ... if we are going to win this fight." For example, "socially responsible investors" in Britain led by Co-operative Asset Management, backed by environmental groups including Greenpeace and WWF-UK, launched a campaign in 2008 for a "moratorium on new investment" in the oil sands by BP and Shell. They also warned investors of financial risks due to the likelihood of stronger climate policies in the future, which could lead to large losses from stranded assets in the tar sands (Crooks 2008) – a problem that came to be known as a "carbon bubble," as overvalued fossil fuel sector assets were based on "unburnable carbon" (Carbon Tracker 2013). The Co-operative's "Stop Tar Sands Expansion" campaign included financial support for a legal battle by the Beaver Lake Cree of northern

Alberta to protect their traditional way of life from further oil sands growth. Documents obtained by journalists revealed Canadian officials' concern over anti–tar sands protests that "have become a regular occurrence in London," with targets including the British oil majors, the Canadian High Commission, and the Royal Bank of Scotland, a significant source of oil sands finance (Lukacs 2011). A network of international environmental groups launched a "Rethink Alberta" campaign encouraging Britons, other Europeans, and Americans to avoid the province as a vacation destination. Disinvestment campaigns also grew in prominence in green-minded Norway. A US diplomatic cable released by Wikileaks revealed Canadian environment minister Jim Prentice's shock at the public sentiment he witnessed in Norway – where debate raged over Statoil's investments in Alberta's "dirty oil" – and his wider concerns over the tar sands' impact on Canada's "historically 'green' standing on the world stage" (Jacobson 2009). With such developments in mind, a Canadian diplomatic document noted that, in Europe, "Oil sands are posing a growing reputational problem … with the oil sands defining the Canadian brand" (Lukacs 2011).

That reputational problem was a key element of the controversy over the EU's Fuel Quality Directive (FQD). As part of its climate policy, the EU required fuel suppliers to reduce GHGs from the fuel production chain by 6 per cent by 2020. When, in 2009, it became clear that the EU was considering labelling the tar sands a high-carbon fuel source – with life-cycle CO_2 emissions some 25 per cent higher than conventional petrol, a distinction that would make tar sands fuel less attractive to buyers – Canada responded with unprecedented European lobbying.

Canada launched its "pan-European oil sands advocacy strategy" in December 2009 – part of a wider Canadian "oil sands advocacy strategy" documented by journalists and environmental organizations using access-to-information requests (CAN Canada 2010; De Souza 2011b; FoE Europe 2011; Lukacs 2011). Led by the Department of Foreign Affairs and International Trade, in collaboration with Natural Resources Canada and Environment Canada, as well as the Alberta government and oil industry, the strategy sought to prevent climate and energy policies in the EU and the US that could limit Canada's ability to export oil from the tar sands. Activities in Europe included monitoring environmental groups, responding to negative media coverage, coordinating trips to Alberta for EU parliamentarians, and feverishly lobbying the European Commission and members of the European Parliament. Friends of the Earth documented 110 lobbying events organized by Canada in Europe from September 2009 to July 2011 – more than one per week. Participants included a number of federal and Alberta government ministers. Lobbying over the FQD took place at the highest levels, including a May 2010 meeting between Prime Minister Stephen Harper and EU Commission president José Manuel Barroso (FoE Europe 2011, 3, 13; P. Harrison and von Reppert-Bismarck 2011).

Canada also threatened the EU with trade conflict unless it dropped plans to label the oil sands a high-carbon fuel source. Canada raised the issue during talks with the EU over a Comprehensive Economic and Trade Agreement (CETA), while Reuters reported that Canada had gone as far as threatening to scrap CETA (P. Harrison and von Reppert-Bismarck 2011). A World Trade Organization (WTO) challenge emerged as a more likely possibility. Canada warned that it would "not hesitate to defend its interests should FQD single out oil sands crude in a disproportionate, arbitrary, and unscientific way" (NRCan 2012), leaving EU officials with little doubt that Canada was prepared to take the issue to the WTO (P. Harrison 2011).

A noteworthy element of Canada's EU strategy was the cultivation of alliances with powerful non-state actors: British and other European-based oil companies. One federal document referred to a "meeting with like-minded allies" in Europe, meaning BP and Shell (De Souza 2011b). Canada maintained close contact and cooperation with these and other European oil majors, including Norway's Statoil and Total of France, the latter of which planned to invest $20 billion in the tar sands by 2020 (Lukacs 2011). Canada also found some support among EU member states, notably the UK, which called for more consultation and research while pushing back a vote on the FQD (EurActiv 2011; see also Carrington 2011c).

Canada's vigorous European lobbying succeeded in delaying the labelling of the oil sands as a high-carbon fuel source. However, environmental campaigners in the UK and the rest of Europe, Canada, and the US kept up pressure on the European Commission to act. Following the commissioning of an independent study confirming that life-cycle emissions from tar sands–derived fuels were significantly greater than conventional oil (Brandt 2011), the EU's climate action commissioner announced in March 2011 that the Commission did, in fact, intend to categorize the oil sands as a high-carbon fuel source. The following month, the European Parliament backed that position. For many members of the European Parliament, the issue had become a credibility test for the EU's much vaunted commitment to climate action (Rankin 2011). Final approval to include tar sands provisions in the FQD required agreement from member states. A committee vote in February 2012 ended in stalemate, with neither enough votes to defeat or approve the provisions. Spain, Italy, Poland and some other new member states voted against the measure, but equally important in temporarily blocking approval were the abstentions of the UK, Netherlands, and France – home to BP, Shell, and Total – as well as Germany (CBC 2012a). The European Commission, seeking to avoid trade friction with both Canada and the US, later proposed removing the FQD from the EU's post-2020 climate package altogether, but the final outcome was still uncertain at the time of writing.

The EU imported minimal quantities of fuel derived from Alberta's tar sands, so the potential loss of European sales did not fully explain Canada's intense reaction to the FQD. One expressed concern of Canadian officials was that a high-carbon classification would strengthen campaigns for disinvestment by European oil companies (Lukacs 2011). Also important was the fear of a precedent that would encourage the spread of low-carbon fuel standards in the US. Alberta officials also expressed concern that the FQD could have an impact further afield, possibly in China and India, potential export markets that had copied EU ecological measures in the past. "Our fear is that if something happens in the EU and it is spread in other countries – not only members of the EU – we could have roughly one-third of the world's population subscribing to regulation or legislation that mitigates against our oilsands," Alberta's international and intergovernmental relations minister Iris Evans told reporters (Gerein 2010).

Canada's battles against low-carbon fuel standards (LCFS) actually began in California, which created the model for the EU FQD. In 2007, California introduced an LCFS, which required reductions in the life-cycle carbon intensity of transportation fuels by at least 10 per cent by 2020. The state was not a major buyer of Alberta oil exports, which flowed mainly to midwestern states. Nevertheless, Canada's federal government feared the possible precedent and intervened numerous times to try to alter California's policy (CAN Canada 2010; Dembicki 2011). Indeed, California's precedent inspired eleven northeast and mid-Atlantic states, who announced tentative plans in 2009 to develop a regional LCFS. Canada and other opponents were successful in getting Wisconsin to withdraw a proposed LCFS from its Clean Energy Jobs Act (Dembicki 2010). Meanwhile, Alberta premier Ed Stelmach praised the role of the province's US representative in defeating Maryland's Oil Sands Responsibility Act, which would have prevented state agencies from using fuels from unconventional oil sources (Alberta 2009). Similar federal proposals were even more worrying for Canada's petroleum interests. Candidate Barack Obama promised a federal LCFS during the 2008 campaign and the idea appeared in versions of the defeated Lieberman-Warner and Waxman-Markey climate bills.

In addition to resisting LCFS proposals, Canada and Alberta lobbied vigorously to exempt the tar sands from Section 256 of the Energy Independence and Security Act of 2007, which prohibited US federal agencies, including the fuel-guzzling military and postal service, from buying alternative fuels with higher life-cycle GHG emissions than conventional petroleum (CAN Canada 2010, 8–9).

The US debate over the $7 billion Keystone XL pipeline linking Alberta to Gulf of Mexico refineries became a particularly high-stakes battle given that the availability of infrastructure to transport fuels to market would be a key determinant of the future rate of oil sands growth. The Sierra Club of Canada's (2011) Prairie Chapter was one group that criticized the pipeline in light of the need for sufficiency with respect to oil consumption while also advocating elements of an EM approach, stating that Keystone XL "simply perpetuates the idea that we must continue to extract more oil and consume more oil, rather than making the changes in our energy use patterns that are required if we are to slow down and reverse climate change ... The time is long overdue for us to be reducing our production and consumption of oil, both through deploying greater energy efficiency technologies, expanding our use of renewable energy and decreasing the need for oil consumption through reduced use of personal automobiles, increased use of public transit, greater local food consumption and a shift from trucks to trains."

On the other side of the debate, Canadian and Alberta government officials lobbied extensively to influence the American decision

(Thomson 2013; Yakabuski 2011). In addition to claims of enhanced energy security and of providing "ethical" oil based on sound environmental stewardship, Canadian officials and TransCanada – the corporation behind the pipeline – highlighted promises of tens of thousands of new jobs from a major "shovel-ready" infrastructure project. Such promises helped win over some US labour organizations, such as the Building and Construction Trades Department of the AFL-CIO and the Teamsters, who welcomed any relief from America's unemployment crisis.

However, other US labour unionists opposed the pipeline on environmental grounds, including the Amalgamated Transit Union and the Transport Workers Union (2011), which stated, "We need jobs, but not ones based on increasing our reliance on Tar Sands oil." They called instead for a version of EM reform: "major 'New Deal' type public investments in infrastructure modernization and repair, energy conservation and climate protection [as] a means of putting people to work and laying the foundations of a green and sustainable economic future for the United States." More widely reported opposition came from Hollywood celebrities – including James Cameron, Robert Redford, Daryl Hannah, and Danny Glover – and from the anti-pipeline protestors that engaged in large-scale civil disobedience outside the White House. They were backed by nine Nobel Peace Prize laureates, including the Dalai Lama, who asked President Obama in September 2011 to reject Keystone XL and fulfill his promises of building a clean energy economy. Meanwhile, all the major US environmental organizations, which often disagreed among themselves on climate strategy, united in calling on the president to block the pipeline.

The forces of sufficiency with respect to oil sands expansion won a significant, albeit provisional victory in November 2011 when the Obama administration decided to delay its decision on Keystone XL. The official reason was to give time to examine an alternative route that would avoid the ecologically sensitive Sand Hills region of Nebraska – deferring the decision until after the 2012 presidential election. The administration said it was responding to bipartisan pressure from Nebraska politicians and landowners. However, many observers believed the most important issue was the president's re-election prospects. Pipeline approval threatened to antagonize green-leaning voters and lead this key part of the Democratic base to sit out the election and withhold donations. This was a case where proponents of sufficiency with respect to a particular form of high-carbon growth were able to win a temporary victory where a political leader needed to bolster his green legitimacy.

Although the decision did not ensure the end of the Keystone XL proposal, supporters of a moratorium on tar sands expansion greeted it enthusiastically. "There are other pipelines to fight and a tar sands monster to slay, but today we can say that we've slowed the expansion and taken another step towards the future we need," proclaimed one group of eco-activists (Ottawa Action Organizing Crew 2011). On the other hand, Canadian government and oil industry interests reacted with dismay and some head scratching about how pipeline approval, which Prime Minister Harper had described as a "no brainer," became derailed. Canadian petroleum interests suddenly faced the prospect of infrastructure bottlenecks and the saturation of existing markets, which threatened their expansion plans. According to energy consultancy IHS CERA, "By 2015, without new pipeline solutions to bring oil sands barrels to markets outside the Midwest (such as the US Gulf Coast), oil sands production growth could stall for lack of new demand" (Snow 2011).

An additional consideration was that Canada was losing tens of billions of dollars per year as it sold oil at discounted prices in the over-supplied US Midwest market (CBC 2012c). By 2012, the US was also feeling less energy insecure as new techniques enabled a boom in domestic shale oil and gas production, adding a further threat to oil sands expansion plans.

While continuing to push for Keystone XL approval, Canada accelerated efforts to export tar sands fuel elsewhere. The proposed Northern Gateway pipeline, which would enable exports to Pacific destinations including China, took on increased urgency for the industry and its government allies. However, that proposal quickly mobilized opposition from environmentalists, Aboriginal people whose land the pipeline would traverse, and political leaders in British Columbia, who saw environmental dangers but little corresponding economic benefit. The possibility that opponents could block Northern Gateway led to renewed interest in an east-west pipeline to bring tar sands crude to Quebec, the Atlantic provinces, and export markets beyond. In the increasingly creative/desperate search to move oil sands products to new markets, other ideas emerged, including building new pipelines up the Mackenzie Valley to the Arctic Ocean or to the port of Churchill, Manitoba, and transporting bitumen by rail to points across North America, by barge down the Mississippi River, or by tanker across the Great Lakes. Such proposals promised to be at the centre of future battles between proponents of expansion and advocates of limits on the growth of tar sands production.

CONCLUSIONS

Given the massive size of everything in the oil sands, it seems strange to speak of them as a microcosm of anything. But they did represent in "miniature" the problems of a growth-based economy and a modern Promethean mindset, which have marshalled considerable ingenuity, powerful technology, and vast amounts of capital and labour to produce great material wealth, while pushing ecosystems to their limits or beyond, and sending vast amounts of carbon skyward. The cost to future generations appears likely to be great, but even in the present, some questioned the benefits in terms of genuine well-being improvements. Some beneficiaries were clear: the corporations reaping vast profits and the political elite that worked closely with them. Much of the general population also owed allegiance to the continuation of business-as-usual expansion for their livelihoods, even as many were also aware of the costs and some asked how to break free from dependence on a high-carbon, high-impact growth model.

Corporate and government advocates of oil sands development were under pressure domestically and internationally to come up with an answer to how to make that break. Not surprisingly, like business and government elites elsewhere, they first reached for a version of ecological modernization, pledging to "green our growth by building a future where prosperity goes hand-in-hand with a deep respect for Alberta's environment" (Alberta 2008a, 4). The main option they were able to come up with for decoupling tar sands growth and GHG emissions was carbon capture and storage, into which large public subsidies were poured, but which was still unproven commercially on the scale contemplated and, according to technical assessments, of limited usefulness in preventing rising oil sands emissions. Alberta embraced an EM rhetoric, but since it refused to put any limits on the particularly carbon-intensive growth it had come to depend on, it could envisage only very minimal climate policy goals. Alberta committed to a move of sorts away from BAU, the continuation of which would lead to even greater emissions increases, but this move still fell far short of the deep GHG cuts in affluent nations that were widely believed necessary to avoid catastrophic warming of greater than 2°C.

Without a convincing strategy for ecologically modernizing the tar sands, Alberta and Canada faced a dilemma of the kind that EM theory does not readily acknowledge: the choice between continuing to pursue high-carbon growth or leaving oil and vast profits in the ground. Some players in the debate proposed a synthesis of sorts between these two positions: significantly slowing the rate of growth, capturing greater value from the resource, creating more high-end processing jobs within Alberta, enhancing efforts to find technological solutions, and better supporting clean energy alternatives. A strategy of this kind might ultimately emerge as dominant from the political confrontations over the issue. However, for the time being, the lack of a viable EM solution and an unwillingness to forgo the high-carbon pot of gold led Alberta and Canada to opt for weak climate policies at home, while fighting green energy policy proposals in the US and EU that threatened their growth strategy.

"Our children may well ask: why the heck didn't you slow things down?" wrote the *Edmonton Journal*'s (2013) editorialists in light of the lack of technological solutions so far to the oil sands' environmental challenges. The inadequacy of an EM response was a key driver leading others to demand, in no uncertain terms, limits on this form of growth. As is typically the case with the idea of sufficiency, daunting obstacles arose from the powerful economic interests at stake in the tar sands. However, those seeking to limit oil sands expansion found allies who had an economic interest in a slowdown, such as organized labour elsewhere in Canada and even, for a time, in Alberta itself.

While a strategy of ecologically modernizing the oil sands had limited prospects on its own, alternative forms of EM, focusing on green growth of Alberta's renewable energy potential and other diversification measures, stood out as an important complement to efforts to limit tar sands growth. In this case and others, sufficiency and EM are not necessarily in conflict, but could work in fruitful synthesis through a "powering down" of carbon-intensive activity and a "powering up" of alternatives (CAT 2013).

The forces within Canada seeking to power down oil sands growth were not powerful enough on their own to achieve their aims, but links with environmental campaigners in the UK, elsewhere in Europe, and in the US gave their efforts a fighting chance of slowing expansion.

Battles were likely to continue for years to come over the policies and infrastructure that either enabled or constrained the access of tar sands fuels to foreign markets. The need for political leaders in the US and EU to bolster their legitimacy on green issues – which was evident in the Obama administration's delay of the Keystone XL pipeline and also one variable in the Fuel Quality Directive debate – was one factor enabling those seeking limits on tar sands growth to make some limited headway in the debate.

Whether or not Canada would eventually accept some degree of sufficiency with respect to the oil sands was likely to have a profound effect on the type of country it would become. Defenders of the sector's expansion could cite significant, albeit unequally distributed, economic benefits, but critics highlighted vulnerabilities. These included the possibilities of a tarnished international image, falling behind in the emerging green economy, a drift toward "petro-state" politics as the boundaries between government and its oil industry allies became blurred, and over-dependence on a single commodity subject to market volatility. The vulnerability to swings in oil prices was evident, for example, as the global economy went into a tailspin in 2008. Oil prices fell from the peak of $147 in July to below $40 a barrel that December. Several tar sands projects were shelved – amounting to a de facto moratorium, at least until oil prices rebounded back to the $100-per-barrel range. The province had to downgrade projections of an $8.5 billion surplus for 2008–09 to a deficit of $852 million. As the provincial economy faltered, journalist Gillian Steward (2008) reminded readers of an Alberta bumper sticker from the 1980s: "Please God, let there be another oil boom. I promise not to piss it away this time." Others were hoping that God could come up with some more creative alternatives in the future.

PART TWO

The Leader

6

Ecological Modernization in Britain:
Coalition around a "Positive Agenda"

07/07/07: It was a lucky day to be alive in London, global alpha-city and a leading centre for the beginnings of a low-carbon economic transition. The floods, heatwaves, and fires dominating headlines around Europe at the time were nowhere in sight – just a perfect blue sky, under which a million people enjoyed the low-carbon pleasures of the Tour de France, as riders sprinted through central London, part of Mayor Ken Livingstone's efforts to boost cycling in the city. Those with more fossil fuel–intensive tastes could enjoy a global spectacle of their own, as British Grand Prix qualifying took place at Silverstone, 80 miles away. The UK's finance-led economy was booming, and would continue to do so – at least for one more month. It was exactly two years earlier that terrorist bombings had killed fifty-two people on the public transport system. And on this day, the Live Earth concert spotlighted the other urgent threat on the lips of Britain's leaders.

By this time, a wide political consensus existed in Britain that something had to be done about climate change. But some confusion and disagreement remained over the type of action needed. "It's so simple, just change a few light bulbs and you can change the world," said one earnest American celebrity on stage at Live Earth. "If you want to save the planet, let me see you jump!" shouted Madonna, a London resident with a mega-celebrity-sized carbon footprint, to the Wembley crowd, inciting an unorthodox response to a warming climate. "It's not enough to be sending the message to change your light bulbs," declared climate activist George Marshall later that night on the BBC. "We need major change to the way we live."

It seemed that almost every group in British society was meeting to debate climate solutions, from the Confederation of British

Industry (CBI) to various Trotskyist tendencies, with ideas ranging from expanded trade in a newly created commodity called "carbon" to organizing an eco-revolutionary movement. The government maintained that deep GHG cuts were perfectly compatible with the pursuit of infinite economic growth and ever-rising consumer aspirations. Two years earlier, in Canada's *Globe and Mail*, British cabinet ministers Margaret Beckett and Patricia Hewitt (2005) claimed that the "U.K. has proved that economic growth does not have to lead to increased greenhouse-gas emissions." Although that claim would be contested, the idea that continued growth and emissions reductions could go hand in hand provided the broad parameters of a newly dominant ecological modernization perspective, voiced by the main political parties, business, trade unions, and many environmentalists. Indeed, an increasingly prominent ecological rationality, or carbon consciousness, was driving considerable social change in a context in which inaction was understood to be economically and ecologically catastrophic in the long term, while climate action was framed as an economic opportunity.

FROM "DIRTY MAN" OF EUROPE TO THE "NEW GREEN INDUSTRIAL REVOLUTION"

The UK was recognized as a relative leader in climate reform. It ranked as high as second on an annual global climate performance index produced by two European NGOs and first on the G8 Climate Scorecards, for reasons including its "strong national climate debate" and "innovative national policies" (Germanwatch 2007; Germanwatch and CAN Europe 2013; WWF-International and Allianz SE 2008, 7). Mind you, the competition for top spot was not so tough – no nation was setting the world on fire, in a good way, in terms of its climate record. In fact, Germanwatch and Climate Action Network (CAN) Europe started leaving the top three spots on their climate performance index empty to emphasize that no state was doing enough. Even so, Canadian environmental groups, among others, pointed to the UK as a model for "proving" that GHG emissions could be decoupled from economic growth (CAN Canada 2008). In fact, the UK appeared to have achieved some of the deepest emissions cuts outside of the former Soviet bloc, with GHGs down 18.4 per cent from 1990 to 2007 while its economy grew 52 per cent in real terms. These figures put the UK well below its Kyoto target of a 12.5 per cent GHG cut by 2008–12 – even before the economic crisis further dampened energy use and emissions. The UK also set itself ambitious future targets. In 2003, it committed to a 60 per cent CO_2 cut by 2050 – then a world-leading target – and later upped the target to 80 per cent. Referring to the ecological transition underway, columnist Jeffrey Simpson (2007) wrote in Canada's *Globe and Mail*, "The last industrial revolution, which began in Britain, was based at first on coal, then on fossil fuels; the next one is beginning, in a halting way, again in Britain."

The UK's role as a climate leader was evident early on. One of the first world leaders to raise the alarm about global warming was none other than Margaret Thatcher. In a speech to the UN, Thatcher (1989) called climate change an "insidious danger" and warned of "the prospect of irretrievable damage to the atmosphere, to the oceans, to earth itself." Like politicians two decades later, she added, "The most pressing task which faces us at the international level is to negotiate a framework convention on climate change." Also very contemporary was her statement that reducing GHGs "should be done in a way which enables all our economies to continue to grow and develop," although Thatcher (1988) did speak in pre-EM terms about environmental action being a significant, albeit necessary, cost. Thatcher's Oxford chemistry degree and work as a research scientist, which gave her a better appreciation than most politicians of the meaning of changes to atmospheric chemistry, was often cited as a factor behind her climate stance.[1] Knowledge that lower-carbon energy would require a shift away from coal gave Thatcher an extra reason to embrace the issue. A chief concern of Thatcher's privatizing, pro-nuclear energy policy was avoiding the fate of her Tory predecessor Ted Heath, who was brought down by coal miner militancy. In light of climate change, her desire to see the coal industry contract "could now be justified on *both* economic and environmental grounds" (Helm 2003, 347). Thatcher was able to appropriate emerging climate concern, diverting it from a potential challenge to neo-liberalism. In her memoirs, Thatcher (1993, 640) rejected environmentalists' use of global warming to "attack capitalism, growth, and industry." Instead, she used climate change to justify increased investment in nuclear power and her broader agenda, notably electricity privatization and the related attack on the coal industry, thereby turning a potential threat to her ideological agenda into a tool of legitimation (Carvalho 2005).

Despite Thatcher's climate statements, the UK was not an early leader in either the discourse or practice of ecological modernization, lagging behind others, including Germany and the Netherlands, and earning the label of the "dirty man" of Europe (Hajer 1995; Hunold and Dryzek 2005). Revell (2005) argues that the increasing prominence of EM discourse in European environmental politics began to influence Britain's Conservative governments of the 1990s; Paterson (2001), however, spots a turning point in 2000, when the Blair government began promoting opportunities for growth and capital accumulation via the emerging renewables industry. Regardless of the precise starting point, the idea that investment in sustainable energy could spur economic growth, profits, jobs, and competitive advantage soon became prominent in key government policy documents (e.g. DETR 2000b, 3; DTI 2003a; HM Government 2005).

With time, an EM language became *de rigueur* in mainstream political debate. An early expression came in a speech to business leaders and environmentalists by Tony Blair (2000), who sought to "push green issues back up the political agenda" by moving beyond the idea of "a trade-off between progress and the environment." This would require engaging consumers and business with "a positive agenda" to create "a coalition that harnesses consumer demand for a better environment, and encourages businesses to see the profit of the new green technologies." Blair concluded with a call to "sell the new insight – we can be richer by being greener; and by being greener we will enrich the quality of our lives." In a major speech emphasizing the "urgency" of climate change and need for a "new green industrial revolution," Blair (2004) stated that the "potential for innovation, for scientific discovery and hence, of course for business investment and growth, is enormous." His successor, Gordon Brown (2007b), similarly spoke of the need for a "fourth technological revolution," which represented "an immense challenge" and "an even bigger opportunity." Not to be out-greened, Conservative leader David Cameron (2006d) spoke of "green growth," calling the idea of conflict between environmental protection and economic growth a "view that belongs to the last century." He added that it was time to move beyond "the battle between the green movement and capitalism," as "responsible" business people and environmentalists understood. Business also came around to the position that strong climate action could, with appropriate policies, be a source of competitive advantage: "With the right focus on R&D, we can be at the forefront of new low carbon technologies that will power the world economy," the CBI announced (2007a). Similarly, for the Trades Union Congress, climate action was "also about employment, jobs and opportunities for millions of workers" (O'Grady 2007), although its particular formulation of EM had a more "central role for the state" than other market-oriented versions (TUC 2009).

Observers of UK environmental politics highlighted an EM discourse's attractions for policy-makers. Barry (2003) noted the appeal to vote-seeking politicians of a discourse that reconciles environmental goals with the prioritization of economic growth, requires no radical structural change, and highlights win-win solutions to competing demands from industry, consumers, and environmentalists. EM thus had a strong affinity with Labour's Third Way politics, which sought to transcend political conflict (Paterson and Barry 2005). The emphasis on "modernization" was attractive to Blair's "New" Labour party, for which modernization was a central concept (Revell 2005; see also Jacobs 1999). EM had the further benefit of focusing on changes in production techniques without questioning growing consumer demand. This had special appeal to New Labour, which explicitly rejected the radical green movement's perceived anti-industry and anti-consumer agenda. Instead, it sought to win over Middle England's swing voters by appealing to their consumer aspirations (Jacobs 1999). In Blair's (2000) words: "We should harness consumer demand, not stifle it. We should not be trying to reduce people's aspirations, but rather find innovative ways of satisfying those aspirations" (see also Revell 2005, 358).

For David Cameron, the desire to lead the Tories back to power provided a strong impetus to embrace EM and distance himself from some conservatives' BAU orthodoxy. After three successive election defeats, the Conservatives saw a need for a thorough "brand decontamination" (Bale 2008; Carter 2009). Party insiders were alarmed by polls showing that "one voter in eight – and one in six swing voters – had such a negative view of the Conservative Party's brand that they would oppose a policy they actually agreed with rather than support a Tory proposal" (Ashcroft 2005, 52). To restore its ability to be heard across the board, the "nasty party" began to talk about "nice things" and take new stances on a range of "caring issues" (Bale 2008, 277; McAnulla 2010, 297). Greening the party was a key element of these efforts to "detoxify" the Tory brand and reposition it as a moderate, centrist alternative (Carter 2009). Cameron rode a dog sled in the Arctic to see the effects of global warming (generating memorable "hugging a husky" images), cycled to work (albeit with a car following with his briefcase), and put a wind turbine on his house. The party adopted a new squiggly tree logo and the slogan "Vote blue, go green." Most importantly, while in opposition, the Tories sought to out-flank Labour on green issues, promising they "would do more to cut carbon" (G. Clark 2009). For example, they came out in support of a Climate Change Act with legally binding annual reduction targets. They also called for a strengthening of the UK's GHG-reduction targets, German-style feed-in tariffs and a smart electricity grid to boost the lagging renewables sector, and emissions standards that would rule out new coal plants without carbon capture and storage (Conservative Party 2007b, 2009b). Such actions helped "sustain the impression that the Conservatives have changed" (Carter 2009, 240). In other words, for the Conservatives, backing EM reform was largely about re-legitimating themselves in the minds of much of the electorate. Although the party's right wing was not enthusiastic about the "bunny hugging" strategy (Bale 2008), Cameron's modernization efforts helped drive EM reform forward, at times forcing the Labour government to catch up to Tory proposals.

NEW LABOUR: STARTING THE LOW-CARBON TRANSITION VIA THE CARBON MARKET

Alongside the EM discourse, considerable policy activity and institutional innovation took place under Labour. The UK's first Climate Change Programme (DETR 2000a) included a set of market-based measures: the Climate Change Levy (CCL), a tax on business energy use; Climate Change Agreements that gave energy-intensive firms an 80 per cent CCL discount if they met negotiated energy efficiency targets; a Renewables Obligation requiring electricity suppliers to source an increasing proportion of power from renewables – 10 per cent by 2010 – with the option of buying or selling Renewables Obligation Certificates (ROCs); tax incentives to encourage low-carbon vehicle purchases; and a voluntary UK Emissions Trading Scheme (UK ETS) that gave firms carbon-trading experience prior to the 2005 launch of the EU ETS. Early measures also included strengthening energy efficiency regulations for buildings and setting up the Carbon

Trust, an independent company that aimed to help business and public sector organizations cut emissions and commercialize low-carbon technologies. Subsequent measures under Labour governments included: a Low Carbon Vehicle Partnership among government, industry, environmental groups, and others to accelerate the shift to greener automobiles and fuels; a Low Carbon Buildings Programme with grants for installation of renewable micro-generation technologies; a Renewable Transport Fuels Obligation to increase biofuel uptake; a requirement that all homes built after 2016 be "zero carbon"; plans to build up to ten zero-carbon "eco-towns"; expanded efforts to encourage lifestyle and behaviour change; a new emissions trading scheme, the Carbon Reduction Commitment, for organizations outside the EU ETS; and a ground-breaking Climate Change Act and new Committee on Climate Change.

The evolving alphabet soup of measures – CCL, CCA, CCC, CRC, EEC, EPC, RO, RTFO, etc. – could be hard to keep straight. Indeed, concerns emerged over these policies' mutual coherence. However, if an overriding theme existed, it was that constructing a carbon market was "at the heart" of the Labour government's approach to climate action, as Gordon Brown (2007b) put it. Carbon pricing would enable cost-efficient GHG cuts, while a multi-billion euro carbon trade promised enormous financial sector profits. In fact, it often appeared that carbon trading, rather than carbon reduction, was the actual goal. The UK ETS received a £215-million subsidy over five years, justified by the argument that this experimental phase would allow London to establish itself ahead of Frankfurt as the centre of carbon trading (Helm 2003, 359). MP Brian Jenkins and Brian Bender, permanent secretary at the Department for Environment, Food and Rural Affairs (Defra) had this exchange about UK ETS subsidies in the House of Commons Select Committee on Public Accounts (2004):

Mr Jenkins: May I put to you that the real priority here was to create a market and not to reduce emissions?

Sir Brian Bender: It was both but creating a market centre in the City of London was a prize. Whether it is 50/50 or 60/40 I think is impossible to answer but it was part of the prize that the City would be the place, and we would look back to the early 2000 years as a time when the decision had taken place where this new commodity trading was centred in the City of London.

With such evidence in mind, Labour MP Colin Challen (2009, 128), chair of the All Party Parliamentary Climate Change Group, criticized the UK ETS as "essentially an R&D scheme on behalf of the City." That said, such efforts to expand carbon trading created a new form of "climate capitalism" that brought the UK's most powerful economic sector into the climate action coalition (Newell and Paterson 2010). Indeed, the CBI (2009a) could soon boast that "London is the global centre of carbon trading, being the location of over 75% of all carbon market trading desks and housing 80% of all carbon market brokering firms."

LOCAL ACTION AND INNOVATION

Some of the most ambitious and innovative measures emerged at the local level. The Mayor of London (2007, 3), "Red Ken" Livingstone, said that climate change was "the number one priority for my administration." London's Climate Change Action Plan raised the bar for world cities, aiming, in light of climate science, for particularly deep and rapid emissions cuts: 60 per cent by 2025, that is, 25 years earlier than the national target at the time. "The prospect of 60 per cent savings in 20 years is easily achievable. It requires no new technology, only political will," said Livingstone (2007). He framed this challenge largely in EM terms, emphasizing efficiency and economic opportunity, albeit with a heavier emphasis on lifestyle change than in many EM formulations. In addition to committing to "make London's business sector a beacon of carbon-friendly commerce" and the "world's leading centre for research and financial development on climate change," Livingstone wrote:

> The simple message is this: to tackle climate change you do not have to reduce your quality of life, but you do have to change the way you live. The present model of huge energy production followed by huge energy waste – in the losses from power stations, from houses, from commercial property, and from transport – is utterly inefficient and is irreparably damaging the planet. There must be a decisive shift to an economy in which energy is conserved, not wasted, and therefore in which far less energy needs to be produced per unit of economic activity.
> The fundamental cause of global warming is the profligacy with which we have exploited global energy resources over the past

century. A strategy to cut carbon emissions is essentially about cutting out waste and improving efficiency. (Mayor of London 2007, 2–3)

The Mayor's "top priority" for reducing emissions was to shift from reliance on the national electricity grid to decentralized energy, including combined cooling heat and power (CCHP) systems, energy from waste, and on-site renewables such as solar panels (16). These decentralized systems allowed the use of waste heat from power production to warm buildings, while avoiding large electricity losses from long-distance transmission. "Centralized power is like having a big leaking pipe," explained Allan Jones (2007), CEO of the London Climate Change Agency. To tackle its main emissions source, London's plan incorporated a "Green Homes" program, including heavily subsidized home insulation and a home-energy audit program inspired by Canadian examples, with estimated potential savings to the average household of £300 per year on fuel bills (Mayor of London 2007, 10–11). Livingstone also played a central role in establishing the C40 Cities Climate Leadership Group, which he chaired. In partnership with the Clinton Foundation, major banks, and energy-service companies, C40 supported major global cities in making job-creating, energy-saving investments such as building retrofits, and established a global purchasing alliance to give cities discounts on energy-saving equipment (e.g. more efficient street lighting). "It's a complete win-win," said Deputy Mayor Nicky Gavron (2007) of the C40 initiative. "It's that kind of thinking and that kind of scale we need."

While emphasizing efficiency and economic benefits, London's initiatives under Mayor Livingstone did stretch the boundaries of EM by incorporating a degree of sufficiency at the micro level. Cutting transport emissions meant more than promoting low-carbon vehicles; it required a modal shift so people drove less (Mayor of London 2007, 18–19). London could boast of being the world's only major city to have seen, in the previous six years, a shift from private car use to public transport, cycling, and walking (6) – a product of the congestion charge on vehicles entering central London and major public transit investments, notably a much expanded bus service. Livingstone also waged war on oversized 4x4s and other high-emission vehicles, questioned the need for further capacity growth at

Heathrow and other UK airports, and urged people to stop buying bottled water (chapter 9).

Livingstone's successor, Boris Johnson, did not have the same carbon-cutting zeal; however, the bicycle-riding, mop-topped Tory moved beyond his earlier comparison of climate concern to a "Stone Age religion." Johnson was one of the few Britons of note to praise George W. Bush's Kyoto Protocol rejection, but as mayor he acknowledged that climate change required "urgent action" and adopted an EM language. "London is well positioned to seize the opportunities coming from this nascent low carbon age, to be one of the world's leading low carbon capitals and the leading carbon finance centre," he wrote. "We don't need to forsake life as we know it and live like cavemen," added Johnson (Mayor of London 2010, 5–6), who rejected "hair-shirt abstinence," instead favouring new technology and reductions in energy waste (TfL 2009). He accepted Livingstone's 60 per cent carbon reduction target by 2025, and pursued several initiatives begun by the previous administration, rolling out a bike hire scheme (using the same Quebec-built bikes as Montreal's Bixi system), continuing energy efficiency retrofit programs, and introducing ten "Low Carbon Zones" aiming to radically cut CO_2 at the community level. He also pledged to make London the plug-in electric vehicle capital of Europe, introduce bicycle superhighways, and put more hybrid buses on the road. However, environmental critics argued that the results of such policies were often limited, and that other of his actions pushed in the opposition direction, such as scrapping the westward extension of the congestion charge, proposing to increase road capacity for cars, supporting a new "Boris Island" airport in the Thames estuary and increased flights from the City airport, abolishing London's Climate Change Agency, slashing climate staff, and leaving half the available climate budget unspent. The contradictory record earned a contradictory assessment from FoE and Greenpeace UK (2012), who said Johnson "does not respect the urgent need to tackle air pollution and climate change" (4) and yet "has been a voice for action on climate change" (24). (Indeed, Johnson's [2013] contradictions continued, as he later returned to themes of climate scepticism in an apparent appeal to right-wing Tories.)

Other municipalities introduced their own carbon-cutting innovations. An early example was the town of Woking, which inspired Livingstone's decentralized energy strategy for London. Woking cut carbon emissions 79 per cent from 1991 to 2006 from municipal operations, and 19 per cent for the community as a whole, through measures including a revolving fund for energy efficiency investment, combined heat and power (CHP) plants providing district heating and electricity, the UK's first fuel-cell CHP facility, and use of solar photovoltaic panels. The borough also installed its own private electricity wires to avoid national grid transmission and distribution fees, allowing green electricity provision at low net cost despite higher upfront production costs. The town of some one hundred thousand people had installed nearly 10 per cent of Britain's solar PV capacity by 2004, before PV became more widely adopted (Climate Group 2006, 2007b; A. Jones 2007).

Innovative local measures included the "Merton Rule," pioneered by the London Borough of Merton in 2003, which required new developments to produce at least 10 per cent of their energy needs from on-site renewable energy. Most UK local authorities, including the Greater London Authority, followed with similar measures that expanded the market for PV cells and other renewable energy equipment. In 2008, the national Planning and Energy Act formally enshrined in law the ability of local councils to adopt such policies, which played a key role in preparing the building sector for the coming era of zero-carbon homes. Adrian Hewitt, Merton's principal environment officer and a key force behind the rule, highlighted its value as a "stimulus to innovation" that would push builders, even recalcitrant ones, to develop solutions to meet higher ecological standards – echoing EM theorists' arguments about the role of smart regulations.

Many grassroots initiatives also emerged. In 2006, Ashton Hayes, a community of 1,000 in Cheshire, set out to become England's first carbon-neutral village through measures ranging from sharing rides to the theatre to building a community-owned renewable power station. By 2010, the village's emissions had fallen some 23 per cent according to University of Chester researchers (Ashton Hayes Going Carbon Neutral 2012; Harrison and Anderson 2007; Stocks-Moore 2008). The local tavern, where residents shared energy-saving tips, similarly set out to be the country's first carbon neutral pub – the Golden Lion reportedly saved £200 a month by drying laundry outside, turning off the cigarette machine at closing time, and lowering the thermostat (Jowit 2007). Ashton Hayes inspired other local groups across the UK and even across the Atlantic; Eden Mills, Ontario sought to follow its example by becoming North America's first carbon-neutral village.

Such examples illustrated initial steps toward the wider social mobilization that would likely be necessary for a low-carbon transition. So, too, did the emergence of scores of Transition Towns, starting with the Devon town of Totnes, which worked toward an "energy descent" in response to the dual challenges of peak oil and climate change. Meanwhile, Carbon Rationing Action Groups (CRAGs), which set ambitious carbon-reduction targets for their members to live within, sprang up across Britain as a way to illustrate the potential of low-carbon living and an eventual nationwide tradable carbon rationing scheme. Transition Towns and CRAGs made full use of the EM staples of greater efficiency and green technology; however, ideas of "energy descent" and "rationing" took the debate well into sufficiency territory.[2] Indeed, Transition Town founder Rob Hopkins (2009) posed this question, via CNN (2009), to the world's business and political elites gathered at Davos: "On a finite planet, is it not impossible for most of us to achieve fulfillment and happiness through material consumption, and will many of our children and grandchildren even have the opportunity to make that choice if we go on with our current ways of being? Is it not time to leave the very concept of 'economic growth' behind?" Such questions are returned to in later chapters. For now, suffice it to say that such thoughts illustrated that the increasingly prominent ecological rationality could not always be contained within the boundaries of an EM framework.

CRADLE-TO-GRAVE CARBON CONSCIOUSNESS

In a land where reform once meant lifelong social protections, signs were emerging of cradle-to-grave carbon consciousness, illustrated in headlines ranging from "The Carbon Neutral Baby: How To Go Green from Day One" to "Crematorium Concern over Carbon Footprint Becomes a Burning Issue." Echoing my impressions about the contrast with North America at the time, Joel Makower (2007), an American green business writer, wrote upon his arrival in London, "The town seems to have gone carbon crazy, offering up a display of initiatives from both the public and private sectors that highlighted how far behind the U.S. has fallen. The consciousness about carbon here seems to be sky-high." For a sports fan, the ubiquity of climate concern was perhaps best illustrated by a column in the *Observer* by England goalkeeper David James (2008), who spoke out against a proposal to play some Premier League matches in other nations. "The environmental impact of 20 teams flying abroad is a negative when football should be promoting a reduced carbon footprint," he wrote. Indeed, a campaign did emerge to "Reduce your carbon footprint with the FA Cup." Ecological rationality, in the form of carbon consciousness, also made its mark on the monarchy ("Queen Seeks to Cut Carbon Footprint"), the Chelsea Flower Show ("gardening in a changing climate"), and even the military, which aimed to cut its own emissions while preparing to operate in a world of more extreme weather and climate-induced conflict (AP 2008; Majendie 2007; RHS 2008).

The "carbon crazy" period was followed by an ebbing of high levels of carbon consciousness – as economic concerns came to dominate the public agenda and climate science faced a renewed challenge in light of the so-called "Climategate" controversy (chapter 7). Some of the initiatives that emerged would turn out to be false starts or dead ends. Nevertheless, the rules of the game were changing. For example, the Advertising Standards Authority stepped up its crackdown on misleading green claims (Ashley-Cantello 2008). Among those rebuked was Shell, which was forced to withdraw an ad showing refinery chimneys emitting flowers. Toyota was ordered to drop commercials with exaggerated claims about the eco-benefits of driving a Prius and its luxury division, Lexus, had to stop claiming its RX 400h hybrid SUV offered: "High performance. Low emissions. Zero guilt." Meanwhile, acting to stop climate change emerged as a possible legal justification for otherwise unlawful behaviour – a sign that ecological rationality was affecting the legal system as well as other social institutions. In 2008, a jury acquitted six Greenpeace activists who occupied the Kingsnorth power station and caused £35,000 of damage by painting Gordon Brown's name on the chimney to protest a proposed new coal-fired plant on the site. Jurors accepted defence arguments that the property damage was lawful to prevent even greater damage to other property from climate change. The ruling did not set a binding precedent – indeed, in 2010, a jury convicted twenty environmentalists for planning to shut down the Ratcliffe-on-Soar power station (Schwarz 2010) – but it did show, according to one bank's legal analysis, "that the 'public' are less willing to accept a lack of action in terms of tackling climate change" (Natwest 2009).

One early impact of growing carbon consciousness was scrutiny of the "climate-busting" lifestyles of the rich and famous, with media exposés of the massive carbon footprints of the likes of David Beckham and Prince Charles (D. Smith and Thompson 2005). Tony Blair was later blasted in the media for his own sizable carbon footprint after a transatlantic holiday flight to former Bee Gee Robin Gibb's Florida beach mansion (Woodward and Watt 2007) – which was not to be the last time that the climate concern he helped unleash came back to challenge his vision of environmentalism reconciled with growing consumer aspirations.

BUSINESS: BEING GREEN TO GROW

"Cut Carbon, Grow Profits." "Carbon Down, Profits Up." "Cleaning Up." "Business must become green to grow." By 2007, this EM language was sweeping through UK business. At that summer's Corporate Climate Response conference in London, a "win-win" theme was in the air as presenters explored the business case behind climate action. Of course, not everyone was equally convinced about the bottom-line benefits of cutting emissions, but it was clear that even the doubters could no longer ignore climate change.

British businesses began to take a wide range of actions to cut their carbon footprints – and encourage or pressure others to do likewise. For many, the first step was to invest in energy efficiency – a cost-saving measure that could fund further greening and/or deliver returns to shareholders. For example, BT, the UK's largest communications service provider, identified redundant computer systems in its data centres and took them out of service, a £50–60,000 investment that saved £1 million – one of several steps that allowed it to reduce emissions 60 per cent below 1996 levels (Tuppen 2007). Other companies invested in on-site renewables or bought green electricity from other suppliers, and/or offset the remaining emissions from unavoidable energy use. Several prominent firms pledged to combine such actions to become "carbon neutral." Among them were HSBC, Marks and Spencer – which reported in 2012 that it had met its target – and even Rupert Murdoch–owned British Sky Broadcasting (BSkyB) (Harvey 2007).[3] Hedge fund manager Man Group Plc upped the ante, pledging to go "carbon neutral plus," by funding a Gold Standard–certified biomass power project in India and a community forestry project in Mozambique (Challis 2007).

Companies also took steps to encourage and enable consumers to cut carbon. Advertising became a prominent source of messages nudging people toward low-carbon behaviour. For example, after discovering that 93 per cent of its shampoo's carbon footprint came from the consumer use phase, Boots's ad for its lower-carbon shampoo included the following words: "Using cooler water to wash your hair cuts CO_2 emissions, reduces your energy bills and is actually better for your hair" (A. Jenkins 2007). Similarly, Marks and Spencer, as part of its "Plan A" ("Because there is no Plan B") greening initiative, advertised the launch of the new "Think Climate – Wash at 30°C" labels sewn into some 70 per cent of the garments it sold. Such messaging was one element of the "We're in This Together" campaign, in which government, major corporations that had committed to reducing their own carbon footprints, environmental NGOs, and the Church of England were participants (Climate Group 2007a). The campaign included the marketing of carbon-reducing products. For example, home improvement retailer B&Q and British Gas offered discount home insulation and green energy tariffs, respectively, while O_2 stepped onto sufficiency territory by encouraging less consumption – of someone else's product – with a £100 credit if customers kept their mobile handsets when renewing their phone plans (Together 2007).

With support from the then-government-funded Carbon Trust, some products began to sport carbon labels to allow consumers to compare carbon as they did calories. Among its eco-initiatives, supermarket giant Tesco pledged to put carbon labels on all 70,000 products it sold (Leahy 2007). Whether carbon labelling would ever play a large role remained to be seen. A major setback to the idea occurred in 2012 when Tesco abandoned its labels after applying them to just five hundred products due to the time-consuming effort involved in calculating product footprints and the slow take-up of the idea by other retailers (Lucas and Clark 2012). Nevertheless, the Carbon Trust noted that more than one hundred firms had applied carbon labels to products worth some £3 billion per year, adding that labelling "enables society to start a series of conversations around carbon" (Messem 2012). Indeed, it seemed that the information given to consumers was less significant than the awareness carbon labelling generated of the GHG impacts of each step in the production process, creating opportunities for firms and suppliers to identify less energy-intensive – and often lower-cost – alternatives (Economist 2011; Upham and Bleda 2009).

Some leading retailers began "choice editing," that is, removing the least ecologically or socially sound options from the shelves and marketing themselves as ethical firms that took the time to make such choices on behalf of consumers. For instance, John Lewis began selling only appliances that received an A rating for energy efficiency, where a sufficient range of models was available.[4] Tesco (2008), for its part, was reluctant to choice edit, but did donate £25 million to a new Sustainable Consumption Institute at the University of Manchester to consider such questions as: "How can we motivate customers to play their part in tackling climate change willingly to deliver a revolution in green consumption?"

Other companies launched curious new products, such as carbon offset mortgages. New types of businesses, such as carbon brokers and consultancies, also emerged. Firms also began to work with and pressure suppliers to provide low-carbon goods. Greening the supply chain, like encouraging customer behaviour change, represented a way for firms to cut carbon with minimal direct cost to themselves or need for investment funds. Richard Gillies (2007), director of store development for Marks and Spencer, noted that his firm's vast procurement budget gave it significant capacity to get suppliers to invest in lower-carbon production. Similarly, BT pledged to require that the energy consumption and environmental impact of any replacement product or service that it purchased be less than its predecessor (Tuppen 2007). Some firms, such as BT (2007), encouraged their own employees to "live lightly," through creation of "carbon clubs" to share ideas and take carbon-reducing actions. Others engaged in food miles and air travel reductions, construction of green buildings and "eco-stores," and high-profile donations to NGOs working on climate change, such as HSBC's US$100 million Climate Partnership.

The most significant aspect of business greening was the call by some leading firms for stronger climate policy. The Corporate Leaders Group on Climate Change (CLG), which consisted of major businesses brought together by the Prince of Wales and the Cambridge Programme for Industry,[5] offered to work in partnership with

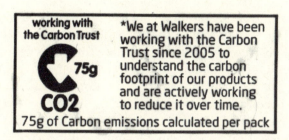

working with
the Carbon Trust

75g
CO2

*We at Walkers have been working with the Carbon Trust since 2005 to understand the carbon footprint of our products and are actively working to reduce it over time.

75g of Carbon emissions calculated per pack

Figure 6.1 Ecological rationality makes its mark on a bag of Walkers Crisps.

government to overcome the following Catch-22: "Governments tend to feel limited in their ability to introduce new policies for reducing emissions because they fear business resistance, while companies are unable to take their investments in low carbon solutions to scale because of lack of long-term policies" (CLG 2005). Critical observers noted the irony that some corporations were calling for stronger regulation while Labour ministers were still reluctant to give up the Third Way idea that "market forces will solve the problem" (Harriss-White and Harriss 2006, 88; Monbiot 2005a). Subsequent CLG statements urged the government to take "ambitious action now to stimulate investment in low carbon technology" (CLG 2006), called for a "cross-party effort" to "deliver deep and rapid cuts in greenhouse gas emissions" (CLG 2008), and urged government and business to "seize the day" and "lead the world down a path of green growth" (CLG 2011). The Aldersgate Group, a coalition that included many firms in the CLG, as well as environmental NGOs and trade unions, similarly put forward demands for ambitious carbon-reduction policies.

While the CLG represented a small number of firms, the CBI, the primary business lobby group, moved beyond an anti-regulation discourse. Its landmark climate report called for the pace and scale of implementation to be "accelerated," adding: "Market forces will drive big changes, but they will not by themselves be enough to do the job. The full range of public policies must be deployed to create the right incentives" (CBI 2007c, 2–3). Similarly, Mark Moody-Stuart, chair of Anglo American mining, stated in the CBI's magazine: "Businesses are pathologically opposed to regulation. But there has to be regulation in this case. We need a regulatory framework for tackling climate change. The market is not going to solve this problem"

(Harvey 2007, 32). Meanwhile, significant business commitment to climate action was evident in statements from the CLG (2008) and CBI (2008) rejecting suggestions that the economic crisis was a reason to abandon carbon-reduction efforts, in the CBI's (2009b) plan for "going the distance" along the "revolutionary road" to the UK's 80 per cent reduction commitment, and in the CBI's (2011) call for the Cameron-led coalition to do more to create profitable conditions for "vital" low-carbon investment. Of course, business was not united behind every climate policy proposal. For example, the EEF manufacturers' organization and the CBI opposed the UK government's call to strengthen the EU's GHG reduction target from 20 per cent to 30 per cent by 2020, arguing that without a binding global deal, such a unilateral move would disadvantage energy-intensive firms – even as some major firms backed the 30 per cent target (Harvey 2010b).

What was driving business to back climate action? To start, companies were operating within the context of a high level of carbon consciousness in UK society – to which many firms were, in turn, contributing through their words and actions. Growing scientific consensus on anthropogenic climate change and the need for strong action was a related factor. "Three to five years ago, there was some debate about climate change. Is it really happening? How urgent is it?" Roger Salomone, energy adviser for EEF, told me in 2007. "Most of society is coalescing around the idea that something is happening and something needs to be done." Similarly, CBI (2007d) director-general Richard Lambert said, upon launching his group's climate task force: "The time for debate about whether human activity is changing the climate has passed. The science is clear. The challenge now is for the business community, Government and society as a whole to decide how to respond." Even when an upsurge of climate scepticism later became evident in Britain around 2009, leading business organizations did not fundamentally retreat from support for a corporate-friendly form of green growth.

Within this context of strong climate concern, many firms experienced internal pressure for action from green-minded employees. Some of these individuals were recognized as activists in their own right, such as Chris Tuppen, BT's director of sustainable development, named one of the *Guardian*'s (2008a) "50 people who could save the planet." Some early expressions of concern came right from the top, in cases such as John Browne (1997) of BP, the first oil major to break from the climate-sceptic camp, gaining the firm considerable environmental credibility – until a series of incidents culminating in the Gulf of Mexico oil spill made a mockery of its "beyond petroleum" claims. Meanwhile, Shell's Ron Oxburgh warned of the "angry beast" of climate change and, at the annual Greenpeace UK (2005) Business Lecture, called for "more determined government action" – a message and venue that was not typical for Calgary or Houston oilmen. Of course, the role of major oil firms in urging climate action was highly contradictory.[6]

In addition to growing ecological concern outside and within firms, something more was needed to change the calculus of whether or not to support climate action. One factor was growing acknowledgment of the economic costs of inaction – a key theme of the *Stern Review on the Economics of Climate Change*. "If we fail to mitigate climate change, the environmental, social and economic consequences will be stark and severe," stated Tesco CEO Terry Leahy (2007). Of greater immediate impact than the broader social costs were the costs for individual firms. BT, for instance, recognized its vulnerability to floods and droughts, forcing it to move key underground equipment away from floodplains (Tuppen 2007). The insurance industry – although slower to emerge as a force in the debate than some greens had originally hoped (Paterson 2005) – presented itself as a "messenger of the costs of climate change." The Association of British Insurers (ABI 2005, 4–6) concluded that climate change could significantly increase the costs of flooding and windstorm damage. These losses could raise capital costs and increase insurance market volatility, with the costs ultimately falling on the wider economy.

The business case for cutting carbon included the desire to avoid several other risks – one of the most notable being the threat of rising energy costs and energy insecurity. Such issues were critical for a company such as BT – which alone consumed 0.7 per cent of total UK electricity (Tuppen 2007) – as they were for corporate Britain more generally. The UK faced real risks of future energy shortages as it needed massive investments to replace aging coal-fired and nuclear plants, while North Sea gas extraction was declining and gas imports increasing. Fears grew of over-dependence on Vladimir Putin's Russia and on Middle East suppliers. "Business has been clear for some years that the priority for energy must be to ensure energy security at an affordable cost, while keeping the UK on track to meet its 2050 carbon targets," wrote the CBI (2010, 2). Among the key ways to improve energy security were greater energy efficiency and investment in low-carbon domestic generation (renewables, nuclear, and CCS) – which were also staples of an EM climate response. Of course, business and greens could disagree over the relative balance between the different options – with the CBI and well-connected firms such as EDF favouring more nuclear and less renewables in the overall mix.

UK companies had little reason to doubt that the climate issue was here to stay and that stronger government policy was coming – possibly in undesirable forms. "It looks to us like governments will act, so it's best to act and win a seat at the table to discuss the details of those policies – always with the belief that the market is the best mechanism to tackle climate change," said Shell chairman James Smith (2007). Pressure also came from investors, through initiatives such as the Carbon Disclosure Project, a not-for-profit organization that demanded that firms measure and report emissions as well as their exposure to climate regulation – and take action to reduce them. Businesses also cited consumer pressure. "Climate change is an issue for us because it's an issue for our customers," said Jon Williams (2007) of HSBC. "We are responding to what we believe our customers want," added Marks and Spencer's Richard Gillies (2007). Customers were not necessarily willing to pay more for low-carbon products and services, but they might withdraw business from firms without a clean climate record; as Gillies put it, the issue had become a "hygiene factor." Customer pressure also applied to business-to-business transactions given the moves, noted above, by many firms to cut carbon throughout their supply chain.

Beyond the risks of not acting were the perceived economic opportunities, which were central to an EM vision. "There is recognition that lots of companies can make money out of it," said Mark Kenber, policy director of the Climate Group, an NGO working in partnership with business and government to achieve a low-carbon economy. "I think the language of opportunity is very important," he added. In addition to cost savings on energy were the possibilities of gaining early mover advantages in international markets for low-carbon goods and services. A review commissioned by UK Trade & Investment (UKTI 2008) found considerable opportunities for Britain's relatively mature eco-industries in markets for renewable energy, carbon finance, and carbon-abatement technologies in countries such as Australia, Brazil, China, India, South Africa, Turkey, and the US. Although the incentives created by the EU ETS were not as strong as first expected, firms that could cut emissions – or were lucky enough to have received a generous allocation – could also profit from selling surplus emissions rights.

Meanwhile, being seen as active on the climate front was a way for some firms to enhance their brand image and reputations in the minds of the public, policy-makers, and potential employees – a form of legitimation. "We survive on our reputation," said one employee of a controversial "carbon-neutral" finance firm at the Corporate Climate Response conference. "This establishes our credibility in commercial space."

In short, the need to reduce vulnerability to risks and the possibility of seizing opportunities were key forces driving business action. For EM theorists, these examples provided many illustrations of ecological rationality transforming business, an emphasis on win-win opportunity, and further evidence that private sector firms and their employees had emerged as key actors contributing to the spread of ecological ideas. However, as critics of EM theory pointed out, highlighting the best cases of corporate practice was not enough to show that such cases were representative of overall trends (York and Rosa 2003).

Indeed, not all firms were equally well-positioned to seize climate-action opportunities. Roger Salomone and Stephen Radley of EEF noted that in manufacturing, win-win opportunities existed, for example, in renewable energy, lightweight composite materials, smart metering, and smart-control technology. But they said a win-win logic did not apply in all cases. "Realistically, investment in carbon efficiency competes for funds with other projects that may have a bigger payback," said Radley. Ensuring that climate policy did not go so far as to erode some firms' competitiveness and drive energy-intensive production abroad remained high among their concerns, suggesting a more mixed picture than upbeat EM advocates often portray. Mixed business positioning was also evident in remarks by Green member of European parliament (MEP) Caroline Lucas (2007), who said that business associations often lobbied her for a slowdown of climate action, even when individual companies within those groups favoured stronger action. Mark Kenber of the Climate Group, an organization that documented many cases of win-win action, acknowledged that carbon-intensive firms exposed to international competition faced considerable challenges. "I think it's important to talk about the opportunities so that people look for it … and part of that is creating conditions for the opportunities to be taken," said Kenber. "But I think there comes a point where we shouldn't believe our rhetoric in every circumstance."

One could also ask whether corporate climate initiatives were as significant as they appeared. Environmental writer Fred Pearce certainly had no shortage of material for his "Greenwash" column on the *Guardian* website, which discussed many of the above-mentioned firms, such as HSBC, Tesco, Shell, and BP. Whatever the merits of the claims and counterclaims about these particular firms, companies did have a tendency to make the easiest and most visible changes – and highlight them through their marketing – without always addressing their most significant climate impacts. For example, HSBC claimed "carbon neutrality" by offsetting the relatively small emissions from its direct operations even as it continued to finance fossil fuel extraction, including high-carbon projects in Alberta's tar sands.

For some on the political left, the business response to climate change was, at best, a slightly greener version of an unsustainable status quo. Although there were grounds to support such criticism – and critics had a valuable role in drawing attention to the limits of business responses – business's embrace of the climate issue did push the agenda significantly forward. It was undoubtedly advantageous for the climate cause to have large corporate players advocating an EM response rather sitting on the sidelines or resisting outright. Every corporate commitment to deep reductions – such as Tesco's pledge to cut GHGs from its stores and distribution centres by 50 per cent by 2020 or BT's goal of 80 per cent cuts by the same date – was another blow to the BAU idea that strong climate action was economically impractical. Corporate action also enabled politicians "to be a bit braver in what they offer the citizens of the UK," said Jonathon Porritt (2007c), Sustainable Development Commission chairman. Although those politicians could have been braver still, in light of the UK's climate-action lead over Canada, one can appreciate the validity of Porritt's statement. Furthermore, as long as corporations were onside and making the case for eco-capitalist reforms such as carbon pricing and carbon trading – for which environmentalists in Canada still found themselves pleading – greens in the UK could worry a little less about battles with BAU advocates and feel a little freer to speak their minds about the more radical changes that many thought were really needed.

THE *STERN REVIEW* AND "THE DAY
THAT CHANGED THE CLIMATE"

Although EM was already the accepted paradigm of the government and main political parties, the Treasury's release of the *Stern Review on the Economics of Climate Change* in October 2006 dealt another blow to a business-as-usual argument and helped cement a wider EM consensus, including more of the corporate sector. This can be considered a "critical discourse moment" marked by events that challenge established discursive positions and help determine the construction of an issue (Carvalho 2005; Gamson 1992). Nicholas Stern (2006), former World Bank chief economist, concluded that it was possible to keep atmospheric GHG concentrations from surpassing 550 ppm CO_2e at a manageable cost of 1 per cent of global GDP per year by 2050, while a BAU path would generate costs of 5 to 20 per cent of global per capita consumption. Given the costs of inaction, Stern argued that "tackling climate change is the pro-growth strategy for the longer term" (ii).

The review's release dominated the front pages, with the *Independent* celebrating "The Day That Changed the Climate." This was more than standard media hyperbole. "The Stern Review is what gave everyone a kick in the UK," a Defra employee told me. It was – at least for some time – no longer possible for high-level politicians to put forward a business-as-usual view, noted Adrian Hewitt, principal environment officer at the London Borough of Merton: "It would be like saying I know more about economics than Stern." Upon hearing Stern's message that "business-as-usual will derail growth" during a cabinet briefing, one minister reportedly said it destroyed the Bush administration's position that cutting carbon emissions was bad for business (McSmith and Brown 2006). Or, as Simon Retallack, head of climate change at the Institute for Public Policy Research, a left-of-centre think tank, put it, "Those who deny climate change have already been smoked out on the science; this report smokes them out on the economics" (BBC 2006b). Similar analysis appeared in the *Times*: "The science debate is effectively over. The Stern review means that the economic debate is all but over. Only the political debate is left" (Cavendish 2006).

The *Stern Review* was not ultimately able to put the final nail in the coffin of the BAU perspective, which later experienced a UK resurgence (chapter 7), but it did perform important tasks that helped government and business to embrace an EM climate response. First, even though Stern acknowledged that "CO_2 emissions per head have been strongly correlated with GDP per head," he presented a reassuring message that "the world does not need to choose between averting climate change and promoting growth and development" (2006, xi). Second, while Stern identified climate change as "the greatest and widest-ranging market failure ever seen" (i), he put forward market-based policies, such as carbon trading, as central elements of the solution. Third, even though Stern concluded that the costs of fighting climate change would be "significant" (xvii), they were also "manageable" and small relative to the estimated cost of inaction. Furthermore, as there were "opportunities for growth," "benefits from innovation," and markets for low-carbon energy products "likely to be worth at least $500bn per year by 2050" (xvi), it was still possible to sustain the idea of win-win climate action. However, Stern's message did represent a subtle darkening of an EM vision. Rather than climate action paying off in a positive sense, generating net increases in economic output, the emphasis was now on avoiding losses. As Environment Secretary David Miliband (2007c) summed up Stern's message: "Yes, it costs to fight climate change, but it costs less to fight it than it does to live with it."

Business generally welcomed the review, albeit with warnings to government not to respond with competitiveness-reducing taxes (S. Shah 2006). A particularly welcome finding, given the UK's economic structure, was that financial markets "face big opportunities to develop new trading and financial instruments across a broad range including carbon trading, financing clean energy, greater energy efficiency, and insurance" (Stern 2006, 269, 271). (The review did find, however, that a few sectors faced large cost increases.)[7] Taking "as its starting point" the "watershed Stern Review," the CBI (2007a, 2007d) set up a task force on the business response, which produced a commitment to "do what it takes to tackle climate change." Paying homage to Stern became common among firms aiming to project an image of ecological responsibility. At the *Guardian*'s Climate

Change Summit, sponsored by Shell, the firm's UK Chairman James Smith (2007) referred to Stern's point that investing 1 per cent of GDP could avoid social costs of 5 to 20 per cent of GDP: "It sounds like good economics to me to take action today."

Many in the green movement also welcomed the *Stern Review*, even if they did not share all its conclusions. SDC chair Jonathon Porritt (2007c) said we "owe thanks to Nic Stern" for the fact that climate change was no longer seen only as an environmental issue, but as a socio-economic one. Stephan Harding, an ecologist and coordinator of Schumacher College's MSc in Holistic Science, stated that, for a work of "conventional thinking," the *Stern Review* was "extremely radical," adding that "within the mainstream, the Stern Review has really helped to consolidate the argument about climate change." Yet Harding and others who saw a need for radical change had concerns that Stern's vision was still "premised on growth" (chapter 7).

THE CLIMATE CHANGE ACT:
BINDING TARGETS AND AN "ECO-CONSTITUTION"

One of the most significant reforms emerging within an EM framework was the Climate Change Act of 2008. With the act, the UK became the first country with legally binding targets for deep medium- and long-term CO_2 reduction. The idea began with Friends of the Earth's "Big Ask" campaign, launched by in 2005, which originally sought a law requiring annual 3 per cent CO_2 cuts – a response to the fact that previous policy had not delivered sustained emissions reductions. Supporters soon came to include the Conservative Party, which criticized the Blair government's "cop-out" on the issue (Cameron 2006c); however, in 2006, the Labour government introduced its own bill. Both the CBI (2007b) and the Trades Union Congress (TUC 2007) welcomed the government's bill, the former citing the "long-term clarity on policy direction" and the latter the expected boost to "energy efficiency in the workplace" and "clean coal and carbon capture and storage."

The original bill set targets of at least 26 per cent by 2020 and 60 per cent by 2050 below 1990 levels; however, widespread demands from sources including the opposition Tories for deeper cuts in light of more alarming climate science led the government, in October 2008, to strengthen the 2050 target to 80 per cent. It later increased the medium-term goal to 34 per cent by 2020 – a target that was still not strong enough for some critics, who argued the science required cuts of at least 42 per cent by 2020.[8] (That target was, in fact, included in Scotland's own Climate Change Act – giving it the world's most ambitious GHG goals, which climate campaigners celebrated by creating a special "2020" whisky with 42 per cent alcohol.)

A key institutional innovation was the UK's new carbon budgeting system, which would cap emissions over five-year periods. The objective was to bind future governments to live within these budgets and to increase certainty about long-term commitment to cutting emissions, which was key to unlocking investment in low-carbon technologies. A new institution, the Committee on Climate Change (CCC), was established to give the government independent expert advice on the size of carbon budgets and how to live within them cost effectively. Its role was to include submitting annual reports to Parliament on the progress toward targets to ensure government accountability. The act also gave the government a variety of new enabling powers, ranging from the relatively trivial power to require a minimum charge for single-use plastic bags to the ability to bring in new carbon trading schemes, which Environment Secretary David Miliband (2007a) said could eventually include tradable personal carbon allowances.

Passage of the act was a "massive victory" for environmental campaigners (FoE 2008). The full significance of these changes would only become evident with time, but they had the potential to play a powerful disciplinary role and fundamentally change government decision-making. According to Chancellor Gordon Brown (2007a), "Just as we manage our financial budgets over the economic cycle with prudence and discipline, so we will have to manage our carbon budgets with the same prudence and discipline. Chancellors of the Exchequer will now count the carbon as they currently count the pounds." Energy and Climate Change Secretary Ed Miliband (2008b) stated, "Once we have the budgets, every major decision taken by government will either have to fit the budget, be accompanied by savings elsewhere or will not be done." He went on, in obligatory EM fashion, to argue that the limits imposed by carbon budgets would not stifle growth, but encourage it: "Carbon budgets must instil discipline in decision-making, ensure greater predictability for business and must also become a platform to drive a green industrial strategy for the UK ... Discipline on government, predictability for business, growth for our economy – used in the right way, carbon budgets can make this happen."

Another very significant aspect of the act was its expression of a multi-party consensus on the need for deep emissions cuts, with only five MPs voting against it. One hoped-for result was to protect the long-term commitment to climate action from the vagaries of partisan politics and cycles of public opinion. "I call this an 'eco-constitution.' It binds all future governments and sets the overall framework," said Environment Secretary David Miliband (2007c). (The fact that all five MPs to oppose the act were Tories indicated where resistance to the cross-party consensus was most likely to emerge, as discussed in chapter 7.)

Such an environmentally induced institutional transformation was well in line with EM theory, and government ministers spoke of the act in EM terms, but it also had the potential to push the UK beyond EM territory. Exactly what would happen in the future if those binding targets began to impinge on economic growth? The potential for a future clash now existed and the end result was unclear. As Tim Jackson, a member of the Sustainable Development Commission, told me in a 2007 interview:

We're in an absolutely fascinating situation … The Climate Change Bill effectively tries to put into legislation those deep environmental cuts. And it has to be said that at this point in time, we have absolutely no idea how to achieve those. In spite of the fact that all the technologies are there, we have no idea how to get them implemented, how to get the economic playing field right, how to create the behavioural changes that will be necessary, and what the institutions look like that would lead to it, or indeed how acceptable ultimately at the social level the necessary changes might be. So that's all got to play out within the next couple of decades. It's like living in the middle of an experiment in some ways, a sort of governance experiment and a social experiment.

Meanwhile, the *Guardian* (2008b) editorialized:

With the law comes a new reality. Parliament has set demanding targets and deserves congratulation for that. But it has barely begun the task of finding a way to meet them … The low-carbon future

always seems to begin tomorrow. If the law works as it should, governments will have no option other than to get it under way today.
It should be a straitjacket, binding departments into policies they
would not otherwise follow: no new third runway at Heathrow, and
no new coal power station at Kingsnorth. But the shame of busting
five-yearly carbon budgets may turn out to be much smaller than
the political pain caused by enforcing emissions reductions. The
call from both main parties for lower petrol prices is just a small
hint of contradictions to come.

Indeed, the Climate Change Act did not prevent the Labour government from approving a third Heathrow runway within weeks of
its passage. The straitjacket, at least for a time, was still a comfortably
loose fit, although it was destined to shrink. The act's carbon constraints would, in fact, soon play a role in the Conservative-led coalition's decision in 2010 to cancel Heathrow expansion plans (chapter
9). One key issue in the future would be the degree to which the government could rely on international credit purchases if it exceeded
its carbon budget. Whether or not the UK could and would buy its
way out of its self-imposed targets – far from a painless option as it
would potentially transfer billions of pounds annually to other nations – was a possible point of contention in years ahead, one that
would influence just how constraining the Climate Change Act would
be in practice. Meanwhile, other challenges to the act would emerge
under the Conservative-led coalition (chapter 7).
   Whatever lay ahead, the act's passage in November 2008, as the
UK's economic gloom deepened, signalled that climate change
was not being entirely pushed off the political agenda by pressing
economic concerns. The act was also accompanied by a subtle shift
in EM discourse. The goal was still to reconcile deep emissions cuts
and economic expansion, but, rhetorically at least, there were suggestions that if something had to give, it might not be the climate
objectives. Business Secretary Peter Mandelson (2009) told the Low
Carbon Industrial Summit: "There is no high carbon future. We've
regulated in the UK to make it inevitable through carbon targets,
vehicle emissions targets and renewables targets. What's not inevitable is that the UK will capture the full industrial and business benefits of this shift – here, and around the world. That will have to be
something we pursue as policy."

PUSHING FOR A LOW-CARBON, GROWING GLOBAL ECONOMY

Britain did considerably more than most nations to push for coordinated global action. This was perhaps only fitting as the UK was estimated to have, after Luxembourg and the US, the highest per capita
responsibility for CO_2 emitted since 1850 (WRI 2012). In 2005, Prime
Minister Blair made climate change a central theme of his G8 and
EU presidencies and tried, with limited success, to shake his White
House allies out of their climate denial. During the 2006 speeches by
world leaders to the UN, Foreign Secretary Margaret Beckett devoted
half of her address to the dangers of climate change, while the UK
used its UN Security Council presidency the following year to chair
that body's first-ever meeting on the threat of climate-induced conflict – attempting to link the climate issue to the security imperative.

Britain encouraged EM-oriented responses in laggard nations
where stronger climate action would be needed for global efforts to
succeed – which also reflected awareness that the UK could face economic costs if it moved too far ahead of others. An early example
was a 2006 climate cooperation pact with California, which included
working toward a joint carbon market, and involved sidestepping
the Bush administration to find a state-level ally. The UK's efforts in
the US included a 2009 grant to the Environmental Defense Fund,
an ENGO, to promote "acceptance among key Texan policymakers
of the science of climate change and the need for urgent action"
and advance the message that "progressive action on global warming
can provide economic benefits to important sectors of the economy"
(L. Hickman 2012). The British High Commission also tried to shift
the Canadian debate by, for example, organizing a visit by Nicholas
Stern, co-sponsoring the 2007 Business of Climate Change conference in Ottawa, and writing op-eds in Canada's press emphasizing
the potential to lower emissions "without reducing growth" (Cary
2008; see also Beckett and Hewitt 2005). Britain later provided funds
to a Canadian project to facilitate a large-scale CCS demonstration,
the launch of an emissions trading scheme in British Columbia in
partnership with the provincial government, and ENGO initiatives
that included a Pembina Institute green jobs report (FCO 2012). The
latter projects grew out of the British Foreign and Commonwealth
Office's Low-Carbon High-Growth Strategic Programme Fund, set up
in 2009, to promote a "low-carbon, high-growth global economy,"

with funds also spent in the US and BRICS, i.e. Brazil, Russia, India, and China (L. Hickman 2012).

Within the EU, the UK stood out as one of the member states most committed to carbon reduction. It was the only country – out of the first ten to submit their national allocation plans – to have its proposed cap for the second phase of the ETS accepted by the European Commission in 2006 without revision downwards. In other words, it was the only state judged not to be over-allocating permits to its own industries – a problem that led to a crash of the EU carbon price. The UK was one of the powerful member states, along with Germany and France, that put its weight behind the EU's 2008 climate and energy package, which included a commitment to cut GHGs 20 per cent below 1990 levels by 2020. Gordon Brown later pushed for the EU to strengthen that target to 30 per cent and the Cameron-led coalition took a similar stance – with the argument again framed in EM terms. "If we stick to a 20 per cent cut, Europe is likely to lose the race to compete in the low-carbon world to countries such as China, Japan or the US – all of which are looking to create a more attractive environment for low-carbon investment," wrote the UK energy secretary with the environment ministers of Germany and France in a *Financial Times* op-ed (Huhne, Röttgen, and Borloo 2010). They added that, "Europe's companies are poised to take advantage of the new opportunities."

The UK's international efforts garnered considerable praise. WWF-International and Allianz SE (2008, 30–1), a German insurance company, credited the UK for "driving the international debate." Even critics of the Blair government's overall climate record tended to give it credit on the international front. "It's right for Blair to have a positive reputation for pushing for serious international engagement with regard to the climate-change challenge," said left-wing Labour MP Alan Simpson. "But its performance and delivery at home is much more patchy." Similarly, while the Quality of Life Policy Group (2007, 13) of the Conservative Party criticized Labour's "contradictory policies" at home, it acknowledged that, "Former Prime Minister Tony Blair must be given credit for forcing [climate change] up the international agenda." Blair's successor, Gordon Brown, likewise received praise for efforts to avoid a complete collapse of the Copenhagen talks – and also for first proposing a $100-billion-a-year fund to support poorer nations in responding to climate change, which became a key element of the global climate agenda (Grice 2009a). Meanwhile, in the early years of the Cameron government, the UK was one of four nations whose international-level efforts received "especially good evaluations," from the Climate Change Performance Index (Germanwatch and CAN Europe 2011, 15).[9] William Hague (2012), the foreign secretary and one of the Conservatives most committed to green growth, asserted that encouraging a low-carbon transition remained "a top priority for our diplomatic network."

The UK's international climate record was not, however, without criticism. Britain lobbied against the EU-wide target of 20 per cent renewable energy by 2020. It later sought maximum flexibility in meeting the target, tried to get electricity from nuclear and carbon-capture coal to count toward it, and tried to block priority access to the electricity grid for renewable sources (Adam 2008; Harrabin 2008b). Lobbying efforts were led by the Department for Business, Enterprise and Regulatory Reform (BERR), which critics labelled the "Department of Business as Usual" (Seager 2008). Critics believed the lobbies representing traditional power suppliers – nuclear, coal, and natural gas – were behind such efforts. Leaked government documents expressed concerns over the "challenging" nature of the targets, given the UK's very low level of renewable energy to start; the perceived danger of reliance on intermittent renewable sources; and electricity price increases that would negatively affect competitiveness and fuel poverty (Adam 2008; BERR 2007; Seager and Milner 2007; Vidal 2007). Even more revealing were concerns that "implementing the renewable energy target may be difficult to reconcile with other measures to tackle climate change" (BERR 2007, 1). Not only did conflict exist between renewables and government plans for more nuclear power, there were fears that successful renewable deployment would make emissions trading "redundant" and undermine the carbon market, in which UK financial interests had a key stake.[10] Economic arguments existed both for and against the BERR position;[11] nevertheless, this was another instance when it appeared that the means, carbon trading, had become an end in itself. The UK ultimately accepted a target for itself of 15 per cent renewable energy by 2020, while negotiating greater flexibility, namely the ability to gain credits toward the target by paying for renewable energy produced in other EU states.

A similar pattern was evident under the Cameron-led coalition. Evidence emerged of UK lobbying to block the next round of proposed renewable energy targets – 30 per cent by 2030 for the EU overall – and to dilute the EU's energy efficiency regulations (Harvey 2012). Meanwhile, the UK – under the influence of Shell, BP, and fierce Canadian lobbying – played a key role in delaying approval of the Fuel Quality Directive that would label tar sands fuel as high carbon (Carrington 2011c), even as it continued to call for stronger EU carbon-reduction targets.

On the international front, the UK's inspiring statements and some cutting-edge efforts stood in contrast to other cases of foot-dragging due to economic interests and political calculation. Such contradictions, discussed in more detail in the following chapter, were a common element of the UK's climate reform efforts.

THE PROMISE OF THE "GREENEST GOVERNMENT EVER"

Upon becoming prime minister, David Cameron (2010a) expressed a desire to lead the "greenest government ever." He added, in typical EM fashion, that, "We've got a real opportunity to drive the green economy, to have green jobs, green growth, and to make sure that we have our share of the industries of the future." The coalition agreement with the Liberal Democrats included a series of pledges with the potential to consolidate Britain's status as a climate leader, such as the launch of a Green Investment Bank; cancellation of Labour's plans for a third Heathrow runway and refusal to permit new runways at Gatwick and Stansted; an emissions performance standard that would prevent new coal-fired power plants without carbon capture and storage (CCS) technology; continued public investment in CCS; a minimum carbon price to provide stronger incentives for low-carbon investment than under the struggling EU emissions trading scheme; a Green Deal to enable businesses and homeowners to improve energy efficiency with no upfront cost, paid for by savings on future energy bills; a reduction of the central government's own carbon emissions by 10 per cent within twelve months; and a reform of "energy markets to deliver security of supply and investment in low carbon energy."

The coalition soon took action on all of the above-mentioned commitments. Indeed, the government surpassed its pledge of cutting its own carbon emissions by 10 per cent in its first year, reaching 14 per cent and promising a 25 per cent reduction by 2015 (DECC 2011). It also introduced a Renewable Heat Incentive to encourage the shift to low-carbon heat sources – according to the government, this was the first such policy in the world (HM Government 2011, 42). It oversaw a rapid expansion of renewable energy generation, up 60 per cent between 2010 and 2012 (DECC 2013b), as the UK prepared for a surge of renewables from 9 per cent of the electricity mix in 2011 to 30 per cent by 2020 to meet EU targets (DECC 2012b, 10–11). Meanwhile, the government's Low Carbon Plan reiterated the commitment to an ambitious decarbonization project, despite the worsening economic situation, with David Cameron and Deputy Prime Minister Nick Clegg stating, "Even in these tough times, moving to a low carbon economy is the right thing to do, for our economy, our society and the planet" (HM Government 2011, 1).

The list of climate-related initiatives compared favourably to that of most governments, although the initial impact of some, such as the Green Deal and Green Investment Bank, fell short of their potential.[12] Environmentalists and the growing low-carbon business sector were far from fully satisfied. Indeed, doubts grew over time about the depth of the coalition's commitment to "green growth" and some reversion to BAU thinking became evident. The various challenges to, and criticisms of, the EM consensus in the UK are the subject of the next chapter, but first it is worth considering key factors that enabled that consensus to emerge.

OPPORTUNITY AND VULNERABILITY: FACTORS DRIVING EM IN THE UK

A number of factors enabled an EM response in the UK – in other words, the linking of climate action to the perceived imperative of economic expansion. The decision about whether to move beyond BAU can be understood in large part by the perceived balance of costs and benefits. As noted above, much of British business embraced EM as it sought to reduce climate and energy vulnerabilities – including vulnerability to further climate policy – and to seize opportunities. For British society more generally, the balance of perceived opportunities and threats was also relatively conducive to climate action. That perception was evident in the cover of a government report, *Investing in a Low Carbon Britain* (HM Government 2009a), the left side of which featured an image of two blokes in hard hats gainfully employed in the new green economy and the remainder showed a massive wave perilously close to swamping them.

One factor that created relatively fertile ground for an EM message was Britain's easy start. It achieved large GHG reductions in the 1990s without much conscious effort, as by-products of the shift from coal to gas-fired electricity and the outsourcing of manufacturing. The relative ease of cutting carbon early on added plausibility to claims that climate action need not be costly, which in turn helped to build a wide EM coalition before difficult choices had to be faced – a situation quite different from the one in Canada.

Of even greater importance was the ability to link climate action to the interests of Britain's dominant economic sector. The UK's finance-heavy economic structure had many drawbacks, including concentration of wealth among a small elite, corrosion of society's ethical foundation by obliterating any evident link between reward and social contribution, and making the country particularly vulnerable to the bursting of the credit bubble; however, on climate change, this economic structure had certain advantages. The finance sector's own direct emissions from keeping the lights on and computers running in City offices were negligible relative to the profits generated – so climate policy was not a direct threat. On the contrary, there was the promise of London's policy-driven emergence as the centre of global carbon finance and trading – a market with the potential to grow considerably as carbon constraints tightened over the long term. At the same time, the financial risks of unchecked climate change, notably the costs to insurance firms, were widely acknowledged within the sector. This is not to suggest that the financial sector's impact on Britain's climate response was entirely positive. The City of London continued to finance high-carbon activity around the globe. Moreover, its power shaped and distorted climate policy to serve its own interests, leading to the prioritization of carbon trading. Still, having the dominant economic sector, among others, onside with the need for climate action gave a key boost to construction of an EM coalition (Newell and Paterson 2010).

Other sectors also had an interest in stronger climate policy, including the nuclear industry, which saw opportunities for revival, the emerging renewables industry, and segments of the diminished manufacturing sector that produced emissions-reducing products. Meanwhile, the decline of British manufacturing since the 1980s contributed to reducing the UK's production-side emissions. It also removed from the scene many energy-intensive operations that might have been threatened by climate policy and complicated the win-win politics of EM coalition building. (Those energy-intensive firms that remained often lobbied for relief from climate policy).

Another economic factor enabling an EM response was the UK's membership in the EU – an entity more conducive to climate action than Canada's comparable trading environment. The EU ensured that the UK's main trading partners also faced some degree of carbon pricing and regulation, while on renewable energy, the EU pushed Britain to invest more than it would have on its own. (That said, looking to the future, questions were emerging over whether the EU as a whole was willing to match Britain's commitment to decarbonizing the economy.)

On the threat side of the equation, the sense of vulnerability to climate change was considerable on a small, crowded island where people had strong attachment to the land as they knew or imagined it. Recent experience of devastating floods and concern over water shortages in the densely populated southeast coincided with climate impact projections of more frequent and intense rain in winters, and hotter and drier summers (G. Jenkins et al. 2009, 30–2; Mayor of London 2010, 9; Pagnamenta 2009b).[13] The Thames Barrier (figure 6.2), which protected some 1.25 million people and £80 billion worth of buildings and infrastructure in at-risk areas of London, needed to be closed more frequently (EA 2008), highlighting the UK's vulnerability to rising seas and higher costs ahead to protect the capital.

Already evident threats to UK landscapes and cultural heritage were documented by a travelling photographic exhibition in 2007, organized by the National Trust, the charity that preserves historic properties. Impacts included stately homes damaged by more intense rainfall, William Morris wallpaper attacked by silverfish thriving in warmer, damper conditions, and historic harbours struggling to keep the sea at bay. Will Snowdon have to be renamed? asked the exhibition. Will British breeds of cows have to be replaced by Southern European varieties? The promise of more English wine, and even the UK's first olive oil, was not necessarily adequate compensation for those, whatever their political stripe, who wanted to conserve the nation's heritage. Meanwhile, Barbara Young (2007), Environment Agency chief executive, warned of a coming debate over whether protecting some coastal towns would be possible.

Figure 6.2 Thames Barrier stands ready to defend the O2 dome, the financiers of Canary Wharf, and others beyond from tidal surges. Photo by author.

Fears of losing beloved territory and of alien invaders were also evident as journalist Andrew Marr (2007, 601) brought his weighty bestseller, *A History of Modern Britain*, to a close. Marr looked ahead to climate change literally reshaping the nation:

> It promised to alter the familiar splatter of Britain as she is seen from space or on any map. Nothing is more fundamental to a country's sense of itself than its shape, particularly when the country is an island. Rising sea levels could make Britain look different on every side. They could eat into the smooth billow of East Anglia, centuries after the wetlands were reclaimed with Dutch drainage, and submerge the concrete-crusted, terraced marshland of London, and drown idyllic Scottish islands and force the abandonment of coastal towns which had grown in Georgian and Victorian times. Wildlife would die out and be replaced by new species – there were already unfamiliar fish offshore and new birds and insects in British gardens.

Consciousness of such threats led to the framing of climate change as a security issue – which gave a significant boost to the economic arguments for action. Indeed, the Cameron Tories depicted climate change as a threat from which the people and nation needed protection – a discursive strategy with potential appeal beyond green and left political circles. Issues of climate and energy policy appeared on the party website under the heading of "Protecting Security," along with this statement: "The primary responsibilities of the British government are to protect our nation from the threats of war, terrorism, climate change, energy insecurity, crime and economic instability" (Conservative Party 2009a). This led to the unusual juxtaposition of the party's commitment to decentralized renewable energy being discussed next to prisons policy. The linkage of climate action to both economic and security concerns was also evident in the title of a Conservative Party (2009b) policy document: *The Low Carbon Economy – Security, Stability and Green Growth*. Other linkages to the security imperative included, as noted above, the Labour government's highlighting of the threat of climate-induced conflict. But the most immediately powerful linkage of climate action to the security imperative was through energy security, which was a priority concern of business and also the British state, and thus investments in energy efficiency and new low-carbon supplies found an additional justification.

CONCLUSIONS

In contrast to Canada and other laggards such as the United States, the degree of policy and societal action in Britain to tackle climate change was noteworthy. The goal, expressed by Tony Blair (2000) in an early EM speech, of "re-awakening the environmental challenge" through a "constructive partnership" between government, business, the green movement, and the public was largely achieved. The idea that climate action could go hand in hand with business opportunity, consumer aspirations, and economic growth became dominant. EM language became the norm in respectable politics and eventually in business, too. Actual practice certainly did not always live up to the language; nevertheless, emergence of a wide EM coalition, including leading voices of business and the Conservative Party leadership, was a significant development. A language of opportunity was centrally important to constructing and maintaining this coalition. So, too, lurking in the background was a sense of vulnerability to the changes that climate change could unleash. Both these elements – the opportunities from action and the costs of inaction – were key themes of the landmark *Stern Review,* which helped consolidate the wide EM consensus and make a BAU stance more difficult for any actor seeking social legitimacy. Indeed, in opposition, David Cameron's Conservatives embraced the language of "green growth" largely as a way to re-legitimate the party in the eyes of voters. Meanwhile, support for climate action not only became linked to the economic imperative through an EM project, it was bolstered by connections to the security imperative – most notably energy security.

In this context, considerable innovation in policy and practice was evident, with a particular emphasis on constructing the carbon market. Exactly how successful these new policies were and would be was a matter of considerable debate. Certainly many critics called for stronger, more urgent measures. Nevertheless, Britain experienced nothing like Canada's federal policy paralysis. Considerable activity also took place at the local level, with London adopting particularly ambitious emissions objectives and other communities providing, in their own ways, glimpses of a low-carbon future. The spread of ecological rationality, in the form of carbon consciousness, was clearly beginning to transform key institutions of British society, making its mark on everything from football to the monarchy and the military.

Of particular importance was change in the corporate sector, as many firms took action to trim their carbon footprints and encourage others – customers, employees, and suppliers – to do so as well. Good reasons existed for scepticism about greenwash, but business initiatives and calls for a stronger, more certain climate policy framework helped expand the space available for government action and push BAU thinking further toward the margins.

Meanwhile, the Climate Change Act of 2008 was a centrally important institutional development. Ministers spoke of the act's legally binding carbon budgets in EM terms, as a boost to economic growth. Indeed the obligatory EM framing enabled support across political parties, as well as from business and labour. However, the act's provisions set the stage for possible future conflict between binding reduction targets and economic growth (or at least certain forms of high-carbon growth), a conflict that could only be avoided with unprecedented carbon-intensity improvements, via efficiency and technology, sustained over decades.

A transformation of British society driven by climate concern – in which EM theorists could find much that resonated with their perspective – was underway. Yet there were indications that change was not happening fast enough and that an EM framework was not sufficient for a successful climate response. If the benchmark was not what existed before, or the limited action of other nations, but what would actually be necessary to make a globally equitable contribution to avoiding catastrophic climate change, then the UK's response no longer appeared to be so positive. The next chapter looks at the limits of an EM project in the UK. It is followed by analysis of how growing recognition of these limits – in light of a climate challenge that grew larger in scale and in urgency – contributed to the reawakening of something Blair and others, including Margaret Thatcher before him, had sought to avoid: a critique of economic growth, ever-expanding consumption, and, for some, capitalism more generally.

7

The Limits of Ecological
Modernization in the UK

Ecological modernization was of great importance in enabling the beginnings of a climate-related reform process backed by powerful actors in government and business. Yet the UK's claims of climate leadership rang hollow to many critics. Britain might very well have been ahead of most other nations, but under Labour governments, a gap between the language of climate urgency and actual political and social responses was evident on many fronts. As MP Colin Challen (2009, 25) concluded, "we – Labour – have not done anything like enough in government to match our rhetoric." A similar gap was also evident under the Conservative-led "greenest government ever" – and indeed, even the rhetoric became less green over time.

On the one hand, EM still faced resistance from backers of business-as-usual and contrarian views on climate science – perspectives that, for a time, appeared to be confined to the margins, but later experienced a revival. Meanwhile, initiatives taken within an EM framework showed serious limits. Government policy often pulled in opposing directions, both limiting and accelerating emissions. One high-profile technological fix, biofuels, promised lower emissions and economic benefits, but was revealed to be deeply problematic on environmental and social grounds. Awareness also grew that energy efficiency was less effective in achieving sustained emissions cuts than had been claimed. The ambitions of some key climate policies were limited to a win-win sphere that would deliver net economic benefits to business, but fell short of the level of emissions reductions that the government itself had acknowledged as necessary. The influential *Stern Review*'s upbeat message about the compatibility of continued economic growth and climate stability similarly turned out to be based on limited emissions reductions goals that left a very high risk of climate catastrophe. Finally, the UK's much vaunted emissions reductions record turned out to be far less impressive than at first glance.

BUSINESS-AS-USUAL AND THE VOICES OF "SCEPTICISM"

Global warming and the human contribution to it "is not an area of political contention here. We've had nothing like the same political debates on the science here as in North America," a Defra official explained in 2007. "There are people who are not persuaded, but they are on the margins." That said, the wide EM political consensus faced rearguard battles with opponents of strong climate action – and such BAU forces later experienced a resurgence.

"The 'consensus' on climate change is a catastrophe in itself," argued Christopher Booker (2008), a leading climate contrarian, in his *Sunday Telegraph* column. More colourful was Jeremy Clarkson (2008), host of *Top Gear*, BBC's popular program for driving enthusiasts, and *Sunday Times* and *Sun* columnist, who wrote: "For years, we've been told that unless we buy a stupid electric car and eat mud for the rest of our lives, the world will boil, our children will be microwaved and all the polar bears will sink ... Everything we've been told for the past five years by the Government, Al Gore, Channel Four News and hippies everywhere is a big bucket of nonsense." Meanwhile, TV presenter David Bellamy (2008) argued that "the way the so-called Greens and the BBC, the Royal Society and even our political parties have handled this [global warming] smacks of McCarthyism at its worst."

Some "sceptics" preferred to accept claims that sunspots were the main driver of any recorded warming or that warming had stopped after 1998, ideas that ricocheted endlessly around the Internet, immune to reasoned refutation. Apart from the scientific claims, many contrarians argued that GHG-cutting efforts would inflict excessive costs without corresponding benefits. Deep emissions cuts threatened "massive reductions in living standards" (Booker and North 2007), accelerated "exodus of industry from the UK and Europe" and even a return to a pre-industrial pastoral existence (N. Lawson 2008b). The argument that growth elsewhere would far outweigh UK GHG cuts became increasingly common. "China and India are laughing at us while they build more coal-fired power stations," said Ryanair CEO

Michael O'Leary (Macalister 2007). Others raised an opposite concern: that the "current, misguided, obsession with reducing carbon emissions could hold back the development of some very poor countries" (Lea 2007; see also N. Lawson 2008b). (Many development NGOs rejected that argument and joined the Stop Climate Chaos coalition out of concern for the vulnerability of developing nations.) In his *Guardian* website column, "Skeptical Environmentalist," Bjørn Lomborg (2008a, 2008b) denounced "scare stories" and "alarmist predictions" that drove a costly short-term focus on emissions cuts rather than a "rational" focus on massive R&D in low-carbon energy technologies to provide long-term solutions. Meanwhile, economist Ruth Lea (2007) claimed that "the old left discovered 'global warming' following the collapse of Communism in order to further their objectives of controlling people's lives and undermining capitalism."

One of the most prominent contrarians was Nigel Lawson (2008a, 2008b), chancellor of the exchequer to Margaret Thatcher. Lord Lawson of Blaby likened the *Stern Review* to Tony Blair's "dodgy dossier" justifying the Iraq war, rejected the "alarmist poppycock" of government ministers who highlighted possible economic and social catastrophe, and cited potential benefits of warmer temperatures for agriculture and fewer deaths from cold. Critical of anti-capitalist and anti-American forces' embrace of climate change as the core of their "new creed," he saw a danger of an "age of unreason" and a spectre of "eco-fundamentalism" haunting Europe.

The ideological stakes were particularly high for the laissez-faire or libertarian political right. While Margaret Thatcher managed in her time to link climate action to her agenda (chapter 6), the possibility that combating climate change would require a greater government role in the economy, or deeper social-structural change, was an anathema to some on the right. As opposition leader, David Cameron frequently took greener positions than Labour, but he did not have his entire party behind him. The polling organization ComRes (2008) asked MPs, "Do you believe climate change is happening and can be directly attributed to greenhouse gas emissions resulting from human activity?" Of the fifty-five Conservatives who responded, ten said no, and another eight that they did not know, while eighty of ninety-one Labour MPs and fifteen of seventeen Liberal Democrats said yes.

The climate sceptics' influence on the Conservatives was limited while the party was in opposition. Cameron, who garnered praise from environmentalists for his impact on public debate, kept his distance from such BAU voices while he was trying to "de-toxify" the party brand. Other Tories, notably Zac Goldsmith and John Gummer, authors of the Quality of Life Policy Group (2007) report, put forward an analysis of climate change that edged into surprisingly radical green territory. Meanwhile, some Tories seemed resigned to the need for something more than a laissez-faire response. "The bad news about climate change is that it involves government taking action," said Shadow Environment Secretary Peter Ainsworth (2007). "I usually believe in government doing as little as possible. But climate change is a major market failure." A more welcoming home for some climate contrarians was the UK Independence Party, an anti-EU, anti-immigration grouping, which in 2010 gave its deputy leadership to the high-profile sceptic Christopher Monckton. "At the moment all the major parties have decided to sign up to the eco-fascist agenda and therefore anyone who does not believe in the eco-fascist agenda has nowhere else to go," said Monckton, explaining what he saw as UKIP's appeal (L. Gray 2010b).

Climate contrarianism was not only present on the right. The Channel 4 documentary *The Great Global Warming Swindle*, aired in 2007, was directed by Martin Durkin, whose political background included ties to the now-defunct Revolutionary Communist Party, which had embraced libertarian opposition to state intervention. Other former RCP members presented a curious mix of Marxism, libertarianism, and anti-environmentalism in the online journal *spiked*. Durkin's documentary gave voice to pro-market climate sceptics, several of them known to have received fossil-industry funds, including Fred Singer, Pat Michaels, and Canadian Tim Ball, while presenting a leftish conspiracy theory that Thatcher funded and politicized climate science to justify a pro-nuclear push to undermine the coal miners' union. According to Nigel Calder, a former *New Scientist* editor quoted in the film, "It was a kind of amazing alliance from Margaret Thatcher on the right through to very left-wing anti-capitalist environmentalists that created this kind of momentum behind a loony idea."

The documentary, which the Royal Society (2008) denounced as "itself a swindle," did not noticeably affect the political class's wide EM consensus at the time, but it did appear to affect public opinion. "It's given a fresh impetus to people who see the thing as a hoax," said

Peter Lockley of the Aviation Environment Federation. "It's been really unhelpful. People are repeating those arguments on blogs and online discussions." My barber in North London was among those who echoed arguments from the film, which had confirmed his fears that government was using climate change to increase taxes – a suspicion shared by 59 per cent of those polled by Ipsos MORI (2008). That same poll showed that a year after the film's broadcast, 60 per cent of Britons agreed that "many scientific experts still question if humans are contributing to climate change." This was an increase from 56 per cent in 2007, even though the IPCC had just released a new assessment with increased certainty that human activities were climate change's main cause.

A bigger boost to climate scepticism came later, in 2009 and 2010. Two weeks before the Copenhagen summit, emails from the University of East Anglia's Climatic Research Unit (CRU) were hacked. They appeared to show, at least to some observers, that researchers had manipulated data and misled the public. Several subsequent inquiries in the UK and US into these "Climategate" events found no evidence of scientific misconduct by the CRU researchers or their American colleagues and no grounds to question the basic science behind climate change; however, they did point to other problems such as a lack of openness with regard to sharing data and responding fully to freedom-of-information requests. Meanwhile, scandal-loving media gave a great deal of attention to revelations of a small number of errors or apparent errors unearthed in the IPCC's three-thousand-page fourth assessment. The most significant was an incorrect statement that Himalayan glaciers would likely disappear by 2035 if warming continued. However, as with "Climategate," none of the revelations undermined the scientific case for taking climate change seriously (e.g. PBL 2010). Nevertheless, these events damaged the public reputation of climate science and gave new life to climate scepticism in the political debate. Indeed, Painter and Ashe (2012) found a marked increase in the presence of climate-sceptic voices in leading UK newspapers between 2007 and 2009–10. After the US, the UK had the greatest media presence for such voices among countries in the study, which also included India, France, China, and Brazil.

Proponents of BAU received an additional boost from the 2009 Copenhagen conference's failure to agree on a Kyoto Protocol successor. If the rest of the world was not similarly committed to climate action, why, some asked, should the UK persist in taking difficult and costly measures? As Nigel Lawson's Global Warming Policy Foundation put it in calling for suspension of unilateral UK climate targets, "It might be possible to make the case for decarbonisation if it were undertaken on a worldwide basis. But the recent Copenhagen Summit showed that there is no prospect of this" (GWPF 2010). The heightened economic insecurity caused by a deep recession undoubtedly contributed to a shift in the public's priorities. Two unusually cold British winters in 2009 and 2010 – which were nevertheless two of the warmest years on record globally – likely also affected public opinion, as research suggested that daily temperature changes influence people's belief in global warming (Li, Johnson, and Zaval 2011).

Opinion polls showed an apparent but not necessarily lasting rise in climate scepticism after these developments. A poll by Populus for the BBC (2010) found that between November 2009 and February 2010, the number of people who said "Climate change is happening and is now established as largely man-made" fell from 41 to 26 per cent, while the number saying "Climate change is not happening" rose from 15 to 25 per cent. As always with polls, the results depended on the exact wording, sampling strategy, and when questions were asked. Polling in January 2011 by ICM Research for the *Guardian*, after the storm of climate controversies had passed, suggested that public concern remained high (Carrington 2011a). Some 83 per cent agreed that climate change was a threat – either a current threat (40 per cent) or one for future generations unless something was done soon (43 per cent) – compared to 14 per cent who said climate change was not a threat. These numbers differed little from August 2009, when, in response to the same question, 85 per cent said climate change was a threat, versus 11 per cent who said it was not. Although the increase in climate scepticism might have been short lived, the salience of climate change as an issue did decline. Newspaper coverage of climate change and the percentage of people saying that pollution/environment was the most important issue facing Britain dropped significantly from 2007 to 2011 (Lockwood 2013, 1342).

Once in power, David Cameron faced significant challenges in managing the sceptic element in his party and other BAU voices – including those who did not necessarily question the science, but expressed concern over the economic costs of climate action. Adding to

Cameron's need to watch his right flank was the shift of support over time to UKIP by some conservative voters who did not approve of his "modernizing" agenda, including its green elements.

An illustration of the challenges came in spring 2011 with a debate over the UK's fourth carbon budget, which revealed a "bloody fight for the green soul of the Conservative Party" (Carrington 2011b). The Committee on Climate Change (CCC 2010b) recommended a carbon budget for 2023 to 2027 with a 50 per cent GHG cut below 1990 levels, generating a split in cabinet. Sources of opposition included the Treasury, Department for Business, and Department for Transport (Harrabin 2011; Monbiot 2011). Cameron ultimately came down in favour of the carbon budget and it was approved, confirming the UK's commitment to some of the world's toughest carbon targets. However, opponents won a review clause that would allow the government to backtrack in 2014 if circumstances (such as the level of commitment of other EU nations) had changed. The conflict within government created a new degree of uncertainty about future policy, which threatened to undermine green energy investment (Harrabin 2011).

Adding to the uncertainty, and one of the most concerning developments for climate-action advocates, was the change in rhetoric, notably from Chancellor George Osborne. In opposition, Osborne (2009) promised that, "If I become chancellor, the Treasury will become a green ally, not a foe." However, by autumn 2011, he had emerged as the key cabinet figure seeking to put the brakes on the UK's carbon reduction ambitions, appealing to party members who preferred more red meat in their conservatism than they were getting from a diet of Cameronism. At the Tory party conference that October, Osborne (2011) shocked green-leaning Tories and environmentalists with his anti-EM rhetoric, stating that "a decade of environmental laws and regulations are piling costs on the energy bills of households and companies." Questioning the UK's climate-leadership ambitions, he added, "Britain makes up less than 2% of the world's carbon emissions to China and America's 40%. We're not going to save the planet by putting our country out of business."

Resistance to wind farms in the countryside added to Cameron's challenges in pursuing an EM project. More than one hundred Tory MPs wrote to the prime minister, calling on him to cut subsidies for onshore wind farms (Heaton-Harris, Pincher, et al. 2012). While

Cameron (2012) responded with a forceful defence of the "perfectly hard-headed reasons," including enhancing energy security and economic opportunity, to build more onshore wind power capacity, his chancellor pushed for deep cuts to support for onshore wind. Meanwhile, in the European Parliament, Tory MEPs ignored the Cameron government's policy and voted against strengthening EU carbon reduction targets to 30 per cent by 2020, arguing that unilateral action would put EU companies at a competitive disadvantage (Meade 2011). Some within conservative circles sought a more substantial green policy U-turn, including repeal of the Climate Change Act and abolition of the Committee on Climate Change (Conservative Home 2012; GWPF 2010; Telegraph 2013; see also Lockwood 2013). The 2012 cabinet shuffle, which downgraded green Tories while boosting some right-wingers, added to uncertainty about future commitment to a green agenda. No fundamental reversals had occurred by 2013, but a weakening of climate laws and targets appeared increasingly possible in the event of a Conservative majority after 2015.

Thanks in large part to the Liberal Democrats, the Conservative-led coalition made some important contributions to EM climate reform. Even some critics conceded that, on energy and climate, "Cameron's government probably has jumped the low bar of being the greenest ever" (Carrington 2013). However, the cross-party consensus of all three main parties had shrunk to at most two-and-a-half parties, and the prime minister's own commitment to climate action was increasingly in doubt.[1]

Responding to resurgent BAU voices, CBI (2012b) Director-General John Cridland stated, "The so-called 'choice' between going green or going for growth is a false one." The fact that Britain's leading business organization was insisting that the "UK must maintain its ambition" on climate change illustrated that a need had emerged to remake the arguments for green growth; however, it also showed that the EM coalition still included some powerful forces.

ONE GOVERNMENT PREVENTING CLIMATE CHANGE, ANOTHER CAUSING IT

In addition to the continued presence of climate sceptics and BAU voices in the debate, BAU practices by business and government persisted. As discussed in chapter 6, while significant climate-driven change in business practice had occurred, problems of greenwash and behind-the-scenes lobbying to thwart policy measures that would compromise corporate interests and competitiveness remained. Meanwhile, government policy frequently pulled in opposing directions. Many critics saw a lack of "joined-up" policy. As the Quality of Life Policy Group (2007, 13) of the Conservative Party put it, "It has often seemed that Britain has had two governments – one committed to preventing climate change, and one committed to causing it."

One of the most glaring examples was the Labour government's airport expansion plans. Contradictions were already evident in the Aviation White Paper of 2003, which endorsed large-scale aviation growth despite the sector's skyrocketing emissions, which, by the government's own admission, could account for 25 per cent of the UK total by 2030 (DfT 2003). Even after the *Stern Review*'s call to action, the government reaffirmed these expansion plans. It went on to approve Heathrow expansion only weeks after passage of its world-leading Climate Change Act, even though a third runway would, according to Friends of the Earth director Tony Juniper (2008), "accommodate enough new air traffic to emit the same carbon dioxide each year as the country of Kenya." Greenpeace's Ben Stewart highlighted the contrast between government talk about climate urgency and its Aviation White Paper that anticipated up to a trebling of passenger volumes. He likened the situation to a smoker who says, "I'm deeply, deeply concerned about the impact this is having on my health and … I have now accepted the science of lung cancer, but I fully intend to move from twenty to sixty a day." Stewart added, in reference to government and industry claims about the potential to reduce impacts per passenger, "but fear not, we're going to invent a new airplane, which is going to be a Marlboro Ultra or something like that."

One reason for dramatic aviation emissions growth was the deregulation of EU air travel in the 1990s, which, rather than making prices reflect full environmental costs, led to an explosion of low-cost flights. With the apparent aim of duplicating such results, in 2007, the UK backed the EU-US Open Skies deal, which was projected, prior to the recession, to increase transatlantic air travel by 50 per cent over five years (Reuters 2007). Such contradictions did not go unnoticed. "Open skies pact 'will worsen climate change,'" read one *Independent* headline (Castle 2007). "Does the left hand know what the right hand is doing?" asked a *Guardian* (2007) editorial, which noted that the transport secretary was hailing the de-regulatory achievement even as the environment secretary was admitting that more air travel was bad for the planet.

Aviation was not the only such contradiction between expressed climate concern and practices resembling business-as-usual. The Labour government also reversed its early pledge to seek sustainable alternatives to new roads and motorway expansion and use demand management to get people to use their cars less (Cahill 2007). Transport 2000, a green transport campaign group, estimated that total road-building expenditure of £13 billion under Labour was more than double that under the Tories, who launched what Margaret Thatcher heralded at the time as the "biggest road-building programme since the Romans" (Leake 2007b; Sadler 2006). The disruptive fuel protests of 2000, which saw the Labour government fall behind the Tories in the polls for the first time, and fears of appearing "anti-motorist" drove Labour to abandon the fuel-duty escalator (annual fuel tax hikes) introduced by John Major's government. Indeed, Labour MP Colin Challen (2009, 186) wrote: "Fear of public opinion has curtailed or at least stunted government policy on climate change since the fuel protests." The political difficulties of increasing the already high cost of driving were illustrated again, in 2007, when an e-petition against a possible national road-pricing scheme received a record number of signatures, some 1.8 million. Abandonment of the fuel-duty escalator was a major reason why green tax revenue as a share of total taxes and social contributions fell from 9.8 per cent in 1999 to 7.4 per cent in 2007, despite the Blair government's pledge in 1997 to "shift the burden of tax from 'goods' to 'bads'" (HOCEAC 2006a; National Statistics 2008). The decision was also a key reason why the cost of travelling by private car fell 8 per cent in real terms from 1997 to 2007, while the cost of travelling by train and bus increased 5 and 13 per cent, respectively (Hansard 2008). In turn, this helped to explain why road transport CO_2 emissions continued their stubborn ascent, rising 4.3 per cent above 2000 levels and 11.0 per cent above 1990 levels by 2007, before tailing off during the recession (DECC 2012a).

Continued construction of out-of-town retail developments also contributed to increased car use, as did policy decisions to reduce services in small towns and rural areas, leading green transport

campaigners to call for carbon audits of such developments and decisions (Joseph 2007). The search for efficiencies by centralizing retail operations and service provision, an aspect of what Weber would
recognize as the modern drive for rationalization, frequently ran
counter to the goal of cutting carbon emissions – an illustration of
how modernization was not necessarily ecological.

Critics also drew attention to spending priorities. For example,
the Low Carbon Buildings Programme's original budget of only £12
million over three years for grants to households to install renewable micro-technologies paled in comparison to the cost of widening
the M1 motorway, estimated at £5.1 billion, or £21 million per mile
(Lynas 2007a; C. Lucas 2007), and to the £20–30 billion to renew
the Trident nuclear weapons system (Juniper 2007a). Meanwhile,
Challen (2009, 78) noted that UK government was not spending
anywhere near its share of the 1 per cent of GDP on climate change
mitigation that Stern advocated.

Even more alarming for those expecting government to live up to
its stated climate concern were proposals for up to eight new coal-
fired power plants, starting with a new facility at Kingsnorth. The
push to build a new generation of coal plants came from power producers such as German-owned E.ON with the support of the UK Department for Business, Enterprise and Regulatory Reform (BERR).
Business Secretary John Hutton (2008) argued that new coal plants
were needed to ensure adequate energy supply, provide the flexibility to respond to fluctuating electricity demand, and enhance energy
security – given that Vladimir Putin's Russia had a growing and
worrying influence over a volatile gas market. The proposed Kingsnorth plant came with the requisite promise of "cleaner coal" – using
"supercritical technology to produce power from coal far more efficiently and far more cleanly than ever before in the UK" (E.ON 2009)
– and being "capture ready," i.e. designed for a CCS retrofit at a later
date. Such promises did little to assuage opponents who argued that
no new coal facilities should be built without CCS being incorporated
from the start, if they were built at all. Among them was NASA scientist
James Hansen (2009), who made a personal plea to Gordon Brown
to put a moratorium on new coal plants without full CCS, calling coal
the "single greatest threat to civilisation and all life on our planet."

The government initially appeared intent on approving the new
unabated coal plants, raising widespread scepticism about the depth

of its climate commitment. A wave of anti-coal activism emerged, including the 2008 Climate Camp at Kingsnorth, the blocking of coal trains, and the direct action of "climate man," who broke into the existing Kingsnorth plant and turned the 500 MW turbine off – single-handedly reducing UK emissions by 2 per cent, at least for a short time (Vidal 2008). Meanwhile, internal cabinet divisions emerged as the conventionally viewed economic benefits of coal clashed with climate objectives, leading to repeated delays in the decision on the new Kingsnorth plant (Grice 2008). In fact, this tension over energy policy went back to the early days of the Labour government, which had struggled to reconcile the provision of low-cost supplies through competitive markets with GHG reduction, given that low prices undermined energy efficiency and the expansion of renewable and nuclear power (Helm 2003).

The climate movement won a victory in April 2009 when the government announced that no new coal-fired plants could be built unless they captured and stored roughly 25 per cent of their GHG emissions from the outset, with the expectation of full use of CCS by 2025. (Another victory followed that October when E.ON postponed plans to build the Kingsnorth coal plant, citing lower energy demand due to the recession.) The government's announcement that "the era of unabated coal is coming to an end" (DECC 2009a) was significant not only for forcing revisions to the proposed new plants but also for taking the government outside of the easy win-win sphere of EM. The costs of such a measure would be significant – an estimated £1 billion in added costs per plant, resulting in increased energy bills (Vidal 2009). Other aspects of EM remained, however, including the predictable promises of "a new high tech industry characterised by more jobs in advanced green manufacturing" (DECC 2009a) and the search for a technological way out of ecological dilemmas.

Climate concern had forced the Labour government to alter its energy plans, but the essence of Monbiot's (2008b) earlier assessment still rang true: "The government's policy is to build more of everything – more coal plants, more nuclear power, more oil rigs, more renewables, more roads, more airports – and hope no one spots the contradictions." To some degree, these contradictions could be explained as a problem of departmental agendas pulling in different directions. In this light, the October 2008 creation of a new Department of Energy and Climate Change (DECC) that took over the energy and climate files from BERR and Defra, respectively, was welcomed by many observers as an important step toward a more "joined-up" approach (BBC 2008a). DECC's Low Carbon Transition Plan was also a step toward reconciling some of these contradictions, as it began to plan for the discipline of meeting binding national carbon budgets in the years ahead and imposed carbon budgets on each department (HM Government 2009b). But there were deeper conflicts still to resolve. Labour's embrace of climate action was premised from the beginning on the idea that emissions reductions did not require questioning an expansionary agenda. Indeed, climate action could generate new economic activity in sectors such as renewable energy; however, it was becoming clear that part of the challenge also involved stopping the growth of sectors that could not be easily decarbonized, and even scaling them back. That was a big stretch for Labour, whose environmental approach, according to Revell (2005, 357), was "to bolt environmental goals onto its existing economic strategies so as to ensure that environmental protection does not jeopardize its central goal of wealth creation."

Meanwhile, those trying to stop high-carbon growth – such as activists in the anti-coal and anti-aviation movements – were subject to police raids, surveillance, and even sexual relationships with undercover officers posing as activists (Lewis and Evans 2011; Rowlatt 2009). These forms of repression represented yet another contradiction, as Ed Miliband (2008a), secretary at the new DECC, had earlier called for a popular movement to push politicians to take the necessary climate action and had praised "utopians" and "agitators."

After the 2010 election, the Conservative-led coalition quickly responded to Labour's biggest climate contradiction by scrapping the Heathrow third runway and pledging to refuse permission for new runways at Gatwick and Stansted (chapter 9). Nevertheless, Cameron's "greenest government ever" had many contradictions of its own, including closing down key environmental bodies, such as its sustainability watchdog, the Sustainable Development Commission, as part of its austerity-driven cuts to taxpayer-funded organizations ("the bonfire of the quangos"). Other actions contradicting the government's commitment to deep GHG reductions included a 2011 U-turn on financial support for large-scale solar power projects; relaxation of environmentally motivated restrictions and charges on parking in towns and cities as part of the transport secretary's pledge to end the "war on motorists" (Millward 2010a); a proposal to increase motorway speed limits to 80 mph despite the negative impact on carbon emissions; working to delay approval of the EU's Fuel Quality Directive that would label Canada's tar sands a high-carbon fuel source; and giving additional tax breaks to the fossil fuel industry.

The biggest potential contradiction was in the government's flagship electricity market reforms. The energy bill, introduced in November 2012 after a bitter battle within the coalition, aimed to stimulate £110 billion in needed electricity investment and accelerate the shift to a low-carbon economy. Among the key features were "contracts for difference" designed to guarantee returns for investors in low-carbon electricity, including renewables and nuclear power. The bill included a major increase in financial support for low-carbon electricity, which would be passed onto consumer bills (Chazan 2012; DECC 2012b). However, in return for this financial support, Chancellor Osborne won a key concession: no commitment to decarbonize the power sector by 2030 (a decision delayed until 2016, after the next election). At the same time, the chancellor won support for up to thirty new gas-fired power plants and a green light for fracking. There were conflicting views on whether the lack of a decarbonization target would erode the certainty that investors needed to make low-carbon energy investments, or whether other provisions would provide sufficient guarantees. The overall package was likely to drive a continued rapid increase in renewables and, at the same time, more carbon-emitting natural gas (Pickard 2012). Many observers, including the CCC (2012a), were concerned that a new dash for gas would lock Britain into carbon-emitting infrastructure at a time when it was necessary to almost entirely decarbonize the electricity supply to meet the country's future carbon budgets and 2050 target.

Meanwhile, concern over rising energy costs grew. While Labour scored political points by attacking the "Big Six" energy companies' excess profits and promising to freeze prices, others zeroed in on the cost of green policies and levies. The government responded, in 2013, by reducing the cost and ambition of the Energy Companies Obligation, a program requiring energy suppliers to deliver energy efficiency improvements, such as home insulation, mainly to low-income customers. To achieve a short-term reduction in electricity bills, the government scaled back one effective way to limit costs and achieve win-win EM gains in the long term.

The coalition's contradictory policies were, in some important respects, very similar to those of the Labour government, which likewise promoted emissions-reducing and emissions-creating activities. A similar process was evident in Scotland, where the Scottish National Party government simultaneously aimed to produce 100 per cent of its electricity needs from renewables and meet the world's most ambitious carbon reduction targets while increasing its oil, coal, and gas production (Carrell 2012). These contradictions, regardless of which party was in charge, reflected EM's lack of a conception of the need to power down high-carbon sectors alongside the powering up of new green activity. But an additional problem existed under the Conservatives, whose contradictions also reflected the growing assertiveness of BAU forces who were never, or were no longer, convinced by the promise of EM reform.

Government was not the only social actor to bolt climate concern onto existing practices in a contradictory way, a fact that constrained how far it could push a green agenda. For example, the website of Brent Cross Shopping Centre, one of London's largest malls, simultaneously invited shoppers to its "Green Matters" sustainability event while urging them to consume voraciously through its "Feed Your Addiction" marketing campaign. In the left-leaning *Observer* newspaper's travel pages, the "Slow Traveller" column by an adventurer (Gillespie 2007) on a flight-free world tour was juxtaposed with ads for cheap transatlantic flights ("Zoom to New York for a spot of retail therapy"). Meanwhile, some polls showed that a significant majority of the public wanted action on climate change but was unwilling to pay higher green taxes for it (Jowit 2008b; Opinium 2008). Such contradictory messages and practices illustrated the challenges ahead in getting actors in a consumer capitalist society – one just beginning to confront the task of decarbonization – to row together in the same low-carbon direction.

CLIMATE PROTECTION PAYS (UP TO A POINT):
THE CARBON REDUCTION COMMITMENT

Even when the government was taking action, the limits of an EM project were often evident. An example was the Carbon Reduction Commitment (CRC) – later renamed the CRC Energy Efficiency Scheme – a policy announced in the Energy White Paper of 2007 and which came into effect in April 2010. In the CRC, one could see several EM themes: the rise of ecological rationality as a force within government and business; the shift from "command-and-control" regulation to more co-operative and market-based policy innovations; a certain degree of common ground among business, government, and moderate environmentalists on potential gains from eco-efficiency; and a rhetoric of reassurance that continued economic expansion and climate stability are compatible. Above all, the CRC illustrated UK policy-makers' working premise that ecological reform could be a positive-sum game with win-win opportunities. Yet it also showed that limiting environmental reform to an uncontentious win-win sphere was unlikely to be enough to put the UK on a path to meet its ambitious GHG targets.

The CRC aimed to fill a policy gap as large non-energy-intensive business and public sector organizations did not have climate policy tools specifically directed at them. These sectors – including retailers, hotels, banks, large offices, universities, large hospitals, government departments, local authorities, and others – were responsible for some 10 per cent of UK carbon emissions. The Climate Change Levy, a business energy tax, had proven inadequate in creating incentives to cut energy use and carbon emissions in these sectors (Defra 2007j, 4), and emissions were projected to rise 11 per cent from 2010 to 2030 without new intervention. To achieve a balanced reduction of emissions across the economy, improve competitiveness, and reduce reliance on imported energy, the government proposed a mandatory cap-and-trade system covering some 5,000 organizations not already included in the EU ETS (Defra 2007a, 2007j).

Considerable intellectual creativity clearly went into the CRC's design, which aimed to create a "light-touch," market-oriented regulation to focus managers' minds on increasing energy efficiency while delivering economic gains to participants (Douglas 2007; Defra 2007c, 2007j). (More critically, the chief executive of the Committee on Climate Change later wondered "who could have come up with this – it's pretty elaborate" [Harvey 2010a].) Unlike the EU ETS in its initial phases – plagued by complex negotiations and lobbying by large emitters, leading to an initial over-allocation of emission rights by national governments eager to protect their firms' competitiveness – the CRC would allow organizations to set their own targets. Through an annual auction, they would be able to buy as

many emission allowances from government as they deemed necessary – within the overall and gradually declining emissions cap set by
the government – and could trade allowances on the CRC market.
Given the large number of organizations involved, auctioning, rather
than negotiated allocations, had particular advantages in minimizing
administrative burdens and the undue influence of politically connected firms.

In response to business concerns over spikes in allowance prices,
and despite some environmentalists' objections, the CRC offered an
extra safety valve: the option of buying emissions rights in the EU ETS
market. To head off critics who feared a stealth tax grab – a charge to
which New Labour was sensitive – the policy was originally planned
to be revenue neutral. Auction proceeds were to be recycled back to
participants, with a bonus or penalty depending on emission trends
and rankings in a performance league table. Organizations with rising emissions would receive less back than those able to cut emissions. League table rankings were to be made public to create an
additional "reputational" incentive, possibly a powerful driver for
firms concerned about brand image. Organizations would also be
responsible for self-certifying their emissions, backed by independent audits, to further limit administrative burdens. Meanwhile, only
organizations with electricity use above a minimum threshold would
be covered, excluding small firms whose administrative costs would
outweigh savings from energy efficiency. (In 2010, the Conservative-
led government cancelled the revenue recycling, opting to keep the
revenues of £1 billion per year to reduce its large budget deficit. In
2013, it replaced the controversial league table – which, according
to critics, failed to recognize earlier carbon-cutting efforts – with reporting of participants' energy use and emissions.)

Collaboration between government and business in shaping the
CRC, with support – and constructive criticism – from environmental
groups, also illustrated EM thinking and processes at work. As one
Defra official put it in 2007: "Some of the big names in the UK economy have been very much engaged in the CRC. Major companies see
the need to be proactive in the light of public opinion and wider government targets. They understand the need for absolute emissions
reductions." But, he added, "At every step of the way, there's a cry,
'Take account of growth.'" Another Defra employee noted that a "cultural shift" had occurred. "Business sees the writing on the wall – the

need for absolute reductions of 60 to 80 per cent. They know that other, less flexible policies – taxes, regulations, etc. – will be brought in if [the CRC] doesn't work. They ask: what's the least worst way of delivering these absolute emissions reductions?"

Business engagement with the CRC process and the wider goal of reducing emissions had made policy-makers' task easier, said a Defra employee: "The political space to do what we're doing has been expanded by the fact that larger, more publicly visible companies are engaged in one-upmanship at the moment over who can do the most environmentally ... They see it as a way to differentiate themselves." He pointed to the example of supermarkets such as Tesco, which expected continued rapid growth yet committed to large absolute emissions reductions. "This helps as a lever. If they can do it, people say, why not others?"

Of course, not all firms were equally enthusiastic about the CRC. A trade association in the food and drink sector, for example, argued during consultation that it was subjected to laws that required energy use, such as minimum fridge temperatures for food safety or the new smoking ban that was "moving inside outside" and supposedly necessitated use of high-carbon patio heaters (Defra 2007g, 14). Businesses raised several other concerns, including the policy's administrative burdens and complexity – indeed, the Conservative-led coalition would later simplify the scheme (Shankleman 2012). Some expressed fears about competitiveness impacts. The need for auctioning and carbon trading expertise was a possible problem for many firms. So, too, was managing their energy use data and the lack of needed IT systems (Gibbs 2010; R. Marshall 2008). Indeed, questions arose about whether a cap-and-trade system was appropriate for these types of organizations. While consultation with business and other stakeholders revealed mixed views on the suitability of the CRC, it did find wide agreement that a new policy was needed for these sectors and, perhaps surprisingly, that it should be mandatory rather than voluntary to ensure sufficient carbon reduction (Defra 2007g, 2–4; DTI 2007, 52; Lindsey Colborne Associates 2007).

The willingness of some leading firms to support the CRC process was reciprocated by policy-makers' considerable efforts to respond to business concerns. "We want to design it together and not have it be us versus them," a Defra official told the Corporate Climate Response conference in 2007, inviting input regarding final policy details. While taking questions from the largely business crowd, he, in turn, asked how large a shift in electricity bills as result of the CRC would have to be to create incentives to cut emissions. Such a question illustrated both a co-operative approach to incorporating business concerns and the simple fact that the state did not have detailed knowledge of enterprise operations.

A Defra employee said in an interview, "Relationship building is a key part of our work. We tell the organizations we're not out to get them. We want better regulation." He added, "We have so far sought deliberately to maintain a progressive coalition of interests. We need to keep some key people on board – for example, the supermarkets – even if we can face down some who put up opposition." He noted that input from key businesses "has been extremely useful in helping us to keep track of what is 'workable,'" adding, "We have received a great deal of praise for the inclusive and constructive way we have worked with our stakeholders." The CRC, he said, "showed the UK is serious about cap and trade, and it helps build business buy-in. For example, it shows that we care about the 'light touch' with regulations."

The complementarity of economic and environmental goals, a core EM idea, was evident in the CRC's development. The policy emerged out of the Energy Efficiency Innovation Review, which found scope for cost-effective energy efficiency improvements in large, non-energy-intensive organizations (Carbon Trust 2005; Defra 2007j). Ian Pearson, climate change and environment minister, said, "Our aim is to reduce absolute carbon emissions whilst growing the economy – and CRC is geared accordingly to help organisations save money through improved energy efficiency" (Defra 2007e, ii). Similarly, a Defra official said in an interview that there is "lots of testing" of the "consistency of environmental policy interventions [such as the CRC] with economic growth and goals of maintaining sectoral or UK competitiveness." In response to concerns that the CRC is "just another burden on business," Defra (2007a) highlighted findings that "the scheme will provide a net benefit to industry" as "any small increase in energy costs would be outweighed by the energy savings promoted by the policy."

This win-win emphasis sounded encouraging; however, a closer look revealed that the CRC's initial environmental ambitions were extremely limited and did not match government expressions of urgency about climate change. When announced in 2007, the policy aimed to cut carbon emissions in the relevant sectors by 1.1 MtC (or 4.0 MtCO$_2$) per year by 2020, equivalent to an 8 per cent reduction. This target fell well short of the UK's nationwide interim goal by that date, en route to the then-target of 60 per cent by 2050. Friends of the Earth characterized the targets as "entirely inadequate," calling for at least a 20 per cent reduction by 2020 (FoE Scotland 2007). The ambition gap only grew when the 2050 target was increased to 80 per cent, which the Committee on Climate Change (CCC 2008, xix) said would require UK-wide GHG reductions of at least 21 per cent below 2005 levels by 2020 (or 34 per cent below 1990 levels). Questioned by participants at the Corporate Climate Response conference about the limited objective, a Defra official said the target was set on the basis of what is truly "win-win" for the organizations involved. Ensuring net gains to the businesses and public sector participants in the CRC was, in fact, the main priority of the cost-benefit analysis supporting the policy (Defra 2007j). When asked, Defra officials acknowledged that if a wider social cost-benefit analysis were used – including the social costs of carbon, benefits of higher air quality, and a lower public discount rate – a more ambitious reduction target would be chosen.[2]

Given the Labour government's desire to appear business friendly and avoid making significant demands on the voting public, it was reluctant to push beyond win-win territory. In fact, a cost-benefit analysis of the CRC showed only one of twenty-seven sub-sectors – mechanical engineering – would experience a slight net loss (Defra 2007j, 34), suggesting that the government was bending over backwards not to inflict costs on the private sector, thus putting a heavy constraint on how far climate policy could go. The government also chose a "cautionary" (in political but not environmental terms) threshold for inclusion of organizations in the scheme, even though it would lead to lower net gains, to reduce the risk that small energy users would experience administration costs that outweighed the economic benefits to them.[3]

"To get approval for the CRC, we had to be very clear it was win-win from a commercial perspective. We stayed very firmly within a win-win box," explained a Defra employee when questioned about the limited targets. "There was a test of regulatory burden that we had to pass," added another Defra official. "There is great resistance and it gets very difficult when you move away from easy wins – for example, when you get to policy that involves rapid change by consumers and businesses."

Limiting the reduction target for the CRC sectors to a level that could pass a conservative win-win test generated another question: which other sectors would have to shoulder a larger share of the burden to meet the nation's 2020 targets? Sectors such as aviation clearly expected that their vast and rapidly rising emissions would be compensated for by even deeper cuts by others. If any sectors were well positioned to take on deeper-than-average cuts, those covered by the CRC would seem strong candidates given that supermarkets, hotels, pubs, government bodies, and the like have relatively low energy costs and are not directly exposed to international competition, unlike energy intensive industry. However, the situation appeared to be the reverse of that in Garrison Keillor's Lake Wobegon (where all the children are above average): all sectors aspired to be below average in terms of required emission cuts. The UK would soon have to confront this untenable situation if its deep reduction targets – legally mandated in the Climate Change Act – were to be met.

The CRC case suggested that claims that "climate protection pays" need to be treated with caution. A more accurate but less catchy slogan might be: only climate protection that pays for business will in practice be pursued, even if it falls well short of what the government recognizes to be ecologically necessary. At least that was the situation at the time the policy was drafted. Defra officials emphasized that the CRC represented an important step in the right direction, one that could be deepened and broadened over time. As one Defra employee put it, "the hard stuff, the biting stuff will take place down the line. We need a process of buy-in first. It's part of a necessary process even if it's a relatively small first step." Another added: "There's an element of the thin edge of the wedge here." The policy was to start with moderate financial rewards and penalties, but these could be increased later to strengthen incentives for a low-carbon transition. "We've got over the initial hurdle, and over time we may see more winners and losers as long as the overall policy is beneficial." Furthermore, it was possible that costs of emissions reductions were being overestimated. A Defra employee noted that their analysis relied on "very static models. It's unlikely they reflect the full potential for innovation … We may find it's easier than the models suggest to hit the targets. But we will get regular feedback in the future and there's scope for tightening the targets over time." Indeed, the new Committee on Climate Change would be able to review the targets and could be expected to strengthen them over time.

Some affected businesses were in fact prepared to go further. For example, the Corporate Leaders Group on Climate Change (CLG 2008) called for a more ambitious CRC target in line with the UK's 2020 goals. Meanwhile, the Environmental Industries Commission (Hyman 2008), which represented the environmental technology and services industry that stood to gain from stronger action, called for the CRC to aim for at least 20 per cent emissions cuts by 2020. A Defra employee stated, "Some of the stakeholders have said, what's this 8 per cent target all about? They see a context in which the rest of the economy will have to meet a higher target. Some prefer to have a more stringent target from the beginning, rather than dilly-dally around and have to tighten up the target later. Some business groups prefer to go for an ambitious target to start. [This is] for certainty reasons – it helps with their planning, and removes some of the regulatory risk of starting out with a target that is likely to change."

At the time, however, the government remained reluctant to push beyond the relatively easy win-win sphere, steering clear where it could of imposing any economic costs on business. Whether that would change in the future through a much tighter CRC emissions cap remained to be seen. The Committee on Climate Change later concluded that the CRC could aim for much greater emissions cuts in the relevant sectors than the government originally proposed – some 30 per cent by 2017 below 2008 levels, although the exact potential was highly uncertain (CCC 2010a). The jury was also still out on the degree to which business could absorb that kind of emissions reduction in a cost-effective way – and much would depend on how quickly the electricity they purchased could be decarbonized. In any case, it was clear that much more stretching targets than those first envisioned – ones that would go beyond an easy win-win sphere and risk imposing economic costs on a wider range of businesses – would be needed.

BIOFUELS: THE EASY WAY TO GO GREEN

Some greens had long warned of the potential disaster of taking land out of food production to feed a voracious automobile fleet travelling longer distances each year. A two-decade-old cartoon on "Future Agriculture" reads: "Acre after acre ... Food for starving children ... Well, actually no ... It's alcohol fuel for our cars" (Plant and Plant 1990, 10). Despite the prophetic warnings, governments in many countries, including Britain, saw biofuels as a win-win climate solution. In 2005, the government announced a Renewable Transport Fuels Obligation (RTFO) requiring fuel suppliers to ensure that a percentage of their sales, starting at 2.5 per cent in 2008 and rising to 5 per cent by 2010, consisted of biofuels. This target was in line with the 2003 EU Biofuels Directive, which later evolved into an EU Renewable Energy Directive target for biofuels to account for 10 per cent of transport fuel by 2020. Since biofuels had matured further than other technologies to displace fossil fuel use in transport, the RTFO was seen as a main tool to curb transport emissions, which accounted for some 25 per cent of the UK total and were stubbornly continuing to grow at the time. The Department for Transport (DfT 2006) highlighted three principal benefits: carbon savings, diversity of energy supply (thereby improving energy security), and benefits to the rural economy. It estimated that attaining 5 per cent biofuel sales would deliver carbon reduction equivalent to taking a million cars off the road – with the added benefit of not actually having to take those cars off the road, cut into auto corporations' sales, or challenge consumers' driving habits. Nor would biofuels require abandoning road-building schemes or confronting the businesses who profit from them. As the Renewable Energy Association (2008) put it: "Biofuels – The Easy Way to Go Green."

One RTFO supporter was the National Farmers' Union, which claimed, "Biofuels are the only way to meet Government and EU emissions targets" (NFU 2005). The biofuels coalition also included big corporate players and workers who would benefit from new jobs. In 2007, the Ensus Group began work on Europe's biggest bioethanol plant, using wheat as a feedstock, in Teesside in northeast England. Major investors included the Carlyle Group, an $81 billion private equity firm "admired" in the City for being "hard-nosed bastards" (Girling 2008), and the subject of many a conspiracy theory given its close ties to senior US Republican Party figures and the military-industrial complex. Shell contracted to take 400 million litres of the facility's annual production. Meanwhile, Vera Baird (2007), local Labour MP in an area ravaged by industrial decline, said "for us locals it is 800 construction jobs and, soon, around 100 permanent jobs at the plant ... a signal contribution ... as we strive to regenerate our area."[4]

The RTFO came into effect in April 2008, which could hardly have been worse timing. At that moment, rising food prices, which had provoked food riots in many lower-income countries from Haiti to Indonesia, were recognized as a global emergency. Some observers, including the US government, downplayed the role of biofuels. However, one World Bank (2008) report publicly identified increased biofuel production, driven by EU and US policies, as a key contributor to the food crisis – and another confidential internal report blamed three-quarters of the 140 per cent increase in food prices over six years on the diversion of grains to fuel, shift of land to biofuel production, and resulting speculation in grains (Mitchell 2008; see also Chakrabortty 2008). Meanwhile, the International Monetary Fund (IMF 2008, 60) blamed almost half the increase in demand for major food crops in 2006–07 on biofuels. For IMF Managing Director Dominique Strauss-Kahn, biofuels "posed a real moral problem," and he warned that "there are people who are going to starve to death." The UN Special Rapporteur on the Right to Food, Jean Ziegler, went further, calling biofuel production "a crime against humanity" (AFP 2008; see also Ziegler 2013). Even Nestlé (2008), whose marketing of baby formula to replace breast milk in the South set the standard for unethical corporate behaviour for a generation, professed to be troubled by the ethics of biofuels. Its chief, Peter Brabeck-Letmathe, said, "It is irresponsible and morally unacceptable to pay enormous subsidies to make biofuels out of foodstuffs." Meanwhile, Swaziland allocated several thousand hectares of farmland to produce ethanol from cassava even as it faced famine. "It would surely be quicker and more humane to refine the Swazi people and put them in our tanks," Monbiot (2007c) suggested. "Doubtless a team of development consultants is already doing the sums."

Evidence emerged at this time to show that, in addition to contributing to hunger, biofuels' net effect on the climate could be minimal or even negative – potentially a lose-lose catastrophe. Two studies in the journal *Science* concluded that direct or indirect (from displacing food production) land use changes due to growing biofuels – such as conversion of rainforests and grasslands into crop production – released vast quantities of GHGs that far outweighed savings from lower fossil fuel use (Fargione et al. 2008; Searchinger et al. 2008). The research consultancy LMC International estimated that if the rest of the world adopted the UK and EU's then-target of a 5 per cent contribution from biofuels, global acreage of cultivated land would expand by 15 per cent to supply this small fraction of oil demand (cited in IMF 2007). If so, remaining tropical forests could be endangered. Righelato and Spracklen (2007), two UK scientists, concluded that rather than using land to grow biofuels, it would be better to reforest that land and continue using fossil fuels. Compared to the carbon emissions avoided by using biofuels, these reforested lands would sequester between two and nine times more carbon over a thirty-year period, at which point other carbon-free transport technologies would be available. Meanwhile, Crutzen et al. (2008) found that nitrous oxide emissions from fertilizer used to produce biodiesel from canola and bioethanol from corn (maize) negated any potential climate benefits from replacing fossil fuels.

In principle, the biofuels boom promised economic opportunities for the rural poor in the global South; however, concern grew over land grabbing, displacement of people from their land, and human rights abuses linked to large-scale monoculture production. For example, a UN Food and Agriculture Organization study concluded that large-scale biofuel production risked further marginalizing rural women in the South as the "marginal lands" they depended on for subsistence were converted to biofuel plantations (Rossi and Lambrou 2008). As Oxfam (2007) policy adviser Robert Bailey put it: "In the scramble to supply the EU and the rest of the world with biofuels, poor people are getting trampled."

Given the harsh reality of first-generation biofuels, demands grew for a moratorium on UK and EU renewable fuel targets. Calls to postpone the RTFO came not only from environment and development NGOs, but also from the House of Commons Environmental Audit Committee, the Conservative Party, former government chief scientist David King, and Defra's chief scientist Robert Watson. The latter told the BBC, "It would obviously be totally insane if we had a policy to try and reduce greenhouse gas emissions through the use of biofuels that's actually leading to an increase in the greenhouse gases from biofuels" (Eaglesham 2008).

The government nevertheless chose to forge ahead with requiring biofuel use. One factor was the need to comply with the EU Biofuels

Directive. Perhaps even more significant was Transport Secretary Ruth Kelly's concern that postponing the RTFO "would put an end to investment in new clean, low-carbon biofuel production facilities in the UK" (Kelly and Ainsworth 2008). She was clearly under pressure from investors to stay the course. One anonymous biofuels investor told the *Guardian* that an RTFO postponement would be disastrous: "People like us will not invest if there is no constancy of purpose and policy in Britain, while the global trade in biofuels will just go on regardless of what happens here." Philip New, BP's global head of biofuels, added, "Ditching the RTFO would clearly make the UK a much more challenging place to invest in both biofuels manufacturing and research capacity" (Macalister 2008). The Renewable Energy Association, which represented biofuel producers including farmers, said a delay would damage the fledgling UK industry while the US, Brazil, and the rest of the EU raced ahead (Jowit 2008a). Having created an EM coalition around biofuels' win-win promise, one including powerful financial and corporate players, the government appeared reluctant to alienate them and risk the profits and jobs at stake, even if it risked contributing to death by starvation and malnutrition in the South. Chancellor Alistair Darling did, however, call for an urgent review of global biofuel programs in April 2008, thereby signalling government concern, but avoiding unilateral action that would risk the UK's falling behind in global capitalist competition in a new "eco" industry.

That July, the government-commissioned Gallagher (2008, 8) review concluded that "there is a future for a sustainable biofuels industry but that feedstock production *must* avoid agricultural land that would otherwise be used for food production" (italics in original). To give time to develop sustainability controls, it advocated slowing down the introduction of biofuels. The government agreed to phase in RTFO targets more slowly – reaching 5 per cent in 2013–14, three years later than planned. The compromise fell short of environmentalists' calls to suspend biofuel targets and shift focus to alternatives, such as improved vehicle efficiency, electric vehicles, and the promotion of walking and cycling.

Many observers – including some critics of first-generation biofuels – saw greater potential in second-generation feedstocks such as dedicated energy crops, agricultural "waste," wood, sewage, or algae rather than food crops. Critics such as Monbiot (2008a) maintained that similar concerns would still be present with many future biofuels, such as dedicated energy crops requiring land and thus competing with food production and contributing directly or indirectly to deforestation (Searchinger et al. 2008). Meanwhile new problems were predictable. For example, removing so-called crop waste would deprive soil of organic material that protects it from erosion, threatening an increase in soil loss of up to one hundred fold (Pimentel and Lal 2007), and would also require replacing lost nutrients with fertilizer, which causes GHG emissions in the form of nitrous oxide (Crutzen et al. 2008). Some biofuel proponents, such as former Shell chairman Lord Oxburgh, who became non-executive chairman of D1 Oils, put high hopes in *Jatropha*, a drought-resistant tree celebrated for its ability to produce an inedible oil on so-called "marginal" land. However, if profitable, *Jatropha* cultivation would be unlikely to stay on marginal land or avoid conflicts with food production and forests. Indeed, it later became increasingly clear to NGOs and even to figures within the industry that *Jatropha* had to be cultivated on high-quality agricultural land with abundant water to generate significant, profitable yields (Action Aid 2010, 22; Carrington and Valentino 2011). More promising biofuel sources, given the lack of on-shore land use conflict, might one day include the organic content of garbage and sewage, as well as algae.

Before non-food biofuels would be viable on a large scale, further technological advances would be needed, such as economical ways to break down cellulose and lignin. Researchers studied the potential contributions of genetically modified enzymes, detritus-loving bugs found in compost piles, Patagonian rainforest tree fungus, and the talents of the gribble, a wood-eating marine creature – among other possible sources of solutions. Some observers asked, however, whether breakthroughs in this area would ultimately be desirable without a strong cultural notion of sufficiency. "If all plant life was seen as potentially convertible for transport fuel, there would be nothing to stop what was left of the planet's biosphere from being strip-mined to keep rich motorists on the road," wrote *New Statesman* environment columnist Mark Lynas (2008a).

Whatever the future for biofuels, the original hopes of a win-win solution – one that could cut transport emissions without having to limit transport demand – were far from being fulfilled. By 2010–11, rising food prices and their threat to people and political stability were back on the global agenda, with renewed demands to end government support for biofuels (e.g. Searchinger 2011). Concerns continued over biofuels' perverse GHG impacts, especially after taking into account impacts on land use such as the clearing of forests (e.g. Bowyer 2010). The UK's implementation in 2011 of EU biofuel "sustainability criteria," which did not take into account indirect land use change, did little to assuage such concerns. NGOs saw even more evidence of land grabbing in the global South (e.g. Action Aid 2010), with British firms leading the way in taking over land in Africa for biofuel plantations (Carrington and Valentino 2011). An eighteen-month inquiry in Britain by the Nuffield Council on Bioethics (2011) concluded that EU and UK biofuel policies were "unethical" and "have backfired badly," and called for a temporary lifting of them until safeguards and better biofuel technologies were developed. The rapid shift in perspective in a few short years was illustrated by the Committee on Climate Change's chief executive, who told a low carbon vehicle conference that there was "not a big role for biofuels in low carbon transport" (Walsh 2011). Indeed, the EU finally acknowledged the problems created by its biofuel policy when, in October 2012, the European Commission proposed capping the use of crop-based biofuels at 5 per cent of total transport fuels and shifting financial support to second-generation fuels – although the biofuels lobby continued to push for a higher cap. Whether the EU would have any biofuels targets at all in the next climate policy package, to take effect after 2020, was in doubt.

Given the limits of real-existing biofuels, many of those seeking a technological fix to transport emissions started pinning their hopes elsewhere, such as on electric vehicles. However, as discussed in the following chapter, evidence of the limits of such easy ways to go green also opened up space for those prepared to advocate more challenging sufficiency-based options.

EFFICIENCY IS NOT ENOUGH

While serious questions emerged about the desirability of biofuel technology, the limits of the other key aspect of an EM project, greater efficiency, were becoming clearer. A key problem was that efficiency gains frequently failed to keep up with growing volumes and sizes, which was evident for example at the micro level. In an interview, a Defra official noted two clear countervailing trends: each product, appliance, or unit had "become much more efficient," but that trend was "overwhelmed" by the general proliferation of ever more units. A typical TV set, for example, may be 50 per cent more efficient than in the past, but people may now have three of them, she noted, or have upscaled from a cathode ray tube to a giant plasma screen. One exception was automobiles, which, for a time, became bigger and heavier, preventing even the per-unit gains that otherwise could have occurred. "Technological potential has increased, but the consumption patterns have shifted as well," she noted. Her analysis was supported by a report, *The Ampere Strikes Back*, showing that the proliferation of household electronic items was the UK's undermining carbon-reduction efforts, and, by 2020, fourteen power stations would be needed just to power home communication and entertainment gadgets (EST 2007). Such awareness within government had not yet translated into policies to limit the proliferation of ever more items, but growing knowledge of these trends did drive proposals for consumption sufficiency by some observers (e.g. Goodall 2007a, 22–3, 75–8).

New evidence on the rebound effect, by which improved energy efficiency leads to new energy demand and hence smaller net gains than expected, also provoked questions about the limits of decoupling growth and emissions through eco-efficiency. Energy efficiency gains make energy services cheaper and thus increase consumption of those services, such as driving more in a fuel-efficient car (direct rebound effect). Some of the monetary savings are also spent consuming other energy intensive goods and services (indirect rebound effect). For example, Labour MP Colin Challen (2009, 197) wrote about a beneficiary of the Warm Front Scheme, which helped low-income earners reduce their heating bills, who told him she could now afford a giant 48-inch plasma-screen TV. Indirect rebound effects are also caused by the fact that the capital needed to achieve energy efficiency – e.g. thermal insulation – itself requires energy to produce and install. The UK Energy Research Centre (UKERC 2007b) reviewed over five hundred studies on the rebound effect and concluded that these effects were significant. Failure of climate policy assessments – the *Stern Review*, the IPCC, and the government's Energy White Paper, among others – to consider these effects threatened climate policy success by overestimating net gains from efficiency (UKERC 2007a).

The UKERC emphasized that "the evidence does *not* suggest that improvements in energy efficiency routinely lead to economy-wide increases in energy consumption" (2007b, vi; emphasis in original), but that did not stop the conservative *Telegraph* from proclaiming "Energy-saving moves could add to emissions" (Eccleston 2007). In fact, the evidence in the report was mixed and inconclusive on this point.[5] The UKERC (2007b) reviewed nine studies of economy-wide rebound effects. The lowest estimate was that 26 per cent of the initial cut in energy use was undone on the rebound; however, most showed large rebound effects of more than 50 per cent and four found a backfire effect (greater than 100 per cent), meaning that more efficiency actually increased energy consumption. The report said that "while little confidence can be placed in the quantitative estimates, the frequent finding that economy-wide rebound effects exceed 50% should be cause for concern" (60). It added that "the available studies suggest that economy-wide effects are frequently large and that the potential for backfire cannot be ruled out" (57).

The UKERC also considered the Khazzoom-Brookes (K-B) postulate, which claims that energy efficiency improvements that are cost effective at the micro level will inevitably increase economy-wide energy consumption above what it would be in the absence of those gains. The UKERC could not verify (or disprove) this provocative claim, but did say the K-B postulate deserved more attention. More generally, the message for those hoping to reconcile economic growth and climate stability mainly through energy efficiency was not good: "Taken together, the evidence reviewed in this report suggests that: a) the scope for substituting other inputs for energy is relatively limited; b) much technical change has historically increased energy intensity; c) energy may play a more important role in economic growth than is conventionally assumed; and d) economy-wide rebound effects may be larger than is conventionally assumed" (UKERC 2007b, vii–viii). Environmental analyst Chris Goodall (2007b) translated the above as follows: "The review is telling us that there is a possibility that improving energy efficiency will simply enhance the rate of global growth, drawing in more energy use. A possible conclusion is ... therefore that improved efficiency in energy use is bad for climate change."

Another troubling conclusion for an EM strategy focused on greater eco-efficiency was that, paradoxically, the bigger the win-win gains from energy efficiency in the first instance, the lower the environmental gain was likely to be after the rebound (UKERC 2007b, viii, ix, 93). The greater the gains in total factor productivity – including capital, labour, and materials – from eco-efficiency investments, the more firms can increase output and lower their prices, thereby contributing to economic expansion and additional energy demands. In other words, the Jevons paradox highlighted by eco-Marxists and others was a real concern.[6] With this in mind, the UKERC noted that it was contradictory for those, such as American eco-efficiency guru Amory Lovins, who used increased total factor productivity to make the business case for energy efficiency investment to simultaneously dismiss the rebound effect's significance (2007b, 70).

Subsequent economic modelling by UK researchers Barker, Dagoumas, and Rubin (2009) estimated that for the global economy as a whole, "no-regrets" energy efficiency investments that pay for themselves through reduced energy consumption would have a total rebound effect of 31 per cent by 2020, rising to 52 per cent by 2030. "The rebound effect is not very welcome to politicians because they have been thinking that energy efficiency programmes are the answer to climate change," Barker told the *Times*. "It's not nearly as good an answer as they thought. Efficiency programmes will have to be ramped up to achieve the same targets" (Jansen 2009). As discussed in the following chapter, some advocates of sufficiency saw in the rebound effect an important reason to go even further and consider more radical alternatives.

THE LIMITS TO THE *STERN REVIEW*

The *Stern Review on the Economics of Climate Change* was a vitally important document in enabling a wide EM consensus in the UK (chapter 6), but it was not free from challenge. Much of the criticism came from fellow economists, who argued the report overestimated the value of climate action, largely due to its use of a relatively low discount rate. That choice, which implied that the costs of climate change to future generations receive prominent consideration in current decision-making, was a relatively enlightened one by the standards of conventional economics and cost-benefit analyses. Others on the radical left criticized what they saw as a contradiction between Stern's (2006, i) statement that climate change was "the greatest and widest-ranging market failure ever seen" and his emphasis on market-based solutions such as carbon trading. Meanwhile, many green-minded critics drew attention to what they considered a dangerously weak GHG concentration target.

One curious feature of the *Stern Review* was the contrast between the evidence it contained showing the dangers of allowing GHG concentrations to surpass 450 ppm CO_2e and the implicit rejection of efforts to keep concentrations below that level. Stern (2006) emphasized two important turning points as temperatures increase, one at a 4 to 5°C increase and the other at much lower levels: "At roughly 2–3°C above pre-industrial, a significant fraction of species would exceed their adaptive capacity and, therefore, rates of extinction would rise. This level is associated with a sharp decline in crop yields in developing countries (and possibly developed countries) and some of the first major changes in natural systems, such as some tropical forests becoming unsustainable, irreversible melting of the Greenland ice sheet and significant changes to the global carbon cycle (*accelerating the accumulation of greenhouse gases*)" (293; italics added).

Due to such concerns over the escalating costs and dangers of climate change at higher temperature levels, as far back as 1996 the EU set a goal of not crossing a 2°C threshold – an objective backed by many NGOs, think tanks, researchers, and eventually, at Copenhagen in 2009, world governments. The UK had long noted the importance of the 2°C threshold in key energy policy documents (DTI 2003a, 24; DTI 2006, 19). The *Stern Review* also acknowledged the dangers of rising temperatures unleashing positive feedback, noting that "climate change itself may accelerate future warming by reducing natural absorption and releasing stores of carbon dioxide and methane" through, for example, the possible loss of tropical rainforests and the thawing of permafrost (Stern 2006, 10–11).

To have a fifty-fifty chance of not exceeding the 2°C threshold, the data Stern and his team had available suggested an atmospheric concentration target of no more than 450 ppm CO_2e (Stern 2006, v, 294). Concentrations of 550 ppm would leave a 63 to 99 per cent probability of exceeding 2°C, and a 30 to 70 per cent chance of exceeding the much more dangerous level of a 3°C increase (194–5). Stern was willing to accept these probabilities despite his own assessment of the possibly devastating consequences. As for stabilizing concentrations at no more than 450 ppm – in other words, a target roughly in line with what many considered to be adequately addressing the problem – Stern concluded that it would be "very difficult and costly" (299; see also xvii). By opting for a maximum 550 ppm target, Stern was able to claim that the cost of dealing with climate change would be just 1 per cent of annual world GDP, a much quoted figure that compared favourably to the estimated costs of inaction of 5 to 20 per cent of world GDP.[7]

Commenting on Stern's analysis, Andrew Simms, policy director of the New Economics Foundation (NEF), said, "On the one hand, it quite openly shows that ... once you go beyond 450 ppm, the probability of hitting major, irreversible climate change becomes much higher quite quickly. And yet at the same time, the spin that was put on the report when it came out was to say, well, the best we can hope for is maybe stabilizing around 550. [But] if you've just said that if you go beyond 450, there's a higher probability of having major, irreversible changes, then how do you envisage stopping at 550 if, having got there, you've triggered major irreversible processes, which you then can't stop?" Similarly, Michael Meacher (2007), a left-wing Labour MP and former environment minister, wrote: "Stern's analysis, though not his conclusion, therefore makes clear that the only real survival scenario is to keep within the global emission limit of 450 ppm. This is achievable, but only if there is a breathtaking change of mindset at all levels. In the case of the UK, there is a precedent: in 1940, when we faced invasion by a powerful enemy, the nation focused single-mindedly on resistance." Meacher's call for a revival of the "Blitz spirit" to face the threat of climate change was based on Stern's (vi, 296) assessment that a 450 ppm concentration target would require global emissions to peak within ten years, then fall very steeply – 5 per cent annually – to achieve a global 70 per cent cut by 2050. That goal implied much deeper emissions cuts in the rich nations and a far greater social transformation than Stern or government leaders envisaged.

Such a critique came not only from the left. Although some on the right, such as Nigel Lawson (2006, 1), attacked Stern for "scaremongering," the Quality of Life Policy Group (2007, 11) of the Conservative Party criticized Stern for being "too complacent, both in terms of the high emissions target he recommended as acceptable and his calculations of the likely cost of climate change impacts," even as it welcomed his central point that the cost of inaction was likely to be greater than the cost of precautionary action. "Don't give up on 2°C" and a 400–450 ppm stabilization target range was its overriding message on climate targets (Quality of Life Policy Group 2007, 378–9; see also Hurd and Kerr 2007). While calling for a "Stern Review 2" to assess the likely economic costs of a more appropriate target, the group asked, "Are our values so warped that we cannot contemplate a pause in our process of wealth creation and consumption in order to safeguard the environment which makes it all possible?" (386–7). This stance was a challenge not only to Stern, but also to the government's chief scientist, David King, who told the BBC a 550 ppm target was "probably the best we can achieve through global agreement" even though it would likely lead to an increase well in excess of 3°C (Quality of Life Policy Group 2007, 379; see also Grice 2006). King took this position despite a report to the UK government showing that such temperatures would increase the number of people at risk of hunger by up to four hundred million and the number at risk of water stress by 1.2 to 3 billion (Warren 2006).

The fact that Stern was effectively giving up on 2°C prompted Andrew Simms to say, "There's no point in building a bridge halfway across the ravine. You've actually got to go the whole way. If your objective is preventing major irreversible climate change, then that's what you've got to do. If the science is telling you that to stay within a reasonable probability of not triggering major irreversible effects means you've got to hold to this level of concentration, then that's what you've got to do. And if your roadmap isn't going to get you to that point, then you need a different roadmap." When asked what kind of response he received to that argument, Simms recounted his experience at the *Stern Review*'s launch, where he put this very issue to the panel, which included Tony Blair, Gordon Brown, David Miliband, and Stern himself. "The response you get is a sort of muffle, evasion, and diversion. And a vague acknowledgement of the importance of what you've said and absolutely no attempt whatsoever to answer it. That's what you get," said Simms. (This phenomenon was evident in other similar situations.)[8] Simms suspected that one factor, among the "variously complicated levels of denial," was that such individuals had convinced themselves they were being pragmatic, strategic, and going as far as they could. "But unfortunately, the atmosphere doesn't really recognize political pragmatism," said Simms. "You can't really negotiate with the weather in the way you can negotiate between political parties, between a government and its institutional civil service about the delivery of policy, and with the public about the acceptability of policy."

Clearly, Stern's message had a strategic upside. "Results like Stern's ... which say we can radically cut emissions and don't have to pay a massive conventional economic penalty, are very positive messages," said a Defra official. "Some people may say, 'That's what they want to hear.' But that makes the choice of tackling climate change emissions a much easier one." Tony Blair, for one, made clear his relief at Stern's message during the press conference releasing the review, according to the *Independent*'s environment editor, who noted that for politicians it represented a welcome alternative to the "deep green" call for "a different type of economic system based on sufficiency rather than growth" (M. McCarthy 2006). Meanwhile, an Environment Agency employee drew attention to another powerful audience: "The Stern Review is all about making climate change more of a comfortable animal for the City."

The question, though, was whether the strategic benefits of soft-pedalling the message outweighed the costs. Paul Baer (2007), of the US-based activist think tank EcoEquity and another critic of Stern's effective dismissal of a 2°C goal, emphasized that the "Stern Review is a highly political document." Baer wrote: "To put the matter bluntly, Stern apparently believes that any suggestion that necessary mitigation might actually significantly reduce economic growth in either poor or rich countries would discredit his argument with the audiences that count. Global environmental policy is still dominated by the neo-liberal consensus that unrestricted economic growth is the solution to whatever ails us, and Stern knows this" (8). Baer speculated that Stern might well have believed that the best way of keeping below 2°C was paradoxically to refrain from advocating such a difficult target, given the resistance that might generate from the outset. However, Baer argued that the kind of "crash program" needed to avoid possible catastrophe required "inconvenient honesty about the urgency of the problem" (3).

For eco-Marxists, the problem was the inability to reconcile capitalism's expansionary drives with climate action on the scale necessary. In arguing that "very rapid emission cuts are unlikely to be economically viable," Stern (2006, 203–4) noted that, "Experience suggests it is difficult to secure emission cuts faster than about 1% per year except in instances of recession," such as the collapse of the former Soviet economies. Foster, Clark, and York (2010, 156) thus interpreted Stern's choice of a weak stabilization target this way: "Any reduction in CO_2e emissions beyond around 1 percent per year would make it virtually impossible to maintain strong economic growth – the bottom line of the capitalism economy. Consequently, in order to keep the treadmill of accumulation going the world needs to risk environmental Armageddon."

Following the release of his landmark report, Stern did in fact speak in more urgent terms, upping his estimate of needed global emissions cuts to 50 per cent by 2050 and at least 80 per cent in wealthy nations (Benjamin 2007; Stern 2009).[9] In an interview with the *Financial Times*, Stern stood his ground against economists and climate "sceptics" who criticized him for overstating the benefits of emissions cuts, but he admitted, "We underestimated the risks ... we underestimated the damage associated with the temperature increases ... and we underestimated the probabilities of temperature increases" (Harvey and Pickard 2008; see also H. Stewart and Elliott 2013). With evidence that emissions were rising more rapidly and the earth's carbon absorption capacity was falling faster than expected, while climate sensitivity to increased GHG concentrations was greater than previously believed, Stern abandoned talk of 550 ppm and called instead for an upper range target of 500 ppm. With this more ambitious target, Stern also had to double his estimate of the costs of fighting climate change to 2 per cent of global GDP (Jowit and Wintour 2008; Stern 2009).

The trouble was that 500 ppm was still extremely risky given the stakes – leaving a 48 to 96 per cent chance of exceeding 2°C and an 11 to 61 per cent probability of exceeding 3°C, according to the models cited by Stern (2006, 195). Retallack (2008) pointed out that to have "a reasonable chance of avoiding dangerous climate change" the target would have to be much deeper, around 400 ppm.[10] As a result, the economic costs would likely be even higher than Stern's new estimate, although would still compare favourably to the costs of inaction.[11] By this point in time, others such as NASA scientist James Hansen were making the case for a much more challenging target: 350 ppm (Hansen et al. 2008). Whatever the ultimate target, as the needed cuts became deeper, Stern's (2006, xiii) conflict-transcending message that strong climate action was "fully consistent with continued growth and development" became more fragile – even if the mainstream EM discourse did not acknowledge it.

Leaving aside the adequacy of his targets, Stern remained a valuable ally of greens in the battle on the other front: taking on the idea that BAU was viable. "Put simply, high-carbon growth will choke off growth," wrote Stern (2008), as he argued that the deepening economic crisis should not be an excuse to avoid climate action, but rather an opportunity to "lay the foundations for a world of low-carbon growth" (see also Jowit 2008c). He also added his voice to calls for some $400 billion, or 20 per cent of estimated global stimulus spending, to go toward green investments (Adam 2009a), and later urged the EU to strengthen its emissions reductions targets from 20 per cent to 30 per cent by 2020, relative to 1990 levels (Stern 2011).

Still, the online comments to Lord Stern's (2008) advocacy of "green routes to growth" in the *Guardian* suggested that his emphasis on endless economic expansion left a dissident segment of the public unimpressed. For example:

> frog2: Obviously, *My Lord,* you have never questioned the Great God "Growth". For many decades now I hear the politicians extolling the virtues and necessity for "Growth". Strangely enough, over that time, I have seen increasing inequality of income and wealth, and a declining quality of life ... The politicians we have cannot conceive of anything else.

> TaghioffDaniel: Nick Stern takes climate change out of its context, which is a more general running up against the limits of growth in natural resource terms ... [B]ecause he needs to present a politically acceptable face, a lot of things that need discussing get swept under the carpet ... Here's a problem to work on Nick, how much will this kind of political dishonesty end up costing us?

> hopefulcyclist: All bow down to the god of growth! ... It is not the human race that needs growth. It is our financial model that will die without growth ... It is dying. Now.

While the low probability that Stern's prescribed targets would avoid climate catastrophe raised questions about the prospects for the growth model in the future, the UK's emissions record also left questions about the reality of decoupling growth and emissions in the present.

THE UK'S EMISSIONS RECORD: A CLOSER LOOK

What did the flurry of carbon-reduction talk and action in the UK deliver in terms of emissions reductions? At first glance, the data put the UK in a positive light, providing grounds for optimism about decoupling economic growth and GHGs. By 2007, prior to the recession, UK emissions of the full basket of GHGs were 18.4 per cent below the 1990 baseline, or 21.7 per cent counting credits purchased via emissions trading, using the standard UN Framework Convention on Climate Change (UNFCCC) accounting method (DECC 2009b). Over the same period, real GDP grew 52 per cent. This trend allowed Defra (2008d) to state that "the UK is continuing to break the historic link between economic growth and growth in emissions." GHGs fell even further in the wake of the economic crisis, standing some 26 per cent below 1990 levels by 2012 (DECC 2013a, 31) – although a recession-driven cut in energy use was hardly what proponents of EM and decoupling had in mind.

The apparent decoupling of emissions and growth masked other less flattering truths. First, the lion's share of GHG reductions during a period of significant growth was actually in the 1990s, before specific climate policy interventions or targets for deep emissions cuts were adopted.[12] For most of its time in power after 1997, the Labour government faced charges that emissions of CO_2, the main GHG, were higher than under the previous Tory government, despite the high profile given to the issue and the establishment of the UK Climate Change Programme in 2000 to target CO_2.[13] Labour's inability to significantly decouple CO_2 emissions and growth during its time in office forced it to acknowledge that it would not achieve its own self-declared target, set out in its 1997 election manifesto, of a 20 per cent CO_2 cut by 2010.

The large CO_2 emissions declines that did occur in the 1990s were widely attributed to two main factors: the "dash for gas" and electricity privatization, which led to a shift from coal to lower-carbon natural gas as a fuel for UK power plants, and the shift of manufacturing out of the UK under globalization (Helm, Smale, and Phillips 2007; HOCECCC 2012a). Neither provided the basis for sustained emissions reductions in the future. Meanwhile, official figures looked artificially good by excluding two emission sources that grew considerably after 1990: international aviation and shipping (Druckman et al. 2008). Concerns about the insufficient action to create a basis for sustained emissions reductions were repeatedly raised by the Committee on Climate Change. For example, the CCC (2012c) pointed out that, while temporary factors such as a mild winter and falling real incomes resulted in big emissions reductions in 2011, the underlying rate of progress was only one quarter of the level needed to meet the UK's future carbon-reduction targets. "As the economy recovers it will be difficult to keep the country on track to meet carbon budgets," said CCC chief executive David Kennedy.

Most damning for the claims that growth and emissions were being decoupled was evidence that emissions linked to goods consumed in the UK had risen substantially due to large increases in carbon embedded in imports from China and the rest of the world (Baiocchi and Minx 2010; Carbon Trust 2011; CCC 2013; D. Clark 2011; Druckman et al. 2008; Helm, Smale, and Phillips 2007). Official UNFCCC statistics obscured this trend since they only counted emissions from production within a country. The government acknowledged the problem, with little fanfare, when Defra (2008b) first published estimates showing that, with net carbon imports included, total UK emissions rose 18 per cent from 1992 to 2004. Later, revised Defra (2012) estimates showed a decline from the 2004 peak, but consumption-based emissions were still 9 per cent higher in 2010 than in 1993. Estimating emissions on the consumption side was much more difficult and imprecise; however, despite some uncertainty over the exact numbers, the Committee on Climate Change noted that "there is a consistent finding across available studies that the UK's carbon footprint has increased" (CCC 2013, 7).[14] Its own estimate was that, from 1993 to 2010, consumption-side GHG emissions had increased 10 per cent, while for CO_2 alone the increase was 15 per cent. In fact, the UK was one of the world's largest net importers of carbon emissions, ranking second after Japan (CCC 2013, 30), or third after the US and Japan (Davis and Caldeira 2010), depending on the study. Meanwhile, the Carbon Trust (2011) concluded that the importance of emissions embedded in imports would rise over time and could negate all of the domestic carbon cuts planned in the UK up to 2025.

The choice of methodology mattered a great deal: a consumption-side perspective led to an estimate of UK CO_2 emissions for 2009 that was 55 per cent higher than the UK territorial emissions figure: 736 versus 474 Mt (HOCECCC 2012b). With similar figures in mind, Helm et al. (2007, 23) wrote, "the decline in greenhouse gas emissions from the UK economy may have been to a considerable degree an illusion." Helm, an Oxford University economist and government adviser, stated, "The implications for the UK are stark: the UK has not yet, as ministers repeatedly claim, emphatically broken the link between economic growth and emissions. To reduce carbon consumption in the UK would demand much more radical policies" (Adam 2007).

Freedom-of-information requests revealed that civil servants repeatedly expressed such concerns internally. One ministerial briefing, which acknowledged a one-fifth increase in UK consumption-based emissions, echoed a main theme of advocates of sufficiency: "While technological efficiency has improved the CO_2 impacts of our products since 1992, the rise in UK consumption has outstripped the improvements achieved" (Shrubsole and Randall 2011). A subsequent report by the House of Commons Energy and Climate Change Committee on consumption-side emissions reached a damning conclusion about the UK's EM project to date: "The rate at which the UK's consumption-based emissions have increased have far offset any emissions savings from the decrease in territorial emissions. This means that the UK is contributing to a net increase in global emissions" (HOCECCC 2012a, 3).

CONCLUSIONS

"Ecological modernization is the only game in town within the policy context that we work," an Environment Agency employee told me. "And it's more about the 'modernization' than the 'ecological' ... We're in a mode of governance that is economically driven." Indeed, the priority given to "modernization" – that is, economic expansion – was evident as a central force behind many of the problems outlined above. It could be seen in the Labour government's continued expansion of aviation, road building, and consideration of new high-carbon electricity supply despite deep emissions reduction commitments – and in the Cameron-led coalition's and Scottish government's own contradictory policies. The prioritization of economic expansion was also evident in the limiting of the Carbon Reduction Commitment's ecological ambitions to a level consistent with economic gains to business; the promotion of a new biofuel industry despite evidence of negative environmental and social impacts; the limited net gains from efficiency once rebound effects and growing production volumes are considered; and the *Stern Review*'s acceptance of a very high risk of climate catastrophe even as it highlighted the costs of inaction.

Of all the limitations of EM reform in Britain, the most significant was that it had yet to deliver unambiguous GHG reduction. The UK's apparent success in delivering on EM's promise of economic growth decoupled from rising emissions depended on an accounting methodology that excluded some of most rapidly growing sources of emissions – international aviation and shipping – and, most importantly, ignored carbon embedded in imports.

An additional problem was the double-edged nature of the coalitions that emerged behind ecological modernization. Corporate players with an interest in climate action could be a powerful force in enabling reform to progress, but they could also distort policy in socially and ecologically destructive ways. The dangers of an "environmental-industrial complex" were clearly illustrated with the powerful forces that had lined up behind the deeply problematic expansion of biofuels. Some critics saw similar dangers with the inclusion in the EM coalition of nuclear power firms and significant elements of the financial sector, which shaped policy to emphasize carbon trading and the opportunities in the controversial new carbon market.

This critical analysis of the limits of Britain's EM project is not meant to suggest that significant change was absent. To the contrary, the rise of EM and its promise of economic opportunity played a central role in pushing a business-as-usual perspective to the margins of debate. When BAU ideas experienced a resurgence, driven in part by anxiety over the UK's stagnating economy, EM arguments about the potential of the green economy were important to fighting these renewed battles. At the same time, experience of both the contributions and limits of EM was a very important step in creating opportunities for the emergence of more radical ideas of sufficiency, to which we turn next.

8

A New Politics of Limits?
Macro-Sufficiency in the UK

We find ourselves in an extraordinary position. This is the first mass political movement to demand less, not more. The first to take to the streets in pursuit of austerity. The first to demand that our luxuries, even our comforts, are curtailed.

George Monbiot, Climate March, London, 2005

Tackling environmental problems gives us an extraordinary chance to pause and rethink the way we live. Facing up to current global challenges could, in fact, propel us towards much better ways of living.

Andrew Simms and Joe Smith, editors,
Do Good Lives Have to Cost the Earth?

That there could be such thing as enough – even too much – production and consumption has long been a central component of green thought. The idea that "infinite growth in a finite system is impossible ... is the foundation-stone of Green political thinking," wrote Andrew Dobson (1991, 13), a leading British ecological political theorist. Such ideas were pushed to the sidelines of mainstream discussion as the limits-to-growth debate of the 1970s gave way to less contentious notions of "sustainable development" in the 1980s and, later, ecological modernization. Yet a growing sense of urgency around climate change, evidence of limits to ecological modernization, and the idea that well-being could be decoupled from growth pushed ideas of sufficiency back into public debate in the UK. A macro-level critique of growth reappeared in mainstream forums, although it continued to run into significant political, economic, and cultural obstacles that prevented it from becoming established as the dominant paradigm of climate response. Driven forward by their apparent necessity, yet blocked by seemingly insurmountable hurdles, sufficiency-based ideas also emerged in other, sometimes contradictory forms that sidestepped a direct confrontation with the societal commitment to endless growth.

TAKING ON ECONOMIC GROWTH HEAD-ON

In March 2007, a sizable crowd filled the Methodist Central Hall in Westminster to support a Sustainable Communities Bill and defend small and rural communities from the drift toward "ghost-town Britain." An impressive coalition had gathered, ranging from the Women's Institute to the Campaign for Real Ale, and including the Communication Workers Union, the Green Party, and the right-of-centre *Evening Standard*, among others trying to save local shops, post offices, pubs, and the planet. I was there to catch my first glimpse of David Cameron, whose green Toryism was a curiosity for a North American used to a more carboniferous conservatism. More than one speaker, including Liberal Democrat leader Menzies Campbell and Tory MP Nick Hurd, noted the illogic of closing public services in small communities, forcing people to drive farther to centralized access sites, at a time when climate change demanded less car use.

During the Q&A, a woman in the crowd interjected a point not on the evening's official agenda: "If we really want to solve climate change, we need to stop economic growth and significantly change our lifestyles." The chair quickly brought the discussion back to something more comfortable for the political leaders onstage. The questioner, Jane Buchanan, was a founder of Shrinking Economies in the Developed World (ShrEc), based in the south London borough of Merton. A few months later, I met with her and Michael Dees, an activist with the group Sustainable Merton. He sketched a graph, showing the need for a steep GHG emissions descent in the coming years, which, he added, resembled estimates of a peak oil production curve. "This emissions descent is not compatible with economic growth," Dees maintained. "We need a managed retreat from current levels of economic output." His group had, among other initiatives, produced a booklet with carbon footprint–reduction tips for individuals. "It's all about using less energy, consuming less," said Dees. "If people did it, it would shrink the economy."

Neither Dees nor Buchanan had much faith in the prospects for decoupling economic growth from GHG emissions, and they were critical of the *Stern Review*'s claims that climate change could be addressed without derailing economic growth. As one of ShrEc's leaflets read, "Surely, if we really want to sustain a habitable planet and life support systems we should be aiming for SHRINKING ECONOMIES and localized activities in the Developed World," accompanied by "avoiding major road building and aviation expansion." But they faced an uphill struggle in their head-on attack on the growth paradigm. "Population reduction and shrinking economies are the unspoken words of sustainability," said Dees. "They're only unspoken because we don't speak them," replied Buchanan, who added that the large environmental groups shied away from an anti-growth message. "Friends of the Earth won't touch economic growth," said Buchanan, who had been trying for years to get the organization to take on growth in its campaigns.

ShrEc tried to put the growth question on the agenda by, for example, holding a public meeting at the House of Commons in July 2006, titled "Growing, Growing, Gone?," which posed the question, "Do we need shrinking economies to save a habitable planet?" The event's chair, Labour MP Colin Challen, an advocate of deep GHG cuts in the context of global contraction and convergence,[1] held back from openly rejecting economic growth, preferring instead to speak of alternative ways to measure growth. Taking on economic growth remained taboo within the three main political parties. However, Green MEP Caroline Lucas (2006), later elected party leader, echoed key aspects of ShrEc's message at their Westminster event. Reiterating the central theme of green thought, Lucas stated, "modern economics is about endless, infinite economic growth. And yet the reality is that growth of this sort is impossible in a finite world."

The call to actually shrink developed world economies was among the more radical expressions of an economic growth critique, some version of which had become "common sense" for many climate activists. "For me, it's obvious. The more you do, the more impact you will have on the environment," said independent protestor Lucy Wills, who criticized the idea of "an economy that is geared for growth and growth alone." At a session called "Can We Avoid Climate Change and Maintain Growth?" at the Campaign against Climate Change's 2007 International Climate Conference, the discussion's dominant tone was that "green growth" and "decoupling" were a myth – the main debate being whether or not climate change could be solved within capitalism. In the conservative *Telegraph*, A-level sociology teacher Paul Sumburn (2007) explained his motivation for joining the direct action Climate Camp at Heathrow: "We can't have an endlessly expanding economy parked on a planet that's not getting any bigger." This echoed the message of the Climate Camp's (2007) *We're Not Toast Yet* information pamphlet: "Governments talk green in one corner and build more airports in another, while corporations cover up their toxic fumes with slick PR campaigns. Both are committed to endless economic growth, making the solutions they offer mere smokescreens for business as usual." Meanwhile the Transition Towns movement was working at the grassroots level toward radical solutions to peak oil and climate change. "The only way forward is very serious energy descent," said Duncan Law, founder of Transition Town Brixton and a long-time climate activist, who saw capitalism, economic growth, and consumerism as "all part of the same disease."

Outside green circles, the anti-growth position was clearly far from dominant in the UK. However, compared to Canada, it appeared with surprising frequency, not merely on the margins of debate, but within mainstream venues. In the media, such views were particularly evident – although certainly not in the majority – among columnists in the left-of-centre *Guardian*, where Monbiot (2007b) went as far as welcoming the economic downturn. "A recession in the rich nations might be the only hope we have of buying the time we need to prevent runaway climate change," he wrote. Monbiot (2009b) later referred to climate change as "a battle to redefine humanity," that is, a "global battle between expanders and restrainers [that] must be won and then the battles that lie beyond it – rising consumption, corporate power, economic growth – must begin." The *Guardian*'s Madeleine Bunting (2007) denounced the "madness at the heart of this economic model" of endless economic growth, adding that some form of state-imposed rationing to restrain hyper-consumerism "will be the stuff of 21st-century politics." In the business pages, the paper's otherwise Keynesian economics editor, Larry Elliott (2007), authored a piece entitled "Spend, Spend, Spend Is Costing the Earth" that criticized the "fantasy that cutting emissions is consistent with a business-as-usual, go-for-growth economic strategy," calling instead for a "new frugality" and "reappraisal of what constitutes the good life." Macro-sufficiency even snuck into a special "Green Business Guide," sponsored by power giant E.ON, in the *Observer*, the Sunday counterpart of the *Guardian*, in which Andrew Simms (2007) of the New Economics Foundation wrote, "The difficult message to government and business is that we need absolute reductions in consumption, not just improvements in efficiency," adding that the scale of necessary change required an "environmental war economy."

The growth critique also found other media expressions. Mark Lynas (2007b), in a column for the centre-left weekly *New Statesman* entitled "How Economic Growth Can Destroy," attacked government airport expansion plans, not only on environmental grounds, but because the promised benefits amounted to little more than perpetuating the growth that "has laid waste to vast areas of southern England," fractured communities, and left people stranded from roots and family. He concluded: "There has to be more to our country than money and tarmac. If materialism is the new *religion*, then I am an atheist." A full-page ad appearing in both the *Independent* and the *Guardian*, from an anti-poverty group called Share the World's Resources (STWR 2007) asked G8 ministers gathering in Heiligendamm, Germany, "For how long must we point out that ... the endless pursuit of economic growth is leading us toward ecological disaster?" Questioning of growth had reached far enough into the mainstream that BBC *Newsnight* devoted a segment to it. "A number of economists and scientists are questioning whether it is possible to tackle climate change while continuing to pursue a go-for-growth economic strategy. So do we need to give up on growth?" asked *Newsnight* (BBC 2008b). The editors of the *New Scientist* (2008), the UK's top science magazine, offered an answer in an issue on "The Folly of Growth." They wrote, "A growing band of experts are looking at [the] figures ... and arguing that personal carbon virtue and collective environmentalism are futile as long as our economic system is built on the assumption of growth."

Such ideas also made headway in the academic world beyond the usual radical green circles. In *The Politics of Climate Change*, Third Way theorist and New Labour adviser Anthony Giddens (2009a) emphasized the need to find convergence between economic and environmental goals to the greatest extent possible, but he moved some distance beyond EM toward a more critical perspective on growth. "Above a certain level of affluence, growth no longer correlates highly with wider criteria of welfare," wrote Giddens. "Economic growth elevates emissions; what is the point of making a fetish of growth if in some large part it diminishes rather than promotes welfare?" (8–9). He added that the "largest and most promising convergence is between climate change policy and an orientation to welfare going well beyond GDP" (69–70). Later, Giddens (2009b) went further, writing, "We are living in an unsustainable society, whose core rationale – the maximising of economic growth – is incompatible with its long-term survival." Meanwhile, respected energy economist and government adviser Dieter Helm (2009, 10) concluded that "the environmentalists are right" in critiquing the conventional growth model and unsustainably high levels of consumption. Taking the necessary steps to tackle climate change would require, in Helm's estimation, North Americans and Europeans to lower their consumption "considerably – and quickly" (9). Even Nicholas Stern expressed doubts about endless growth, stating that robust growth was compatible with avoiding dangerous GHG levels until at least 2030, but rich nations might eventually have to consider an alternative path. "At some point we would have to think about whether we want future growth," said Stern, before getting back on message. "We don't have to do that now" (Watts 2009). These and other examples were certainly not enough to suggest any imminent large-scale cultural breakthrough for sufficiency, but they did illustrate the presence of considerable counter-hegemonic sand in the wheels of the dominant ecological modernization approach.

The economic growth critique also found organizational and institutional backing. One source was the New Economics Foundation (NEF), a self-described "think-and-do tank." NEF was a key producer of ideas critical of economic growth on environmental, well-being, and poverty-reduction grounds, and its interventions often garnered considerable media attention (e.g. Abdallah et al. 2012). "There's an inconvenient relationship between growth and rising greenhouse gases," said NEF policy director Andrew Simms, who expressed scepticism that "in the real world" delinking growth and emissions would ever happen on an adequate scale. Such concerns were at the core of a NEF report concluding that "growth isn't possible" if humanity is to keep temperature increases from exceeding 2°C (Simms, Johnson, and Chowla 2010). Meanwhile, the Green Party (2010, 8), as noted above, was a home for critical views on growth – calling in its election manifesto for the UK to "move to a zero-carbon economy [and] move away from an obsession with growth" – although different currents existed within the party regarding how to approach the question.

One key institutional incursion for the growth critique occurred at the Sustainable Development Commission (SDC), which brought such ideas into the margins of the state. The SDC (2003), an independent government watchdog and advisory body, sought to generate critical reflection on growth, starting with its document *Redefining Prosperity*. So, too, did its chair Jonathon Porritt, who was particularly critical of growing consumerism. "I think capitalism is patently unable to go on growing the size of the consumer economy for any more people in the world today because levels of consumption are already undermining life support systems on which we depend – so if we do it for any more people, the planet will go pop," warned Porritt in the *Observer* (D. Smith 2007). He added, "it's almost inevitable we will learn to have more elegant, satisfying lives, consuming less. I can't see any way out of that in the long run." At times, as discussed below, Porritt (2007b) left an ambivalent message about the feasibility of further economic growth, arguing for a vision of "capitalism as if the world really mattered." Yet subsequent work by the SDC continued to develop the critique of growth, with the aim of putting "prosperity without growth" on the agenda (chapter 10). Meanwhile, the UK's science academy, the Royal Society (2012, 105–6), highlighted the need to limit both population and per capita consumption growth. Its landmark report on *People and the Planet* called on governments "to develop socio-economic systems and institutions that are not dependent on continued material consumption growth" and to "explore alternative models to the growth-based economy."

The Church of England was another institution that brought questioning of economic growth and consumerism into public debate. Its report *Sharing God's Planet* (CofE 2005) noted that the "force behind the increase in [greenhouse] gas emissions is economic growth" (7) and that "for Christians there must be a recognition that the project of growth without limit has to be curtailed" (15).[2] The Archbishop of Canterbury echoed that view as he called in the press for a "new spiritual politics of limits" to address climate change, adding that "endless trajectories of growth are not realistic" (R. Williams 2008).

Later, in his parting book, the Archbishop returned to the theme of "living within limits" and highlighted "the dangers of 'growth' as an unexamined good … A goal of growth simply as an indefinite expansion of purchasing power is either vacuous or malign – malign to the extent that it inevitably implies the diminution of the capacity of others in a world of limited resource" (R. Williams 2012, 219). For his part, the Bishop of London caused a stir when he said, "There is now an overriding imperative to walk more lightly upon the earth and we need to make our lifestyle decisions in that light. Making selfish choices such as flying on holiday or buying a large car are a symptom of sin" (Leake 2006).

Yet, as discussed below, the Church of England was not always consistent in directly critiquing a growth-based culture and civilization, sometimes emphasizing decoupling economic growth from carbon emissions and ideas such as contraction and convergence, a proposal which is agnostic on economic growth. The Church was certainly not the only source of mixed messages on growth. The significant obstacles to a strong critique of growth led many to reframe their message, return to hopes for decoupling, or to advance their ideas in other ways.

"IT'S LIKE THE THIRD RAIL": OBSTACLES TO THE GROWTH CRITIQUE IN BRITAIN

A head-on critique of growth encounters numerous obstacles and challenges. "It's like the third rail," said Adrian Hewitt, principal environment officer with the London Borough of Merton, who preferred instead to focus on technical solutions. Some reasons why many people would rather not touch it – preferring instead to put forward an EM vision – were evident during the appearance of Derek Wall, the UK Green Party's principal male speaker, on BBC's (2007e) *Hard Talk*. Wall, an eco-socialist, criticized the three main parties' obsession with economic growth, proposing instead a vision of prosperity decoupled from a "blind accumulation of GNP." On economic matters, his interrogator grilled him on two main points: the impact of zero growth on jobs and, with even greater persistence, people's aspirations to earn more. "What people don't understand is that they see a party that talks about zero growth as an aspiration and they think, do you want to go back a hundred years?" asked the journalist, somewhat exaggerating the point, given that zero growth would only take one back to the previous year in terms of income. She added, "People are ambitious. They want to be successful. One of their measures of success is that they want to be paid more next year. Is that something that should be ruled out under the Green vision of Britain?" Wall, in turn, argued that many people could be better off materially through redistribution of financial sector excess – one element of a Green vision of progress focused on quality over quantity, new measures of standard of living, production of longer-lasting goods, more shared provision, better public services, and a full employment policy in which job sharing plays a prominent role. None of this satisfied his inquisitor, who continued to hammer away at the idea that people "would like to earn more" and think "that perhaps there are going to be more jobs available." Wall concluded by saying that, "Above all, we need to say green politics is difficult, and actually bring in some of [these] debates," clearly distancing himself from an easy win-win EM rhetoric. Although Wall held his heretical ground, this exchange highlighted two principal questions that critics of growth must confront: can a turn away from growth have broad public appeal in democratic societies? And can it address key macroeconomic challenges?

These questions appeared in both the UK and Canada, where the call to move away from a growth-oriented economy to combat climate change ran into several serious obstacles, including the strength of consumerist values and the growth ideology, business resistance, government dependence on growth, labour's concerns over employment, and a need for more fully developed economic alternatives. The following section explores particular ways that these issues played out in the UK context.

Political Viability: "The Deep Green Trap That Spells Isolation"?

Drawing on the ideas of Italian revolutionary Antonio Gramsci, who argued that capitalism in advanced nations was sustained not only through coercion but also the consent of the working-class majority, one can see the growth economy's first line of defence being the population's consent to a society that promises to fulfill their consumer aspirations. These aspirations are relatively well served, at least for most people in non-recessionary times, in advanced capitalist societies. Politicians who question these consumer aspirations step onto very treacherous political terrain given the hegemonic role of consumer culture, and most are very hesitant to do so. That was the case with the New Labour governments, which rejected the idea that zero growth could appeal to the public. (The fact that Labour politicians felt compelled to explicitly address the growth critique did, however, suggest that such ideas were prominent enough in the UK that mainstream politicians could not do as their Canadian counterparts did and simply ignore them.) Labour's return from nearly two decades in opposition was achieved, in large part, by appealing to the consumerist aspirations of middle- and working-class people. After a fourth straight defeat in 1992, Tony Blair concluded, "Labour has not been trusted to fulfil the aspirations of the majority of people in the modern world" (Marr 2007, 503). This general conclusion had particular relevance to Labour's approach to environmental matters. In a Fabian Society pamphlet on "Environmental Modernization" shortly after Tony Blair's rise to power, Michael Jacobs (1999, 9–10), an environmental economist and later an adviser to Gordon Brown, wrote that New Labour was "fundamentally suspicious of environmentalism," seeing it as "anti-aspirational," due to its challenge to consumerist lifestyles, as well as "anti-poor" given its advocacy of higher costs for energy and other resources (see also Revell 2005). These themes remained evident in a speech by Environment Secretary David Miliband (2006b), who argued that by "challenging our interest in economic growth and material progress, and advocating a return to simpler living, personal sacrifice, and spiritual rather than material progress," the green movement gained "a deep appeal, but also a narrow one." Miliband criticized greens for "exaggerating the trade off between economic dynamism and environmental protection, between human welfare and nature," a view, he said, that resulted in a failure of environmental politics to gain broad legitimacy. Similarly, Hilary Benn (2007b), then International Development Secretary and later Miliband's successor in the environment portfolio, argued that "It is the 'deep green' trap that spells political isolation."

New Labour's social objectives, although more modest than in earlier decades, continued to depend on a growing economy to fund higher public spending – as large-scale distribution was deemed politically off limits. Raising people out of poverty, both domestically and globally, is "much easier ... in a context of more general growth of incomes than by making it a zero-sum game or a negative-sum game," noted a Defra official. While advocates of sufficiency in the global North were typically motivated by concern for global justice and the need to leave "ecological space" for economic expansion and poverty reduction in the South (e.g. McLaren 2003; Schor 2001; Simms and Smith 2008a), David Miliband (2006b) alleged that critics of growth were insensitive to the South's legitimate development aspirations: "Arguing for zero growth, particularly to rapidly industrializing and developing countries, plays to the worst fears of those in China and India who believe that the debate about climate change is an excuse to cement the existing disparities of wealth and power between the industrialized countries and the industrializing countries. If we are to gain a consensus here and abroad that climate change is soluble, it has to be an ally of aspiration, progress, and economic growth. Zero growth is in my view impractical, but it's also immoral." Miliband added that "the Stern report shows it is pro-growth to be green" and "equally, unless we are pro-growth, especially for developing countries, we will end up not being pro-green."

Undoubtedly, an even more significant obstacle to a sufficiency politics than concern for Southern poverty was the fierce business resistance to the idea that climate solutions would involve reduced output or sales. All mainstream political parties were sensitive to such concerns, but Labour put a particularly strong emphasis on maintaining its recently won business-friendly credentials. As a Defra official put it, "It's much easier to engage the business community on a better-product or substitutes agenda than on a reduced-sales agenda." Similarly, in his experience working with business representatives on the Sustainable Consumption Round Table, in which he raised sufficiency-oriented ideas, Tim Jackson, chair of the SDC's economics steering group and professor of sustainable development at the University of Surrey, found that, "If you're actually talking about less output, either at the macroeconomic level or at the level of individual companies, you immediately invoke scepticism. You immediately invoke resistance. Sometimes you won't even finish the conversation. It's almost *de rigueur*. And this is even with quite enlightened business people. That's not something that enters the business mind." He added, however, that "the most environmentally enlightened" business people were receptive to the idea of creating value in different ways. For example, one business person told him, "As an oil extraction company, we're not interested in oil. We're interested in bubbles of value. You show us where value lies in the economy and we're quite happy to go and extract it." This eco-modernizing revision of the role of business was, according to Jackson, important in enabling firms to consider diversifying out of extractive industries and into services, renewable energy, and other new activities. "That's where companies are happy to go, at best," said Jackson. "Where they are very, very unhappy to go is the idea of lost output."

Given the Labour Party's desire to maintain support among middle- and working-class consumers, its left-leaning urge to raise living standards of those at the bottom, and its right-leaning desire to cultivate friendly relations with business, tied together by a market-oriented Third Way ideology, it was not fertile ground for a low- or no-growth politics. Neither its "new" and "modernizing" current, for whom environmentalism was most easily digested in the form of EM, nor the "Old" Labour wing rooted in the trade union movement, which tended to see low growth as a threat to workers' jobs, had an instinctive pull toward macro sufficiency. "The real interest actually is in environmentally driven technological change as an enhancer of economic performance rather than as an alternative to conventionally measured economic growth," said a Defra official, assessing most government ministers' views. "They find the win-win model [EM] – much more appealing. And if you were a politician, you would, too."

The situation was not greatly different within David Cameron's Tory opposition or the Liberal Democrats, who pledged to worship the same "trinity" of the broad centre ground as Labour: "social justice, economic growth, and environmental sustainability" (Benn 2007b). Indeed, when the Conservatives and Liberal Democrats took power at a time of economic contraction, the emphasis on boosting growth – ideally "green growth" – became even more intense.

Macroeconomic and Social Stability: Fears of "Shark-Infested Seas of Collapse"

Alongside questions of the political appeal of low- or no-growth were fears of macroeconomic and related social instability. In his SDC work, Jackson experienced "fierce or dismissive" reactions on many occasions from business people, Treasury officials, and others to the idea of "redefining prosperity" with less emphasis on growth. He referred to a meeting where a Treasury official ridiculed that idea as essentially

being about "going back to living in caves" (see also Jackson 2008).
He added, "You can see where that comes from. It comes in part
from an understanding that economic structure is such that the alternative to growth is not stability. And yet it is immensely frustrating
that it isn't even, in some contexts, possible to ask those questions."
Jackson noted that the Treasury sought to manage the economy so
as to avoid the "shark-infested seas of collapse," which it perceived to
be the "horrible alternative to growth." For Jackson, macroeconomic
questions were "the trickiest issue" for notions of sufficiency: "The
implications of consuming less in the economy are that producers
will produce less, and the implications of that are that the economy
doesn't grow so fast … Everywhere you look, you see that becoming
an impediment to a realistic sufficiency strategy." Nevertheless, he
maintained that such questions had to be wrestled with, starting with
opening up space for more serious reflection on the current progress
ideology and growth imperative.

The SDC (2003, 21–2), in its initial attempt to stimulate such reflection, acknowledged the "significant macro-economic implications in any low-consumption economic model." Among them, lower
economic growth would – all other things being equal – mean lower
tax revenues, resulting in less public spending on services such as
health and education, which, in turn, raised concerns about negative
impacts on society and individuals' quality of life. Employment concerns were also prominent for the SDC and for a Defra official, who
asked, "What happens to your economy with technological progress
and increasing productivity if you don't have growth?" Steady labour
productivity increases without economic growth would – at least without compensatory but politically contentious measures to reduce
work hours – lead to steadily rising unemployment, putting downward pressure on real wages. That, in turn, would raise challenging
questions for political and social stability. Even if ecological reasons
for stepping off the treadmill of production were evident, much work
was still needed to develop full answers about how to do so.

Easier Ways Out

A further obstacle to sufficiency was the perceived availability of less
demanding solutions – namely, an EM project of eco-efficiency (or
resource productivity) and new technology, supported by tools such

as carbon trading and offsetting. As the SDC (2003, 16) pointed out, the government's preferred approach – "improving resource productivity" – was "a seductive strategy in that it appears to offer an almost pain-free route to a 'cleaner environment' without in any way jeopardising macroeconomic priorities. One of the hardest tasks any democratically elected politician can be asked to perform is to call for curbs on forms of consumption." Technologies such as carbon capture and storage (CCS), nuclear power, and biofuels also promised lower emissions without having to push consumers to change their behaviour, confront business with limits on their activity, or cope with the macroeconomic consequences of demand reduction.

And why consume less, stop flying, or give up your 4×4 – let alone shrink the economy – when you could simply offset your emissions for a small fee? Land Rover, for example, continued to make large fuel-inefficient SUVs but, through collaboration with the firm ClimateCare, promised, in the words of critic Andrew Simms (2007), "guilt-free motoring through the miracle of carbon offsetting." A representative of a carbon offsetting firm at the June 2007 Corporate Climate Response conference criticized those in the environmental movement who seemed to believe that solutions had to be expensive and difficult, or painful and personal. As evidence of just how easy it could be, a speaker at the same event from the travel agency lastminute.com noted that a flight from London to Athens generated as much carbon as leaving your kettle on for twenty-six days, but pointed out that this could be offset for only £3.92. (To which my immediate reaction was that I might as well go back to my flat and leave the kettle on for a month. Why not, if I could put things right again for roughly the cost of a single Tube fare?)

The principal obstacles to a macro-level vision of sufficiency could be summarized in two related questions: Could it gain enough public acceptance to be politically viable? Would the macroeconomic implications be socially acceptable? It was hard to imagine affirmative answers to those questions, at least within the ideological and institutional frameworks of contemporary neo-liberal capitalism, in which consumer culture was hegemonic and any slowdown of the treadmill of production generated a sense of social crisis. Furthermore, the apparent availability of easier options held the promise of avoiding difficult questions about growth.

Given the powerful obstacles to sufficiency, particularly when formulated as a macro-level critique of economic growth, one might expect it to fade away. That was the expectation of EM theorist Arthur Mol (2003, 49–52), who argued that ideas of limits to growth were part of environmentalism's second wave in the 1970s, but were superseded in the late 1980s by EM. Yet ideas of sufficiency and limits to growth showed signs of a comeback in the UK as the scale of necessary carbon reduction became clearer, further signs of EM's limits emerged, and some found hope in evidence that growth was not strongly associated with well-being.

Deep and Deeper Reduction Targets

It was one thing for Britain to achieve the Kyoto Protocol's relatively modest targets – helped by some one-time luck in the 1990s and a favourable accounting method – while its economy grew significantly. It would be quite another to sustain exponential GDP growth while achieving the far deeper GHG cuts needed in light of increasingly alarming climate science.

In 2003, the UK set a unilateral goal of a 60 per cent GHG cut by 2050 – judged to be its equitable contribution to avoiding dangerous temperature increases of more than 2°C. This goal was believed at the time to be compatible with atmospheric CO_2 concentrations of 550 ppm. Reaching the 60 per cent goal would clearly be difficult, but was not in itself enough to shake the faith in endless economic growth. As the Confederation of British Industry (CBI 2007a), for whom GDP growth was a top priority, put it, the "2050 goals, whilst stretching, can be achieved at a manageable cost – provided a greater sense of urgency is now adopted."

The once-ambitious 60 per cent target was soon challenged as inadequate due to evidence of greater sensitivity of the earth's temperature to increased atmospheric GHG concentrations, a decline in the absorptive capacity of the earth's carbon sinks, and more rapid emissions growth than expected. The Tyndall Centre for Climate Change Research, the UK's leading source of academic research on the issue, told the government its targets were "more likely to contribute to a world 4°C or 5°C warmer than pre-industrial, than they are to constrain warming to no more than 2°C" (Anderson and Bows

2007). Four or five degrees of warming were the stuff of nightmares, widely believed to be well beyond the point at which positive feed-back mechanisms – such as methane release from permafrost and the loss of the Amazon rainforest from drought and fire – could create runaway climate change that humanity would be powerless to limit (e.g. Lynas 2007c; Stern 2006, v; see also IPCC 2007, 15). To avoid such a future, a wide range of voices demanded a stronger 2050 target,[3] and, in October 2008, the government accepted the need for an 80 per cent cut. In its report leading to the initial 60 per cent target, the Royal Commission on Environmental Pollution (RCEP 2000, 4) had suggested 80 per cent reductions might be needed by 2100, im-plying "massive changes." The fact that, within a few years, this target had been moved up a half century illustrated the growing sense of scientific urgency.

But would even 80 per cent be enough? Not according to the Tyn-dall Centre, which, as early as 2006, called for a 70 per cent cut by 2030 and 90 per cent by 2050 if the UK was to make a fair contri-bution to avoiding a 2°C increase (Bows et al. 2006). Many climate activists followed Monbiot (2006b), who estimated a 90 per cent re-duction in rich countries would be needed by 2030, and later called for 100 per cent cuts in light of more alarming science (2007a). Similarly, the Centre for Alternative Technology in Wales proposed an emergency plan for a "zero carbon Britain" by 2030 (CAT 2007, 2013). Such ideas were not confined to radical greens: IPCC data prompted the Liberal Democrats (2007) to put forward their own plan for a zero-carbon Britain, albeit with a later target date of 2050. Some observers even suggested that 100 per cent emissions reduc-tions might not be enough, as crossing the threshold of "safe" atmos-pheric GHG concentrations would require humanity not only to stop all net emissions, but to achieve negative emissions by sequestering GHGs already in the atmosphere (H.D. Matthews 2006, cited in CAT 2007, 23; see also Hansen, Sato, et al. 2008; Rockström et al. 2009).

What would such targets mean? "Ninety per cent by 2030 – people can't get their heads around it. They have no idea what it means. They think if you buy a Prius, it'll do the job," said Duncan Law of Transition Town Brixton. Several reports that thought through how to achieve emissions cuts of 80 per cent or more could not avoid, at a minimum, calling for limits on growth of certain carbon-intensive activities, notably aviation (CAT 2007, 2013; Quality of Life Policy

Group 2007; WWF-UK, IPPR, and RSPB 2007). And the deeper and more rapid the target, the less unthinkable it became to question economic growth itself. Tyndall Centre researchers (Bows et al. 2006) noted that even deeper cuts, in line with achieving a target of 400 ppm, would give better odds of avoiding catastrophe, in which case options would include a "phased reduction in economic growth and a corresponding shift in the balance between materialism and alternative forms of value" (164).

Growing understanding of the inconvenient math of decarbonization led to arguments that limiting GDP growth was not merely one option among others, but a necessity. For example, writing in the *Observer*, growth critic Andrew Simms (2007) highlighted the unprecedented 11.5 per cent annual carbon-intensity improvements needed to meet the Tyndall Centre's proposed 70 per cent emissions cuts by 2030 if the economy was to keep growing 2.5 per cent per year (Bows et al. 2006, 165) – which would require an almost six-fold increase in the UK's underlying annual carbon-intensity improvement of 2.1 per cent from 1970 to 2000 (Helm, Smale, and Phillips 2007; DTI 2003b, 5).

A subsequent, more alarming Tyndall Centre report that incorporated carbon-cycle feedbacks and new empirical emissions data had little optimism about reconciling growth and climate goals – or, for that matter, avoiding climate catastrophe at all (Anderson and Bows 2008). It concluded that stabilization at the still risky 450 ppm CO_2e level was only possible with very deep and fast emissions cuts under the most optimistic scenarios. Even stabilization at a far more dangerous 650 ppm would require a "radical reframing" of "the economic characterization of contemporary society," with absolute emissions declines in excess of 6 per cent annually in OECD nations. The report warned, "Unless economic growth can be reconciled with unprecedented rates of decarbonization ... it is difficult to envisage anything other than a planned economic recession being compatible with stabilization at or below 650 ppmv CO_2e" (18) – a message conveyed to the public in the *Sunday Times* (Leake 2008).

Meanwhile, the SDC concluded that stabilization at 450 ppm would require global carbon intensity to improve ten times faster than at present – and by an unlikely factor of twenty-one by 2050 – if trend levels of income growth continued. Even more rapid and unlikely decarbonization rates would be needed if incomes in the global

South were to match rich-world levels (Jackson 2009, 54–7). Other researchers came to similar conclusions (e.g. Li 2008; Sorrell 2010, 1795–6).

Faith in the potential for unprecedented decarbonization was still the official line of government, but the arithmetic clearly made it hard for some informed observers to avoid questioning the viability of continued economic growth. Indeed, in a later paper, Tyndall Centre researchers Anderson and Bows (2012, 639–40) were even more explicit in emphasizing the need for a "new paradigm for climate change," which amounted to moving beyond EM to sufficiency. They criticized the "misguided belief" that avoiding warming of 2°C was still possible with "incremental adjustments to economic incentives. A carbon tax here, a little emissions trading there and the odd voluntary agreement thrown in for good measure will not be sufficient." To the contrary, "the threshold of 2°C is no longer viable, at least within orthodox political and economic constraints." They added: "Acknowledging the immediacy and rate of emission reductions necessary to meet international commitments on 2°C illustrates the scale of the discontinuity between the science (physical and social) underpinning climate change and the economic hegemony. Put bluntly, climate change commitments are incompatible with short- to medium-term economic growth."

Evidence of the Limits of EM and Decoupling

Not only was the emerging scientific evidence driving understanding of the need for even deeper emissions cuts – ones that challenged the faith in the possibility of endless growth – but many other limits to the UK's EM project were also evident, as discussed in the previous chapter. Claims that the UK had decoupled economic growth and GHG emissions did not stand up to critical scrutiny. Contradictory government policies simultaneously worked to limit and increase GHGs. Policies such as the Carbon Reduction Commitment did not go far enough to match the government's rhetoric and commitments. Some observers were also aware that behind the *Stern Review*'s upbeat message about climate action and growth going hand in hand were relatively weak and risky climate targets. Limits to energy efficiency were also evident. Taken together, such factors contributed to driving the argument that more radical change going beyond the

parameters of EM would be needed – although they could also produce other responses.

Take, for example, evidence of limits to efficiency. Research that
shined the spotlight on the rebound effect (UKERC 2007b) – the idea
that improved energy efficiency produces lower net gains than expected and possibly even negative "backfire" effects – led to various
reactions. *Guardian* columnist Leo Hickman (2007a) expressed concern that "a rebound effect of the rebound effect will be that it is
now added to the growing list of reasons and excuses some people
cite for not actually doing anything to tackle our profligate energy
consumption." (This response was evident in Canada, as discussed in
chapter 2, where some turned the rebound effect into an argument
for business-as-usual.) Others urged redoubled efforts to increase efficiency given that some gains will be lost on the rebound, complementary policies to dampen those effects (such as increased carbon/
energy prices or encouraging the use of savings from efficiency to
make green investments), and a major push to decarbonize energy
supplies altogether so that GHGs fall regardless of the rebound effect.
Knowledge of the rebound effect also opened further space for sufficiency by challenging EM's core assumptions about the relationship
between more eco-efficient technology (T in the I=PAT, or Ehrlich,
equation) and environmental impacts (I).

SDC Commissioner Tim Jackson (2007) noted that backfire effects
from efficiency represented a "situation in which the overall effect
of improving T in the Ehrlich equation, leads to an overall increase
in I – something quite unforeseen by the ecological modernist." He
added:

> The challenge here for the conventional position is enormous.
> Whether or not my cavity wall insulation engenders backfire, the
> fact is that with constant or rising income, I am looking to spend
> my money somewhere. If I save it on energy in the home, it will be
> spent on other goods and services; all of them with some energy
> impact. Even if I am taxed more heavily – and have less to spend
> myself – the government will be happy to spend the excess, on my
> behalf, somewhere in the economy. If they choose to spend it on
> roads, say, or on military defence – each of which induces more
> energy demand, more carbon – then the upshot will be some re-
> bound, possibly even backfire.

One way out of this predicament, some have argued, is to pursue a strategy of "sufficiency" – a voluntary curtailment of income growth. The Ehrlich equation certainly suggests this route as a quite legitimate way of reducing impact.

Although Jackson went on to note that a sufficiency response might be complicated by a potential for its own rebound effect,[4] evidence of the efficiency rebound effect strengthened the case for exploring ways to cap the growth of A – Affluence – in the I=PAT equation. Indeed, the main author of UKERC's rebound effect report, Steven Sorrell (2010, 1794), went on to argue that "Recognising the importance of rebound effects and the role of energy in driving economic growth ... re-opens the debate about limits to growth." He concluded that "the pursuit of improved efficiency needs to be complemented by an ethic of sufficiency" and that, as a result of the limited potential for decoupling emissions from economic growth, "sustainability is incompatible with continued economic growth in rich countries" (1784; see also Santarius 2012).

Awareness of the rebound effect propelled other variations on sufficiency. For some, such as *Guardian* columnist Leo Hickman (2007a), the direct rebound effect in transport – fuel efficiency making travel cheaper and enabling people to travel more and farther – was a further reason to stop airport and road expansion. The rebound effect also provided a strong argument for carbon rationing, a.k.a. personal carbon allowances (PCAs), an idea incorporating a strong dose of sufficiency. The RSA Carbon Limited (2007) project, which examined PCAs' feasiblity, noted that it "may be that where emissions are capped policies are less susceptible to such rebounds." That argument was put forward forcefully by Monbiot (2006b), who criticized environmentalists who "blissfully ignored" micro- and macro-level rebound effects.[5] "If efficiency is to work for us rather than against us, the amount of carbon the economy uses must be capped. And the only fair means of capping it is to give everyone an equal share," concluded Monbiot. "Only then does energy efficiency make sense" (62–3).

THE HISTORICAL RECORD. The longer-term historical record also supported the idea that sufficiency in some form would be needed. In an analysis of carbon emissions since 1870, submitted to the

Treasury as part of the *Stern Review*, economic historians Tooze and Warde (2005) wrote that "the most fundamental conclusion for policy from the historical experience to date is simple: The 'normal,' 'background' processes of increasing efficiency in energy use and thus diminishing carbon-intensity, are nowhere near large enough to offset the overall dynamic of economic growth" (5). In the UK, carbon intensity had fallen 80 per cent since 1920, while in the US the figure was 75 per cent. In other words, factor-four efficiency improvements, of the kind that some believed to be the answer to humanity's environmental predicament, had already occurred, yet carbon emissions skyrocketed anyway. Tooze and Warde concluded that the "existing framework of private and public governance both at a national and international level has not produced change on the scale that would be necessary to allow continued expansion in the global economy to be reconciled with stabilizing, let alone, reducing CO_2 output, certainly not in the medium term. To achieve that goal will require actions that are quite literally without historical precedent" (6). Although Stern's overall message steered away from any suggestion that economic growth might overwhelm carbon-intensity improvements, his review did indirectly acknowledge such evidence submitted to it by stating that annual emissions cuts of more than 1 per cent have "historically been associated only with economic recession or upheaval" (2006, 8.6, 204).

In a subsequent paper, Warde (2007) showed similar trends in energy efficiency and energy consumption: consistent "dematerialization" of the average unit of economic output since the 1880s but not enough to counter the effects of even greater increases in production. Warde noted that "expansion in energy consumption has accompanied all periods of economic growth since the 16th century." Given these trends – and the unprecedented effort that would be required to replace fossil fuels with low-carbon renewable alternatives – the historical evidence suggested, for Warde, that meeting climate change targets would likely require direct restrictions on energy use, or rationing. That proposal, which incorporates a strong element of sufficiency, made its way into mainstream policy discussion, as discussed in the following chapter.

DISCREDITING OF EASIER WAYS OUT. Whether or not sufficiency is considered essential depends largely on the perceived adequacy of less demanding options. At least two easier ways out linked to an EM project – carbon offsetting and biofuels – faced considerable negative scrutiny soon after moving into mainstream consciousness. The scepticism generated about such solutions widened the space available for advocacy of more radical sufficiency-based responses.

The idea for one of the first UK-based offsetting organizations, Future Forests, was born around a campfire at the 1996 Glastonbury music festival, with punk icon Joe Strummer of The Clash, among others, playing a key role (Carbon Trade Watch 2007). By 2005, the idea had moved well into the mainstream. Not only had bands such as Coldplay, Pink Floyd, and Atomic Kitten made "carbon-neutral" albums by paying for trees to be planted on their behalf, but large carbon-intensive corporations were also getting in on the act. British Airways launched a scheme allowing passengers to voluntarily offset their emissions and, in 2006, BP and Land Rover followed. BP's scheme let someone keep driving a mid-size saloon (sedan) 10,000 miles a year claim to be "carbon neutral" for a mere £20 (Telegraph 2006).

Media reports soon appeared with titles such as "The Inconvenient Truth about The Carbon Offset Industry" (Davies 2007), the "Great Green Smokescreen" (C4 2007), and "The Great Carbon Con" (Morris 2008), exposing a "dodgy," "Wild West" industry populated by "carbon cowboys" and "snake oil salesman" (Gutcher 2007; D. Milmo 2007). Activists produced their own detailed critiques (Carbon Trade Watch 2007; Lohmann 2006). One concern was outright scams in an unregulated market, such as unscrupulous firms selling the same offset credits to several different buyers. Beyond the bad apples, more fundamental objections arose. Tree-planting projects, the mainstay of pioneering offset firms, came under early criticism. Reasons included the inability to ensure that any carbon absorbed by growing trees would be locked away over the long term and the displacement of local people in the South from their lands to make room for trees to soak up the affluent North's emissions (Carbon Trade Watch 2007). But even as offsetters moved away from tree planting, they still faced difficulties in precisely measuring the emissions saved by particular projects and in showing additionality – that is, that the money was spent on emissions reductions that would not have otherwise occurred. As journalist Dan Welch put it, "Offsets are an imaginary commodity created by deducting what you hope happens from what you guess would have happened" (Davies 2007).

Meanwhile, those seeking deeper social, political, and/or techno-logical change argued that offsetting delayed the transition to truly low-carbon alternatives, while keeping the focus on individual rather than social solutions (e.g. Carbon Trade Watch 2007). Critics main-tained that corporations used it to greenwash carbon-tainted prod-ucts and practices. Similarly, offsetting allowed consumers to continue their sins of emission, while cleansing their consciences at minimal cost – resembling the medieval practice of papal indulgences. The most creative critique along these lines came from the two young creators of Cheatneutral, who, for £2.50, offered those who cheated on their partners the opportunity to neutralize the pain and unhappy emotion by funding someone else to stay faithful.

Offsetting's defenders typically responded that it was not an al-ternative to taking responsibility for reducing one's emissions dir-ectly, but a good way to deal with unavoidable emissions that re-mained.[6] The House of Commons Environmental Audit Committee (HOCEAC 2007) reached a similar conclusion in its report on the vol-untary offset market, which called for a code of practice to increase confidence in the industry.[7] Whether or not that was a reasonable middle-ground position, it did not stop activists – dressed as red her-rings – from occupying the offices of ClimateCare and the Carbon-Neutral Company, as part of the Camp for Climate Action's direct action efforts to protest Heathrow expansion (BBC 2007b). Activists from London Rising Tide (2007) explained that a similar occupation aimed to "highlight the damage that offset companies are doing in promoting climate complacency." For many anti-aviation campaign-ers and other greens, a clear choice existed between offsetting and scaling back climate-damaging activity.[8]

Biofuels were another light-green climate solution that promised to sidestep any need to reduce transportation demand – an attract-ive option for governments seeking to avoid imposing any difficult changes on automakers, airlines, and road builders eager for future construction contracts, not to mention voters who happened to be motorists or vacationers. As discussed in the previous chapter, this proposed solution was widely discredited due to concerns about ris-ing food prices and hunger, limited (or negative) climate benefits over the full life cycle of production, and human rights abuses and land grabbing in the South.

Whatever the future for next-generation biofuels, their evident limitations in the present opened up space to question consumption and growth, at least with regard to transport. The *Independent*'s environment editor noted that biofuels had not been the promised "free lunch" that once seemed to be "the very way to keep our ever-expanding number of cars on the road, and planes in the sky, without contributing to climate change" (M. McCarthy 2008). Another *Independent* reporter wrote, "To save us from difficult decisions about our consumption, we are told that a transition is possible in which we grow the fuel we need, rather than drill for it. The reason this sounds too good to be true is because it is" (Howden 2008). Problems with biofuels did not inevitably lead to calls for sufficiency. Many looked to alternative technological and efficiency-based solutions – such as electric vehicles – or, in the case of environmental NGOs calling for a moratorium on mandated use of biofuels, a combined response of "more efficient engines, smaller vehicles, and better public transport so people want to drive less" (Jowit 2008a; see also Greenpeace UK, FoE, and Oxfam et al. 2008). But there was something about the biofuels controversy that made it harder to ignore the excesses of affluent-world consumption. When one's transport footprint falls directly on the land, and when one is faced with the knowledge that the "amount of grain needed to fill the tank of an SUV with ethanol just once can feed one person for an entire year" (EPI 2010), the impact of current consumption practices on the earth and others becomes – at least for those receptive to such information – just a little more obvious.

Equally contentious technologies such as nuclear power and CCS had key similarities to biofuels. Many people looked to them as a way to allow continued economic expansion in a carbon-constrained world, while others saw them as diversions – with potentially harmful unintended consequences – from the challenge of reining in consumption demands. "The persistent claim that a [technological] solution is just around the corner has allowed politicians and corporations to cling to the mantra that tackling climate change will not impact on economic growth," wrote UK-based Corporate Watch (2008, 11–12) in its critique of "techno-fixation." Without reviewing the nuclear and CCS debates, suffice it to say that the degree to which they can overcome public scepticism and questions about their economic viability to supply large quantities of low-carbon power will be a key variable in the years ahead in determining the extent to which sufficiency-oriented responses are considered necessary.

Hope for Decoupling Well-Being from Growth

The above-mentioned factors driving sufficiency onto the agenda – growing urgency of deep emissions cuts and evidence of limits to EM and decoupling – had a whiff of doom and gloom about them. So, too, did demands for "less, not more" and taking "to the streets in pursuit of austerity" (Monbiot 2005b). This was politically problematic as a negative message and calls for austerity had a limited capacity to mobilize people, particularly with an issue like climate change, as it was possible to ignore threats of future catastrophe in the present given the gradually escalating nature of the problem. Monbiot (2007a) acknowledged this issue, telling a Campaign against Climate Change gathering in London, "Unfortunately, most people aren't like us and we have to accept that we have to make life as easy as possible for people. And we have to be able to maintain to the greatest possible extent a level of comfort if we are going to win this extraordinary and extremely taxing battle."

An opportunity did in fact emerge to present a more positive sufficiency vision courtesy of the public debate on the determinants of well-being, which opened space for the idea that turning away from endless economic growth need not reduce quality of life, and might even leave people better off. That was the contention of many sufficiency advocates, who could marshal a significant part of the emerging well-being evidence to promote their cause.

The prominence of well-being and happiness as public issues began to grow with a review by senior government advisers of the evidence on life satisfaction and its implications for government (Donovan and Halpern 2002). Among the findings was that, despite large GDP increases, the percentage of Britons saying they were fairly or very satisfied with life was practically unchanged since 1970 (figure 8.1). (Other polling showed a marked shift since the 1950s from "very happy" to only "fairly happy" as the largest category [Easton 2006a].) The review did find an association between per capita GDP and life satisfaction when nations were compared at the same point

Figure 8.1 UK life satisfaction and GDP per capita, 1973–97

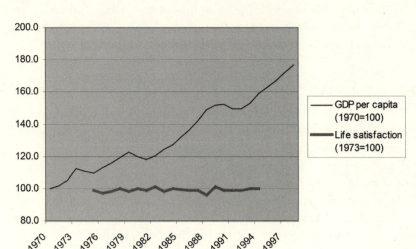

Source: Cabinet Office Strategy Unit (Donovan and Halpern 2002, 17).

in time, but that association largely broke down for nations with per capita incomes above us$10,000 annually – a level the UK reached in the 1950s (Donovan and Halpern 2002, 9, 17). Lest anyone get the wrong idea about the government's intentions in exploring such findings – and others showing the happiness-boosting potential of prioritizing the economic development of poor nations over rich ones, progressive taxation, more leisured work-life balance, and more equitable income distribution – the words "This is not a statement of government policy" featured prominently atop each page of the report. Some advocates, however, did begin to call on government to prioritize well-being rather than economic growth, as the New Economics Foundation did in its "Well-Being Manifesto" (Shah and Marks 2004).

The book *Happiness: Lessons from a New Science* by Richard Layard (2005), an LSE economist and member of the House of Lords, took such findings to a wider public. The impact of an establishment figure such as Layard putting the determinants of happiness on the agenda was significant – not unlike Nicholas Stern bringing the economic case for climate action into the mainstream. Layard – who went on to convene the Happiness Forum, a group of academics, psychologists, and top civil servants, and later to co-found the NGO Action for Happiness – did not emphasize links between happiness and environmental sustainability. However, several of his ideas were consistent with a sufficiency perspective, such as his critique of the "hedonic treadmill" which drives people to keep running towards higher incomes and consumption just to keep their happiness standing still. "If we do not foresee that we get used to our material possessions, we shall overinvest in acquiring them, at the expense of our leisure," wrote Layard (2005, 49). "As a result, our life can get distorted towards working and making money, and away from other pursuits." In later writing, Layard (2011) criticized the role of advertising – whose "overall effect is to make people want more" or, in other words, to be "less contented with what we have" – and argued that every country should learn from Sweden's ban on advertising directed at children under twelve. Layard (2005, 179–80) also challenged some strategies to promote economic growth, such as high labour mobility, which disrupts many things associated with happiness – people's ties to their families, friends, neighbours, and networks of social support – while also reducing happiness by producing more criminality.

Debate over the causes of well-being became something of a cultural phenomenon. It gave rise, for example, to the *The Happiness Formula*, a TV series that explored issues such as why Britain's happiness was in decline, and *Making Slough Happy*, in which six "happiness specialists" descended on the town that was a running joke in *The Office* and proceeded to increase residents' measured happiness levels by one-third (BBC 2005). Meanwhile, a poll for the BBC found that when asked whether the government's prime objective should be the "greatest happiness" or the "greatest wealth," 81 per cent favoured the former (Easton 2006a).

With such polling results, it was not surprising that politicians picked up the well-being discourse. Most notable was David Cameron, for whom embracing well-being was part of his efforts to "detoxify" the Conservative Party. Cameron (2006b) stated: "We have always known that money can't buy happiness. But politics in Britain has too often sounded as though it was just about economic growth." He added that politics "needs to find the words to articulate, and the means to fulfil, the nation's longing for a General Well-Being that goes beyond economic prosperity." Cameron set up the Quality of Life Policy Group to "investigate all aspects of the quality of life agenda" and work out how to deliver economic growth that was "sustainable" and "green" (Conservative Party 2005). Tony Blair (1999) had previously made similar statements that "money isn't everything ... delivering the best possible quality of life for us all means more than concentrating solely on economic growth." Meanwhile, Defra began examining the well-being evidence and its policy implications. This followed the government's commitment in its 2005 Sustainable Development Strategy to better understand the causes of well-being – reflecting a shift toward defining sustainable development, in part, as "promoting personal well-being" (HM Government 2005, 16, 23). Some local authorities, which now had a legislated duty "to promote well-being," also saw their role in increasing citizens' happiness (Easton 2006c).

The well-being agenda could be taken in any number of political directions. Emerging evidence on happiness was used, for example, to back conservative stances on issues such as marriage and multiculturalism (Easton 2006b), New Labour priorities such as active labour policies to move people from welfare to work, calls for mental health support to become a core element of the welfare state (Layard 2012), as well as a radical critique of consumerism, growth, and capitalism. Psychologist Oliver James (2007, 2008) argued that "selfish capitalism" was generating "affluenza" – increased mental illness amid growing consumerism and material wealth, particularly in the neo-liberal English-speaking nations – as well as environmental destruction. He added that this economic model could not continue indefinitely due to climate change, peak oil, and other ecological constraints. While welcoming James's critique of consumerism and "selfish capitalism," some on the radical felt that his proposed solutions – such as "Consume what you need, not what advertisers want you to want" – did not go far enough beyond individual lifestyle change toward political and structural change (Ferguson 2008).

According to Tim Jackson, well-being emerged as a focal point that "doesn't necessarily threaten the [dominant] ideology. It asks questions in different ways about what progress and what society is about. And it could potentially provide the platform for opening out political space on the questioning of growth." One group trying to use that platform was the New Economics Foundation, which linked a growth critique to the argument that "good lives don't have to cost the earth" (Simms and Smith 2008b, 21). Building on evidence of flatlining life satisfaction despite GDP growth, NEF conducted a web-based survey of thirty-four thousand people in Europe that showed no relationship between life satisfaction and ecological footprint. Whether a person's lifestyle required the equivalent of seven planets if matched by everyone on the globe or just one planet made no difference in terms of self-reported life quality (see figure 8.2). While indicating the extent of European over-consumption of planetary resources, the data also represented an opportunity. According to NEF, the findings "suggest that well-being has little to do with consumption; which, in turn, allows for the possibility that footprint could be reduced significantly without leading to widespread loss in well-being" (Thompson et al. 2007, 28–9).

This research stemmed from NEF's work formulating a Happy Planet Index (HPI) – a measure of efficiency in converting resource consumption into long and happy lives. The index consisted of the product of the mean national average of life satisfaction multiplied by average life expectancy, divided by either per capita carbon footprint or ecological footprint. The HPI suggested that Europe had actually become much less carbon efficient in the last forty years: while subjective well-being had increased little and life expectancy somewhat, per capita carbon footprints had risen dramatically, by some 70 per cent (Thompson et al. 2007, 22). Andrew Simms, NEF's policy director, was quoted in the conservative *Telegraph* as saying, "These findings question what the economy is there for. What is the point if we burn vast quantities of fossil fuels to make, buy and consume ever more stuff, without noticeably benefiting our wellbeing?" (T. Stevenson 2007). According to NEF's Nic Marks (2007), the HPI's launch garnered "huge media coverage" – with headlines such as "Happiness Doesn't Cost the Earth" (BBC 2006c) and 250,000 downloads within a month. With the HPI, NEF had found an attention-getting way to highlight the wealthiest nations' waste and excess, while reframing the idea of eco-efficiency to serve a sufficiency agenda and support the case for an alternative vision of progress.

The HPI showed that the nations most efficient in turning their resource consumption into good lives were in the global South. In the first HPI report, in 2006, the top spot was taken by Vanuatu, while a later version in 2012 put Costa Rica on top. Only one high-income Western country, Malta, made it into the top forty in 2006 (Marks et al. 2006), whereas only four countries with a GDP per capita of over US$15,000 reached the top forty in 2012 (Abdallah et al. 2012). The

Figure 8.2 Life satisfaction and ecological footprint in Europe

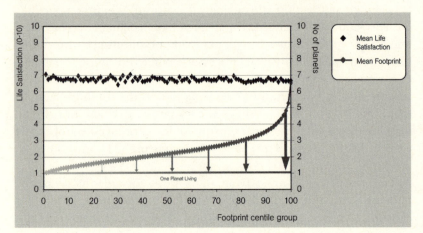

Source: New Economics Foundation and Friends of the Earth (Thompson, Abdallah et al. 2007, 28).

HPI was, to repeat, a measure of efficiency, not an indicator of absolute levels of well-being – a distinction lost in media reports hailing Vanuatu as the "happiest nation on earth" (e.g. BBC 2006c). However, that media misconception about the HPI was itself revealing of the spread of the idea that income and well-being were not closely related once core material needs were met.

That idea had, at least in the UK, become "the new conventional wisdom" in Coyle's (2011, 23) estimation. "It's widely accepted as fact by media commentators and many academics that GDP has gone up but happiness hasn't increased," wrote Coyle, before challenging this perspective. Some academic studies did, in fact, push back against the idea of a satiation point beyond which higher GDP no longer increases well-being (e.g. Stevenson and Wolfers 2008). In turn, new evidence emerged to show that while a short-term happiness-income association may exist, higher economic growth does not produce greater happiness over the long term (Easterlin et al. 2010). Weighing in on the evidence, Adair Turner (2012, 11), chair of both the Financial Services Authority and the Committee on Climate Change, concluded, "We certainly do not have good reason for believing that further growth in measured per capita GDP will *necessarily* deliver further significant increases in human contentment."

Whatever the academic debate's ultimate conclusion, the idea that abandoning the obsession with growth could help shrink carbon footprints without reducing well-being created opportunities to link sufficiency to a positive vision – one with a fighting chance of competing with EM's win-win promise. Green MEP Caroline Lucas (2007; 2008, 224–5) argued that linking the politics of well-being to the climate challenge was an "extraordinary opportunity" as the "policies we need to live good lives are precisely the policies we need to tackle climate change." According to Lucas (2006), "If we can communicate effectively the message that not only is endless economic growth environmentally impossible, it is also failing to deliver the improvements in our wellbeing which policy makers have assumed would follow, then we'll have a better chance of persuading both the public and other politicians that they can afford to be much bolder when it comes to challenging our economic system. Lower growth doesn't have to mean lower quality of life. To the contrary, it could deliver a better quality of life."

Sufficiency advocates had varying ideas about how quality of life could improve with less consumption. "We shouldn't tell people we need sacrifice and to give something up," George Marshall (2007a) founder of the Climate Outreach and Information Network, told the International Climate Conference in London. He sketched one possible vision of a better life in a less consumptive, climate-friendly society. Its features included pride in your hometown because it is unique; your friends and everything you need close at hand; a comfortable home that generates its own power; car-free streets alive with people on bicycles and others stopping to talk; fresh food from local farms; not having to drive to the gym because you are already fit; freedom to work less because you only have things that you really value and need; no traffic jams or fighting for parking places; travel that occurs more rarely, but when it does, it is special and you are welcomed as an honoured guest; technologies that are appreciated and not taken for granted; and no rock musicians flying in personal jets lecturing on what to do to save the earth. Similarly, Lucas (2008, 228) wrote that a "low carbon future doesn't have to be a future of shivering around a candle in a cave." The move away from endless consumerism and materialism within neo-liberal growth-oriented economies could, Lucas maintained, create opportunities for "secure and meaningful work" in a low-carbon economy based on repair, recycling, and re-use; "strong local communities, with greater local production and consumption, and thriving local economies"; and a "much safer world" as greater energy self-sufficiency reduced the threat of resource conflicts in unstable regions.[9]

Translating such visions into reality was clearly not simple, as it challenged many established practices, ideas, and interests. Some research also suggested that, at least with regard to some practices, "sustainability and happiness may actually be in conflict," as one Defra official said. For example, a deep attachment to flying on holiday was revealed at Defra's Citizens' Summit on Climate Change, where, out of a range of suggested behaviour changes, participants were particularly resistant to the idea of flying less. "This is not a popular idea with lots of people feeling that the highlight of their year is under threat. Cheap flights to a place in the sun are perceived as a well-deserved treat," concluded Defra (2007d, 65).

The Defra official also criticized the "growth doesn't matter brigade" for taking the wrong conclusions from the flatlining of life satisfaction. While economic growth might have done little to increase happiness, she said, "It's not at all clear that bringing the growth line down boosts the happiness line up." She expressed concern about rising unemployment and real wage cuts with a lower growth rate, adding that, according to the literature, unemployment and economic insecurity are major causes of unhappiness (see Defra 2007h). "All of the experience with things like the fall of the Soviet Union suggests that with negative growth you get serious losses of happiness," she said. Indeed, the subsequent onset of a deep recession had negative impacts on many lives, from young people blocked in starting their careers to older workers consigned to a premature retreat from the formal economy – which certainly added to the challenges of those hoping to make the case that growth and well-being were not strongly linked.

An intellectual answer to such criticism existed. One could distinguish the need to avoid cyclical economic downturns and the unhappiness they clearly cause from the overriding pursuit of endless economic growth. Layard and his colleagues with Action for Happiness argued, "the top priority should be economic stability and full employment which are crucial to happiness rather than long-term economic growth, which has a much more limited effect" (Layard, Seldon, and Williamson 2011; see also A. Turner 2012, 74–5).

Indeed, one could argue that it was the promise of faster growth that provided the justification for the financial sector liberalization and excessive, risky lending that produced the recent devastating economic crisis. One could also identify features of a social environment where a managed low- or no-growth economy could coincide with high levels of employment, economic security, and well-being more generally (Victor 2008). However, much political and intellectual work still remained to establish such an environment – and to show that it differed from the "shark-infested seas of collapse."

The significant obstacles to moving beyond a growth economy co-existed with potential openings for the idea of sufficiency created by the rise of the well-being discourse, commitment to deep environmental targets, and evidence of EM's limits. Tim Jackson argued that such factors combined to create a window of opportunity for sufficiency, amounting to a "moment of cultural change which might just be swept away tomorrow by some strengthening of the ideology itself, but might be the seed of thinking in a different way about how society is structured, how progress works, and how the economy operates." It was too early to tell how this would play out in the long term. Indeed, some of the drivers of macro-level sufficiency mentioned in this chapter could be used to argue for other responses. For example, limited "green growth" successes could lead back to business-as-usual, awareness of rebound effects could produce a stepped-up drive to decarbonize energy supplies, and the need for deep GHG cuts could provoke despair in the face of a seemingly overwhelming challenge. Whatever the ultimate fate of a head-on critique of economic growth, sufficiency was making inroads in a range of more limited and sometimes contradictory ways.

THE "ECONOMIC GROWTH DANCE"

A number of voices presented what at first resembled a radical growth critique – pushing growth away – only to pull it back and embrace it again within a version of EM. The most significant was the Conservative Party, or at least its Quality of Life Policy Group (2007), led by former Environment Secretary John Gummer and Zac Goldsmith, editor of the *Ecologist*, son of late billionaire Sir James Goldsmith, and nephew of radical anti-industrialist green Edward Goldsmith. The group's report, *Blueprint for a Green Economy*, proposed non-binding policy recommendations to the party's Shadow Cabinet, with an emphasis on climate change and "social unease." To a surprising degree, sufficiency-oriented thinking infiltrated the document.

"The great Error of our Nature is not to know where to stop; not to be satisfied with any reasonable Acquirement; not to compound with our Condition; but to lose all we have gained by an insatiable Pursuit after more." This observation by conservative political philosopher Edmund Burke begins the *Blueprint*'s opening chapter (Quality of Life Policy Group 2007, 8). The sense that the affluent world has failed in judging the appropriate point to stop was driven home by citation of the alarming findings of the Millennium Ecosystem Assessment, the most comprehensive scientific analysis yet of global ecosystem degradation. Gummer and Goldsmith noted that "economic growth, like all human activities, operates within environmental limits," adding that, "When our demand for resources and environmental services starts to outstrip the planet's capacity to provide them, then the problems we are storing up for ourselves become exceptionally serious. *We have reached that point, and moved beyond it* ... The underlying cause is a way of life which is out of step with the long-term health of the planet. The solution requires us to dig deep into our reserves of human ingenuity: to challenge our own cultural beliefs, economic assumptions, and policy frameworks" (10; italics added).

The report's radical green message continued with a discussion of "the problem with growth," emphasizing that economic growth's benefits had come at great environmental cost. The authors quoted deep-green American writer and activist Bill McKibben, who characterized fossil energy as "a one-time gift that underwrote a one-time binge of growth" (Quality of Life Policy Group 2007, 12). The document questioned the social purpose of economic growth: "material prosperity has not made us a contented society" and "beyond a certain point – a point which the UK reached some time ago – ever increasing material gain can become not a gift but a burden" (8). The point was illustrated by the graph (figure 8.1) showing rising GDP and unchanged life satisfaction (43). Not only does growth fail to satisfy, it threatens to undermine real sources of satisfaction: "Modern economies are organised specifically to elevate the pursuit of economic growth above all other national goals. Because of this, they have a structural need to promote the values that sustain consumption growth. This, in turn, weakens the social glue that binds people together in communities" (26–7). Among the consequences of the dogged pursuit of material gains are "status anxiety" driven by the pursuit of positional goods and a "deteriorating work-life balance" (20), taking time away from one's family, community activity, exercise, or leisure and resulting in the contemporary malady of "affluenza" (41). The report similarly critiqued the "hedonistic treadmill" of endless dissatisfaction in pursuit of ever-escalating wants (41), while referring favourably to the downshifting movement and the "growing thirst in society to slow things down, for the sake of our wellbeing" (21).

Another key theme of sufficiency theorists echoed in the document was the following: "The problem with relying solely upon 'green growth' is that it deals primarily with mitigating the *relative* impacts of consumption, but fails to respect *absolute* environmental limits" (24; italics in original). Furthermore, "If … our appetite for material goods continues on its current trajectory, it is unlikely that resource-use efficiency in and of itself will halt or reverse our impacts on the planet, and in particular its ability to maintain a stable climate. It is also crucial to understand that in some circumstances increasingly efficient or 'greener' production processes can lower the costs to business and thus, paradoxically, ultimately lead to higher total rates of production and consumption … Simply cleaning up existing lifestyles and patterns of economic growth will not take us far enough" (24–5).

This passage and others like it sounded like a deep critique of economic growth and the limits of decoupling. However, they were embedded within a more conventional message about the continued viability of economic growth: "If society at large can shift its thinking away from 'what can I buy?' to 'what do I want from life?' or 'what needs do I have?' then perhaps we can decouple economic growth from resource input. This is our challenge" (25). The report's ultimate message was not the need to shift focus to improving well-being without economic growth, but that growth remained essential as long as it could be decoupled from environmental resource demands, redefined to focus on well-being, and put on an equal footing with social and ecological goals. Moreover, social progress should be measured by indicators other than GDP. In the end, an EM language prevailed: "In truth there is no either/or between environmental protection, social stability and sustainable economic growth" (22). Similarly, "the need to transform the world's energy and transport infrastructures represents one of the greatest wealth creation opportunities since the Industrial Revolution" (23). By putting "greater resource productivity at the heart of our value system," Britain can "prove the principle of Green Growth – to show that we can grow our economy without damaging the environment" (24). Indeed, the Conservative Party (2007a) news release on the report ignored the "problem with growth" to emphasize an "agenda to make Britain a world leader on green growth."

The *Blueprint* pushed an economic growth critique perhaps as far as one could go within mainstream electoral politics at the time, yet ultimately it could not escape the perceived need for growth. It was in some sense a synthesis – not necessarily a fully coherent one – between sufficiency and EM, in which a strong critique of economic growth on well-being and environmental grounds coexisted with calls for continued, albeit dematerialized and "green," growth. Despite the initial challenge to confront the "great Error of our Nature" in not knowing where to stop, it seemed that the "insatiable Pursuit after more" and the "one-time binge of growth" could continue after all, as long as growth took a different form. Yet at a micro level, the report did call for strong limits on some carbon-intensive activities: a moratorium on airport expansion (356), taxation of short-haul domestic flights to discourage them (354), and an end to "grandiose programmes of road-building" as part of a need "to challenge the ascendancy of the motor car" (309). These micro-sufficiency proposals were contentious enough, running counter to a separate Conservative report on economic competitiveness by MP John Redwood, who urged expanded airport capacity and new, privately funded motorways, both of which were deemed vital to continued economic success (Economic Competitiveness Policy Group 2007).

While much media commentary on the *Blueprint* focused on specific policy proposals – with right-wing tabloids choosing, for example, to attack suggestions that local councils could end free parking at supermarkets (Merrick 2007) – environmental groups praised the Tory document's broader significance. Friends of the Earth director Tony Juniper called it an "enormously important report," adding that the party had a choice between this "blueprint for a greener future" and "John Redwood's outdated proposals for an old-fashioned economic policy hell-bent on growth at any cost" (FoE 2007). Green-peace UK director John Sauven (2007) welcomed the report for starting "from the basic premise that humans across the planet are consuming too much given the realities of climate change" and for attempting to answer the "defining question of the 21ˢᵗ century": how we humans can change the way we live. "In essence, it is trying to change the mentality of world economics by decoupling economic growth from resource input; to break the link that the only way for people to improve their lot in life is to earn more, own more and con-sume more. It is radical stuff, but vitally important," wrote Sauven, bringing together EM's focus on decoupling economic growth from resource use and a sufficiency-based call to decouple well-being from growth. Sauven praised the report as a step toward a fundamental shift in economic thinking, comparable to the shift from Keynesian-ism to monetarism in the 1970s.

Whether or not that ultimately turns out to be the case, key ele-ments of the Quality of Life Policy Group report were judged not to be ready for political primetime. At the October 2007 party confer-ence, David Cameron (2007a) put aside the well-being focus and the critique of excessive materialism. This followed considerable criti-cism of the report within the party. One Tory MEP, Roger Helmer, dismissed many of the proposals as "absolute anti-Conservative non-sense," adding, "We really have to make up our mind as Conservatives whether we're actually supply-side tax-cutters or whether we're socio-environmental tinkerers and interventionists" (Tory Radio 2007). Meanwhile, Tim Montgomorie (2007), editor of the Conservative-Home website, wrote, "Let's have a debate about 'the good life,' but Conservative politicians ... shouldn't be lecturing low-income fam-ilies that there's too much materialism in Britain." Indeed, having the son of a billionaire deliver the message that too much material wealth can be a burden, or that plane tickets were too inexpensive, was probably not tactically wise. Montgomorie added, in reaction to the report's sufficiency-based flavour, "What I don't like in the tone of the Gummer-Goldsmith report is an apparent embrace of the be-lief at the heart of the green movement that growth, material acquisi-tion and sometimes even humanity itself are enemies of the planet."

A similar tension regarding economic growth and whether it must be abandoned or merely reformed was evident in *Capitalism as if the World Matters* by SDC chairman Jonathon Porritt (2007b). In this book,

Porritt said a great deal about why economic growth was problematic and almost nothing about why it was desirable in itself, favourably citing the pantheon of growth critics from John Stuart Mill to Herman Daly and other contemporaries. He wrote, for example, "Politicians' near obsessive pursuit of increased growth, year after year, regardless of increasingly negative consequences, might be justifiable (albeit in a somewhat morally defective way) if people were genuinely getting happier – if all that planet-trashing, consumptive economic activity resulted in more and more people feeling more and more content with their lot every year. But this is absolutely not happening" (61).

Porritt also poured cold water on hopes that human ingenuity and dematerialization of the economy could keep pushing limits to growth away and "indefinitely defer the day of reckoning," suggesting that such responses were "crucial" but "do not constitute a panacea" (2007b, 71). He attacked the "institutionalized denial about the limits to growth" (72) and the overemphasis on technology as lower population and consumption had wrongly been ruled "off-limits" (185), while criticizing, among others, the progressive left for being "largely co-opted by the myth of permanent economic growth as the answer to everything" (327). Moreover, he referred to the "self-evident oxymoron of 'sustainable growth'" only to catch himself at this point and add: "assuming that we are talking about conventionally determined growth ... rather than (to put it somewhat laboriously) growth in levels of welfare derived from growth in economic value decoupled from biophysical throughput!" (72). So, once again, maybe sustainable growth was possible after all as long as it took a different form.

Like the Tory Quality of Life Policy Group, Porritt's ultimate message was that "conventional GDP-driven economic growth" (52) was leading us into the abyss, yet we still needed economic growth in some form. Why did we need it if it was so destructive and ineffective in generating greater well-being? Porritt spelled out the source of the conundrum (249):

All the evidence suggests that a capitalist economy that is not growing at all may not be economically viable. Nor is it necessarily even environmentally benign. This suggests that "no growth" under capitalism would not further the cause of environmental sustainability as such ...

In the broad sweep of human history, it seems most improbable that capitalism will prove to be the last word in humanity's organization of its economic affairs. But it is all that is credibly on offer at present, and if capitalism needs economic growth, then the only chance for social and environmental sustainability in the coming decades is to make that growth consistent with sustainability, rather than conjuring fanciful visions of how to do without it.

On this point, eco-socialists and some others reached a different conclusion: that if the climate and environmental challenge was as urgent and actually existing economic growth as destructive as Porritt made it out to be, then the answer was to work toward replacing the system that required it. Having considered but rejected the viability of that radical option (87), Porritt was left trying to reconcile ecological goals with capitalist imperatives – a task he took up in his work with major corporations to reduce their carbon and ecological footprints. However, he did not seem fully convinced about the prospects: "This tension between the imperative of a biophysical 'steady state' (albeit with some room for manoeuvre around what science determines as the limits) and the life blood of capitalism at its best remains hugely problematic" (312).

The conflicting messages prompted one reader, Richard, to write on Porritt's (2007a) blog, "This is an excellent book. Enlightening and progressive. Perhaps it is me not being perceptive enough but, on the crux point of economic growth, I don't feel any clearer on the answer. Do we say: OK GDP is high enough (no more growth) and will that mean mass unemployment and an increase in poverty OR do we continue with the growth policy but make it truly sustainable?" No, Richard, it's not you. Mixed messages on this difficult issue were common when people raised critical questions about economic growth and the project of decoupling it from ecological impacts, but then had to wrestle with the heretical implications.

Other participants in the "economic growth dance" included the Church of England. As noted above, the Church's statement on the environment, *Sharing God's Planet* (CofE 2005), contained a radical critique of "growth without limit," identifying it as the culprit behind rising greenhouse gas emissions, among other social and environmental problems, and stating very clearly that the "project of growth without limit has to be curtailed" (15). However, subsequent

statements stemming from that analysis downplayed the need to cur-
tail economic growth itself, shifting focus to contraction and convergence (a policy proposal that remains agnostic on the growth question), broader economic indicators to replace GDP, and "de-coupling
of economic growth from carbon emissions" (e.g. CofE 2007, 6).
That said, the Archbishop of Canterbury later returned to sufficiency
themes, stating, as noted above, that "endless trajectories of growth
are not realistic" as part of his call in the press for a "new spiritual
politics of limits" to address climate change (R. Williams 2008). This
suggested that the next move in the economic growth dance could
be to push it away again.

Indeed, Porritt (2009) was later to return to a more critical perspective, praising the SDC's report on "prosperity without growth"
(Jackson 2009). On the other hand, writer Mark Lynas (2007b),
who, among interviewees, was one of the most forceful in questioning the "religion" of growth, later rejoined the faith. In *The God Species*, Lynas (2011) rejected green calls to restrain economic growth,
saying that "increasing prosperity – measured in material consumption – is non-negotiable both politically and socially" (67–8). He also
criticized the Green left's "dead-end ideology" of sacrifice and "communitarian austerity" (214), which he judged partly responsible for
the political backlash of climate deniers (210) and the failure so far
to achieve adequate climate change mitigation (227–8). Meanwhile,
energy economist Dieter Helm (2009; 2012, 114), who concluded
that "the environmentalists are right" in critiquing economic growth
and consumption-driven economies, later added that, although they
may be right, the no-growth position "shows no sign of gaining any
political traction. If the answer to climate change is no growth, we are
not going to crack the problem." The pointing out of these shifting
positions should not be taken as criticism of the individuals involved.
Rather, the point is to highlight the great difficulties faced in coming
to terms with the apparent political-economic necessity of endless
growth and the likely ecological impossibility of it – or what Jackson
(2009) called the "dilemma of growth."

NUANCED, PARTIAL CRITIQUES OF GROWTH

Other ways of partially challenging economic growth in the context
of climate change and the broader ecological predicament were

evident. One version of a nuanced growth critique involved distinguishing between those things that must not grow and those whose growth would be welcome. After noting that "high levels of resource consumption, waste generation and greenhouse-gas emissions [are] all correlated with high GDP growth," FoE executive director Tony Juniper (2007b, 186) wrote: "All this is not to say that growth policies should not be pursued ... The point is to be more careful about *what* we are measuring as growth. The important thing is the *type* of economic activity that is going on."[10] Similarly, Green MEP Jean Lambert drew on a distinction made by ecological economist and former party member Paul Ekins: "You have the growth of children, which we all think is very important and very positive, and then you have the growth of cancer, which we all think is very negative. But they're both growth." So, rather than talking about a "steady state," which was the original Green formulation, Lambert preferred to present it as a debate is about quality: "What do you think you want to grow? And what is it you don't want to grow?"

Stephan Harding, coordinator of Schumacher College's MSc in Holistic Science, made a similar distinction after concluding that it was essential to allow space for discussion of growth in some form. Harding (2006b) welcomed the contributions of the *Stern Review*, which said action to stop climate change was the "pro-growth strategy," but criticized its failure to distinguish between "intelligent growth" and the "suicidal growth that our mainstream culture is so hell-bent on pursuing, predicated on the limitless extraction of our Earth's wild resources and the continual disabling of her ability to absorb pollution, stabilize soils, regulate the world's climate and operate a whole gamut of 'ecosystem services.'" In contrast, intelligent growth "recognises that we must move towards a steady-state economy in which the living standards in the south could grow whilst those of the north decline until both converge on a steady and equitable per capita share of what the earth can spare us." Harding (2006a) added, "Intelligent growth recognises that certain things must be encouraged to grow – the development and deployment of renewable technologies, the restoration of degraded ecosystems, the recreation of vibrant local communities and economies, and the adoption of ecologically diversified farming practices. Policies inspired by intelligent growth would stimulate those non-material things that can grow without limit – strength of community, love of the earth, creativity and spirituality. These are, after all, the sources of our deepest satisfactions and of our sense of well-being."

Harding's vision amounted to a radical call for a steady state economy in which certain things would be allowed to grow within strong limits on material throughput "rationally determined through our best science" (2006c). Yet, over time, Harding moved away from talking about a steady state, concluding that, "I don't think it's very clever to be anti-growth because certain things are going to have to grow." When asked in an interview about the importance of the language used to talk about growth, Harding said it was "very important." In his experience, talking about a steady state "puts people off." When he first started speaking out on these issues, he encountered business people who told him they agreed with him, but the term "steady state" was an obstacle to discussion. "Tell us what can grow and what can't grow," they told him. "You have to emphasize the growth aspect," said Harding. "That's why I use the phrase 'intelligent growth and suicidal growth.'" Harding said that after he adopted that language, reactions to his public talks improved. Now "everyone nods in agreement basically. And then they throw up their hands and say, well, you're right, but what can we do about this? How can we change such a massive economic system? It's a good point, really." To begin that process of change, Harding (2006b) advocated a sufficiency-inspired reform: tradable energy quotas to ration fossil fuel use, set at "a level low enough to ensure that the economy does as little harm to the natural world as possible whilst ensuring that citizens enjoy a simple but comfortable standard of living."

Eco-socialists put forward a vision that was similar in distinguishing between what ought and ought not to grow. Michael Löwy (2007a; see also 2007b) told the Marxism 2007 conference in London that, under a democratically planned eco-socialism, some economic sectors would grow – e.g. solar energy, organic agriculture, public transport, health, education – while others, such as the production of "gadgets" and military hardware, would cease growing or be discontinued. He argued that zero growth should not be seen as the goal: it was not the quantity of growth that mattered, but its qualitative dimension. In other words, use values need to be prioritized over exchange values, and "being over having." With the qualitative dimension in mind, he noted that the growth of free time was "most important" for Marx, whether to play football, make love, get involved in self-management

of workplaces and communities, create culture, or participate in any-
other freely determined activity.

Another variation on the partial growth critique was that economic growth, even if it continues in the future, should cease to be
the dominant social priority. "Greens aren't against economic growth
in principle. There are ways growth can happen without increasing
inequalities, harming our health, or accelerating climate change,"
Green Party Principal Female Speaker Siân Berry (2007) said in a
debate over whether a then-booming London could also be green,
taking a somewhat more growth-friendly line than sometimes heard
from her party. But Greens do "question growth for growth's sake."
Berry added that "Greens aren't trying to stop growth," but had a
"different sense of priorities emphasizing health and quality of
life."[11] Her words were echoed at the same event by Sunand Prasad
(2007), president-elect of the Royal Institute of British Architects,
who argued that "growth in itself is not a problem ... It's the fetish for
growth that is the problem."

A more surprising and politically significant source of such arguments – given his establishment credentials and power to influence
climate and economic policy – was Adair Turner. The former director-general of the Confederation of British Industry and member
of the House of Lords was also chair of the UK's Financial Services
Authority and the Committee on Climate Change. "I believe we can
continue to have classic measured GDP growth," Turner told the *Observer* (Mathiason 2008). "I just believe we shouldn't make a fetish of
it, and we must not end up believing it's the thing we must at all costs
maximise."

Turner (2008) elaborated on these views in *Do Good Lives Have to
Cost the Earth?*, a book compiled by the pro-sufficiency NEF (Simms
and Smith 2008a). He wrote, "the very fact that beyond a certain
level increased prosperity does not drive increased happiness is in itself a clue to one step we should take to make it more likely that good
lives do not cost the Earth – which is to dethrone the idea that maximizing the growth in measured prosperity, GDP per capita, should be
an explicit objective of economic and social policy" (93). Increased
prosperity as measured by GDP per capita could still occur as a likely
by-product of the pursuit of other desirable ends, such as full employment, innovation, and creativity. But dethroning economic growth
as an objective would eliminate the need to maximize GDP as the

"clinching argument" in public policy debates. For example, "The pros and cons of further road development, or of tighter environmental standards, should be debated without introducing a confused economic concept of 'competitiveness,' which mistakenly asserts that we cannot choose to sacrifice a sliver of future GDP per capita growth without risking an actual fall in prosperity and employment in the face of low wage competition. And if one country falls behind another in GDP per capita not because it has higher unemployment, or less freedom to innovate, but simply because its citizens choose to take the benefits of new technology in more leisure not more material consumption, that should be welcomed for its beneficial impact on environmental sustainability not denigrated as an unaffordable choice" (94). He added that even if the cost of mitigating climate change were as high as 5 per cent of GDP in rich nations, "Given that there is no strong correlation between GDP per capita growth and human well-being, even this much higher cost than Stern has estimated could not be considered a conclusive argument against action" (95; see also A. Turner 2012, 77–9).

Turner (2012, 68) later clarified that his position would disappoint "radical green egalitarians." He supported a market economy based on the "human desire for change and economic freedom as ends in themselves," which would tend to produce growth and non-trivial levels of inequality. However, "economic growth should not be the overriding objective." Turner's "neutral" (73) position toward growth was not a full embrace of sufficiency, nor was it dominant in the mainstream, but it did suggest that the growth critique was making some inroads into establishment circles as people informed about the scale of the climate challenge – as well as the limits of growth in improving well-being – wrestled with the implications.

CONCLUSIONS

A critique of the limits to economic growth, long a mainstay of green thought, showed signs of a renaissance in the UK, contrary to the expectations of EM theory and representing an emerging challenge to an EM political project. Factors that created opportunities for a sufficiency perspective included a broad political consensus (at least for a time) on the need for deep emissions cuts, emerging evidence of the limits of the EM response to date, and the prominent public discussion of economic growth's faltering capacity to improve well-being in rich nations – which opened up space to put forward a positive, sufficiency-oriented vision of well-being. The latter point was of particular importance given the limited ability of a negative vision to mobilize popular support. Such driving factors were weak or non-existent in Canada, where similar consensus was lacking, EM had yet to be seriously tried, and public discussion of the determinants of well-being was muted. In effect, advocates of sufficiency in the UK operated within a significantly different set of political opportunities (Tarrow 1998, chap. 5), one that was somewhat more open to their ideas.

In addition to being the "common sense" of many climate activists and radical greens, the growth critique found institutional support from organizations such as the New Economics Foundation, the Green Party, the Sustainable Development Commission, the Royal Society, and the Church of England. However, given that macro-level sufficiency conflicts with contemporary capitalism's imperative for economic growth and related cultural expectations for high and growing consumption – which play a key role in legitimizing the existing socio-economic order – significant questions remained about its political viability. In addition, more work was needed on the issue of how a low- or no-growth society could maintain economic and social stability. Ideas of macro-level sufficiency, although present in mainstream media and public debate, were still a long way from becoming established as the dominant perspective of government and the three main political parties – let alone business.

The notion of sufficiency made greater inroads into the mainstream when formulated in more limited and sometimes contradictory ways. In some cases, critics of growth participated in an "economic growth dance," pushing the idea of growth away by denouncing its ecological destructiveness and limited social benefits, yet quickly re-embracing it in light of the difficulties of living without it in capitalism. The most politically significant source of such ideas was the Conservative Party's Quality of Life Policy Group, which produced a radical growth critique while simultaneously promoting an EM "green growth" message. It was not entirely surprising that people who attempted to wrestle with such issues had difficulty forging a clear, coherent message given the apparent conflict between the economic imperative of growth and ecological need. Others put forward nuanced growth critiques of a different sort, focusing on what ought and ought not to grow (one possible way to achieve an EM-sufficiency synthesis), or calling for a downgrading of economic growth as a social priority. Such ideas were heard, as might be expected, from Green politicians, environmentalists, and eco-socialists. However calls to "dethrone growth" also emerged from elite, establishment voices – indicating that the growth critique was making inroads beyond radical green circles and helping to make such thoughts just a little less heretical.

Sufficiency also emerged in less expansive forms at the micro level and managed to make limited inroads within the state sphere, which are the subjects of the next two chapters.

9

Enough of That Already:
Micro-Sufficiency in the UK

With the macro-level critique of economic growth running counter to the perceived imperative of GDP expansion, the idea of sufficiency found more favourable – but still challenging – ground in the UK when channelled toward specific products, practices, or sectors deemed to be ecologically excessive. Climate concern led to calls for reduced consumption or phase-out of a number of modern goods and services ranging from plastic bags to air travel. These demands for sufficiency at the micro level were part of an emerging moral conversation about consumption in the UK, which included issues of ethical consumer choice and the responsibilities of retailers to provide sustainably produced and fairly traded items. Such demands for micro-sufficiency challenged economic interests that depended on sales of the product or activity in question, but the social challenge was much less fundamental than questioning economic growth as a whole. The politics of taking on a single product, practice, or sector were always contentious. Yet the task was somewhat easier in cases where minimal if any sacrifice by consumers was required, the economic interests under threat were not especially powerful, and calls for sufficiency could overlap with an efficiency agenda or create economic opportunities for suppliers of less carbon-intensive alternatives. The need for political legitimation in a context where climate action was seen as necessary also drove politicians to embrace some of these micro-level calls for sufficiency, a phenomenon evident in the most significant micro-sufficiency victory: the cancellation, at least for a time, of plans to expand Heathrow airport.

RELATIVELY EASY TARGETS:
BANISHING BAGS AND BOTTLED WATER

As in Canada, the plastic bag was vulnerable to attack, as evidenced by the fact that not only Gordon Brown, but even the *Daily Mail*, a right-wing tabloid with a large circulation across middle England, singled it out for extinction. In his first climate change speech as prime minister, Brown (2007b) committed to work with retailers to "eliminate single-use disposable bags altogether." He referred to disposable plastic bags as "one of the most visible symbols of environmental waste," undoubtedly a key reason why targeting them was politically appealing at a time of high levels of eco-angst. The prime minister said climate change required urgent action on the scale of the Marshall Plan, but as for action during his own term of office, the main headline-grabber in the speech was the plastic bag announcement. The measure had some environmental merits, but fell short of a bold, Churchillian response to the gathering storm of climate change. Environmental writer George Marshall (2007b, 127) noted that plastic bags accounted for 5 kg of the 12,500 kg of CO_2 emitted by the average Briton each year, equal to thirty-six seconds of a day's total emissions. Brown's plastic bag announcement illustrated the potential tokenistic use of micro-sufficiency to give the appearance of climate action, but it was still noteworthy that a ubiquitous item of everyday life was on death row.

In the 2008 budget, Chancellor Alistair Darling pledged to tax retailers if they did not significantly reduce the number of single-use bags on a voluntary basis. Other countries had shown that a tax could cut the number of bags by some 90 per cent. Plastic bag manufacturers denounced the "discriminatory proposal," warned of big output reductions, and threatened legal action (Polymer Age 2008). The British Retail Consortium (2008) said, with some justification, that "emphasis on carrier bags as a cause of climate change is outrageous" and denounced the "green smokescreen" that "hides a tax grab." Nevertheless, in a 2008 deal with government, the consortium and its supermarket members agreed to reduce distribution of single-use bags by 50 per cent below 2006 levels by 2009.

Negative reactions from firms facing lost sales and limits on their autonomy were predictable, so why would a government aspiring to be "the natural party of business," in the words of Business Secretary John Hutton (Eaglesham 2007), risk such action? One factor was that the political popularity of reducing the visible waste of plastic bags had become evident, starting with grassroots campaigns that opened up space and increased pressure for government action. In 2007, Modbury in Devon, home to fifteen hundred people, became Europe's first community to banish plastic bags. This inspired many similar local campaigns, mobilizing people across the country and across traditional political lines. Successes included a vote by all thirty-three local authorities in the London Councils group in favour of an Act of Parliament enabling them to prevent shops from handing out free plastic bags. The *Daily Mail*'s "Banish the Bags" campaign followed in February 2008 (Poulter and Derbyshire 2008). The tabloid devoted ten pages to the campaign on its first day. The focus was not on climate change, but the sheer excess of 13.4 billion bags per year used on average for a mere twenty minutes each, overflowing landfills and kitchen drawers, visual insults to England's "green and plastic land," and agonizing deaths of charismatic wildlife. ("No escape: the corpse of the gannet ... strangled by the handle of a carrier bag" read the caption under one of many disturbing photos.) On the campaign's second day, with another seven pages of coverage, the tabloid could already claim an impact as Marks and Spencer said it would charge 5 pence per bag, and some other retailers later followed. By the third day, the *Daily Mail* declared victory as Gordon Brown (2008) pledged in its pages to act, using "compulsion" against recalcitrant businesses if needed, while re-linking the issue to climate change.

A few factors helped explain the rapid progress of efforts to bin the bags. Not only were plastic bags a highly visible form of excess, but alternatives were easily available and the change involved was relatively simple for individuals, requiring minimal sacrifice. These factors increased the willingness of people to accept and even demand change. Once support for banishing bags became clear, and a segment of the right-wing press that often whipped up opposition to policy interventions was onside, politicians were emboldened to face down the inevitable opposition from affected businesses. The fact that the firms most at risk, the plastic bag suppliers, were not core contributors to the economy was certainly a factor, as was the Labour government's need for a high-profile measure to regain ground in the green one-upmanship with the Tories and Liberal Democrats.

Plastic bag numbers soon fell. In 2009–10, UK retailers gave out almost 5 billion fewer single-use bags than in 2006, a 41 per cent decline (WRAP 2013b). Although the government had given itself the power in the Climate Change Act to introduce a charge on plastic bags, it held off on threats to tax retailers given the progress made through voluntary efforts (M. Hickman 2009). To encourage further plastic bag reduction, in April 2009, the British Retail Consortium joined the government in launching a "get a bag habit" campaign – leaving the packaging industry on its own to feel victimized by "token gesture" politics (J. Brooks 2009). However, the limits of voluntary action became evident when the number of single-use bags distributed in the UK began to increase again. Although still well below 2006 levels, the numbers rose 12 per cent from 2009 to 2012. In contrast, in Wales, which introduced a tax of 5 pence in October 2011, the number of bags fell 76 per cent the following year (WRAP 2013b). These figures led to renewed demands for a plastic bag tax across the UK – which came into effect in Northern Ireland in 2013, with similar measures later announced for Scotland and England.

Would plastic bag reduction be the start of something bigger or a distraction from more significant action to address core causes of climate change? Politicians could certainly use it as a form of symbolic climate politics. Others might see bringing their own bags to the shops as proof that they had done their part – what Marshall (2007b, 127) called "diversionary good behaviour." One critic called using fewer carrier bags "the tiny – and entirely cosmetic – commitment to the survival of the planet that the Daily Mail, and therefore everyone, would consider" (Gold 2012). However, Rebecca Hosking, the Modbury resident who launched the anti-bag movement, wanted to go further, envisaging a wider campaign against disposable consumer culture. "It's our consumption of everything – whether it's petrol, water or consumer goods – that is driving virtually every environmental problem on the planet and it needs to stop. We have shown that individual people can make a difference," said Hosking (M. Hickman 2007b).

Campaigns also successfully targeted bottled water. The *Evening Standard* (Prigg 2008) and the mayor of London launched efforts to promote tap water in restaurants, cafes, and pubs and to embolden customers to ask for it instead of more costly bottled water. During the "London on Tap" (2008) campaign, Mayor Livingstone told residents, "Don't be embarrassed to ask for tap water when you eat out. You will save money and help the planet." That message was backed by *Times* restaurant critic Giles Coren (2008), who gave penalty points in his reviews for serving bottled water and mocked customers who paid £4 or £5 "for stuff no different, no different at all, from what you brushed your teeth in that morning." Anti–bottled water campaigns also had well-resourced allies in the privatized water firms, such as Thames Water, which joined as a partner in the London campaign. The for-profit water companies saw bottled water as a competitor, and their marketing budgets could support the cause. This was a case where micro-level sufficiency could create opportunities for one business while taking them away from another. A shift to tap water would nevertheless involve – in the first instance at least – less consumption in both environmental and economic terms.[1] Thames Water stated that the tap water it provided was "up to 500 times cheaper than bottled water" while "emitting 300 times less CO_2 to process" (London on Tap 2008).

Politicians backing the London on Tap campaign used particularly harsh language against the bottled water industry, a sign that it risked becoming a pariah sector. Jenny Jones, Green Party member of the London Assembly, said the campaign's goal was to "help Londoners take a stand against one of the biggest con jobs of the last two decades. Selling water in bottles and burning massive quantities of fossil fuels for its transportation does not make economic or environmental sense" (London on Tap 2008). The tough talk came not only from Greens: Labour environment minister, Phil Woolas, condemned the industry as "daft" during BBC *Panorama*'s investigation of "Bottled Water: Who Needs It?" He added that it "borders on being morally unacceptable to spend hundreds of millions of pounds on bottled water when we have pure drinking water, when at the same time one of the crises that is facing the world is the supply of water." A predictably furious response ensued from the £2-billion-per-year industry, which demanded a retraction of the minister's remarks, while pointing out the estimated twenty thousand jobs at stake in the sector. However, Conservative Party shadow environment secretary Peter Ainsworth took his Labour counterpart's side. "I don't think Phil Woolas is wrong," he said. "Huge amounts are imported from other countries – some now ludicrously from the Far East. This is an ecological nightmare and it doesn't make economic sense either. It certainly raises questions about the basis on which we have constructed our economic lives" (L. Smith 2008).

Bottled water also came under fire in the elite press: depicted in the left-leaning *Observer* as "the ultimate symbol of unsustainable profligacy" (Siegle 2008) and in the right-wing *Telegraph* as "completely crazy" (Hailes 2008). Meanwhile, the government cut its own bottled water consumption when the cabinet secretary told departments to serve tap water at meetings (Cabinet Office 2008). The Victorian-era demand for the provision of safe public drinking fountains also returned, to which Livingstone's successor, Boris Johnson, gave his support; although progress was slow, some new fountains appeared for the first time in decades and plans emerged to restore others (Gallagher 2009; Mayor of London 2011, 65–6). A "Find-a-Fountain" (2011) campaign – backed by the maker of refillable, collapsible pocket-bottles – also emerged to "increase the number of free water sources across the nation and make them easier to find."

Bottled water did have defenders, such as libertarian bloggers who denounced "control freak ravings from UKGov" and "morally unacceptable" attempts to "to tell people how to spend their own damn money" (De Havilland 2008). The leading bottled water firms, Nestlé, Danone, and Highland Spring, joined forces in 2008 to fight back against falling sales and re-legitimate their product through a new Natural Hydration Council, "dedicated to researching the science and communicating the facts about healthy hydration" (NHC 2012). To regain the moral high ground, the NHC argued that bottled water was better than sugary drinks linked to obesity.

Bottled water had much in common with plastic bags: both were highly visible, environmentally profligate products that large numbers of people perceived, or could be persuaded to see, as unnecessary. As well, in both cases, alternatives were easily available to consumers, and campaigners were able to find a populist angle to critique business-driven excess. Furthermore, the businesses directly at risk from lower consumption were not core economic sectors. Other economic interests also stood to gain from providing alternatives, such as the private water firms and, in the case of reusable bags, their producers and the retailers that sold them. The sense that consumption was out of control thus found favourable terrain in campaigns against these items.

That said, it was not clear that the anti–bottled water campaigns' initial achievements would be sustained. After more than a decade of rapid growth, UK bottled water consumption appeared to peak at

2.21 billion litres in 2006. When the campaigns against the product took off, consumption fell sharply, by 10 per cent, to 2.00 billion litres in 2008; however, consumption crept back up to 2.14 billion litres by 2012 (British Bottled Water 2013). The industry was optimistic about renewed growth, with forecasts of 2.4 million litres in sales by 2016. It appeared the industry's efforts to restore its reputation and promote "convenient and healthy hydration on-the-go" were having some impact (Zenith International 2012). Like many other sufficiency campaigns, victories in reducing bottled water consumption were provisional and had to overcome determined forces seeking sustained growth. One could still consider bottled water a *relatively* easy target, but little was easy in an absolute sense for a sufficiency approach.

As in Canada, the trio of vulnerable targets also included energy-guzzling incandescent light bulbs, although the light bulb issue was more easily understood as being about efficiency than sufficiency. In 2005, a "Ban the Bulb" campaign began in the UK and soon saw results. At the March 2007 European Council meeting, Tony Blair and other EU leaders called on the European Commission to develop plans to scrap incandescent light bulbs as part of a new climate and energy package. By September 2007, major UK retailers voluntarily agreed to begin phasing out sales of the bulbs. In 2009, the EU announced that the ban would start with 100W bulbs later that year, with the final step – phase-out of 40 and 25W bulbs – in September 2012. These measures led to media reports that lighting traditionalists were "incandescent" (Randall 2009), and provoked grumblings among ideologues and the Eurosceptic right about "nanny state" controls over consumers and subjugation to Brussels. The *Telegraph* even "revealed" that the man behind the EU ban, Energy Commissioner Andris Piebalgs of Latvia, was a "former communist" (R. Gray 2009). Despite media opposition, change occurred quickly, with the Ban the Bulb campaign achieving its aim only seven years after it began. Alternatives for consumers were readily available and profitably provided by firms that produced the old bulbs – indeed, critics of the ban even denounced the "Unholy Alliance between Philips and the Greens" (Kasteren and Tennekes 2010). Banning the bulb was a low-cost way for political leaders to signal their commitment to climate action – not to mention actually cut carbon – while it did not represent a major challenge to any powerful group's economic interests.

FOOD: CUTTING WASTE, DISTANCES, AND MEAT AND DAIRY

As the food supply chain accounted for an estimated 22 per cent of UK GHG emissions (Defra 2009a, 46), the stakes with respect to food were much higher than with plastic bags or bottled water. While potential GHG reductions from limiting food waste, food miles, and meat and dairy product consumption were considerable, so too were the obstacles and complexities.

Food Waste: Efficiency Sliding into Sufficiency

Food waste, a core government concern during years of wartime rationing, returned to the public agenda. It provided an example of how EM's focus on increased efficiency and waste reduction could slip into a sufficiency-based critique of over-consumption.

In 2007, the Waste & Resources Action Programme (WRAP), a government-funded, not-for-profit company whose core goal was "to accelerate resource efficiency," launched the "Love Food Hate Waste" campaign. Food diary studies showed that UK consumers threw away about one third of all food purchased, at least half of which could have been eaten. In other words, "for every three bags of shopping we bring home, we effectively put one straight in the bin" (WRAP 2007a). Since rotting food in landfills generates methane, a potent GHG, and the embedded energy involved in production, packaging, transport, and delivery of wasted food resulted in some 15 MtCO$_2$ per year, cutting food waste could "make a big impact – the same as taking 1 in 5 cars off UK roads" (WRAP 2007a). In addition to highlighting such ecological benefits, the campaign could tap into the strong social stigma against throwing away food, which many participants in Defra's (2007d) Citizen's Summit on Climate Change considered morally "wrong" (62). Yet significant obstacles to reducing food waste were also evident, including the need for better planning when shopping and cooking which, in turn, involved changing ingrained habits (58).

WRAP's (2007a) media release on the campaign launch did its best to stick to an EM message about potential environmental and economic gains, emphasizing that needless food waste cost £8 billion a year. The agency added, "We also need the food industry to change," promising to "work with them to improve their environmental, social and economic performance." Meanwhile, language on the Love Food Hate Waste campaign's website (WRAP 2008), a useful source of tips to better plan one's shopping and use of food, was positively Ben Franklinesque in promoting efficiency: "get the most out of the food we buy," "save time and money," "save pennies and the planet," "shortcuts for making food go further," and "cook once, eat twice" with recipes for British leftover specialities such as bubble and squeak.

In 2009, the government launched a "war on waste." In addition to funding anaerobic digestion plants to turn food waste into energy, the program included working with retailers on new, more optimal food packaging sizes and ending misleading "best before" labels that led cautious consumers to throw out food unnecessarily (Defra 2009b; Shields 2009). Its "Food 2030" strategy listed "reducing, reusing, and reprocessing waste" as one of six priorities – one with economic and environmental benefits (HM Government 2010, 53–6). A win-win EM message was also evident in the Committee on Climate Changes's (CCC 2010b, 307) *Fourth Carbon Budget*; citing the billions of pounds spent on wasted food, it saw potential for 10 $Mtco_2e$ in GHG reduction while saving households money.

The food waste discussion could not, however, be contained within the bounds of an EM focus on efficiency. "Britons must swap their wasteful habits with food for the thrifty approach of previous generations by buying less," began the *Independent*'s report on the Love Food Hate Waste campaign (M. Hickman 2007a). It noted that Joan Ruddock, minister for climate change, biodiversity and waste, had called for a "'cultural' move against overshopping." In a speech on diverting waste from landfill, Ruddock (2007) stated, "We should begin by reducing the amount of food we buy. We need to plan beforehand. We buy too much in the first place. Then we cook too much ... I think it's an extraordinary comment on our times that that the average household feels able to waste £250–400 each year on food it throws away." While the public messaging in WRAP's initial campaign press release avoided talk of "overshopping" and the need to buy less, these were recurring themes in its more detailed summary of food waste research (WRAP 2007b, 5, 9, 10, 12, 17). One concern was "BOGOF" (buy one get one free) marketing, which led to unnecessary food purchases. Similarly, the Love Food Hate Waste website's official message skirted any explicit call to buy less, but that conclusion was hard to avoid – although one could conceivably stop throwing out one of every three bags of food by eating 50 per cent more. Many comments on the site from the public reflected an understanding of the issue that went beyond ideas of efficiency. As Toni Spain from Folkestone put it, "We all need to learn to buy only what we need" (WRAP 2008). Wendy Tooke from Stevenage added: "My Dad used to use a lovely phrase from the war for dinners made from left overs – 'make do and mend.' He used it as an apology when money was tight but in my family it now stands for wholesome family dinners made with love and a bit of creativity … A lot of people have lost touch with what food is and what it does to your body and soul – they just treat it as another commodity. More is not better."

Participants in the food waste debate also highlighted other important sufficiency themes: the negative impacts on the global South of excessive consumption by rich nations and the need to confront consumption growth more generally. Author Tristram Stuart (2009, 9), who exposed the scandalous levels of food waste, argued that with globally traded food commodities such as cereals, "putting food in the bin really is equivalent to taking it off the world market and out of the mouths of the starving." He added that wasted cereal-based foods in the UK and USA could alleviate the hunger of more than 224 million people. Tom MacMillan (2009), executive director of the Food Ethics Council, concurred on the need to stop food waste, but went further. He argued that in an inequitable, growth-based economy, land and resources freed up by cutting food waste would likely be used to produce other things for rich-world consumption, such as more resource-intensive and expensive foods, bio-energy, textiles, or industrial products. MacMillan said, "Consumption growth and persistent inequalities look set to undo the good that cutting food waste does in reducing our overall use of natural resources and improving food security. Now is the moment all parties should be searching out ways to define prosperity that get away from runaway consumption" (Food Ethics Council 2009).

Efforts to cut food waste produced results. WRAP (2013a, 3, 6) reported that, from 2007 to 2012, avoidable household food and drink waste fell by 21 per cent to 4.2 million tonnes – reducing emissions by some 4.4 million tonnes of CO_2e per year. In addition to the Love Food Hate Waste initiative, factors leading to the decline in waste included higher food prices, lower disposable incomes due to the recession, and the efforts of grocery retailers that had signed the voluntary Courtauld Commitment to cut waste and carbon. While retailers might have been happy to save money on their own food waste – e.g.

by using new packaging to keep produce on the shelf longer before having to pay for disposal (Tesco 2012) – they likely had mixed feelings, at best, over the full implications of the "war on waste." As evidence of success, WRAP (2011, 11–12) pointed to reduced purchases of food and drink – one million tonnes less in 2009 than 2006. Although an EM emphasis on greater efficiency was WRAP's mandate, the ultimate implication of its work, and a key sign of its success, was sufficiency with respect to food purchases.

Fewer Food Miles, More Local Production, Less Carbon?

"Use spades, not ships: Grow your own food," urged one Second World War home-front poster at a re-created "Dig for Victory" allotment in St. James's Park in 2007. The poster display was timely as reducing food transport, or food miles, was another wartime concern that was back on the public agenda. Like food-waste reduction, cutting food miles intertwined elements of efficiency and sufficiency. Lowering the ratio of miles travelled per unit of food was, from one angle, a form of eco-efficiency. However, saying "enough" with respect to the distances travelled by food also challenged the modern trend toward ever-longer supply lines in search of gains from specialization, economies of scale, and lower labour costs, made possible by seemingly abundant fossil fuels (e.g. Sachs, Loske, and Linz 1998, 145; SERI et al. 2006, 13).

Advocates of food-miles reduction saw considerable potential from partially reversing the (ir)rationalization of modern agriculture. As Stephan Harding of Schumacher College noted, "We do things like make butter here and send it to Denmark and then import their butter. It's just absurd." Beyond countering such absurdities, eating food grown closer to home held the promise of a fresher, healthier diet. It also had a political advantage that sufficiency-based proposals often lack: support from domestic producers who would gain economically. The National Farmers' Union was an early supporter of reducing food miles. For example, it backed an ad campaign against the eleven-thousand-mile voyage of butter from New Zealand and launched a "local food finder" online (Mercer 2006; NFU 2007). The UK-based *Farmers Weekly* (2006a, 2006b) ran an influential "Local food is miles better" campaign, endorsed by Environment Secretary David Miliband, Foreign Secretary Margaret Beckett, and Tory leader David

Cameron, among many others. Media attention to the circuitous global travels of food (e.g. Ungoed-Thomas 2007) and public concern led supermarkets to launch food-miles-reduction initiatives, including moves by Tesco and Marks and Spencer to label air-freighted products. Meanwhile, Defra (2005) found that CO_2 emissions from food transport rose 12 per cent from 1992 to 2002. Moving food accounted for 25 per cent of all heavy-goods vehicle traffic in Britain, generating environmental, social, and economic costs of over £9 billion annually, mostly from increased road congestion.

However, just as proposed EM solutions such as biofuels and offsetting were at least partially discredited in short order, so too was the concept of food miles called into question. Defra (2005) concluded early on that food miles were not an adequate sustainability indicator. "How the Myth of Food Miles Hurts the Planet," read one *Observer* headline as the media began to catch onto problems with an idea that had been hailed as "the means to empower the carbon-conscious consumer" (McKie 2008). The basic problem was that food miles only considered one element – not necessarily the most important one – of food's full carbon footprint. Indeed, transport accounted for only an estimated 9 per cent of the food chain's overall GHGs (HM Government 2010, 7). Another complication was the impact on foreign producers, including farmers in the global South, who Oxfam noted were among the most vulnerable to climate change, had done the least to create it, and were seeing livelihoods threatened by rich-world initiatives to mitigate it (D. Green 2008). Defenders of air-freighted Kenyan green beans pointed out that agricultural goods produced in distant lands by manual labour on fields enriched with manure could have a smaller footprint than UK production using diesel tractors and chemical fertilizers (Gareth Edwards-Jones, quoted in McKie 2008). Items grown in heated greenhouses in the UK or nearby nations – such as Dutch flowers (A. Williams 2007) – fared particularly badly compared to the South's lower-input production. Concern over the air freight debate led to a Valentine's Day intervention by International Development Secretary Hillary Benn (2007a), who encouraged Britons to keep buying African flowers, while the Department for International Development (DFID 2007) sought to discourage the Soil Association, Britain's leading organic advocacy group, from withdrawing organic certification from air-freighted produce.

Other research emerged to question the food miles concept, although it was sometimes hard to disentangle objective analysis from economic interest. A Carbon Trust–approved study concluded that shipping UK-caught langoustines to Thailand for manual de-shelling, before they were sent all the way back for sale and consumption – a practice environmentalists denounced as "madness" when first revealed (BBC 2006a) – was no worse than having fossil fuel–fed machines do the work in Britain (Enviros and Carbon Trust 2007). That conclusion depended on the accuracy of the data provided by the company, Young's, which might have felt some temptation to shine the best light possible on its decision to cut 120 jobs at a plant in Scotland. Meanwhile, the Green Party of Aotearoa New Zealand (2006), sharing their compatriots' alarm over potential eco-protectionism, wrote to the UK Greens "to correct misinformation on food miles." They appealed to their British counterparts not to support a campaign against Kiwi dairy and lamb, which a study by New Zealand researchers concluded were less emissions-intensive than homegrown British products despite the shipping involved, once factors such as fertilizer requirements, sources of animal feed, and the UK's more carbon-intensive electricity were considered (Saunders, Barber, and Taylor 2006). A subsequent study for Defra found that that food imports from New Zealand, Brazil, Israel, and Spain were not always more GHG-intensive than local UK produce, depending on factors such as the yield per hectare and need for refrigerated storage, as well as distance from the consumer (Williams et al. 2009).

The complexities of food miles led Tesco to remove its air freight labels as it worked on more comprehensive carbon labels (which also later had to be dropped due to their complexity and cost). Kenyan producers even added their own "Grown Under the Sun" label to distinguish their exports to the UK from European greenhouse produce (Oyuke 2007). The Labour government continued to distance itself from the concept of food miles, saying it was "not a helpful measure of food's environmental footprint" in its Food 2030 strategy (HM Government 2010, 47). Likewise, a guide for "food and drink: greener choices" informed citizens that "Food from a long way away doesn't necessarily have a big carbon footprint" (DirectGov 2010).

Reducing food miles still had a role to play. Buying local produce in season was the lowest carbon option for many items, while Defra (2007i) worked with the food industry to cut unnecessary food transport within Britain. Food and grocery companies would later proclaim that over 200 million food miles had been removed from UK roads as a result of their "Efficient Consumer Response" program set up in 2007 to reduce food transport impacts, primarily through more efficient management of the vehicle fleet and some shift from road to rail (IGD 2012).

The idea that local food was better remained "common sense" to many people and political actors. "Localisation and Local Food" remained a key priority of the Green Party (2012), whose "Policies for a Sustainable Society" included commitments to "minimise transportation of food" and "promote a 'local food culture.'" Shortly after becoming the coalition government's environment secretary, Conservative Caroline Spelman (2010), expressed her ambition "to lead the way in encouraging public procurement to choose food which is local and involves the fewest food miles." Although her department did not act to prioritize local food, the National Health Service's Sustainable Development Unit (NHS SDU 2011) did propose a shift to more seasonal and local food in hospitals, and the Prince of Wales and the Soil Association (2011) congratulated several hospitals for their efforts to source locally and cut food miles.

It was somewhat surprising that there was not more government backing of efforts to localize the food supply, given the possible linkage with the economic imperative by expanding the local food sector, as had occurred in Ontario. Environment Secretary Spelman (2010) did refer positively to cases of local food sourcing that saved jobs among producers on the verge of bankruptcy. However, uncertainties over the ecological benefits and concern over the impacts on farmers in developing countries provided reasons for government to back away from a localization agenda. In addition, the dominant political parties shared a wider commitment to neo-liberal principles of open global markets. In the background was also the question of whether a "buy local" effort would comply with EU rules. In 2009, Sweden announced a buy local campaign as part of its Climate Smart Food program. The European Commission (2011; see also Barclay 2012, 8–9), which in the past had objected to "Buy British" and "Buy Irish" campaigns, considered this incompatible with the principle of free movement of goods, leading to the policy's withdrawal. Even with a possible linkage to the UK farm sector's economic interests, in this case, sufficiency-based ideas continued to struggle to make a bigger breakthrough.

Reducing Demand for Meat and Dairy

Meat and dairy consumption was also called into question, not only by environmental and animal rights campaigners, but also, to a limited degree, by organizations within government. Accumulating evidence of the climate impacts of livestock helped push this issue onto the public agenda. One of the most prominent studies came from the UN Food and Agriculture Organization, which concluded that livestock generated 18 per cent of global GHGs, even more than transport (Steinfeld et al. 2006) – with most estimates ranging from 10 to 25 per cent (UNEP 2012). In the UK, the Food Climate Research Network (FCRN) found that meat and dairy consumption accounted for 8 per cent of consumption-related GHGs, largely methane and nitrous oxide (Garnett 2007). Given such numbers, if the target of an 80 per cent GHG cut by 2050 was serious, emissions linked to meat and dairy consumption had to be confronted.

In the long run, techno-fixes for the problem were not unimaginable, especially if humanity could overcome scientific and cultural obstacles to lab-grown "manufactured meat." Indeed, the In Vitro Meat Consortium was working on it, and Dutch scientists produced the first strips of lab-grown muscle derived from stem cells in 2012. Researchers were also hard at work on changes to animal diets and vaccines to curb livestock belching and flatulence, as well as on understanding better pasturing strategies that could increase soil capture of carbon.

However, such efficiency- and technology-based solutions had limited prospects for the foreseeable future, adding weight to calls for cuts in animal-product consumption. The FCRN concluded that an EM-like "maximizing productivity" scenario – increasing "value for burp" through technologies such as "methane inhibitors" (Garnett 2007, 162) – would be inadequate to lessen livestock impacts. It called instead for livestock to be reared only on marginal land unsuited for other purposes, which required a shift from taking demand growth for granted toward policies to reduce dairy and meat demand (9–11). "Technology alone will not be sufficient to keep us to an emissions pathway that prevents a rise of more than 2 °C," wrote Garnett (2008, 147) of the FCRN. "This is as true of the food chain as it is for transport, and for other areas of commercial and individual consumption ... If we are all to eat, while keeping within required emissions limits, then we have to eat differently." The limited technological options to reduce per unit livestock emissions were also highlighted in a study in the UK-based medical journal the *Lancet*, which called for large cuts in rich nations' meat consumption for both health and environmental reasons, following a contraction-and-convergence logic (McMichael et al. 2007).[2] A subsequent Canadian study estimated that, given projected growth rates for livestock production, this one sector alone would account for some 70 per cent of humanity's "safe operating space" for GHG emissions by 2050 – even with generous assumptions about efficiency and technology improvements. The researchers concluded that, "Across the board reductions in per capita consumption of livestock products should ... be a policy priority" (Pelletier and Tyedmers 2010, 3; see also E. Davidson 2012).

Other analysis found that global reduction of meat consumption, in line with healthier eating recommendations, would cut the cost of meeting a 450 ppm CO_2e stabilization target by roughly 50 per cent in 2050 (Stehfest et al. 2009) – a finding that "clearly shows the value that dietary change could have on reducing GHG emissions," according to an OECD report (Stephenson 2010, 12). Meanwhile, a report for the Committee on Climate Change found that a 50 per cent reduction in livestock product consumption would reduce GHGs from primary food production by 19 per cent, while reducing the land area needed to feed the UK population (Audsley et al. 2011). That level of reduction in meat and dairy consumption would, in turn, improve public health – with an estimated 36,910 fewer deaths per year in Britain (Scarborough et al. 2012) – illustrating that sufficiency with respect to meat consumption had potential "win-win" benefits by improving well-being (see also Aston et al. 2012).

Armed with such analyses, campaigners stepped up efforts to cut meat and dairy consumption. "Go Vegan, Fight Climate Change," urged Animal Aid (2006). Celebrity Heather Mills helped the vegan/animal-rights group Viva! (2007) make the case that "the most effective action individuals can take to reduce global warming and other environmental catastrophes is to change their diet." While Viva! sought to catch eyes with its "Hey Meaty, you're making me so hot!" billboards featuring Mills looking sultry and dehydrated on a parched-earth backdrop, the Vegetarian Society (2007) appealed to different senses with "Silent But Deadly" ads dominated by the rear view of a cow. In 2009, Paul McCartney, backed by several celebrities, businessman Richard Branson, former chief scientist David King, and others, launched a "Meat-Free Mondays" campaign to appeal to those who were unlikely to give up meat completely, but might do so once a week. Friends of the Earth proclaimed that eating less meat could "save lives and the planet" under the banner of "Healthy Planet Eating" (FoE 2010), while WWF-UK launched a "Livewell 2020" campaign urging people to eat more plants and less meat.

The climate benefits of less consumption of animal products also entered the minds of some in government. A leaked email from an Environment Agency (EA) official to Viva! revealing government interest in the issue caused a minor media storm (Clover 2007; Ormsby 2007; Poulter 2007). The group had entered a comment on the EA website, asking why, when veganism had significant climate benefits, the agency was not promoting this message. An EA official wrote back: "Whilst potential benefit of a vegan diet in terms of climate impact could be very significant, encouraging the public to take a lifestyle decision as substantial as becoming vegan would be a request few are likely to take up." The official added: "You will be interested to hear that the Department of Environment, Food and Rural Affairs is working on a set of key environmental behaviour changes to mitigate climate change. Consumption of animal protein has been highlighted within that work. As a result the issue may start to figure in climate change communications in the future. It will be a case of introducing this gently as there is a risk of alienating the public majority ... Future Environment Agency communications are unlikely to ever suggest adopting a fully vegan lifestyle, but certainly encouraging people to examine their consumption of animal protein could be a key message" (Clover 2007).

While Viva! expressed dismay that the EA was aware of a vegan diet's ecological benefits but was not prepared to argue the case for it (Clover 2007), the *Daily Mail* whipped up alarm over the "secret plans to turn us all vegetarian" (Poulter 2007). While the paper played a "pro-environment" role when it turned its scandal-making machinery on plastic bag excess, its reaction to the Defra email demonstrated that the press could be a significant obstacle, not only to policy, but even to rational discussion of the need for sufficiency with respect to meat and other items. A spokesperson from Defra had to calm fears, saying, "The Government is not telling people to give up meat. It isn't the role of Government to enforce a dietary or lifestyle change on any individual" (Clover 2007).

That said, Defra did suggest that participants in its Citizens' Summit on Climate Change try to reduce dairy and meat consumption, among other GHG-reducing changes. This was "perhaps the least popular behaviour change with only a handful of people supporting it" (Defra 2007d, 58). Unlike with food waste, people had difficulty understanding why meat and dairy consumption was "bad," an idea that contradicted other long-held health and nutrition beliefs. Beyond that, many people undoubtedly would experience major diet change as a greater sacrifice than, say, using reusable bags or consuming clean water from a tap rather a costly bottle.

The government did provide, for a time, online suggestions for "greener choices" for food and drink that encouraged the choice of "climate-friendly foods" and noted that "meat and dairy foods have a much bigger effect on climate change and the environment than most grains, pulses, fruit and vegetables" (DirectGov 2010). However, the government's Food 2030 strategy did not encourage diets with less meat, claiming "the evidence to inform appropriate consumer choices and policy responses is currently unclear" (HM Government 2010, 48).

One noteworthy public initiative came from the National Health Service (NHS 2009, 45), the UK's largest public sector contributor to GHGs, which pledged "a reduction in the reliance on meat, dairy and eggs" in its carbon-reduction strategy. "We should not expect to see meat on every menu," said the director of the NHS Sustainable Development Unit (Jowit 2009).[3] Exaggerated headlines followed. The *Daily Mail*, for example, proclaimed: "Ban meat from hospital menus? That's just tripe!" (J. Clarke 2009). The NHS SDU (2011) clarified that "there are no plans to remove meat fully from NHS menus." It did, however, reiterate a commitment to "more seasonal food, more local food, and more use of sustainable and nutritionally valuable produce such as sustainably sourced fish," which "will reduce the reliance on meat and other products." It added that the NHS could "promote a meat-free day in hospitals."

At the local level, the UK's first Green Party–led council in Brighton and Hove promised Meat-Free Mondays in council cafeterias. It encountered a setback, however, when binmen rebelled against the lack of lamb and bacon butties on the menu. One worker spoke of "general disgust at being told no meat would be served in the staff canteen." The backlash forced a policy reversal, at least in that particular workplace (Ridgway 2011).

Sufficiency with respect to meat and dairy had great emissions reduction potential but faced considerable resistance. In addition to potentially alienating the meat-eating majority, the threat to economic interests was, as usual, an obstacle to sufficiency-oriented policy. The National Farmers' Union called the idea of state discouragement of meat consumption "simplistic" and "a cause for concern" (Clover 2007), and likewise dismissed McCartney's Meat-Free Mondays (Ford 2009). The FCRN, while advocating demand-reduction policies for animal products, also acknowledged potential negative impacts on farmers: "At current profit levels, a decline in production and consumption could terminally damage UK farmers and so a demand reduction scenario needs to be considered very carefully. But in our view it *does* need to be considered. Serious efforts to tackle climate change mean that we may be forced to consider options that we now find unthinkable. Such options may include reassessing current economic systems and ways of doing business" (Garnett 2007, 11; italics in original). Some groups gave thought to how to protect farmers' interests during a transition to climate-friendly diets. WWF and the Food Ethics Council argued, for example, that promoting "'less but better' (i.e. premium quality) meat and dairy could, in principle, preserve or boost profitability for producers by increasing margins" (MacMillan and Durant 2009). Potential opportunities also existed for producers of less-GHG-intensive meat, such as chicken, rather than beef and lamb.

As with other sufficiency-based ideas, commitment to deep GHG cuts – which pushed the state and others to scrutinize all GHG-intensive social practices – was a key driver of calls to cut animal product consumption, even in the face of serious obstacles. Or, as the *Daily Mail* described the alleged plot to get Britons to give up meat, "The extreme policy is being examined on the basis it could make a major contribution to slowing climate change" (Poulter 2007).

The UK was still a long way from any "extreme" policy on the issue. However, the government and its advisers – including the Sustainable Development Commission (SDC 2009) and the Chief Medical Officer (2010, 59) – were aware that curbing meat and dairy consumption could bring major climate and social benefits. The Committee on Climate Change recommended that the government seriously consider "the full range of measures" to encourage less emissions-intensive diets – from awareness raising to a carbon tax on food (CCC 2010b, 315, 322–3). Even Nicholas Stern, a key voice behind a pro-growth macroeconomic strategy, saw the need for sufficiency with respect to meat. "Meat is a wasteful use of water and creates a lot of greenhouse gases," Stern told the *Times*. "A vegetarian diet is better" (Pagnamenta 2009a).

CHELSEA TRACTORS: WAGING WAR ON THE SUV

Attempts to delegitimate high-carbon consumption made significant progress against 4×4 vehicles. The trend toward bigger, heavier vehicles was one reason why, despite greater engine efficiency, CO_2 from UK road transport rose 11 per cent from 1990 to 2007 (DECC 2012a). GHGs and other problems caused by 4×4s led to calls for sufficiency with respect to vehicle size and weight, first from ecological activists and later from some political and even business leaders. Indeed, both trends – bigger vehicles and rising transport emissions – were eventually broken, at least for the time being.

In Britain, urban 4×4s (SUVs) were vulnerable to a populist critique of elite excess in a way that differed from North America. During their fashionable phase, 4×4s were more of a badge of class in the UK, said Blake Ludwig, a transplanted American and co-founder of the Alliance Against Urban 4×4s. "People are trying to look like countrified gentry, posh, and like they've arrived." The label "Chelsea tractor" evoked the elite privilege of one of London's most exclusive neighbourhoods and the excesses of a commodity that was, to many eyes, out of place in the UK's cramped cities. "When I see a farmer going over rugged terrain in their four-wheel drive, I think that's a reasonable decision to have made. When you see someone trying to manoeuvre it round the school gates, you have to think 'you are a complete idiot,'" said Mayor Ken Livingstone, an early critic of such vehicles who was less afraid of insulting potential voters than most politicians, during his 2004 campaign (White and Muir 2004).

Seeing 4×4s proliferating on London streets after the start of the Iraq war, at a time of growing climate concern, prompted Ludwig and other eco-activists to act. The Alliance Against Urban 4×4s emerged in 2004 "to make driving a big 4×4 as socially unacceptable as drink-driving." Its initial actions included issuing mock parking tickets outlining the social and ecological costs of a "poor vehicle choice" infraction. Ludwig acknowledged such tactics were unlikely to change the minds of 4×4 drivers, who often reacted defensively at the intrusion into their personal space and decision-making, but said the main target was elsewhere: those who could see the tickets when walking by. The group's media work generated significant coverage, contributing, in Ludwig's estimation, to a perceptible shift in public opinion. "It's seen as un-cool to drive a 4×4. You're kind of labelled as a social pariah more and more now if you're seen driving a 4×4," he said. Others promoted a similar message, including Greenpeace UK (2006), which produced a none-too-subtle online video, featuring a pleasant, good-looking 4×4 driver ostracized by his co-workers ("What does your car say about you?" Answer: "I am a prick.") The impact of such campaigns was hard to quantify, but they did prompt the industry to defend SUVs and their drivers from "unhelpful stereotypes and inaccurate statistics," and to point, for example, to falling CO_2 emissions from SUVs over time (SMMT 2007).

Changing public attitudes enabled policy changes, including local measures such as CO_2-based parking fees. In the London Borough of Richmond (2007), the first local authority to introduce such fees, owners of the most-polluting cars faced increases from £100 to £300 per year, while Band A vehicles with the lowest emissions parked for free. Other London boroughs followed, including Islington, where residents backed the change in a referendum (D. Williams 2010). The idea spread to other cities, including Newcastle, Edinburgh, York, and Brighton. Rather than highlighting a punitive increase for high-carbon vehicles, some councils framed the policy as rewarding drivers of low-emissions cars with discounted parking, such as Manchester City Council's (2012) call to "Pollute Less, Pay Less." Richmond's new Conservative council scrapped CO_2-based parking after campaigning to stop the "fanatical hostility to the family car" (D. Williams 2011), but the idea continued to spread elsewhere – including the University of Nottingham (2011), which set parking fees based on CO_2 emissions and salary level.

Mayor Livingstone also accepted the Alliance's call for a CO_2-based congestion charge. He pledged to increase the daily fee for the biggest footprint vehicles – which accounted for 17 per cent of cars entering the Congestion Charge zone – from £8 to £25, or some £6,000 annually (GLA 2008). Low-emitting Band A and B vehicles, still few in number, were to be exempt. "Nobody needs to damage the environment by driving a gas guzzling Chelsea Tractor in central London," said Livingstone as he declared "war" on this vehicle class (GLA 2008;

Hines 2008). For a mayor facing a tight electoral race, this critique of excess was not necessarily a liability, given the target. One *Times* columnist likened 4×4s to tax-avoiding non-domestic residents, or non-doms, "with their moneyed, arrogant disregard for the city and wider humanity. Yeah, stiff them – and the Ferraris, Rollers and Bentleys – then reward the little guy" (J. Turner 2008).

Predictably, threatened businesses, such as UK-based Land Rover, attacked the CO_2-based charge. Porsche, fearing an 11 per cent drop in UK sales if the policy were enacted, took legal action, alleging an infringement of the free movement of goods and even of human rights (Porsche 2008; Sibun 2008). Its plight was unlikely to garner the same sympathy as, say, underdog African growers of air-freighted produce. However, the charge would hit some people who could be depicted as the "little guy," including families with people carriers (minivans), whose situation the measure's opponents highlighted (Porsche 2008; see also Crerar 2008).

Despite the opposition, this move against ecologically excessive consumption had a fighting chance to be an electoral winner since the revenues raised were earmarked for improved public transit, walking, and cycling infrastructure – potentially improving daily life for the average voter. Livingstone certainly made the CO_2-based charge a high-profile part of his 2008 campaign. However, Conservative Boris Johnson, who opposed the congestion charge reform, was victorious and cancelled it – with other factors appearing to drive the election result.[4] It was nevertheless significant that such a policy was on the verge of implementation.

Delegitimation of 4×4s and other gas guzzlers spread well beyond the usual green suspects. For example, Mark Moody-Stuart, Anglo American mining group chair and former Shell chairman, urged the EU to simply ban cars that go under 35 miles per gallon. Echoing Livingstone, he said, "Nobody needs a car that does 10–15 mpg." In fact, Moody-Stuart's proposal was more radical than Red Ken's: "When we eliminated coal fires in London we didn't say to people in Chelsea you can pay a bit more and toast your crumpets in front of an open fire – we said nobody, but nobody, could have an open fire" (Harrabin 2008a). The forces behind such an intervention require further exploration, but it appeared that, at least for some in the business class, climate change costs had become a more significant concern than the benefits of such vehicles in fuelling the "automobile-petroleum complex's" profits. Meanwhile, UK consumers were turning away from 4×4s (BBC 2007c; Massey 2008) – a trend that only accelerated with the large rise in fuel prices in late 2007–2008, road-tax increases, and the economic downturn.

For the Labour government, the gas guzzler issue involved a balancing act. In 2003, it set up the Low Carbon Vehicle Partnership (Low-CVP 2008) with industry and other stakeholders, giving it a mission to "accelerate a sustainable shift to low carbon vehicles and fuels in the UK and thereby stimulate opportunities for UK businesses." Ideally, economic and environmental gains would go hand-in-hand. In practice, some tension existed between the greener vehicle production of the future and the profits and jobs dependent on building gas guzzlers today, and between the goal of emissions cuts and political concerns about alienating motorists by penalizing past choices or future aspirations. Ludwig said the Department for Transport officials he encountered through the LowCVP were "lukewarm," fearing the Alliance would target UK firms such as Land Rover. Tensions between different goals came to the fore in the Labour government's own choices, as two-thirds of cabinet ministers continued driving cars in the top two emissions bands despite Britain's CO_2 targets. The issue created a split between ministers favouring a shift to lower-emission Prius hybrids and others defending British firms and workers, not to mention their own right to sit behind the wheel of a Jaguar (Russell 2008).

Anti-4×4 activists eventually made national level policy gains despite resistance from the auto industry and some drivers. The goals of the Alliance Against Urban 4×4s included increases in vehicle excise duty (VED), or road tax, on gas guzzlers. A graduated VED, with rates linked to CO_2 emissions, had existed since 2001, but tax differentials were too small to have much impact on consumer choices. That was to change with the 2008 budget, which widened the differentials in annual rates from £0 to £400 depending on the emissions band – with the difference reaching £475 by 2012. The 2008 budget also increased the number of graduated VED bands and introduced a "showroom tax," a hefty first-year registration charge of £950 on the most-polluting vehicles, which came into effect in 2010. The measures – although falling short of Liberal Democrat calls for an annual £2,000 "Chelsea tractor tax" – strengthened incentives for consumers not to lock themselves into costly high-carbon choices, while sending a signal to manufacturers about the likely evolution of demand.

In addition to financial incentives for greener vehicle choices, the government's market-oriented playbook included providing more complete information to consumers (DfT 2008, 11). For example, detailed fuel economy labels were developed to inform buyers of a vehicle's CO_2 emissions, fuel efficiency, and average yearly running costs – including fuel and CO_2-based road tax (LowCVP 2009).[5] Meanwhile, the strengthening of EU-level CO_2 regulations for vehicles, which the government supported, also promised to lead to a shift away from gas guzzlers.

The movement against oversized vehicles was a borderland where EM and sufficiency perspectives overlapped. An element of sufficiency was inherent in the critique of cars that had grown too big, but some framed the issue as a matter of greater efficiency. Moody-Stuart's call for a gas guzzler ban was part of a vision of doing "more for less" (Harrabin 2008a; Moody-Stuart 2008). Similarly, when asked about the alternatives backed by the Alliance Against Urban 4×4s, Ludwig said the main focus was to encourage people to buy more efficient, lower-carbon vehicles. To reward such choices, the Alliance put on its "good cop" hat, giving out "We Love Your Car" Valentines that thanked drivers of lower-emissions vehicles. The group's blog proclaimed, "We're not anti-car ... What we do find more interesting is redirecting the current trajectory of personal mobility away from large gas-guzzling, clumsy and poorly designed vehicles to something new, graceful and a harmonious part of our environment" (Alliance Against Urban 4×4s 2008). Although Ludwig criticized the government's timidity in demanding the industry improve its performance, his vision of lower-carbon vehicles and "taking the industrial revolution to the next stage" was not fundamentally different from the government's EM objectives. Others, while accepting the need for lower-carbon vehicles, framed the issue differently. Siân Berry, an Alliance co-founder who had become Green Party principal female speaker, outlined a transport vision that included "cycling and walking more and – crucially – reducing the demand for travel" (Green Party 2007a). Similarly, at a Low Carbon Vehicle Partnership conference, Green MEP Caroline Lucas spoke out against a narrow efficiency focus. "We have to be much more radical about reducing the need to travel," said Lucas, who called for "accessibility" to replace "mobility" as a goal (see also Green Party 2007b).

Those calling for action to rein in transport demand received support from the European Environment Agency (EEA). It reported that, while GHGs from most other sectors dropped after 1990 in the EU, transport emissions rose significantly due to higher transport volumes. Success in limiting CO_2 and other impacts from transport "still hinges on limiting (growth in) transport volumes," noted the EEA (2007, 4). It later concluded that the greatest potential for GHG-reduction came "from a combined package, in which technological improvements that reduce fuel consumption are used alongside measures to shift journeys to lower emission modes and to avoid the need to travel altogether. Achieving the desired reductions requires that we implement a package of policy measures that does not rely solely upon technology" (EEA 2010, 5).

The potential of such a package – a form of EM-sufficiency synthesis – was becoming evident in the UK. After rising steadily from 1990 to 2007, transport emissions fell in each of the next four years (DECC 2013c). The average new car became more efficient, with CO_2 emissions falling from 181.0 g/km in 2000 to 138.1 in 2011 – reflecting technological advances and a shift in market share from gas guzzlers to lower-emissions vehicles (SMMT 2012b, 3–4). New registrations of 4×4s/SUVs peaked in 2005, falling 29 per cent by 2009, before rebounding to 11 per cent below their peak in 2011 (SMMT 2012a, 26). Another factor was that vehicle kilometres travelled declined after 2007 – whereas previously their growth had eroded the gains from improved fuel efficiency (DECC 2013c). The number of cars on the roads also grew more slowly due to the economic crisis (SMMT 2012b, 10) – and actually fell in absolute terms in 2009 for the first time since the Second World War (Millward 2010b). Speculation emerged over whether the UK was on the verge of "peak car" (Goodwin 2012). If this combination of sufficiency – in vehicle size, numbers, and distance travelled – and greater efficiency could be sustained, there was indeed potential for significant reductions in road transport emissions in the years ahead.

AIR TRAVEL: HALTING HEATHROW EXPANSION

Air travel was the best of candidates and the worst of candidates for sufficiency. In no other sector were the limits of an EM strategy and the case for sufficiency so clear. At the same time, it was particularly difficult to convince people that living better could go hand in hand with flying less. Despite the obstacles, the aviation sector saw one of the most significant victories for sufficiency-oriented ideas with the cancellation of Heathrow's third runway.

The Aviation Battle Begins under Labour

Britons had, according to one estimate, the world's highest per capita CO_2 emissions from air travel (TGI 2007, 9). Yet the UK also became home to one of the planet's most significant anti-aviation campaigns, which took aim at the country's "binge-flying" culture.

These contradictions were evident shortly after I arrived in 2007. Coming from Canada, where there was minimal mainstream discussion of aviation's climate impact, I felt as if I had walked (ok, I flew) into an unfamiliar battle zone. "Green Lobby Launches War to Curb Domestic Flights," reported the *Independent*, which proclaimed on its March 17 cover that "The Battle of Newquay" was on. In the *Guardian* two days later, a full-page, back-cover ad from Greenpeace denounced British Airways (BA) for launching a new short-haul route from London to the Cornish resort town and offered passengers a free train ticket instead. In the same issue, other messages tempted would-be travellers: Ryanair advertised one-way flights to Germany, Croatia, and Mallorca for £9.99. Monarch Airlines offered price cuts on one million flights and six inches extra legroom. Online travel retailer lastminute.com proclaimed "Long Live the Short Break" and "Get Your 5 a Year" flights with bank-holiday deals to Copenhagen, Barcelona, and Dubai.

Anti-aviation forces struck another blow in the *Independent* on March 21. Three campaign groups took out a full-page ad on "The True Cost of Flying" (equivalent to 18.5 per cent of UK CO_2 emissions and rising fast, they estimated), urging people to tell Gordon Brown to "put the brakes on airport expansion," fly less, use video conferencing, and take trains instead. Another full-page ad from "Spurt" airlines launched a spoof Gordon Brown frequent flyer card with the slogan "Screw Global Warming. Let's Fly!" In the same issue, a real airline, EasyJet, asked, "Care about the environment? We do too." It claimed aviation only accounted for 1.6 per cent of global GHGs, "but we are not complacent." The *Independent* itself, whose editorials criticized aviation expansion, advertised two reader offers: a twelve-day tour of Peru and an "Aircraft Enthusiasts Day" with behind-the-scenes access at Manchester Airport and a fifty-five-minute flight with full in-flight commentary from pilots and air traffic control. (Apparently, the separation of editorial and marketing offices was still alive and well.)

Before arriving in the UK, I sensed the intensity of feeling on the issue. "Can you reassure me that you won't be flying to London purely to carry out the interviews?!" wrote one eco-activist in response to my email. Once I was in Britain, an interviewee spoke with disgust of the "monstrous" flying habits of his neighbours, who had just travelled to India and Australia, but he was kind enough not to bring up the matter of how I had appeared before him. Others were less subtle. "So, do you feel guilty about flying here?" asked a trade unionist at a TUC climate event. "I suppose I do, now that you mention it," I thought to myself. Back home, my only source of grief over flying was my own conscience. In Britain, at least in certain circles, flying was "the new farting loudly," as the *Economist* (2007b) put it, or "the new smoking."

Among the groups seeking to curb the sector's growth was the Aviation Environment Federation (AEF), which called for policies such as additional taxes on flights and a moratorium on airport expansion. In effect, it urged a combination of incentives for greater efficiency and a dose of sufficiency to bridge the gap between demand-side growth, then running at 6 per cent per year, and supply-side efficiency gains of about 2 per cent annually. "We think both of those are going to be necessary to close that gap between six and two so that it comes to something like four and four, at which point you stabilize the emissions from the industry," explained Peter Lockley, an AEF policy analyst, in 2007. "We're not asking for them to close down the industry or even stop its growth – just slow down the growth."

Others used more radical methods, such as the direct action group Plane Stupid. It sought to emulate the anti-road protests of the 1990s, which forced the government to scale back road-building plans. "What we're trying to do is get enough direct activists together to pose a threat to airport expansion – a financial threat. We're non-violent," Graham Thompson of Plane Stupid told me in 2007. The group's first action in 2005 targeted an airline conference that had failed to include climate change on the agenda. Activists entered the hall with rape alarms attached to helium balloons, set off the alarms, let go of the balloons, and brought a BA executive's speech to

Flying Causes Melting Ice Caps and Species Extinction	Health Warning Government impotence against aviation industry lobbying causes climate damage	Protect Your Children's Planet. Cut Down On Flying.
www.flyingsthenewsmoking.com	www.flyingsthenewsmoking.com	www.flyingsthenewsmoking.com

Figure 9.1 These proposed warning labels for flights from enoughsenough, World Development Movement, Greenpeace, and Plane Stupid appeared as ads in the *Guardian* on 2 July 2007.

a screeching halt. "The idea was for them to think, 'Ok, we're a target – and we're a target over climate change," explained Thompson. In 2006, the group occupied a taxiway at Nottingham East Midlands Airport, where Baptist minister Malcolm Carroll held a "sermon on the runway," including a remembrance of climate change victims and a reminder of the Bishop of London's comments that "Flying is a symptom of sin" (Plane Stupid 2006). Other targets included the British Airports Authority (BAA), airline offices, travel agents, and the roof of Parliament, from which activists hung two large banners reading "No third runway" and "BAA HQ." The former referred to Heathrow expansion plans and the latter to the "extraordinary level of collusion between the aviation industry and government" (Plane Stupid, 2008). The group was also one of many involved in the Climate Camp at Heathrow in 2007 to protest airport expansion plans.

Anti-aviation campaigners showed they were not only capable of being disruptive; they were well armed with scientific findings. Press reports commented on the number of people with graduate degrees at the Heathrow Climate Camp. A Canadian participant told the *Toronto Star*, "One thing that was obvious is the level of education within this movement. It's a bit scary when three quarters of the people around you have PhDs. You realize, 'These aren't dangerous people. These are people who have studied science'" (Potter 2007). Insisting that aviation executives read peer-reviewed science was one of Plane Stupid's demands, turning the tables on the tired stereotype of ill-informed environmentalists confronting scientifically literate, rational industry. On Tony Blair's tenth anniversary in power, Plane

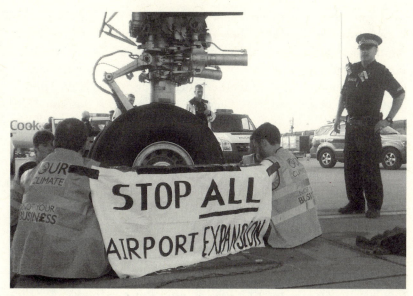

Figure 9.2 Activists occupy Manchester Airport, May 2010. Photo courtesy of Plane Stupid.

Stupid (2007) symbolically chained shut the revolving door to BAA headquarters and refused to allow staff to leave until they had read IPCC and Tyndall Centre for Climate Change Research reports. In fact, it was the Tyndall Centre's projections of UK emissions, backed by similar findings from Oxford University's Environmental Change Institute (ECI) (Cairns and Newson 2006), that provided "the key argument" Plane Stupid used to convince people, said Thompson.

The Tyndall Centre showed – using government projections of emissions growth that included generous estimates of potential efficiency and technology gains – that aviation alone would account for 25 to 51 per cent of the UK's 2050 carbon budget, assuming a weak 550 ppm stabilization target (figure 9.3). However in the context of a 450 ppm target, giving better odds, but still no guarantee, of staying below a 2°C increase, aviation would account for between 50 and 112 per cent of the UK's 2050 carbon budget (Bows and Anderson 2007, 106–7). All other sectors would have to dramatically, and perhaps completely, decarbonize to make room.

Thompson gave me a graph with even more worrying Tyndall Centre estimates (Bows and Anderson 2006), assuming faster emissions growth than the government predicted. It showed that even with a weak 550 ppm target, aviation would consume the full UK carbon budget by 2050. The data "show the untenable nature of the government's plans, if we accept their figures. And if you have independent figures, it's just nonsensical. Aviation growth and meeting the targets for emissions cuts – it's just mathematically impossible," said Thompson. Brenda Boardman from Oxford's ECI echoed his position, "Unless the rate of growth in flights is curbed, the UK cannot fulfil its commitments on climate change. If government wants to be confident about achieving its targets, it has to undertake demand management. Relying on technological fixes alone is totally unrealistic" (Oxford 2006; see also Cairns and Newson 2006).

Predictably, the industry put forward a different view. Ryanair CEO Michael O'Leary took the confrontational path, rejecting proposals to tax plane tickets to dampen demand as "the usual horseshit" and claiming aviation accounted for a "Mickey Mouse" percentage of GHGs (D. Milmo 2006). But most industry actors showed environmental concern by, for example, joining the Sustainable Aviation group. One member, EasyJet (2007), advertised that it used "the latest generation aircraft" and packed in more people per plane, which was a good thing – for the climate – as it reduced emissions per passenger kilometre. Under the banner of "Low cost, but not at any cost," Flybe (2007) claimed to be a leader in responsible flying. It trumpeted "the world's first aviation eco labelling scheme," a $2-billion investment in efficient planes, use of regional airports "which means less travel by car before you fly," and "the UK's leading carbon off-setting scheme." Meanwhile, Virgin Atlantic's Richard Branson heralded a new era of eco-flying with a biofuel test flight. Using 20 per cent biofuel in one of four fuel tanks required some 150,000 coconuts to take a single 747 on a short hop from Heathrow to Amsterdam. Extrapolating from these figures, critics noted that a fully biofuel-powered flight to New York would devour forty-five million coconuts, highlighting doubts about whether biofuels could be scaled up to meet global aviation demand (J. Jacobsen 2008; Virgin 2008). Branson did recognize the limits of first-generation biofuels and funded research into possible future sources, such as algae.

The industry also promised operating efficiencies from air traffic control improvements to allow more direct routing of flights, while it considered towing aircraft on the ground at airports to save fuel. It pointed to new aircraft designs over the long term: concepts such as

Figure 9.3 UK allowable carbon emissions and projected aviation emissions, 2000–2050.

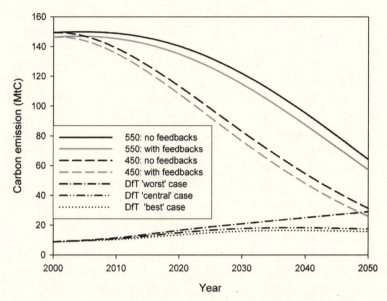

Based on Department of Transport projections of UK aviation emissions compared to contraction and convergence scenarios for 450 and 550 ppmv, with and without the incorporation of biogeochemical feedbacks.
Source: Tyndall Centre for Climate Change Research (Bows and Anderson 2007).

blended-wing bodies, use of lighter composite materials, contra-rotating fan engines mounted above the wing, and perhaps one day hydrogen power. Boeing (2007), which had a lucrative market in sales to discount British airlines, took out full-page ads in the UK press trumpeting the new 747-8 that emitted 15 per cent less CO_2 than the current 747-400 and claiming to bring "technology to new heights, environmental impact to new lows."

Speaking on the theme of "Maintaining Growth in a Low-Carbon Economy," Donal Dowds (2007), BAA's director of safety, security, and services, highlighted the airline industry's 70 per cent increase in fuel efficiency in the previous forty years and its target of a 50 per cent efficiency increase by 2020 over 2000 levels. This aspiration sounded impressive at first, but the industry's own Advisory Council for Aeronautics Research in Europe admitted it would require going beyond refining current engine design to "breakthrough technologies" that did not yet exist (HOCEAC 2004; Monbiot 2006b, 178; Quality of Life Policy Group 2007, 351). The efficiency target also only applied to new aircraft. Given the aircraft fleet's slow turnover, it would take decades for new efficient planes to displace older ones – unless airlines were prepared to scrap valuable capital with years of profitable life remaining. Even if achieved, a 50 per cent efficiency gain by 2020 would fall far behind growing passenger numbers.[6]

As the political battles heated up in 2007–08, aviation found itself without adequate technological solutions to its emission problems for the foreseeable future, making it different from other key sectors. Technologies for zero-carbon electricity and road transport already existed or were visible on the horizon. Some combination of renewables, nuclear power, and perhaps CCS could be used to power homes, businesses, and eventually electric or hydrogen vehicles – even if significant obstacles existed to deploying these technologies at the necessary pace and control of demand was likely also needed. In contrast, not only were projected efficiency gains in aviation far too small to keep up with demand, neither biofuels nor hydrogen yet offered scalable, sustainable alternatives to get planes off the ground. As the government acknowledged in its Aviation White Paper, "There is no viable alternative currently visible to kerosene as an aviation fuel" (DfT 2003, 40, par. 3.38; see also RCEP 2002, 26–8).

Aviation's limited technological options were emphasized by Monbiot (2006b, 182), who concluded that, uniquely among key sectors, "no technofix" was imaginable to cut air travel emissions deeply in the necessary time frame. As Ben Stewart, Greenpeace's chief media officer, put it, "The aviation industry is in a cul-de-sac. They have absolutely no way out apart from reducing the amount of planes that take off and land. And that's a huge leap for them because we're in a situation where economic growth is the golden egg of all corporations and they have to totally and utterly change their mindset. And they're not ready to do it."

Politicians could not ignore the lack of a technological fix. Ken Livingstone (2007) stated, "All the technology we need [to solve climate change] is there, with one exception: air traffic." David Miliband (2007c) admitted, "Critically there's no technological fix to replace kerosene." The Conservative Quality of Life Policy Group (2007, 351) noted that, "Only very modest efficiency gains are likely to be delivered, at least on a timescale compatible with the urgency of averting dangerous climate change … This leads us to conclude that some form of demand management is inevitable if the growth in aviation is to be squared with action to cut greenhouse gas emissions." Beyond the political sphere, even *Popular Science*, a US publication prone to seeing gee-whiz solutions to all problems, confessed that there was no obvious technical fix capable of keeping up with skyrocketing demand. Behind a cover hailing a "Hydrogen Hyper-Jet: New York to London in 2 Hours – Emissions-Free" was the admission that "the core of the greenhouse-gas problem" is "growth," and that "any solution is going to struggle to overcome the added carbon from the projected doubling of passenger aircraft in service by 2025" (Gaffney 2008, 41, 46). The industry could not fully hide from these realities. BAA (2007b) acknowledged that "aviation is growing at a faster rate than technology can reduce emissions and at present there is currently no significant alternative to burning kerosene" (see also Barkham 2008). The industry would, however, later return to themes of techno-optimism.

The industry also had other cards to play. "Emissions trading is key for BAA and aviation," said Dowds (2007; see also BAA 2007a, 14). The carbon market was also the preferred solution of the Labour government, which successfully pushed to include aviation in the EU ETS by 2012. The idea was backed by some airlines, including BA, Virgin, and the Sustainable Aviation group they were a part of, as long as the trading system met certain conditions, such as free allocation of allowances, to limit the cost burden. If public concern over climate change required action by governments and business to maintain legitimacy, then trading could allow aviation to keep growing, compensated for by emissions cuts in other sectors. "If we're going to keep flying more, we'll need less pollution from other sectors," said Environment Secretary David Miliband (2007c). "It's not such a bad thing if aviation accounts for 50 per cent of our emissions, as long as the total falls. These are social choices." The logic behind this was sound in principle: if people highly value flying, then it could be socially optimal to cut emissions in other sectors, while still respecting the overall cap.

In practice, however, it was doubtful whether other sectors could reduce emissions fast enough and would accept bearing that burden – and a much higher carbon price – to allow aviation to keep growing. As the House of Commons Environmental Audit Committee warned,

"Power companies, manufacturers, retailers, households, motorists and hauliers are already going to have to make significant efforts to decarbonise their lives and livelihoods. If the Government continues in its policy of allowing just this one industry to grow, it will either cause severe pain to all other sectors or provoke so much opposition as to fatally undermine its 2050 target" (HOCEAC 2006b, 61; see also Cairns and Newson 2006, 4).

The wide gap between the expected emissions reduction in aviation and other sectors was evident when, in 2009, the Labour government set a target that UK aviation emissions of CO_2 in 2050 should not exceed 2005 levels – that is, *122 per cent above 1990 levels*. The implication was that other sectors would have to cut their CO_2 emissions by roughly 90 per cent below 1990 levels to meet the overall 80 per cent reduction target (table 9.1).

Plane Stupid spokesperson Leo Murray (2009) saw the issue this way: "The government plans to let air travel stick at emissions levels that are already double what they were in 1990, and force every other person and every other sector of the economy to make even bigger cuts to accommodate this special treatment." Likewise, Tory shadow transport secretary Theresa Villiers (2009) noted that "it will be virtually impossible to keep [our climate change] promises without a slower long term aviation growth rate ... Nor would it be fair to ask other sectors to make much deeper cuts to give aviation the head room for continuing levels of very high growth."

Indeed, it seemed unlikely that other domestic sectors could free up enough room under the cap to accommodate unfettered aviation growth; however, the aviation industry could still hope that emissions trading would allow them to reach into the European and global markets to buy allowances. Perhaps this would delay the need to rein in aviation growth, but other nations, including poor developing ones, would likely face their own challenging reduction targets at some future point. It was thus doubtful whether other nations could provide large carbon credit supplies over the medium to long term (Cairns and Newson 2006, 8–9).

It was unclear how these issues would play out in the future. Over time, with a strict and gradually tightened cap, the cost of emissions credits would likely increase and eventually drive up the price of flying enough to slow and even stop demand growth – a way of bringing sufficiency through the back door. In fact, by May 2008, BA's support

Table 9.1 UK greenhouse gas emissions and targets

	1990 (Mtco₂e)	2050 (Mtco₂e)	Change from 1990 to 2050
GHGs (incl. IA&s)*	797	159	–80%
Aviation (domestic and international)	16.9	37.5	+122% (equal to 2005 levels)
GHGs (excl. IA&s)	774	118	–85%
Non-CO₂	183	55	–70%
CO₂ (excl. IA&s)	591	60–70	~ –90%

* IA&s = international aviation and shipping
Data sources: Committee on Climate Change (CCC 2010b,118); Department for Transport (DfT 2009,174).

for emissions trading was already being "severely tested" by the EU parliament's proposals to tighten the cap and make airlines pay for their allowances (Challen 2009, 120–1; A. Osborne 2008).[7] For politicians, there were political advantages in setting up an architecture that might address the issue in a long-term, indirect way, allowing them, during their own term of office, to escape the need to directly challenge people's desire to fly. However, there were potentially large long-term costs of skirting the issue through emissions trading rather than confronting head-on the immediate need to restrain demand. According to Cairns and Newson (2006, 73), "By initially transferring the onus for carbon reduction to other sectors, the air industry is encouraged to grow further before the brakes of demand restraint are applied ... If, in the long term, demand restraint for aviation will be necessary, then it will be more difficult to achieve this reduction at some future date when lifestyles have become more air dependent ... Demand restraint applied now is consequently likely to be a 'better buy' than demand restraint applied later."

In the face of doubts about the ability to reconcile aviation growth with deep GHG cuts, the old BAU argument also reappeared: the economy needed aviation growth and that consideration had to take precedence. Such arguments had evolved to include the requisite acknowledgment that climate change was serious, and often included the assurance that the ETS would take care of things, but the upshot that environmental concerns had to give way was still the same. This position was in abundant supply in November 2007 when, only a week after Gordon Brown suggested that the UK's GHG target might have to be tightened from 60 to 80 per cent by 2050, the government released proposals for a third Heathrow runway. Willie Walsh, BA's chief executive warned, "If we as a country turn our back on expanding Heathrow, we are throwing in the economic towel – and must prepare ourselves for the consequences of a low-growth, or perhaps no-growth, economy in the future" (BBC 2007a). Virgin Atlantic's Steve Ridgway added, "Limiting growth at Heathrow wouldn't prevent climate change because that growth would only go elsewhere. It would serve to damage the UK's competitiveness" (BBC 2007f). Speaking on behalf of a wider range of UK business, the CBI's Richard Lambert said, "Good air links are vital to UK businesses operating in a global economy, and Heathrow, as our national hub, has been constrained for too long" (Future Heathrow 2007).

Government leaders sang from the same hymnbook. Transport Secretary Ruth Kelly said Heathrow was "our main gateway to the global economy" and, without expansion, "jobs will be lost and the economy will suffer" (DfT 2007). Meanwhile, Gordon Brown (2007c) said, "Our prosperity depends on [Heathrow expansion]: Britain as a world financial centre must be readily accessible from around the world." Not only did the aviation industry and Labour present similar arguments; the revolving door between them was well travelled.[8] The *Sunday Times* also revealed government and BAA collusion in "reforecasting" noise and pollution levels near an expanded Heathrow after the original estimates would have breached maximum limits (Woolf and Ungoed-Thomas 2008). In the words of John McDonnell, a rebel Labour MP critical of aviation expansion, "BAA dominates the government's aviation policy" (Ungoed-Thomas 2008).

The aviation-expansion coalition included trade unions. The TUC was part of the aviation lobby groups Future Heathrow and Flying Matters. The latter was a coalition – including BAA, airlines, aerospace manufacturers, travel agents, and even the African Organic Farming Foundation – launched in 2007 to fight back against the anti-aviation campaign. TUC secretary Brendan Barber stated, "Aviation supports around 500,000 jobs in the UK, and many others in support services, so the future of Heathrow is crucial to our economy" (Future Heathrow 2007). Also backing Heathrow expansion were the Transport and General Workers' Union, GMB-Britain's General Union, and

Unite. The latter, the main union representing civil aviation workers, argued that expansion would create "quality jobs" – of the kind
that were no longer as abundant in the wake of manufacturing's
decline – and restore Heathrow's position in the face of competition
from Frankfurt, Amsterdam, and Paris (Unite 2007). Alternative
views on aviation did, however, exist within the trade unions – and
would become more prominent with time.[9]

Aviation interests had another line of defence, perhaps their
most powerful one: the attachment of most of the public to flying.
Although Tony Blair caught a great deal of media flak for the contrast between his own transatlantic holiday travel and his grand pro-
nouncements on climate change, a significant part of the public undoubtedly welcomed his remarks that it was "a bit impractical actually
to expect people to [holiday closer to home]." Blair added, "I'm still
waiting for the first politician who's actually running for office who's
going to come out and say [cancel all the cheap air travel] – and
they're not" (10 Downing Street 2007). The prime minister's stance
might not have been the kind of bold leadership needed in a carbon-
constrained world, but Blair was as skilled as anyone in knowing how
to win an election. "It is difficult for politicians because, despite the
high level of debate, there isn't really a general public acceptance
that they might have to curb their lifestyles," acknowledged Lockley.
As noted above, people had come to see foreign holidays as a well-
deserved treat (Defra 2007d). A government-funded study by University of Exeter researchers, using focus groups and questionnaires,
concluded that flying had become so embedded in people's lifestyles
that even the most environmentally minded were reluctant to fly less
(Black 2007). Anti-aviation campaigners also had to contend with
accusations of being "miserabilist" and guilty of "plane snobbery" by
criticizing growth of mass leisure travel (B. O'Neill 2008). Clearly, air
travel was a considerable challenge for advocates of sufficiency who
sought a win-win linkage between cuts in high-carbon consumption
and greater well-being.

Some mainstream politicians nevertheless did begin to question
people's attachment to frequent holiday travel. "It's nice to have
four or five flights a year, but at what price to the planet?" asked Ken
Livingstone (2007), who was otherwise inclined to emphasize GHG-
cutting actions that did not require people to sacrifice. He backed a
proposal floated briefly by the Tories: a "green air miles allowance" of

one tax-free flight per year, with all flights beyond that taxed at progressively higher rates – a measure that would reverse the ecologically perverse practice of rewarding frequent flyers. "We should maintain the present level of flights in London and the southeast, and price air travel to stop the growth," Livingstone added. Labour MP Colin Challen, chair of the All Party Parliamentary Climate Change Group, said policies were needed to encourage "people to appreciate their own country more ... rather than thinking 'we must fly abroad on holiday every time we want to go on holiday – that's our right.'" Meanwhile, the Conservatives' Quality of Life Policy Group (2007, 57) wrote: "Of course there will not always be easy 'win-wins.' Managing demand for aviation or motoring is strongly justified on environmental grounds, but is assumed to be detrimental to personal wellbeing. This conflict – if indeed there is one – has to be resolved through public information and debate. We would like to see the Conservative Party lead a focused discussion on what it means to lead a happy, satisfied life, and how this can be reconciled with environmental limits."

The popularity of travel was one reason campaigners emphasized stopping short-haul flights, for which trains were a viable low-carbon alternative. "The airlines will say we're trying to stop you from travelling and take away your democratic right to go where you want. But the fact of the matter is that a huge amount of flying is low utility," said Graham Thompson of Plane Stupid. He added: "Short-haul flights are the soft target. If you say to people, you just cannot fly, then they're going to be resistant to that message. And understandably. People like to travel. And there are certain places where travelling any other way, if you really must go there, is a bit of a hassle. But with short-haul flights ... it's pretty much as fast to get the train ... So if you can find these areas where the flight isn't really giving you a huge amount of benefit ... then that's the place to start trimming down the industry. The industry is not very happy about it because it's those areas where they have had big growth recently. And it's those areas where they are hoping to continue growing. But that's where we're destroying the climate without really benefiting."

Heathrow's top destinations included Manchester and Paris, both of which had frequent rail connections. Thompson noted that Paris-to-Brussels flights no longer existed since the train links were so good: "That's the model that we should follow. Not causing people to suffer in any way, but giving them a comfortable, quick, easy way of getting from A to B that does 10 per cent of the damage of flying." With such ideas in mind, Plane Stupid blockaded Manchester Airport's domestic departures area in October 2007 to demand an end to domestic and short-haul flights. The following month, Tory MP John Gummer brought such ideas into the House of Commons: "Nearly one quarter of the flights out of London's airports go to places that are easily reached in the same time by train. For example, what are we going to do about the thirty-odd flights a day to Manchester? There is no reason to have those" (Hansard 2007).

The rail option showed that it was not entirely true that technological solutions were lacking for aviation emissions. Video conferencing was another proven idea promoted by climate campaigners, one that could spare business people from the ordeals of air travel, notably a particular circle of hell called Heathrow. Meanwhile, Prince Charles raised the high-tech bar, appearing, like Obi-Wan Kenobi, by hologram at a conference in Abu Dhabi (Jacob 2008). But these technological solutions embraced and enabled sufficiency with respect to aviation.

Alternative technological options were a threat to aviation firms, but offered cost savings to other businesses. WWF-UK (2008), which challenged business to eliminate one in five flights, commissioned a survey of the FTSE 350, Britain's biggest firms, and found that 89 per cent expected to reduce air travel in the next ten years, 85 per cent saw video conferencing as a way to do so, and 77 per cent planned more train travel. One company to take up the challenge, Lloyds, later reported 143,000 fewer journeys compared to 2008 (2020 Climate Group 2012). Unlike the individual on holiday, for whom flying was a treat, business saw flying as a cost – one that was rising with fuel prices, but which it could often avoid with little downside. Firms also increasingly reported and scrutinized their carbon footprints, and business travel was often the biggest factor for non-manufacturing firms (WWF-UK 2008, 4). According to WWF-UK, "Twenty-first century business will operate in an increasingly carbon-constrained environment, and less air travel achieved through greater use of videoconferencing already looks like a key strategy for enabling continued growth and competitiveness" (5). In this case, the call for less air travel to enable more growth blurred the boundaries between sufficiency and ecological modernization.

That blurring of paradigmatic boundaries was also evident in the fact that the firms providing alternatives saw economic opportunities in slower aviation growth. Eurostar (2009) noted that while airlines

pledged to cut emissions 50 per cent by 2050, its high-speed rail services to the continent offered "an immediate 90% cut in journey emissions." It also predicted that domestic air travel would lose millions
of passengers if a British high-speed network were built (D. Milmo
2009a). Likewise, BT marketed its video conferencing services as a
carbon-cutting, cost-saving alternative to flying, and offered itself as
an example, claiming that lower travel costs and higher productivity
saved £238 million in 2007 (J. Murray 2008). Thanks to anti-aviation
activists, BT (2009) could also highlight the following legitimation
benefit for businesses: "Prevent bad publicity by being socially responsible, don't be shamed by pressure groups."

The anti-aviation campaign made significant inroads in a short
time. Campaigners increased awareness of aviation's impacts, opened
up space for critical debate about the sector, and challenged its very
legitimacy. Examples included the decision of Standard Life Investments to drop airline stocks from their ethical fund portfolios after
surveying their investors – illustrating that, in some eyes, airlines were
now "akin to arms dealers" and cigarette makers (Jamieson 2008). In
the *British Medical Journal*, doctors debated whether flying to international medical conferences was "an outdated luxury the planet
can't afford" (M. Green 2008). Passenger numbers also began to fall
from their peak of 240 million in 2007 to 211 million in 2010, before
rebounding to 221 million in 2012, according to Civil Aviation Authority statistics. However, these figures were heavily affected by the
recession. Whether passenger numbers would remain below peak
levels if and when steady economic growth resumed would be a key
indicator of how successful the anti-aviation campaigns had been in
reshaping attitudes and practices. Meanwhile, the campaign's most
significant victory was to come with a change of government.

The Coalition's Cancellation of Heathrow Expansion

In May 2010, the new Conservative–Liberal Democrat coalition cancelled the Heathrow third runway and said it would refuse permission for new runways at Gatwick and Stansted. For Gatwick Airport's
chairman, it was "mildly extraordinary" that a Tory-led government
had blocked aviation expansion in southeast England (D. Milmo
2010). Indeed, one Tory lobby group, Conservatives for International
Travel, had earlier posted on its website a mock "Wanted" poster of

Theresa Villiers, shadow transport secretary, with the caption, "For the crime of turning the Conservative Party into an anti-capitalist, eco-campaigning arm of Greenpeace" (Dale 2008).

Although the Tories were a long way from a green-left revolutionary force, they did deliver a major victory to a campaign motivated largely by sufficiency-based analysis. It is worth considering the forces that enabled this to happen. (For a more detailed account, see Hayden 2014b). The Conservative-led government clearly had not been won over by sufficiency-based thinking – even if currents of such thought existed in the party, as expressed in the Quality of Life Policy Group (2007) report. That document included calls for demand management with respect to aviation and a moratorium on airport expansion (351, 353–6) and, according to anti-aviation campaigner John Stewart (2010, 29), "revealed that new thinking on aviation might well be emerging within the Conservative Party."

Construction of a broad anti-expansion coalition was a key factor behind the Heathrow campaign's success – one emphasized by campaign activists (Garman 2010; J. Stewart 2009, 464). It was, in Monbiot's (2006a) words, "a coalition of homeowners and anarchists, of Nimbys and internationalists." The campaign actually began with local groups such as the No Third Runway Action Group (NoTRAG) and HACAN Clear Skies,[10] along with local councils resisting noise, air pollution, and the threatened bulldozing of communities. The local campaign went beyond NIMBY-ism by joining forces with airport expansion opponents across Britain, including groups such as Plane Stupid and the Aviation Environment Federation. Over time, the coalition came to include large environmental groups, such as Greenpeace, WWF, and the Royal Society for the Protection of Birds, as well as development NGOs such as Oxfam and Christian Aid concerned about climate impacts in the global South. According to Stewart (2009, 464), "To make possible this coalition, the campaign had to be about more than local concerns such as noise and community destruction. Above all, it had to be about climate change." This wider coalition united around a "new rhetoric of protest" centred on the sufficiency-based concept of "demand management" (Griggs and Howarth 2004, 2012).

Given the local unpopularity of the third runway, the Tories saw potential to win some Labour-held constituencies in 2010 by opposing it; however, the stakes were higher than simply winning votes under the flight path. The nationwide coalition ultimately turned the local Heathrow struggle into what Labour MP John McDonnell called the "iconic battleground for the campaign around climate change" (Mehr 2008; see also J. Stewart 2009, 464).

In the new cultural context of heightened awareness of aviation growth's climate costs, political positions on Heathrow became a matter of establishing legitimacy on environmental matters. "If you were a politician, how you felt about the third runway became a test of your commitment to dealing with climate change," said Ben Stewart of Greenpeace UK (Rosenthal 2010). Although Tony Blair and Gordon Brown did much to give the UK a global reputation as a climate leader, Labour's approval of Heathrow expansion – which the *Guardian* (2009a) called a "rare moment of truth for government" – undermined its green credibility at home. The Conservatives and Liberal Democrats were not alone in denouncing the failure to pass this green credibility test. Among the wide range of critics was actress Emma Thompson (2009), who stated, "They're asking all of us to reduce our energy consumption while they build another runway at Heathrow. I think it's the most egregious piece of hypocrisy I've seen in a long time."

For the Conservatives, opposing Heathrow expansion was particularly important to their wider efforts to re-legitimate themselves in the eyes of the electorate and "decontaminate" their brand. According to Carter (2009, 234), environmental issues in general had "great symbolic importance within Cameron's wider strategy of party renewal." Opposition to Heathrow's third runway was, along with rejection of new coal-fired power plants, one of two specific "symbolically important policy commitments," which, "by setting the party firmly against dominant business interests ... help sustain the impression that the Conservatives have changed" (Carter 2009, 240). Likewise, Tory MP Tim Yeo (2012) attributed Cameron's opposition to expanding Heathrow to the fact that he was "anxious to make the Conservatives greener and help detoxify their brand." After taking power, the Conservatives would have quickly lost their hard-won green credibility and image of being a changed party had they not lived up to their Heathrow pledge – a position buttressed by their coalition partners' anti-expansion position. (That said, the Tories later distanced themselves from opposition to new runways in the southeast as political conditions changed, as discussed below.)

Economic arguments would typically trump concerns over green legitimacy, but campaigners were also able to challenge the economic case. "We reasoned that we would make little headway unless we challenged the prevailing assumptions that airport expansion was essential for the economy," recounted campaigner John Stewart (2010, 8). Lockley of the AEF saw it this way: "The economic card is played very hard by the airlines. But you need to ask whether they are talking about *their own* economic self-interest, or the general health of UK plc."

A key weakness of claims that Heathrow expansion would bring multi-billion pound benefits was the failure to account for the costs of added carbon emissions, noise, air pollution, and traffic congestion. The Liberal Democrats, using the government's revised shadow price for carbon, showed that counting the climate costs all but eliminated the third runway's expected benefits (Adam 2009b). A WWF-commissioned study concluded that proper costing of carbon, among other tweaks in assumptions, would turn the government's estimated £5 billion benefit from Heathrow expansion into a £5 billion loss (K. Buchan 2008). The New Economics Foundation, which produced similar numbers, concluded that "building a Runway 3 would destroy rather than create value" (Kersley and Lawlor 2010, 3). These analyses suggested that, in a carbon-constrained world, Heathrow expansion was a case of "uneconomic growth," to use ecological economist Herman Daly's terminology. The Labour government did not go that far, but new environmental cost calculations did force the Department for Transport to downgrade its estimate of the benefits from £5.5 billion to less than £1 billion (L. Gray 2010a).

Other aspects of the economic case also came under scrutiny. Observers questioned the value of international transfer passengers "who never leave the airport" (Economist 2008) and the need for Heathrow to expand to serve as the UK's aviation hub, given that some of the most successful airlines had abandoned a hub-and-spoke model to focus on direct flights (Ayling 2008). A study commissioned by HACAN Clear Skies concluded that the models behind the government's case for expansion vastly overestimated the net benefits; for example, if aviation did not expand, people would find jobs in other sectors as consumers would spend their money on other goods and services (Boon et al. 2008). Mayor Ken Livingstone (2007) insisted that "we don't need to increase air traffic to maintain London's economic position" since only 15 to 18 per cent of London air traffic was business related. Given the predominance of holiday flying, critics maintained that more airport capacity would worsen the UK's multi-billion-pound tourism deficit by enabling more Britons to vacation abroad (Quality of Life Policy Group 2007, 355; Sewill 2009, 4, 17; J. Stewart 2009, 466). The *Sunday Times* (2009) and Monbiot (2009a) found common ground, questioning whether air travel would grow as fast as the Labour government assumed. It was not only a matter of the recession putting a dent in passenger numbers. The "huge efforts being made to reduce business travel" to cut costs and carbon helped make the economic case for the third runway "unconvincing" for Theresa Villiers, Tory shadow transport secretary, who referred in parliamentary debate to WWF-UK's study documenting business plans to reduce flying (Hansard 2009).

Doubts about the economic case enabled the Conservatives to take increasingly strong positions against Heathrow expansion. "There are now increasing grounds to believe that the economic case is flawed, even without addressing the serious environmental concerns," said David Cameron in June 2008 (Eaglesham and Done 2008). Three months later, the Tories declared that they would scrap the third runway if they came to power (Villiers 2008).

The work done to counter the economic case, along with concerns over climate and the public legitimacy of expansion, brought out more business opposition. In May 2009, thirteen business leaders from finance, media, and high-street retail – including James Murdoch of News Corporation – wrote a letter to the *Times* entitled "Business can do without a third runway." It stated that "the business case for the third runway simply does not stack up. Moreover, millions of people in the UK oppose the new runway. They are our customers and our colleagues. The business community must take account of the strongly held views of those living in the broader community in which we operate" (Armstong et al. 2009). The letter added that, "our approach to transport must reflect the seriousness with which we take our Climate Act target to cut emissions by 80 per cent by 2050." Leading business organizations such as the CBI still backed Heathrow expansion, but this rift in the corporate world had an impact. "The business opposition, when it eventually did come, was very important to the campaign," recalled Stewart (2010, 39).

An alternative current within the labour movement also became more vocal. Breaking with the TUC's support for aviation expansion, six trades unions, including the public service union Unison and the National Union of Rail, Maritime and Transport Workers (RMT), joined anti-aviation campaigners in taking out a full-page ad in the *Times*. "If the government pushes ahead with expanding our airports, including Heathrow, the UK will never be able to meet the new target of cutting emissions by at least 80% by 2050 and play its part in fighting climate change," said the ad. Calling the economic case for a third runway "unproven," the ad said the £13 billion cost would "be better spent on a low carbon and efficient high speed rail network linking the UK's major cities with the rest of Europe" (Unison, TSSA, et al. 2008).

The Climate Change Act also contributed to the third runway's defeat, as the need to live within its tight carbon constraints provided key arguments for sufficiency with respect to aviation. The act's impact was also evident in a March 2010 ruling by a High Court judge that the Labour government's approval of Heathrow expansion was without basis and its claims to the contrary were "untenable in law and common sense." Lord Justice Carnwath (2010; see also RBWM 2010) argued that increased estimates of the social cost of CO_2 had not been properly taken into account. Most significantly, he ruled that government could no longer base policy on its 2003 Aviation White Paper (DfT 2003), which emphasized expanding airport capacity to cater to projected demand growth. The judge in effect told the government to produce an aviation policy in line with the Climate Change Act and other key developments since 2003.

The act's carbon constraints also gave some in business a direct interest in blocking Heathrow expansion. As discussed above, given a fixed carbon budget and the lack of adequate technological solutions for aviation emissions, the greater the expansion of aviation, the greater the emissions reductions burden faced by other sectors. In the future, conflict between aviation and other sectors over shares of the limited carbon pie was likely to intensify, but a more immediate impact was within the aviation sector itself. This became evident after the release of a Committee on Climate Change report on how to achieve the aviation emissions target of not exceeding 2005 levels in 2050 (CCC 2009c). Lord Turner, chair of the CCC, summed up a key conclusion: "Given the likely pace of technological progress a demand increase of up to 60% but no more could be compatible with the government's target. Aviation policies should be consistent with this overall limit on demand growth, unless and until more rapid technological progress than currently anticipated makes any greater increase compatible with the target" (ccc 2009a). The need to limit demand growth to 60 per cent – well below the projected level of 200 per cent – did not necessarily rule out Heathrow's third runway; however, it did mean that Heathrow expansion would require some other airports to abandon growth plans, as the Campaign for Better Transport pointed out (cbt 2009; Webster 2009). Plane Stupid (2009) summed up the implications: "It's regional airports versus Heathrow in the fight to expand, because once we hit 60%, forget it." Fearing just such a scenario, Birmingham Airport's chief executive backed the Conservative Party's pledge to block expansion at Heathrow, Gatwick, and Stansted, stating, "Regional airports will be up in arms if Heathrow is allowed to expand while they are frozen" (Webster 2009; see also D. Milmo 2009b).

While advocates of sufficiency with respect to aviation faced great obstacles given the support for the third runway from powerful economic actors and claims that UK economic growth depended on the project, they were able to win an important victory. A broad anti-expansion coalition was able to turn Heathrow expansion into a test of ecological legitimacy and seriousness about the expressed commitment of all main political parties to deep carbon reduction – a test the Conservatives had a particular need to pass at that time. Meanwhile, anti-expansion campaigners were able to cast doubt on the claims that the third runway served the perceived imperative of economic growth. In this case, sufficiency-oriented campaigners did not have to challenge the overriding economic imperative or to link their cause to it; it was enough to show that the economic case for expansion was inconclusive, allowing the decision to be made on other grounds. However, the durability of this victory was not guaranteed.

Third Runway Rising from the Dead?

By 2012, the Tories were again open to expanding airport capacity in the southeast and considering, but reluctant to commit to, a Heathrow U-turn. The aviation industry and other key players in business had continued their forceful lobbying and revived arguments that London, and the UK more generally, risked losing out economically due to airport capacity constraints. Increasingly prominent was the claim that the UK lacked connections to rapidly growing Chinese cities (CBI 2012a; Matthews, McClusky, et al. 2012). Expansion proponents within government also claimed that the ecological issues had changed now that the ETS gave Heathrow expansion "environmental cover," as cuts in other sectors covered by the emissions cap would compensate for aviation emissions increases (Merrick and Chorley 2012; Yeo 2012).[11] However, no consensus existed among expansion supporters over whether the solution was a third or even fourth Heathrow runway, new capacity at Gatwick or Stansted, Mayor Johnson's proposed "Boris Island" airport in the Thames estuary, or other proposals. Meanwhile, a new Aviation Policy Framework also expressed the government's belief that "aviation needs to grow," albeit with the standard EM pledge to do so "whilst respecting the environment" (DfT 2013, 6).

Economic and political calculations had changed. As the government's anxiety grew over sluggish GDP growth, it became more open to the claims that airport expansion would boost the UK's economic prospects. The prolonged recession also gave proponents a new line of argument: the potential economic stimulus provided by a large infrastructure project, one financed privately rather than by the debt-crippled Treasury (Watt 2012). The primacy of economic concerns, and the increasing challenge to David Cameron from his political right, both from within his party and from UKIP, also reduced the political benefits of holding to a strong green position on Heathrow (and other issues). That said, the political costs of an "off-the-scale betrayal," as green Tory MP Zac Goldsmith described a potential Heathrow U-turn (BBC 2013), would be significant. The prospect of such a reversal not only raised the possibility of direct action by activists to block construction; it provoked tensions within the coalition and the Tory party itself, while it threatened the Conservatives' hold on Heathrow-area constituencies. Without easy options, the government devised a classic "solution." It kicked the issue into the long grass by launching a new commission to examine airport capacity options and deliver its final report after the 2015 election. This would allow the Conservatives to avoid a rupture with the Lib Dems, stay silent on Heathrow in their next election manifesto, and have the option of reviving Heathrow expansion if they were to win a majority government.

The aviation industry also pushed back against arguments that limited technological options required measures to dampen aviation growth. New high-tech ideas emerged, such as planes launched sky-ward by green-energy-powered catapults (Airbus 2012). However, the emphasis was on slightly more established ideas such as global carbon trading and biofuels, which had seen advances for use in avi-ation. In its "CO_2 road map," the Sustainable Aviation (2012) group claimed that efficiency, technology, and trading could cut UK avi-ation emissions 50 per cent below 2005 levels by 2050, with little need to limit growing demand.

Critics of aviation growth had to remake their case on a range of issues. These included the economic arguments (e.g. Monbiot 2012); the incompatibility of Britain's climate commitments with additional airport capacity (e.g. AEF 2013); the limited prospects for technologi-cal improvements when airplane designs were already optimized in aerodynamic and structural terms (Lister 2013); problems with bio-fuels, including evidence that more advanced algae-based fuels could not yet meet even a small fraction of fuel demand without unsustain-able ecological impacts (Committee on the Sustainable Development of Algal Biofuels 2012); the limits of emissions trading and shifting the burden onto other sectors; and the need to be wary of promised tech solutions before they had materialized and their tradeoffs had been assessed. "We are being sold a lot of promises," said Jean Leston of WWF-UK in response to the Sustainable Aviation group's roadmap. "They should not be allowed to expand until it has been demon-strated these efficiencies can be achieved" (Carrington 2012). "Those in favour of endless airport expansion must finally accept that there are ecological limits to aviation growth," maintained Green Party MP Caroline Lucas (2012). That was precisely what the industry was un-willing to accept, promising ongoing battles in the years ahead.

CONCLUSIONS

In the UK, sufficiency-based calls for reduced output and consump-tion targeted an extensive range of products, practices, and sectors. Other targets not mentioned above included patio heaters, which Energy Minister Malcolm Wicks labelled "environmental obscen-ities" due to their high CO_2 emissions serving little genuine need, and some major retailers stopped selling them (Brignall 2008). Critics of "fast fashion" argued that having fewer items lasting longer could cut the carbon footprint of clothing. Greens and others challenged the modern emphasis on speed by proposing lower speed limits to cut fuel use and emissions. Demands for sufficiency with respect to energy consumption were among the most far reaching in their implications – and Transition Towns took such ideas furthest with their work toward an "energy descent."

Sufficiency found some of its most favourable territory in debates over plastic bags and bottled water, which were high-profile symbols of excess for which alternatives were readily available, and whose consumption most people could reduce with minimal sacrifice. The firms threatened by lower consumption of these items were also of relatively limited importance to the UK economy. By supporting limits on these specific items, political actors needing to illustrate climate action could thus gain green legitimacy without running into insurmountable opposition or threatening the wider perceived imperative of economic growth.

Sufficiency made inroads in a number of cases where the boundaries between it and ecological modernization were blurred. The widely shared belief in the need to stamp out inefficiency, a staple of EM reform, could bring to the fore issues that ended up on sufficiency terrain. This was most evident with action to reduce food waste, which was presented as a way to improve efficiency and cut GHGs, but the message that people ought to buy less food was hard to avoid. Indeed, less spending on food was an indicator of these efforts' success. Meanwhile, urban 4×4s were attacked for their fuel inefficiency, but also for symbolizing the supersized consumption standards that, in some eyes, were no longer legitimate in a society aiming for deep GHG reductions. Food miles reduction similarly intertwined elements of efficiency (less transport per unit of food) and sufficiency (living within local limits). Environmentalists' appeals to businesses to reduce air travel also emphasized efficiency gains that could cut costs, carbon, and lost time. Meanwhile, micro-sufficiency and promotion of low-carbon technology – another key element of an EM program – could also overlap, which was evident in efforts to cut air travel through video conferencing and high-speed rail.

The idea of sufficiency received a boost, as in Canada, in cases where less of one thing coincided with economic opportunities to provide more of an alternative. In the case of air travel, rail services and video conferencing providers were among those urging people to fly less. British anti–bottled water campaigns could draw on the resources of the privatized water suppliers that saw bottled water as a competitor. There were also potential economic benefits to British farmers from reducing food miles; however, the UK government chose not to emphasize localization of the food supply for reasons including concern over the impacts on developing country farmers, uncertainties over the ecological benefits, and a neo-liberal commitment to open global markets.

Sufficiency was most necessary for types of consumption where large GHG volumes were at stake and limited scope existed for technological and efficiency-based solutions – meat and dairy products as well as air travel being two key examples. Yet these were two issues where resistance to consuming less was particularly strong – not only among influential economic interests, but equally if not more significantly among the general public, whom vote-seeking politicians were loath to alienate. Modest public sector initiatives nevertheless emerged to curb meat and dairy consumption, notably in the National Health Service. In the case of air travel, one of the most significant victories for sufficiency-based ideas came with the cancellation of Heathrow's third runway – a victory made possible by campaigners' successful efforts to cast doubts on the economic case for expansion and the need, at a particular political moment, for the Conservative Party to achieve green legitimacy as part of its wider brand "detoxification" efforts.

The various advances for sufficiency at the micro level were often provisional, with battles against those seeking sustained growth having to be fought and re-fought. Campaigns against plastic bags and bottled water were followed by falling consumption levels for a time, but numbers later started to rebound. Meanwhile, a third runway at Heathrow and other ways to expand airport capacity in the southeast were being considered once again. Nevertheless, these examples illustrated that, despite the odds, sufficiency-based ideas were making some inroads – in the minds of the public and even, to a very limited degree, within the state sphere. It is to the theme of sufficiency and the state that we turn next.

10

Sufficiency and the State in the UK:
Setting the Stage for Deeper Change?

This is the shortest chapter in this book, which is appropriate given that promoting macroeconomic growth and the capital accumulation it enables remains a core state priority. Nevertheless, UK state agencies and government leaders did play a role in some of the micro-sufficiency campaigns discussed previously, on issues such as cutting food waste and the use of plastic bags and bottled water, while policies were introduced to discourage purchases of urban 4x4s and other high-emissions vehicles. Although it did not do so from within a sufficiency paradigm, the Cameron-led coalition delivered a significant (although perhaps temporary) victory to opponents of aviation growth when it cancelled the Heathrow third runway.

Other state actions, which are the subject of this chapter, emerged out of an ecological modernization framework, but took the climate debate forward in a way that had the potential to end up on sufficiency terrain. These actions included embrace of a new language of living within limits, backed by deep carbon-reduction targets, as well as a turn toward promoting behaviour and lifestyle change. Without abandoning its commitment to GDP growth, the government gave the critics of growth one of their long-standing demands when it announced plans for a new well-being indicator. The Labour government floated the idea of tradable carbon rations (personal carbon allowances), generating significant interest and intellectual support for some form of carbon rationing to mobilize the "home front" to combat climate change. Perhaps most striking, the government's own sustainable development watchdog and adviser concluded that ecological modernization did not go far enough and the time had come to seek prosperity without growth.

LIVING WITHIN LIMITS AND ONE-PLANET LIVING

A degree of sufficiency infiltrated the language of government, which acknowledged the finite nature of the planet's resources, notably its carbon sinks, and the point that growth must take place within these limits. In 2005, the UK's Sustainable Development Strategy (HM Government 2005) explicitly acknowledged for the first time the principle of "living within environmental limits," which was put at the heart of the strategy. "We've moved the language here," said a Defra official. She added, however, that such changes in language did not represent a fundamental shift in the balance between economic growth and ecological/climate stability as government priorities.

Another language change was Environment Secretary David Miliband's (2006a) adoption of "one-planet living" as Defra's mission. The concept built on the ecological footprint analysis that Canadian William Rees originally developed to put limits to growth back on the agenda. In a speech entitled "Towards a One-Planet Economy," Miliband (2007c) referred to WWF's calculation that if "everyone in the world were to consume natural resources and generate carbon dioxide at the rate we do in the UK, we'd need three planets to support us." Miliband (2007b) added that "the science tells us that we are living well beyond our environmental means." He also framed the government's Climate Change Bill, with its legal framework for deep CO_2 reductions, as "in effect legislating to become a one-planet economy in relation to carbon," and gave initial support to personal carbon allowances (tradable carbon rations) as a future tool to "enable people to move towards one-planet living" (D. Miliband 2006c). The Tories' Quality of Life Policy Group (2007, 20) also embraced the concept, referring to the need for "One Nation Conservatism" to "walk hand-in-hand with One Planet Conservatism."

Moving from three-planet living – or four-planet living for Canadians – to one-planet living could conceivably be achieved without sufficiency, through eco-efficiency and green technology. Miliband (2007b) was clear about his preferred path: "We must achieve it not by cutting our consumption by two-thirds, but by dramatically increasing the productivity with which we use natural resources." Still, establishing one-planet living as a goal represented another partial inroad, albeit one that did not challenge economic growth directly, for the idea of sufficiency with respect to ecological demands. As a Defra employee explained, "The bet is still on sustainable growth." Having said that, he acknowledged that ideas such as one-planet living represented a "shift to a concept of strong sustainability with respect to climate change. Whether at some point that forces you to reconsider economic growth as sustainable, that's a possibility."

It was difficult to know what one-planet living would require in the future, but one could get some idea from initial attempts to create one-planet communities. Completed in 2002, the Beddington Zero Energy Development (BedzED), which consisted of one hundred dwellings in the south London borough of Sutton, was a groundbreaking eco-residential development. The attractive homes were super-insulated and built to maximize passive solar heating – a tour guide noted that many residents had purchased space heaters but did not need to use them. Many design features aimed to minimize electricity use; BedzED used energy efficient appliances and lighting, put living space upstairs and bedrooms downstairs to minimize lighting needs, and encouraged residents to have light-coloured walls. The site included space for a car-sharing club, London's first. Photovoltaics generated some 11 per cent of the residents' electricity needs. A community hot-water system, combined with aerated taps and showers, minimized energy needs for water heating. Although not 100 per cent zero carbon as originally hoped, the design and technology features reduced carbon emissions by 56 per cent compared to similar homes built at the same time (BioRegional 2006). This specially built eco-community had pushed eco-efficiency and green technology considerably further than one could realistically expect in the conventional housing stock that most people would live in for decades to come; yet even here, one-planet living was hard to achieve. "One planet-living is possible at BedzED, but only if you adhere to a sustainable lifestyle strategy," a guide explained. Given real-existing technology, that meant no flying and minimal driving, among other changes. On a display of BedzED residents' eco-footprints, "Nicole" came out best at 1.2 planets, while "Steve" consumed 2.8 planets worth of resources, roughly the UK average, due largely to a trans-Atlantic flight. The fact that one-planet living required lifestyle changes, in addition to greener technology, was not lost on government.

BEHAVIOUR AND LIFESTYLE CHANGE:
AN OPPORTUNITY, WITH PITFALLS, FOR SUFFICIENCY

Now that you've found your paradise
This is your kingdom to command
You can go outside and polish your car
Or sit by the fire in your Shangri-la
Here is your reward for working so hard
Gone are the lavatories in the back yard
Gone are the days when you dreamed of that car
You just want to sit in your Shangri-la

                           The Kinks, "Shangri-La," 1969

To the haunting sounds of the Kinks' critique of consumerist con-
formity, images appeared of middle-class Britons making use of a
patio heater, an electric clothes dryer, a family car, a video game con-
sole, a warm bath, an open fridge, and a busy airport terminal – leaving behind, with each step they take, a thick, tarry footprint. "We all
have a carbon footprint which contributes to climate change," says
a child's voice, before directing viewers to the government's "Act on
CO_2," website "to discover yours and how to reduce it" (Defra 2007b).

The ad, produced for the government's launch of an online carbon calculator, reflected the increasing emphasis on lifestyle change.
Government interest in influencing behaviour to combat climate
change went back at least as far as 1993 under Conservative PM John
Major, when the Department of the Environment ran a primetime ad
with a cartoon thermostat and a child's voice saying, "turning down
the heat by just one degree slows down global warming and saves
energy" (L. Hickman 2011). However, more intense promotion of
low-carbon behaviour change was to emerge under New Labour. According to Tony Blair, "Making the shift to a more sustainable lifestyle is one of the most important challenges for the 21st century.
The reality of climate change brings home to us the consequences
of not facing up to these challenges" (2006). Similarly, the intellectual most closely associated with the Blairite Third Way, Anthony
Giddens, argued, in his set of prescriptions for Gordon Brown's government, that "lifestyle change is at the heart of the environmental
agenda" and a "basic response to climate change" (2007, 133, 122).
Despite New Labour's hostility to anti-consumerism and Giddens's
derision of the green movement's "hair-shirt philosophy of everyday

life" (138), this turn toward lifestyle and behaviour change presented openings for the idea of sufficiency – as well as some pitfalls.

Transported to the UK, I was struck by the greater prominence of communications encouraging low-carbon lifestyle change. Much of this came from government departments and quasi-public agencies: "Pull the plug on your carbon footprint" (Defra), "Save your 20%" (Energy Saving Trust), "Less clutter in your boot means less CO_2," and "Less rev, rev, rev, rev, rev means less CO_2" (Department for Transport). Similarly, the Mayor of London's "DIY Planet Repairs" campaign encouraged residents to make simple changes such as switching off unused lights and appliances on standby, unplugging unused mobile phone chargers, turning down thermostats, and only boiling "what you need" when making a "cuppa." Mayor Livingstone (2007) told the *Guardian*'s Climate Change Summit that such actions could save the average family £100 per year and cut London's emissions by 3 per cent, without reducing quality of life. The mayor added, "You shouldn't flush the toilet when you've only had a pee." Livingstone noted the vast energy requirements to treat water to drinking standard, while offering reassurance that plague had yet to break out at City Hall under the new flushing regime.

The private sector also encouraged low-carbon behaviour change. Marks and Spencer ("Introducing our new designer labels: Designed to help you wash at 30°C") and Ariel detergent ("Turn to 30°: One way to help keep the world's temperature down") both sought to change the ways of a nation obsessed with hot-water washing. British Gas offered ominously named "Green Survival Packs" as part of its "make it greener where you are" campaign that encouraged a standard set of energy-saving changes. Meanwhile, several high-profile retailers, banks, media outlets and service providers joined the "We're in this Together" campaign that provided advice to consumers on reducing household emissions, along with related products and services. For corporations, promotion of low-carbon behaviour helped them brand themselves as carbon conscious and also helped market their green products, from eco-kettles to credit cards with lower rates on green spending – although it could also provoke allegations of greenwash unless accompanied by meaningful changes in the firms' own environmental practices.

Within government, lifestyle and behaviour change had become a "huge area," said a Defra official, who added that the environmental

debate had shifted away from simply controlling point-source pollutants: "Now it's about influencing the behaviour of multiple actors."
Defra's initial approach included giving people better information
and increasing carbon literacy, backed by some mild fiscal incentives,
to help them make better choices. The Act on CO_2 campaign and
online carbon calculator fit within that framework, which was consistent with standard economic theory about well-functioning markets.
Within this broad effort, one area of interest for Defra was influencing
people at the moment of key consumption choices that lock them
into specific patterns of energy use. "When you are buying a house,
let's give you an incentive to demand a more energy efficient house
where you can have a lower impact, so then we don't have to nag you
on a daily basis about light bulbs, turning things off, insulating, and
things like that," explained the Defra official. "Or if you are buying a
car, buy a fuel-efficient car and then we don't have to try to price you
out of ever using it." Government also set up a research program to
investigate more effective ways to promote pro-environmental behaviour change. "What we're trying to do is to create a dynamic change
of social norms and of default behaviour," said the Defra official. She
added that they were trying to change "what's normal" and "raise the
bar" for behaviour such as recycling, car use, and the degree to which
people insulate their homes.

The factors driving government toward a behaviour-change strategy were similar to those pushing others toward sufficiency: the combination of ambitious green targets and recognition of the limits of
existing approaches to meeting them. Tim Jackson, whose work on
"motivating sustainable consumption" (2005) created an initial basis
for government to approach these questions, said behaviour change
was "pushed to the front" because the Blair government had committed to aggressive carbon-reduction goals, yet struggled to find
conventional policies that could meet them. New Labour's market-
oriented ideology was averse to command-and-control regulation,
but green taxes – economists' textbook response to environmental
market failure – would have to reach seemingly politically impossible
levels to overcome inelastic demand for carbon-based energy. The
result was that "Third Way governance" had "nowhere to go in relation to carbon," said Jackson, other than asking people to change.
This problem was "painfully evident," he added, after the *Stern Review*'s release. Journalists pressed political leaders on how they would

respond: Which green taxes would they raise and by how much? Politicians were reluctant to commit to anything beyond modest green-tax increases with little potential impact. However, "the one single thing that came very clearly out of the media reaction and the policy response to the Stern report was behaviour change – we need people to change," said Jackson.

The way that behaviour change gained prominence as a "Third Way" alternative to taxes and command-and-control regulation left Jackson with reservations. One problem, he said, was that changing behaviour requires more than exhortation by governments; it requires changes in structure, access to different ways of operating, and ultimately different institutions: "What the behaviour change literature tells you ... is that you're not talking about a non-interventionist government – it just doesn't work. The interventions are not necessarily command-and-control interventions, but they are as much about building government, building governance as they are about thinning it out." Subsequent government documents did acknowledge the need to address a wide range of influences on behaviour, such as social norms, values, and the institutional framework and infrastructure, as well as the need for an "integrated package of measures to mobilise action" with a full "spectrum of policy and communication tools," including "coercive and non-coercive" ones (Defra 2008a; 2011, 8, 9). Some interventions did go beyond exhortation, such as grants and loans for energy efficiency and renewables. However, government was still some way from aggressively promoting the full range of social and policy changes – e.g. combining the discouragement of automobile use with urban form and infrastructure enabling people to live well without an automobile – that could enable wider lifestyle change.

Many other criticisms of the focus on individual behaviour appeared across the eco-political spectrum. At the Promethean end, James Woudhuysen (2007b) of De Montfort University rejected "the whole attempt to make us feel guilty about what we are doing" and the alleged reduction of politics to "if it's yellow let it mellow." Woudhuysen (2006) stated, "Really what we ought to be doing is focusing on supply-side innovations, rather than finger-wagging every time you boil a cup of tea." His vision of "transformative technological and social innovation" rather than "meddling micro-action" focused on aggressive promotion of big energy solutions: large-scale renewables, city-wide combined heat and power schemes, extensive cultivation of biofuels (possibly genetically modified), and a "can-do attitude" toward nuclear fission and fusion. "We should be more thoughtful about energy supply so that we can be more thoughtless about our own consumption," said Woudhuysen (2007a, 2007b). For different reasons, green policy analyst Mayer Hillman also rejected an emphasis on persuading people to adopt ecological practices voluntarily. "We should stop engaging in wishful thinking that sufficient people will make a sufficient reduction in their use of fossil fuels in sufficient time to prevent ecological catastrophe," said Hillman. He referred to the Second World War, when encouraging individual action was clearly insufficient: "You need conscription and my definition of conscription in this context is carbon rationing." Green MEP Caroline Lucas (2007) similarly said there was not enough time to wait for everyone "to have his or her own personal Green conversion on the way to ecological Damascus." She urged government to focus on creating a minimum floor of standards applying to all businesses and citizens. Socialists were especially likely to see lifestyle change as an individualization of responsibility that distracted from broader systemic change. "There is an enormous ideological offensive saying not to blame governments, and part of that is the emphasis on personal solutions," said Jonathan Neale at a gathering of Marxists in London. Neale (2007) argued that everyone should still make personal changes, but the key was to push for "social solutions." One study found that many of those trying to make low-carbon lifestyle change similarly concluded that social and structural change was needed to enable themselves, and others, to do so (Evans and Abrahamse 2009, 496–9).

In addition to intellectual criticisms, practical obstacles existed to behaviour-change promotion capable of nudging people beyond "consumption as usual" (Webb 2012, 117). These included suspicion that government was using the climate issue to increase taxes, doubts about the impact if others – whether next door, in America, or in China – did not change as well, resentment at being made to feel guilty over everyday actions, and scepticism about government and corporate hypocrisy. "It's 'Do as I say,' isn't it – not 'Do as I do,'" said a participant in one study – with Labour's simultaneous promotion of low-carbon lifestyle change and a third Heathrow runway an often-cited example (Platt and Retallack 2009, 5, 16–18; see also Defra

2007d, 14–15; Webb 2012, 115). Part of the challenge was to develop more effective communication strategies to reach segments of the public that had yet to adopt lower-carbon behaviour to a significant degree (Platt and Retallack 2009). Indeed, officials within the environment department were working on this issue (Defra 2008, 2011), although it was an uphill struggle to promote low-carbon behaviour in a culture that stoked the fires of consumer desire. One critic of these strategies maintained that, "With multiple sources of messages, conveying contradictory messages, and low levels of trust in government, social marketing and behaviour change campaigns are likely to fail simply by being ignored by the vast majority of those whose conduct is targeted" (Webb 2012, 115). A further obstacle to success was the rebound effect; a key attraction of lower-carbon behaviour was the cost savings on energy, which could enable people to spend more on other carbon-emitting goods and services. One participant in a deliberative workshop described her vision: "If I was to build a house tomorrow, it would have anything energy saving that I could possibly ram in it to make it as energy efficient as I could – and then I could have my Audi TT" (Platt and Retallack 2009, 5, 19; see also Druckman et al. 2011).

Although valid reasons existed for scepticism over government interest in behaviour-change promotion and its prospects for success, it did open up space to discuss the idea of consuming differently and the more challenging notion of consuming less – thereby creating opportunities (although no guarantees) for the discussion to move in a more radical direction. Jackson suggested that "lifestyle change" could be "a way of eliding the distinction between different consumption and less consumption," allowing a discussion of living differently without first having to register the need to consume less. To the extent that government was prepared to address the idea of less consumption, Jackson noted that it tried to keep this discussion within the bounds of an EM vision of decoupling ecological impacts from ever-rising economic value. It did so by distinguishing between consuming fewer materials (desirable) and consuming fewer goods and services (a problematic challenge to economic growth). Yet – as seen previously with the issue of food waste – it was not always easy to stop at that boundary once embarking on this path. Jackson gave the example of Defra's (2007d) Citizens' Summit on Climate Change, where participants were asked to try a range of different carbon-cutting behaviours. Suggested changes went beyond "just buying a more efficient car" to include driving less, repairing something rather than throwing it away, avoiding throwing away uneaten food, and cutting down on meat and dairy consumption (see also Defra 2011, 13). Behaviour change of this type, noted Jackson, "by implication, would mean consuming less in economic terms as well. So there's a bit of the agenda that quite clearly recognizes that there's a role for behaviour change which is dedicated towards sufficiency." Jackson pointed, however, to "a kind of doublethink that goes on" due to the inadequate reflection on the broader economic impacts and infrastructure needs – collapsing car markets, much greater demands on the public transport system, failures of businesses that provide unsustainable services, etc. – if everybody actually did what they were asked to do.

The government's Act on CO_2 calculator similarly illustrated how talk of behaviour change could slip from consuming differently into consuming less, despite official reticence about the latter. After entering details of one's home, appliances, and travel behaviour, the website not only estimated one's carbon footprint, but also provided a personalized action plan to reduce it. The first items in my top six tips were very specific, including "fit draught-proofing around doors and windows," "double glaze your windows," and "consider investing in an A-rated dishwasher." So far, there was nothing but encouragement to buy more goods, i.e. energy efficient ones. But when it came to the dominant factor behind my excessive footprint – air travel – the British state suddenly seemed less sure of its prescriptions. It offered only the following information on the summary page: "Air travel is making a growing contribution to CO_2 emissions" and "Just one long haul return flight can give a footprint similar to a year's use for a typical car." Digging a little deeper into my "full action plan," the first tentative suggestions that avoiding a major purchase might be the answer crept in: "Consider the need for a flight and the alternatives to taking a plane." More surprising was to receive HM Government's seal of approval for my main act of non-consumption: "You state you do not own a vehicle. Congratulations, by not owning a car or motorbike you are reducing your CO_2 footprint by about 3 tonnes compared to the typical footprint for a household with a car." This was a small and still rare example of state encouragement of less consumption, but that message was hard to avoid if the goal was to promote lifestyle change through carbon footprinting. The more successful the government was in its aims of increasing carbon literacy – of producing individuals who "internalize the logic of carbon reduction" as part of the emerging imperative of "carbon control" (While, Jonas, and Gibbs 2010, 85)[1] – the more widespread would be the realization that some of the most effective ways to limit one's footprint went beyond consuming differently to include consuming less. Avoiding car ownership and flying, limiting the number of electricity-consuming gadgets, buying not only an efficient home but a modestly sized one, sharing living space with others or – for a certain part of the population – doing without a second home, were among the ideas that followed logically from serious scrutiny of one's carbon footprint.

At least some members of the public were already reaching such conclusions. Ways to bypass consumption dominated a feature in the *Independent* (2007) with ten ideas from readers on how to lead a "less carbon-heavy lifestyle." The list included: "reduce your meat consumption"; "join a car club" (car-sharing system); "reuse and refuse plastic bags"; "holiday in the UK" ("Holidays are among our biggest sources of CO_2 emissions and the main element is the flight"); "don't bin things: reuse, Freecycle and buy second-hand"; and "keep your clothing footprint small" ("A low-carbon wardrobe is also a small wardrobe. Buy second-hand whenever possible and when you buy new, ensure they're things you really like and will wear for years.")[2] Taking lifestyle change further beyond the boundaries of EM was author Neil Boorman, who, after diagnosing himself as a victim of "obsessive branding disorder," burnt all his branded possessions in a bonfire in central London to start a year of living brand free. "If you believe carbon reduction is a necessity in safeguarding the planet, leading a less branded life is a good place to start. By turning off the TV and binning the glossy magazines we expose ourselves to less advertising and feel less compelled to consume," wrote Boorman (2007) on BBC's website.

Public agencies also became inadvertent conduits for anti-consumerist lifestyle messages. In the Environment Agency's survey of "25 experts" on "50 things that will save the planet," ranking ninth was "buying less, buying better" (EA 2007). For a government agency, this was "quite a bold statement, given that we are constantly told that avid consumption improves our lives and fuels the economy," noted the *Guardian*'s Leo Hickman (2007b). "My hope is that we come to see consumption as slightly naff, something you only do when you have to," said Chris Goodall, author of *How to Live a Low-Carbon Life*, in the Environment Agency's report.

Some powerful figures clearly did not want such anti-consumerist low-carbon lifestyle lessons to spread. While announcing £25 million in funding for a Sustainable Consumption Institute at the University of Manchester, Tesco chief executive Terry Leahy stated, "We need to move from a high-carbon to a low-carbon economy, but the answer is not 'do not consume.' It is intelligent consumption" (Attwood 2007). These mixed messages about whether or not to consume represented a significant cultural contradiction. A participant in a BBC (2007d) *Newsnight* climate change focus group stated, "You've got all these goods being chucked at you – you know, 'buy this, buy me, buy me, buy me.' You know, 'consume, consume, consume.' And on the other hand, you're getting 'don't do this, don't buy, be less wasteful.' And it's really very difficult to manoeuvre around this whole issue." It seemed likely to get more difficult, for individuals and society, too, in the years ahead to manage these contradictions as deep carbon-reduction targets encoded in law would begin to be felt.[3]

ALTERNATIVE WELL-BEING AND ECONOMIC INDICATORS

Public debate over the divergence between economic growth and stagnant measures of life satisfaction was a key factor pushing the idea of sufficiency onto the agenda (chapter 8). The call for alternative well-being and economic indicators to replace or supplement GDP was also a relatively uncontroversial outlet toward which doubts about economic growth could be channelled. This long-standing demand of the green movement entered the mainstream, eventually to become a matter of policy under the Conservative-led coalition. The debate over indicators produced a significant advance for sufficiency-oriented thinking, although it also served as a proxy for a more direct and controversial critique of growth.

The importance of alternative well-being measures to the green movement was illustrated, for example, by the Scottish Green Party's (2005, 5) Westminster Election Manifesto, which began with a quotation from Robert F. Kennedy, who concluded that gross national product "measures everything, in short, except that which makes life worthwhile." The manifesto said the Greens were "the only party

to challenge the measurement of economic well-being as Gross Domestic Product" (5), and pledged to replace GDP with a "genuine
progress indicator based on quality of life, distribution of income
and protection of environmental resources" (7). The New Economics Foundation likewise made new indicators the top demand in
their 2004 "well-being manifesto." Others calling for new measures
included Friends of the Earth, the Sustainable Development Commission (SDC 2003), and its chairman Jonathon Porritt (2007b), who
devoted a chapter of his book on the eco-reform of capitalism to
"changing the metrics."

On several occasions when I asked whether it was time to question the emphasis on economic growth, given that growth was outpacing carbon-intensity gains in many nations, respondents steered
their answers toward the safer ground of critiquing GDP as a measure.
For example, Friends of the Earth's executive director Tony Juniper
responded by highlighting his group's work with NEF on the Happy
Planet Index, which showed, for example, that Germany achieved
similar well-being to the US, but required only half the carbon to
do so.[4] Similarly, when asked whether growth should still be the top
social priority, Labour MP Colin Challen said, "We should have a well-
being index rather than an economic measure alone," adding, "We
do need to have more policies which top up quality of life not just in
materialistic terms."

Demands for new progress indicators were much less radical than
calls to stop pursuing economic growth, and become safe enough for
some business leaders (e.g. Prince of Wales Business and Environment Programme 2006, 11, 35) and mainstream politicians to embrace. Most notable was David Cameron (2006a), who spoke of the
need to look beyond GDP and was soon (2007b) quoting the same
Robert Kennedy speech as the Greens. Cameron (2006b) called for
a focus on "General Well-Being that goes beyond economic prosperity." Peter Madden (2006), chief executive of the sustainable development organization Forum for the Future, responded enthusiastically:
"Many of us in the British environmental movement have been campaigning for wider measures of progress for years. Few of us would
ever have expected a Conservative to be the first leader of a major
political party to propose this."

When it came to specifying an alternative indicator, the Conservatives at first hesitated. In September 2007, the Conservatives' Quality

of Life Policy Group was ready to propose use of the New Economics Foundation's Happy Planet Index (HPI) as a national well-being measure. Days before the group launched its groundbreaking report, the *Times* reported that "For some, the most controversial idea may be the proposed abandonment of GDP ... as the main measure of the nation's success" (Leake 2007a). It also cited "insiders" who said party chiefs feared that the group's ideas on well-being, such as replacing GDP with HPI, might be too "woolly" and "easily lampooned." In the end, the HPI recommendation was dropped in favour of a more general call to use broader measures of progress (Quality of Life Policy Group 2007, 21–2).

While there was a false start for the HPI within Conservative ranks, the government was working behind the scenes on national well-being accounts to supplement GDP. Initial steps in this area dated back at least as far as 1998, when Deputy Prime Minister John Prescott launched a "quality of life" barometer that included a set of thirteen economic, social, and environmental indicators (BBC 1998). In 2005, Defra set up the Whitehall Wellbeing Working Group (a.k.a. the Department of Happiness) and the Wellbeing Indicator Group to coordinate work across departments, including the Treasury, while the Sustainable Development Commission had its own work on "redefining progress" (SDC 2007). The Office of National Statistics (ONS) said well-being emerged as one of its analytical priorities in 2007 (Thomas and Evans 2010, 30). Meanwhile, international recognition grew of the need to look beyond GDP. The European Commission and the OECD were among those developing alternative indicators, while French president Nicholas Sarkozy pushed this agenda forward by commissioning two Nobel laureate economists, Joseph Stiglitz and Amartya Sen, to produce recommendations on new, comprehensive well-being measures.

David Cameron's enthusiasm for "General Well-Being" appeared to wane for a time, but he returned to the issue shortly after gaining power. Cameron instructed the ONS to devise a new well-being measure to complement, but not replace, GDP. In fact, the ONS was already working on it (Toynbee 2010), but political backing at the highest level raised the profile and potential impact of this work. In making the announcement, Cameron (2010b) noted that GDP had risen steadily in the west while "levels of contentment have remained static or even fallen." He added that the new measure "will open up a national debate about what really matters" and "reaffirms the fact that our success as a country is about more than economic growth." At the same time, he addressed fears in some quarters that "government is somehow sidelining economic growth as our first concern" by saying, "let me be very, very clear: growth is the essential foundation of all our aspirations." Indeed, as he was recognizing the failure of growth to improve well-being, Cameron (2010c) was promising business a "relentless focus on growth."

Cameron (2010b) tried to head off criticism that the new well-being initiative was "airy-fairy" and "impractical," but much cynical punditry predictably ensued: "Happiness Police are on the way," "Cameron sees himself as the Messiah of happiness," etc. (Naish 2010; Odone 2010). More serious were doubts about the timing, as Cameron rediscovered his softer, "detoxifying" side just as a harsh round of public sector austerity began. As one supporter of the new measure acknowledged, "It is of course difficult to trust a government that claims a commitment to wellbeing while simultaneously slashing funding for public services that contribute to it" (Williamson 2012; see also Toynbee 2010). "It plays well to people who have a lingering sense of the Tory Party as the nasty party that favours big business," added sociologist David Bartram (Wardell 2011). "This gives a veneer of interest in well-being."

Whether driven by a need to shore up government legitimacy during a renewed assault on the welfare state, a genuine long-term interest of Cameron's, or a shift in societal priorities (Williamson 2012), the initiative did give a boost to a sufficiency-based growth critique. Indeed, some critics reacted against precisely that; for example, one *Telegraph* columnist saw little evidence that the science of happiness behind the new measure was "anything other than a strategy for declining growth" (Johnston 2010). On the other hand, Christian groups – CAFOD, Theos, and Tearfund – welcomed the measure, which was consistent with their message that "life is about more than quarterly growth figures" (Lyle 2010). A favourable response in the *New Scientist* reflected the views of many greens, pointing to a "strong case" that "slavish devotion to growing GDP is unsustainable, and that new measures of social and environmental progress are needed" (Aldhous 2010). Meanwhile, David Harvie (2011), a lecturer in finance and political economy, saw "exciting" potential to build on this growing questioning of economic value – as a first step toward "transforming an economy in which the profit motive is dominant" and in which inequality, hours of work, global temperatures, and other threats to well-being are rising.

New economic indicators were one way that green concerns about economic growth were making inroads – or, alternatively, being absorbed by state institutions. But questions remained. How much of a difference would alternative measures make? Would they merely amount to a symbolic concession to concerns over the focus on GDP growth, while government and business remained committed to status quo practices that prioritized capitalist expansion? Or would they be a "short, sharp statistical shock to the system" (Porritt 2007b, 255), leading to a questioning of current policies and strengthening political forces calling for a real change of priorities?

The answers were not yet clear, but some policy change appeared likely. The top civil servant, Cabinet Secretary Gus O'Donnell, enthusiastically backed the new statistics and incorporated the need to consider well-being impacts in the "Green Book," the policy evaluation guide for bureaucrats. Again, there was no official downplaying of the importance of growth; the new measures were presented in neutral terms as "a way to deliver better policy outcomes" (O'Donnell 2011). Political battles over whether this would mean a policy shift to the left, right, or in a green direction were still to come. Cameron (2010b) himself suggested that the "immigration free-for-all" and the "irresponsible ... marketing free-for-all," both of which were "meant to be good for growth," were among the things that one could question on well-being grounds. Whatever the future outcomes, a new well-being measure represented an opportunity for the forces of sufficiency and a step toward dethroning growth as the top societal priority.[5]

FLOATING THE IDEA OF CARBON "RATIONING"

One proposal that embodied ideas of "one-planet living" and "living within limits" and would, in effect, "institutionalise behavioural change" (Challen 2009, 196) was tradable carbon rations, also referred to as domestic tradable quotas, tradable energy quotas, personal carbon credits, or personal carbon allowances (PCAs). Minor variations existed among specific proposals, but the basic idea was similar. Each individual would receive a carbon allowance to cover emissions from home heating, electricity, and transportation – and possibly other purchases as carbon footprinting techniques evolved in the future. People whose emissions exceeded the allowance would have to buy credits from others, resulting in income transfers from the carbon profligate to those living within their carbon means. Over time, allowances would shrink in line with the nation's carbon-reduction targets. Since higher-income individuals typically have bigger carbon footprints, the measure would – on the whole – lead to income redistribution from rich to poor, although not all low-income earners would come out ahead.[6]

As with one-planet living, PCAS are agnostic on the economic growth question, even if they incorporate a strong dose of sufficiency-based thinking. They would establish a hard limit on personal carbon emissions, within a national and ideally global cap, but economic growth could still occur within those limits if decarbonization advanced quickly enough. Some advocates clearly saw the idea through a sufficiency lens. In arguing in his book *How We Can Save the Planet* that carbon rationing was key, Mayer Hillman (2004, 178) criticized the "daydreams that economic growth can be sufficiently 'decoupled' from current levels of carbon dioxide emissions so that it can be maintained in perpetuity." "Rationing is the opposite of today's consumerist free-for-all, where economic growth is the highest objective of government policy," wrote *New Statesman* columnist Mark Lynas (2006). "But that is precisely the point. It is because carbon rationing represents a total break with business as usual that it is the only climate-change policy that will work." Yet Environment Secretary David Miliband, who planted his feet firmly in EM territory, also championed the idea. In a much publicized speech, Miliband (2006c) stated, "Imagine a country where carbon becomes a new currency. We carry bank cards that store both pounds and carbon points. When we buy electricity, gas and fuel, we use our carbon points, as well as pounds ... Imagine your neighbourhood. Each neighbour receives the same free entitlement to a certain number of carbon points. The family next door has an SUV and realise they are going to have to buy more carbon points. So instead they decide to trade in the SUV for a hybrid car. They save 2.2 tonnes of carbon each year. They then sell their carbon points back to the bank and share the dividends of environmental growth."

For those hoping to frame the idea as something palatable to political-economic elites and mainstream voters, PCAS were about bringing the established practice of carbon trading to the individual level. Indeed, Paterson and Stripple (2010, 358) saw in PCAS "a logical extension of the premise of neoliberal climate governance," albeit with a more egalitarian logic than carbon taxes. "Carbon trading is not rationing, it's about individual choices as to what relative value you place on income versus consumption," said Miliband. "Everyone gets the same allocation of emissions. And then we all have huge choice about how we either live within that or how we buy our way out of it" (D. Lawson et al. 2008).

Green-minded policy analysts had long advocated personal carbon rationing and trading. Hillman first proposed carbon allowances in 1990, while David Fleming, formerly the Ecology (Green) Party's economics spokesperson, was credited with proposing Domestic Tradable Quotas in 1996. The idea had a strong affinity with the concept of contraction and convergence, proposed by Aubrey Meyer at the Global Commons Institute in the early 1990s, in which nations would converge on equal per capita carbon allowances over time, with trading between them.

In 2004, MP Colin Challen presented the PCA idea to the House of Commons in a private member's bill. Challen recounted that, at the time, he would have been satisfied if the government took the idea seriously within five years. Yet the proposal made a surprisingly quick ascent. As Challen (2009, 190–1) described it, "in the absence of other solutions" and as a result of a favourable study of the issue by the Tyndall Centre, the idea "began to gain traction." By 2005, Defra included it in a list of ideas to tackle climate change that it presented to Cabinet. Elliot Morley, climate change minister, told the *Daily Telegraph* that we should "not be afraid to think the unthinkable" with regard to ideas such as PCAS (Clover 2005). Meanwhile, starting in 2005, Carbon Rationing Action Groups (CRAGS) began to appear, setting their own carbon allowances and exploring, on a small scale and voluntary level, the possibilities of personal carbon trading, while providing a structure to support members in adopting low-carbon lifestyles.

Once David Miliband became environment secretary, the idea's prominence grew. Miliband first floated the idea publicly in July 2006. He then commissioned a scoping study, which concluded that PCAS, with each citizen receiving a carbon "credit card," could be possible in five years, although unanswered questions remained (Roberts and

Thumim 2006).[7] Miliband praised PCAs for "a simplicity and beauty that would reward carbon thrift" (Wintour 2006). The following year, the Climate Change Bill included enabling powers for government to launch new carbon trading schemes, including at the personal level (D. Miliband 2007a).

However, as Challen (2009, 191) explained, "Outside of Defra's curtilage, more powerful forces would have none of it." He noted a meeting with a Treasury special adviser who said "the idea was going nowhere." Other observers highlighted Gordon Brown's opposition to PCAs (Toynbee 2008). Whatever the exact details of the internal politics, once Brown moved from the Treasury to 10 Downing Street, the momentum behind PCAs was lost. With Miliband promoted to foreign secretary, Defra (2008c, 4) produced a "pre-feasibility study" that concluded personal carbon trading was "a potentially important way to engage individuals" in acting to combat climate change, but was "an idea currently ahead of its time in terms of its public acceptability and the technology to bring down the costs."

Although the government wound down its research work, the idea did not disappear. The House of Commons Environmental Audit Committee (HOCEAC 2008) criticized the government for shelving the idea, which "has the potential to drive greater emissions reductions than green taxation" (3). The committee made clear that the commitment to deep carbon reductions and the limits of existing approaches – two key forces that were driving sufficiency more generally onto the agenda – were behind its interest in personal carbon trading:

It is quite clear that if the Government is to stand the slightest chance of meeting its 2050 target it cannot afford to neglect the domestic and personal sector ... This is *a matter of urgency*. Ambitious targets must be accompanied by equally ambitious emissions reduction trajectories and bold policies ...

... *Existing initiatives are unlikely to bring about behavioural change on the scale required*, with many individuals choosing to disregard the connection between their own emissions and the larger challenge. We conclude that *more radical measures must be introduced* if emissions reductions from the individual and household sector are ever to make a meaningful contribution to UK targets. Personal carbon trading might be the kind of measure needed to bring about behavioural change. (HOCEAC 2008, 9; italics added)

The Committee's chairman, Conservative MP Tim Yeo, told the press, "We found that personal carbon trading has real potential to engage the population in the fight against climate change and to achieve significant emissions reductions in a progressive way." The *Daily Mail* translated this to middle England through the following headline: "Every Adult in Britain Should Be Forced To Carry 'Carbon Ration Cards,' Say MPs" (Derbyshire 2008) – and later cited unnamed critics who labelled a similar proposal "lunatic" (Chapman 2011). Clearly, gaining public support would not be straightforward in the face of media spin and concerns about yet more "Orwellian" state data gathering on citizens, among other objections.

Yet the idea continued to find support. The Royal Society for the encouragement of Arts, Manufactures and Commerce (RSA) concluded from its trials of personal carbon trading that operating costs could be much less than government claimed, using existing technology such as bank or retail loyalty cards (Prescott 2008).[8] The Environment Agency chair, Lord Smith, called PCAs the fairest and most effective way to meet the UK's GHG targets (Everett 2009). On a leading Conservative website, Yeo (2010) urged the Cameron government to introduce personal carbon trading, praising it as "the only green market instrument which redistributes costs from poor people to richer ones," and later volunteered his constituency for a pilot project (Nelsen 2012). A report for the All Party Parliamentary Group on Peak Oil concluded that Tradable Energy Quotas were needed to achieve two key goals: accelerating GHG reduction to meet the UK's 80 per cent target and ensuring access for all Britons to a fair share of energy if fossil fuels grew scarcer (Fleming and Chamberlin 2011). The report argued that such quotas would incentivize low-carbon living and create first-mover advantages in markets for carbon-saving technology. It would also create a sense of "common purpose" to achieve an "energy revolution" (17) – a subtle reference to Second World War rationing, which was key to ensuring equitable access to scarce basic goods, shared sacrifice, and sustained morale on the home front.

Whether or not PCAs were the most desirable policy instrument remained a matter of debate. Groups such as Carbon Trade Watch, which opposed carbon trading at EU and global levels, also objected to it at the personal level. Some former proponents shifted allegiance to other carbon-reduction tools that did not require managing millions of personal accounts, such as upstream "cap-and-share" or "cap-and-dividend" systems in which fossil fuel suppliers would have to purchase emissions permits, with revenues given to citizens on an equal per capita basis (Lynas 2008b; Monbiot 2008b; Starkey 2012).[9] On the other hand, Fawcett (2010) concluded that personal carbon trading was "promising and timely" on the basis of studies showing it to be at least as acceptable to the public as other options, such as carbon taxation, to meet the government's radical GHG targets. (That said, all options faced considerable challenges in winning public support.) Among its potential carbon-reduction benefits would be the psychological effect of having an allowance to live within, while it would put "conscious consideration of carbon emissions at the heart of many purchasing decisions" (Fawcett 2010, 6874).

The fact that such a radical idea found support from individual politicians in all major parties, including a prominent cabinet minister, was studied by government, backed by a parliamentary committee, and trialled in local pilot projects indicated how much further the boundaries of acceptable thought on climate responses had been extended in the UK than in Canada. At the same time, the official shelving of the proposal for the foreseeable future illustrated that considerable political obstacles remained to putting such ideas into practice.

Other similar cases of sufficiency "false starts" included the Conservative Party's floating of a "green air miles allowance" of one tax-free flight per year and Ken Livingstone's proposed CO_2-based congestion charge. Commitment to deep emission cuts and the shortcomings of existing responses were allowing once-radical ideas to become the subject of mainstream political discussion in Britain, although that was hardly enough to satisfy those who felt it well past time to move beyond the debate and start implementing such measures.

If sufficiency were to play a greater future role, one likely path would be through measures such as PCAs, similar hard caps on business, or government carbon budgets. By targeting carbon emissions and not GDP per se, such measures sidestep a direct challenge to growth and have the potential to win support as well from EM supporters optimistic about technological possibilities. It is only over time that it will become clear whether or not they serve as a constraint on economic growth. Some were already thinking ahead to such an eventuality.

PROSPERITY WITHOUT GROWTH?

Perhaps the most significant incursion of sufficiency-based thought into the broad state sphere was the exploration of low- or no-growth scenarios by the government's sustainability watchdog and adviser. In 2008, the Sustainable Development Commission's "Redefining Prosperity" project began investigating "how the economy would function if a lower priority was given to economic growth" (Defra 2008e). The objective: "taking the arguments against continuing growth seriously and thinking through the consequences," including the implications of no- or low-growth for "unemployment, tax revenue, the ability to repay debt and pay interest, company profits and economic competitiveness" (SDC 2008). These questions were part of a broader investigation into the links between growth, sustainability, and well-being, which included the prospects for EM and the question "can 'decoupling' work?"

This initiative led to an SDC report by Tim Jackson (2009) entitled *Prosperity Without Growth?* and a subsequent book – without the question mark. The report emphasized the "dilemma of growth": economic growth may be ecologically unsustainable, but a lack of it appears to be socially unstable (Jackson 2009, 9). However, based on the evidence to date, it characterized the conventional way out of the dilemma – decoupling – as a myth and hence argued that it was necessary to confront the issue of how to achieve a socially stable economy without growth. The report argued that "simplistic assumptions that capitalism's propensity for efficiency will allow us to stabilise the climate and protect against resource scarcity are nothing short of delusional. Those who promote decoupling as an escape route from the dilemma of growth need to take a closer look at the historical evidence – and at the basic arithmetic of growth" (8).[10] It concluded that "there is an urgent need to develop a resilient and sustainable macroeconomy that is no longer predicated on relentless consumption growth. The clearest message from the financial crisis of 2008 is that our current model of economic success is fundamentally flawed. For the advanced economies of the Western world, prosperity without growth is no longer a utopian dream. It is a financial and ecological necessity" (12).

SDC Chairman Jonathon Porritt (2009) hailed the release of the commission's "magnum opus," and emphasized that for too long politicians had used talk of "decoupling" as a "get-out clause" to avoid "any intellectual encounter" with the difficult problem of economic growth. "Politicians may not want to hear these messages. But it's our task to broadcast them much more loudly and much more clearly than we've done over the last 20 years." This could be seen as another move in the economic growth dance (chapter 8). Porritt (2007b, 249) had earlier acknowledged capitalism's need for growth and therefore promoted the idea of making "growth consistent with sustainability, rather than conjuring fanciful visions of how to do without it." The political and economic imperative for growth had not disappeared, but with the emerging ecological imperative speaking more loudly, and hopes for a happy reconciliation of these imperatives in doubt, it was apparently time to make those visions of doing without growth less fanciful.[11]

Ironically, Tony Blair (2000) launched the SDC in one of his first EM speeches, which called for a new environmental coalition in tune with consumer aspirations and business's drive for profit as an alternative to the green critique of unconstrained growth and consumption. Less than a decade later, things had come full circle. The SDC, in effect, concluded that Blair's "central theme" of "a more productive use of environmental resources," albeit important, was not enough, and that rethinking society's reliance on economic growth was no longer avoidable.

A further irony illustrated Jackson's point about the dilemma of growth. In July 2010, facing a deep budget deficit after the debt-driven growth bubble burst, Cameron's "greenest government ever" axed the SDC as part of its public sector austerity program. There was clearly still some way to go – intellectually and politically – to manage without growth while preserving the public services and agencies needed for a transition to a low-carbon, high–well-being society.

CONCLUSIONS

The sufficiency paradigm made some limited headway in the UK state sphere. In a way unseen in Canada, the British state had to confront sufficiency-based ideas and to some extent opened further space for them. Continued economic growth and capital accumulation remained central state priorities. Yet a sufficiency-based language of "one-planet living" and "living within limits" crept into government discourse. This language was given some substance by a commitment to deep carbon-reduction targets in the Climate Change Act that, depending on how quickly economic output could be decarbonized, had the potential to constrain future economic growth – even if government leaders did not admit to any such conflict. The commitment to deep reduction targets and acknowledgment of limits to conventional policy instruments to achieve them also pushed government into promoting behaviour and lifestyle change – thereby encouraging a scrutiny of carbon-intensive practices that did not easily stop at the boundary of "consuming differently," sometimes spilling over onto the terrain of "consuming less." One way to institutionalize the requirement for behaviour change and give concrete substance to ideas of one-planet living was through proposals for personal carbon allowances. PCAs resided in the conceptual borderland between sufficiency and EM, and moved from the green margins to serious consideration by government with the backing of a prominent cabinet minister, before being deemed ahead of their time. A more significant victory for the forces of sufficiency was the announcement of a new well-being indicator, which they had long demanded due to GDP's failings as a measure of progress. Meanwhile, the Sustainable Development Commission acted as a heretical adviser to the state, as it urged creation of new economic structures that would allow prosperity without growth. None of these developments implied any lessening of the political commitment to ecological modernization and economic growth more generally, but they did suggest that the ground underneath that commitment was shifting.

The British government arguably contributed, inadvertently, to encouraging ideas of sufficiency in one other way. Critics maintained that the coalition's decision to respond to the economic crisis through deep spending cuts undermined and delayed the UK's economic recovery. As this book went to press, signs of renewed economic growth in Britain were finally evident, long after the initial downturn; however, it was not yet clear whether that growth would be sustained or simply be a blip in a long period of economic stagnation. If the stagnation scenario were to prevail, most people would be left with no choice but to come to terms with an end to consumption growth. In such a context, potential existed for necessity-induced cultural innovation leading to less consumption-oriented norms and practices. Indeed, Cohen (2012, 5) suggested that austerity policies would likely hasten the transition to "post-consumerism" by damp-ening purchasing power. Meanwhile, the economic crisis and slow recovery contributed to a sharp GHG emissions drop in Britain after 2007. Despite the possible ecological upsides, this amounted to suf-ficiency by disaster, not design – the opposite of what most sufficiency supporters were seeking (e.g. Victor 2008).

Comparison and Conclusions

"There is no high carbon future." What exactly these words would come to mean was still up for grabs, but it was significant that Labour government ministers in Britain, including Business Secretary Peter Mandelson (2009) and Energy and Climate Change Secretary Ed Miliband (Grice 2009b), promoted this message. It was still far from clear that the British government would in fact do enough to rule out a high-carbon future, but the idea that this had to happen was enshrined in law with cross-party support. Canada, in contrast, was unable to make a comparable national commitment to a low-carbon future, torn by a choice between the planet or the gold, or, more precisely, the black gold.

If the high-carbon option could be ruled out as something that simply had to be avoided – that is, if we did not pick the planet, we would also lose the gold and much else, as Nicholas Stern concluded – then the focus could shift to the question of what a low-carbon path required. The dominant answer, at least in the UK, was an ecological modernization approach that assumed that continued economic growth and deep emissions cuts were compatible – a perspective embraced by key political and business actors who had moved beyond business-as-usual thinking. However, the new consensus on ecological modernization was fragile. On the one hand, there was evidence that more radical change was likely necessary to avoid a high-carbon future. The idea of rethinking a growth-based economy and culture of consumption was struggling to break through, and beginning to make inroads in various ways. At the same time, proponents of climate action had to fight rearguard battles against a resurgence of BAU ideas. Meanwhile, in Canada, where EM was unable to gain an upper hand over BAU, more radical sufficiency-based ideas faced an even greater struggle to make headway.

Before turning to the inroads and the prospects for sufficiency, this chapter considers in more detail some contrasts and similarities between Canada and the UK, as well as the appeal, importance, and limits of ecological modernization. Comparison of these countries – which share many similarities and yet differ significantly in their progress on EM reform – allows for insight to be gained into the conditions in which a sufficiency approach may find political opportunities.

SHARED COMMITMENT TO GROWTH,
DIVERGING STRATEGIES

In both nations, proposed political and social responses to climate change had to contend with the perceived imperative of economic growth. Canada was committed to a growth strategy focused on high-carbon sectors, which was a formidable obstacle to strong climate policy. The prioritization of growth was reflected, for example, in the preference of the federal and Alberta governments, as well as business, for intensity-based rather than absolute GHG-reduction targets – a choice designed to ensure that climate policy did not impinge on economic expansion of the tar sands and other sectors. Canada's political climate was such that no federal government officially took a stance against the need for climate action, but the desire to avoid disrupting a carbon-intensive growth path led Liberals and Conservatives alike to delay, time and time again, significant policy action capable of delivering large GHG reductions. The Conservatives did eventually introduce limited regulatory measures and some significant provincial action emerged, but overall, Canada remained stuck between business-as-usual and ecological modernization at the level of discourse, and closer still to BAU in practice.

In contrast, in the UK, political and business leaders more widely embraced an EM rhetoric that economic growth and carbon reduction could go together – without growth being any less of a priority. An EM discourse was backed by considerable innovation in British government policy and business practice. A particularly important focus was construction of the carbon market. The UK had established a voluntary UK emissions trading scheme, participated in two phases of the EU ETS, and later initiated the CRC, a trading system for businesses and organizations outside the ETS – during which time Canada still had not managed to launch its long-promised regulatory and trading scheme for large emitters. In fact, by 2011, Canada's Conservative government had taken the idea of cap-and-trade off the table. The UK also introduced a business energy tax, the Climate Change Levy, in 2001, and later a minimum carbon price for firms covered by the ETS, while Canada's federal government had yet to introduce any price incentives to lower emissions. (Quebec and British Columbia did, however, introduce provincial carbon taxes, and Alberta had a low carbon price for some industrial emissions.) Canada had no equivalent to a number of other policy and social developments in Britain, such as carbon labelling projects, plans to require all new housing to be zero-carbon, a Green Investment Bank, a major national push to expand renewable and other low-carbon energy sources – to name a few examples. Likely most significant of all in the long term would be the UK's Climate Change Act, which received all-party support and was hailed as an "eco-constitution" binding future governments to meet deep carbon-reduction targets (albeit one that faced challenges from some on the political right).

The UK's wide range of policy initiatives, advanced social debate on necessary actions, contributions to international efforts, and apparent emissions trends were reasons why various observers considered it to be a relative leader on climate change. Meanwhile, Canada ranked near the back of the pack, in the unfamiliar company of countries such as Saudi Arabia. That said, the UK was not ahead on every front. For example, Canada had inherited a lower-carbon electricity system due mainly to its vast hydroelectric resources, and some local and provincial initiatives offered lessons for others. Nevertheless, carbon consciousness clearly had become a more significant force in the UK, even if Britain's actions were still wanting in various ways. Labour MP Colin Challen (2009) argued that the UK had only begun the "phoney war" stage of climate response, still reluctant to launch a "total war," but if the Second World War analogy were appropriate, then Canada had barely gone beyond "denial" into the "appeasement" phase. Such differences were particularly evident in comparing the Conservative parties in the two countries.

Carboniferous Conservatives and Green Tories

In the late 1980s, both Canada and the UK had Tory prime ministers that were early leaders in taking climate change seriously and putting

Figure 11.1 Conservative Party table at Camden Green Fair, London, 2 June 2007. Photo by author.

it on the global agenda. Two decades later, the UK Conservatives under David Cameron were, while in opposition and the early days of government, champions of "green growth," while a small segment of the party even spoke like radical greens in raising critical questions about the relentless pursuit of ever more output. When Cameron entered 10 Downing Street, he committed to lead the "greenest government ever." In contrast, Canada's Conservatives came to power steeped in climate scepticism, rejected the country's Kyoto Protocol commitments and later withdrew from the treaty, scrapped the previous Liberal government's limited climate programs, fought against absolute emission targets in favour of intensity targets in international negotiations for a post-Kyoto deal, and muzzled Environment Canada scientists. Canada's Conservative government consistently acted as if the first priority of climate policy and diplomacy was to ensure that nothing got in the way of becoming a carbon-based "energy superpower."

Canada's Conservatives did, however, move some distance from their position when elected in 2006. Public opinion forced the Harper government to re-evaluate its climate stance and commit to

GHG-reduction targets, albeit ones that were very limited compared to the UK's commitments and the levels called for by the IPCC and other scientists. Canada's Conservatives also hesitantly used an EM discourse at times – for example, to justify their 2007 Turning the Corner plan and their 2010 announcement of new regulations on coal-fired power – even if they frequently reverted to an emphasis on the costs of climate action and the need to "balance" economic and environmental goals. Yet despite the slight shift over time, nothing in the federal Canadian Conservative universe compared to David Cameron's "vote blue, go green" rebranding or his efforts to stake out ground to the green side of the Labour Party.[1] The equivalent of Cameron's launch of his party's energy policy at the office of Greenpeace UK (2007), for example, was frankly unimaginable in Canada – except perhaps as a set up for a comedy skit.

In the UK, the greening of the Conservatives while they were in opposition and their competitive one-upmanship with Labour and the Lib Dems helped to drive forward the debate over how to combat climate change. Rather than acting as a brake on strong climate policy as in Canada, the opposition Tories in Britain pushed for a more extensive EM project – often forcing the Labour government to catch up to their proposals. The UK Conservatives had their own unique way of framing their green policy ideas, which appeared on their website under the banner of "Protecting Security," next to a report on prisons policy.[2] Another way that Conservatives could integrate climate action into existing priorities was the use of an anti-bureaucratic-state rhetoric of "power to the people" to support its decentralized renewable energy proposals (Conservative Party 2007b) – linkages that Canadian Tories had not made. Meanwhile, the Conservative opposition's rhetoric bolstered the EM cause in a way wholly unfamiliar to Canadians. For example, Cameron (2008b) continued to back a green agenda even as the economic crisis deepened, saying, "It's not that we can't afford to go green – it's that we can't afford not to go green." The Cameron Tories had demonstrated enough climate commitment in opposition that even a green radical such as Monbiot (2009c) brought himself to cautiously praise them for making "the right noises about the environment."

In opposition, the Cameron Conservatives, although committed to economic growth, also gave a surprising boost to a sufficiency perspective, contributing to the questioning of the prioritization of

GDP growth and of particular high-carbon products and sectors. A remarkably critical perspective on growth appeared in the Quality of Life Policy Group (2007) report, whose non-binding recommendations included forms of micro-sufficiency such as a moratorium on airport expansion and an end to large-scale road building. In 2008, the Conservative Party as a whole took a position against Heathrow expansion. This stance won the party credibility points in green circles, contributed to the perception that it was a changed party, and likewise added mainstream credibility to the efforts of anti-aviation campaigners. It also opened the party to unfamiliar criticism from some business leaders and party members, one of whom asked, "When did the Conservative Party become the bulwark against consumer demand?" (Normille 2009; see also Malmo 2008). Tory flirtation with "General Well-Being" rather than GDP also contributed to the prominence of the debate over determinants of happiness, which sufficiency advocates took advantage of to put forward their own visions of better ways of life. In fact, Cameron (2008a) contributed a chapter "In Praise of General Well-Being" in *Do Good Lives Have to Cost the Earth?*, a book compiled by the pro-sufficiency New Economics Foundation. Such Tory association with the voices of sufficiency was hard to imagine in Canada.

In government, the Conservatives and their Liberal Democrat coalition partners built on the EM reforms begun under Labour – albeit, like Labour, with a gap between their green rhetoric and many of their actions. They also delivered two notable, if partial, victories for the cause of sufficiency: the cancellation of the Heathrow third runway and the announcement of a new well-being indicator to complement GDP. However, Cameron faced increasing difficulties in managing the resurgent BAU voices in his party, whether they were outright climate sceptics or others, such as Chancellor George Osborne, who in 2011 dropped the win-win EM rhetoric and warned of the economic costs of Britain's carbon-reduction ambitions. As long as they needed the Liberal Democrats to govern, there was little chance of a fundamental U-turn on issues such as Heathrow airport or, most significantly, the Climate Change Act and its deep GHG reduction targets; however, there were intense battles between EM and BAU forces over the details of specific policies, such as electricity market reforms and the relative balance between renewables and a new "dash for gas." Looking ahead, in the event of a Conservative majority after

2015, it was unclear whether the UK's commitment to ambitious carbon reduction would survive. Nevertheless, during the time period covered by this study, overall, the UK Conservatives played a key role in advancing EM reform in way unseen in Canada.

Factors behind the UK's Ecological Modernization Lead over Canada

The differences between Conservative parties reflected wider political-economic differences that enabled an EM project to advance further in the UK than in Canada. These included greater ease in the UK – due to differences in economic structure – in linking climate action to the perceived economic imperative of growth, as well as additional linkages to the security and legitimacy imperatives that did not occur in the same way in Canada.

LINKING CLIMATE ACTION TO THE ECONOMIC IMPERATIVE. Canada's economic structure created significant obstacles to an EM linkage of economic and climate strategies. Calls for a strong national climate policy were not easily reconciled with the dominance of high-carbon sectors, most notably Alberta's petroleum sector and, to a lesser degree, Ontario's automotive sector, which long saw higher fuel efficiency standards as a threat. The lack, at least for the foreseeable future, of adequate technological solutions to the oil sands' GHG problems created an intense conflict between an economic strategy based on rapidly expanding extraction of this highly profitable resource and emissions reduction goals.

Some sectors of Canada's economy – e.g. renewable and nuclear energy, biofuels, forest products, production of public transit vehicles and lightweight materials – did see opportunities in strong climate policy. However, they were not yet able to counterbalance the power of dominant high-carbon sectors. These dominant economic sectors faced the prospect of major economic costs right from the outset of climate policy discussions. The relative lack of easy, cost-free GHG reductions to start the climate reform process also worked against the EM idea of win-win carbon reduction. Combined with regional disparities in climate action costs, the result was that Canada faced many tough decisions right from the outset of its carbon-reduction debate, hobbling efforts to take initial steps and generating a great deal of "policy agony."

One could argue, as many environmentalists and others did, that Canadian political and business leaders exaggerated the costs of action and showed a lack of foresight in understanding the country's long-term interest in making the transition to a low-carbon economy. That lack of foresight was one factor in the costly near-death experience in 2008–09 of an automobile sector overly dependent on producing gas-guzzling vehicles (after which the revived North American auto industry was less resistant to EM initiatives). Risks related to overdependence on petroleum, a commodity with volatile price swings, were also growing. These risks included the possibility that Canadian petroleum and other exports could face limits in US and other markets due to their high carbon content and Canada's weak climate policy, and the threat of falling behind in emerging low-carbon industries (De Souza 2012a; NRTEE 2012). In any case, whether acting from self-interest or foolishly misinterpreting it, Canada's federal leaders acted as if strong climate policy, not climate change, was the greater threat for the foreseeable future.

In the UK, the sense of threat and opportunity differed, resulting in greater openness to EM. Nicholas Stern's message that the costs of inaction exceeded the costs of action fell on relatively fertile ground. Britain's easy start in achieving large GHG cuts in the 1990s gave plausibility early on to claims that climate action need not be costly. Benefiting from the windfall gains from the dash for gas and offshoring of manufacturing, and with a finance-led economy that was less carbon intensive than Canada's, the UK could build a coalition of interests around win-win emissions cuts before having to face painful choices. Particularly significant was the fact that climate policy was less of a direct threat to the UK's finance-heavy economy than it was to Canada's powerful oil and automobile sectors. Some sectors and firms in Britain did face serious challenges in limiting emissions, but it was easier than in Canada to see the opportunities for the dominant sector – notably in London becoming the centre of global carbon finance and trading – and to bring it into an EM coalition. There was also considerable awareness of the financial risks of climate change, such as rising costs to the insurance sector.

It is worth emphasizing that the main difference between the two countries was not that business had any lesser degree of influence over UK policy. True, Britain's Labour government did introduce the Climate Change Levy in 2001 despite business opposition (which led to concessions to trade-exposed, energy-intensive firms). Later, the Conservative-led coalition also cancelled Heathrow expansion despite considerable business opposition. However, on the whole, the Labour government went to great lengths to prove its business-friendly credentials, while critics pointed to many signs that business interests shaped and distorted policy on issues such as aviation and the balance between renewables and other energy sources. Meanwhile, Britain's Conservative-led coalition clearly had close ties to business. In both countries, there were abundant signs that the dominant sectors had an important impact on climate policy. The key difference, to reiterate, was the nature of these dominant sectors and the capacity to integrate them into an EM coalition, not their degree of influence over policy. (Indeed, the power of finance had problematic aspects for British climate policy; for example, evidence existed that carbon trading was not merely a means – and a contentious one at that – to GHG reduction, but an end in itself.)

Beyond the differences in the key economic sectors, the degree of business-led EM activity also suggested that a large segment of British business, at an earlier point and to a greater degree than its Canadian counterparts, came to see its own interests differently, with the future lying in an EM strategy based on efficiency, a shift to low-carbon technologies, and the financing of such a transition. As *Globe and Mail* columnist Jeffrey Simpson (2007) put it, "In contrast to Canada, British industries are getting with the program … By integrating environmental considerations into their most basic calculations, instead of treating the environment as an afterthought or 'externality,' companies are groping toward rethinking how they do business, and from that rethinking will come the first steps of the next industrial revolution." Indeed, by the time the Conservative-led government's commitment to green growth was wavering, the leading voice of UK business was encouraging the coalition to maintain its carbon-reduction ambitions (CBI 2012b).

Differing regional trade environments also affected the ability to link climate and economic agendas. One constraint on Canada's ability to deliver on its Kyoto Protocol and post-Kyoto commitments was concern that the climate policy cost burden would put its firms at a competitive disadvantage relative to those from the US, its core trading partner, which never ratified Kyoto and was unable in the first Obama administration to pass climate legislation. One could argue that such fears were exaggerated, and that first-mover advantages existed in acting before the US to seize low-carbon economic opportunities. Nevertheless, these fears were a reason why Canadian federal governments repeatedly delayed imposing GHG limits on trade-exposed sectors. In contrast, the UK was part of the European Union, which had its own carbon-reduction targets and policies. Competitiveness concerns relative to the rest of the globe remained, but the existence of EU-wide climate action limited the pressures in relation to the UK's nearest trading partners.[3] Moreover, the EU occasionally pushed the UK further than it would have gone on its own – e.g. on renewable energy targets – whereas NAFTA provided no such impetus, and even created obstacles to scaling back carbon-intensive energy exports were Canada to try to do so.

THE SECURITY/ENERGY SECURITY IMPERATIVE. In the UK, calls for climate action were linked to security concerns, bolstering the economic arguments for EM reform. As noted above, climate change could be framed as a threat from which the people and nation needed protection (e.g. Conservative Party 2009a). Indeed, there appeared to be a greater sense of vulnerability to climate change on a small, crowded island where a larger percentage of the land and population, including parts of central London, were at risk of rising waters – among other changes that threatened the landscape and cultural heritage. Especially important in extending the base of support for climate action was the linkage of such action to enhancing energy security – a core concern of business and the state – as investments in energy efficiency and low-carbon supplies promised to reduce dependence on fossil fuel imports from Russia and the Middle East.

In contrast, the idea that Canada could face energy supply shortages or be vulnerable to rising costs of imported energy was not a prominent theme in mainstream debate at the federal level, even if some observers argued that Canadians should in fact be concerned about their energy security (e.g. Laxer and Dillon 2008), and energy security concerns did appear in some provinces (e.g. Nova Scotia 2009, 17). To the contrary, there was much talk of Canada becoming an "energy superpower" – the nation to which others, particularly the US, turned to enhance their energy security. Concerns over energy security thus served as a key force behind the expansion of Alberta's tar sands and continuation of Canada's high-carbon growth path.

THE LEGITIMACY IMPERATIVE. The need to maintain the legitimacy of the wider political-economic order and for political leaders to legitimate themselves played differing roles in Canada and the
UK. In Canada, where deep emissions reductions threatened core
carbon-intensive industries and regions, climate action represented a
significant challenge to the unity and legitimacy of the Canadian federation. Ambitious climate policies threatened intense political confrontation given the concentration of the costs of action in certain
provinces, notably Alberta, where danger existed of reawakening the
strong historical sense of alienation from the federal government, a
sentiment caused in large part by past energy sector interventions. Regardless of the party in power, fears of delegitimating the federation
in the eyes of Albertans and other westerners represented an important constraint on federal government carbon-reduction ambitions.

In the UK, there was no comparable threat to the legitimacy of
the union over the regional costs of climate action. Indeed, Britain's
great regional concern, Scotland, which was holding a vote on independence in 2014, was equally or more committed than the rest
of the UK to climate action, as it boasted the world's most ambitious
carbon-reduction goals and plans to generate 100 per cent of its own
electricity needs from renewables. The legitimacy imperative did,
however, play a role in another way. David Cameron's use of commitment to climate action to relegitimate the Conservative Party, i.e.
to "detoxify" the brand among the general public, played a key role
in the initial establishment of a cross-party consensus on EM reform.

To recap, in the UK, climate action was more easily linked to the
perceived imperative of economic growth than in Canada, while security (particularly energy security) concerns and the legitimation
needs of key political actors pointed toward climate action in the UK
and toward continuation of a high-carbon growth path in Canada.
That said, the way in which these imperatives interacted with climate
action was in flux. In the UK, BAU voices were increasingly vocal
in claiming that Britain faced economic costs from moving more
quickly on carbon reduction than other nations. A new "dash for
gas" emerged as an alternative, fossil fuel–based solution to Britain's
energy security concerns, raising doubts about the future commitment to decarbonizing the power supply. Meanwhile, Cameronism
faced a growing challenge from the right – both inside and outside
the Conservative Party – for which strong green policies were less of

an asset than a liability. As a result, new battles had emerged over maintaining the commitment to EM reform and deep GHG reductions. Meanwhile, in Canada, the obstacles to EM reform were substantial, but it was possible to imagine scenarios leading to stronger climate action. Provincial EM efforts and the growth of a green energy sector could over time expand the coalition of businesses and workers with an economic interest in stronger climate policy. Those efforts might be bolstered by a reframing of the energy security discourse to acknowledge the vulnerabilities faced in parts of the country dependent on fossil energy imports – or by a reassessment of energy security in the US, leading to reduced interest in Canada's tar sands. Meanwhile, erosion of Canada's legitimacy in the international arena could increase external pressure on the country to act, especially if economic interests were jeopardized by restrictions on the export of Canada's high-carbon fuels or carbon tariffs on Canadian goods.

OTHER FACTORS. Leaving aside questions about the future level of commitment to EM in both countries, we can consider other factors that contributed to the UK's EM lead in the period covered by the study.

Canada's vast, sparsely populated land contributed to a frontier mentality and worked against a sense of limits to BAU expansion. Speculatively, Canada's size and northern latitude may also have limited its residents' sense of vulnerability to climate change, although further research would be needed to confirm this point. Unlike in Britain, in Canada, even the loss of some coastal areas would not change the fact that a lot of elbowroom would remain, and some of it could be more hospitable in a warmer world. Climate change not only promised less harsh winters, but also to open the Arctic to further resource extraction and new shipping possibilities, which some voices in the debate depicted as veritable bonuses. That said, northern nations were ill equipped to deal with extreme heat and the potential for unprecedented forest fires, as illustrated by Russia's experience in 2010. However, the Conservative government did its part to keep reports on the negative impacts of climate change out of the limelight, efforts that might have contributed to limiting the breadth and depth of the public's sense of vulnerability.

One should also not exclude the role of individual agency and leadership in enabling the UK to advance further toward EM reform.

Examples at the elite level included Tony Blair's highlighting of climate change's importance domestically and internationally, David Cameron's greening of the Conservative Party, Ken Livingstone's championing of climate change when he was mayor of London, and decisions by UK business leaders to turn away from a BAU approach and urge stronger climate action. This is not to say that such elite leadership was always adequate to the challenge or without contradiction, only that it played a role in advancing and legitimating strong climate action at key moments. In contrast, the lack of elite leadership in advancing the cause of climate action was notable at the federal level in Canada, especially under the Harper government. Meanwhile, the actions of Britain's relatively strong climate movement – in which not only environmentalists, but international development NGOs, religious groups, and the Women's Institute, among others, played a prominent role – were another relevant factor in achieving a national commitment to deep emissions reductions.

Preference for Easy Ways to Go Green

One key similarity between Canada and the UK was a political preference in both countries for easy ways to go green and, to the extent possible, avoid hard choices. Canadian environmentalists expressed frustration at the lack of political will to make the "tough decisions" needed on climate change, and to create "winners and losers" if necessary (e.g. Bramley 2007b). In Canada, climate policy, such as it existed, was not designed to achieve deep GHG reductions but "to avoid undermining of competitive position," which was how the Canadian Association of Petroleum Producers favourably described proposed federal targets for large industrial emitters and Alberta's 2007 climate measures (Alvarez 2007, 3, 5). A desire to maintain economic competitiveness was also evident in the UK. For example, British policy-makers explicitly designed the Carbon Reduction Commitment to ensure net economic gains to the business and public sector organizations involved. To avoid imposing costs on companies, only a modest level of emissions cuts was required to begin – one that was far lower than the UK had acknowledged as necessary nationwide by 2020. The UK was clearly doing much more than Canada in terms of EM reform, but it was not obviously doing a lot more that was difficult – at least not in the early phases of climate action.[4]

Another sign of the preference for easy options was the high priority given to biofuels, whose inclusion in fuel supplies was mandated in both Canada and the UK. Governments could claim to be taking strong climate action, farmers would benefit, and a new agrofuel industry could grow. Politicians could boast of emissions cuts equivalent to taking however many millions of cars off the road, even as drivers kept driving and no additional regulations would have to be imposed on a resistant auto industry. The only trouble was that actually existing biofuels had, according to several studies, little if any net climate benefit and contributed to global hunger through rising food prices. Governments in both countries nevertheless went ahead with biofuel expansion policies, which had short-term political advantages over a more difficult, sufficiency-based scaling back of transport demand.

Carbon capture and storage also had considerable political appeal, offering the potential for continued fossil energy expansion and new export opportunities – with $ and £ signs appearing in many eyes with thoughts of all those new Chinese coal plants needing CCS. Meanwhile, without CCS, meeting emissions reductions targets would almost certainly require a more significant sacrifice of future economic growth. CCS was central to key Canadian scenarios to meet deep emissions targets (NRTEE 2006, 2007), even those put forward by environmental groups (Pembina Institute and Suzuki Foundation 2008, 2009), as it was to Nicholas Stern's (2006) vision of climate action being the pro-growth strategy. Canada was particularly aggressive in supporting CCS, budgeting $650 million of federal funds over five years – nearly two thirds of a $1 billion Clean Energy Fund announced in 2009 – with another $2 billion pledged by Alberta. Since CCS was arguably Canada's best shot at fulfilling its "energy superpower" dreams while doing its part to address climate change, it was not surprising that Canada – even under Conservative governments ostensibly committed to small government and market solutions – was so willing to find billions of dollars to spend on the matter. However, the technology had yet to be proven viable on the scale needed and for the uses contemplated, such as power plants and oil sands extraction and upgrading facilities. Significant setbacks to CCS development schemes also occurred in both Canada and the UK. Meanwhile, even if technical obstacles could be overcome, CCS would inevitably add to energy bills (or tax burdens, if subsidized). This was due to the additional energy it would require – as it would cannibalize a significant percentage of a power plant's output – in addition to the cost of the technological infrastructure itself.

Although a shared preference for easy ways out of the climate conundrum was evident in both countries, some costly actions could not be avoided. Indeed, the UK put in place a framework of legally binding carbon budgets in the Climate Change Act that promised to make it more difficult for British governments to sidestep hard choices in the future – an institutional change with no equivalent in Canada. Indeed, the Committee on Climate Change created by the act repeatedly called for a "step change" in the pace of carbon reduction and the strength of policy to meet the UK's commitments (CCC 2009b; 2012b, 7). Some difficult choices began to be made, such as the 2009 decision to rule out new coal-fired plants without some use of CCS, and the coalition's subsequent electricity market reforms, which would increase electricity prices in the years ahead. Meanwhile, the decision to cancel Heathrow airport expansion despite claims it was necessary for prosperity was also driven, in part, by the new political and economic dynamics of tight carbon constraints. For its part, Canada also introduced measures to rule out new coal-fired power without CCS despite the higher costs for CCS-equipped plants, one of the limited cases of federal action. Although such actions were often introduced with an EM language of opportunity, they illustrated the limits of EM's search for cost-free, win-win solutions.

THE APPEAL, IMPORTANCE, AND LIMITS OF ECOLOGICAL MODERNIZATION

An EM discourse and reform strategy could sometimes serve to mask the need for more difficult choices – i.e. it could function as a "mass tranquilizer," as Harriss-White and Harriss (2006, 83) called the Blair government's "aspirational discourse" on climate change. There was clear political appeal to sidestepping a confrontation with business's drive for endless expansion of sales and profits, consumer aspirations for more, or the thorny question of how to construct a socio-economic system not dependent on growth. However, EM's appeal went beyond serving as a way to avoid difficult choices. EM could be presented as a "positive agenda," as Tony Blair (2000) did in his call for a new environmental coalition including business and in line with consumer aspirations. Potential for green job creation was also vitally important in broadening the political base for climate action, and became even more so during the economic recession. Many observers argued that focus on limits and doom-and-gloom failed to motivate people to act, and EM's upbeat message was thus important. Sufficiency advocates, too, were conscious of the need to frame their own vision in a positive way, as discussed below.

The appeal of an EM language was evident in the fact that almost all key actors in the climate debate used it to some degree. In the UK, it became the language of choice among the major political parties – at least until some Tories, including Chancellor George Osborne (2011), reverted to a BAU framing – and among leading voices of business, such as the Confederation of British Industry (CBI 2007c, 2012b), which became a strong advocate of "green growth." Among greens, even a steady state–economy advocate such as Stephan Harding spoke of how he was better able to reach people when he presented his ideas under the term "intelligent growth." In Canada, no broad EM consensus emerged, but there were moments of convergence on an EM discourse. When the federal Tories announced their limited climate initiatives, they justified them with an EM language of opportunity and economic benefits, while green critics of growth, such as David Suzuki and Elizabeth May, reached for a similar language of economic opportunity at key political moments.

In the UK, where the EM process had advanced further, an EM discourse and program allowed government and mainstream political parties, business, moderate environmentalists, and others to find some common ground, enabling the beginning of a society-wide climate-related reform process for which the UK was recognized as a relative leader. In line with EM theory, considerable evidence existed that ecological rationality (or carbon consciousness) was transforming the state, business and the market, and other key institutions of British society, making its mark on everything from football to the monarchy and the military. Also consistent with EM theory were these prominent elements of UK climate politics: the integration of climate policy with strategies to boost economic growth, technological innovation, and export opportunities; the fact that key actors driving these changes included not only the state, pressured by environmental groups, but private sector businesses, consumers, and other economic actors; and, above all, a dominant rhetoric of reassurance about the compatibility between continued economic expansion and climate stability.

A significant, environment-induced social transformation had begun in the UK. A sphere also clearly existed in which GHG reduction could go hand-in-hand with some degree of further economic growth, while greater eco-efficiency and the deployment of low-carbon technologies were urgently needed. However, it was far from obvious that the EM process was happening fast enough or that an EM framework could encompass a full and adequate response to climate change. EM only recently emerged in the UK – becoming a prominent aspect of government policy around the turn of the century and delivering a near knockout blow to a business-as-usual stance with the *Stern Review*. Yet anomalies and limits quickly appeared in this paradigm as the climate challenge began to look more daunting than previously thought, emissions progress had not occurred as steadily or rapidly as needed, government policy simultaneously encouraged low-carbon transition and high-carbon expansion, and economic growth itself was called into question for not delivering increased well-being. There were also signs that the economic win-win sphere was not large enough to deliver the level of emissions cuts required, as evidenced, for example, by the limited ecological ambitions of the Carbon Reduction Commitment and the doubling of Nicholas Stern's estimates of the costs of climate action soon after his landmark report. One could still convincingly argue that the costs of action compared favourably to inaction, but the idea that "climate action pays" subtly took on a darker tone, being more about disasters avoided than additional net economic benefits generated.

Critical political economists could point to several aspects of the UK case in line with their challenges to EM theory. Most notably, success in cutting emissions was overstated due to the transfer of high-carbon production abroad, discussed in more detail below. The state's role in promoting economic growth and capital accumulation faced contradictions with its environmental protection role in the UK (and this was even more evident in Canada). Carbon-intensity improvements struggled to outpace growing output and consumption volumes (a fact that was most evident with consumption-side statistics), in part due to the rebound effect, a variation on the Jevons paradox. The UK's biggest GHG reductions occurred in the 1990s as a result of one-off changes that did not provide a foundation for future

GHG cuts, and again in the period after 2007, when economic output declined sharply and recovered very slowly – hardly what EM supporters had in mind. EM strategies showed a bias toward efficiency- and technology-based solutions, while ignoring more far-reaching and arguably equally essential societal changes. Meanwhile, the emerging "ecological-industrial" complex was a force whose impacts were not all benign – most evident in the push for expanded biofuel use despite the negative social and ecological consequences.

In Canada, an EM political program was much less advanced and EM theory less relevant to understanding the state of climate efforts. Certainly one could point to signs of growing ecological rationality and pockets of EM reform at the level of some provinces, cities, businesses, and consumers (and even, on occasion, the federal Conservative government), but they had not yet become central to Canada's economic strategy. Even at the level of discourse, EM was not able to establish dominance in Canada, where many asked, "Where is the win-win?" and climate action was frequently seen in terms of economic cost and trade offs. To the extent that an EM discourse was present at the federal level, under both Liberal and Conservative governments, it often amounted to little more than a form of symbolic politics masking the continuation of business-as-usual, as seen with respect to other environmental issues in Canada (Davidson and MacKendrick 2004). EM theory had little to offer in terms of understanding the relentless pursuit of carbon-intensive growth by the state and business even in the face of widespread climate awareness and concern, which could be better understood through treadmill-of-production theory or eco-Marxian perspectives that emphasize the endless drive for growth and capital accumulation regardless of ecological cost. Meanwhile, John Bellamy Foster's (2002) discussion of the "automobile-petroleum" complex's role in resisting transitions to greener forms of energy, transport, and economic development was particularly relevant to understanding Canada, given its economic structure.

If one minimal test of EM's success was the decoupling of economic growth from environmental impacts in absolute terms, then the evidence showed that EM was failing so far to meet the climate challenge. Neither the EM laggard nor the leader had convincingly broken the link between economic growth and GHGs. In Canada, this was obvious as official emissions figures rose 28 per cent from 1990 to 2007 – the worst record of any G8 country. Emissions did fall in subsequent low-growth years, but were still 19 per cent above 1990 levels in 2011 (despite a major fall in emissions per unit of GDP between those years). Environment Canada (2013a, 19) acknowledged that "a strong connection still remains between economic growth and GHG emissions." Even though some Canadian environmentalists and others celebrated the UK as a model of decoupling GDP and GHGs, and the official UN accounting methodology suggested this was indeed the case, a closer look showed that emissions reductions in Britain were less impressive after including international aviation and shipping. Worse, several studies showed that emissions linked to goods consumed in the UK grew significantly after 1990, a phenomenon masked in official production-side figures that did not count the high-carbon production that had been transferred abroad. In fact, the UK was, by one estimate, the world's second largest net importer of emissions (CCC 2013, 30). This process was in line with a key element of world-system theorists' critique of EM theory – namely that the apparent greening of core nations' economies often involved a transfer of ecological impacts to nations in the periphery or semi-periphery.

World-system analysis also shed light on Canada's GHG challenges as a hybrid core/semi-periphery exporter of high-carbon resources, which had to take responsibility for production-related emissions (e.g. in the tar sands) even when consumption occurred elsewhere, while at the same time it imported carbon-intensive manufactured goods. Indeed, consumption-side figures put Canada in a slightly better light than conventional figures. In 2011, Canada's per capita GHG emissions were 126 per cent more those in Britain and 5 per cent less than the US on the production side, but according to one consumption-side dataset, Canadian emissions were only 35 per cent higher per person than in the UK and 23 per cent less than the US.[5] In fact, Canada's petroleum industry had long preferred a consumption-side methodology, which, ironically, put it on the same side of that question as many greens in the UK and Marxian world-system theorists.[6] However, even with a different way to tally the numbers, one that showed that Canada was a small net exporter of emissions, the country still had the fifth highest per capita emissions on the consumption side (Davis and Caldeira 2010).

The limited achievements of EM climate reform to date, even in a relative leader such as the UK, did not in themselves prove that EM was incapable of providing adequate climate solutions in the future.

However, even some pioneers of EM theory acknowledged that this paradigm did not have all the answers. Jänicke (2008), while maintaining that EM had much greater potential to deliver environmental improvements than any other approach including sufficiency (563), acknowledged that EM faced limits where technological solutions were not available and that incremental eco-efficiency gains "tend to be easily wiped out by subsequent growth processes" (562). In addition to advocating more radical technological innovations, he called for "structural" solutions including changes in the structure of industry (scaling back ecologically intensive sectors) as well as lifestyle change. Jänicke concluded that win-win reform would not be enough: "Industrial transformation will inevitably clash with vested interests. Governance for sustainable development must therefore, mobilise the will and capacity to win this struggle. This is not going to be easy. Sorry about that" (2008, 564).

Despite its limits, an EM discourse and program – it is worth reiterating – is an important initial step in enabling climate action to begin. Of particular importance was the role that an EM message of economic opportunity played in the UK in pushing a BAU perspective to the political margins, and later in fighting rearguard battles to keep it there. The inability to push BAU aside in this way in Canada severely limited the climate-related reform process and the space available for public debate over future requirements. Some initial changes occurring within an EM framework also had potential to extend the range of future possibilities. For example, the rise of new ecological actors, such as investors committed to low-carbon reform, began to play a role in trying to limit carbon-intensive forms of growth by withdrawing their financial backing for British oil firms' investments in Canada's oil sands and for aviation in the UK. Meanwhile, developments such as the Climate Change Act and its apparently binding carbon budgets, as well as lifestyle-change promotion, introduction of new well-being measures other than GDP, and initial debate over personal carbon allowances, were consistent with EM, but had the potential to lead to a greater role for sufficiency in the future.

SUFFICIENCY: INROADS AND PROSPECTS

In both countries, a sufficiency-based critique of economic growth faced a staggering set of obstacles. Even before confronting fierce business resistance to the idea of less output, a critique of growth faced a more immediate line of defence: the consumerist aspirations of the population, which were linked to a wider ideology assuming growth to be essential and good, and were buttressed by a social logic that pressured individuals to keep up with rising consumption standards. Governments had come to depend on an ever-accelerating treadmill of production to meet a range of goals, most notably ensuring continued capital accumulation, but also including reducing poverty, limiting unemployment, moderating class conflict, and providing the revenues needed to satisfy voters and win re-election. The labour movement, for the most part, saw lower growth as a threat to jobs. Even environmentalists were often reluctant to raise a critique of growth out of concern for remaining "credible," among other constraints. Lying beneath many of these obstacles was a capitalist system dependent – or at least is widely perceived to depend – on never-ending growth for endless cycles of capital accumulation. Indeed, many questions remained about how a low- or no-growth economy could be organized to cope with a range of macroeconomic challenges, maintain social stability, and generate high levels of well-being.

With EM offering a less demanding alternative, one that was in line with the perceived growth imperative and the ideological and institutional structures of contemporary capitalism, EM theorists and others had reasons to expect sufficiency to fade away. Yet similar factors in both countries continued not only to keep a sufficiency perspective alive, but also to give it new relevance: the need for deep emissions cuts (even deeper than previously imagined), evidence of limits of an EM response, evidence of economic growth's limited capacity to improve well-being in affluent nations, and concerns for global justice in an ecologically constrained world. These factors, however, played out differently in Canada and the UK.

Struggling to Gain Traction, but More Opportunities in the UK

In both nations, sufficiency struggled to make its way onto the public agenda. In Canada, there was very little if any recognition by government or corporate leaders that a turn away from endless growth and expanding consumption was an option anyone with a full set of mental faculties would seriously consider, whereas in the UK, political and business leaders had to contend occasionally with the idea, even if they rejected it. But away from the centres of power, the idea of sufficiency was voiced in both countries by those who were critical of the absence of discussion of endless growth and consumption on the official agenda. (A similar process appeared to be at play in other countries such as Germany, according to Wolfgang Sachs, one of the world's leading sufficiency theorists.)[7] Meanwhile, in the UK, where the space available for a critique of endless economic expansion was greater than in Canada, sufficiency was not only the common sense of many climate activists, it also showed signs of getting closer to those centres of power, although there were still many lines of defence to overcome.

A growth critique appeared – to some interviewees and to myself – to have a greater presence in the UK media than in Canada, although a content analysis would be needed to confirm this conclusion. Meanwhile, in Canada, it was most often lone individual voices – supplemented by a range of small, radical organizations – who struggled by a variety of means to launch a discussion about growth. Although doing so was also an uphill battle in the UK, there was more significant backing for the growth critique from organizations capable of injecting it into mainstream discussion, such as the New Economics Foundation, the Church of England, the Sustainable Development Commission, and the Royal Society. Doubts about growth were also expressed by some surprising British sources, such as the Conservative Party's Quality of Life Policy Group (2007), which – although it never ultimately broke with the language of "green growth" – raised serious questions about the "insatiable pursuit after more" and the failure of growth to deliver well-being. The group's report would not only be unimaginable coming from Canadian Conservatives, it actually went further than the Green Party of Canada's (2007b) Vision Green document, released at roughly the same time, in wrestling with "the problem with growth" and the limits of efficiency. Meanwhile, the call by Adair Turner (2008, 93), chair of the Committee on Climate Change and former CBI head, to "dethrone" GDP growth as "an explicit objective of economic and social policy" suggested that the growth critique was making some limited inroads into UK establishment circles in a way not seen in Canada. So, too, did the expression of doubts about the viability of continued prioritization of growth by sociologist and New Labour adviser Anthony Giddens (2009a, 2009b), energy economist and government adviser Dieter Helm

(2009), and even, to a limited degree, Nicholas Stern (Watts 2009). In Canada, it was not unusual to hear that deep emissions cuts would require reductions in growth and consumption, but more often than not, this was an argument that BAU critics used against calls for deep emissions cuts. In the UK, such BAU arguments certainly existed, but space had also opened up for establishment figures – not only greens and others on the margins – to take a position on the other side of EM and voice the idea that climate action was not easily reconciled with economic growth yet it had to happen regardless.

As discussed in more detail below, in both countries, sufficiency made greater inroads at the micro level, targeting specific goods, sectors, or practices rather than economic growth more generally. However, in the UK, there was a more extensive range of targets for prominent campaigns, including food waste, meat and dairy consumption, gas-powered patio heaters, and SUVs. Most notable was the high-profile and contentious campaign to limit aviation expansion, which achieved a key victory for sufficiency supporters with the cancellation of plans for Heathrow's third runway – a victory which had no equivalent in Canada.

Sufficiency also made greater incursions into the state sphere in the UK, although one should not overstate this point, as growth remained an overriding state priority. In both countries, the national state promoted (at least for a time in Canada) individual lifestyle change, which opened a small window for the idea not only of consuming differently, but also of consuming less. However, in the UK, government also embraced a sufficiency-based language of "living within limits" and "one-planet living," and gave some substance to this language with its legal framework for deep CO_2 reductions in the Climate Change Act. The goal of "one-planet living" also took shape in the idea of tradable carbon rations or personal carbon allowances, which was promoted by a prominent cabinet minister, studied by government, and trialled in local projects. The UK government did eventually shelve the idea as "ahead of its time," but in Canada, personal carbon allowances were not even on the mainstream radar as an option. An additional contrast was the type of work by government advisory bodies that was considered groundbreaking. Canada's National Round Table on the Environment and the Economy pushed the boundaries of politically acceptable thought when, in 2008, it called for a carbon tax (and/or cap-and-trade). However, that hardly compared with the boundary pushing by the

UK Sustainable Development Commission, which concluded that an urgent need existed to develop an economy capable of "prosperity without growth" (Jackson 2009). (One similarity, however, was that both these advisory boundaries were later shut down by their respective governments – as part of the austerity-driven "bonfire of the quangos" in the case of the UK's SDC, and an apparently more politically motivated desire to silence the messenger in the case of Canada's NRTEE.)

Why Did Sufficiency Advance Further in the UK?

Greater space for sufficiency-based ideas opened up in the UK, at least for a time, in a context marked by three key factors, which were either non-existent or weaker in Canada.

First, a broad (although not necessarily permanent) political consensus was constructed in Britain on the need for deep GHG cuts consistent with avoiding warming of 2°C – with targets that became even deeper in light of new climate science. In Canada, no comparable consensus existed across the political spectrum and across regions. Although the Harper government did come around to the need for relatively modest emissions cuts, the targets it established bore no relation to scientific estimates of what rich nations had to do to avoid warming of 2°C.

Second, in the UK, increasing awareness and experience of the limits of an EM response to date contributed to the emergence of arguments that more radical steps were needed to meet the nation's commitments. The fact that Canada had yet to seriously embark on the easier path of ecological modernization made it hard to see the limits of "green growth," and did not leave much space to argue that a move to the next, more difficult step was necessary.

Third, prominent public discussion in the UK of evidence that economic growth did little, if anything, to improve well-being in rich nations gave sufficiency advocates an opportunity to promote an alternative vision of a higher quality of life that would not "cost the earth." Indeed, the idea that there was no strong connection between GDP growth and well-being in already rich nations had become, to some UK observers, "the new conventional wisdom" (Coyle 2011, 23). In contrast, debate in Canada about the determinants of well-being was relatively muted, and sufficiency advocates spoke of the lack of space in which to have such a public conversation.

A fourth driving factor behind sufficiency-based arguments was concern for global equity and social justice in an ecologically constrained world, but it was not clear that this was a stronger force in the UK than Canada.[8]

Commitment to deep emissions cuts in the UK – the first factor described above – helped drive scrutiny of all major GHG sources and made it difficult to sidestep questions about the volumes of high-carbon activity. This was most obvious in the case of aviation, where even assuming considerable efficiency improvements, growing passenger volumes would, under some projections, lead this single sector to consume the nation's entire carbon budget within decades. That fact did not stop the Labour government from continuing its airport expansion plans, but it caused many people, ranging from direct action protestors to forces within the Conservative Party, to question aviation growth – ultimately contributing to the Cameron-led coalition's cancellation of Heathrow expansion. Meanwhile, meat and dairy consumption came under scrutiny – not only from activists, but also, even, from branches of government, which began to consider how to raise this delicate issue with the public, while the NHS proposed cutting the amount of meat on its menus. The goal of cutting GHGs by 60 and later 80 per cent also led to consideration of radical policy ideas such as personal carbon allowances. Commitment to deep emissions cuts did not guarantee implementation of radical, sufficiency-based ideas to achieve them, but it did extend the boundaries of what was thinkable. For some, that included questioning the commitment to economic growth itself in light of the inconvenient math of decarbonization, which showed that unprecedented reductions in carbon intensity would have to be achieved – and sustained for decades – to reconcile continued GDP growth with strong carbon-reduction targets.

In light of the above factors, advocates of sufficiency in the two countries faced a different set of political opportunities, with greater openness to such ideas in the UK. The political opportunity perspective within social movement theory (e.g. McAdam 1996; Meyer 2004; Tarrow 1998) emphasizes that the prospects for advancing particular claims, mobilizing supporters, or influencing political outcomes depend on the political context. That context greatly influences the issues around which activists mobilize, advantages some claims over others, and affects the costs, dangers, and possible payoffs of various options for social movement action (Meyer 2004). In effect, the political opportunity structure in Canada presented only very minimal openness to claims that sufficiency-based responses were needed. Even activists who thought they were necessary emphasized the obstacles to raising such issues, given pressures to appear "credible" and "respectable," while others reached for less contentious EM arguments at key political moments. The extent of openness to sufficiency in the UK was greater, although that degree of openness should not be overstated, as there were still major difficulties in gaining political traction for proposals to shift away from a growth-based society. Indeed, in both countries, there was greater opportunity for sufficiency when defined in more limited forms, rather than as a head-on critique of economic growth.

The national commitment to deep GHG cuts – combined with experience of the limits of EM and prominent debate over the limits of economic growth in improving well-being – provided *relatively* favourable conditions in the UK for the emergence of sufficiency-based ideas. However, with time, doubts about the strength and durability of the consensus on carbon reduction in the UK became more evident. By 2011, opposition had grown within the Conservative Party to an EM project of green growth to the point that the chancellor was voicing BAU ideas, with one possible outcome in the future being an erosion of the UK's strong carbon-reduction commitments in the Climate Change Act. It also became necessary for supporters of climate action to remake the case for an EM project of green growth (D. Clark 2012). A further drift away from a strong national consensus on climate action would likely reduce the space available for sufficiency-based ideas as pressures would grow, as in Canada, for green-leaning forces to unite around a less controversial EM project. Indeed, in the UK, some critics already blamed green calls for sacrifice and "communitarian austerity" for contributing to a backlash by climate deniers and other BAU proponents (Lynas 2011, 210, 214, 227–8). The future prospects for sufficiency in the UK will likely depend, to a large degree, on whether or not that backlash can be weathered and political consensus on the need for deep carbon cuts consolidated.

Mixed Messages and Changing the Metrics

One limited, contradictory way that sufficiency appeared in political debates was through mixed messages about economic growth. In Canada, two leading environmentalists, David Suzuki and Green

Party leader Elizabeth May, at times denounced growth as a cancer; at others, notably when battling a BAU perspective, they and their organizations promoted an EM message celebrating economic opportunities from climate action (even if they did not necessarily celebrate growth per se). In the UK, similar mixed messages were evident in work by the Conservative Party's Quality of Life Policy Group (2007) and SDC chairman Jonathon Porritt (2007b), both of whom pushed a radical critique of growth and the limits of decoupling quite far, yet re-embraced growth as long as it was "green." In Porritt's (2009) case, later statements backing the SDC's work on "prosperity without growth" put him back more squarely in the growth critic camp. One could understand such mixed messages and the rhetorical contortions that often came with them in the context, on the one hand, of evidence of an ecological need to move beyond growth and, on the other, the seeming impossibility of doing so in contemporary capitalism.

Another outlet for doubts about economic growth was the demand for new well-being indicators as an alternative to GDP, an idea that did not require a direct challenge to a growth-based system. A longstanding demand of greens in both countries, the idea moved into the mainstream in the UK. Prime Minister Cameron later launched a new national well-being indicator to complement GDP in 2010 – possibly a step toward dethroning GDP growth as the dominant social priority. A Canadian Index of Well-Being was also developed, although it remained an under-the-radar measure without government backing or national debate over its significance. Like other indirect ways of raising doubts about a growth-based system, the question remained whether new economic and social indicators would lead to a fundamental rethinking of priorities or simply allow dominant institutions to absorb a growth critique without wider structural change.

Micro-Sufficiency: Enough, within Limits

With a macro-level growth critique facing daunting obstacles, the idea of sufficiency found more favourable prospects at the micro-level in both nations, although, as noted above, in the UK there was a wider range of products and practices on the receiving end of the challenge and a greater prominence for such questioning.

LINKING TO CORE POLITICAL IMPERATIVES. Sufficiency at the micro level did not always make the most progress where its carbon-reduction potential was greatest. In Canada and the UK, plastic bags and bottled water were vulnerable because they were highly visible symbols of consumption excess, consumers had readily available alternatives, and their producers were not centrally important to the economy. Progress in such campaigns still had to overcome resistance, but these products were more vulnerable than many others. In both countries, politicians facing the imperative of establishing legitimacy on environmental matters could support reduced use of plastic bags and bottled water without encountering overwhelming opposition or endangering economic expansion. (Incandescent light bulbs were another relatively easy target, although that issue was more easily understood in terms of efficiency rather than sufficiency.) The question also arose as to whether campaigns against such targets represented initial steps toward a broader challenge to high-carbon consumption growth, or merely a distraction allowing politicians and ordinary citizens to claim and even believe they were doing their part.

Particularly noteworthy were cases where sufficiency was able to make inroads at the micro level and GHG reductions were potentially large. In some cases, this became possible where micro-sufficiency coincided with the economic interests of influential actors, helping overcome a key structural disadvantage that this paradigm usually faces. Campaigns to reduce food miles benefited from the interest of local farmers, agri-business, and the state in expanding sales of local foods (albeit at the expense of producers elsewhere), resulting in local food promotion policies in some Canadian municipalities and provinces, including the largest province, Ontario. Meanwhile, the main driver of Ontario's conservation campaign to reduce electricity consumption was state and business fear that excessive demand could overwhelm the power system's capacities and, in turn, undermine the functioning and growth of the broader economy. The Canadian Council of Chief Executives also came to support a broad national effort to "get serious about energy conservation, for the health of our economy as well as the environment" (CCCE 2011, 31). These were special cases where the idea of less could overlap, up to a point, with state and business interests in general economic expansion. Sufficiency with respect to certain goods or practices appeared to face better prospects, paradoxically, when it could be linked to increased economic output in some other form. In other words, there were instances where sufficiency, narrowly defined, attached itself to the economic growth imperative.

Other cases existed where the idea of sufficiency could coincide with the economic interests of actors who could benefit from less consumption and output – of somebody else's product. Campaigns against bottled water consumption benefited, at least in Britain, from the resources of the privatized water suppliers, who saw bottled water as a competitor. In both countries, telecommunications firms encouraged other businesses to travel less by using their video conferencing services. In addition to such opportunities to profit from providing alternative products, some firms had an interest in making their own record look greener by highlighting their efforts to cut high-carbon consumption, such as Aeroplan publicizing its encouragement of employees to stop driving to work. Such cases illustrated the potential for micro-sufficiency campaigns to gain additional support and resources through temporary alliances with corporate and other economic interests. Whether such alliances help or hinder the emergence of a broader social movement to create a very different economy, one informed by the idea of sufficiency – and under what conditions they might do so – is another matter, one worthy of further research and debate. Meanwhile, labour union support for micro-sufficiency could also be found when there was a connection to economic interests: calls to limit tar sands expansion received backing from Canadian unions largely due to concern over negative impacts of a rising petro-currency on manufacturing jobs in other regions (i.e. "Dutch disease").

Scaling back consumption demand and output is particularly relevant for products, practices, and sectors that are significant GHG sources and for which adequate technological solutions are not immediately available nor on the horizon. Key examples are aviation, meat and dairy consumption, and Alberta's oil sands. The obstacles to sufficiency with these issues were great. Political action to curb air travel and meat and dairy consumption was complicated not only by resistance from powerful economic interests but also by public attachment to these forms of consumption. Indeed, in Canada, neither aviation nor meat and dairy consumption had become prominent public issues. However, in the UK, the need to scrutinize all major GHG sources as result of the legislated commitment to deep GHG reductions and the efforts of campaigners helped push these two issues onto the agenda. The most significant outcome was the Cameron-led coalition's cancellation of the Heathrow third runway. This victory for a sufficiency approach was made possible, in part, by the Conservative Party's need at the time for green legitimacy as part of its efforts to shed its image as "the nasty party" (in addition to political calculations that this position would help win votes under the Heathrow flight path). Anti-third-runway campaigners also cast doubt on the idea that Heathrow expansion would enhance economic growth – a case of successfully neutralizing claims of a linkage between aviation expansion and the wider economic imperative. That said, the victory was a provisional one – as was often the case for sufficiency at the micro level – as controversial proposals to expand Heathrow and other airports in southeast England returned to the public agenda.

At some point in the future, an ecological imperative to do whatever it takes to address climate change and other sustainability challenges – as discussed in more detail below – could conceivably become a powerful enough force of its own to enable a more comprehensive critique of economic growth to gain influence. However, until then, these cases suggested that some of the best prospects for ideas of sufficiency could be found in limited circumstances, at the micro level, where linkages could be made to the political imperative of legitimation or, paradoxically, the perceived need for economic growth – and possibly the (energy) security imperative.[9]

BORDERLANDS AND HIDING PLACES. When sufficiency is limited to the micro level, the boundaries between it and ecological modernization can become blurred. In both countries, sufficiency managed to make inroads in many such instances. In some cases, efforts to improve efficiency, a widely shared value, spilled over into less mainstream sufficiency territory – as with UK government–backed efforts to cut food waste, which could not avoid becoming linked to calls to buy less food. Demands for fewer suvs on the road were framed as a way to boost fuel efficiency but also as a matter of consumption norms having grown beyond reasonable limits. Food miles reduction was similarly a matter of both reducing unnecessary transport and living within local limits. State efforts to encourage energy conservation in Ontario incorporated calls to get more out of each unit of electricity and for less consumption of energy services. Meanwhile, micro-sufficiency could involve use of advanced technology – another staple of EM reform – as in the case of reducing air travel through video conferencing and high-speed trains.

Sufficiency-based ideas were also lurking within concepts with greater mainstream acceptability. "Conservation," as just mentioned, was a concept that included less consumption of energy services. Meanwhile, most observers accepted lifestyle and behaviour change as a necessary part of any climate response, and indeed states and some businesses in both countries promoted such change to varying degrees. Opening up the question of lifestyle change at a minimum raised the issue of consuming differently, but it was not easy to stop at that threshold and avoid the issue of consuming less. Indeed, in the UK, there were signs of contradictions between the long-prevalent cultural message to consume more and the recent emphasis on the importance of low-carbon behaviour. Conceptual hiding places such as conservation and lifestyle/behaviour change could amount to cells in which the idea of sufficiency was confined, but also refuges from which it might emerge to play a broader role.

Given the obstacles facing a radical sufficiency approach, the overlap with elements of a more mainstream EM agenda provided important cover for it. Those seeking to advance a sufficiency perspective might find some of their best prospects in these borderlands. The boundary zones also included policy measures that embraced the idea of limits, but remained agnostic with respect to economic growth – measures that could provide one of the more likely avenues for sufficiency to play a greater role in the future, as discussed in more detail below.

Neither EM nor Sufficiency? An EM-Sufficiency Synthesis?

In the UK, EM supplanted BAU as the dominant paradigm of climate response, but that status was fragile. As the emergence of an EM consensus, coupled with recognition of its limits, opened up space for more radical sufficiency ideas, one could theorize that EM might be like a gateway drug to a harder-core variety of green politics.[10] That potential existed, but there was certainly no guarantee, even if doubts about EM continued to grow, that sufficiency would emerge as the main alternative. Other potential responses were evident on the landscape, including backsliding into business-as-usual. In both countries, many voices justified inaction by pointing fingers at growing emissions in China and India that would swamp emissions reduction efforts elsewhere. High-risk geo-engineering options gained adherents, including scientists deeply concerned about possible side effects but losing patience with inadequate political and social responses. Others called for a more explicitly anti-capitalist, revolutionary project. With the possibility that tipping points into runaway positive feedback were near, some suggested that efforts to mitigate climate change through emissions reductions had already failed and argued that adaptation was the only option left. (However, it was doubtful that humanity could successfully adapt to the ever-changing and worsening climate conditions that would result without mitigation efforts). A further option was despair and resignation in the face of a seemingly overwhelming task, or as influential British scientist James Lovelock suggested, "Enjoy life while you can" (Aitkenhead 2008; see also Lovelock 2008). That led to consideration of another, less hopeful path to sufficiency – one resulting from climate disruption, as the unravelling of the ecological conditions that enabled capitalist expansionism could force a reduction of consumption and put a full stop to the modern utopian vision of endless economic growth (e.g. Gilding 2011; Hamilton 2010; McKibben 2010). Others foresaw an end of growth arising out of the end of cheap fossil energy, forcing a shift to less consumptive lifestyles (Rubin 2012).

Looking ahead, if solutions are to be found and debilitating despair avoided, a certain degree of both sufficiency and EM are likely needed. As noted above, even some EM theorists began to acknowledge the limits of EM alone. Initial efforts toward a synthesis of the two paradigms were evident in both countries. However, the challenge remains to synthesize the two perspectives in a more coherent way than presenting double messages on growth depending on the context or an "economic growth dance," in which growth's destructiveness and the limits of decoupling are criticized, before returning to the argument that growth is still needed as long as it is "green."

EM's appeal derives from its positive vision promising green jobs, economic opportunity, and technological innovation – all of which are vitally important to building support for strong climate action. There is clearly no way of resolving the problem without considerable reliance on technology – a point that becomes even clearer the deeper the needed emissions cuts become. (Take, for example, the call in some quarters for 100 per cent emissions cuts, which would be impossible solely by cutting consumption on that scale.) It is equally clear that there can be some "green growth" in line with EM, as more nuanced growth critiques also acknowledge. Significant opportunities for new economic activity and job creation do exist, notably in transforming the energy system. Indeed, the recent sharp fall in the cost of power from photovoltaics could give a major boost in the years ahead to the green energy sector and to carbon-cutting efforts. However, the growth of other high-impact activities will almost certainly need curtailing – including significant components of modernity and globalization, such as air travel – a task that requires going beyond EM. As the Centre for Alternative Technology in Wales put it, the challenge is to "power down" high-carbon activities and "power up" a low- or zero-carbon energy system and society (CAT 2007, 2013). Whether the net effect will be higher GDP is unclear in advance, but – as voices ranging from radical greens to the Confederation of British Industry's former head (A. Turner 2008) have suggested – good reasons exist why that should no longer be the clinching factor in the debate.

Embryonic versions of such a synthesis – which could be considered a strong form of EM (Christoff 1996) – were evident. For example, under Ken Livingstone, the Greater London Authority framed its ambitious climate efforts largely in EM terms – emphasizing efficiency, decentralized energy technologies, and economic opportunity – but also incorporated a significant dose of sufficiency, at least at the micro level. This included promotion of a modal shift to reduce car use (which coincided with business's need to reduce congestion), efforts to restrict oversized 4×4 vehicles, rejection of further capacity growth at UK airports, and a campaign encouraging people to stop buying bottled water. The potential impact of such an EM-sufficiency synthesis could already be seen, for example, with UK transport emissions. For years, these emissions had risen stubbornly, but began falling after 2007 due to improved vehicle technology, a shift in consumer demand from gas guzzlers to smaller and/or more efficient vehicles, fewer vehicle miles travelled, and a significant slowdown in growth of the number of cars on the road.

Agnosticism on Growth and a New Ecological Imperative

The examples in the previous paragraph represented a still quite limited role for sufficiency. Some observers saw a need for a more comprehensive, head-on critique of and movement against economic growth. In addition to Canadian and UK examples discussed in this book, these included, for instance, Gus Speth, an adviser to Jimmy Carter and Bill Clinton and a founder of mainstream environmental groups such as the Natural Resources Defense Council and World Resources Institute. Speth (2012) concluded that "rich countries should abandon their growth fetish and move toward no growth or degrowth," in light of the "implausibly high" rates of carbon-intensity reduction needed in a fast-growing economy. While warning that the economic slowdown was no excuse to delay climate action, the European Union's chief scientific adviser, Anne Glover, added, "The simplest way to think about increasing jobs is to make more stuff and get people to buy more stuff. But my point is that we can't do that, because we're running out of resources" (Dunmore 2012). Meanwhile, a global survey of nearly one thousand "qualified sustainability experts" in business, government, NGOs, academia, and media found a roughly even split between those who agreed (40 per cent) and disagreed (43 per cent) that "there is an inherent conflict between economic growth and sustainable consumption" (SustainAbility and Globescan 2011) – a ratio that was certainly not matched by the proportionate representation of such views in mainstream media or political debate.

Yet the core dilemma remained that, although a direct challenge to economic growth might be ecologically necessary, massive political-economic obstacles left it with poor prospects for success in the near future. A more likely scenario in which sufficiency-based ideas rise to greater prominence is as a consequence of the imposition of hard caps on emissions – in other words, limits set with respect to GHGs rather than GDP. Demands for deep GHG reductions in line with climate science can remain agnostic about the potential for continued GDP growth. Whatever economic growth is possible within tight carbon constraints – and other similarly defined limits relevant to the range of other pressing ecological problems – can be welcomed. Concepts such as "one planet living" and "contraction and convergence" are likewise agnostic about growth – which is a key reason why some mainstream political figures, at least in the UK, were able to endorse them. For the foreseeable future, approaches that are agnostic about growth – i.e. which represent "a-growth," focusing on meeting core ecological and social goals, regardless of the impact on GDP (van den Bergh and Kallis 2012) – are undoubtedly more politically viable than the pursuit of degrowth (intentionally aiming to downscale the size of the economy).

In effect, the challenge is to shift from a situation where there is as much climate protection as possible as long as there is little or no cost to the economy to one allowing as much economic growth as is compatible with a stable climate (and respect for other ecological limits). In economists' terms, maximizing growth would become a "constrained optimization problem," as Mark Kenber of the Climate Group put it – or, in the terms of climate protestors in the photo (figure 11.2), "Planet 1st, Economy 2nd."

In this light, the UK Climate Change Act's legally binding targets stood out as a very significant reform. The act was initiated within an EM framework but had already contributed to a greater role for sufficiency at the micro level (e.g. in the cancellation of Heathrow expansion) and might eventually become a key driver of sufficiency at the macro level. The act's impact in the future would, of course, depend on whether its carbon-reduction targets were indeed respected – or, in other words, whether the act truly represented the emergence of an ecological imperative to ensure the attainment of core climate goals. It was still too early to tell if this was the case, especially given the signs of a wavering of climate commitment among Conservatives. Assuming that the commitment to tight emissions limits is consolidated and respected, then interesting times lie ahead. If efficiency gains and progress toward low-carbon technologies accelerate dramatically, substantial GDP growth could still occur within those limits, but if not, EM's inadequacy and the requirement for sufficiency with respect to economic growth will become all the more apparent.

IMPORTANCE OF A POSITIVE, ALTERNATIVE VISION

The degree to which sufficiency plays a part in future climate responses will also likely depend on the extent to which it can be shown to be an attractive option that, like EM, can offer a positive agenda and its own language of opportunity. Whereas EM holds out the promise of win-win economic gains, sufficiency seeks to shift the emphasis to quality-of-life improvements, and to develop and deploy not only new technologies, but also new visions of the good life. Many sufficiency advocates in both countries were clearly aware of the need to present a vision of the future with greater political appeal than an emphasis

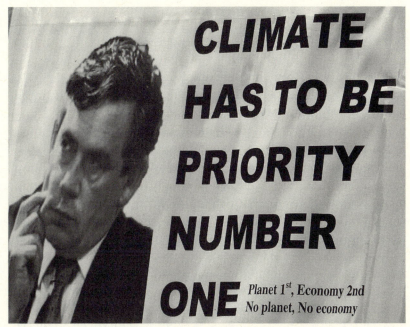

Figure 11.2 Protester's placard, Climate Rally, 30 June 2007, Parliament Square, London. Photo by author.

on austerity or sacrifice – or even calls for an economic recession – sometimes voiced by, or attributed to, adherents of their perspective. They spoke with conviction of their belief that life could be better in a less consumption- and growth-centred society, with a range of benefits from less stress and better health to greater global justice and security. The debate over the politics of well-being provided, at least in Britain, an important opening for these arguments. Of course, much work still lay ahead to go beyond showing that growth was failing to improve well-being and to create social conditions in which the converse were true: constant or rising well-being decoupled from flat (or falling) economic output.

A sufficiency perspective faces a particular challenge in maintaining employment and protecting workers displaced in a transition to a low-carbon, low- or no-growth society – which is vitally important to ensuring high levels of well-being. In a context of continued labour productivity growth driven by market competition and the relentless quest for profit, output expansion has been a central tool to maintain employment and social stability within capitalism. A long-term solution may very well require alternatives to the basic dynamics of capitalism, but other, more immediate potential answers were evident in the debate. One was, yet again, to return to the search for "green growth," or at least some degree of it, as an alternative to destructive high-carbon growth. An example was the call by some prominent growth critics in the UK, such as Andrew Simms of NEF and Green Party leader Caroline Lucas, for a Green New Deal, with massive renewable energy investment to help the country escape its economic downturn. As important as such measures were in the short term, using a green stimulus to put the economy back on a growth path, even a lower-carbon growth path, did not represent a full response to the problems of a growth-based system (Jackson 2009). An option that could represent a bigger step away from a growth paradigm was work-time reduction, an idea commonly voiced by sufficiency advocates in both the UK and Canada as a way to maintain employment levels and provide a basis for improved quality of life without consumption growth (e.g. Coote and Franklin 2013). Meanwhile, just transition policies to enable workers to move from high-carbon sectors that must contract into other activities were an important piece of the puzzle.

Evidence of limits to an EM response to climate change – and other key ecological challenges – suggests that much more learning is needed about how to step off the treadmill of production while protecting well-being and social stability. As Giddens (2009a, 113) points out, public enthusiasm for policy issues rarely lasts unless problems can be connected to clear solutions. If more people were to reach the conclusion that continued prioritization of economic growth is not compatible with climate stability, there would be a risk that climate change could slip from the agenda, replaced by a sense of fatalism – at least as long as the perception reigns that there is no prospect of a socially viable low- or no-growth alternative. Hence carrying forward the initial work in Canada on "managing without growth" (Victor 2008) and in the UK on "prosperity without growth" (Jackson 2009) is of great importance. Indeed, others have followed by outlining changes needed to achieve an "economy of enough" (Dietz and O'Neill 2013). Such work is an important step toward one day moving beyond the widely accepted notion that there is an imperative of economic growth.

Not only is further intellectual work, backed by much greater societal resources commensurate with the stakes, urgently needed in this area. Equally if not more important is a far-reaching societal debate on the path for the future, as many sufficiency advocates have pushed for. Beyond that lies the challenge of constructing through political and social action an economy that does not need growth to function adequately. That may sound utopian, but the depth of the climate challenge, not to mention a host of other pressing ecological concerns, suggest that it may be more realistic than the idea that growth can continue indefinitely.

APPENDICES

Methods

To understand the prominence of the three paradigms of interest – business-as-usual, ecological modernization, and sufficiency – in the UK and Canada, I began by identifying several categories of mainstream groups in order to analyze their proposed responses to climate change. These included government departments and agencies, politicians and political parties, business (conventional and environmentally oriented), environmental groups, labour unions, and others prominent in the public debate (e.g. think tank researchers, engaged academics, writers, and journalists). Since a theoretical goal was to gain insight into the obstacles and opportunities for sufficiency-based ideas, advocates of sufficiency were also identified, regardless of their organizational affiliation, following a logic of purposive sampling.

Multiple sources of evidence were used: interviews, direct observation, and documents. Semi-structured interviews – thirty in the UK and twenty-eight in Canada – were conducted with key informants covering the range of groups mentioned above. An initial sample of individuals was identified through their writing and public statements on climate change responses, and later expanded upon through snowball techniques and contacts made at conferences and public events. Interviews took place in person, with the exception of one phone interview in the UK and five in Canada – necessitated by the greater distances and wider geographic distribution of key actors in the climate debate in Canada.

In addition, direct observation of climate debates occurred through attendance at a wide range of public events and conferences discussing climate solutions: thirty-three in the UK (primarily in London) and thirty-six in Canada (mainly in Toronto, but also in

Appendices

Montreal, Ottawa, and Edmonton). These events ranged from meetings of radical greens and socialist groups to corporate gatherings on the "business of climate change." Attendance allowed a greater number of voices, and a more complete range of perspectives, to be heard than through interviews alone. In the UK, it was relatively difficult to set up interviews with business leaders and – surprisingly – climate campaigners with large environmental organizations, hence they were under-represented in interviews. Communications with the latter group suggested they were receiving many similar requests from researchers and felt a high sense of urgency about devoting their time to serving the climate action cause. However, business and large environmental organizations were well represented at conferences and public events, as was a broad range of views across the political spectrum – other than groups to the right of the Conservative Party.

Documents analyzed included policy statements, press releases, op-eds, speeches, and position papers by actors within the various groups identified above. Mainstream media websites – covering a range of ideological perspectives in both countries – were also a source for the positions of key actors, leads toward more detailed documents and primary sources, and information on emerging developments. For the UK, the principal sources were the BBC, the *Guardian* (left-of-centre), the *Independent* (left-of-centre), the *Times* (right-of-centre), and the *Daily Telegraph* (right-of-centre). Additional items were drawn from the *Financial Times* (right-of-centre) and the *Daily Mail* (right-of-centre tabloid). For Canada, the CBC, the *Toronto Star* (centre/left-of-centre), the *Globe and Mail* (centre/right-of-centre), the *National Post* (right-of-centre), and the *Edmonton Journal* (right-of-centre, local paper in a centre of Canada's oil industry) were key sources. Other items were drawn from other local papers in the PostMedia chain. Daily email updates from the United Nations Environment Programme's "Earth Wire Climate" also alerted me to relevant news items, particularly in the UK press. Given the tendency of journalistic accounts to distort information to some degree – often in pursuit of an eye-catching headline – I traced statements and information back to their original source (e.g. reports, transcripts of speeches, press releases, data sources) wherever possible.

Analysis of the data from these different sources focused on identifying the presence of the major paradigms of response to climate change, i.e. BAU, EM, and sufficiency (either at the macro- or micro-level). In the case of sufficiency advocates, analysis included identification of the opportunities and obstacles they experienced with respect to their ideas.

The variety of data sources was not only useful in ensuring that a full range of perspectives was considered. It also provided opportunities for triangulation by ensuring that key conclusions were supported by multiple sources of evidence.

A first round of research took place in 2007–08, when the attendance at public events and climate conferences, as well as the bulk of the interviews, took place. This led to the first draft of this text, in the form of a doctoral dissertation. Later revisions and updates, taking into account events up to the end of 2012, drew primarily on an analysis of documents and media sources. This second phase of research offered an opportunity to assess and reflect on the evolution of policies and proposed climate responses that emerged during the earlier round of research.

Interviews and Events Attended in the UK

Occupational titles listed represent the individual's position at the time of the interview or event.

INTERVIEWS

UK interviews took place in 2007, unless otherwise indicated. The names of officials from national government departments and agencies have been kept anonymous.

Government Departments or Agencies – National (4)

Two officials from the Environment Agency
Official from the Department of Food, Environment and Rural Affairs (Defra)
Four Defra employees
Two officials from the Department of Energy and Climate Change (2010)

Government Departments or Agencies – Local (1)

Adrian Hewitt, Principal Environment Officer, Environment & Regeneration Department, London Borough of Merton

Politicians / Political Parties (4)

Shahrar Ali, London Federation of Green Parties, Policy Coordinator
Colin Challen, Labour Party MP (chair of All Party Parliamentary Group on Climate Change)
Jean Lambert, Green Party Member of European Parliament
Alan Simpson, Labour Party MP (left wing of Labour Party)

Business – *"Mainstream" (1)*

Stephen Radley, Chief Economist, and Roger Salomone, Energy Adviser, EEF (the manufacturers' organization)

Business – *"Environmentally Oriented" (1)*

Aled Jones, Development Director, Corporate Leaders Group on Climate Change, and Emma Dowen, Project Manager, University of Cambridge Programme for Industry

Labour Unions (2)

Paul Noon, General Secretary, Prospect (union for professionals), and Joint Chair of Trade Union Advisory Committee on Sustainable Development
Sean Geoghegan, National Union of Rail, Maritime and Transport Workers (RMT)

Environment – Large Mainstream Organizations (1)

Ben Stewart, Head of Media, Greenpeace UK

Environment – Grassroots and Other Climate Activists (8)

John Ackers, Islington Carbon Rationing Action Group
Duncan Law, Coordinator and Chair, Transition Town Brixton
Peter Lockley, Policy Analyst, Aviation Environment Foundation
Blake Ludwig, Co-Founder, Alliance Against Urban 4x4s (and member of Camden Greenpeace)
George Marshall, Founder and Director of Projects, Climate Outreach and Information Network
Jessica Rayburn, Islington Carbon Rationing Action Group
Graham Thompson, Plane Stupid
Lucy Wills, independent protestor

Sufficiency Advocates (5)

(Others listed elsewhere may also fit in this category)
Jane Buchanan, Founder, "Shrinking Economies in the Developed World"
Stephan Harding, Resident Ecologist, Schumacher College

Tim Jackson, Professor of Sustainable Development, University of
 Surrey, and Chair of UK Sustainable Development Commission
 Economics Steering Group
Wolfgang Sachs, Senior Researcher, Wuppertal Institute, Germany
Andrew Simms, Policy Director, New Economics Foundation

Other (5)

Mayer Hillman, Senior Fellow Emeritus, Policy Studies Institute,
 University of Westminster, and independent policy analyst
Mark Kenber, International Policy Director, The Climate Group
Mark Lynas, journalist and author
Ed Mayo, Chief Executive, National Consumer Council
Aubrey Meyer, author and originator of the "Contraction & Conver-
 gence" concept

INDIVIDUALS HEARD AT CONFERENCES OR PUBLIC EVENTS
(PARTIAL LIST)

Government Departments or Agencies – National

Mike Anderson, Director General, Climate Change Group, Depart-
 ment for Environment, Food and Rural Affairs (Defra)
Philip Douglas, National Climate Change Policy Division, Defra
Terence Ilott, Head of Business and Consumers, Defra
David King, Chief Scientific Advisor to HM Government, Head of
 Office of Science and Innovation
Graham Pendlebury, Director, Environment and International Dir-
 ectorate, Department for Transport
Barbara Young, Chief Executive, Environment Agency

Government Departments or Agencies – Regional and Local

Simon Bilsborough, Sustainable Futures Division, Welsh Assembly
 Government
Allan Jones, CEO, London Climate Agency

Politicians / Political Parties – National

Peter Ainsworth, Conservative MP, Shadow Secretary of State for
 Environment, Food and Rural Affairs

Norman Baker, Liberal Democrat MP
Siân Barry, Green Party Principal Female Speaker
Menzies Campbell, Liberal Democratic Party Leader
Chris Huhne, Liberal Democrat MP, Shadow Secretary of State for
    Environment, Food and Rural Affairs
Nick Hurd, Conservative MP
Chris Keene, Climate Policy Adviser, Green Party
Caroline Lucas, Green Party Member of European Parliament
David Miliband, Labour MP, Environment Secretary
Elliot Morley, Labour MP, Prime Minister's Special Representative
    on Climate Change
Derek Wall, Green Party Principal Male Speaker
Tim Yeo, Conservative MP, Chair of Environmental Audit
    Committee

Politicians / Political Parties – Local

Nicky Gavron, Deputy Mayor of London
Ken Livingstone, Mayor of London

Business – Mainstream

Ian Armstrong, Manager of Customer Communcations, Honda
Ian Blythe, Head of Corporate Social Responsibility, Alliance Boots
    plc
Rob Challis, Global Head of Corporate Responsibility, Man Group
    plc
Donal Dowds, Director of Safety, Security and Services, BAA (airport
    authority)
Richard Gillies, Director of Store Design, Development and Pro-
    curement, Marks and Spencer
Joe Greenwell, Ford of Britain
Abyd Karmali, Managing Director, ICF International
Paul Jefferiss, Director of Environmental Policy, BP
Andrew Jenkins, Sustainable Development Manager, Boots
Jason Leonard, Group Head of Health, Safety & Environment, Stan-
    dard Chartered Bank
Simon Lewis, Group Director of Corporate Affairs, Vodafone
Paul Monaghan, Head of Ethics and Sustainability, Co-operative
    Group

David North, Community and Government Affairs Director, Tesco
Ronald Oxburgh, Chair, D1 Oils, former chair of Shell
James Smith, Chairman, Shell UK
Ben Stimson, Director of Corporate Responsibility, BSkyB
Chris Tuppen, Head of Sustainable Development and Corporate
    Accountability, BT
Jon Williams, Head of Group Sustainable Development, HSBC Hold-
    ings plc
RebeccaWoodward, Technical Manager, Burts Potato Chips
Daniel Yates, Strategy and Business Development Manager, last-
    minute.com

Business – Environmentally Oriented

Gary Freedman, Head of Business, Ecotricity
Alan Knight, Founder, Single Planet Living
Jeremy Leggett, CEO, Solarcentury
Mike Mason, Founder, ClimateCare
Andrew Morris, Managing Director, dcarbon8
Jonathan Shopley, Managing Director and External Affairs, The
    CarbonNeutral Company
Phillip Paddington, Director, Combined Heat and Power
    Association

Labour Unions

Gail Cartmail, Assistant General Secretary, Amicus
James Croy, Political Officer, RMT (transport union)
Mike Farley, Director, Doosan Babock, and Chair of TUC Clean Coal
    Task Group
Sue Ferns, Head of Research and Specialist Services, Prospect (pro-
    fessionals union)
Frances O'Grady, Deputy General Secretary, Trades Union Congress
Dave Prentis, General Secretary, Unison

Environment – Large Mainstream Organizations

Keith Allott, Head of Climate Change, WWF
Jos Dings, Director, European Federation for Transport and
    Environment

Tony Juniper, Executive Director, Friends of the Earth
Ed Matthews, Head of the New Economics Team, Friends of the
   Earth

Environment – Grassroots and Other Climate Activists

Mike Fairfield, Stop Stansted Expansion
Joss Garman, Plane Stupid
Guy Taylor, Globalise Resistance
Phil Thornhill, National Coordinator, Campaign against Climate
   Change

Sufficiency Advocates / Growth Critics

(Others listed elsewhere may also fit in this category)
Tom Hodgkinson, author
William Rees, Professor, University of British Columbia
Mathis Wackernagel, President, Global Footprint Network

Marxist Perspectives on Climate Change

Pete Ashley
Adam Buick, Socialist Party of Great Britain
Martin Empson
Michael Löwy, eco-socialist, Emeritus Research Director in Social
   Sciences at the French National Center of Scientific Research
Jonathan Neale
Derek Wall, Green Party Principal Male Speaker (and eco-socialist)

Other

David Fleming, originator of tradable energy quotas / carbon ra-
   tioning idea
Stephen Joseph, Director, Transport 2000
Robert May, Chief Scientific Advisor to the Government, 2000–05
Euan Murray, Strategy Manager, The Carbon Trust
Jonathon Porritt, Chair of Sustainable Development Commission
   and Founder/Director of Forum for the Future
Matt Prescott, Project Director, RSA Carbon Limited, proponent of
   personal carbon allowances

Graham Smith, Chair, Low Carbon Vehicle Partnership
James Woudhuysen, Professor of Forecasting and Innovation at De
    Montfort University, Leicester
Joanna Yarrow, broadcaster and founder of Beyond Green

CONFERENCES AND OTHER PUBLIC EVENTS ATTENDED

20 March 2007: "Sustainable London: Addressing Climate Change
    in the Capital," Exhibition at New London Architecture,
    London
21 March 2007: Allan Jones, MBE, Chief Executive Officer, London
    Climate Change Agency "Decentralised Energy and Climate
    Change," talk organized by New London Architecture, London
22 March 2007: "A Warming Meal: How Climate Change Will Affect
    What's On Your Plate," Dana Centre, Science Museum, London
23 March 2007: "How Do We Change Climate Change?" Sunday
    Times Oxford Literary Festival, Oxford
26 March 2007: Rally for Sustainable Communities Bill, Methodist
    Central Hall, London
8–10 May 2007: International Ecological Footprint Conference,
    Cardiff, Wales
11 May 2007: "Exposed: Climate Change in Britain's Backyard."
    Photo Exhibition by National Trust, Hoopers Gallery, London
12–13 May 2007: International Climate Change Conference, Or-
    ganized by Campaign Against Climate Change, London School
    of Economics and Political Science
16 May 2007: Tour of BedZED (model low-carbon housing develop-
    ment), London Borough of Sutton
17 May 2007: Tom Hodgkinson (editor of "The Idler," author of
    "How to be Idle" and "How to be Free"), "Medieval Values: Why
    Going Back Will Make Us Free," Royal Society for the encour-
    agement of Arts, Manufactures and Commerce (RSA), London
21 May 2007: "Preventing Climate Change: What Individuals and
    Communities Can Do." Reception organized by RSA Carbon
    Limited and the Cooperative Party at Portcullis House (Parlia-
    ment), Westminster
23 May 2007: "Global Warming: Who's to Blame?" The Socialist
    Party, Plough Pub, London
29–30 May 2007: Corporate Climate Response Conference,

Confederation of British Industries Conference Centre, Centre Point Tower, London

30 May 2007: "Punk Science: Climate Change," Dana Centre, Science Museum, London

3 June 2007: Camden Green Fair, Regent's Park, London

3 June 2007: Climate Change Walk, Brixton, Transition Town Brixton, London

4 June 2007: "On Target? Environment Policy and the Climate Change Bill," conference organized by the Trades Union Congress, Congress House, London

4 June 2007: Jeremy Leggett, "Climate Change Meets Peak Oil: Mega-Problems Needing Local Bottom-Up Solutions," hosted by Transition Town Brixton, Lambeth Town Hall, Brixton (London)

6 June 2007: Andrew Simms and Nic Marks, "From Economic Growth to Well-Being," Schumacher College Open Evening, Totnes

11 June 2007: The Guardian Climate Change Summit 2007 – "How to Succeed in a Low-Carbon Economy," Victoria Park Plaza, London

12 June 2007: Jonathon Porritt, Chair of Sustainable Development Commission, and Joanna Yarrow, broadcaster, Royal Borough of Kensington and Chelsea Environment Day, Kensington Town Hall, London

13 June 2007: Oliver James, "Affluenza: Can We Be Successful And Stay Sane?" Primrose Hill Lecture, St. Mary's Church, London

16 June 2007: "Energise London," workshop for climate activists organized by London21 and Planet Positive in partnership with Blackout Britain and Climate Outreach and Information Network, King's College, London

18 June 2007: Islington Carbon Rationing Action Group (I-CRAG) meeting

20 June 2007: Mark Lynas, "Carbon Conscience: Time to Face the Truth," Primrose Hill Lectures, St Mary's Church, London

24 June 2007: "How Can a Boom Town Be Green?" Debate London, series organized by The Architecture Foundation, Turbine Hall, Tate Modern, London

25 June 2007: Wolfgang Sachs, "Fair Futures: Resource Conflicts, Security and Global Justice," in conversation with Andrew

Simms, New Economics Foundation, Book Launch, Mary Ward Centre, London

28 June 2007: "Cutting Carbon Through Greener Motoring Marketing and Other Approaches," Low Carbon Vehicles Partnership Fourth Annual Conference, Department of Trade and Industry, London

30 June 2007: Demonstration for a Climate Bill That Really Works, Parliament Square, London

1 July 2007: Derek Wall (Green Party Principal Male Speaker), "Can Eco-Socialism Save the Planet?" Permanent Revolution Conference (Trotskyist), Conway Hall, London

2 July 2007: Dr. Alan Knight (business consultant), "If Products Could Talk!" Breakfast Briefing on Sustainability, Wallacespace, London

3 July 2007: Environmental Audit Committee Hearing, "Government and the Challenge of Climate Change," Palace of Westminster, London

6–8 July 2007: "Marxism 2007: A Festival of Resistance," Conference hosted by Socialist Workers Party, University of London

APPENDIX THREE

Interviews and Events Attended in Canada

Occupational titles listed represent the individual's position at the time of the interview or event.

INTERVIEWS

Canadian interviews took place in 2007 or 2008, with subsequent follow-up by email in some cases.

Government Departments or Agencies – Federal (2)

Senior Executive, Environment Canada
Peter Salonius, Research Scientist, Natural Resources Canada

Politicians – Federal (2)

Lynn McDonald, former NDP MP
Grant Mitchell, Liberal Senator

Politicians – Local (1)

Gord Perks, Toronto City Councillor

Business – "Mainstream" (4)

Gordon Brown, Canadian Chemical Producers Association, and
    Claude-Andre Lachance, Dow Chemical
John Dillon, Vice President, Canadian Council of Chief Executives
Rick Hyndman, Senior Policy Advisor, Canadian Association of Pet-
    roleum Producers

David Lewin, Senior VP IGCC Development, EPCOR, and Mike Smith, Director, Environment, EPCOR

Business – "Environmentally Oriented" (2)

Randal Goodfellow
Kyle Kasawski, President, Conergy Sales Canada

Labour Unions (1)

Nick DeCarlo, National Representative for Health, Safety, and Environment, Canadian Auto Workers (2008)

Environment – Large Mainstream Organizations (5)

Kim Fry, Boreal Forest Campaigner, Greenpeace
Mike Hudema, Climate and Energy Campaigner, Greenpeace, Edmonton office
Dale Marshall, Climate Change Policy Analyst, David Suzuki Foundation
Lindsay Telfer, Prairie Chapter Director, Sierra Club
Dan Woynillowicz, Senior Policy Analyst, Pembina Institute

Environment – Grassroots and Other Climate Activists (1)

Chris Winter, Executive Director, Conservation Council of Ontario

Sufficiency Advocates (6)

(Others listed elsewhere may also fit in this category)
David Hallman, Climate Change Programme Co-ordinator, World Council of Churches / United Church of Canada
Thomas Homer-Dixon, Professor, University of Toronto
Mike Nickerson, Executive Director, Sustainability Project
Kris Orantes, Founder, Make Affluence History
William Rees, Professor University of British Columbia
Peter Victor, Professor, York University

Other (1)

Larry Lohmann, scholar and activist, The Corner House, and Co-Founder, Durban Group for Climate Justice

INDIVIDUALS HEARD AT CONFERENCES OR PUBLIC EVENTS
(PARTIAL LIST)

Government Departments or Agencies – National

Brigid Barnett, Responsible Investing Manager, Canada Pension
Plan Investment Board
David McLaughlin, President & CEO, National Round Table on the
Environment and the Economy
Robert Page, Vice-Chair, National Round Table on the Environment
and the Economy
Vicky Sharpe, President and CEO, Sustainable Development Tech-
nology Canada

Government Departments or Agencies – Provincial

Jennifer Keyes, Manager, Renewables Section, Ontario Ministry of
Natural Resources
Peter Love, Chief Energy Conservation Officer, Ontario

Government Departments or Agencies – Local

Lawson Oates, Director, Toronto Environment Office

Politicians / Political Parties – National

Stéphane Dion, Liberal Leader
Jack Layton, NDP Leader
Gary Lunn, Minister of Natural Resources, Conservative
Bob Mills, Conservative MP
Elizabeth May, Green Party Leader

Politicians / Political Parties – Provincial

Michael Bryant, Ontario Attorney General, Liberal
Donna Cansfield, Ontario Minister of Natural Resources, Liberal
Jean Charest, Quebec Premier, Liberal
Cheri diNovo, Ontario MPP, NDP
John Gerretsen, Ontario Minister of Environment, Liberal
Lillyann Goldstein, Ontario election candidate, Progressive
Conservative
Gerry Phillips, Ontario Minister of Energy, Liberal
Peter Tabuns, Ontario MPP, NDP

Politicians/Political Parties – Local

David Miller, Mayor of Toronto
Gord Perks, Toronto City Councillor
Adam Vaughan, Toronto City Councillor

Business – "Mainstream"

Elyse Allan, President and CEO, GE Canada
Thierry Berthoud, Vice President International Relations and Government Affairs, Alcan Inc.
Sam Boutziouvis, Canadian Council of Chief Executives
Michael Dancison, Director of New Generation Development, American Electric Power
Mark Demchuk, Team Lead, Weyburn Eastern Oil Business Unit, EnCana
Claude Demers, Science Communicator, Hydro-Québec
Marc Duchesne, Director, Corporate Responsibility and Environment, Bell Canada
Murray Elston, President and CEO, Canadian Nuclear Association
Richard Evans, President and CEO, RioTinto Alcan
Peter Frise, Scientific Director and CEO, Auto 21
Johanne Gélinas, Partner – Enterprise Risks, Deloitte
Gord Lambert, Vice President of Sustainable Development, Suncor
Avrim Lazar, President and CEO, Forest Products Association of Canada
Clive Mather, former CEO, Shell Canada
Gregor Robinson, Vice President, Policy and Economic Analysis, Ontario Energy Association
Ian Shaw, Energy Manager, Corporate Technology, ArcelorMittal
Patrick Tobin, Director, Corporate and Government Affairs, Alcan
Keith Trent, Group Executive and Chief Strategy, Policy and Regulatory Officer, Duke Energy
Thierry Vandal, President and CEO, Hydro-Québec
Adam White, President, Association of Major Power Consumers in Ontario

Business – "Environmentally Oriented"

Corinne Boone, Managing Director, CantorCO2e

Leon Bitton, Vice-President, Research and Development, Montreal
    Climate Exchange
Rod Bryden, President and CEO, Plasco Energy Group
How-Sen Chong, Founder and Senior Project Manager, Carbon
    Zero
Scott Harrison, President and CEO, Azure Dynamics Inc.
Tom Heintzman, Co-Founder and Director, Bullfrog Power
Kate Holloway, President and CEO, Carbonzero
Robert Hornung, President, Canadian Wind Energy Association
Kyle Kasawski, President, Conergy Sales Canada

Labour Unions

John Cartwright, President, Toronto and York Region Labour
    Council
Nick DeCarlo, National Representative for Health, Safety, and En-
    vironment, Canadian Auto Workers
Hugh Mackenzie, Research Associate, Canadian Centre for Policy
    Alternatives (former Research Director, United Steelworkers of
    America)
Mike Seaward, United Steelworkers of America

Environment – Large Mainstream Organizations

Jose Etcheverry, Research and Policy Analyst, David Suzuki
    Foundation
Stephen Hazell, Executive Director, Sierra Club of Canada
Mark Lutes, Climate Change and Energy Policy Analyst, David Su-
    zuki Foundation
Dave Martin, Climate & Energy Coordinator, Greenpeace
Matt Price, Climate Change Project Manager, Environmental
    Defence

Environment – Grassroots and Other Climate Activists

Tony Clarke, Founder and Director, Polaris Institute, and activist,
    Tar Sands Watch
Franz Hartmann, Executive Director, Toronto Environmental
    Alliance
Clayton Thomas-Muller, member of the Mathais Colomb Cree

Nation and organizer with the Indigenous Environmental
    Network
Sheila Watt-Cloutier, former International Chair, Inuit Circumpolar
    Council
Chris Winter, Executive Director, Conservation Council of Ontario

Sufficiency Advocates

Thomas Homer-Dixon, Professor, University of Toronto
William Rees, Professor, University of British Columbia
Jack Santa-Barbara, Director, Sustainable Scale Project
Peter Victor, Professor, York University

Marxist Perspectives on Climate Change

Ian Angus, Editor, "Climate and Capitalism" blog
Joel Kovel, Editor-in-Chief, *Capitalism, Nature, Socialism*

Other

David Bell, Professor Emeritus, York University, and former mem-
    ber of the National Round Table on the Environment and the
    Economy
Thomas J. Courchene, Senior Scholar, Institute for Research on
    Public Policy
Danny Harvey, Professor, University of Toronto, IPCC contributor
Toby Heaps, Co-Founder and President, *Corporate Knights* magazine
Mark Jaccard, Professor, Simon Fraser University
Bryan Karney, Professor, University of Toronto
Doug Macdonald, Senior Lecturer, University of Toronto
Lynn McDonald, former NDP MP, sociologist, and activist
John Nyboer, Simon Fraser University
Finn Poschmann, Director of Research, C.D. Howe Institute
Judy Rebick, CAW-Sam Gindin Chair in Social Justice and Democ-
    racy, Ryerson University
Jeffrey Simpson, National Affairs Columnist, the *Globe and Mail*
John Strong, IPCC scientist
Ralph Torrie, Vice-President, ICF International
Mark Winfield, Assistant Professor, York University

Other – Non-Canadians Speaking at Canadian Events

Don Chen, Founder and Executive Director, Smart Growth America
Eileen Claussen, President, Pew Center on Global Climate Change
Ross Gelbspan, journalist and author
John Holdren, Director, Woods Hole Research Center
Daniel Kammen, Director, Renewable and Appropriate Energy Laboratory, University of California, Berkeley
David Korten, author and political activist
Larry Lohmann, scholar and activist, The Corner House, and Co-Founder, Durban Group for Climate Justice
Scott Minos, Senior Policy and Communications Specialist, Office of Energy Efficiency and Renewable Energy, US Department of Energy
George Monbiot, journalist, UK
Martin Nesbit, Director, Climate and Energy: Business and Transport, UK Department for Environment, Food and Rural Affairs
Franklin M. Orr, Director, Global Climate and Energy Project, Stanford University
Henri Proglio, President and CEO, Veolia Environnement
John Seed, Founder and Director, Rainforest Information Centre, Australia
Truman Semans, Director for Markets and Business Strategy, Pew Center on Global Climate Change
David Vincent, Director, Projects, UK Carbon Trust

CONFERENCES AND OTHER PUBLIC EVENTS ATTENDED

13 October 2006: George Monbiot, "Heat: How to Stop the Planet from Burning." Hart House, University of Toronto
1 December 2006: "Climate Change Solutions." Panel Discussion. University of Toronto
3 April 2007: Joel Kovel, "A Really Inconvenient Truth: The Left Beyond Kyoto," University of Toronto
22 April 2007: Earth Day Climate Change Rally, Metro Hall, Toronto
26 April 2007: Elizabeth May, "Kyoto: How Do We Get There from Here?" organized by the Sierra Club of Canada Peel Region Group, Mississauga, ON

27–29 April 2007: Green Living Show, Canadian National Exhibition Grounds, Toronto

30 April 2007: "Out of Afghanistan and Into Kyoto," Davenport Neighbours for Peace, Concord Café, Toronto

2 May 2007: John Seed, "Climate Change: Despair and Empowerment," OISE Auditorium, Toronto

5 September 2007: Climate Change panel, Public Affairs Association of Canada, Albany Club, Toronto

11 September 2007: "Our Energy Future: Where Have We Been and Where Are We Going?" Post-Carbon Institute, City Council Chamber, Toronto

25 September 2007: Mike Nickerson, "Life, Money, Illusion," Tinto Café, Toronto

26 September 2007: All Candidates Meeting on Energy and Climate Change, St. Paul's Riding, Organized by Green Neighbours 21, Holy Rosary Parish Hall, Toronto

14 October 2007: Second Annual Shirley Shipman Memorial Lecture, A Life Institute Event, "Open the Green Door to Facts, Challenges, Solutions," Ryerson University, Toronto

24–26 October 2007 : "Climate 2050" Conference, Palais des congrés, Montreal

30 October 2007: "Business of Climate Change," Fairmont Chateau Laurier, Ottawa

1–2 November 2007: "A Globally Integrated Climate Policy for Canada," Conference, Hart House, University of Toronto

3 November 2007: "Climate Change: Global Problem, Local Action. What You As a Student Can Do," Hart House, University of Toronto

8 November 2007: "Convenient Solutions for an Inconvenient Truth," Organized by Green Neighbours 21, Oakwood Collegiate, Toronto

12 November 2007: Lynn McDonald, "Social Change to Meet Climate Change," Toronto Dollar Supper Club, Hot House Restaurant, Toronto

16 November 2007: "False Solutions: The Canadian Tar Sands, A Nightmare in the Making," Organized by Kairos, Pharmacy Building, University of Toronto

17 November 2007: "From Climate Crisis to Climate Justice," Teach-In, Steelworkers Hall, Toronto

18 November 2007: Danny Harvey, Professor of Geography and
contributor to IPCC, "Climate Change: A Scientific and Political
Overview," Hart House, University of Toronto
30 November 2007: Tom Heintzman of Bullfrog Power, Interviewed
by Gill Deacon, Toronto Reference Library
8 December 2007: Kyoto Now, Climate Change Demonstration,
Parliament Hill, Ottawa
8 January 2008: Stop the Tar Sands, Organizing Meeting,
Edmonton
13 January 2008: Larry Lohmann, "Keeping Fossil Fuels Flowing:
The Carbon Trading Approach to Climate Change," University
of Alberta, Edmonton
22 January 2008: "Carbon Trading or Carbon Cheating? Can Carbon Trading and Offsets Work?" Larry Lohmann and How-Sen
Chong, Founder and Senior Project Manager, Carbonzero,
University of Toronto
21 February 2008: Screening of "Escape from Suburbia" and Panel
Discussion, York University, Toronto
20 March 2008: "If Not Us, Who?" Thomas Homer-Dixon and Ross
Gelbspan, Isabel Bader Theatre, University of Toronto
9 April 2008: "Tax Shifting for a Greener Future," St. Lawrence
Centre Forum, Toronto
15 April 2008: Carbon Offsets Debate, Organized by Young Environmental Professionals, Bahen Centre, University of Toronto
20 April 2008: Reclaim Earth Day: U-Turn on Climate Change,
Rally, Yonge-Dundas Square, Toronto
22–23 April 2008: "Energy 2100 – Making the Lakes Great: Energy
Options that Sustain the Great Lakes," Hosted by Dofasco Centre for Engineering and Public Policy, McMaster University, at
MaRS Discovery Centre, Toronto
17 June 2008: "Thinking Through Carbon Taxes: Competitiveness
and Federalism Challenges," Institute for Research on Public
Policy Working Lunch, Royal York Hotel, Toronto
20 June 2008: Society for Environmental Journalists Conference,
Hart House, University of Toronto
18 September 2008: Climate Change panel, Public Affairs Association of Canada, Albany Club, Toronto

Notes

1 Conceptual confusion can arise from the failure to distinguish between different types of growth. By "growth," I mean conventionally defined economic growth, i.e. rising Gross Domestic Product (GDP). I specify in the text when I am referring to other forms of growth (e.g. growth in emissions, material throughput, or well-being).

2 Considerable debate exists over the meaning of "sustainable development," but most formulations of the concept share EM's belief that there is no inherent conflict between economic growth and environmental sustainability. However, different emphases exist in the EM and sustainable development literatures. EM has tended (at least until recently) to focus primarily on the global North and to lack the emphasis on social equity that is prominent in much of the sustainable development debate (see, e.g., Dryzek 2013).

3 Two innovative examples Jänicke (2008) gives are the Japanese "Top-Runner" approach, under which the most energy efficient products available on the market become in a short time the minimum standard for all producers, and Germany's feed-in tariffs that require energy distributors to pay premium rates to renewable energy suppliers.

4 Evidence for the EKC has been limited and contentious (Cavlovic et al. 2000; Dinda 2004; Stern 2004). There has been some evidence that growing affluence has enabled wealthy nations to mitigate some environmental problems with local impacts, particularly those that harm human health, including sulphur emissions and some other forms of water and air pollution. However, for such forms of pollution, the evidence appears less robust than initial studies suggested. Nor is there strong evidence for an EKC with regard to biodiversity conservation (Mills and Waite 2009) or, as noted in the main text, key indicators of a nation's global impacts, such as GHGs and ecological footprint.

5 UN Framework Convention on Climate Change data showed that UK emissions were 18.5 per cent below 1990 levels in 2008 (followed by

further GHG reductions during the subsequent recession). Other notable cases were Germany (–22.2 per cent) and Sweden (–11.7). Smaller reductions occurred in Belgium (–7.1), France (–6.1), and the Netherlands (–2.4). However, such reductions did not represent an overall trend of decoupling GDP and GHGs. Not including former state-socialist economies in central and eastern Europe (which saw large GHG declines as the Soviet-era economy collapsed), GHG emissions increased in seventeen of twenty-seven wealthy Annex I nations from 1990–2008. Emissions in the non-Annex I countries of the global South more than doubled in this time period. Meanwhile, the records of nations such as Germany and the UK are much less positive when one looks at emissions linked to consumption of goods within a country rather than production (e.g. CCC 2013, 19, 30; Davis and Caldeira 2010; Hertwich and Peters 2009), a point I discuss in more detail in chapter 7.

6 Some climate analysts refer to atmospheric concentrations in parts per million of CO_2, while others refer to the carbon dioxide equivalent (CO_2e), which includes the warming effect of other greenhouse gases. These additional gases are often estimated to add roughly 50 ppm CO_2e, thus a long-term stabilization target of 400 ppm of CO_2 would equal 450 ppm CO_2e. However, the relationship between CO_2 and CO_2e is complicated and depends on the time period and range of effects included in the analysis. Some analysts estimate that, for the time being, CO_2 and CO_2e are roughly equivalent (as cooling aerosols counteract the warming effect of other GHGs), while others maintain that non-CO_2 gases already add another 78 ppm of CO_2e (Hassol 2011; Monastersky 2013).

7 Li (2008) considered nine scenarios for stabilizing atmospheric concentrations at 445 ppm CO_2e, a level estimated to be equivalent to a 2°C increase above pre-industrial levels. In the least optimistic scenario for emissions- and energy-intensity improvements (which are still well in excess of historical trends from 1973–2005), the world economy would have to decline 3.4 per cent per year from 2010–50. In the most optimistic scenario, with annual emissions- and energy-intensity improvements of 2.7 and 2.0 per cent, respectively, the global economy would still have to decline 0.7 per cent per year. Li concludes that "under no plausible scenario could the objective of climate stabilization be compatible with the endless expansion of the global capitalist economy" (59).

CHAPTER TWO

1 An Environment Canada executive pointed out in 2008 that Canada's then-target of a 20 per cent GHG cut from 2006 to 2020 was similar to EU targets over that period. Defenders of Canada's position also noted

that its BAU emissions trajectory was more carbon intensive than the EU's, so comparable targets required greater effort in Canada. That said, since Canada had not acted to prevent rising emissions, despite international commitments to do so dating back to 1992, it was not unfair to expect Canada to make greater effort to make up for lost ground.

2 The Canadian Association of Petroleum Producers told energy and environment ministers that "targets for industry should be an achievable stretch beyond the historical or anticipated 'business as usual' rate of improvement in energy efficiency and emission intensity. Targets beyond that would simply be a tax on production in Canada to be met by paying other countries for emission credits or shifting production outside Canada" (CAPP 2002).

3 Canada's 1998 National Climate Change Process had estimated a marginal abatement cost of $250 per tonne to reduce domestic emissions by 200 Mt, less than needed to comply with the Kyoto target (K. Harrison 2007, 109). Other estimates of the cost per tonne of complying with Kyoto were lower, but a $15 carbon price clearly would not have sufficed.

4 The first page alone of the executive summary used phrases like "reductions in GHG emissions while ensuring continued economic growth"; "meet our Kyoto target while maintaining a productive and growing economy"; "boosting our economic competitiveness," "encouraging innovation and the development of environmental technology"; "reduce GHG and other harmful emissions while enjoying the benefits of a competitive economy"; "spur innovative and technological advancement, situating Canada's industries for a competitive advantage in the 21st century"; and "enable Canada's largest emitters to contribute to national climate change objectives in a manner that facilitates growth and competitiveness" – all made possible by "harnessing market forces" (Government of Canada 2005, iii).

5 Intensity targets were not necessarily a weaker policy instrument than absolute targets. Intensity-based targets, if strong enough, could also lead to absolute emissions reductions, while absolute targets did not necessarily guarantee real reductions beyond what would have occurred anyway. Rick Hyndman of CAPP pointed to the World Resources Institute's analysis of intensity targets, which, in his words, showed that, "It's not how you do it, it's how much you are actually doing. You can have easy intensity and tight absolute or easy absolute and tight intensity targets." He added, "Unfortunately, the Bush administration gave a bad name to intensity targets because they used it to justify a business-as-usual policy. But if I look at the European phase I [of the emissions

trading scheme] ... they had absolute targets. How good was this? Well, actually, on an intensity basis, those were piddling. They didn't do anything. They were worse than business-as-usual. They actually had an over-allocation."

6 Cap and trade involves the establishment of an overall limit on emissions within a jurisdiction. The governing authority then allocates the limited number of emissions allowances to polluters, either through an auction or by distributing them free of charge. Polluters are then able to buy and sell emissions allowances among themselves, an option that gives those with high emissions-reduction costs the ability to buy allowances from others facing lower costs.

7 The tax was to begin at $10 per tonne of GHG emissions and rise an additional $10 per tonne each year, reaching $40 per tonne within four years. In contrast, environmental groups called for a minimum $30 per tonne to start (Tomorrow Today 2008) and the Green Party of Canada (2007b, 52) called for a carbon tax starting at $50 per tonne.

8 It may seem a distant memory, but Republicans such as John McCain once had carbon-reduction plans, too.

9 These organizations were the Canadian Parks and Wilderness Society, the David Suzuki Foundation, Ecojustice, Environmental Defence, Equiterre, Greenpeace Canada, Nature Canada, the Pembina Institute, Pollution Probe, the Sierra Club of Canada, and WWF-Canada.

10 The document did not endorse "economic growth" per se, or refer to the term at all, except in quotations from other sources, which suggested uneasiness within the environmental movement about endorsing growth as a goal.

11 The Sierra Club (2007) presented ten steps to Kyoto implementation, focused on efficiency, technology, and conventional policy – with a small degree of sufficiency in calls to reduce investments in road and air infrastructure.

12 The forestry sector had already experienced damage likely linked to climate change: a large-scale pine beetle infestation. It also saw opportunities, hoping to gain credit for early action in cutting emissions and profit from carbon trading, while also becoming a source of green power (FPAC 2007a, 2007b).

13 Alberta was the first North American jurisdiction to regulate large industrial emitters, requiring cuts in emissions intensity (GHGs per unit of output) of 12 per cent. Firms unable to meet the target could purchase credits from others that exceeded their target, buy credits from offset projects in Alberta, or pay $15 per tonne (but only on excess emissions) into a technology fund. The net effect was, in typical cases, a weak price signal amounting to a maximum cost of $1.80 for each

tonne of a firm's emissions ($15 × 12% = $1.80) (Partington 2013a; see also Leach 2012). For oil companies, the cost equalled roughly 10 cents per barrel of oil (Alberta Department of Energy 2013; CBC 2013b). The policy's limited impact led the province to consider increasing the intensity reduction target to 40 per cent and the penalty on excess emissions to $40 per tonne (McCarthy and Vanderklippe 2013).

14 In an analysis of future energy scenarios, the International Energy Agency concluded that with current climate policies, world demand would support 4.6 million barrels per day (mbd) of oil sands production in 2035, while its central "new policies" scenario foresaw 4.2 mbd of output by that date. However, under a 450 ppm scenario with policy aiming to limit warming to 2°C, tar sands production would be just 3.3 million barrels per day by 2035, much less than the 5.2 mbd of output that Alberta had already approved (IEA 2010, 144; see also Huot 2012).

15 Hyndman argued that, to avoid wealth transfers between regions, the provinces should levy the tax and control the revenues. Other elements of "well-designed carbon tax" from his perspective included border adjustments to add the tax to imports and rebate it on exports for trade-exposed sectors; recycling of tax revenues to support new energy technologies such as CCS and other investments in mass transit, auto industry retooling, etc.; and measures to offset its regressive impact (Hyndman 2007; see also Burrows 2007). "If it isn't done right, then we will be adamantly opposed to it," Hyndman said, but if designed in this way, "you can put any level of tax you want that the Canadian consumer is willing to pay for."

CHAPTER THREE

1 One could argue that limiting immigration would not help the climate problem as people will emit GHGs whether in Canada or elsewhere. Critics of immigration would counter that since per capita emissions are particularly high in Canada, the average immigrant's carbon footprint will increase substantially after coming to Canada. A full analysis of these issues is beyond the scope of this book; suffice it to say that they are deeply controversial.

2 Similarly, Homer-Dixon (2007, 217) wrote, "The defenders of the economic status quo can marshal an overwhelming onslaught of attacks and ridicule against anyone who dares to publicly challenge capitalism's logic – much the way an organism's immune system launches an attack against an incoming pathogen, with its macrophages and T-cells finding, identifying, and destroying the intruder."

CHAPTER FOUR

1 The 2011 document was similar on these issues, with minor revisions such as the addition of the wording, "Greens know that the notion of unending economic growth is a dangerous illusion" (Green Party of Canada 2011, 8).

2 In 2008, the Vancouver Humane Society wrote to ten Canadian environmental groups to ask them support an "Eat Less Meat" campaign. Only two replied – Greenpeace and the David Suzuki Foundation – both organizations that did mention meat consumption on their websites, but had not made the issue a campaign priority despite its high GHG impact (Read 2008; see also Toronto Vegetarian Society 2007; Vancouver Humane Society 2008). EarthSave, a Vancouver-based NGO that promotes a plant-based diet, the Toronto Vegetarian Society, and Montreal-based Lundi sans Viande later launched a Meatless Monday campaign.

3 Cynthia Dunsford, a member of Prince Edward Island's legislative assembly, told the CBC (2008), plastic bags "are made out of petroleum products, and we know what those kinds of products do to our environment. We can talk about global warming and climate change and we can talk about how it affects wildlife, how plastic bags can get mixed up with nature, and the results are never positive."

4 Reducing food miles made less progress federally. The governing Tories emphasized export-oriented agriculture; however, the four opposition parties urged more support for local food (see, e.g., Leeder 2011; Liberal Party 2010).

5 Brooks and Paehlke's (1980) set of proposed actions included not only a strong commitment to energy efficiency, but also several sufficiency-oriented ideas at the micro level that later reappeared: reducing car and plane travel while favouring buses, trains, and video conferencing; more compact urban form; cutting food miles through "careful decentralization of food production"; and "a modest shift in eating habits from animal to vegetable protein" (449). They also raised the idea of tradable gasoline rations, foreshadowing later UK debates about tradable carbon rations.

6 Similarly, the Sierra Club of Canada (2007, 9) envisioned a 35 per cent cut in electric power production by 2030 through demand-side efficiency gains and co-generation.

7 The Conservation Bureau's responsibilities were later reallocated within the Ontario Power Authority, as well as to local distribution companies and the Environmental Commissioner of Ontario. Meanwhile, the province's 2009 Green Energy Act included provisions to strengthen the commitment to conservation.

8 In addition to "conservation of use," the Ontario Conservation Bureau
   (2008) identified "energy efficiency" (investing in lower-energy appliances, equipment, and buildings), "demand management" (shifting
   electricity demand to off-peak hours), "fuel switching" (switching from
   electricity to alternate energy sources), and "self-generation" (generating electricity using on-site renewable or co-generation to reduce
   demand on the power grid).
9 Personal communication, May 24, 2011 (see also OPS 2011).
10 The Science Council of Canada (1977, 14) defined a conserver society
   as one that "promotes economy of design of all systems, i.e., 'doing
   more with less'; favours re-use or recycling and, wherever possible,
   reduction at source; [and] questions the ever-growing per capita demand for consumer goods, artificially encouraged by modern marketing techniques." The Council added: "As inhabitants of a 'consumer
   society,' most Canadians have lived through a period when materials
   seemed plentiful, energy cheap, and growth in size and quantity,
   whether of cities, automobiles, monuments, or lawnmowers, was the
   natural order of things. Status, of individuals or societies, was measured by conspicuous consumption, and economic prosperity was demonstrated by what you could afford to throw away. Designers, engineers, architects tended to be caught up in it too, placing the emphasis
   on the 'more' and forgetting 'with less' ... Now, as we become aware
   of constraints and uncertainties in the future, we question our implicit
   assumption that 'bigger is better'" (28).

CHAPTER FIVE

1 "Well-to-wheel" figures show a narrower differential since the lion's
   share of life-cycle emissions occurs when fuel is burned in a vehicle,
   and combustion emissions are similar for tar sands and conventional
   fuels. The federal and Alberta governments cited studies by Cambridge Energy Research Associates (CERA), an oil industry consultancy,
   which concluded that the tar sands fuels were 5 to 15 per cent greater
   emissions on a "well-to-wheel" basis than conventional crude. However, the European Union commissioned an independent analysis by
   Adam Brandt (2011) of Stanford University's department of Energy
   Resources Engineering, who rejected the oil sands defenders–favoured
   CERA study since it lacked methodological transparency. Brandt concluded that a "most likely estimate" was that tar sands fuel was 23 per
   cent more GHG intensive than conventional fuel on a "well-to-wheel"
   basis, with, as noted above, a much larger difference when only extraction and upgrading are considered.
2 Canada's GHG emissions in 2011 were 702 Mt (Environment Canada

2013a). Subtracting 55 Mt leaves 647 Mt from sources other than the tar sands. This is 16.0 per cent above Canada's Kyoto target of 558 Mt and 9.7 per cent above the 1990 level of 590 Mt. In comparison, the US saw total GHGs rise 8.4 per cent from 1990 to 2011, according to the Environmental Protection Agency.

3   Based on IPCC estimates, many observers argued that wealthy nations must cut GHGs by 80 per cent below 1990 levels by 2050. For Canada, that would require reducing GHGs to 118 Mt by 2050. Environment Canada (2013a, 24, 25) projected that tar sands emissions would reach 101 Mt by 2020 based on output of 3.3 million barrels per day. Assuming output rises to 5 million barrels per day by 2030, and emissions rise proportionately, the tar sands will generate roughly 153 Mt by 2030. Perhaps technologies might emerge to reverse such trends by 2050; nevertheless these figures highlight the incompatibility of current trends with strong climate targets. Even deeper reduction targets – such as those consistent with the call to reduce atmospheric concentrations of CO_2 to 350 ppm – would make oil sands emissions growth appear even more problematic. For example, if Monbiot (2006b) was right that at least 90 per cent emission cuts were needed in rich nations by 2030, the tar sands alone were on track to account for 2.6 times more than Canada's corresponding carbon budget of 59 Mt by that date.

4   While the province did require large industrial emitters to reduce their GHG *intensity* or pay a small carbon price – indeed it was the first North American jurisdiction to establish a carbon price – Alberta's targets left much to be desired from an environmental perspective, as discussed in more detail later in this chapter.

5   The Edmonton GPI figures were 100 in 1981, 103.8 in 1983, 83.8 in 1998, 94.7 in 2006, and 94.8 in 2008 (Anielski and Johannessen 2009, 55).

6   Among the concerns expressed by Lougheed (2006): the unwise use of natural gas, failure to provide necessary infrastructure given the rate of development, inflated costs of goods and housing, inadequate royalty returns to the people of the province, and the incentives for young people to forgo further education and training to take high-paying, relatively unskilled jobs in the tar sands.

7   ICO_2N participants by 2012 included many corporations active in Alberta's tar sands and coal-powered electricity sectors: BP Canada, Canadian Natural Resources, ConocoPhillips, Enbridge, Husky Energy, Shell Canada, Statoil, Suncor, Syncrude, Total, and TransAlta. Firms previously listed on the network's website as participants included Chevron Canada, EPCOR, and Imperial Oil.

8   Upgraders transform bitumen into synthetic crude, which can then be transported to refineries that make gasoline and other petroleum

products. ccs has greater potential at upgraders since their CO_2 emissions are more concentrated and easier to capture than at other oil sands operations.

9　This statement is contained in a document, obtained by Greenpeace's Keith Stewart under freedom-of-information legislation, sent to Alberta environment ministry officials by capp (2013a) in response to a proposal to strengthen ghg-reduction requirements by increasing the carbon price (see also cbc 2013b).

10　Other possible technological options to reduce ghgs were proposed. The most seriously discussed was replacing natural gas with nuclear power to produce steam, although that option faced resistance from environmentalists and limited industry enthusiasm due to the significantly higher cost.

11　For details, see chapter 2, note 13.

12　Alberta emitted 171 Mt of ghgs in 1990 and 231 Mt in 2005 (Environment Canada 2010b, 87). A 14 per cent reduction below 2005 levels by 2050 thus equals 198.7 Mt, well above 1990 levels.

13　Another conceivable option was the purchase of carbon offsets or emissions credits from abroad. Even though it allowed the oil industry and government to buy their way out of the ghg problem, it was not an option that either the Alberta government or the Conservative federal government supported. The transfer of development funds to poorer nations through purchases of emissions credits and offsets was a key part of the vision behind the Kyoto Protocol, and a point to which conservative political and industry forces in Alberta specifically objected. It was this provision that led Stephen Harper (2002), then leader of the opposition Canadian Alliance, to state that, "Kyoto is essentially a socialist scheme to suck money out of wealth-producing nations."

14　Hudema of Greenpeace argued that once the one-time spurt of construction was over, many thousands would find themselves looking for work: "You are looking at a massive recession that's coming from a massive bubble that is eventually going to burst." Instead, he advocated "avoiding these boom-and-bust cycles by actually creating a sustainable industry that is healthy for our planet."

CHAPTER SIX

1　In an earlier speech to the UK Royal Society, Thatcher (1988) noted that "in today's world it is no bad thing for a politician to have had the benefit of a scientific background." She went on to express concern over the possibility that "we have unwittingly begun a massive experiment with the system of this planet itself," highlighting changes to atmospheric chemistry – the increase in ghgs, ozone depletion, and acid rain. Meanwhile, the roles of Crispin Tickell, Britain's outgoing UN ambassador, and Chris Patten, then environment secretary, in persuading Thatcher of the worrying nature of the climate data are also cited as a factor in her decision to give the issue a high profile (Helm 2003, 346; Marr 2007, 480; Thatcher 1993, 640). In retirement, Thatcher showed more sympathy for climate scepticism, criticizing Al Gore for his "doomist" predictions in her 2002 memoirs (Vidal 2013).

2   I did encounter CRAG members who felt that technology and efficiency could allow deep GHG reductions without questioning economic growth; however, the overall ethos of CRAGS, inspired by Monbiot's (2005b) call for a movement for "austerity" to cut GHGs 90 per cent, ran counter to the dominant growth paradigm.

3   Rupert Murdoch's embrace of the green cause was "one of the most unexpected conversions since Saul of Tarsus hit the road to Damascus" in one journalist's estimation (Lean 2007), but that did not stop his media outlets from later contributing to the upsurge of climate scepticism.

4   Other retailers that practiced choice editing with regard to issues beyond climate change included B&Q, which chose to stock only Forest Stewardship Council–certified timber, and Marks and Spencer, which sold only fair trade coffee, free-range eggs, and Marine Stewardship Council fish. Meanwhile, a number of retailers removed patio heaters from their stores in response to environmentalists' demands.

5   The UK CLG's members included Anglian Water Group, BAA, B&Q, BSkyB, BT, Doosan Power Systems, EDF Energy, Johnson Matthey, Lloyds Banking Group, Philips, Shell, Tesco, Thames Water, and Unilever.

6   As Harriss-White and Harriss (2006, 86) point out, BP, Shell, and their former leaders were influential advocates of climate action, while accounting between them for some 40 per cent of the CO_2 emissions of the leading one hundred companies on the Financial Times Stock Exchange (FTSE) listing. These firms continued to invest primarily in fossil fuel extraction, including making subsequent major investments in Alberta's tar sands.

7   Six sectors out of 123 would face an increase in variable costs of 5 per cent or more due to carbon pricing of $30/tonne of CO_2. These were gas supply and distribution (25 per cent cost increase); refined petroleum (24 per cent); electricity production and distribution (16 per cent); cement (9 per cent); fertilizers (5 per cent); and fishing (5 per cent) (Stern 2006, Sect. 11.2, 254).

8   In 2008, the new Committee on Climate Change recommended a target of 34 per cent by 2020, but rising to 42 per cent if a sufficiently strong global agreement on GHG reductions were reached.

9 Canada's assessment was, in contrast, "especially bad," according to the same source.

10 According to a document produced by BERR (2007) and leaked to the *Guardian* (Seager and Milner 2007, 1), "If the EU has a 20% GHG target for 2020, the GHG emissions savings achieved through the renewables target and energy efficiency measures risk making the EU ETS redundant, and prices to [*sic*] collapse. Given that the EU ETS is the EU's main existing vehicle for delivering least cost reductions in GHG, and the basis on which the EU seeks to build a global carbon market to incentivise international action, *this is a major risk*" (italics added).

11 A DECC official noted in an interview that some in government and the bureaucracy saw the renewable targets as an unnecessary burden since the core objective of GHG reduction was optimally addressed by emissions trading. A risk also existed that the renewable target would, by lowering the carbon price, reduce incentives to invest in other forms of low-carbon power and negatively affect long-run GHG reductions. On the other hand, the target had possible benefits in stimulating a new job-creating renewable energy industry and enhancing energy security (D. Buchan 2009, 140).

12 The initial take-up of the Green Deal was low, with a key factor being the high interest rate facing homeowners who made energy efficiency investments through the scheme. The Green Investment Bank was capitalized with £3 billion in public funds, but its initial impact was limited because the government did not allow it to borrow from capital markets until the national debt was reduced.

13 On the other hand, fewer deaths from cold was one benefit of climate change – a significant issue in a country where fuel poverty afflicted many low-income people in drafty homes.

CHAPTER SEVEN

1 The *Sun* reported that, as public concern over electricity prices grew, Cameron told aides to "get rid of all the green crap" (i.e. green levies) that added to household energy bills (Schofield 2013); however, official representatives denied that the prime minister had done so.

2 The Partial Regulatory Impact Assessment (RIA) of the CRC concluded that the policy would result in net present value (NPV) benefits of £755 million to participants. This involved a strict test using a 10 per cent commercial discount rate, without counting the social benefits of lower carbon emissions and improved air quality. When a 3.5 per cent public discount was used, the NPV rose to £1.919 billion, and increased further to an estimated £3.245 billion once the social cost of carbon and

air quality benefits were considered (Defra 2007j, 34). This suggested that the emissions reductions objectives could be pushed considerably further and still produce a net social benefit, but at the risk of creating losses for some firms and sub-sectors.

3   With a threshold of 3,000 MWh/year for inclusion in the scheme, net present value (NPV) private benefits were estimated to be £786 million. However, a 6,000 MWh/year threshold was chosen even though it would deliver a lower private NPV of £755 million (Defra 2007j, 34). The government said it took this "cautionary" approach to "further reduce the risk of including participants for whom the administrative cost of participating in the scheme might outweigh the benefits" (Defra 2007a).

4   The Ensus plant opened in 2010 but faced periodic shutdowns due to adverse market conditions.

5   Estimates of rebound effects varied widely by technology, sector, and income group. The UKERC found that direct rebound effects were usually less than 30 per cent for household energy use and lower still for personal transport (2007b, vi, 87), but estimates of indirect rebound effects were more varied, making it difficult to reach solid conclusions on the economy-wide effect (the sum of the direct and indirect effects).

6   The UKERC (2007b, viii, 89) added that the K-B postulate was more likely to hold for eco-efficiency gains associated with "general-purpose technologies" adopted by producers rather than final consumers – past examples being nineteenth-century steam engines and electric motors in the early twentieth century. However, "the K-B postulate seems less likely to hold for dedicated energy efficiency technologies such as thermal insulation, particularly when these are used by consumers or when they play a subsidiary role in economic production. These technologies have smaller effects on productivity and economic growth, with the result that economy-wide energy consumption is likely to be reduced" (iv).

7   Stern did not flatly rule out a 450 ppm target. He referred to stabilization of atmospheric concentrations "in the range of 450–550ppm CO_2e" (2006, xi, 299). However, he made clear that he believed stabilization at 450 ppm was "already almost out of reach," adding that "Efforts to reduce emissions rapidly are likely to be very costly" (xv). His cost estimate of 1 per cent of global GDP by 2050 was based on stabilization at around 550 ppm CO_2e (xiv).

8   With similar concerns in mind, Colin Challen, Labour MP and chair of the All Party Parliamentary Climate Change Group, challenged Stern at a public meeting: "I have to say that when the report was released

there was a huge sigh of relief around Whitehall and I suspect that that's partly because in my opinion you've played rather fast and loose with the precautionary principle ... Where the *Stern Review* is taking us is the upper end, the probability that we'll fail to avoid dangerous climate change or as some people now prefer to say a catastrophic climate change" (RSA 2007). In his response, Stern clarified that the review was not based on the precautionary principle, but a standard expected utility approach used in cost-benefit analyses, and defended the robustness of his conclusion that the costs of inaction were much higher than the costs of action; however, he did not address the point that his chosen targets would likely fail to avoid dangerous climate change.

9 The *Stern Review* (2006, xii, xxiii) originally referred to the need for global emissions cuts of "25% or more" and cuts of 60 to 80 per cent in rich countries.

10 The models cited by Stern (2006, 195) showed that a 400 ppm target would leave an 8 to 57 per cent probability of exceeding 2°C.

11 The IPPR previously estimated that an 80 per cent cut in UK emissions by 2050 would slow down economic growth by 2–3 per cent of GDP by that date, but said that 80 per cent was "probably the least that the UK needs to achieve in order to make a fair contribution to a global effort to avoid dangerous climate change" (WWF-UK, IPPR, RSPB 2007, 8). With a global emissions cut of 70 to 80 per cent needed by 2050 to achieve 400 ppm, Retallack (2008) noted that, like all developed countries, the UK would likely have to cut even deeper than 80 per cent, implying higher economic costs. He added that "the sums involved in meeting an 80% target are significant and it would be counterproductive to be anything other than honest about that," although those sums were still less than the costs of inaction, estimated by Stern to be between 5 and 20 per cent of GDP.

12 The UK's baseline emissions figure for Kyoto Protocol reporting was 779.9 million tonnes CO_2 equivalent. By 1999, GHG emissions were down 107.2 million tonnes, whereas the period from 1999 to 2007 only took another 36.1 million tonnes off the total (DECC 2009b, 2009c).

13 Only in 2006 did official CO_2 emissions return to 1997 levels, before falling further in later years (DECC 2009c).

14 One exception later emerged. A revised estimate from Defra (2013) showed a fall in consumption-based emissions between 1997 and 2011 of 11 per cent for CO_2 and 14 per cent for all GHGs. Defra's revised data showed a significant increase in emissions from 1997 to 2004, a slight decline from 2004 to 2007, and a big drop after the onset of the

economic crisis in 2007; therefore, the data did not provide strong evidence of a decoupling of consumption-based emissions and economic growth. In addition, Defra moved up the base year from 1993 in previous studies to 1997, eliminating four years of rising emissions from the analysis.

CHAPTER EIGHT

1 "Contraction and convergence" was developed by Aubrey Meyer of the Global Commons Institute. The idea is to contract global emissions to a level compatible with climate stability. Each nation's emissions rights would over time converge on an equal per capita level, implying that emissions in rich nations would have to fall sharply while many poorer nations would still have room to increase their emissions to allow for poverty reduction.

2 *Sharing God's Planet* (CofE 2005) associated "the project of growth without limit" in the twentieth century with the rise of secularism in the West, which saw happiness as "something to enjoy now, on this earth, and not beyond it" (2). In summarizing the human impact on the environment, it stated: "The twentieth century can be seen as a time of tremendous human prodigality, a project of growth without limit. The project has favoured some and hurt far more others. The solution to inequality has been seen as yet more growth, but if humanity cannot restrain its own exuberance it may be that the earth is forced to do it" (15). Furthermore, acknowledging a link between "human encroachment on the earth's systems" and "so-called natural disasters that harm the two-thirds world," the document stated, "Even if ecological devastation is not on the horizon, for Christians there must be a recognition that the project of growth without limit has to be curtailed" (15).

3 Among them: the House of Commons Environmental Audit Committee, London Mayor Ken Livingstone, Nicholas Stern, SDC Chairman Jonathon Porritt, the Conservative Party Quality of Life Group, the Liberal Democrats, the Green Party, and the fifty-plus NGOs in the Stop Climate Chaos coalition.

4 Sufficiency could lead to its own rebound effect as reduced demand for resources in one location lowers global prices, allowing increased consumption by others (Alcott 2008). In other words, "my 'carbon sacrifice' makes it easier for others to indulge their own 'carbon sins'" (Jackson 2007). A later study by Druckman et al. (2011) also found

evidence of rebound effects for lower-carbon behaviour changes – turning down the thermostat, eliminating food waste, and walking or cycling instead of using a car for short trips – encouraged by the UK government. The researchers estimated that the rebound effect would undo 34 per cent of the expected GHG reductions from these abatement actions, although the figure could be lower or well above 100 per cent (i.e. "backfire") depending on assumptions about how individuals spend the savings from these changes.

5 For example, Hawken, Lovins, and Lovins (1999) advocated cost-saving measures to improve efficiency in air travel, which, by lowering costs and increasing convenience, successfully increased airline profits – by attracting more flying customers. "Somehow they contrive to overlook this consequence," noted Monbiot (2006b, 63).

6 This common line was satirized by Cheatneutral: "First you should look at ways of reducing your cheating. Once you've done this you can use Cheatneutral to offset the remaining, unavoidable cheating." However, ClimateCare (2007) attempted a different line of defence, arguing that offsetting was not actually a last resort after one has tried every other means of carbon reduction, but an "essential" action because "a credible offset will direct your money wherever in the planet it makes the biggest impact."

7 The Committee stated that "the principal need is to reduce emissions directly through changes in behaviour or technological improvements," but that offsetting should be encouraged for unavoidable emissions "because robust and credible offsetting can have a useful if limited role" (HOCEAC 2007, 3). It added another key point behind state support for offsetting: "The UK's financial and carbon markets have much to gain from a rapid growth in what is increasingly seen as a vital component of commercial activity and corporate responsibility" (3).

8 Lynas (2011, 191–2) later argued that the green movement made a great mistake in opposing offsetting, which was "completely derailed as a climate-mitigation strategy." He maintained that greens succeeded in convincing people that offsetting was a "con," but failed to convince people to fly less or reduce other carbon-intensive activity.

9 Meanwhile, Tom Hodgkinson (2007) proposed an anarchist vision of a low-carbon good life, based on (somewhat idealized) "medieval values," to counter the "individualist-expansionist-Protestant-capitalist experiment" that had "caused gloom, despondency and servitude for individuals, and potential environmental disaster for the planet" (2008, 27). His vision entailed "enjoyable work, lots of sitting around doing nothing,

lots of parties and dancing and beer and wine" (27–8). He added, "When you stop working and stop spending you start living" (33).

10 Juniper (2007b, 186–7) continued: "If growth leads to high levels of greenhouse-gas emissions and deforestation and benefits only a few already wealthy people, then many people might judge the quality of the economy to be low. At present, the tendency is to regard all growth as good, and largely to ignore the type of economy that produced it."

11 Similarly, Green MEP Caroline Lucas (2007) told the Guardian Climate Change Summit: "Some quantity and quality of economic growth is not necessarily incompatible with tackling climate change – and indeed there are some real business opportunities in a low carbon world. But if we think we can avoid the worst of climate change by using the same economic paradigm that caused the crisis in the first place – the dominant economic paradigm of progress through exponential economic growth at any cost – then we're setting ourselves up for failure."

CHAPTER NINE

1 One question is what people do with money saved on bottled water. If they spend it on carbon-intensive items, then net environmental gains would be reduced – a version of the rebound effect with regard to micro-sufficiency.

2 Global average meat consumption is roughly 100 g per person per day. In high-consuming populations, the average is 200–250 g per day, about ten times higher than in low-consuming populations. If the rich were to reduce their high levels of meat consumption, while the poor world increased average meat intake, each converging on 90 g per person per day, GHG emissions would decline and both groups' health would improve (McMichael et al. 2007).

3 Referring to the wider GHG-reduction challenge, the NHS SDU director noted, "This is not just about doing things more efficiently, it's about doing things differently, because efficiency is not going to get us to big cuts" (Jowit 2009b). The NHS (2009, 8) found that, despite efficiency gains, its carbon footprint grew 40 per cent since 1990.

4 These factors included some scathing media attacks on Livingstone's management and character, voters seeking change after eight years, and the massive nationwide shift away from Labour to the Tories. In fact Livingstone fared better than Labour more generally in holding onto voter support.

5 The recommendations of the King Review of low-carbon cars included another information tool to encourage consumers to choose "best in class" vehicles or to "downsize": colour-coded road-tax discs following a

traffic light scheme (King 2008, 10–11). High-emission vehicles would in effect be required to sport a kind of scarlet letter for all to see. Potential uses by municipalities and retailers included reserving the best parking spots for low-emission vehicles. However, the government rejected this idea, in part due to possible public opposition to such visual stigmatization of those with less fuel-efficient vehicles (DfT 2008, 13).

6   Annual passenger growth of 6 per cent – the UK average from the mid-1970s to 2005 (Cairns and Newson 2006, 30) – would lead to 220 per cent growth over twenty years. Even a much lower 3 per cent annual rate would swamp a 50 per cent efficiency gain with an 80 per cent increase in volumes – meaning higher total emissions.

7   As it became clear that the EU ETS would impose costs on the sector, BA and Virgin joined an Aviation Global Deal Group calling instead for a global trading scheme that would cover all their competitors (Climate Group 2009).

8   Among many examples: Gordon Brown chose former CBI leader Digby Jones, then chairman of the pro-aviation coalition Flying Matters, as his trade minister. Jones was replaced at Flying Matters by former Labour cabinet minister Brian Wilson. Tom Kelly, Tony Blair's former Downing Street spokesman, became BAA's director of public affairs. Meanwhile, Joe Irvin, a special adviser at Downing Street, was a former director of public affairs at BAA. Another former director of public affairs at BAA, Stephen Hardwick, was a former policy adviser to ex-deputy prime minister John Prescott. Lord Soley, campaign director of Future Heathrow, which pushed for a third runway, was former chairman of the parliamentary Labour party (Woolf and Ungoed-Thomas 2008; Ungoed-Thomas 2008; see also Plane Stupid 2008).

9   For example, when a questioner at the June 2007 TUC Climate Change event asked about airport expansion, Dave Prentis, general secretary of Unison, representing public service workers, stated that aviation growth threatened to negate all the other work to reduce emissions in other sectors.

10 HACAN Clear Skies was originally the Heathrow Association for the Control of Aircraft Noise.

11 This was a curious argument since that cover existed as far back as 2008, when the EU confirmed aviation's inclusion in the ETS.

CHAPTER TEN

1   Critics saw potential for the internalization of such ideas to take authoritarian forms – a new way for political-economic elites to discipline

and control people and their desires (Webb 2012, 112; While, Jonas, and Gibbs 2010, 85–6).

2   The other items on the readers' tip list were also about avoiding excess, rather than technology or efficiency, even if not clearly implying less consumption: "buy local produce," "avoid over-packaged goods," "cut down on junk mail," and "be eco when staying in hotels" (Independent 2007).

3   As Webb (2012, 119) put the issue, "The 'split mind' of the public, construed as simultaneously individualized hedonistic consumer and responsibilized carbon-calculating citizen, is reflected in the structural 'split mind' of a government model committed to economic growth driven by consumerism on the one hand, and shared obligations for transition to a sustainable society on the other."

4   This exchange occurred at the Sunday Times Oxford Literary Festival in March 2007 (see also Juniper 2007b, 183–7). At the same event, Robert May, former Royal Society president and chief government scientist, backed Layard's (2005) calls to measure happiness and not only GDP, adding that redefining measures of well-being was needed since our consumption exceeds available planetary resources.

5   As NEF (2010) put it, "it's likely that we have reached the end of what GDP can do for us. Economic growth in the rich world is not improving life satisfaction. Instead it is increasing inequality and pushing our planetary life-support systems to their breaking point. That's why we welcome Mr. Cameron's plans."

6   Thumim and White (2008, 3) found that, in the lowest three income deciles, 71 per cent of households would gain monetarily from personal carbon trading. In contrast, in the top three deciles, 55 per cent of households would have to buy allowances if they did not cut emissions. However, some low-income households were above-average emitters and would lose economically, due to factors such as living in less energy efficient homes. Thumim and White's analysis excluded air travel, which is highly concentrated among the wealthy, and the net effect would likely be more progressive with air travel included (Fawcett 2010, 6870–1).

7   The study concluded that Tesco's loyalty card had already shown the feasibility of collecting data on billions of personal transactions, and that personal carbon trading would, unlike carbon taxes, be moderately progressive.

8   The RSA argued that, although barriers had to be overcome, personal carbon trading could play a "critical role," and suggested a community-level approach, in which local authorities, employers, or other groups conducted carbon trading on behalf of individuals.

9 Meanwhile, some supporters of carbon rationing objected to the trading of credits, which would allow the rich to continue their high-carbon consumption. Former left-wing Labour minister Tony Benn, for example, said trading undermined the fair sharing of scarce resources, noting that trading rations was illegal during the war (Boase 2007).

10 Jackson (2009, 8) noted: "In a world of nine billion people, all aspiring to a level of income commensurate with 2% growth on the average EU income today, carbon intensities (for example) would have to fall on average by over 11% per year to stabilise the climate, 16 times faster than it has done since 1990. By 2050, the global carbon intensity would need to be only six grams per dollar of output, almost 130 times lower than it is today."

11 In response to the report, the *Guardian*'s (2009b) editors wrote, "The solution, say optimists, is green growth; but that appears ever more optimistic." The near impossible math of decarbonizing economic growth quickly enough "could leave Europeans and Americans with little option but to ease off the economic accelerator, even while Africans and Asians keep developing," but a bright side existed. "Instead of working feverishly while accumulating and consuming ever more, we could live at a slower pace and have more time for socialising and interests."

CHAPTER ELEVEN

1 In Canada, a version of green conservatism was evident provincially. British Columbia premier Gordon Campbell embraced climate action and, in 2007, committed to cut emissions one third by 2020, which had the potential to win over some of the province's environmentally minded electorate from the NDP. In 2008, Campbell introduced a carbon tax. Although leader of the Liberal party – which in BC is a broad tent for those to the right of the NDP – Campbell's government had been considered one of Canada's most conservative on social and economic issues.

2 "The primary responsibilities of the British government are to protect our nation from the threats of war, terrorism, climate change, energy insecurity, crime and economic instability," stated the Conservative Party (2009a).

3 At least that was the case in the initial stages of climate reform; however, competitiveness concerns relative to other EU nations with a lesser commitment to post-Kyoto carbon reduction were an emerging issue. The Cameron government's establishment of a minimum carbon price, for example, raised concerns that British firms would

face higher costs than competitors elsewhere in the EU, where the ETS price languished at very low levels.

4 Another example of competitiveness concerns constraining Britain's climate ambitions was provided by Canada's petroleum producers, who did their own review of UK policy. CAPP noted that – other than electricity, which did not face international competition – all other sectors covered by the EU ETS in the second allocation phase were given emission allowances based on BAU projections for output and intensity improvements (Hyndman 2007). In other words, the UK did not demand anything more from most firms than they would have done anyway – at least nothing more than earlier policies required. In fact, the UK's "National Allocation Plan" was clear in saying that due to competitiveness concerns, no additional costs would be imposed outside the electricity sector (Defra 2007f, 6, 20, 23).

5 Author's calculation using consumption-side emissions of CO_2 (excluding land use, land use change, and forestry) from the Eora World MRIO database and World Bank population figures for 2011. Production-side figures are from the OECD. Similar variations in consumption-side emissions among Canada, the UK, and US are evident in figures produced by Hertwich and Peters (2009, 6416).

6 Rick Hyndman of CAPP made this point about the oil industry's interest in consumption-side accounting in an interview. The call for a consumption-side analysis of emissions was not the only case of a curious overlap of position between greens and other radical voices in the UK and some conservatives in Canada, including people within the petroleum industry. Another was the critique of carbon trading as an opportunity for the finance sector to make huge profits while doing little to encourage development of long-term solutions. Furthermore, neither group had much patience for the gap between the UK government's high-minded climate rhetoric and its actual practice.

7 "The closer you get to official discourses – be it of politics or academics – the more sceptical people are of the sufficiency approach," said Wolfgang Sachs, a senior research fellow at Germany's Wuppertal Institute for Climate, Environment and Energy, with whom I spoke in London in 2007. In his experience in Germany, the assumption among policy-makers and experts was that it was not possible to bring people around to accept sufficiency, nor did they feel it was within their competence to do that: "Their competence is to run systems, but not to change people." Sachs added, however, that among a "less expert public" there is a "certain feeling that many things in everyday life have been characterized by excess." Sachs's (2007) description of the dominant message in Germany about how to respond to climate

change was familiar: "Go for renewed growth, a third industrial revolution, and embrace opportunities for new technology and new sectors of the economy." He noted that "from that perspective, questioning growth is very old." However, he added, "Many people who aren't experts and don't have to show respectability see that there's some potential for some time of renewed growth, but ask: 'Is it possible in the long term to have an economy that works well without growth?'"

8 This may be a factor worthy of further consideration and research given that, unlike Canada and other G8 nations, the UK lived up to the long-standing UN target of providing 0.7 per cent of GDP on development aid – a target that was reached in 2013 at a time of economic austerity under a Conservative-led government.

9 Sufficiency-based calls to reduce energy consumption could, in principle, be linked to the security imperative, i.e. enhancing energy security by reducing dependence on imported supplies. Government efforts in the UK (and also in the Canadian province of Nova Scotia) to improve energy security by increasing energy efficiency were part of an EM reform program, but one could interpret the push to cut energy consumption as having an element of sufficiency.

10 Thanks to Sarah Babb for the gateway drug metaphor.

Bibliography

10 Downing Street. 2007. "PM's Climate Change Interview with Sky." January 9. London: 10 Downing Street. Accessed May 26, 2008. http://www.number-10.gov.uk/output/Page10715.asp.

2020 Climate Group. 2012. *Cutting Business Travel at Lloyds Banking Group*. Stirling, Scotland: 2020 Climate Group. Accessed December 3, 2012. http://www.2020climategroup.org.uk/leading-by-example/cutting-business-travel-at-lloyds-banking-group/.

Abdallah, Saamah, Juliet Michaelson, Sagar Shah, Laura Stoll, and Nic Marks. 2012. *The Happy Planet Index: 2012 Report*. London: New Economics Foundation.

ABI. 2005. *Financial Risks of Climate Change*. London: Association of British Insurers.

Action Aid. 2010. *Meals per Gallon: The Impact of Industrial Biofuels on People and Global Hunger*. London: ActionAid.

Adam, David. 2007. "UK's Official CO_2 Figures an Illusion – Study." *Guardian*, December 10, 1.

– 2008. "Britain Tries to Block Green Energy Laws." *Guardian*, July 24, 1.

– 2009a. "$400bn Demand for Green Spending." *Guardian*, February 12, 9.

– 2009b. "Economic Case for Heathrow Third Runway Flawed, Figures Show." *Guardian*, September 18, 13.

Adams, Michael, and Keith Neuman. 2006. "It's Not Easy Being Green." *Globe and Mail*, October 20, A21.

Adbusters. 2009. "Man of the Year." *Adbusters*, January.

AEF. 2013. *How the Latest DfT Forecasts Show That Any New Runways Would Be Incompatible with the Climate Act*. London: Aviation Environment Federation.

AER. 2013. "Crude Bitumen (Datasheet)." Calgary: Alberta Energy Regulator. Accessed December 1, 2013. http://www.aer.ca/documents/sts/ST98/ST98-2013_CrudeBitumen.xls.

AFL. 2007a. "Climate Change Policy Paper." Edmonton: Alberta Federation of Labour. Accessed November 9, 2008. http://www.afl.org/upload/climatechange2007.pdf.

– 2007b. Presentation to Multi-Stakeholder Committee on Oil Sands. Calgary, April 24. Edmonton: Alberta Federation of Labour. Accessed November 9, 2008. http://www.afl.org/upload/oilsandspresent.pdf.

– 2007c. *Temporary Foreign Workers: Alberta's Disposable Workforce.* Edmonton: Alberta Federation of Labour.

AFP. 2007. "Nobel Climate Panel Chief Raps Canada on Carbon Cuts." *Agence France-Presse,* December 6. Accessed August 18, 2009. http://afp.google.com/article/ALeqM5hjgJAYTz1867ZFCzPoIQIDnFdDcA.

– 2008. "EU Defends Biofuel Goals amid Food Crises." *Agence France-Presse,* April 18. Accessed April 22, 2008. http://afp.google.com/article/ALeqM5gp1nkJeC-IhlYkVtsvPfp3u7mOWQ.

Agrell, Siri. 2011. "Traffic Jams May Force Oil Sands Workers to Stop Driving." *Globe and Mail,* August 23, A10.

Ainsworth, Peter. 2007. Speech to Guardian Climate Change Summit, June 11, London.

Airbus. 2012. "Eco-Climb." Toulouse, France: Airbus. Accessed December 2, 2012. http://www.airbus.com/innovation/future-by-airbus/smarter-skies/aircraft-take-off-in-continuous-eco-climb/.

Aitkenhead, Decca. 2008. "'Enjoy Life While You Can.'" *Guardian,* March 1, 33.

Alberta. 2008a. *Alberta's 2008 Climate Change Strategy: Responsibility/Leadership/Action.* Edmonton: Alberta Government.

– 2008b. "Alberta's Oil Sands: Protecting the Environment." Edmonton: Government of Alberta. Accessed November 15, 2008. http://oilsands.alberta.ca/4.cfm.

– 2009. *Alberta Hansard.* April 7. Edmonton: Province of Alberta.

– 2012. "Fact Sheet: Climate Change." Edmonton: Government of Alberta. Accessed January 10, 2013. http://www.oilsands.alberta.ca/FactSheets/CChange_FSht_June_2012_Online.pdf.

Alberta Department of Energy. 2013. Spreadsheet Analyzing Four Greenhouse Gas Reduction Scenarios. Sent to Canadian Association of Petroleum Producers, March 28. Edmonton: Department of Energy. Accessed December 2, 2013. http://pubs.pembina.org/reports/foip-oil-and-gas-ghg-regs-nov13.pdf.

Alberta NDP. 2006. "Health Concerns Must Trump Development." Press Release, November 11. Edmonton: Alberta New Democratic Party. Accessed November 19, 2008. http://www.ndpopposition.ab.ca/site/index.cfm?fuseaction=page.details&ID=7239&t=8&i=1.

Alcott, Blake. 2008. "The Sufficiency Strategy: Would Rich-World Frugality Lower Environmental Impact?" *Ecological Economics* 64 (4):770–86.

Aldhous, Peter. 2010. "How Will the UK's Well-Being Index Shape Up?" *New Scientist*, November 16. Accessed July 12, 2012. http://www. newscientist.com/blogs/shortsharpscience/2010/11/how-the-uks-wellbeing-index-wi.html.

Alexander, Samuel. 2012. "Planned economic contraction: the emerging case for degrowth." *Environmental Politics* 21(3):349–68.

Allan, Elyse. 2007. Speech by President & CEO of GE Canada to Climate 2050 Conference, Montreal, October 10.

Alliance Against Urban 4×4s. 2008. "We're Not Anti-Car, But …" London: Alliance Against Urban 4×4s. Accessed April 14, 2008. http://stop urban4×4s.blogspot.com/search?updated-max=2008-02-24To 8%3A41%3A00Z&max-results=4.

Alvarez, Pierre. 2007. "Fears, Myths & Realities Regarding Canada's Climate Change and Clean Air Policies." CAPP Symposium, June 18. Calgary: Canadian Association of Petroleum Producers. Accessed December 18, 2007. http://membernet.capp.ca/raw.asp?x=1&dt=PDF&dn=123010.

– "Industry's Reply." Letter to Miami Mayor Manuel A. Diaz, President, United States Conference of Mayors, June 25. Accessed November 16, 2008. http://www.canadasoilsands.ca/en/forum/topic.aspx?id=35.

Amalgamated Transit Union and Transport Workers Union. 2011. "ATU & TWU Oppose Approval of the Keystone XL Pipeline and Call for End of Increased Use of Tar Sands Oil." Washington, DC: Amalgamated Transit Union. Accessed November 12, 2011. http://www.atu.org/media/releases/atu-twu-oppose-approval-of-the-keystone-xl-pipeline-and-call-for-end-of-increased-use-of-tar-sands-oil.

Anderson, Kevin, and Alice Bows. 2007. "A Response to the Draft Climate Change Bill's Carbon Reduction Targets." Manchester: Tyndall Centre for Climate Change Research. Accessed April 27, 2008. http://www .tyndall.uea.ac.uk/publications/briefing_notes/bn17.pdf.

– 2008. "Reframing the Climate Change Challenge in Light of Post-2000 Emission Trends." *Philosophical Transactions of the Royal Society A* 366 (1882):3863–82.

– 2012. "A New Paradigm for Climate Change." *Nature Climate Change* 2 (9):639–40.

Angus, Ian. 2011. "Beyond Growth or beyond Capitalism?" *Climate & Capitalism*, January 4. Accessed December 18, 2012. http://climateand capitalism.com/2011/01/04/beyond-growth-or-beyond-capitalism/.

Anielski, Mark, and Heather Johannessen. 2009. *The Edmonton 2008 Genuine Progress Indicator Report*. Edmonton: Anielski Management Inc.

Animal Aid. 2006. "Go Vegan, Fight Climate Change!" Tonbridge, Kent: Animal Aid. Accessed April 3, 2008. http://www.animalaid.org .uk/h/n/NEWS/news_veggie/ALL/1395.

AP. 2008. "British Military Reacting to Climate Change." *Associated Press*, September 3. Accessed October 31, 2009. http://www.sfchronicle marketplace.com/cgi-bin/article.cgi?f=/n/a/2008/09/03/ international/i093325D58.DTL.

Armstrong, Martin, Russell Chambers, Ian Cheshire, Jeremy Darroch, Charles Dunstone, Sir Roy Gardner, Justin King. 2009. "Business Can Do without a Third Runway." *Times*, May 6, 25.

Ashcroft, Michael A. 2005. *Smell the Coffee: A Wake-up Call for the Conservative Party.* London: Michael A. Ashcroft.

Ashley-Cantello, Will. 2008. "Advertising Watchdog Receives Record Complaints over Corporate 'Greenwash.'" *Guardian*, May 1. Accessed May 1, 2008. http://www.guardian.co.uk/environment/2008/may/01/ corporatesocialresponsibility.ethicalliving.

Ashton Hayes Going Carbon Neutral. 2012. "Ashton Hayes Going Carbon Neutral." Accessed June 28, 2012. http://www.goingcarbonneutral .co.uk/.

Aston, Louise M., James N. Smith, and John W. Powles. 2012. "Impact of a Reduced Red and Processed Meat Dietary Pattern on Disease Risks and Greenhouse Gas Emissions in the UK: A Modelling Study." *BMJ Open* 2 (5). doi:10.1136/bmjopen-2012-001072. http://bmjopen.bmj.com/ content/2/5/e001072.

Athanasiou, Tom, Sivan Kartha, Paul Baer, and Eric Kemp-Benedict. 2009. *Canada's Fair Share in a Climate Constrained World.* EcoEquity, Stockholm Environment Institute, and Heinrich Böll Stiftung.

Attwood, Karen. 2007. "Tesco Funds 'Green Consumption' Studies." *Independent*, September 13. Accessed September 13, 2007. http:// www.independent.co.uk/news/business/news/tesco-funds-green- consumption-studies-402217.html.

Audsley, Eric, Julia Chatterton, Anil Graves, Joe Morris, Donal Murphy-Bokern, Kerry Pearn, Daniel Sandars, and Adrian Williams. 2011. "Food, Land, and Greenhouse Gases: The Effect of Changes in UK Food Consumption on Land Requirements and Greenhouse Gas Emissions." London: Committee on Climate Change.

Ayling, Bob. 2008. "Third Runway Is a Flight of Fallacy." *Sunday Times*, May 4, 21.

BAA. 2007a. *BAA Corporate Responsibility Report 2007.* London: British Airports Authority.

– 2007b. "Heathrow and Climate Change." London: British Airports Authority. Accessed May 21, 2008. http://www.baa.com/portal/page/CR micrositesLHR07%5EOverview%5EHeathrow+and+climate+change/4 882b9ce2bc63110VgnVCM10000036821coa____/448c6a4c7f1b0010 VgnVCM200000357e120a____/.

Baer, Paul. 2007. "The Worth of an Ice-Sheet: A Critique of the Treatment of Catastrophic Impacts in the Stern Review." EcoEquity. Accessed February 11, 2009. http://www.ecoequity.org/docs/WorthOfAnIceSheet.pdf.

Baiocchi, Giovanni, and Jan C. Minx. 2010. "Understanding Changes in the UK's CO_2 Emissions: A Global Perspective." *Environmental Science & Technology* 44 (4):1177–84.

Baird, Vera. 2007. "Ensus Bioethanol Opening – 11 May 2007." Website of Vera Baird, MP for Redcar. Accessed April 19, 2008. http://www.labouronline.org/wibs/166155/cf7789c4-63a7-3a34-bd2b-14f06d23e35e?PageId=9f93df6c-fa3d-52a4-898d-f39eff1d820a.

Bale, Tim. 2008. "'A Bit Less Bunny-Hugging and a Bit More Bunny-Boiling'? Qualifying Conservative Party Change under David Cameron." *British Politics* 3(3):270–99.

Barclay, Christopher. 2012. "Food Miles." London: House of Commons Library. Accessed November 20, 2012. http://www.parliament.uk/briefing-papers/SN04984.pdf.

Barker, Terry, Athanasios Dagoumas, and Jonathan Rubin. 2009. "The Macroeconomic Rebound Effect and the World Economy." *Energy Efficiency* 2(4):411–27.

Barkham, Patrick. 2008. "Virgin's Biofuel Is a PR Stunt Says BA Boss." *Guardian*, March 15, 11.

Barry, John. 2003. "Ecological Modernisation." In *Environmental Thought*, edited by E. Page and J. Proops, 191–214. Cheltenham: Edward Elgar.

– 2012. *The Politics of Actually Existing Unsustainability: Human Flourishing in a Climate-Changed, Carbon Constrained World.* Oxford: Oxford University Press.

BBC. 1998. "Prescott Defends 'Quality of Life' Barometer." *BBC News*, November 23. Accessed May 14, 2008. http://news.bbc.co.uk/1/hi/uk_politics/220317.stm.

– 2005. "BBC TWO's Making Slough Happy Reveals Final Happiness Levels to Be up by a Third." Press Release, December 5. London: BBC Press Office. Accessed May 5, 2008. http://www.bbc.co.uk/pressoffice/pressreleases/stories/2005/12_december/05/slough.shtml.

– 2006a. "12,000-Mile Scampi Trip Condemned." *BBC News*, November 15. Accessed April 6, 2008. http://news.bbc.co.uk/1/hi/scotland/south_of_scotland/6150240.stm.

– 2006b. "Expert Reaction to Stern Review." *BBC News*, October 30. Accessed February 13, 2009. http://news.bbc.co.uk/1/hi/business/6098612.stm.

– 2006c. "Happiness Doesn't Cost the Earth." *BBC News*, July 12. Accessed May 7, 2008. http://news.bbc.co.uk/1/hi/sci/tech/5169448.stm.

– 2007a. "BA Boss Urges Heathrow Expansion." *BBC News*, November 20.

Accessed May 23, 2008. http://news.bbc.co.uk/2/hi/business/ 7104458.stm.

– 2007b. "Campaigners Leave Heathrow Camp." *BBC News*, August 20. Accessed April 16, 2008. http://news.bbc.co.uk/1/hi/uk/6954428.stm.

– 2007c. "Car Bosses Say 4×4 Demand Falling." *BBC News*, January 4. Accessed April 13, 2008. http://news.bbc.co.uk/1/hi/business/ 6229695.stm.

– 2007d. "Do Voters Care about the Climate?" Accessed May 15, 2008. http://news.bbc.co.uk/player/nol/newsid_7000000/newsid_7006300 /7006310.stm.

– 2007e. "Hard Talk." *BBC News*. Accessed May 20, 2007. http://www.bbc .co.uk/newsa/n5ctrl/progs/07/hardtalk/wall21feb.ram.

– 2007f. "Reaction: Heathrow Expansion Plan." *BBC News*, November 22. Accessed May 23, 2008. http://news.bbc.co.uk/2/hi/uk_news/ politics/7107549.stm.

– 2008a. "Greens Welcome New Climate Dept." *BBC News*, October 3. Accessed October 4, 2009. http://news.bbc.co.uk/1/hi/sci/tech/ 7650669.stm.

– 2008b. "Should We Stop Caring about Growth?" *Talk about Newsnight*, December 23. Accessed May 12, 2008. http://www.bbc.co.uk/blogs/ newsnight/2008/01/wednesday_23_january_2008.html.

– 2010. "BBC Climate Change Poll – February 2010." Accessed July 4, 2011. http://news.bbc.co.uk/nol/shared/bsp/hi/pdfs/05_02_10climate change.pdf.

– 2013. "Zac Goldsmith Challenges Leaders over Heathrow Expansion." *BBC News*, December 14, sec. UK. Accessed December 17, 2013. http:// www.bbc.co.uk/news/uk-25375563.

BBC World Service, PIPA, and GlobeScan. 2007. "All Countries Need to Take Major Steps on Climate Change: Global Poll." London: BBC World Service. Accessed August 9, 2009. http://www.worldpublicopinion.org/ pipa/pdf/sep07/BBCClimate_Sep07_rpt.pdf.

BC. 2008. *Climate Action Plan*. Victoria, BC: Government of British Columbia.

Beaudin, Monique. 2009. "Canada Should Put Oil Sands on Hold: Climate Change Expert." *Montreal Gazette*, September 21.

Beckett, Margaret, and Patricia Hewitt. 2005. "Naysayers, Take Note: Britain Is Pro-Kyoto and Prospering." *Globe and Mail*, March 15, A19.

Belfry Munroe, Kaija. 2010. *Business, Risk, and Carbon Pricing: Business Preference for Climate Change Instruments in Canada*. Ottawa: Sustainable Prosperity.

Bell, Daniel. 1976. *The Cultural Contradictions of Capitalism*. New York: Basic Books.

Bell, Sonya. 2011. "Megan Leslie Calls for Pause – Not Moratorium!

– on Keystone." *iPolitics*, October 4. Accessed November 25, 2011.
http://www.ipolitics.ca/2011/10/04/megan-leslie-calls-for-pause-
%E2%80%94-not-moratorium-%E2%80%94-on-keystone/.

Bellamy, David. 2008. "BBC Shunned Me for Denying Climate Change."
Daily Express, November 5. Accessed November 5, 2008. http://www
.dailyexpress.co.uk/posts/view/69623.

Benjamin, Alison. 2007. "Stern: Climate Change a 'Market Failure.'" *Guardian*, November 29. Accessed February 11, 2009. http://www.guardian
.co.uk/environment/2007/nov/29/climatechange.carbonemissions.

Benn, Hilary. 2007a. "Air Miles: Roses and Ending Poverty." Speech,
February 13. London: Department for International Development."
Accessed April 6, 2008. http://www.dfid.gov.uk/News/files/Speeches/
trade/hilary-valentine-speech.asp.

– 2007b. "The Environmental Revolution: How Green Politics Can Renew
Labour." Speech to Socialist Environment and Resources Association,
March 20. Accessed February 14, 2008. http://hilarybenn.org/2007/
speeches-articles/the-environmental-revolution-how-green-politics-can-
renew-labour/.

Bennett, Dean. 2007a. "Alberta Minister Says Post 9-11 Oil Fears Are Fuelling Hyper-Inflated Economy." *Canadian Press*, April 30. Accessed May
1, 2007. http://www.redorbit.com/news/science/919835/alberta_
minister_says_post911_oil_fears_are_fuelling_hyperinflated_economy/
index.html.

– 2007b. "Albertans Not Happy Campers." *Globe and Mail*, October 14. Accessed November 3, 2008. http://www.theglobeandmail.com/servlet/
story/RTGAM.20071014.wgrumpy1014/BNStory/National/home.

Bernstein, Steven, and Benjamin Cashore. 2002. "Globalization, Inter-
nalization, and Liberal Environmentalism: Exploring Non-Domestic
Sources of Influence on Canadian Environmental Policy." In *Canadian
Environmental Policy: Context and Cases*, edited by R. Boardman and D.L.
VanNiijnatten, 212–233. Toronto: Oxford University Press.

BERR. 2007. "Draft Options Paper on Renewables Target." London: Department for Business, Enterprise & Regulatory Reform." Accessed
February 17, 2009. http://image.guardian.co.uk/sys-files/Guardian/
documents/2007/08/13/RenewablesTargetDocument.pdf.

Berry, Siân. 2007. "How Can a Boom Town Be Green?" Address to Debate
London Event, June 24, London.

Biello, David. 2013. "How Much Will Tar Sands Oil Add to Global Warming?"
Scientific American, January 23. Accessed December 1, 2013. http://www
.scientificamerican.com/article.cfm?id=tar-sands-and-keystone-xl-pipeline-
impact-on-global-warming.

BioRegional. 2006. "BioRegional's Response to UK Government's

Announcements on Zero Carbon Homes." December 20. Accessed
March 8, 2008. http://www.bioregional.com/news%20page/news_
stories/ZED/zerocarbon%20201206.htm.

Birch, James I. 2011. "An Open Letter from a Climate Science Researcher/
Student about Impact of Environment Canada Staff and Program
Cuts." Accessed October 12, 2011. http://www.cleanbreak.ca/2011
/09/22/an-open-letter-from-a-climate-science-researcherstudent-
about-impact-of-environment-canada-staff-and-program-cuts/.

Black, Richard. 2007. "Brits 'Addicted' to Cheap Flights." *BBC News*, August
30. Accessed May 25, 2008. http://news.bbc.co.uk/2/hi/science/
nature/6970730.stm.

Blair, Tony. 1999. "Foreword." In *A Better Quality of Life – Strategy for Sustainable Development for the United Kingdom – 1999*. London: The Stationery
Office.

– 2000. "Speech to CBI/Green Alliance. London, February 4." London: 10
Downing Street." Accessed February 19, 2009. http://www.number10.
gov.uk/Page1530.

– 2004. "Full Text: Blair's Climate Change Speech." *Guardian*, September
15. Accessed February 17, 2009. http://www.guardian.co.uk/politics
/2004/sep/15/greenpolitics.uk.

Bloc Québécois. 2008. "Kyoto et les gaz à effet de serre: Ce que nous pro-
posons." Montreal: Bloc Québécois. Accessed August 12, 2009. http://
www.blocquebecois.org/dossiers/environnement/kyoto_propositions
.asp.

Blue Green Canada. 2012. *More Bang for Our Buck: How Canada Can Create
More Energy Jobs and Less Pollution*. Toronto: Blue Green Canada.

BMU. 2006. *Climate Protection Pays*. Berlin: BMU Public Relations Division.

Boase, Nell. 2007. "Carbon Credits Are 'Wrong' Says Benn." *Guardian*,
May 31. Accessed May 29, 2009. http://www.guardian.co.uk/
environment/2007/may/31/climatechange.climatechange.

Boeing. 2007. "It Represents a Simple Philosophy: Technology to New
Heights, Environmental Impacts to New Lows." Advertisement. *Guardian*, July 2, 17.

Booker, Christopher. 2008. "The 'Consensus' on Climate Change Is a
Catastrophe in Itself." *Telegraph*, August 31, 25.

Booker, Christopher, and Richard North. 2007. "The Deceit behind Global
Warming." *Telegraph*, November 4. Accessed May 27, 2008. http://
www.telegraph.co.uk/earth/earthnews/3312921/The-deceit-behind-
global-warming.html.

Boon, Bart, Marc Davidson, Jasper Faber, Dagmar Nelissen, and Gerdien
van de Vreede. 2008. *The Economics of Heathrow Expansion*. Delft, Netherlands: CE Delft.

Boorman, Neil. 2007. "My Brand New Life." *BBC News*, September 4. Accessed September 4, 2007. http://news.bbc.co.uk/go/pr/fr/-/1/hi/magazine/6977844.stm.

Bouchard, Luc-André. 2009. "The Integrity of Creation and the Athabasca Oil Sands." St. Paul, AB: Diocese of St. Paul. Accessed January 28, 2009. http://www.dioceseofstpaul.ca/index.php?option=com_content&task=view&id=135&Itemid=11.

Bows, Alice, and Kevin Anderson. 2006. "Contracting UK Carbon Emissions: Implications for UK Aviation." Manchester: Tyndall Centre for Climate Change Research. Accessed May 22, 2008. http://www.biee.org/downloads/index.php?dir=Energy+Policies+In+a+Global+Context%2F&download=biee+presentation+tyndall+2006.pdf.

– 2007. "Policy Clash: Can Projected Aviation Growth Be Reconciled with the UK Government's 60% Carbon-Reduction Target?" *Transport Policy* 14(2):103–10.

Bows, Alice, Sarah Mander, Richard Starkey, Mercedes Bleda, and Kevin Anderson. 2006. *Living within a Carbon Budget*. Manchester: Tyndall Centre for Climate Change Research.

Bowyer, Catherine. 2010. "Anticipated Indirect Land Use Change Associated with Expanded Use of Biofuels and Bioliquids in the EU – An Analysis of the National Renewable Energy Action Plans." London: Institute for European Environmental Policy.

Boyd, David R. 2003. *Unnatural Law: Rethinking Canadian Environmental Law and Policy*. Vancouver: UBC Press.

Bramley, Matthew. 2007a. "Analysis of the Government of Canada's April 2007 Greenhouse Gas Policy Announcement." Ottawa: Pembina Institute. Accessed August 16, 2009. http://pubs.pembina.org/reports/Reg_framework_comments.pdf.

– 2007b. Interview on CBC Radio, *Sunday Edition*. CBC Radio, May 27.

Brandt, Adam R. 2011. "Upstream Greenhouse Gas (GHG) Emissions from Canadian Oil Sands as a Feedstock for European Refineries." Accessed August 9, 2011. https://circabc.europa.eu/d/d/workspace/SpacesStore/db806977-6418-44db-a464-20267139b34d/Brandt_Oil_Sands_GHGs_Final.pdf.

Brechin, Steven R, and Medani Bhandari. 2011. "Perceptions of Climate Change Worldwide." *Wiley Interdisciplinary Reviews: Climate Change* 2(6): 871–85.

Brignall, Miles. 2008. "B&Q to End Sale of Patio Heaters." *Guardian*, January 22. Accessed April 2, 2009. http://www.guardian.co.uk/environment/2008/jan/22/carbonemissions.climatechange.

British Bottled Water. 2013. "Water's Vital Statistics: Industry Data." London: British Bottled Water Producers. Accessed November 22, 2013. http://www.britishbottledwater.org/vitalstats2.html.

British Retail Consortium. 2008. "Green Smokescreen Hides Tax Grab."
    March 12. London: British Retail Consortium. Accessed December 20,
    2013. http://www.brc.org.uk/brc_news_detail.asp?id=1336.

Broadhead, Lee-Anne. 2001. "Canada as a Rogue State: Its Shameful Per-
    formance on Climate Change." *International Journal* 56(3):461–80.

Brooks, David B. 1981. *Zero Energy Growth for Canada.* Toronto: McClelland
    & Stewart.

Brooks, David B., and Robert C. Paehlke. 1980. "Canada: A Soft Path in
    a Hard Country." *Canadian Public Policy / Analyse de Politiques* 6(3):
    444–53.

Brooks, Josh. 2009. "Monbiot's Voice of Reason Helps Battle Plastic Bag
    Scandal." *Packaging News*, April 8. Accessed November 17, 2012.
    http://www.packagingnews.co.uk/environment/monbiots-voice-of-
    reason-helps-battle-plastic-bag-scandal/.

Brooymans, Hanneke. 2009. "Fort Mac to Ban Plastic Bags." *Edmonton
    Journal*, March 14, B4.

Brower, Derek. 2006. "In Search of the Key." *Petroleum Economist*, Septem-
    ber. Accessed November 21, 2008. http://www.petroleum-economist.
    com/default.asp?page=14&PubID=46&ISS=22387&SID=648065.

Brown, Gordon. 2007a. "Speech by the Chancellor of the Exchequer, the
    Rt Hon Gordon Brown MP, to the Green Alliance, London." March
    12. London: HM Treasury. Accessed February 5, 2009. http://www.hm-
    treasury.gov.uk/speech_chex_120307.htm.

– 2007b. "Speech on Climate Change." November 19. London: 10 Down-
    ing Street. Accessed November 19, 2007. http://www.number10.gov
    .uk/Page13791.

– 2007c. "Speech to the CBI." November 26. London: 10 Downing Street.
    Accessed May 23, 2008. http://www.number-10.gov.uk/output/
    Page13851.asp.

– 2008. "Why Sarah and I Know This Is Right: Prime Minister Gordon
    Brown Backs the Daily Mail's Banish the Bags Campaign." *Daily Mail*,
    February 29, 21.

Browne, John. 1997. "Addressing Global Climate Change." Speech to
    Stanford University, Palo Alto, California, May 19. London: BP Global.
    Accessed April 5, 2009. http://www.bp.com/genericarticle.do?categor
    yId=98&contentId=2000427.

BT. 2007. "Climate Change – What's BT Doing? Our People." London: BT.
    Accessed April 2, 2009. http://www.btplc.com/ClimateChange/Whats
    BTdoing/Ourpeople/index.htm.

– 2009. "Reduce CO$_2$ Emissions with BT Conferencing." London: BT. Ac-
    cessed May 9, 2009. https://www.conferencing.bt.com/infocentre/
    conferencing/reduce_co2_emissions.jsp.

Buchan, David. 2009. *Energy and Climate Change: Europe at the Crossroads.*
    Oxford: Oxford University Press & Oxford Institute for Energy Studies.

Buchan, Keith. 2008. *Alchemy Economics – the UK Government's Conjuring Trick
    to Justify Airport Expansion.* London: WWF-UK.

Buck, Daniel. 2006. "The Ecological Question: Can Capitalism Prevail?" In
    Socialist Register 2007: Coming to Terms With Nature, edited by L. Panitch
    and C. Leys, 60–71. New York: Monthly Review Press.

Bunting, Madeleine. 2007. "Eat, Drink and Be Miserable: The True Cost of
    Our Addiction to Shopping." *Guardian,* December 3, 30.

Burrows, Matthew. 2007. "Petro-Giants Will Accept a Carbon Tax." *Georgia
    Straight,* December 6. Accessed December 18, 2007. http://www
    .straight.com/article-123594/petro-giants-will-accept-a-carbon-tax.

Butler, Don. 2007. "Reality Check on Climate Change." *Ottawa Citizen,*
    February 18. Accessed January 30, 2009. http://www.canada.com/
    ottawacitizen/news/arts/story.html?id=b434b3d7-dd08-4af2-9f10-
    e84ab816968f&k=81151.

Buttel, Frederick H. 2000. "Ecological Modernization as Social Theory."
    Geoforum 31(1):57–65.

C4. 2007. "The Great Green Smokescreen." Dispatches, July 16. *Dispatches.*
    London: Channel 4.

Cabinet Office. 2008. "Cabinet Secretary Announces Phasing out of Bottled
    Water across Government Estate." News Release, March 6. London:
    Cabinet Office. Accessed March 31, 2008. http://www.cabinetoffice.gov
    .uk/newsroom/news_releases/2008/080306_bottled_water.aspx.

Cahill, Michael. 2007. "Why the U-Turn on Sustainable Transport?" *Capital-
    ism, Nature, Socialism* 18(4):90–103.

Cairns, Sally, and Carey Newson. 2006. *Predict and Decide: Aviation, Climate
    Change, and UK Policy.* Oxford: Environmental Change Institute.

Camcastle, Cara. 2007. "Survey Says: Green Party Members Overwhelm-
    ingly Accept Limits-to-Growth and Believe Nature Has an Intrinsic
    Value." *Alternatives Journal* 33(1):25–6.

Cameron, David. 2006a. "Full Text: David Cameron's Speech to Google
    Zeitgeist Europe 2006." *Guardian,* May 22. Accessed May 5, 2008.
    http://www.guardian.co.uk/politics/2006/may/22/conservatives.
    davidcameron.

– 2006b. "General Well-Being Speech." Speech, July 20. London: Conserva-
    tive Party." Accessed May 12, 2008. http://www.conservatives.com/
    News/Speeches/2006/07/David_Cameron_General_Well-Being_
    speech.aspx.

– 2006c. "Labour's Carbon Targets Amount to a Cop-Out." *Independent,*
    October 27. Accessed February 19, 2009. http://www.independent
    .co.uk/opinion/commentators/david-cameron-labours-carbon-targets-
    amount-to-a-copout-421777.html.

– 2006d. "The Planet First, Politics Second." *Independent,* September 3. Accessed December 19, 2006. http://www.independent.co.uk/opinion/commentators/david-cameron-the-planet-first-politics-second-414401.html.
– 2007a. "Cameron Speech in Full." *BBC News,* October 3. Accessed March 16, 2008. http://news.bbc.co.uk/1/hi/uk_politics/7026435.stm.
– 2007b. "Full Text of David Cameron's Speech: The Conservative Party Leader's Speech at the Royal Society of Arts in London Entitled: Civility and Social Progress." *Guardian,* April 23. Accessed May 12, 2008. http://www.guardian.co.uk/politics/2007/apr/23/conservatives.davidcameron.
– 2008a. "In Praise of General Well-Being." In *Do Good Lives Have to Cost the Earth?,* edited by A. Simms and J. Smith, 207–13. London: Constable.
– 2008b. "The Choice Isn't between Economy and Environment." London: Conservative Party. Accessed May 7, 2009. http://www.conservatives.com/News/Speeches/2008/06/David_Cameron_The_choice_isnt_between_economy_and_environment.aspx.
– 2010a. "Cameron Commits Government to 10:10." Speech at Department of Energy and Climate Change, May 14. Accessed September 4, 2010. http://vimeo.com/11737406.
– 2010b. "PM Speech on Wellbeing." London: 10 Downing Street. Accessed June 26, 2011. http://www.number10.gov.uk/news/speeches-and-transcripts/2010/11/pm-speech-on-well-being-57569.
– 2010c. "PM's Speech on Creating a 'New Economic Dynamism.'" London: 10 Downing Street. Accessed July 11, 2012. http://www.number10.gov.uk/news/creating-a-new-economic-dynamism/.
– 2012. "Letter to Chris Heaton-Harris on Wind Power." February 13. Accessed June 9, 2012. http://www.scribd.com/doc/82548604/David-Cameron-wind-letter.
CAN Canada. 2008. "UK Uncouples GHG Pollution from Economic Growth." Ottawa: Climate Action Network Canada. *Climate Action News,* February 6. Accessed February 7, 2008. http://www.climateactionnetwork.ca/e/news/climate-action/can-2008-02-06.pdf.
– 2010. *The Tar Sands' Long Shadow: Canada's Campaign to Kill Climate Policies Outside Our Borders.* Ottawa: Climate Action Network Canada.
Canada.com. 2011. "Harper Opens Door to Cash for Other Provinces after Lower Churchill Outrage." *Canada.com,* April 5. Accessed December 10, 2011. http://blogs.canada.com/2011/04/05/harper-opens-door-to-cash-for-other-provinces-after-lower-churchill-outrage/.
Canada-Alberta Carbon and Capture Storage Task Force. 2008. "Key Messages for Ministers." Accessed November 29, 2011. http://www.cbc.ca/news/pdf/foip-scan.pdf.

Canada-US Monitor. 2009. "The Economy and Climate Change." *Canada-US Monitor*, March. Accessed April 1, 2009. http://www.connect2 canada.com/resources/newsletters.jhtml?id=35885.

Canadian Press. 2006a. "Ontario, CAW Slam Green Plan." *Toronto Star*, October 3. Accessed October 3, 2006. http://www.thestar.com/NASApp/cs/ContentServer?pagename=thestar/Layout/Article_Type1&call_pag eid=971358637177&c=Article&cid=1159869427369.

– 2006b. "Think-Tank Takes Issue with Stelmach's Stance on Oil Sands." *Globe and Mail*, December 8. Accessed November 12, 2008. http://www.theglobeandmail.com/servlet/story/RTGAM.20061208.woilsands1208/BNStory/Business/?cid=al_gam_nletter_maropen.

– 2007. "Al Gore Says Tories' Green Plan a 'Fraud.'" *Globe and Mail*, April 28. Accessed April 29, 2007. http://www.globeandmail.com.

– 2008. "Vote on Environmental Issues, Scientists Urge." *Toronto Star*, October 7. Accessed October 7, 2007. http://www.thestar.com/FederalElection/article/513053.

CanWest. 2007. "Survey Finds Canadians Want Greener Lives." *Canada.com*, October 18. Accessed August 9, 2009. http://www.canada.com/topics/news/story.html?id=0b15bc38-3215-45f7-89a5-85af5f9db878&p=2.

– 2008. "New Harper Spokesman Expected to Make PMO More Political." *Canada.com*, July 4. Accessed August 24, 2009. http://www.canada.com/topics/news/national/story.html?id=5b4a27f0-a92c-4e3d-8012-7d62eebd3272.

CAPP. 2002. "Letter to Minister of Energy, Government of Nova Scotia; Minister of Fisheries, Aquaculture and Environment, Government of Prince Edward Island; and Other Canadian Ministers of Energy and Environment." November 18. Calgary: Canadian Association of Petroleum Producers. Accessed December 18, 2007. http://www.capp.ca.

– 2011. *Statistical Handbook for Canada's Upstream Petroleum Industry*. Calgary: Canadian Association of Petroleum Producers.

– 2013a. "CAPP Concerns and Questions for AB and Consultants: Model Assumptions and Comments." Calgary: Canadian Association of Petroleum Producers. Accessed December 2, 2013. http://pubs.pembina.org/reports/foip-oil-and-gas-ghg-regs-nov13.pdf.

– 2013b. "Greenhouse Gases." Calgary: Canadian Association of Petroleum Producers. Accessed December 6, 2013. http://www.capp.ca/rce/oil-sands/air/greenhouse-gases/.

– 2013c. *Responsible Canadian Energy: 2013 Progress Report Summary*. Calgary: Canadian Association of Petroleum Producers.

Carbon Tracker. 2013. *Unburnable Carbon 2013: Wasted Capital and Stranded Assets*. London: Carbon Tracker and the Grantham Research Institute, LSE.

Carbon Trade Watch. 2007. *The Carbon Neutral Myth: Offset Indulgences for Your Climate Sins.* Amsterdam: Transnational Institute.

Carbon Trust. 2005. *The UK Climate Change Programme: Potential Evolution for Business and the Public Sector.* London: Carbon Trust.

– 2011. *International Carbon Flows – Global Flows.* London: Carbon Trust.

Carrell, Severin. 2012. "Alex Salmond Hits Back at Critics of Scotland's Energy Policies." *Guardian,* October 10. Accessed January 19, 2013. http://www.guardian.co.uk/environment/2012/oct/10/alex-salmond-scotland-energy-policies.

Carrington, Damian. 2011a. "Public Belief in Climate Change Weathers Storm, Poll Shows." *Guardian,* January 31. Accessed July 14, 2011. http://www.guardian.co.uk/environment/2011/jan/31/public-belief-climate-change.

– 2011b. "The Bloody Fight for the Green Soul of the Conservative Party." *Guardian,* June 22. Accessed June 8, 2012. http://www.guardian.co.uk/environment/damian-carrington-blog/2011/jun/22/green politics-davidcameron.

– 2011c. "UK Secretly Helping Canada Push Its Oil Sands Project." *Guardian,* November 28, 1.

– 2012. "Can the UK Fly More without Breaking Climate Change Targets?" *Guardian,* September 6. Accessed December 2, 2012. http://www.guardian.co.uk/environment/2012/sep/06/uk-fly-climate-change-targets.

– 2013. "Government Might Clear Low Bar for Greenest Ever, but Is It Green Enough?" *Guardian,* November 22, 19.

Carrington, Damian, and Stefano Valentino. 2011. "Biofuels Boom in Africa as British Firms Lead Rush on Land for Plantations." *Guardian,* June 1, 1.

Carter, Neil. 2009. "Vote Blue, Go Green? Cameron's Conservatives and the Environment." *Political Quarterly* 80(2):233–42.

Carvalho, Anabela. 2005. "Representing the Politics of the Greenhouse Effect: Discursive Strategies in the British Media." *Critical Discourse Studies* 2(1):1–29.

Cary, Anthony. 2008. "Time to Ease up on the Climate Agenda? No Way." *Globe and Mail,* July 7, B2.

Castle, Stephen. 2007. "Open Skies Pact 'Will Worsen Climate Change.'" *Independent,* March 22, 24.

CAT. 2007. *Zero Carbon Britain: An Alternative Energy Strategy.* Machynlleth, Powys, Wales: Centre for Alternative Technology.

– 2013. *Zero Carbon Britain: Rethinking the Future.* Machynlleth, Powys, Wales: Centre for Alternative Technology.

Catton, William R., and Riley E. Dunlap. 1980. "A New Ecological

Paradigm for Post-Exuberant Sociology." *American Behavioral Scientist* 24(1):15–47.

Cavendish, Camilla. 2006. "The Only Argument Left on Emissions Is Political." *Times*, October 31. Accessed April 15, 2009. http://www .timesonline.co.uk/tol/news/politics/article619829.ece.

Cavlovic, Therese A., Kenneth H. Baker, Robert P. Berrens, and Kishore Gawande. 2000. "A Meta-Analysis of Environmental Kuznets Studies." *Agricultural and Resource Economics Review* 29(1):32–42.

CAW. 2007. *Climate Change and Our Jobs: Finding The Right Balance.* Discussion Paper for CAW Canada-Quebec Joint Council. Toronto: Canadian Auto Workers.

CBC. 2006. "Renegotiate NAFTA, New Green Party Leader Says." *CBC News*, August 26. Accessed October 24, 2008. http://www.cbc.ca/canada/story/2006/08/26/greens.html.

– 2007a. "Resist Temptation to Spend on 'Buy Nothing Day,' May Says." *CBC News*, November 23. Accessed November 24, 2007. http://www.cbc.ca/canada/british-columbia/story/2007/11/22/bc-buynothing.html.

– 2007b. "U.S. Urges 'Fivefold Expansion' in Alberta Oilsands Production." *CBC News*, January 18. Accessed January 19, 2007. http://www.cbc.ca/canada/story/2007/01/17/oil-sands.html.

– 2008. "MLA Wants Restriction on Plastic Bags." *CBC News*, June 23. Accessed January 2, 2008. http://www.cbc.ca/canada/prince-edward-island/story/2008/06/23/plastic-dunsford.html.

– 2012a. "EU at Stalemate on Canada's Oilsands Ranking." *CBC News*, February 22. Accessed April 24, 2012. http://www.cbc.ca/news/world/story/2012/02/22/oilsands-european-union-vote.html.

– 2012b. "NDP Leader Considers Northern Gateway Pipeline Dead." *CBC News*, August 18. Accessed January 1, 2013. http://www.cbc.ca/news/politics/story/2012/08/18/pol-mulcair-northern-gateway.html.

– 2012c. "Oil Price Gap Costing Canada Billions." *CBC News*, December 13. Accessed January 19, 2013. http://www.cbc.ca/news/business/story/2012/12/13/oil-price-spread-report.html.

– 2013a. "Energy Industry Letter Suggested Environmental Law Changes." *CBC News*, January 9. Accessed February 3, 2013. http://www.cbc.ca/news/politics/story/2013/01/09/pol-oil-gas-industry-letter-to-government-on-environmental-laws.html.

– 2013b. "Greenhouse Gas Reduction Called Threat to Oil Industry." *CBC News*, November 8. Accessed December 2, 2013. http://www .cbc.ca/news/politics/greenhouse-gas-reduction-called-threat-to-oil-industry-1.2418990/.

CBC Radio. 2007. "The Current." April 27. Toronto: CBC Radio. Accessed August 21, 2009. http://www.cbc.ca/thecurrent/2007/200704/20070427.html.

– 2008. "The Current." October 10. Toronto: CBC Radio. Accessed
     September 22, 2009. http://www.cbc.ca/thecurrent/2008/200810/
     20081010.html.
CBI. 2007a. "British Business Commits To 'Do What It Takes' To Tackle
     Climate Change – Major New Report." Press Release, November 26.
     London: Confederation of British Industries. Accessed November 26,
     2007. http://climatechange.cbi.org.uk/press_release/00083/.
– 2007b. "Climate Change Bill Strikes Right Balance." Press Release, March
     13. London: Confederation of British Industry. Accessed April 11,
     2009. http://www.cbi.org.uk/ndbs/press.nsf/0363c1f07c6ca12a8025
     671c00381cc7/c89c2266d47c69128025729d003952ef?OpenDocum
     ent.
– 2007c. *Climate Change: Everyone's Business.* London: Confederation of Brit-
     ish Industries.
– 2007d. "Top Business Leaders Join CBI Climate Change Task Force."
     Press Release, January 11. London: Confederation of British Indus-
     tries. Accessed February 13, 2009. http://www.cbi.org.uk/ndbs/press
     .nsf/0363c1f07c6ca12a8025671c00381cc7/dae438b2afoe64c280257
     25foo6a6318?OpenDocument.
– 2008. "Don't Give up on Climate Change during Recession, Urges CBI."
     Press Release, December 2. London: Confederation of British Indus-
     try. Accessed February 2, 2009. http://climatechange.cbi.org.uk/
     latest_news/00092/.
– 2009a. "Barclays: Helping London Lead in Carbon Finance." Lon-
     don: Confederation of British Industries. Accessed June 28, 2012.
     http://www.cbi.org.uk/media-centre/case-studies/2009/05/
     barclays-helping-london-lead-in-carbon-finance/.
– 2009b. "CBI Calls for UK to Take Revolutionary Road to Low-Carbon
     Economy. News Release, April 6. London: Confederation of British
     Industry. Accessed April 11, 2009. Nhttp://climatechange.cbi.org.uk/
     latest_news/00177/.
– 2010. *No Time to Lose: Deciding Britain's Energy Future.* London: Confedera-
     tion of British Industries.
– 2011. *Risky Business: Investing in the UK's Low-Carbon Infrastructure.* Lon-
     don: Confederation of British Industries.
– 2012a. "CBI Urges Government to Act Now on Aviation Capacity to Boost
     UK Exports and Remain Competitive." Press Release, March 26. Lon-
     don: Confederation of British Industries. Accessed December 1, 2012.
     http://www.cbi.org.uk/media-centre/press-releases/2012/03/cbi-
     urges-government-to-act-now-on-aviation-capacity-to-boost-uk-exports-
     and-remain-competitive/.

– 2012b. "Green or Growth Is a 'false Choice' – CBI Chief." Press Release,
    July 5. London: Confederation of British Industries. Accessed January
    18, 2013. http://www.cbi.org.uk/media-centre/press-releases/
    2012/07/green-or-growth-is-a-false-choice-%E2%80%93-cbi-chief/.
CBT. 2009. "Response to the Transport Select Committee's Inquiry 'The
    Future of Aviation.'" Campaign for Better Transport. Accessed April
    30, 2011. http://www.bettertransport.org.uk/system/files/Select_
    Committee_response_Future_of_Aviation.pdf.
CCC. 2008. *Building a Low-Carbon Economy – the UK's Contribution to Tackling
    Climate Change.* London: Committee on Climate Change.
– 2009a. "Committee on Climate Change Sets out Options to Meet the
    UK's Aviation Emissions Target." Press Release, December 8. London:
    Committee on Climate Change. Accessed May 1, 2011. http://
    downloads.theccc.org.uk/Aviation%20Report%2009/AviationReport
    PRESSRELEASE08.12.09.pdf.
– 2009b. *Meeting Carbon Budgets – the Need for a Step Change.* London: Com-
    mittee on Climate Change.
– 2009c. *Meeting the UK Aviation Target – Options for Reducing Emissions to
    2050.* London: Committee on Climate Change.
– 2010a. *CRC Energy Efficiency Scheme – Advice to Government on the Second
    Phase.* London: Committee on Climate Change.
– 2010b. *The Fourth Carbon Budget – Reducing Emissions through the 2020s.*
    London: Committee on Climate Change.
– 2012a. "CCC Says Early Decarbonisation of the Power Sector Should Be
    Plan A – and the Dash for Gas Plan Z." Press Release, December 5.
    London: Committee on Climate Change." Accessed April 10, 2013.
    http://www.theccc.org.uk/news-stories/ccc-says-early-decarbonisation-
    of-the-power-sector-should-be-plan-a-and-the-dash-for-gas-plan-z/.
– 2012b. *Meeting Carbon Budgets – 2012 Progress Report to Parliament.* London:
    Committee on Climate Change.
– 2012c. "Pace of Measures to Reduce Emissions Needs to Increase Four-
    fold Says Committee on Climate Change." Press Release, June 29.
    London: Committee on Climate Change. Accessed April 10, 2013.
    http://www.theccc.org.uk/pressreleases/pace-of-measures-to-reduce-
    emissions-needs-to-increase-fourfold-says-committee-on-climate-
    change/.
– 2013. *Reducing the UK's Carbon Footprint.* London: Committee on Climate
    Change.
CCCE. 2002. *Kyoto Protocol Revisited: A Responsible and Dynamic Alternative for
    Canada.* Ottawa: Canadian Council of Chief Executives.
– 2007a. *Backgrounder: Clean Growth.* Ottawa: Canadian Council of Chief
    Executives.

– 2007b. "CEO Council Offers New Year's Resolutions for a Greener, More
    Sustainable 2008." Press Release, December 19. Ottawa: Canadian
    Council of Chief Executives. Accessed January 27, 2008. http://www
    .ceocouncil.ca/en/view/?document_id=1088&area_id=1.
– 2007c. *Clean Growth: Building a Canadian Environmental Superpower.* Ot-
    tawa: Canadian Council of Chief Executives.
– 2010. *Clean Growth 2.0: How Canada Can Be A Leader In Energy And En-
    vironmental Innovation.* Ottawa: Canadian Council of Chief Executives.
– 2011. *Energy-Wise Canada: Building a Culture of Energy Conservation.* Ottawa:
    Canadian Council of Chief Executives.
CCME. 1990. "National Action Strategy on Global Warming." Winnipeg:
    Canadian Council of Ministers of Environment.
CCO. 2008a. "Ontario's Fourth Conservation Summit: Shifting to a Con-
    server Economy." Toronto: Conservation Council of Ontario. Accessed
    December 30, 2008. http://weconserve.ca/summit/index.html.
– 2008b. "We Conserve." Toronto: Conservation Council of Ontario. Ac-
    cessed December 30, 2008. http://weconserve.ca/.
CCRES. 2002. "Coalition Formed to Advance 'Made In Canada' Strategy on
    Climate Change." Press Release, September 26. Canadian Coalition for
    Responsible Environmental Solutions." Accessed December 17, 2007.
    http://www.capp.ca/default.asp?V_DOC_ID=802.
Chakrabortty, Aditya. 2008. "Secret Report: Biofuel Caused Food Crisis."
    Guardian, July 4, 1.
Challen, Colin. 2009. *Too Little, Too Late: The Politics of Climate Change.* Hove,
    UK: Picnic Publishing Ltd.
Challis, Rob. 2007. "Offsetting Plus." Presentation by Man Group Plc's
    Global Head of Corporate Responsibility to Corporate Climate Re-
    sponse Conference. London, May 30.
Chapman, James. 2011. "PM's Plan for Fairer Fuel Tax 'Won't Work.'" *Daily
    Mail,* January 25. Accessed July 9, 2012. http://www.dailymail.co.uk/
    news/article-1350021/David-Camerons-fairer-fuel-tax-plan-wont-work
    .html.
Chase, Steven. 2011. "Peter Kent's Plan to Clean up the Oil Sands' Dirty
    Reputation." *Globe and Mail,* January 7, A8–9.
Chazan, Guy. 2012. "Green Groups See Red over Energy Bill." *Financial
    Times,* November 23, 2.
Chen, Yiqun. 2009. "Cancer Incidence in Fort Chipewyan, Alberta 1995–
    2006." Edmonton: Alberta Cancer Board, Division of Population
    Health and Information Surveillance. Accessed December 18, 2013.
    http://www.ualberta.ca/~avnish/rls-2009-02-06-fort-chipewyan-study
    .pdf.
Chief Medical Officer. 2010. *2009 Annual Report.* London: Department of
    Health.

Christoff, Peter. 1996. "Ecological Modernisation, Ecological Modernities."
    Environmental Politics 5(3):476–500.
– 2005. "Out of Chaos, A Shining Star? Toward a Typology of Green
    States." In *The State and the Global Ecological Crisis*, edited by J. Barry and
    R. Eckersley, 26–52. Cambridge, MA: MIT Press.
CIW. 2012. *How Are Canadians Really Doing?* Waterloo, ON: Canadian Index
    of Wellbeing and University of Waterloo.
Clark, Campbell. 2008. "Dion's Carbon Tax Would 'Screw Everybody,' PM
    Says." *Globe and Mail*, June 21, A6.
Clark, Duncan. 2011. "New Data on Imports and Exports Turns Map of
    Carbon Emission on Its Head." *Guardian*, May 3. Accessed July 17,
    2011. http://www.guardian.co.uk/environment/datablog/2011/
    apr/28/carbon-emissions-imports-exports-trade#data.
– 2012. "Protesters Call on George Osborne to Recognise Green Economy's
    Potential." *Guardian*, October 18. Accessed March 7, 2013. http://www
    .guardian.co.uk/environment/2012/oct/18/protest-george-osborne-
    green-economy.
Clark, Greg. 2009. "Tories Would Do More to Cut Carbon." *Guardian*, July
    15. Accessed June 28, 2012. http://www.guardian.co.uk/commentis
    free/cif-green/2009/jul/15/low-carbon-strategy-climate-change.
Clarke, Jane. 2009. "Ban Meat from Hospital Meals? That's Just Tripe!"
    Daily Mail, February 3. Accessed November 6, 2012. http://www.daily
    mail.co.uk/health/article-1134413/JANE-CLARKE-Ban-meat-hospital-
    meals-Thats-just-tripe.html.
Clarke, Tony. 2008. "Toronto Stood up to Bottled Water Industry." *Toronto
    Star*, December 11. Accessed May 27, 2011. http://www.thestar.com/
    comment/article/551909.
Clarke, Tony, Diana Gibson, Brendan Haley, and Jim Stanford. 2013. *The
    Bitumen Cliff: Lessons and Challenges of Bitumen Mega-Developments for
    Canada's Economy in an Age of Climate Change*. Ottawa: Canadian Centre
    for Policy Alternatives / Polaris Institute.
Clarkson, Jeremy. 2008. "Ignore the End of the World." *Sun*, April 18.
    Accessed April 18, 2008. http://www.thesun.co.uk/sol/homepage/
    news/columnists/clarkson/article1062588.ece.
CLC. 2008. *Climate Change and Green Jobs: Labour's Challenges and Opportun-
    ities*. Document No. 9, 25th CLC Constitutional Convention. Ottawa:
    Canadian Labour Congress.
CLG. 2005. "2005 Letter to the Prime Minster." Cambridge, UK: The Prince
    of Wales's UK Corporate Leaders Group on Climate Change. Accessed
    April 4, 2009. http://www.cpi.cam.ac.uk/programmes/energy_and_
    climate_change/clgcc/uk_clg/2005_letter_to_uk_pm.aspx.
– 2006. "2006 Letter to the Prime Minster." Cambridge, UK: The Prince

of Wales's UK Corporate Leaders Group on Climate Change."
Accessed April 4, 2009. http://www.cpi.cam.ac.uk/programmes/
energy_and_climate_change/clgcc/uk_clg/2006_letter_to_uk_pm
.aspx.

– 2008. "UK CLG Letter to UK Party Leaders." Cambridge, UK: The Prince
of Wales's UK Corporate Leaders Group on Climate Change." Accessed April 4, 2009. http://www.cpi.cam.ac.uk/pdf/UK%20CLG%20
letter%20to%20Party%20Leaders%20PM.pdf.

– 2011. *Seize the Day: A Call to Action for UK Climate Leadership*. Cambridge,
UK: The Prince of Wales's UK Corporate Leaders Group on Climate
Change.

Climate Camp. 2007. "We're Not Toast Yet." Information Brochure. Leeds:
Camp for Climate Action." Accessed November 8, 2007. http://www
.climatecamp.org.uk/toast.PNG.

ClimateCare. 2007. "Q&A: Carbon Offsetting. Offset Firm Climate Care
Debunks Some Myths about the Industry." *Guardian*, September 7.
Accessed April 16, 2008. http://www.guardian.co.uk/environment/
2007/sep/07/carbonoffsetprojects.

Climate Group. 2005. "Low Carbon Leader: Cities." Toronto: Climate
Group. Accessed August 16, 2009. http://www.theclimategroup.org/
assets/resources/low_carbon_leader_cities.pdf.

– 2006. "Woking – Municipal Government." London: Climate Group. Accessed September 24, 2006. http://www.theclimategroup.org/index
.php?pid=548.

– 2007a. "Businesses Come 'Together' to Help Consumers Tackle Climate
Change." London: Climate Group. Press Release. April 23." Accessed
June 17, 2007. http://theclimategroup.org/index.php/news_and_
events/news_and_comment/businesses_come_together_to_help_
consumers_tackle_climate_change/.

– 2007b. *Carbon Down, Profits Up*. London: Climate Group.

– 2009. "Airlines Tell UN, Include Us in a Post-Kyoto Deal on Climate
Change." Press Release, April 6. London: Climate Group. Accessed
May 8, 2009. http://www.theclimategroup.org/assets/resources/
060409_Airlines_tell_UN,_include_us_in_a_post-Kyoto_deal_on_
climate_change_FINAL.pdf.

Climate Justice Now! 2007. "What's Missing from the Climate Talks? Justice!" Accessed August 30, 2010. http://www.climate-justice-now.org/
category/events/bali/.

Clover, Charles. 2005. "Energy Ration Cards for Everyone Planned." *Telegraph*, July 2, 1.

– 2007. "Go Vegan to Help Climate, Says Government." *Telegraph*, May 30, 7.

CNN. 2009. "Dear Davos." *CNN*, January 30. Accessed March 14, 2009. http://

www.cnn.com/2009/WORLD/europe/01/07/davos.deardavos/#cnn
STCText.

CofE. 2005. *Sharing God's Planet: A Christian Vision for a Sustainable Future.*
London: Church of England (CofE) Mission and Public Affairs Coun-
cil/Church House Publishing.

– 2007. "Climate Change – Not Just A Green Issue: A Mission And Public
Affairs Briefing Paper." London: Church of England (CofE) Mission
and Public Affairs Council. August 28." Accessed February 18, 2008.
http://www.cofe.anglican.org/info/socialpublic/international/
climatechange/climatechange.pdf.

Cohen, David. 2007. "Rational Solutions (Letter)." *Globe and Mail,* February 5, A14.

Cohen, Maurie. 2012. "Overcoming Cultural Dissonance in the Transition
to a Postconsumerist Future." In "SCORAI Europe Workshop Proceedings: Sustainable Consumption During Times of Crisis." First Trans-Atlantic SCORAI Workshop, May 1. Bregenz, Austria, 107–124. Accessed
April 10, 2013. http://scorai.org/wp-content/uploads/SCORAI-
20Europe-20-20Proceedings-20Bregenz-20May-2020121.pdf.

Committee on the Sustainable Development of Algal Biofuels. 2012. "Sustainable Development of Algal Biofuels in the United States." Washington, DC: National Academy of Sciences.

ComRes. 2008. "Parliamentary Panel Survey – MPs – April 2008." London:
Local Goverment Association. Accessed July 17, 2008. http://www.lga
.gov.uk/lga/aio/830449.

Conservative Home. 2012. "The Committee on Climate Change Should Be
Abolished." *Conservative Home.* Accessed June 9, 2012. http://conservative
home.blogs.com/localgovernment/2012/05/the-committee-on-climate-
change-should-be-abolished.html.

Conservative Party. 2005. "Cameron Launches Quality of Life Policy
Group." News Release, December 9. Accessed May 5, 2008. http://
www.conservatives.com/News/News_stories/2005/12/Cameron_
launches_Quality_of_Life_Policy_Group.aspx.

– 2007a. "Blueprint for a Green Economy." News Release. September 13.
London: Conservative Party. Accessed September 13, 2007. http://
www.conservatives.com/News/News_stories/2007/09/Blueprint_
for_a_green_economy.aspx.

– 2007b. *Power to the People: The Decentralised Energy Revolution.* London:
Conservative Party.

– 2009a. "Protecting Security." London: Conservative Party. Accessed May
8, 2009. http://www.conservatives.com/Policy/Security_Agenda.aspx.

– 2009b. *The Low Carbon Economy: Security, Stability and Green Growth.* London: Conservative Party.

Conservative Party of Canada. 2008. "Why Is Jack Layton Threatening
    Thousands of Good Union Jobs Right Across Canada?" Ottawa: Con-
    servative Party of Canada. Accessed November 5, 2008. http://www
    .conservative.ca/EN/2874/104454.

Coote, Anna, and Jane Franklin. 2013. *Time on Our Side: Why We All Need a
    Shorter Working Week.* London: New Economics Foundation.

Copps, Sheila. 2004. *Worth Fighting For.* Toronto: McClelland & Stewart.

Corcoran, Terence. 2008. "Economics Only Thing Shifting." *National Post,*
    June 28, A6.

Coren, Giles. 2008. "These Water Drinkers Are the New Smokers. Thank
    Me." *Times,* February 16, 33.

Corporate Watch. 2008. *Techno-Fixes: A Critical Guide to Climate Change Tech-
    nologies.* London: Corporate Watch.

Coward, Harold G., and Andrew J. Weaver. 2004. *Hard Choices: Climate
    Change in Canada.* Waterloo, ON: Wilfrid Laurier University Press.

Coyle, Diane. 2011. *The Economics of Enough: How to Run the Economy as If the
    Future Matters.* Princeton, NJ: Princeton University Press.

CPAWS, Sage Centre, David Suzuki Foundation, Sierra Club of Canada –
    National, Dogwood Initiative, Sierra Club of Canada Prairie Chapter,
    Greenpeace Canada, et al. 2005. "Canadian Environmental Groups
    Issue Declaration on Oil Sands Development." Accessed November 17,
    2008. http://www.sierraclub.ca/en/node/487.

Crerar, Pippa. 2008. "Go-Ahead for £25 C-Charge." *Evening Standard,* Feb-
    ruary 12, 1.

Crooks, Ed. 2007. "'America's Energy Security Blanket.'" *Financial Times,*
    May 21. Accessed November 14, 2008. http://www.ft.com/cms/s/0/
    e27386fc-0737-11dc-93e1-000b5df10621.html?nclick_check=1.

– 2008. "Investors Warned of Risk to Oil Sands Plans." *Financial Times,*
    September 15, 19.

Crosby, Shanese et al. 2013. *Transporting Alberta Oil Sands Products: Defin-
    ing the Issues and Assessing the Risks.* Seattle, WA: National Oceanic and
    Atmospheric Administration.

Crutzen, P.J., A.R. Mosier, K.A. Smith, and W. Winiwarter. 2008. "N2O
    Release from Agro-Biofuel Production Negates Global Warming
    Reduction by Replacing Fossil Fuels." *Atmospheric Chemistry and Physics*
    8(2):389–95.

CTV. 2007. "Baird Accused of Scare Tactics on Kyoto." *CTV News,* April 19.
    Accessed December 17, 2007. http://www.ctv.ca/servlet/ArticleNews/
    story/CTVNews/20070419/kyoto_senate_070419/undefined.

Curran, Giorel. 2009. "Ecological Modernisation and Climate Change in
    Australia." *Environmental Politics* 18(2):201–17.

Curry, Bill, and Dawn Walton. 2009. "Climate Change Report 'Irrespon-
    sible,' Prentice Says." *Globe and Mail,* October 30, A1.

D'Aliesio, Renata, and Jason Markusoff. 2008. "No Brakes on Oilsands."
    Edmonton Journal, February 26. Accessed November 7, 2008. http://
    www.canada.com/edmontonjournal/story.html?id=0529ba89-d54e-
    4f9c-a050-b57b5fd019c3&k=81516.
Dale, Iain. 2008. "Tory Concerns Grow Over Villiers Airports Policy." *Iain
    Dale's Diary.* Accessed May 1, 2011. http://iaindale.blogspot.com/
    2008/11/tory-concerns-grow-over-villiers.html.
Daly, Herman E. 1996. *Beyond Growth: The Economics of Sustainable Develop-
    ment.* Boston: Beacon Press.
Dauncey, Guy. 1988. *After the Crash: The Emergence of the Rainbow Economy.*
    Basingstoke, Hants, UK: Green Print.
David Suzuki Foundation. 2006. "Economy Needs a Better Goal than
    'More'." Vancouver: David Suzuki Foundation. Accessed October
    24, 2008. http://www.davidsuzuki.org/about_us/Dr_David_Suzuki/
    Article_Archives/weekly02240601.asp.
– 2007a. "Sir Nicholas Stern and David Suzuki at the TSX." February 19.
    Toronto. Accessed October 24, 2008. http://www.davidsuzuki.org/
    Climate_Change/stern.asp.
– 2007b. "Sir Nicholas Stern and Dr David Suzuki Release Joint Statement."
    News Release, February 19. Vancouver: David Suzuki Foundation.
    Accessed October 24, 2008. http://www.davidsuzuki.org/latestnews/
    dsfnews02190701.asp.
Davidson, Debra J., and Norah A. MacKendrick. 2004. "All Dressed Up with
    Nowhere to Go: The Discourse of Ecological Modernization in Alberta,
    Canada." *Canadian Review of Sociology and Anthropology* 41(1):47–65.
Davidson, Eric A. 2012. "Representative Concentration Pathways and
    Mitigation Scenarios for Nitrous Oxide." *Environmental Research Letters*
    7(2):024005.
Davies, Nick. 2007. "The Inconvenient Truth about the Carbon Offset
    Industry." *Guardian,* June 16, 14.
Davis, Steven J., and Ken Caldeira. 2010. "Consumption-Based Account-
    ing of CO_2 Emissions." *Proceedings of the National Academy of Sciences*
    107(12):5687–92.
De Graaf, John, David Wann, and Thomas H Naylor. 2014. *Affluenza: How
    Overconsumption Is Killing Us – and How We Can Fight Back.* 3rd ed. San
    Francisco: Berrett-Koehler.
De Havilland, Perry. 2008. "Bottled Water Is … a Damn Fine Idea." *Samiz-
    data,* February 17. Accessed March 31, 2008. http://www.samizdata
    .net/blog/archives/2008/02/bottled_water_i.html.
De Souza, Mike. 2007a. "Nobel Scientists Blast Government on Environ-
    ment." *Victoria Times-Colonist,* November 5, A3.
– 2007b. "Scientists Puzzled at Tories Not Releasing Climate Report." *Van-
    couver Sun,* December 4, A9.

– 2008. "Ottawa Was Warned of Biofuel Problems." *Vancouver Sun*, November 12, B3.
– 2010. "Climate-Change Scientists Feel 'Muzzled' by Ottawa: Documents." *Montreal Gazette*, March 15, A10.
– 2011a. "Oilsands Carry Steep Ecological Price: Report." *Victoria Times-Colonist*, December 22, B5.
– 2011b. "Ottawa Considers PR Firm for Oilsands." *Calgary Herald*, May 31, A4.
– 2012a. "Canada Needs Energy Diversity: Federal Documents." *Vancouver Sun*, August 23. Accessed February 2, 2013. http://www.vancouver sun.com/technology/Canada needs energy diversity federal documents /7043979/story.html.
– 2012b. "Oilsands Pipeline Development Was 'Top of Mind' in Budget Bill." *Vancouver Sun*, September 26, B2.
DECC. 2009a. "No New Coal without CCS – Miliband." Press Release, April 23. London: Department of Energy and Climate Change." Accessed June 20, 2009. http://www.decc.gov.uk/en/content/cms/news/ pn050/pn050.aspx.
– 2009b. "UK Climate Change Sustainable Development Indicator: 2007 Greenhouse Gas Emissions, Final Figures." Statistical Release, February 3. London: Department of Energy and Climate Change." Accessed February 17, 2009. http://www.defra.gov.uk/ENVIRONMENT/ statistics/globatmos/download/ghg_ns_20090203.pdf.
– 2009c. "UK Greenhouse Gas Emissions 1990-2007: Headline Results (Data Table)." London: Department of Energy and Climate Change. Accessed March 21, 2009. http://www.defra.gov.uk/ENVIRONMENT /statistics/globatmos/download/xls/ghg_annex_a_20090203.xls.
– 2011. "Whitehall Exceeds PM's 10% Carbon Target." News Release, July 6. London: Department of Energy and Climate Change. London: Department of Energy and Climate Change. Accessed June 7, 2012. http://www.decc.gov.uk/en/content/cms/news/pn11_059/ pn11_059.aspx.
– 2012a. "2010 UK Greenhouse Gas Emissions, Final Figures." London: Department of Energy and Climate Change. Accessed November 13, 2012. http://www.decc.gov.uk/assets/decc/11/stats/climate-change/4282-statistical-release-2010-uk-greenhouse-gas-emissi.pdf.
– 2012b. *Electricity Market Reform: Policy Overview*. London: Department of Energy and Climate Change.
– 2013a. "2012 UK Greenhouse Gas Emissions, Provisional Figures and 2011 UK Greenhouse Gas Emissions, Final Figures By Fuel Type and End-User." London: Department of Energy and Climate Change. Accessed December 8, 2013. https://www.gov.uk/government/uploads/

system/uploads/attachment_data/file/193414/280313_ghg_national
_statistics_release_2012_provisional.pdf.

– 2013b. "Table 6.1. Renewable Electricity Capacity and Generation".
London: Department of Energy and Climate Change. https://www
.gov.uk/government/uploads/system/uploads/attachment_data/
file/244901/et6_1.xls.

– 2013c. "Transport: GHG Inventory Summary Factsheet." London: Department of Energy and Climate Change. Accessed November 22,
2013. https://www.gov.uk/government/uploads/system/uploads/
attachment_data/file/210499/9_Transport.pdf.

DeCloet, Derek. 2008. "Why Big Oil Discovered Its Love of Trees." *Globe
and Mail*, February 26, B2.

Defra. 2005. *The Validity of Food Miles as an Indicator of Sustainable Development.* London: Department of Environment, Food and Rural Affairs.

– 2006. "Government Signals a Step-Change on Environmentally Sustainable Behaviour." London: Department for Environment, Food
and Rural Affairs. Accessed March 21, 2008. http://nds.coi.gov.uk/
Content/Detail.asp?ReleaseID=207052&NewsAreaID=2&print=true.

– 2007a. "Action in the UK – Carbon Reduction Commitment: Key Questions." London: Department of Environment, Food and Rural Affairs.
Accessed June 20, 2007. http://www.defra.gov.uk/environment/
climatechange/uk/business/crc/qanda.htm.

– 2007b. "ActonCO₂." TV ad. London: Department for Environment, Food,
and Rural Affairs." Accessed February 15, 2008. http://www.youtube
.com/watch?v=hCJotacAmo4.

– 2007c. "Carbon Reduction Commitment." London: Department of Environment, Food and Rural Affairs." Accessed June 20, 2007. http://
www.defra.gov.uk/environment/climatechange/uk/business/crc/
index.htm.

– 2007d. *Citizen's Summit on Climate Change.* London: Department of Environment, Food and Rural Affairs.

– 2007e. *Consultation on Implementation Proposals for the Carbon Reduction Commitment.* London: Department of Environment, Food and Rural Affairs.

– 2007f. *EU Emissions Trading Scheme: Approved Phase II National Allocation
Plan 2008–2012.* London: Department for Environment, Food and
Rural Affairs.

– 2007g. *Measures to Reduce Carbon Emissions in Large Non-Energy Intensive
Organisations: Review of Consultation Responses.* London: Department of
Environment, Food and Rural Affairs.

– 2007h. "New Statistics on Life Satisfaction Shed Light on Wellbeing." Statistical Release, July 27. London: Department for Environment, Food
and Rural Affairs. Accessed May 7, 2008. http://www.defra.gov
.uk/news/2007/070727b.htm.

– 2007i. *Report of the Food Industry Sustainability Strategy Champions' Group on Food Transport.* London: Department of Environment, Food and Rural Affairs.

– 2007j. *Updated Partial Regulatory Impact Assessment on the Carbon Reduction Commitment.* London: Department of Environment, Food and Rural Affairs.

– 2008a. *A Framework for Pro-Environmental Behaviours.* London: Department for Environment, Food and Rural Affairs.

– 2008b. "Identifying Climate Change Impacts of Global Imports." News Release, July 2. London: Department for Environment, Food and Rural Affairs." Accessed July 5, 2008. http://www.defra.gov.uk/news/2008/080702a.htm.

– 2008c. *Synthesis Report on the Findings from Defra's Pre-Feasibility Study into Personal Carbon Trading.* London: Department for Environment, Food and Rural Affairs.

– 2008d. "UK Emissions Figures Down, But 'Much More Must Be Done': Benn." News Release, January 31. London: Department for Environment, Food and Rural Affairs. Accessed February 22, 2008. http://www.defra.gov.uk/news/2008/080131c.htm.

– 2008e. "Wellbeing: Government Departments and Other Organisations: Sustainable Development Commission." London: Department of Environment, Food and Rural Affairs. Accessed May 13, 2009. http://www.defra.gov.uk/sustainable/government/what/priority/wellbeing/ogds.htm#sdc.

– 2009a. *Food Statistics Pocketbook 2009.* London: Department for Environment, Food and Rural Affairs.

– 2009b. "War on Waste: Anaerobic Digestion Demonstration Projects Get the Go-Ahead from DEFRA." London: Department for Environment, Food and Rural Affairs. Accessed November 19, 2012. http://www.whitehallpages.net/news/archive/204264.

– 2011. "The Sustainable Lifestyles Framework." London: Department for Environment, Food and Rural Affairs. London: Department for Environment, Food and Rural Affairs. Accessed July 22, 2012. http://archive.defra.gov.uk/environment/economy/documents/sustainable-life-framework.pdf.

– 2012. "UK's Carbon Footprint 1993–2010." London: Department of Environment, Food, and Rural Affairs. Accessed December 30, 2012. http://www.defra.gov.uk/statistics/files/release-carbon-footprint-dec2012.pdf.

– 2013. "UK's Carbon Footprint 1997–2011." London: Department of Environment, Food, and Rural Affairs. Accessed December 8, 2013. https://www.gov.uk/government/uploads/system/uploads/attachment_data/file/261692/Consumption_emissions_28_Nov_2013.pdf.

Delacourt, Susan. 2006. "PM Denies Climate-Change Shift." *Toronto Star*, December 21, A6.

Dembicki, Geoff. 2010. "'I Was Disappointed With the Canadians.'" *The Tyee*, December 9. Accessed September 3, 2011. http://thetyee.ca/News/2010/12/09/DisappointedWithCanadians/.

– 2011. "The Battle to Block Low Carbon Fuel Standards." *The Tyee*, March 17. Accessed August 15, 2011. http://thetyee.ca/News/2011/03/17/LowCarbonFuelFight/.

Demerse, Clare. 2009. "Denying Canada's Environmental Truths." *Toronto Star*, November 8, A15.

Derbyshire, David. 2008. "Every Adult in Britain Should Be Forced to Carry 'Carbon Ration Cards,' Say MPs." *Daily Mail*, May 27, 8.

DETR. 2000a. *Climate Change: The UK Programme*. London: Department of the Environment, Transport and the Regions.

– 2000b. "Climate Change: The UK Programme (Summary)." London: Department of the Environment, Transport and the Regions.

DFID. 2007. "Balancing the Cost of Food Air Miles: Listening to Trade and Environmental Concerns." London: Department for International Development. Accessed April 6, 2008. http://www.dfid.gov.uk/news/files/foodmiles.asp.

DfT. 2003. *The Future of Air Transport*. London: Department for Transport.

– 2006. "RTFO Biofuels Benefits." London: Department for Transport. Accessed April 23, 2008. http://www.dft.gov.uk/pgr/roads/environment/rtfo/biofuelsbenefits.

– 2007. "Public Invited to Have Their Say on the Future of Heathrow." News Release, November 22. London: Department for Transport. Accessed May 23, 2008. http://nds.coi.gov.uk/environment/fullDetail.asp?ReleaseID=332639&NewsAreaID=2&NavigatedFromDepartment=True.

– 2008. *The Government Response to the King Review of Low-Carbon Cars*. London: Department for Transport.

– 2013. *Aviation Policy Framework*. London: Department for Transport.

Dietz, Rob, and Daniel O'Neill. 2013. *Enough Is Enough: Building a Sustainable Economy in a World of Finite Resources*. San Francisco: Berrett-Koehler.

Dinda, Soumyananda. 2004. "Environmental Kuznets Curve Hypothesis: A Survey." *Ecological Economics* 49(4):431–55.

Dion, Stéphane. 2007. "Economy and Environment: Smart Money Is Going Green." Speech to the Economic Club of Toronto and the Toronto Board of Trade, January 16. Accessed January 16, 2007. http://www.liberal.ca.

DirectGov. 2010. "Food and Drink: Greener Choices." Accessed November 6, 2012. http://ia201120.eu.archive.org/tna/20100914161545/

http://direct.gov.uk/en/Environmentandgreenerliving/Greener homeandgarden/Greenershopping/DG_064434.

Dobson, Andrew. 1991. *The Green Reader*. London: Andre Deutsch Ltd.

Doern, G. Bruce. 2005. "Canadian Energy Policy and the Struggle for Sustainable Development: Political-Economic Context." In *Canadian Energy Policy and the Struggle for Sustainable Development*, edited by G.B. Doern, 3–51. Toronto: University of Toronto Press.

Donovan, Nick, and David Halpern. 2002. "Life Satisfaction: The State of Knowledge and Implications for Government." London: Cabinet Office Strategy Unit.

Douglas, Philip. 2007. "The Carbon Reduction Commitment (CRC) and Other Measures." Presentation to Corporate Climate Response Conference, Confederation of British Industries Conference Centre, London, May 30.

Dowds, Donal. 2007. "Maintaining Growth in a Low-Carbon Economy." Speech to Guardian Climate Change Summit, June 11, London.

Druckman, Angela, P. Bradley, E. Papathanasopoulou, and Tim Jackson. 2008. "Measuring Progress towards Carbon Reduction in the UK." *Ecological Economics* 66(4):594–604.

Druckman, Angela, Mona Chitnis, Steven Sorrell, and Tim Jackson. 2011. "Missing Carbon Reductions? Exploring Rebound and Backfire Effects in UK Households." *Energy Policy* 39(6):3572–81.

Dryzek, John S. 1996. "Political Inclusion and the Dynamics of Democratization." *The American Political Science Review* 90(3):475–87.

– 2013. *The Politics of the Earth: Environmental Discourses*. Third edition. Oxford: Oxford University Press.

Dryzek, John S., David Downes, Christian Hunold, David Schlosberg, and Hans-Kristian Hernes. 2003. *Green States and Social Movements: Environmentalism in the United States, United Kingdom, Germany, and Norway*. Oxford: Oxford University Press.

Dryzek, John S., Christian Hunhold, David Schlosberg, David Downes, and Hans-Kristian Hernes. 2002. "Environmental Transformation of the State: The USA, Norway, Germany and the UK." *Political Studies* 50(4):659–82.

DTI. 2003a. *Energy White Paper: Our Energy Future – Creating a Low Carbon Economy*. London: Department of Trade and Industry.

– 2003b. "Sectoral Energy and Emissions Projections in the Energy White Paper." London: Department of Trade and Industry Energy Strategy Unit. Accessed April 29, 2008. http://www.berr.gov.uk/files/file21354.pdf.

– 2006. *Our Energy Challenge: Securing Clean, Affordable Energy for the Long-Term (Energy Review Consultation Document)*. London: Department of Trade and Industry.

– 2007. *Meeting the Energy Challenge: A White Paper on Energy*. London: Department of Trade and Industry.

Duncan, Dwight. 2004. "Choosing What Works For a Change." Speech to the Empire Club, Toronto, April 15. Toronto: Ontario Ministry of Energy. Accessed January 10, 2009. http://www.energy.gov.on.ca/index.cfm?fuseaction=about.speeches&speech=15042004.

Dunmore, Charlie. 2012. "Europe's Chief Scientist Warns against Climate Delays." *Reuters*, March 16. Accessed March 30, 2013. http://in.reuters.com/article/2012/03/16/us-eu-scientist-idINBRE82F15920120316.

EA. 2007. "The 50 Things That Will Save the Planet." *Your Environment*. Accessed November 1, 2007. http://publications.environment-agency.gov.uk/pdf/GEHO0907BNFQ-e-e.pdf?lang=_e.

– 2008. "Thames Barrier Closures against Tidal Surges, 1983 to 2007." London: Environment Agency. Accessed April 15, 2009. http://www.grdp.org/research/library/data/58613.aspx.

Eaglesham, Jean. 2007. "Labour Wants to Be the Party of Business." *Financial Times*, July 4, 28.

– 2008. "Call to Delay Biofuels Obligation." *Financial Times*, March 25, 1, 2.

Eaglesham, Jean, and Kevin Done. 2008. "Cameron Queries Heathrow Expansion." *Financial Times*, June 17, 2.

Easterlin, Richard A., Laura Angelescu McVey, Malgorzata Switek, Onnicha Sawangfa, and Jacqueline Smith Zweig. 2010. "The Happiness–income Paradox Revisited." *Proceedings of the National Academy of Sciences* 107(52):22463–8.

Easterlin, Richard A., Robson Morgan, Malgorzata Switek, and Fei Wang. 2012. "China's Life Satisfaction, 1990–2010." *Proceedings of the National Academy of Sciences*. 109(25):9775–80.

Easton, Mark. 2006a. "Britain's Happiness in Decline." *BBC News*, May 2. Accessed May 7, 2008. http://news.bbc.co.uk/1/hi/programmes/happiness_formula/4771908.stm.

– 2006b. "Does Diversity Make Us Unhappy?" *BBC News*, May 30. Accessed May 5, 2008. http://news.bbc.co.uk/1/hi/programmes/happiness_formula/5012478.stm.

– 2006c. "The Survival of the Happiest." *New Statesman*, April 24. Accessed April 22, 2009. http://www.newstatesman.com/200604240016.

EasyJet. 2007. "Care about the Environment? We Do Too." Advertisement. *Independent*, March 21, 4.

Eccleston, Paul. 2007. "Energy Saving Moves Could Add to Emissions." *Telegraph*, November 1. Accessed November 3, 2007. http://www.telegraph.co.uk/earth/earthnews/3312520/Energy-saving-moves-could-add-to-emissions.html.

ECO. 2010. *Re-Thinking Energy Conservation in Ontario – Results: Annual*

Energy Conservation Progress Report – 2009 (Volume One). Toronto: Environmental Commissioner of Ontario.

– 2013. *Building Momentum – Results: Annual Energy Conservation Progress Report 2012 (Volume Two).* Toronto: Environmental Commissioner of Ontario.

Economic Competitiveness Policy Group. 2007. "Freeing Britain to Compete: Equipping the UK for Globalisation." Submission to the Shadow Cabinet. London: Conservative Party.

Economist. 2007a. "Canada's Oil Sands: Boomtown on a Bender." *Economist,* June 28. Accessed September 26, 2011. http://www.economist.com/node/9410672.

– 2007b. "Planes, Prizes and Perfect PR." *Economist,* February 13, 18.

– 2008. "Heathrow's Future: The Right Side of the Argument." *Economist,* November 8, 18.

– 2011. "Following the Footprints." *Economist,* June 2. Accessed April 9, 2013. http://www.economist.com/node/18750670.

Edelman, Murray. 1964. *The Symbolic Uses of Politics.* Urbana, IL: University of Illinois Press.

Edemariam, Aida. 2007. "Mud, Sweat and Tears." *Guardian,* October 30, 4.

Edmonton Journal. 2013. "The Risks of Rushing the Oilsands." *Edmonton Journal,* December 11, A20.

EEA. 2007. *Transport and Environment: On the Way to a New Common Transport Policy.* Copenhagen: European Environment Agency.

– 2010. *Towards a Resource-Efficient Transport System.* Copenhagen: European Environment Agency.

EIA. 2013. "International Energy Statistics: Total Carbon Dioxide Emissions from the Consumption of Energy." Washington, DC: Energy Information Administration. Accessed December 8, 2013. http://www.eia.gov/cfapps/ipdbproject/iedindex3.cfm?tid=90&pid=44&aid=8.

Elgie, Stewart, and Jessica McClay. 2013. "BC's Carbon Tax Shift Is Working Well after Four Years (Attention Ottawa)." *Canadian Public Policy* 39:S1–S10.

Elliott, Larry. 2007. "Spend, Spend, Spend Is Costing the Earth." *Guardian,* May 21, 24.

Environment Canada. 1995. *Canada's National Action Program on Climate Change.* Ottawa: Environment Canada.

– 2006. *Evaluation of the One-Tonne Challenge Program.* Ottawa: Environment Canada.

– 2007. "Canada's New Government Announces Mandatory Industrial Targets to Tackle Climate Change and Reduce Air Pollution." News Release, April 26. Ottawa: Environment Canada." Accessed February

28, 2008. http://www.ec.gc.ca/default.asp?lang=En&n=714D9AAE-1&news=4F2292E9-3EFF-48D3-A7E4-CEFA05D70C21.

– 2010a. "Government of Canada to Regulate Emissions from Electricity Sector." News Release, June 23. Ottawa: Environment Canada. Accessed January 10, 2012. http://www.ec.gc.ca/default.asp?lang=En&n=714D9AAE-1&news=FD27D97E-5582-4D93-8ECE-6CB4578171A9.

– 2010b. *National Inventory Report 1990–2008: Greenhouse Gas Sources and Sinks in Canada, Part 1.* Ottawa: Environment Canada.

– 2012. *Canada's Emissions Trends.* Ottawa: Environment Canada.

– 2013a. *Canada's Emissions Trends.* Ottawa: Environment Canada.

– 2013b. *National Inventory Report 1990–2011: Greenhouse Gas Sources and Sinks in Canada (Executive Summary).* Ottawa: Environment Canada.

Environmental Defence. 2008. *Canada's Toxic Tar Sands: The Most Destructive Project on Earth.* Toronto: Environmental Defence.

Enviros and Carbon Trust. 2007. "Report on Young's Langoustine." Executive Summary. Accessed April 6, 2008. http://www.youngsseafood.co.uk/web/pdfs/carbon-trust-report.pdf.

E.ON. 2009. "Kingsnorth Cleaner Coal Plant." London: E.ON UK. Accessed March 7, 2009. http://www.eon-uk.com/generation/supercritical.aspx.

EPI. 2010. "U.S. Feeds One Quarter of Its Grain to Cars While Hunger Is on the Rise." Washington DC: Earth Policy Institute. Accessed October 9, 2102. http://www.earth-policy.org/data_highlights/2010/highlights6.

Esping-Andersen, Gøsta. 1990. *Three Worlds of Welfare Capitalism.* Princeton, NJ: Princeton University Press.

EST. 2007. "The Ampere Strikes Back: How Consumer Electronics Are Taking over the World." London: Energy Saving Trust.

EurActiv. 2011. "Britain Accused of Stalling EU Tar Sands Regulation." *EurActiv,* October 26. Accessed November 22, 2011. http://www.euractiv.com/climate-environment/britain-accused-stalling-eu-tar-sands-regulation-news-508576.

European Commission. 2011. "Answer to a Written Question – Commission Opposition to Climate-Smart Dietary Recommendations – E-008421/2011." Brussels: European Parliament. Accessed November 21, 2012. http://www.europarl.europa.eu/sides/getAllAnswers.do?reference=E-2011-008421&language=EN.

Eurostar. 2009. "High-Speed Rail Streaks Ahead in Race to Cut Carbon Dioxide Emissions from Travel." Accessed December 20, 2013. http://www.eurostar.com/uk-en/about-eurostar/press-office/press-releases/2009/high-speed-rail-streaks-ahead-in-race-cut-carbon#.UrO9AScsDa1.

Evans, David, and Wokje Abrahamse. 2009. "Beyond Rhetoric: The Possibilities of and for 'Sustainable Lifestyles.'" *Environmental Politics* 18(4):486–502.

Everett, Cath. 2009. "Environment Agency to Propose Individual Carbon Ration Cards." *Business Green*, November 9. Accessed October 11, 2011. http://www.businessgreen.com/bg/news/1803386/environment-agency-propose-individual-carbon-ration-cards.

Executive Forum on Climate Change. 2005. "Canadian business leaders issue call to action to Prime Minister in advance of Montreal Conference on Climate Change." Press Release and Letter, November 17. Montreal: Executive Forum on Climate Change. Accessed March 16, 2008. http://www.prnewswire.com/news-releases/canadian-business-leaders-issue-call-to-action-to-prime-minister-in-advance-of-montreal-conference-on-climate-change-55664422.html.

Fargione, Joseph, Jason Hill, David Tilman, Stephen Polasky, and Peter Hawthorne. 2008. "Land Clearing and the Biofuel Carbon Debt." *Science* 319(5867):1235–8.

Farmers Weekly. 2006a. "Food Miles Endorsements." Accessed April 8, 2008. http://www.fwi.co.uk/gr/foodmiles/endorsements.html.

– 2006b. "Local Food Is Miles Better." Campaign Website. Accessed April 7, 2008. http://www.fwi.co.uk/gr/foodmiles/index.html.

Fawcett, Tina. 2010. "Personal Carbon Trading: A Policy ahead of Its Time?" *Energy Policy* 38(11):6868–76.

FCO. 2012. "The Foreign and Commonwealth Office's Climate Projects – Document." *Guardian*, April 3. Accessed June 22, 2012. http://www.guardian.co.uk/environment/interactive/2012/apr/03/fco-climate-projects.

Ferguson, Iain. 2008. "Neoliberalism, Happiness and Wellbeing." *International Socialism* 117 (Winter). Accessed May 5, 2008. http://www.isj.org.uk/?id=400.

Find-a-Fountain. 2011. "About Find-a-Fountain." London: Find-a-Fountain. Accessed November 17, 2012. http://www.findafountain.org/about.

Flannery, Tim. 2008. "A Cavalier Country, with Much to Fear." *Globe and Mail*, March 29, F7.

Fleming, David, and Shaun Chamberlin. 2011. *TEQs (Tradable Energy Quotas): A Policy Framework for Peak Oil and Climate Change*. London: All Party Parliamentary Group on Peak Oil and The Lean Economy Connection.

Flybe. 2007. "Low Cost, but Not at Any Cost." Advertisement. *Guardian*, June 5, 42.

FoE. 2007. "Quality of Life: Cameron Urged to Adopt Blueprint for a Green Future." Press Release, September 13. London: Friends of the

Earth. Accessed March 16, 2008. http://www.foe.co.uk/resource/
   press_releases/quality_of_life_cameron_ur_13092007.html.
– 2008. "History of The Big Ask." London: Friends of the Earth. Accessed
   February 5, 2009. http://www.foe.co.uk/campaigns/climate/news/
   big_ask_history_15798.html.
– 2010. *Healthy Planet Eating: How Lower Meat Diets Could Save Lives and the
   Planet.* London: Friends of the Earth.
FoE and Cooperative Bank. 2006. "The Future Starts Here: The Route
   to a Low-Carbon Economy." London: Friends of the Earth. Accessed
   September 18, 2006. www.foe.co.uk/resource/reports/low_carbon_
   economy.pdf.
FoE Europe. Undated. "Eco-Efficiency and Sufficiency." Brussels: Friends
   of the Earth Europe." Accessed September 5, 2009. http://www
   .foeeurope.org/sustainability/foeapproach/efficiency/t-frame-effic
   .htm.
– 2011. *Canada's Dirty Lobby Diary: Undermining the EU Fuel Quality Directive.*
   Brussels: Friends of the Earth Europe.
FoE and Greenpeace UK. 2012. "London's next Mayor: Who Is the Green-
   est Candidate?" London: Friends of the Earth and Greenpeace UK.
FoE Scotland. 2007. "Consultation on the Proposed Energy Performance
   Commitment." Edinburgh: Friends of the Earth Scotland. Accessed
   December 18, 2007. http://www.foe-scotland.org.uk/publications/
   EPC_response_final.pdf.
Food Ethics Council. 2009. "Government Food Waste Strategy – a Missed
   Opportunity?" Brighton: Food Ethics Council. Accessed November 19,
   2012. http://www.foodethicscouncil.org/node/325.
Ford, Richard. 2009. "Beef Industry Gives Meat Free Mondays Short
   Shrift." *The Grocer,* June 20. Accessed November 21, 2012. http://www
   .thegrocer.co.uk/fmcg/beef-industry-gives-meat-free-mondays-short-
   shrift/200887.article.
Foster, Jason. 2007. "Labour, Climate Change, and Alberta's Oil Sands."
   Our Times, June 6. Accessed December 20, 2008. http://www.ourtimes
   .ca/Features/printer_19.php.
Foster, John Bellamy. 2002. *Ecology Against Capitalism.* New York: Monthly
   Review Press.
– 2009. *The Ecological Revolution: Making Peace with the Planet.* New York:
   Monthly Review Press.
– 2012. "Planetary Emergency." *Monthly Review* 64(7):1–25.
Foster, John Bellamy, Brett Clark, and Richard York. 2010. *The Ecological
   Rift: Capitalism's War on the Earth.* New York: Monthly Review Press.
Foster, Peter. 2010. "Yellow Brick Road to Green Serfdom." *Financial Post,*
   November 9, 17.

FPAC. 2007a. "Canadian Forest Products Industry Aims to Be First Carbon-Neutral Sector." Press Release, October 30. Ottawa: Forest Products As-sociation of Canada. Accessed November 4, 2007. http://www.fpac.ca/en/media_centre/press_releases/2007/2007-10-30_carbonNeutral.php.

– 2007b. "New Green Plan Fails to Substantially Recognize Early Action-Punishes Proactive Industries, Says Forest Products Industry." Press Release, April 26. Ottawa: Forest Products Association of Canada." Accessed August 13, 2009. http://www.fpac.ca/en/media_centre/press_releases/2007/2007-04-26_emissionsRegulations.php.

Frey, Bruno S, and Alois Stutzer. 2002. "What Can Economists Learn from Happiness Research?" *Journal of Economic Literature* 40(2):402–35.

Friedman, Benjamin M. 2005. *The Moral Consequences of Economic Growth.* New York: Alfred A. Knopf.

Future Heathrow. 2007. "Heathrow Growth to Bring UK £10 Billion a Year." News Release, November 22. London: Future Heathrow. Accessed May 23, 2008. http://www.futureheathrow.com/press-releases/Master%20Consultation%20launch%20release%20%20Nov22%2007%20(1).txt.

Gaffney, Dennis. 2008. "Fly the Eco-Friendly Skies." *Popular Science*, February, 40–6.

Galbraith, John Kenneth. 1958. "How Much Should a Country Consume?" In *Perspectives on Conservation: Essays on America's Natural Resources*, edited by H. Jarrett, 89–99. Baltimore, MD: Johns Hopkins University Press.

Gallagher, Ed. 2008. *The Gallagher Review of the Indirect Effects of Biofuels Production.* London: Renewable Fuels Agency.

Gallagher, Paul. 2009. "London's New Drinking Fountains a Challenge to Bottled Water Industry." *Observer*, October 4, 18.

Galloway, Gloria. 2008. "Layton Targets Tar Sands." *Globe and Mail*, September 8. Accessed September 8, 2009. www.theglobeandmail.com/servlet/story/RTGAM.20080908.welexndp0908/BNStory/politics/homewww.theglobeandmail.com/servlet/story/RTGAM.20080908.welexndp0908/BNStory/politics/home.

Gallup. 2011. "Worldwide, Blame for Climate Change Falls on Humans." Accessed January 14, 2012. http://www.gallup.com/poll/147242/Worldwide-Blame-Climate-Change-Falls-Humans.aspx?version=print.

Gamson, William A. 1992. *Talking Politics.* Cambridge, UK: Cambridge University Press.

Garman, Joss. 2010. "The Crucial Role of Activism in Scrapping Heathrow's Third Runway." *Guardian*, May 17. Accessed May 2, 2011. http://www.guardian.co.uk/environment/cif-green/2010/may/17/heathrow-third-runway-activism.

Garnett, Tara. 2007. "Meat and Dairy Production & Consumption: Explor-
    ing the Livestock Sector's Contribution to the UK's Greenhouse Gas
    Emissions and Assessing What Less Greenhouse Gas Intensive Systems
    of Production and Consumption Might Look Like." Working Paper.
    Food Climate Research Network, Centre for Environmental Strategy,
    University of Surrey.
– 2008. "Cooking up a Storm: Food, Greenhouse Gas Emissions and Our
    Changing Climate." Surrey, UK: Centre for Environmental Strategy,
    University of Surrey.
Gavron, Nicky. 2007. "Remarks to 'On Target? Environment Policy and the
    Climate Change Bill.'" Conference hosted by Trades Union Congress.
    London, June 4.
Gerein, Keith. 2010. "EU Delegation Visit Crucial to Oilsands." *Edmonton
    Journal*, November 2, A1.
Germanwatch. 2007. *The Climate Change Performance Index: A Comparison of
    Emissions Trends and Climate Protection Policies of the Top 56 CO$_2$ Emitting
    Nations*. Berlin: Germanwatch.
Germanwatch and CAN Europe. 2011. *The Climate Change Performance Index:
    Results 2012*. Bonn / Brussels: Germanwatch / Climate Action Network
    Europe.
– 2013. "The Climate Change Performance Index: Results 2014. Bonn/
    Brussels: Germanwatch / Climate Action Network Europe.
Gibbs, David. 2010. "Business Fears over Impending CRC Scheme." *Edie*,
    August 10. Accessed July 11, 2011. http://www.edie.net/news/news_
    story.asp?id=18528.
Giddens, Anthony. 2007. *Over to You, Mr Brown: How Labour Can Win Again*.
    Cambridge, UK: Polity.
– 2009a. *The Politics of Climate Change*. Cambridge, UK: Polity Press.
– 2009b. "Walking the Climate Talk." *Guardian*, September 4, 30.
Gilding, Paul. 2011. *The Great Disruption*. New York: Bloomsbury Press.
Gillespie, Ed. 2007. "The Slow Traveller." *Observer*, November 18, 14.
Gillies, Richard. 2007. "The Business Case Behind Climate Change."
    Presentation by Marks and Spencer's Director of Store Development to
    Corporate Climate Response Conference. London, May 29.
Girling, Richard. 2008. "Biofuels: Fields of Dreams." *Sunday Times*, March
    9, 52.
GLA. 2008. "Mayor Gives Green Light to CO$_2$ Charge to Tackle Climate
    Change." Press Release, February 12. London: Greater London
    Authority. Accessed April 12, 2008. http://www.london.gov.uk/view_
    press_release.jsp?releaseid=15632.
Goar, Carol. 2008a. "Contemplating Life without Growth." *Toronto Star*,
    December 8, A6.

– 2008b. "Curbing Conspicuous Consumption." *Toronto Star*, August 4, AA4.

Gold, Tanya. 2012. "This Plastic Bag Conspiracy Is a Truly Deadly Distraction." *Guardian*, August 4, 40.

Gonzalez, George A. 2005. "Urban Sprawl, Global Warming and the Limits of Ecological Modernisation." *Environmental Politics* 14(3):344.

Gonzalez, George A. 2009. *Urban Sprawl, Global Warming, and the Empire of Capital.* Albany: State University of New York Press.

Goodall, Chris. 2007a. *How to Live a Low-Carbon Life: The Individual's Guide to Stopping Climate Change.* London: Earthscan Publications Ltd.

– 2007b. "The Rebound Effect." *Carbon Commentary*, November 11. Accessed April 29, 2008. http://www.carboncommentary.com/2007/11/11/51.

Goodwin, Phil. 2012. "Three Views on 'Peak Car.'" *World Transport Policy and Practice* 17 (4):8–17.

Gorrie, Peter. 2010. "When Consumption's in the Red, We're in Trouble." *Toronto Star*, May 28, IN3.

Gould, Kenneth A., David N. Pellow, and Allan Schnaiberg. 2004. "Interrogating the Treadmill of Production: Everything You Wanted to Know about the Treadmill but Were Afraid to Ask." *Organization Environment* 17(3):296–316.

– 2008. *Treadmill of Production: Injustice and Unsustainability in the Global Economy.* Boulder, CO: Paradigm Publishers.

Government of Canada. 2002. *Climate Change Plan for Canada.* Ottawa: Government of Canada.

– 2004. "Your Guide to the One-Tonne Challenge." Ottawa: Government of Canada." Accessed December 21, 2008. http://dsp-psd.pwgsc.gc.ca/Collection/M144-27-2003E.pdf.

– 2005. *Project Green: Moving Forward on Climate — A Plan for Honouring Our Kyoto Commitment.* Ottawa: Government of Canada.

– 2007. *The Cost of Bill C-288 to Canadian Families and Business.* Ottawa: Environment Canada.

– 2008. "From Impacts to Adaptation: Canada in a Changing Climate 2007." Ottawa: Natural Resources Canada.

Graedel, Thomas E., and Braden R. Allenby. 1995. *Industrial Ecology.* Englewood Cliffs, NJ: Prentice Hall.

Gray, Louise. 2010a. "Heathrow Third Runway Has Fewer Benefits than We Thought, Admits Government." *Telegraph*, March 24. Accessed May 2, 2011. http://www.telegraph.co.uk/earth/environment/climatechange/7506674/Heathrow-third-runway-has-fewer-benefits-than-we-thought-admits-Government.html.

– 2010b. "UKIP Would Ban Al Gore Film in Schools." *Telegraph*, February 25. Accessed July 17, 2011. http://www.telegraph.co.uk/earth/environment/climatechange/7309204/UKIP-would-ban-Al-Gore-film-in-schools.html.

Gray, Richard. 2009. "Official Responsible for Light Bulb Ban Is a Former Communist." *Telegraph*, September 12. Accessed November 18, 2012. http://www.telegraph.co.uk/news/worldnews/europe/eu/6178082/ Official-responsible-for-light-bulb-ban-is-a-former-communist.html.

Green, Duncan. 2008. "The Rights and Wrongs of Food Miles." *From Poverty to Power (Oxfam)*. Accessed November 20, 2012. http://www.oxfam blogs.org/fp2p/?p=7.

Green, Malcolm. 2008. "Are International Medical Conferences an Outdated Luxury the Planet Can't Afford? Yes." *British Medical Journal* 336(June 28):1466.

Green Party. 2007a. "Can a Boom Town Be Green?" News Release, June 24. London: Green Party. Accessed April 12, 2008. http://www.greenparty .org.uk/news/3047.

– 2007b. "More Roads, More Aviation, More Carbon Emissions." News Release, October 30. Accessed April 12, 2008. http://www.greenparty .org.uk/news/3047.

– 2010. *UK Green Party 2010 Election Manifesto*. London: Green Party.

– 2012. "Policies for a Sustainable Society: Food and Agriculture." London: Green Party. Accessed November 21, 2012. http://policy.greenparty .org.uk/fa.

Green Party of Aotearoa New Zealand. 2006. "NZ Greens Write to British Greens to Correct Misinformation on Food Miles." Wellington, NZ: Green Party of Aotearoa New Zealand. Accessed March 3, 2008. http://www.greens.org.nz/node/14720.

Green Party of Canada. 2007a. "Do Something! Buy Nothing, Says Green Party Leader." Press Release, November 22. Ottawa: Green Party of Canada. Accessed November 27, 2008. http://www.greenparty.ca/en/ releases/22.11.2007.

– 2007b. *Vision Green*. Ottawa: Green Party of Canada.

– 2011. *Vision Green*. Ottawa: Green Party of Canada.

– 2012. "G12-P06 On Limits to Growth." Ottawa: Green Party of Canada. Accessed December 22, 2012. http://www.greenparty.ca/node/20581.

Greenpeace UK. 2005. "January 25th 2005: Lord Ron Oxburgh, Chairman of Shell UK, Delivers the Latest Greenpeace Business Lecture." London: Greenpeace. Accessed April 4, 2009. http://www.greenpeace .org.uk/about/greenpeace-business-lecture-series.

– 2006. "What Does Your Car Say about You?" London: Greenpeace UK. Accessed May 5, 2009. http://www.greenpeace.org.uk/blog/climate/ what-does-your-car-say-about-you.

– 2007. "Here Come the Tories to Launch Their Green Energy Policy." London: Greenpeace UK." Accessed May 7, 2009. http://www .greenpeace.org.uk/blog/climate/here-come-the-tories-to-launch-their -green-energy-policy-20071206.

Greenpeace UK, FoE, Oxfam et al. 2008. "Letter to Ruth Kelly Regarding Biofuels and the RTFO." March 24. London: Greenpeace UK. Accessed April 20, 2008. http://www.greenpeace.org.uk/files/pdfs/forests/kelly-rtfo-letter-20080324.pdf.

Greenpeace USA. 2010. "Koch Industries: Secretly Funding the Climate Denial Machine." Washington, DC: Greenpeace USA. Accessed August 29, 2010. http://www.greenpeace.org/usa/campaigns/global-warming-and-energy/polluterwatch/koch-industries/.

Grice, Andrew. 2006. "'Millions at Risk' from Escalation in Global Warming." *Independent*, April 15, 2.

– 2008. "Cabinet Split on Kingsnorth Power Station." *Independent*, September 26, 12.

– 2009a. "A Flawed Deal, but Credit to Brown for His Efforts." *Independent*, December 19, 6.

– 2009b. "Emissions Targets to Be Part of the Budget." *Independent*, April 18, 10.

Griggs, Steven, and David Howarth. 2004. "A Transformative Political Campaign? The New Rhetoric of Protest against Airport Expansion in the UK." *Journal of Political Ideologies* 9(2):181–201.

– 2012. "Phronesis, Logics, and Critical Policy Analysis: Heathrow's 'Third Runway' and the Politics of Sustainable Aviation in the UK." In *Real Social Science: Applied Phronesis*, edited by Bent Flyvbjerg, Todd Landman, and Sanford Schram, 163–203. Cambridge, UK: Cambridge University Press.

Guardian. 2007. "Air Travel Deal: Plane Wrong." *Guardian*, March 24, 36.

– 2008a. "50 People Who Could Save the Planet." *Guardian*, January 5, 17.

– 2008b. "Turning up the Heat." *Guardian*, October 28, 34.

– 2009a. "Air Sickness (editorial)." *Guardian*, January 12, 28.

– 2009b. "Economy and the Environment: Growing Pains." *Guardian*, May 18, 30.

Gupta, Sujata et al. 2007. "Policies, Instruments and Co-operative Arrangements." In *Climate Change 2007: Mitigation. Contribution of Working Group III to the Fourth Assessment Report of the Intergovernmental Panel on Climate Change*, edited by B. Metz, O.R. Davidson, P.R. Bosch, R. Dave, and L.A. Meyer, 745–807. Cambridge, UK and New York: Cambridge University Press. Accessed December 11, 2008.

Gutcher, Lianne. 2007. "Offering a Passport to a Greener Planet." *Sunday Herald* (Scotland), September 16. Accessed April 16, 2008. http://www.sundayherald.com/business/businessnews/display.var.1691611.0.offering_a_passport_to_a_greener_planet.php.

Guy, Anna. 2011. "Going Green Into the Black: Can Elizabeth May Show Canadians That Going Green Is Profitable?" *Canadian Business Journal* 4(8):12–21.

GWPF. 2010. "GWPF Calls for Suspension and Review of Unilateral Climate Targets." London: Global Warming Policy Foundation. Accessed July 14, 2011. http://www.thegwpf.org/press-releases/945-gwpf-calls-for-suspension-and-review-of-unilateral-climate-targets.html.

Hague, William. 2012. "Climate Change: Why the Government Must Meet the Challenge." *Huffington Post UK*, April 25. Accessed June 23, 2012. http://www.huffingtonpost.co.uk/william-hague/climate-change-government-challenge_b_1450562.html.

Hailes, Julia. 2008. "Bottled Water – Eau No!" *Telegraph*, February 19. Accessed March 31, 2008. http://www.telegraph.co.uk/earth/earthcomment/3325973/Bottled-water-eau-no.html.

Hajer, Maarten A. 1995. *The Politics of Environmental Discourse: Ecological Modernization and the Policy Process.* Oxford: Oxford University Press.

Haley, Brendan. 2011. "From Staples Trap to Carbon Trap: Canada's Peculiar Form of Carbon Lock-In." *Studies in Political Economy* 88:97–132.

Hallman, David. 2002. "Globalization and Climate Change." Geneva, Switzerland: World Council of Churches. Accessed November 1, 2007. http://www.oikoumene.org/en/resources/documents/wcc-programmes/justice-diakonia-and-responsibility-for-creation/climate-change-water/02-globalization-and-climate-change.html.

– 2005. "Climate Change: A Challenge for Faith Communities." Presentation to Catholic Earthcare Australia Conference, November 18–20. Accessed January 28, 2009. catholicearthcareoz.net/pdf/David_Hallman.doc.

Hamilton, Clive. 2010. *Requiem for a Species: Why We Resist the Truth About Climate Change.* London: Earthscan.

Hansard. 2007. "House of Commons Hansard Debates for 22 November 2007." Accessed May 24, 2008. http://www.publications.parliament.uk/pa/cm200708/cmhansrd/cmo71122/debtext/71122-0011.htm#07112239001239.

– 2008. "House of Commons Hansard Written Answers for 22 July 2008." London: House of Commons. Accessed February 28, 2009. http://www.publications.parliament.uk/pa/cm200708/cmhansrd/cmo80722/text/80722w0015.htm#column_1049W.

– 2009. "House of Commons Hansard Debates for 28 Jan 2009." Accessed May 2, 2011. http://www.publications.parliament.uk/pa/cm200809/cmhansrd/cmo90128/debtext/90128-0004.htm#09012857000001.

Hansen, James. 2009. "Coal-Fired Power Plants Are Death Factories. Close Them." *Observer*, February 15, 29.

Hansen, James, Makiko Sato, et al. 2008. "Target Atmospheric CO_2: Where Should Humanity Aim?" *The Open Atmospheric Science Journal* 2: 217–31.

Harding, Stephan. 2006a. "Doomed to Failure." *Guardian*, November

13. Accessed May 20, 2007. http://environment.guardian.co.uk/
print/0,,329626414-121568,00.html.

– 2006b. "Growing Pains." *The Ecologist*, December 7. Accessed May 20,
2007. http://www.theecologist.co.uk/archive_detail.asp?content_
id=689.

– 2006c. "It's Time We Learned to Live in Peace with Our Planet." *Guardian*, September 27, 8.

Hargrove, Buzz. 2002. "Kyoto Is an Automobile Opportunity for Canada."
December. Toronto: Canadian Auto Workers." Accessed January 15,
2007. http://www.caw.ca.

Harper, Stephen. 2002. "Letter to Members of Canadian Alliance." Repub-
lished on *Toronto Star* website, January 30, 2007. Accessed January 30,
2007. http://www.thestar.com/article/176382.

– 2006. "Address by the Prime Minister at the Canada-UK Chamber of
Commerce." London, July 14. Ottawa: Prime Minister's Office. Accessed November 11, 2008. http://pm.gc.ca/eng/media.asp?id=1247.

– 2008. "Prime Minister Harper Addresses the Canada-U.K. Chamber of
Commerce in London." London, May 29. Ottawa: Prime Minister's
Office. Accessed August 18, 2009. http://pm.gc.ca/eng/media.
asp?id=2131.

Harrabin, Roger. 2008a. "EU 'Should Ban Inefficient Cars.'" BBC *News*,
February 4. Accessed April 12, 2008. http://news.bbc.co.uk/1/hi/sci/
tech/7225451.stm.

– 2008b. "UK Opposes Green Aviation Target." BBC *News*, September 26.
Accessed September 30, 2008. http://news.bbc.co.uk/1/hi/sci/
tech/7636780.stm.

– 2011. "Cameron Intervenes to Settle Row over Emissions Targets." BBC
News, May 16. Accessed June 8, 2012. http://www.bbc.co.uk/news/
uk-politics-13409404.

Harrison, Kate, and Ros Anderson. 2007. "My Village Is Going Carbon-Neutral." *Guardian*, June 2. Accessed June 12, 2007. http://www.guardian
.co.uk/environment/2007/jun/02/ethicalliving.lifeandhealth.

Harrison, Kathryn. 2007. "The Road Not Taken: Climate Change Policy
in Canada and the United States." *Global Environmental Politics*
7(4):92–116.

– 2010. "The Struggle of Ideas and Self-Interest in Canadian Climate
Policy." In *Global Commons, Domestic Decisions: The Comparative Politics
of Climate Change*, edited by K. Harrison and L. McIntosh Sundstrom,
169–200. Cambridge, MA: MIT Press.

Harrison, Kathryn, and Lisa McIntosh Sundstrom. 2007. "The Comparative
Politics of Climate Change." *Global Environmental Politics* 7(4):1–18.

Harrison, Pete. 2011. "Canada Warns EU over Oil Sands." *Edmonton Journal*, April 5, D3.

Harrison, Pete, and Juliane von Reppert-Bismarck. 2011. "Tar Sand Row Threatens Canada-EU Trade Deal – Sources." *Reuters*, February 21. Accessed June 5, 2011. http://www.reuters.com/article/2011/02/21/us-eu-canada-trade-idUSTRE71K2FL20110221.

Harriss-White, Barbara, and Elinor Harriss. 2006. "Unsustainable Capitalism: The Politics of Renewable Energy in the UK." In *Socialist Register 2007: Coming to Terms With Nature*, edited by L. Panitch and C. Leys, 72–101. New York: Monthly Review Press.

Harvey, Fiona. 2007. "Carbon Neutral, Cash Positive?" *Business Voice: The CBI Magazine*, February, 28–34.

– 2010a. "Carbon Scheme Is 'Overcomplex.'" *Financial Times*, September 23, 4.

– 2010b. "CBI Attacks Plan to Tighten Emissions Targets." *Financial Times*, July 28, 3.

– 2012. "Leaked Documents Reveal UK Fight to Dilute EU Green Energy Targets." *Guardian*, June 4, 1.

Harvey, Fiona, and Jim Pickard. 2008. "Stern Takes Bleaker View on Warming." *Financial Times*, April 17, 3.

Harvie, David. 2011. "Good Life, Good Living and National Wellbeing." University of Leicester. Accessed July 12, 2012. http://leicester exchanges.com/2011/02/16/good-life-good-living-and-national-well-being/.

Hassol, Joy. 2011. "Questions and Answers: Emissions Reductions Needed to Stabilize Climate." Presidential Action Climate Project. Accessed April 23, 2014. http://www.climatecommunication.org/wp-content/uploads/2011/08/presidentialaction.pdf.

Hawken, Paul, Amory Lovins, and L. Hunter Lovins. 1999. *Natural Capitalism: Creating the Next Industrial Revolution*. Boston: Little, Brown & Co.

Hayden, Anders. 1999. *Sharing the Work, Sparing the Planet: Work Time, Consumption, & Ecology*. London: Zed Books.

– 2014a. "Enough of That Already: Sufficiency-Based Challenges to High-Carbon Consumption in Canada." *Environmental Politics* 23(1):97–114.

– 2014b. "Stopping Heathrow Airport Expansion (For Now): Lessons from a Victory for the Politics of Sufficiency." *Journal of Environmental Politics and Planning*. doi: http://dx.doi.org/10.1080/1523908X.2013.873713.

Hayden, Anders, and John M. Shandra. 2009. "Hours of Work and the Ecological Footprint of Nations: An Exploratory Analysis." *Local Environment* 14(6):575–600.

Health Canada. 2008. "Health Canada Releases New Report on Climate Change." Press Release, July 31. Accessed August 20, 2009. http://www.hc-sc.gc.ca/ahc-asc/media/nr-cp/_2008/2008_122-eng.php.

Heaton-Harris, Chris, Christopher Pincher, et al. 2012. "Full Letter from MPs to David Cameron on Wind Power Subsidies." Accessed June 9,

2012. http://www.telegraph.co.uk/earth/energy/windpower/9061554
/Full-letter-from-MPs-to-David-Cameron-on-wind-power-subsidies.html.

Helm, Dieter. 2003. *Energy, the State, and the Market: British Energy Policy since 1979*. Oxford: Oxford University Press.

– 2009. "Environmental Challenges in a Warming World: Consumption, Costs and Responsibilities." Tanner Lecture, New College, Oxford, February 21. Accessed October 12, 2012. http://www.dieterhelm .co.uk/sites/default/files/TANNER_LECTURE_Feb09.pdf.

– 2012. *The Carbon Crunch: How We're Getting Climate Change Wrong – and How to Fix It*. New Haven: Yale University Press.

Helm, Dieter, Robin Smale, and Jonathan Phillips. 2007. "Too Good To Be True? The UK's Climate Change Record." Accessed January 18, 2008. http://www.dieterhelm.co.uk/publications/Carbon_record_2007.pdf.

Henton, Darcy. 2008. "Albertans Support Slower Growth." *Calgary Herald*, February 28. Accessed November 17, 2008. http://www.canada .com/calgaryherald/features/albertavotes/story.html?id=61dccc87 -5cea-454a-85e2-b92c847fd683&k=89329.

Hertwich, Edgar G., and Glen P. Peters. 2009. "Carbon Footprint of Nations: A Global, Trade-Linked Analysis." *Environmental Science & Technology* 43(16):6414–20.

Hey, Christian. 2010. "The German Paradox: Climate Leader and Green Car Laggard." In *The New Climate Policies of the European Union: Internal Legislation and Climate Diplomacy*, edited by Sebastian Oberthür and Marc Pallemaerts, 211–30. Brussels: Brussels University Press.

Hickman, Leo. 2007a. "Are You on the Rebound?" *Guardian*, November 11. Accessed April 29, 2008. http://blogs.guardian.co.uk/ethicalliving /2007/11/are_you_on_the_rebound.html.

– 2007b. "How to Save the Planet." *Guardian*, November 1, 18.

– 2011. "The Mystery of the 1993 Global Warming TV Ad." *Guardian*, March 29. Accessed July 22, 2012. http://www.guardian.co.uk/environment/ blog/2011/mar/28/global-warming-1993-ad.

– 2012. "Rick Perry Criticises UK Initiative to Influence US Climate Sceptics." *Guardian*, April 3. Accessed June 23, 2012. http://www.guardian.co.uk /environment/2012/apr/03/rick-perry-climate-sceptic-policymakers.

Hickman, Martin. 2007a. "Britain's Colossal Food Waste Is Stoking Climate Change." *Independent*, November 2. Accessed April 2, 2008. http:// www.independent.co.uk/environment/climate-change/britains- colossal-food-waste-is-stoking-climate-change-398664.html.

– 2007b. "London Joins National Campaign to Banish the Curse of the Plastic Bag." *Independent*, November 14, 2.

– 2009. "Billions Fewer Plastic Bags Handed Out." *Independent*, February 26, 8.

Hillman, Mayer. 2004. *How We Can Save The Planet*. First edition. Penguin UK.

Hines, Nico. 2008. "Ken Livingstone Declares War with £25 Congestion Charge." *Times*, February 12. Accessed April 11, 2008. http://driving.timesonline.co.uk/tol/life_and_style/driving/news/article3356455.ece.

HM Government. 2005. *Securing the Future: The UK Government Sustainable Development Strategy*. London: HM Government.

– 2009a. *Investing in a Low Carbon Britain*. London: HM Government.

– 2009b. *The UK Low Carbon Transition Plan: National Strategy for Climate and Energy*. London: HM Government.

– 2010. *Food 2030*. London: Department for Environment, Food and Rural Affairs.

– 2011. *The Carbon Plan: Delivering Our Low Carbon Future*. London: HM Government.

HOCEAC. 2004. *Environmental Audit – Third Report*. London: House of Commons Environmental Audit Committee.

– 2006a. *Pre-Budget 2006: Shifting the Burden of Taxation*. London: House of Commons Environmental Audit Committee.

– 2006b. *Reducing Carbon Emissions from Transport: Ninth Report of Session 2005–06*. London: House of Commons Environmental Audit Committee.

– 2007. *The Voluntary Carbon Offset Market*. London: House of Commons Environmental Audit Committee.

– 2008. *Personal Carbon Trading*. London: House of Commons Environmental Audit Committee.

HOCECCC. 2012a. *Consumption-Based Emissions Reporting*. London: House of Commons Energy and Climate Change Committee.

– 2012b. "Government Should Be Open about 'Outsourced Emissions' according to Committee." London: House of Commons Energy and Climate Change Committee. Accessed April 10, 2013. http://www.parliament.uk/business/committees/committees-a-z/commons-select/energy-and-climate-change-committee/news/consumption-published/.

Hodgkinson, Tom. 2007. "Medieval Values: Why Going Back Will Make Us Free." Address to Royal Society for the Encouragement of Arts, Manufactures & Commerce (RSA), London, May 17.

– 2008. "The Art of Doing Nothing." In *Do Good Lives Have to Cost the Earth?*, edited by A. Simms and J. Smith, 27–33. London: Constable.

Hoekstra, George. 2013. "B.C. Losing Its Position as Climate-Change Leader." *Vancouver Sun*, October 13. Accessed October 4, 2013. http://www.vancouversun.com/technology/losing+position+climate+change+leader/8989493/story.html.

Homer-Dixon, Thomas. 2001. *The Ingenuity Gap: Can We Solve the Problems of the Future?* Toronto: Vintage Canada.
– 2006. "The End of Ingenuity." *New York Times*, November 29, A29.
– 2007. *The Upside of Down: Catastrophe, Creativity, and the Renewal of Civilization.* Toronto: Vintage Canada.
– 2008. "Remarks to 'If Not Us, Who?' Event. Victoria College Environmental Festival. University of Toronto, March 3.
– 2011. "Economies Can't Just Keep on Growing." *Foreign Policy*, January. Accessed July 28, 2012. http://www.foreignpolicy.com/articles/2011/01/02/unconventional_wisdom?page=0,1.
Hopkins, Rob. 2009. "The Transition Culture Question for the Business Leaders at DAVOS." *Transition Culture*. Accessed March 14, 2009. http://transitionculture.org/2009/01/23/the-transition-culture-question-for-the-business-leaders-at-davos/.
House of Commons. 2007. "Legislative Committee on Bill C-30: Thursday, February 8, 2007." Ottawa: House of Commons. Accessed August 16, 2009. http://www2.parl.gc.ca/HousePublications/Publication.aspx?DocId=2679623&Language=E&Mode=1&Parl=39&Ses=1.
House of Commons Select Committee on Public Accounts. 2004. "Select Committee on Public Accounts Minutes of Evidence." May 12. London: House of Commons Select Committee on Public Accounts. Accessed April 12, 2009. http://www.parliament.the-stationery-office.com/pa/cm200304/cmselect/cmpubacc/604/4051205.htm.
Howden, Daniel. 2008. "Brazil's Experience Testifies to the Downside of This Energy Revolution." *Independent*, April 15, 2.
Huhne, Chris, Norbert Röttgen, and Jean-Louis Borloo. 2010. "Europe Needs to Reduce Emissions by 30%." *Financial Times*, July 15, 7.
Hunold, Christian, and John S. Dryzek. 2005. "Green Political Strategy and the State: Combining Political Theory and Comparative History." In *The State and the Global Ecological Crisis*, edited by J. Barry and R. Eckersley, 75–95. Cambridge, MA: MIT Press.
Huot, Marc. 2012. "Oilsands Emissions Lie at the Core of Canada's Climate Challenge." Drayton Valley, AB: Pembina Institute. Accessed December 7, 2013. http://www.pembina.org/blog/668.
Huot, Marc, and Jennifer Grant. 2012. *Clearing the Air on Oilsands Emissions: The Facts about Greenhouse Gas Pollution from Oilsands Development.* Drayton Valley, AB: Pembina Institute.
Hurd, Nick, and Claire Kerr. 2007. *Don't Give up on 2 °C.* London: Quality of Life Commission (Conservative Party).
Hussain, Yadullah. 2012. "Oil Explorers' New Challenges." *Financial Post*, May 3. Accessed December 7, 2013. http://business.financialpost.com/2012/05/03/oil-explorers-face-new-challenges/.

Hutton, John. 2008. "The Future of Utilities – Speech to the Adam Smith Institute." London, March 10. London: Department for Business, Enterprise & Regulatory Reform. Accessed February 28, 2009. http://www.berr.gov.uk/aboutus/ministerialteam/Speeches/page45211.html.

Hyman, Merlin. 2008. "Getting Commitment on Carbon." *Water & Wastewater Treatment,* January, 28.

Hyndman, Rick. 2007. "The Canadian Approach to Industry GHG Policy." Presentation to CIBC World Markets Toronto, April 18. Calgary: Canadian Association of Petroleum Producers." Accessed December 18, 2007. http://membernet.capp.ca/raw.asp?x=1&dt=PDF&dn=119902.

ICO₂N. 2007. "Carbon Capture & Storage: A Canadian Environmental Superpower Opportunity." Calgary: Integrated CO₂ Network. Accessed November 22, 2008. http://www.ico2n.com/docs/media/ICO2N%20Report_Carbon%20Capture%20and%20Storage_A%20Canadian%20Environmental%20Superpower%20Opportunity.pdf.

– 2008. "The Vision." Calgary: Integrated CO₂ Network. Accessed November 22, 2008. http://www.ico2n.com/docs/tech/ICO2N_The%20Vision_%204pg%20overview.pdf.

IEA. 2010. *World Energy Outlook 2010.* Paris: International Energy Agency. Accessed December 7, 2013. http://www.worldenergyoutlook.org/media/weo2010.pdf.

IESO. 2013. "Demand Overview." Toronto: Independent Electricity System Operator. Accessed December 1, 2013. http://ieso-public.sharepoint.com/Pages/Power-Data/Demand.aspx.

IGD. 2012. "Over 200 Million Food Miles Removed from UK Roads." Watford, Hertfordshire: Institute of Grocery Distribution. Accessed November 20, 2012. http://www.igd.com/Media/IGD-news-and-press-releases/Over-200-million-food-miles-removed-from-UK-roads/.

IMF. 2007. *World Economic Outlook – October 2007: Globalization and Inequality.* Washington, DC: International Monetary Fund.

– 2008. *World Economic Outlook – April 2008.* Washington, DC: International Monetary Fund.

Independent. 2007. "Ten Readers' Ways to Cut Your Carbon Footprint." *Independent,* August 9. Accessed August 19, 2007. http://www.independent.co.uk/environment/climate-change/ten-readers-ways-to-cut-your-carbon-footprint-460822.html.

IPCC. 2007. *Climate Change 2007: Climate Change Impacts, Adaptation and Vulnerability – Summary for Policy Makers.* Working Group II Contribution to the Intergovernmental Panel on Climate Change Fourth Assessment Report. Intergovernmental Panel on Climate Change.

Ipsos MORI. 2008. "Public Attitudes to Climate Change, 2008: Concerned but Still Not Convinced." London: Ipsos 5. Accessed February 16, 2013.

http://www.ipsos-mori.com/Assets/Docs/Publications/sri-environment-
    public-attitudes-to-climate-change-2008-concerned-but-still-unconvinced
    .pdf.
Jaccard, Mark. 2006. *Sustainable Fossil Fuels: The Unusual Suspect in the Quest for
    Clean and Enduring Energy.* Cambridge, UK: Cambridge University Press.
– 2007. "The Second Inconvenient Truth." *Vancouver Sun,* October 24, A15.
Jaccard, Mark, Nic Rivers, Chris Bataille, Rose Murphy, John Nyboer, and
    Bryn Sadownik. 2006. "Burning Our Money to Warm the Planet: Can-
    ada's Ineffective Efforts to Reduce Greenhouse Gas Emissions." *C.D.
    Howe Institute Commentary* 234. Accessed April 10, 2013. http://www
    .cdhowe.org/pdf/Commentary_234.pdf.
Jackson, Tim. 2005. "Live Better by Consuming Less?: Is There a 'Double
    Dividend' in Sustainable Consumption?" *Journal of Industrial Ecology*
    9(1-2):19–36.
– 2007. "Rebound Launch: Keynote Presentation." Keynote Speech for
    Launch of UK Energy Research Centre Rebound Effect Report. Octo-
    ber 31. Accessed April 30, 2008. http://www.ukerc.ac.uk/Downloads/
    PDF/07/0710ReboundEffect/0710TJKeynote.pdf.
– 2008. "What Politicians Dare Not Say." *New Scientist,* October 18, 42–3.
– 2009. *Prosperity without Growth? The Transition to a Sustainable Economy.* Lon-
    don: Sustainable Development Commission.
Jacob, Catherine. 2008. "HRH: His Royal Hologram's Virtual Speech." *Sky
    News,* January 22. Accessed May 25, 2008. http://news.sky.com/skynews
    /article/0,,30100-1301500,00.html.
Jacobs, Michael. 1999. "Environmental Modernisation." Fabian Pamphlet
    591. London: Fabian Society.
Jacobsen, Jackie. 2008. "Virgin on Disaster." *Red Pepper,* April. Accessed
    May 22, 2008. http://www.redpepper.org.uk/Virgin-on-disaster?var
    _recherche=virgin%20on%20disaster.
Jacobson, David. 2009. "Ottawa: Ambassador Jacobson and Environment
    Minister Prentice Discuss Continental Carbon Market and Oil Sands."
    Diplomatic Cable Released by Wikileaks. Accessed August 17, 2011.
    http://www.aftenposten.no/nyheter/iriks/article3959849.ece.
James, David. 2008. "Mr Capello Treats Us as Equals. How Refreshing."
    Observer, February 10, 24.
James, Oliver. 2007. "Affluenza: Can We Be Successful And Stay Sane?"
    Primrose Hill Lecture, St. Mary's Church, London, June 13.
– 2008. *The Selfish Capitalist: Origins of Affluenza.* London: Vermillion.
Jamieson, Alistar. 2008. "Airlines 'Are Akin to Arms Dealers' in Ethics
    Stakes." *Scotsman,* February 6, 4.
Jang, Brent. 2007. "Aeroplan Launches Carbon Offset Initiative." *Globe and
    Mail,* December 7, B2.

Jänicke, Martin. 2005. "Trend-Setters in Environmental Policy: The Character and Role of Pioneer Countries." *European Environment* 15(2):129–42.

– 2008. "Ecological Modernisation: New Perspectives." *Journal of Cleaner Production* 16(5):557–65.

Jänicke, Martin, and Klaus Jacob. 2004. "Lead Markets for Environmental Innovations: A New Role for the Nation State." *Global Environmental Politics* 4(1):29–46.

Jansen, Mark. 2009. "Rebound Effect Will Raise Fossil Fuel Use." *Sunday Times*, May 31, Business 1.

Jenkins, Andrew. 2007. "Product Life-Cycle Emissions: Low Carbon Shampoo." Presentation by Boots' Sustainable Development Manager to Corporate Climate Response Conference. London, May 29.

Jenkins, Geoff, James Murphy, David Sexton, Jason Lowe, Phil Jones, and Chris Kilsby. 2009. *UK Climate Projections: Briefing Report.* Exeter, UK: Met Office Hadley Centre.

Johnson, Boris. 2013. "It's Snowing, and It Really Feels like the Start of a Mini Ice Age." *Telegraph*, January 21, 18.

Johnston, Philip. 2010. "How Can We Measure Happiness?" *Telegraph*, November 16, 23.

Jones, Allan. 2007. "Decentralised Energy and Climate Change." Speech to Event Organized by New London Architecture, March 21.

Jones, Terry. 2007. "Hey, Buddy. Can You Spare a Room?" *Edmonton Sun*, June 25. Accessed November 2, 2008. http://www.edmontonsun.com/Sports/Eskimos/2007/06/25/4288078-sun.html.

Jorgenson, Andrew K. 2003. "Consumption and Environmental Degradation: A Cross-National Analysis of the Ecological Footprint." *Social Problems* 50:374–94.

– 2006. "Global Warming and the Neglected Greenhouse Gas: A Cross-National Study of the Social Causes of Methane Emissions Intensity, 1995." *Social Forces* 84:1779–98.

– 2012. "The Sociology of Ecologically Unequal Exchange and Carbon Dioxide Emissions, 1960–2005." *Social Science Research* 41(2):242–52.

Jorgenson, Andrew K., and Thomas J. Burns. 2007. "The Political-Economic Causes of Change in the Ecological Footprints of Nations, 1991–2001: A Quantitative Investigation." *Social Science Research* 36(2):834–53.

Jorgenson, Andrew K., and Brett Clark. 2012. "Are the Economy and the Environment Decoupling? A Comparative International Study, 1960–2005." *American Journal of Sociology* 118(1):1–44.

Jorgenson, Andrew K., James Rice, and Jessica Crowe. 2005. "Unpacking the Ecological Footprint of Nations." *International Journal of Comparative Sociology* 46:241–60.

Joseph, Stephen. 2007. Remarks to Workshop on Transport and Climate Change. "On Target? Environment Policy and the Climate Change Bill" Conference Hosted by the Trades Union Congress, June 4, London.

Jowit, Juliette. 2007. "Village That's Saving the World." *Observer*, March 25, 23.

– 2008a. "Biofuels 'Do More Harm than Good.'" *Observer*, April 28, 2.

– 2008b. "British Public 'Unwilling' to Pay for Environmental Agenda." *Guardian*, September 24. Accessed March 11, 2009. http://www.guardian.co.uk/environment/2008/sep/24/climate.change.science.ofclimatechange.

– 2008c. "Stern: Financial Crisis Could Promote Clean Energy." *Guardian*, October 7. Accessed October 10, 2008. http://www.guardian.co.uk/environment/2008/oct/06/climatechange.carbonemissions.

– 2009. "Hospitals Will Take Meat off Menus in Bid to Cut Carbon." *Guardian*, January 26, 1.

Jowit, Juliette, and Patrick Wintour. 2008. "Cost of Tackling Global Climate Change Has Doubled, Warns Stern." *Guardian*, June 26, 2.

Juniper, Tony. 2007a. "Remarks to Session on 'How Do We Change Climate Change?'" Sunday Times Literary Festival, Oxford, March 23.

– 2007b. *How Many Lightbulbs Does It Take to Change a Planet?* London: Quercus.

– 2008. "Virgin Territory." *Guardian*, February 25. Accessed February 28, 2009. http://www.guardian.co.uk/commentisfree/2008/feb/25/virginterritory.

Kahn, Herman. 1976. *The Next 200 Years: A Scenario for America and the World.* William Morrow & Co.

Kallis, Giorgos. 2011. "In Defence of Degrowth." *Ecological Economics* 70(5):873–80.

Kasser, Tim. 2003. *The High Price of Materialism.* Cambridge, MA: MIT Press.

Kasteren, Joost van, and Henk Tennekes. 2010. "The Unholy Alliance between Philips and the Greens." *Climate Science: Roger Pielke Sr.* (Blog), March 17. Accessed November 18, 2012. http://pielkeclimatesci.wordpress.com/2010/03/17/the-unholy-alliance-between-philips-and-the-greens-a-guest-weblog-by-joost-van-kasteren-and-henk-tennekes/.

Kaufman, Stephen. 2007. "We Come to Bury Carbon, Not to Praise It." *Globe and Mail,* July 23. Accessed July 24, 2007. http://www.theglobeandmail.com/servlet/story/RTGAM.20070723.wwcomment23/BNStory/Front/.

Keepers of the Athabasca. 2008. "Unanimous Passing of No New Oil Sands Approvals Resolution at the Assembly of Treaty Chiefs Meeting." Press Release, February 25. Calgary: Keepers of the Athabasca. Accessed November 7, 2008. http://www.aenweb.ca/node/2131.

Kelly, Erin N., David W. Schindler, Peter V. Hodson, Jeffrey W. Short, Roseanna Radmanovich, and Charlene C. Nielsen. 2010. "Oil Sands Development Contributes Elements Toxic at Low Concentrations to the Athabasca River and Its Tributaries." *Proceedings of the National Academy of Sciences* 107(37):16178-16183.

Kelly, Ruth, and Peter Ainsworth. 2008. "Biofuels: A Blueprint for the Future?" *Guardian*, April 14, 26.

Kersley, Helen, and Ellis Lawlor. 2010. *Grounded: A New Approach to Evaluating Runway 3*. London: New Economics Foundation.

Ki-moon, Ban, and Al Gore. 2009. "Green Growth Is Essential to Any Stimulus." *Financial Times*, February 16. Accessed February 17, 2009. http://www.ft.com/cms/s/0/0fa98852-fc45-11dd-aed8-000077b07658.html.

King, Julia. 2008. *The King Review of Low-Carbon Cars. Part II: Recommendations for Action*. London: HM Treasury.

Klaus, Václav. 2008. "From Climate Alarmism to Climate Realism." *Environment & Climate News*, May. Chicago: Heartland Institute. Accessed August 24, 2010. http://www.heartland.org/policybot/results/23073/From_Climate_Alarmism_to_Climate_Realism.html.

Klein, Naomi. 2011. "Capitalism vs. the Climate." *The Nation*, November 28. Accessed June 10, 2012. http://www.thenation.com/article/164497/capitalism-vs-climate.

Knight, Kyle W., and Eugene A. Rosa. 2011. "The Environmental Efficiency of Well-Being: A Cross-National Analysis." *Social Science Research* 40(3):931-49.

Kolbert, Elizabeth. 2007. "Unconventional Crude: Canada's Synthetic-Fuels Boom." *New Yorker*, November 12, 46-51.

Kovel, Joel. 2008. "Ecosocialism, Global Justice, and Climate Change." *Capitalism, Nature, Socialism* 19(2):4-14.

Krauss, Clifford. 2005. "In Canada's Wilderness, Measuring the Cost of Oil Profits." *New York Times*, October 9, 3.

Kurek, Joshua, Jane L. Kirk, Derek C. G. Muir, Xiaowa Wang, Marlene S. Evans, and John P. Smol. 2013. "Legacy of a Half Century of Athabasca Oil Sands Development Recorded by Lake Ecosystems." *Proceedings of the National Academy of Sciences*. Accessed January 10, 2013. http://www.pnas.org/content/early/2013/01/02/1217675110.

Laghi, Brian. 2007. "Climate Concerns Now Top Security and Health." *Globe and Mail*, January 26, A1.

Latouche, Serge. 2009. *Farewell to Growth*. Cambridge, UK: Polity.

Lawson, Dominic, Robert Cooper, Kishwer Falkner, David Goodhart, and Richard Reeves. 2008. "David Miliband (Interview)." *Prospect*, October. Accessed May 20, 2009. http://www.prospect-magazine.co.uk/article_details.php?id=10395.

Lawson, Nigel. 2006. "The Economics and Politics of Climate Change: An Appeal to Reason." London: Centre for Policy Studies. Accessed June 1, 2008. http://www.cps.org.uk/cpsfile.asp?id=641.

– 2008a. *An Appeal to Reason: A Cool Look at Global Warming.* London: Gerald Duckworth & Co Ltd.

– 2008b. "The REAL Inconvenient Truth: Zealotry over Global Warming Could Damage Our Earth Far More than Climate Change." *Daily Mail,* April 5. Accessed March 19, 2009. http://www.dailymail.co.uk/news/ article-557374/The-REAL-inconvenient-truth-Zealotry-global-warming-damage-Earth-far-climate-change.html.

Laxer, Gordon, and John Dillon. 2008. "Canada Freezing in the Dark?" *Peace Review* 20(4):426–34.

Layard, Richard. 2005. *Happiness: Lessons from a New Science.* New York: Penguin Press.

– 2011. "Happiness and Public Policy." London: Action for Happiness. Accessed October 12, 2012. http://www.actionforhappiness.org/news/ happiness-and-public-policy.

– 2012. "Mental Health: The New Frontier for the Welfare State." Presentation at the London School of Economics and Political Science, March 6. Accessed October 12, 2012. http://www2.lse.ac.uk/publicEvents/ pdf/20120306%20Layard%20Transcript.pdf.

Layard, Richard, Anthony Seldon, and Mark Williamson. 2011. "Putting Happiness before Growth." *Times,* November 5. Accessed October 12, 2012. http://www.actionforhappiness.org/news/putting-happiness-before-growth.

Layton, Jack. 2007. "Green-Collar Jobs: NDP Leader Jack Layton's Speech to the B.C. Federation of Labour." Ottawa: New Democratic Party, November 26. Accessed July 2, 2008. http://www.ndp.ca/page/5939/.

– 2008. "In Praise of Cap-and-Trade." *National Post,* June 4.

Lea, Ruth. 2007. "Fred Flintstone Didn't Drive a Gas Guzzler ..." *New Statesman,* May 21. Accessed March 19, 2009. http://www.newstatesman .com/environment/2007/05/global-warming-climate-change.

Leach, Andrew. 2012. "Alberta's Specified Gas Emitters Regulation." *Canadian Tax Journal* 60(4):881–98.

Leahy, Terry. 2007. "Tesco, Carbon and the Consumer." Speech to Joint Forum for the Future and Tesco Event, London, January 18. Accessed April 6, 2009. http://www.tesco.com/climatechange/speech.asp.

Leake, Jonathan. 2006. "It's a Sin to Fly, Says Church." *Sunday Times,* July 23, 1–2.

– 2007a. "Cameron to Offer Green Tax Cuts." *Sunday Times,* September 9, 1.

– 2007b. "Labour's 'Stealth' Road Schemes." *Sunday Times,* April 8, 5.

– 2008. "The Fool's Gold of Carbon Trading." *Sunday Times,* November 30, 8.

Lean, Geoffrey. 2007. "Murdoch: I'm Proud to Be Green." *Independent,* May
13. Accessed May 15, 2007. http://www.independent.co.uk/environ
ment/murdoch-im-proud-to-be-green-448652.html.

Leeder, Jessica. 2011. "Something to Chew on: A Party-by-Party Breakdown
of Food Policy." *Globe and Mail,* April 10, A3.

Lefebvre, Ben, and Ben Kesling. 2013. "Dustup Grows over Refinery
Byproduct." *Wall Street Journal,* November 26. Accessed December 1,
2013. http://online.wsj.com/news/articles/SB100014240527023042
8100457922082772971704

Leger Marketing. 2008. "Albertans Divided on Public Auto Insurance Issue."
Press Release, February 27. Montreal: Leger Marketing. Accessed
November 17, 2008. http://www.legermarketing.com/documents/POL
/080227ENG.pdf.

Leggett, Jeremy. 2001. *Carbon War: Global Warming and the End of the Oil Era.*
New York: Routledge.

Levant, Ezra. 2010. *Ethical Oil: The Case for Canada's Oil Sands.* Toronto:
McClelland & Stewart.

Lewenza, Ken. 2010. "After the Meltdown: What Comes Next?" Toronto:
Canadian Auto Workers. Accessed September 26, 2011. http://www
.caw.ca/assets/pdf/After_the_Meltdown_Ken_Lewenza_Feb_24_2010
.pdf.

Lewis, Paul, and Rob Evans. 2011. "Tricked, Betrayed, Violated: Did Police
Spy Use Sex to Win Activists' Trust?" *Guardian* (Environment Blog),
January 11, 6.

LFP. 2011. "About LFP." Toronto: Local Food Plus. Accessed May 24, 2011.
http://localfoodplus.ca/about.

Li, Minqi. 2008. "Climate Change, Limits to Growth, and the Imperative
for Socialism." *Monthly Review* 60(3):51–67.

Li, Ye, Eric J. Johnson, and Lisa Zaval. 2011. "Local Warming: Daily Temperature Change Influences Belief in Global Warming." *Psychological
Science* 22(4):454–9.

Liberal Democrats. 2007. *Zero Carbon Britain: Taking a Global Lead.* London:
Liberal Democrats.

Liberal Party. 2008a. "NDP Threatens to 'Shut down Tar Sands.'" Media
Release, September 26. Ottawa: Liberal Party of Canada. Accessed November 5, 2008. http://www.liberal.ca/story_14953_e.aspx.

– 2008b. *The Green Shift: Building a Canadian Economy for the 21st Century.*
Ottawa: Liberal Party of Canada.

– 2010. "Michael Ignatieff Commits to Canada's First National Food
Policy." Press Release, April 26. Accessed April 26, 2010. http://www
.liberal.ca/en/newsroom/media-releases/18007_michael-ignatieff-
commits-to-canadas-first-national-food-policy.

– 2011. *Your Family. Your Future. Your Canada.* Ottawa: Liberal Party.

Libin, Kevin. 2009. "Carbon Report's Bloody Portent." *National Post,* October 30, A1.

Liepens, Larissa. 2006. "Fort McMurray Votes to Put Brakes on Oil Sands." *Globe and Mail,* June 14. Accessed November 7, 2008. http://www.theglobeandmail.com/servlet/story/RTGAM.20060614.woilsandso614/BNStory/National/home.

Lin, J. 2008. "Trends in Employment and Wages, 2002 to 2007." *Canadian Economic Observer* (October). Accessed November 5, 2008. http://www.statcan.ca/english/freepub/11-010-XIB/01008/feature.htm.

Lindsey Colborne Associates. 2007. *UK Energy Performance Commitment, Voluntary Benchmarking and Reporting & Other Options. Stakeholder Workshops January 2007: London, Edinburgh, Belfast, Cardiff, Manchester. Summary Report of Key Findings.* London: Department of Environment, Food, and Rural Affairs.

Lister, Kevin. 2013. "Response to Discussion Paper 01: Aviation Demand Forecasting." Cirencester, UK: Cirencester People and Plane Stupid. Accessed November 22, 2013.

Livingstone, Ken. 2007. Speech to Guardian Climate Change Summit, June 11, London.

Lockwood, Matthew. 2013. "The Political Sustainability of Climate Policy: The Case of the UK Climate Change Act." *Global Environmental Change* 23(5):1339–48.

Lohmann, Larry. 2006. "Carbon Trading: A Critical Conversation on Climate Change, Privatization, and Power." Development Dialogue No. 48. Uppsala, Sweden: Dag Hammarskjöld Foundation.

Lomborg, Bjørn. 2001. *The Skeptical Environmentalist: Measuring the Real State of the World.* Cambridge, UK: Cambridge University Press.

– 2007. *Cool It: The Skeptical Environmentalist's Guide to Global Warming.* New York: Knopf.

– 2008a. "The Green Inquisition." *Guardian,* July 14. Accessed March 19, 2009. http://www.guardian.co.uk/commentisfree/2008/jul/14/climatechange.

– 2008b. "Warming Warnings Get Overheated." *Guardian,* August 15. Accessed March 19, 2009. http://www.guardian.co.uk/commentisfree/2008/aug/15/carbonemissions.climatechange.

– 2010. *Smart Solutions to Climate Change: Comparing Costs and Benefits.* Cambridge, UK: Cambridge University Press.

London Borough of Richmond Upon Thames. 2007. "Council Launches CO_2 Parking Charges." Press Release, April 2. Accessed April 11, 2008. http://www.richmond.gov.uk/press_office/press_releases/march_2007_press_releases/council_launches_co2_parking_charges.htm?viewmode=pr.

London on Tap. 2008. "Thames Water and Mayor of London Launch New Campaign to Promote Tap Water in London's Restaurants, Cafes and Pubs." Press Release, February 19. London: London on Tap. Accessed March 31, 2008. http://www.londonontap.org/press.php.

London Rising Tide. 2007. "Three Go Digging for the Heart of the Carbon Neutral Con on 21.2.07." London: London Rising Tide. Accessed April 17, 2008. http://www.londonrisingtide.org.uk/node/69.

Lord Justice Carnwath. 2010. "London Borough of Hillingdon & Ors, R (on the Application Of) v Secretary of State for Transport & Anor [2010] EWHC 626 (Admin) (26 March 2010)." London: Royal Courts of Justice. March 26. Accessed May 1, 2011. http://www.bailii.org/ew/cases/EWHC/Admin/2010/626.html.

Lougheed, Peter. 2006. "Sounding an Alarm for Alberta" (Interview). *Policy Options* (September): 5–9.

Lovelock, James. 2008. "Medicine for a Feverish Planet: Kill or Cure?" *Guardian*, September 1. Accessed September 3, 2008. http://www.guardian.co.uk/environment/2008/sep/01/climatechange.scienceofclimatechange.

Lovins, Amory. 1976. "Energy Strategy: The Road Not Taken?" *Foreign Affairs* 55(1):65–96.

Lovins, L. Hunter, and Boyd Cohen. 2011. *Climate Capitalism: Capitalism in the Age of Climate Change.* New York: Hill and Wang.

LowCVP. 2008. "Mission, Aims and Objectives." London: Low Carbon Vehicles Partnership. Accessed April 14, 2008. http://www.lowcvp.org.uk/about-lowcvp/mission-and-objectives.asp.

– 2009. "Background to the Fuel Economy Label." London: Low Carbon Vehicle Partnership. Accessed November 14, 2012. http://www.lowcvp.org.uk/fuel-economy/label-background.asp.

Löwy, Michael. 2007a. "Eco-Socialism and Democratic Planning." In *Socialist Register 2007: Coming to Terms With Nature*, 43:294–309. Halifax, NS: Fernwood Publishing.

– 2007b. "Ecosocialism: The Alternative to Capitalist Environmental Crisis." Address to Marxism 2007: A Festival of Resistance, July 6, London.

Lucas, Caroline. 2006. "Shrinking Economies in the Developed World." Speech to Event Hosted by Shrinking Economies in the Developed World, July 17, London. Accessed May 31, 2007. http://www.carolinelucasmep.org.uk/speeches/ShrinkingEconomies_170706.htm.

– 2007. "The Current Situation: Working with Central Government." Speech to Guardian Climate Change Summit, June 11, London. (Transcript of Remarks Provided by Caroline Lucas's Office).

– 2008. "The Real Deal?" In *Do Good Lives Have to Cost the Earth?*, edited by A. Simms and J. Smith, 223–30. London: Constable.

– 2012. "Heathrow Expansionists Must Drop Their Third Runway Obsession."
    Guardian, August 29. Accessed December 2, 2012. http://www.guardian
    .co.uk/environment/blog/2012/aug/29/heathrow-expansionists-third-
    runway.
Lucas, Louise, and Pilita Clark. 2012. "Tesco Steps Back on Carbon Foot-
    print Labelling." *Financial Times,* January 31, 4.
Lukacs, Martin. 2011. "Canada on Secret Oil Offensive: Documents." *The
    Dominion,* May 25. Accessed August 15, 2011. http://www.dominion
    paper.ca/articles/3991.
Lyle, Jenna. 2010. "Christian Leaders Welcome Cameron's Plans to Meas-
    ure Happiness." *Christian Today,* November 16. Accessed July 12, 2012.
    http://www.christiantoday.com/article/christian.leaders.welcome
    .camerons.plans.to.measure.happiness/27084.htm.
Lynas, Mark. 2006. "Why We Must Ration the Future." *New Statesman,*
    October 23. Accessed May 21, 2009. http://www.newstatesman.com/
    200610230015.
– 2007a. "Belching Chimneys instead of Solar Panels." *New Statesman,* May
    21, 20.
– 2007b. "How Economic Growth Can Destroy." *New Statesman,* January
    15. Accessed February 17, 2008. http://www.newstatesman.com/
    environment/2007/01/economic-growth-lynas-airport.
– 2007c. *Six Degrees: Our Future on a Hotter Planet.* London: Fourth Estate.
– 2008a. "How the Rich Starved the World." *New Statesman,* April 17, 24.
– 2008b. "If the Cap Fits, Share It." *New Statesman,* January 31. Accessed
    May 29, 2009. http://www.newstatesman.com/environment/2008/01
    /carbon-cap-lynas-share-price.
– 2011. *The God Species.* London: Fourth Estate.
Macalister, Terry. 2007. "Record Profit and Green Raspberry from Ryanair."
    Guardian, November 6, 28.
– 2008. "Undercut and under Fire: UK Biofuel Feels Heat from All Sides."
    Guardian, April 1, 28.
Macdonald, Douglas. 2007. *Business and Environmental Politics in Canada.*
    Peterborough, ON: Broadview Press.
– 2008. "Explaining the Failure of Canadian Climate Change Policy." In
    Turning Down the Heat: The Politics of Climate Policy in Affluent Countries,
    edited by H. Compston and I. Bailey, 223–40. New York: Palgrave
    Macmillan.
Macdonald, Douglas, and Debora VanNijnatten. 2005. "Sustainable
    Development and Kyoto Implementation in Canada: The Road Not
    Taken." *Policy Options* July-August (July):13–19.
Mackenzie, Hugh, Hans Messinger, and Rick Smith. 2008. *Size Matters: Can-
    ada's Ecological Footprint, By Income.* Ottawa: Canadian Centre for Policy
    Alternatives.

MacMillan, Tom. 2009. "What's Wrong with Waste?" *Food Ethics* 4(3):3.

MacMillan, Tom, and Rachael Durant. 2009. "Livestock Consumption and Climate Change: A Framework for Dialogue." Brighton/Godalming: Food Ethics Council and WWF-UK. Accessed November 20, 2012. http://assets.wwf.org.uk/downloads/fec_report_.pdf.

Madden, Peter. 2006. "Brit's Eye View: Britain's Conservatives Challenge Labour for Mantle of Greenest Party." *Grist*, September 29. Accessed May 11, 2008. http://gristmill.grist.org/story/2006/9/29/105338/543.

Magdoff, Fred. 2008. "The Political Economy and Ecology of Biofuels." *Monthly Review* 60(3):34–50.

MAH. 2007. "Make Affluence History." Toronto: Make Affluence History. Accessed November 8, 2007. http://www.globalaware.net/affluence/affluence.html.

Majendie, Paul. 2007. "Queen Seeks to Cut Carbon Footprint." *Reuters*, April 3. Accessed September 16, 2008. http://uk.reuters.com/article/reutersEdge/idUKNOA34774820070403.

Makin, Kirk. 2007. "High-Stakes Battle Looms over Oil-Sands Pollution." *Globe and Mail*, August 15, A1.

Makower, Joel. 2007. "London Goes Carbon Crazy." *Two Steps Forward.* Accessed April 12, 2009. http://makower.typepad.com/joel_makower/2007/06/london_goes_car.html.

Malmo, Dan. 2008. "Tory Aviation Policy 'All over the Place', Declares BA Chief." *Guardian*, October 2. Accessed May 8, 2009. http://www.guardian.co.uk/politics/2008/oct/02/transport.conservatives.

Manchester City Council. 2012. "Green Badge Parking: Pollute Less, Pay Less." Accessed November 14, 2012. http://www.manchester.gov.uk/info/500117/green_city/3835/green_badge_parking/1.

Mandelson, Peter. 2009. "Building a Successful Low Carbon Economy." Speech to Low Carbon Industrial Summit, London: Department of Business, Enterprise & Regulatory Reform, March 6. Accessed April 13, 2009. http://www.berr.gov.uk/aboutus/ministerialteam/Speeches/page50378.html.

Manno, Jack. 2002. "Commoditization: Consumption Efficiency and an Economy of Care and Connection." In *Confronting Consumption*, edited by T. Princen, M. Maniates, and K. Conca, 67–99. Cambridge, MA: MIT Press.

Marks, Nic. 2007. Presentation to What's an Economy For Anyway? Conference, Washington DC, October 6.

Marks, Nic, Andrew Simms, Sam Thompson, and Saamah Abdallah. 2006. *The Happy Planet Index.* London: New Economics Foundation.

Marr, Andrew. 2007. *A History of Modern Britain.* London: Macmillan.

Marsden, William. 2007. *Stupid to the Last Drop: How Alberta Is Bringing Environmental Armageddon to Canada.* Toronto: Knopf Canada.

Marshall, Dale. 2006. "The Gap Between Rhetoric and Action: Canada's Climate Change Plan." *Canadian Dimension,* January. Accessed September 4, 2006. http://canadiandimension.com/articles/2006/01/01/288/.

Marshall, George. 2007a. Address to International Climate Change Conference, London School of Economics, London, May 12.

– 2007b. *Carbon Detox.* London: Gaia Books.

Marshall, Rosalie. 2008. "UK Firms Ill-Prepared for Cap-and-Trade." *Business Green,* July 30. Accessed March 27, 2009. http://www.businessgreen.com/business-green/news/2222806/uk-firms-ill-prepared-cap-trade.

Martin, Mike. 2002. "Unions Urge Ratification of Kyoto." *Straight Goods,* December 6. Accessed August 9, 2009. http://www.straightgoods.ca/ViewFeature.cfm?REF=776.

Massey, Ray. 2008. "4×4 Sales down as Green Cars Soar 120%." *Daily Mail,* June 6, 31.

Mathiason, Nick. 2008. "Interview: Adair Turner – From Blue Chips to the Green Dream." *Observer,* February 3, 9.

Matthews, Colin, Len McClusky, et al. 2012. "Heathrow in Crisis: Letter in Full." *Telegraph,* March 3. Accessed December 1, 2012. http://www.telegraph.co.uk/finance/newsbysector/transport/9120943/Heathrow-in-crisis-letter-in-full.html.

Matthews, H. Damon. 2006. "Emissions Targets for CO_2 Stabilization as Modified by Carbon Cycle Feedbacks." *Tellus B* 58(5):591–602.

May, Elizabeth. 2006. "When Canada Led the Way: A Short History of Climate Change." *Policy Options* October: 49–53.

Mayor of London. 2007. *Action Today to Protect Tomorrow: The Mayor's Climate Change Action Plan – Executive Summary.* London: Greater London Authority.

– 2010. *Delivering London's Energy Future: The Mayor's Draft Climate Change Mitigation and Energy Strategy.* London: Greater London Authority.

– 2011. *Securing London's Water Future: The Mayor's Water Strategy.* London: Mayor of London.

McAdam, Doug. 1996. "Political Opportunities: Conceptual Origins, Current Problems, Future Directions." In *Comparative Perspectives on Social Movements,* edited by D. McAdam, J.D. McCarthy, and M.N. Zald, 23–40. Cambridge, UK: Cambridge University Press.

McAnulla, Stuart. 2010. "Heirs to Blair's Third Way? David Cameron's Triangulating Conservatism." *British Politics* 5(3):286–314.

McCarthy, Michael. 2006. "So What Does the Stern Report Mean for the World?" *Independent,* October 31, 6.

– 2008. "'Free Lunch' That Could Cost the Earth." *Independent*, February 8, 24.

McCarthy, Shawn. 2008. "A Lobby Machine That Runs on Ethanol." *Globe and Mail*, May 30.

– 2011. "Oil Sands Emissions Rules Stalled, despite Vows to EU." *Globe and Mail*, March 22, B4.

McCarthy, Shawn, and Nathan Vanderklippe. 2013. "Alberta Cranks up Carbon Levy." *Globe and Mail*, April 1, A1.

McCright, Aaron M, and Riley E Dunlap. 2010. "Anti-Reflexivity: The American Conservative Movement's Success in Undermining Climate Science and Policy." *Theory, Culture, and Society* 27(2–3):100–33.

McCulloch, Matthew, Marlo Raynolds, and Rich Wong. 2006. *Carbon Neutral by 2020: A Leadership Opportunity in Canada's Oil Sands*. Drayton Valley, AB: Pembina Institute.

McCullum, Hugh. 2006. *Fuelling Fortress America: A Report on the Athabasca Tar Sands and U.S. Demands for Canada's Energy*. Ottawa/Edmonton: Canadian Centre for Policy Alternatives, Parkland Institute, and Polaris Institute.

McDonald, Lynn. 2007. "Social Change to Meet Climate Change." Presentation to Toronto Dollar Supper Club, November 12.

– 2008. "Social Change to Address Climate Change." Centre for Constitutional Studies, University of Alberta, Edmonton, February 7. Accessed October 23, 2008. http://www.justearth.net/publications/socialchange.html.

McDonough, William, and Michael Braungart. 2002. *Cradle to Cradle: Remaking the Way We Make Things*. New York: North Point Press.

McGrath, Matt. 2009. "Climate Scenarios 'Being Realised.'" BBC News, March 12. Accessed March 12, 2009. http://news.bbc.co.uk/2/hi/science/nature/7940532.stm.

McKibben, Bill. 2010. *Eaarth: Making a Life on a Tough New Planet*. Toronto: Knopf Canada.

McKie. 2008. "How the Myth of Food Miles Hurts the Planet." *Observer*, March 23, 30.

McLaren, Duncan. 2003. "Environmental Space, Equity and the Ecological Debt." In *Just Sustainabilities: Development in an Unequal World*, J. Agyeman, R.D. Bullard, and B. Evans, edited by J. Agyeman, R.D. Bullard, and B. Evans, 17–37. Cambridge, MA: MIT Press.

McMichael, Anthony J., John W. Powles, Colin D. Butler, and Ricardo Uauy. 2007. "Food, Livestock Production, Energy, Climate Change, and Health." *The Lancet* 370 (9594): 1253–1263.

McSmith, Andy, and Colin Brown. 2006. "Climate Change: US [*sic*] Economist's Grim Warning to Blair's Cabinet." *Independent*, October 27, 2.

Meacher, Michael. 2007. "Blitz Spirit Needed to Face Threat of Climate Change." *Guardian*, May 9, 8.

Meade, Geoff. 2011. "Conservative MEPs Defeat New Climate Change Targets." *Independent*, July 6, 22.

Meadowcroft, James. 2007. "Building the Environmental State." *Alternatives Journal* 33(1):11–17.

Meadows, Donella H., Dennis L. Meadows, Jørgen Randers, and William W. Behrens III. 1972. *Limits to Growth: A Report to the Club of Rome.* New York: Universe Books.

Mech, Michelle. 2011. *A Comprehensive Guide to the Alberta Oil Sands: Understanding the Environmental and Human Impacts, Export Implications, and Political, Economic, and Industry Influences.* Accessed August 17, 2011. http://greenparty.ca/files/attachments/a_comprehensive_guide_to_the_alberta_oil_sands_-_may_20111.pdf.

Mehr, Nathaniel. 2008. "Interview: John McDonnell MP Talks to London Progressive Journal." *London Progressive Journal*, January 11. Accessed May 1, 2011. http://londonprogressivejournal.com/article/8/interview-john-mcdonnell-mp-talks-to-london-progressive-journal.

Mercer, Chris. 2006. "Anchor Butter Attacked by Dairy Crest, NFU." *Dairy Reporter*, July 18. Accessed April 29, 2009. http://www.dairyreporter.com/Products/Anchor-butter-attacked-by-Dairy-Crest-NFU.

Merrick, Jane. 2007. "Now Tories Want Us to Pay for Parking at the Supermarket." *Daily Mail*, September 11. Accessed April 4, 2008. http://www.dailymail.co.uk/pages/live/articles/news/news.html?in_article_id=481113&in_page_id=1770.

Merrick, Jane, and Matt Chorley. 2012. "Heathrow: Tories' Secret Plot to Build Third Runway." *Independent*, March 25. Accessed December 1, 2012. http://www.independent.co.uk/news/uk/politics/heathrow-tories-secret-plot-to-build-third-runway-7584591.html.

Messem, Darran. 2012. "Why We Need Carbon Footprinting and Labelling." *Guardian*, February 7. Accessed June 22, 2012. http://www.guardian.co.uk/sustainable-business/carbon-footprinting-labelling-information-access.

Meyer, David S. 2004. "Protest and Political Opportunities." *Annual Review of Sociology* 30:125–45.

MGI. 2008. *The Carbon Productivity Challenge: Curbing Climate Change and Sustaining Economic Growth.* McKinsey & Company.

Michaelson, Juliet. 2010. "Cameron's Well-Being Index Could Help Transform Lives for the Better." London: New Economics Foundation. Accessed December 21, 2012. http://www.neweconomics.org/blog/2010/11/26/cameron%E2%80%99s-well-being-index-could-help-transform-lives-for-the-better.

Miliband, David. 2006a. "My Priorities for Defra." Letter to the Prime Minister, London: Department for Environment, Food and Rural Affairs, July 11. Accessed May 14, 2008. http://www.defra.gov.uk/corporate/ministers/pdf/milibandtopm-letter060711.pdf.

– 2006b. "Red-Green Renewal." Lecture in Fabian Society's 'Next Decade' Series, London: Fabian Society, December 14. Accessed September 29, 2008. http://www.fabians.org.uk/events/speeches/red-green-renewal-the-future-of-new-labour.

– 2006c. "The Great Stink: Towards an Environmental Contract." Speech at the Audit Commission Annual Lecture, London: Department for Environment, Food and Rural Affairs, July 19. Accessed September 29, 2008. http://www.defra.gov.uk/corporate/ministers/speeches/david-miliband/dmo60719.htm.

– 2007a. "Get Ready to Be a Carbon Trader." *Sunday Times*, March 11. Accessed March 29, 2009. http://www.timesonline.co.uk/tol/comment/columnists/guest_contributors/article1496877.ece.

– 2007b. "One-Planet Security." Speech to the WWF One Planet Living Summit, London, March 27. Accessed March 22, 2008. http://www.defra.gov.uk/corporate/ministers/speeches/david-miliband/dmo70327.htm.

– 2007c. "Towards a One-Planet Economy." Speech to the 'On Target? Environment Policy and the Climate Change Bill' Conference Hosted by the Trades Union Congress, London, June 4.

Miliband, Ed. 2008a. Speech to the Environment Agency, London: Department of Energy and Climate Change. Accessed May 11, 2009. http://nds.coi.gov.uk/content/Detail.asp?ReleaseID=385391&NewsAreaID=2.

– 2008b. Speech to the CBI, London: Department of Energy and Climate Change, December 2. Accessed February 5, 2009. http://www.decc.gov.uk/pdfs/miliband-speech-cbi-021208.pdf.

Miller, David. 2007. "Climate Change and the City of Toronto: Facts – Challenges – Solutions." Speech to 'Open the Green Door to Facts, Challenges, Solutions' Event Organized by the Life Institute. Toronto, October 14.

Miller, Gord. 2013. Remarks by Gord Miller, Environmental Commissioner of Ontario, Upon Release of "Building Momentum: Results – Annual Energy Conservation Progress Report, 2012 (Volume Two)." Accessed December 14, 2013. http://www.eco.on.ca/uploads/Reports-Energy-Conservation/2013v2/Remarks.pdf.

Mills, Julianne H., and Thomas A. Waite. 2009. "Economic Prosperity, Biodiversity Conservation, and the Environmental Kuznets Curve." *Ecological Economics* 68(7):2087–95.

Millward, David. 2010a. "Labour's War on Motorists Is Over, Says Minister." *Telegraph*, May 14, 7.

– 2010b. "Number of Cars Declines for the First Time since Second World War." *Telegraph*, April 7. Accessed November 15, 2012. http://www.telegraph.co.uk/motoring/news/7563297/Number-of-cars-declines-for-the-first-time-since-Second-World-War.html.

Milmo, Cahal. 2007. "The Biggest Environmental Crime in History." *Independent*, December 10. Accessed December 11, 2007. http://www.independent.co.uk/environment/the-biggest-environmental-crime-in-history-764102.html.

Milmo, Dan. 2006. "O'Leary Pooh-Poohs Green Tax Idea." *Guardian*, November 2, 26.

– 2007. "EasyJet Slams 'Snake Oil Sellers' in Offset Market and Goes It Alone." *Guardian*, April 30. Accessed April 30, 2007. http://www.guardian.co.uk/environment/2007/apr/30/frontpagenews.the airlineindustry.

– 2009a. "Plane to Train: The Ultra-Fast Route to a Travel Revolution." *Guardian*, August 5, 10.

– 2009b. "Tories under Pressure to Rethink Airport Expansion Policy." *Observer*, December 13, 2.

– 2010. "Gatwick Chairman Blasts Airport Expansion Ban." *Guardian*, December 3, 43.

Mitchell, Donald. 2008. "A Note on Rising Food Prices." April 8. Washington, DC: World Bank (Internal Report). Accessed July 10, 2008. http://image.guardian.co.uk/sys-files/Environment/documents/2008/07/10/Biofuels.PDF.

MKJA. 2009. "Exploration of Two Canadian Greenhouse Gas Emissions Targets: 25% below 1990 and 20% below 2006 Levels by 2020". Vancouver: M.K. Jaccard and Associates Inc.

Mol, Arthur P. J. 1995. *The Refinement of Production: Ecological Modernization Theory and the Chemical Industry*. Utrecht, The Netherlands: Van Arkel.

– 2003. *Globalization and Environmental Reform: The Ecological Modernization of the Global Economy*. Cambridge, MA: MIT Press.

– 2011. "Ecological Modernization as a Social Theory of Environmental Reform." In *The International Handbook of Environmental Sociology*, edited by M. Redclift and G. Woodgate, 63–76. London: Edward Elgar.

Mol, Arthur P. J., and Martin Jänicke. 2009. "The Origins and Theoretical Foundations of Ecological Modernisation Theory." In *The Ecological Modernisation Reader: Environmental Reform in Theory and Practice*, edited by A.P.J. Mol, D.A. Sonnefeld, and G. Spaargaren. London: Routledge.

Mol, Arthur P. J., David A. Sonnenfeld, and Gert Spaargaren. 2009. *The Ecological Modernisation Reader: Environmental Reform in Theory and Practice*. London: Routledge.

Monastersky, Richard. 2013. "Global Carbon Dioxide Levels Near Worrisome Milestone." *Nature* 497(7447):13–14.

Monbiot, George. 2005a. "It Would Seem That I Was Wrong about Big Business." *Guardian*, September 20, 27.

– 2005b. "The Struggle Against Ourselves." Speech to Climate March, December 3, London. Accessed May 24, 2007. http://www.monbiot .com/archives/2005/12/05/the-struggle-against-ourselves/.

– 2006a. "For the Sake of the World's Poor, We Must Keep the Wealthy at Home." *Guardian*, February 28, 27.

– 2006b. *Heat: How to Stop the Planet From Burning*. Toronto: Doubleday Canada.

– 2007a. "How Can We Win the Race against Climate Catastrophe?" Address to Public Meeting. Friends Meeting House, London, November 8. Accessed November 20, 2007. http://www.youtube.com/ view_play_list?p=E20B7F6B5E814E7D.

– 2007b. "In This Age of Diamond Saucepans, Only a Recession Makes Sense." *Guardian*, October 9, 31.

– 2007c. "The Western Appetite for Biofuels Is Causing Starvation in the Poor World." *Guardian*, November 6, 33.

– 2007d. "This Crisis Demands a Reappraisal of Who We Are and What Progress Means." *Guardian*, December 4, 29.

– 2008a. "Apart from Used Chip Fat, There Is No Such Thing as a Sustainable Biofuel." *Guardian*, February 12, 27.

– 2008b. "This Economic Panic Is Pushing the Planet Right Back down the Agenda." *Guardian*, July 1, 29.

– 2009a. "Government Insists on Business as Usual despite Heavy Losses at BA." *Guardian*, May 22. Accessed May 2, 2011. http://www.guardian .co.uk/environment/georgemonbiot/2009/may/22/ba-heathrow-airlines-recession.

– 2009b. "This Is Bigger than Climate Change. It Is a Battle to Redefine Humanity." *Guardian*, December 15, 33.

– 2009c. "Tories Make the Right Noises about the Environment but Are Lacking in Detail." *Guardian*, April 17. Accessed May 7, 2009. http:// www.guardian.co.uk/environment/georgemonbiot/2009/apr/17/ george-monbiot-conservative-energy-plans.

– 2011. "This 'Greenest Government Ever' Is the Greatest Threat Yet to Our Environment." *Guardian*, May 9, 27.

– 2012. "The Case for Expanding UK Airports Is Based on Fallacy." *Guardian*, September 28. Accessed December 2, 2012. http://www.guardian.co .uk/environment/georgemonbiot/2012/sep/28/expanding-uk-airports-runways.

Montgomerie, Tim. 2007. "Too Much Materialism?" *ConservativeHome*,

September 13. Accessed March 16, 2008. http://conservativehome.
  blogs
  .com/torydiary/2007/09/too-much-materi.html.

Moody-Stuart, Mark. 2008. "Society Depends on More for Less." *BBC News*,
  February 4. Accessed April 12, 2008. http://news.bbc.co.uk/1/hi/sci/
  tech/7218002.stm.

Morris, Sophie. 2008. "The Great Carbon Con: Can Offsetting Really Help
  to Save the Planet?" *Independent*, April 3. Accessed April 17, 2008.
  http://www.independent.co.uk/environment/green-living/the-great-
  carbon-con-can-offsetting-really-help-to-save-the-planet-803933.html.

Mouvement québécois pour une décroissance conviviale. 2007. "Manifeste
  pour une décroissance conviviale." Montreal: Mouvement québécois
  pour un décroissance conviviale. Accessed December 7, 2008. http://
  www.decroissance.qc.ca/documents/manifeste.pdf.

Moyers, Bill. 2004. "Battlefield Earth." *Alternet*, December 8. Accessed December 15, 2004. http://www.alternet.org/story/20666/.

Munro, Margaret. 2008. "Environment Canada 'Muzzles' Scientists' Deal-
  ings with Media." *Ottawa Citizen*, February 1, A1.

Murphy, Joseph. 2000. "Ecological Modernisation." *Geoforum* 31(1):1–8.

Murphy, Rex. 2009. "So How Do You like Our Green World?" *Globe and
  Mail*, April 3, A19.

Murray, James. 2008. "BT Saves £238m with Video Conferencing." *Business
  Green*, January 15. Accessed May 9, 2009. http://www.businessgreen
  .com/business-green/news/2207288/bt-saves-238m-video.

Murray, Leo. 2009. "Rip up Aviation Policy and Start Again." *Guardian*,
  December 8. Accessed May 1, 2011. http://www.guardian.co.uk/
  commentisfree/cif-green/2009/dec/08/aviation-heathrow-runway-
  climate-change.

Naish, John. 2010. "Don't Ask Us How Happy We Are Mr Cameron ... It'll
  Only Make Us Feel Miserable." *Daily Mail*, November 16. Accessed July
  12, 2012. http://www.dailymail.co.uk/debate/article-1330059/David-
  Cameron-asking-happy-willl-make-feel-miserable.html.

Nanos, Nik. 2010. "Global Warming Most Important Issue For Canadians at
  G8 and G20 Summits." *Policy Options*, June, 22–5.

National Energy Policy Development Group. 2001. *National Energy Policy*.
  Washington, DC: White House. Accessed November 21, 2008. http://
  www.whitehouse.gov/energy/National-Energy-Policy.pdf.

National Statistics. 2008. "Environmental Taxes." London: National Statistics. Accessed February 27, 2009. http://www.statistics.gov.uk/cci/
  nugget.asp?id=152.

Nature. 2008. "Editorial: Science in Retreat." *Nature* 451:866.

Natwest. 2009. "Case Law – The Greenpeace Kingsnorth 6 Case." *NatWest
  Mentor*, February. Accessed June 30, 2012. http://www.natwestmentor
  .co.uk/news/articles/2009-02/greenpeacekingsnorth6case.aspx.

NCCP. 2000. *Canada's National Implementation Strategy on Climate Change.* Ottawa: National Climate Change Process.

NDP. 2008a. "NDP Challenges Conservatives to Deliver on the Environment." Ottawa: New Democratic Party. Accessed November 4, 2008. http://www.ndp.ca/page/4376.

– 2008b. "NDP Platform: The New Energy Economy: Cutting Pollution and Creating Jobs." Ottawa: New Democratic Party of Canada. Accessed November 5, 2008. http://www.ndp.ca/platform/environment/newenergyeconomy.

– 2011. *Giving Your Family a Break.* Ottawa: New Democratic Party.

Neale, Jonathan. 2007. "Stop Global Warming – Change the World!" Address to Marxism 2007: A Festival of Resistance, July 8, London.

NEB. 2013. *Canada's Energy Future 2013: Energy Supply and Demand Projections to 2035.* Ottawa: National Energy Board.

NEF. 2010. "Cameron's Well-Being Index Must Inform Policy, Says NEF." London: New Economics Foundation. Accessed July 13, 2012. http://www.neweconomics.org/press-releases/cameron%E2%80%99s-well-being-index-must-inform-policy-says-nef.

Nelsen, Arthur. 2012. "Tory MP Calls for Personal Carbon-Trading Scheme." *EurActiv,* July 6. Accessed July 11, 2012. http://www.euractiv.com/specialreport-prods-green-planet/pioneering-tory-mp-calls-persona-news-513659.

Nestlé. 2008. "Then There Will Be Nothing Left to Eat." English Translation of Interview with Nestlé Chief Peter Brabeck-Letmathe in Swiss Newspaper NZZ Am Sonntag, March. Vevey, Switzerland: Nestlé. Accessed April 24, 2008. http://www.nestle.com/MediaCenter/SpeechesAndStatements/AllSpeechesAndStatements/Then+there+will+be+nothing+left+to+eat.html.

New Scientist. 2008. "Why Our Economy Is Killing the Planet and What We Can Do about It." *New Scientist,* October 16, 40–1.

Newell, Peter, and Matthew Paterson. 1998. "A Climate for Business: Global Warming, the State and Capital." *Review of International Political Economy* 5(4):679–703.

– 2010. *Climate Capitalism.* Cambridge, UK: Cambridge University Press.

NFU. 2005. "The Renewable Transport Fuels Obligation – Introduction." Stoneleigh, Warwickshire: National Farmers' Union. Accessed April 25, 2008. http://www.nfuonline.com/x3510.xml.

– 2007. "New Local Food Finder Service for NFU Members." Media Release, October 9. Stoneleigh, Warwickshire: National Farmers' Union. Accessed April 5, 2008. http://farmingfutures.org.uk/x24307.xml.

NHC. 2012. "About Us." London: Natural Hydration Council. Accessed November 17, 2012. http://naturalhydrationcouncil.org.uk/about-us/.

NHS. 2009. *Saving Carbon, Improving Health: NHS Carbon Reduction Strategy for*

England. Fulbourn, Cambridge: National Health Service Sustainable Development Unit.

NHS SDU. 2011. *Quality Food for a Sustainable Healthcare Service.* Fulbourn, Cambridge: National Health Service Sustainable Development Unit.

Nickerson, Mike. 2008. "Sustainability – A Choice to Consider." Accessed January 14, 2009. http://www.sustainwellbeing.net.

– 2009. *Life, Money, and Illusion: Living on Earth as If We Want to Stay.* Second Edition. Lanark, ON / Gabriola Island, BC: Seven Generations Publishing / New Society Publishers.

Nikiforuk, Andrew. 2007. "Boom, Busts." *Canadian Business,* April 23. Accessed November 17, 2008. http://www.canadianbusiness.com/markets/commodities/article.jsp?content=20070423_85419_85419.

– 2008. *Tar Sands: Dirty Oil and the Future of a Continent.* Vancouver: Douglas & McIntyre.

No New Approvals for Tar Sands Development. 2008. "No New Approvals for Tar Sands Development." Accessed November 7, 2008. http://nonewoilsands.wordpress.com/some-of-our-signatories/.

Normille, Babz. 2009. "Heathrow Expansion Will Provide a Runway to Recovery for British Business." *ConservativeHome,* May. Accessed May 7, 2009. http://conservativehome.blogs.com/platform/2009/05/heathrow-expansion-will-provide-a-runway-to-recovery-for-british-business.html.

Nova Scotia. 2009. *Toward a Greener Future: Nova Scotia's 2009 Energy Strategy.* Halifax, NS: Nova Scotia Department of Energy.

– 2010. *Renewable Electricity Plan.* Halifax, NS: Department of Energy.

NRCan. 2012. "Fuel Quality Directive: Backgrounder." Ottawa: Natural Resources Canada. Accessed January 19, 2013. http://www.nrcan.gc.ca/media-room/news-release/2012/30a/6062.

NRTEE. 2006. *Advice on a Long-Term Strategy on Energy and Climate Change.* Ottawa: National Round Table on the Environment and the Economy.

– 2007. *Getting to 2050: Canada's Transition to a Low-Emission Future.* Ottawa: National Round Table on the Environment and the Economy.

– 2012. *Framing the Future: Embracing the Low-Carbon Economy.* Ottawa: National Round Table on the Environment and the Economy.

Nuffield Council on Bioethics. 2011. "Current Biofuels Policies Are Unethical, Says Report." Press Release, April 13. Accessed July 9, 2011. http://www.nuffieldbioethics.org/news/current-biofuels-policies-are-unethical-says-report.

O'Connor, James. 1994. "Is Sustainable Capitalism Possible?" In *Is Capitalism Sustainable?: Political Economy and the Politics of Ecology,* edited by M. O'Connor, 152–75. New York: Guilford.

O'Donnell, Gus. 2011. "Wellbeing Statistics: How Will Whitehall Respond?" November 2, All Party Parliamentary Group on Wellbeing Economics.

Portcullis House, London. Accessed July 10, 2012. http://soundcloud
.com/neweconomicsfoundation/sir-gus-odonnell-on-well-being.

O'Grady, Frances. 2007. Speech to the 'On Target? Environment Policy
and the Climate Change Bill' Conference Hosted by the Trades Union
Congress, London, June 4.

O'Hara, Bruce. 2005. "Why I'm Running for the Work Less Party." Vancouver: Work Less Party. Accessed January 25, 2009. http://www.work
lessparty.org/index.php?option=com_content&task=view&id=28&Ite
mid=54.

O'Neill, Brendan. 2008. "Plane Snobbery." *Guardian*, February 27. Accessed February 20, 2013. http://commentisfree.guardian.co.uk/
brendan_oneill/2008/02/plane_conservative.html.

– 2009. "'Low Carbon' Is Code for Low Ambitions." *spiked*, July 16. Accessed September 3, 2009. http://www.spiked-online.com/index.php/
site/article/7160/.

O'Neill, Juliet, and Sheldon Alberts. 2009. "Ignatieff Defends Canada's
'World Leader' Oil Sands." *National Post*, February 25. Accessed November 25, 2011. http://www.nationalpost.com/related/topics/Ignatie
ff+defends+Canada+world+leader+sands/1329069/story.html.

Obama, Barack. 2013. "Remarks by the President on Climate Change."
June 25. Washington: White House. Accessed November 28,
2013. http://www.whitehouse.gov/the-press-office/2013/06/25/
remarks-president-climate-change.

OCC. 2005. "Power Shortages Continue to Worry Business." Press Release,
August 12. Toronto: Ontario Chamber of Commerce. Accessed May
26, 2011. http://occ.on.ca/2005/08/power-shortages-continue-to-
worry-business/.

– 2007. "Energy & Environment Policies 2007–2008." Toronto: Ontario
Chamber of Commerce. Accessed February 1, 2009. http://occ.on.ca/
private/460.

Occupy Ottawa. 2011. "Finite Planet Cannot Have Infinite Growth." *Occupy
Ottawa*. Accessed December 14, 2012. http://www.occupyottawa.org/
forum-topic/finite-planet-cannot-have-infinite-growth.

OCI. 2013. *Petroleum Coke: The Coal Hiding in the Tar Sands*. Washington, DC:
Oil Change International.

Odone, Cristina. 2010. "David Cameron Has a Messianic Mission to Make
Britain Happy." *Telegraph*. Accessed July 12, 2012. http://blogs
.telegraph.co.uk/news/cristinaodone/100063815/david-cameron-has-
a-messianic-mission-to-make-britain-happy-will-he-boost-marriage-and-
dismantle-the-culture-of-victimhood/.

OECD. 2013. "Greenhouse Gas Emissions: Total GHG, T. per Capita." Paris:
Organisation for Economic Cooperation and Development. Accessed
December 19, 2013. http://stats.oecd.org/.

Office of the Premier of Ontario. 2007. "Jackets And Ties Optional This
    Summer For Ontario Government Employees." Toronto: Office of the
    Premier of Ontario. Accessed January 9, 2009. http://ogov.newswire
    .ca/ontario/GPOE/2007/06/07/c9963.html?lmatch=&lang=_e.html.
OMAFRA. 2008. "Local Groups Create Buzz For Local Food." Toronto:
    Ontario Ministry of Agriculture, Food, and Rural Affairs. Accessed
    January 7, 2009. http://www.omafra.gov.on.ca/english/infores/
    releases/2008/073008.htm.
– 2013. "Local Food." Ontario Ministry of Agriculture, Food and Rural
    Affairs. Accessed November 30, 2013. http://www.omafra.gov.on.ca/
    english/about/localfood.htm.
ONDP. 2011. "Stop Stalling on Local Food Procurement, Hampton Tells
    McGuinty." Press Release, February 9. Toronto: Ontario New Demo-
    cratic Party. Accessed May 27, 2011. http://ontariondp.com/en/
    stop-stalling-on-local-food-procurement-hampton-tells-mcguinty/.
Ontario. 2004. "Ontario Conserves." Toronto: Government of Ontario. Ac-
    cessed January 10, 2009. http://www.ontla.on.ca/library/repository
    /mon/9000/246177.pdf.
– 2009. "McGuinty Government's Plan Will Lead to Green Jobs and Green
    Energy." Press Release, May 14. Toronto: Ontario Ministry of Energy
    and Infrastructure. Accessed August 13, 2009. http://news.ontario.ca/
    mei/en/2009/05/ontario-legislature-passes-green-energy-act.html.
– 2010. Ontario's Long-Term Energy Plan. Toronto: Ontario Ministry of Energy.
– 2013. Conservation First: A Renewed Vision for Conservation in Ontario. To-
    ronto: Ministry of Energy.
Ontario Conservation Bureau. 2008. "What Is Conservation." Toronto: On-
    tario Conservation Bureau. Accessed January 10, 2009. http://www
    .conservationbureau.on.ca/Page.asp?PageID=1248&SiteNodeID=176
    &BL_ExpandID=143.
Ontario Green Energy Act Alliance. 2008. "Green Energy Act." Toronto:
    Ontario Green Energy Act Alliance. Accessed January 10, 2009.
    http://www.greenenergyact.ca/.
OPA. 2012. 2011 Conservation Results. Toronto: Ontario Power Authority.
Opinium. 2008. "How Green Are We?" London: Opinium Research LLP.
    Accessed March 11, 2009. http://www.opinium.co.uk/surveyreports/
    report_independentGreen.pdf.
OPS. 2011. "Dressing for Warmer Temperatures." OPS Weekly, May 18.
Ormsby, Avril. 2007. "Eat Less Meat to Save Planet: British Official." Reuters,
    May 30. Accessed April 4, 2008. http://www.reuters.com/article/
    scienceNews/idUSL3044053120070530.
Osborne, Alistair. 2008. "British Airways Warns Carbon Trading Will
    Cripple Europe's Airlines." Telegraph, May 24, 33.

Osborne, George. 2009. "The Treasury Should Lead the Fight against Climate Change." *Independent*, November 24, 26.

– 2011. "Conservative Party Conference 2011: George Osborne Speech in Full." *Telegraph*, October 3. Accessed June 7, 2012. http://www.telegraph.co.uk/news/politics/georgeosborne/8804027/Conservative-Party-Conference-2011-George-Osborne-speech-in-full.html.

Ottawa Action Organizing Crew. 2011. "Keystone XL: Time to Celebrate!" Accessed December 2, 2013. https://www.facebook.com/notes/bruce-borland/keystone-xl-time-to-celebrate-c%C3%A9l%C3%A9brons-ensemblefromthe-ottawa-action-organizing/10150400347698421.

Oxfam. 2007. "Biofuelling Poverty – EU Plans Could Be Disastrous for Poor People, Warns Oxfam." Press Release, November 1. Oxford: Oxfam. Accessed April 19, 2008. http://www.oxfam.org.uk/applications/blogs/pressoffice/2007/11/biofuelling_poverty_eu_plans_c.html.

Oxford. 2006. "Are the UK's Aviation and Climate Change Policies Impossible Bed-Fellows?" News Release, October 17. Oxford: Oxford University. Accessed May 19, 2008. http://www.eci.ox.ac.uk/research/energy/downloads/predictdecide-pressrelease.pdf

Oyuke, John. 2007. "Kenya: Flower Exporters Launch New UK Market Campaign." *The Standard* (Nairobi), July 11. Accessed April 30, 2009. http://allafrica.com/stories/200707101021.html.

Paehlke, Robert C. 2008. *Some Like It Cold: The Politics of Climate Change in Canada.* Toronto: Between the Lines.

Pagnamenta, Robin. 2009a. "Climate Chief Lord Stern: Give up Meat to Save the Planet." *Times*, October 27, 1.

– 2009b. "Floods and 40C – Britain's Climate of the Future." *Times*, June 19, 26–7.

Painter, James, and Teresa Ashe. 2012. "Cross-National Comparison of the Presence of Climate Scepticism in the Print Media in Six Countries, 2007–10." *Environmental Research Letters* 7(4):1–8.

Partington, P.J. 2013a. "How Carbon Pricing Currently Works in Alberta." Drayton Valley, AB: Pembina Institute. Accessed October 2, 2013. http://www.pembina.org/blog/708.

– 2013b. "Tales from the National Inventory: A Look at Canada's Latest Greenhouse Gas Emissions Report." Drayton Valley, AB: Pembina Institute. Accessed December 1, 2013. http://www.pembina.org/blog/712.

Partington, P.J., and Matthew Bramley. 2010. "Pembina Institute Comments on Canada's Proposed Passenger Automobile and Light Truck Greenhouse Gas Emission Regulations." Drayton Valley, AB: Pembina Institute. Accessed December 20, 2011. http://www.pembina.org/pub/2055.

Paterson, Matthew. 2001. "Climate Policy as Accumulation Strategy: The

Failure of cop6 and Emerging Trends in Climate Politics." *Global Environmental Politics* 10(2):10–17.

– 2005. "Insuring the Climate." *Alternatives Journal*, September, 21.

Paterson, Matthew, and John Barry. 2005. "Modernizing the British State: Ecological Contradictions in New Labour's Economic Strategy." In *The State and the Global Ecological Crisis*, edited by J. Barry and R. Eckersley, 53–74. Cambridge, MA: MIT Press.

Paterson, Matthew, and Johannes Stripple. 2010. "My Space: Governing Individuals' Carbon Emissions." *Environment and Planning D: Society and Space* 28(2):341–62.

Payne, Michael. 2007. "Project Oil Sands, Alberta's Experience with the Atomic Bomb." Edmonton: Innovation Alberta. Accessed November 20, 2008. http://www.innovationalberta.com/article.php?articleid=90.

PBL. 2010. *Assessing an IPCC Assessment: An Analysis of Statements on Projected Regional Impacts in the 2007 Report.* The Hague: Netherlands Environmental Assessment Agency.

PBS. 2012. "Robert Brulle: Inside the Climate Change 'Countermovement.'" *Frontline.* Accessed February 7, 2013. http://www.pbs.org/wgbh/pages/frontline/environment/climate-of-doubt/robert-brulle-inside-the-climate-change-countermovement/.

Pelletier, Nathan, and Peter Tyedmers. 2010. "Forecasting Potential Global Environmental Costs of Livestock Production 2000–2050." *Proceedings of the National Academy of Sciences* 107(43):18371–4.

Pembina Institute. 2004. "One Less Tonne." Drayton Valley, AB: Pembina Institute. Accessed January 29, 2009. http://www.onelesstonne.ca/home.cfm.

– 2005. "Energy Sector Employees Reduce Personal Greenhouse Gas Emissions." Drayton Valley, AB: Pembina Institute. Accessed December 30, 2008. http://climate.pembina.org/media-release/1144.

– 2007a. "Albertans' Perceptions of Oil Sands Development: Poll." Drayton Valley, AB: Pembina Institute. Accessed November 17, 2008. http://pubs.pembina.org/reports/Poll_Env_mediaBG_Final.pdf.

– 2007b. "Oil Sands Fever: Blueprint for Responsible Oil Sands Development." Drayton Valley, AB: Pembina Institute. Accessed December 1, 2007. http://pubs.pembina.org/reports/OS_Blueprint_FINAL_lc.pdf.

Pembina Institute and David Suzuki Foundation. 2008. *Deep Reductions, Strong Growth.* Drayton Valley, AB and Vancouver: Pembina Institute and David Suzuki Foundation.

– 2009. *Climate Leadership, Economic Prosperity.* Drayton Valley, AB and Vancouver: Pembina Institute and David Suzuki Foundation.

Perks, Gord. 2007a. Address to 'From Climate Crisis to Climate Justice' Teach-In. Toronto, Steelworkers Hall, November 17.

– 2007b. "Out of Afghanistan and Into Kyoto." Address to Public Meeting on 'Out of Afghanistan and Into Kyoto,' Toronto, Concord Cafe, April 30.

Peters, Glen P., Jan C. Minx, Christopher L. Weber, and Ottmar Eden-hofer. 2011. "Growth in Emission Transfers via International Trade from 1990 to 2008." *Proceedings of the National Academy of Sciences* 108(21):8903–8.

Pickard, Jim. 2012. "Renewables and Gas Likely to Fuel UK Future." *Financial Times*, December 9. Accessed January 19, 2013. http://www .ft.com/intl/cms/s/0/54e96f80-3fa4-11e2-b2ce-00144feabdc0.html #axzz2ISaTwA3b.

Pimentel, David, and Rattan Lal. 2007. "Letters: Biofuels and the Environ-ment." *Science* 317 (5840):897–8.

Plane Stupid. 2006. "Sermon on the Runway." Press Release, September 24. London: Plane Stupid. Accessed May 20, 2008. http://www .planestupid.com/?q=content/sermon-runway-24th-september-2006.

– 2007. "Climate Campaigners Mark 10 Years of Blair." Press Release, May 1. London: Plane Stupid. Accessed May 20, 2008. http://www .planestupid.com/?q=content/climate-campaigners-mark-10-years-blair-1st-may-2007.

– 2008. "Climate Campaigners Hang 'NO 3rd RUNWAY' Banner before PMQs." Press Release, February 27. London: Plane Stupid. Ac-cessed May 20, 2008. http://www.planestupid.com/?q=content/plane-stupid-scales-parliament-27th-february-2008.

– 2009. "CCC Hides Killing Blow behind Polite Veneer." *Plane Stupid* (Ri-chard's Blog). Accessed May 1, 2011. http://www.planestupid.com/blogs/2009/12/8/ccc-hides-killing-blow-behind-polite-veneer.

Plant, Christopher, and Judith Plant. 1990. *Green Business: Hope or Hoax? Toward an Authentic Strategy for Restoring the Earth.* Gabriola Island, BC: New Society Publishers.

Platt, Reg, and Simon Retallack. 2009. *Consumer Power: How the Public Thinks Lower-Carbon Behaviour Could Be Made Mainstream.* London: Insti-tute for Public Policy Research.

Polymer Age. 2008. "Budget Pledge on Action against Plastic Bags." *Polymer Age*, March 12.

Porritt, Jonathon. 2007a. "Capitalism as If the World Matters." *Jonathon Porritt* (blog), October 22. Accessed March 13, 2008. http://www.jonathon porritt.com/pages/2007/10/capitalism_as_if_the_world_matters.html.

– 2007b. *Capitalism As If The World Matters.* Revised. London: Earthscan Publishers.

– 2007c. "Energy Now and for the Future." Speech to Guardian Climate Change Summit, June 11, London.

– 2009. "Prosperity Without Growth?" *Jonathon Porritt* (blog). Accessed May

13, 2009. http://www.jonathonporritt.com/pages/2009/03/prosperity
_without_growth.html.

Porsche. 2008. "Our Case: Why We Believe the Increased Charge Is Bad for
London." Porsche Cars Great Britain. Accessed April 11, 2008. http://
www.porschejudicialreview.co.uk/our_case.htm.

Porter, Douglas. 2012. "Canadian Dollar Renaissance: 10 Years After." *Focus*
(BMO Nesbitt Burns), March 2.

Post Carbon Toronto. 2008. "What We Must Do." Toronto: Post Carbon
Toronto. Accessed December 7, 2008. http://www.postcarbontoronto
.org/energy-descent/what-we-must-do/.

Potter, Mitch. 2007. "Heathrow Rally Hailed as Success." *Toronto Star*, August 21, 1.

Poulter, Sean. 2007. "The Secret Plans to Turn Us All Veggie." *Daily Mail*,
May 29, 20.

Poulter, Sean, and David Derbyshire. 2008. "Banish The Bags: The Mail
Launches a Campaign to Clean up the Country ... and the Planet."
Daily Mail, February 27, 2.

Prasad, Sunand. 2007. Address to Debate London Event, "How Can a
Boom Town Be Green?" June 24, London.

Pratt, Larry. 1976. *The Tar Sands: Syncrude and the Politics of Oil.* Edmonton:
Hurtig.

Pratt, Sheila. 2012. "Oilsands Must Be Balanced with Other Sectors, Mulcair Says in Visit to Edmonton." *Edmonton Journal*, September 23. Accessed January 1, 2013. http://www.edmontonjournal.com/business/
Oilsands+must+balanced+with+other+sectors+Mulcair+says/7285767/
story.html.

Prescott, Matthew. 2008. *A Persuasive Climate: Personal Trading and Changing
Lifestyles.* London: Royal Society for the Encouragement of Arts, Manufactures and Commerce.

Prigg, Mark. 2008. "Water on Tap at Every Restaurant." *Evening Standard*,
February 25, A8.

Prince of Wales Business and Environment Programme. 2006. *The Sustainable Economy Dialogue.* Cambridge, UK: University of Cambridge
Programme for Industry.

Princen, Thomas. 2005. *The Logic of Sufficiency.* Cambridge, MA: MIT Press.
– 2010. *Treading Softly: Paths to Ecological Order.* Cambridge, MA: MIT Press.

Princen, Thomas, Michael Maniates, and Ken Conca. 2002. *Confronting
Consumption.* Cambridge, MA: MIT Press.

Quality of Life Policy Group. 2007. *Blueprint for a Green Economy.* London:
Conservative Party.

Radio Canada. 2012. "Les Québécois ont réduit de moitié leur utilisation
de sacs en plastique." *Radio Canada*, July 24. Accessed July 29, 2012.

http://www.radio-canada.ca/nouvelles/societe/2012/07/23/001-reduction-sacs-quebec.shtml.

Rajotte, James. 2008. "Saving the Planet, without Killing Jobs." *Edmonton Journal,* August 30, A19.

Randall, David. 2009. "The Battle of the Bulbs: A Very British Conflict." *Independent,* January 11. Accessed January 11, 2009. http://www.independent.co.uk/environment/green-living/the-battle-of-the-bulbs-a-very-british-conflict-1299412.html.

Rankin, Jennifer. 2011. "Row over Green Status of Oil from Tar Sands." *European Voice,* February 3. Accessed August 14, 2011. http://www.europeanvoice.com/article/imported/row-over-green-status-of-oil-from-tar-sands/70112.aspx.

RBWM. 2010. "Third Runway 'Effectively Dead' after High Court Ruling." Accessed May 1, 2011. Royal Borough of Windsor and Maidenhead. Press Release, March 26. http://www.rbwm.gov.uk/web/news_26509_heathrow-High_court_ruling_third_runway.htm.

RCEP. 2000. *Energy – The Changing Climate: Summary of the Royal Commission on Environmental Pollution's Report.* London: Royal Commission on Environmental Pollution.

– 2002. *The Environmental Effects of Civil Aircraft in Flight.* London: Royal Commission on Environmental Pollution.

RCM. 2008. "Sorting through Plastic Grocery Bags." Winnipeg, MB: Resource Conservation Manitoba. Accessed January 2, 2009. http://www.resourceconservation.mb.ca/news/Policy/bags_jan08.html.

Read, Nicholas. 2008. "Climate Panel Has a Beef with Meat Lovers." *Victoria Times-Colonist,* November 2, B4.

Renewable Energy Association. 2008. "Biofuels – The Easy Way to Go Green." Press Release, April 16. London: Renewable Energy Association. Accessed April 24, 2008. http://www.r-e-a.net/article_default_view.fcm?articleid=3123.

Rennie, Steve. 2008. "Federal Climate Change Report Warns of Health Problems." *Globe and Mail,* July 24. Accessed July 24, 2008. http://www.theglobeandmail.com/news/national/federal-climate-change-report-warns-of-health-problems/article699303/.

Retallack, Simon. 2008. "Nicholas Stern May Be Underestimating the Cost of Climate Change." *Guardian,* June 28. Accessed June 27, 2008. http://www.guardian.co.uk/commentisfree/2008/jun/26/carbonemissions.scienceofclimatechange.

Reuters. 2007. "EU Backs U.S. Air Pact in New Era for Travellers." *Reuters,* March 22. Accessed February 27, 2009. http://www.reuters.com/article/tnBasicIndustries-SP/idUSL2210360420070323?sp=true.

Revell, Andrea. 2005. "Ecological Modernization in the UK: Rhetoric or Reality?" *European Environment* 15:344–61.

RHS. 2008. "RHS Chelsea Flower Show 2008." London: Royal Horticultural Society. Accessed March 12, 2009. http://www.rhs.org.uk/chelsea/2008/continuous-learning.asp.

Rice, James. 2007. "Ecological Unequal Exchange: Consumption, Equity, and Unsustainable Structural Relationships within the Global Economy." *International Journal of Comparative Sociology* 48(1):43–72.

Ridgway, Tim. 2011. "Brighton and Hove Binmen Get 'Meat-Free Monday' the Chop." *The Argus*, July 28. Accessed November 7, 2012. http://www.theargus.co.uk/news/9165595.Brighton_and_Hove_binmen_get___meat_free_Monday___the_chop/.

Righelato, Renton, and Dominick V. Spracklen. 2007. "Carbon Mitigation by Biofuels or by Saving and Restoring Forests?" *Science* 317(5840):902.

RMI. 2007. "Soft Energy Path." Snowmass, CO: Rocky Mountain Institute, Accessed January 23, 2007. http://www.rmi.org/sitepages/pid292.php.

RMWB. 2012. *Municipal Census 2012*. Fort McMurray, AB: Regional Municipality of Wood Buffalo.

Roberts, Simon, and Joshua Thumim. 2006. "A Rough Guide to Individual Carbon Trading: The Ideas, the Issues and the next Steps." London: Centre for Sustainable Energy / Department for Environment, Food and Rural Affairs.

Rockström, Johan, Will Steffen, Kevin Noone, Asa Persson, F. Stuart Chapin, Eric F. Lambin, Timothy M. Lenton. 2009. "A Safe Operating Space for Humanity." *Nature* 461(7263): 472–5.

Rosa, Eugene A., Richard York, and Thomas Dietz. 2004. "Tracking the Anthropogenic Drivers of Ecological Impacts." *Ambio: A Journal of the Human Environment* 33(8):509–12.

Rosenthal, Elisabeth. 2010. "Britain Curbing Airport Growth to Aid Climate." *New York Times*, July 1, A1.

Rossi, Andrea, and Yianna Lambrou. 2008. "Gender and Equity Issues in Liquid Biofuels Production: Minimizing the Risks to Maximize the Opportunities." Rome: Food and Agricultural Organization.

Rowberry, Ian. 2008. "No Real Miracles in Tar Sands (Letter)." *Globe and Mail*, February 7, A18.

Rowlatt, Justin. 2009. "The Politics of Tackling Climate Change." *BBC News* (Ethical Man Blog), April 29. Accessed May 11, 2009. http://www.bbc.co.uk/blogs/ethicalman/2009/04/tackling_climate_change_is_a.html.

Royal Society. 2008. "Royal Society Response to OFCOM Decision on 'The Great Global Warming Swindle.'" Press Release, July 21. London: Royal Society. Accessed March 19, 2009. http://royalsociety.org/news.asp?id=7901.

– 2012. *People and the Planet.* London: Royal Society.

Royal Society of Canada. 2010. *Environmental and Health Impacts of Canada's Oil Sands Industry.* Ottawa: Royal Society of Canada.

RSA. 2007. "The Economics of Climate Change." Transcript of Public Event, January 15. London: Royal Society for the Encouragement of Arts, Manufactures and Commerce.

RSA Carbon Limited. 2007. "Emissions Bounce Back." November 2. London: Royal Society for the Encouragement of Arts, Manufactures & Commerce. Accessed April 29, 2008. http://www.rsacarbonlimited.org/viewarticle.aspa?pageid=829.

Rubin, Jeff. 2012. *The End of Growth.* Toronto: Random House Canada.

Rubin, Jeff, and Benjamin Tal. 2007. "Does Energy Efficiency Save Energy?" *CIBC World Markets – StrategEcon,* November 27, 4–7.

Ruddock, Joan. 2007. "Speech by Joan Ruddock MP on Food Waste and Anaerobic Digestion to the ESA (Environmental Services Association) Conference, London." London: Department for Environment, Food, and Rural Affairs. Accessed April 2, 2008. http://www.defra.gov.uk/corporate/ministers/speeches/joan-ruddock/jr071016.htm.

Russell, Ben. 2008. "Ministers Keep Their Gas-Guzzling Cars despite CO_2 Targets." *Independent,* March 20, 14.

Sachs, Wolfgang. 2001. "Development Patterns in the North and Their Implications for Climate Change." *International Journal of Global Environmental Issues* 1(2):150–62.

– 2007. "Fair Futures: Resource Conflicts, Security and Global Justice." Book Launch and Conversation with Andrew Simms, NEF. Mary Ward Centre, London, June 25.

Sachs, Wolfgang, Reinhard Loske, and Manfred Linz. 1998. *Greening the North: A Post-Industrial Blueprint for Ecology and Equity.* London: Zed Books.

Sachs, Wolfgang, and Tilman Santarius. 2007. *Fair Future: Resource Conflicts, Security and Global Justice.* London: Zed Books.

Sadler, Richard. 2006. "Roads to Ruin." *Guardian,* December 13, 11.

Salleh, Ariel, ed. 2009. *Eco-Sufficiency & Global Justice: Women Write Political Ecology.* London: Pluto Press.

Sallot, Jeff. 2006. "Kyoto Plan No Good, Minister Argues." *Globe and Mail,* April 8, A5.

Santarius, Tilman. 2012. "Green Growth Unravelled: How Rebound Effects Baffle Sustainability Targets When the Economy Keeps Growing." Berlin: Heinrich Böll Foundation.

Saunders, Caroline M., Andrew Barber, and Greg Taylor. 2006. *Food Miles – Comparative Energy/Emissions Performance of New Zealand's Agriculture Industry.* AERU Research Report No. 285, July. Accessed April 6, 2008. http://www.lincoln.ac.nz/story_images/2328_RR285_s13389.pdf.

Saunders, Doug. 2008. "Getting Ready for a No-Growth Future." *Globe and Mail,* January 5, F3.

Sauven, John. 2007. "A Quality Report." *Guardian,* September 13. Accessed September 13, 2007. http://commentisfree.guardian.co.uk/john_sauven/2007/09/a_quality_report.html.

Scarborough, P., S. Allender, D. Clarke, K. Wickramasinghe, and M. Rayner. 2012. "Modelling the Health Impact of Environmentally Sustainable Dietary Scenarios in the UK." *European Journal of Clinical Nutrition* 66 (6):710–15.

Scherer, Glenn. 2003. "Religious Wrong: A Higher Power Informs the Republican Assault on the Environment." *E Magazine,* May. Accessed September 27, 2004. http://www.emagazine.com/view/?757.

Schmidt-Bleek, Friedrich. 2000. "Factor 10 Manifesto." Carnoules, France: The Factor Ten Institute. Accessed September 6, 2009. http://www.ima.kth.se/im/3c1395/pdf/Manifesto.pdf.

Schnaiberg, Allan. 1980. *Environment: From Surplus to Scarcity.* New York: Oxford University Press.

Schnaiberg, Allan, and Kenneth Alan Gould. 1994. *Environment and Society: The Enduring Conflict.* New York: St. Martin's Press.

Schnaiberg, Allan, David N Pellow, and Adam S Weinberg. 2002. "The Treadmill of Production and the Environmental State." In *The Environmental State Under Pressure,* edited by A.P.J. Mol and F.H. Buttel, 15–32. London: JAI.

Schofield, Kevin. 2013. "Get Rid of the Green Crap." *The Sun.* Accessed December 12, 2013. http://www.thesun.co.uk/sol/homepage/news/politics/5275026/David-Cameron-orders-aides-to-cut-green-taxes.html.

Schoof, Renee. 2008. "U.S. Taps Canada's Oil Sands — but at What Cost?" *McClatchy Newspapers,* October 12. Accessed November 16, 2008. http://www.mcclatchydc.com/226/story/53653.html.

Schor, Juliet B. 2001. "The Triple Imperative: Global Ecology, Poverty and Worktime Reduction." *Berkeley Journal of Sociology* 45:2–17.

– 2005. "Sustainable Consumption and Worktime Reduction." *Journal of Industrial Ecology* 9(1–2):37–50.

– 2010. *Plenitude: The New Economics of True Wealth.* New York: Penguin Press.

Schwarz, Mike. 2010. "Why Did Ratcliffe Defence Fail Where Kingsnorth Six Succeeded?" *Guardian,* December 16. Accessed June 30, 2012. http://www.guardian.co.uk/environment/cif-green/2010/dec/16/ratcliffe-trial.

Science Council of Canada. 1977. *Canada as a Conserver Society: Resource Uncertainties and the Need for New Technologies.* Ottawa: Supply and Services Canada.

Scoffield, Heather. 2013. "Pipeline Industry Pushed Environmental Changes Made in Omnibus Bill, Documents Show." *Globe and Mail*, February 20. Accessed November 30, 2013. http://www.theglobeandmail.com/news/politics/pipeline-industry-pushed-environmental-changes-made-in-omnibus-bill-documents-show/article8894850/.

Scott, Norval. 2008. "Oil Patch Split over Proposal for Partial Moratorium." *Globe and Mail*, February 25, A1.

Scottish Green Party. 2005. *People, Planet, Peace: Westminster Election Manifesto 2005*. Edinburgh: Scottish Green Party.

SDC. 2003. *Redefining Prosperity: Resource Productivity, Economic Growth and Sustainable Development*. London: Sustainable Development Commission.

– 2007. *Redefining Progress: Consultation*. London: Sustainable Development Commission.

– 2008. "Redefining Prosperity." London: Sustainable Development Commission. Accessed September 13, 2008. http://www.sd-commission.org.uk/pages/redefining_prosperity.html.

– 2009. *Setting the Table: Advice to Government on Priority Elements of Sustainable Diets*. London: Sustainable Development Commission.

Seager, Ashley. 2008. "Reasons to See Red over Green Energy." *Guardian*, February 18, 26.

Seager, Ashley, and Mark Milner. 2007. "Revealed: Cover-up Plan on Energy Target." *Guardian*, August 13, 1.

Searchinger, Timothy. 2011. "A Quick Fix to the Food Crisis." *Scientific American*, July, 14.

Searchinger, Timothy, Ralph Heimlich, R. A. Houghton, Fengxia Dong, Amani Elobeid, Jacinto Fabiosa, Simla Tokgoz, Dermot Hayes, and Tun-Hsiang Yu. 2008. "Use of U.S. Croplands for Biofuels Increases Greenhouse Gases Through Emissions from Land-Use Change." *Science* 319(5867):1238–40.

SERI (Sustainable Europe Research Institute), UNI-MERIT (United Nations University), and FFRC (Finland Futures Research Centre). 2006. *Environment and Innovation: New Environmental Concepts and Technologies and Their Implications for Shaping Future EU Environmental Policies*. IP/A/ENVI/ST/2005-84. Brussels: European Parliament.

Sewill, Brendon. 2009. *Airport Jobs: False Hopes, Cruel Hoax*. London: Aviation Environment Foundation.

Shah, Hetan, and Nic Marks. 2004. *A Well-Being Manifesto for a Flourishing Society*. London: New Economics Foundation.

Shah, Saeed. 2006. "Business Backs Stern but Warns of 'Penalising' Taxation Burden." *Independent*, October 31, 36.

Shankleman, Jessica. 2012. "Autumn Statement: Businesses Call for Clarity as CRC Avoids the Chop." *Business Green,* December 5. Accessed December 12, 2013. http://www.businessgreen.com/bg/news/2229860/autumn-statement-businesses-call-for-clarity-as-crc-avoids-the-chop.

Sharpe, Andrew, Jean-Francois Arsenault, Alexander Murray, and Sharon Qiao. 2008. "The Valuation of the Alberta Oil Sands." Ottawa: Centre for the Study of Living Standards. Accessed August 28, 2011. http://www.csls.ca/reports/csls2008-7.pdf.

Shi, Anqing. 2003. "The Impact of Population Pressure on Global Carbon Dioxide Emissions, 1975–1996: Evidence from Pooled Cross-Country Data." *Ecological Economics* 44 (1): 24–42.

Shields, Rachel. 2009. "Kitchen Bin War: Tackling the Food Waste Mountain." *Independent,* June 7. Accessed November 19, 2012. http://www.independent.co.uk/environment/green-living/kitchen-bin-war-tackling-the-food-waste-mountain-1698753.html.

Shrubsole, Guy, and Alex Randall. 2011. "The UK Must Own up to the Full Scale of Its Emissions Problem." *Guardian,* February 8. Accessed July 8, 2011. http://www.guardian.co.uk/environment/cif-green/2011/feb/08/uk-emissions-problem.

Shupac, Jodie. 2009. "Fort McMurray Passes Plastic Bag Ban." *National Post,* December 11. Accessed May 24, 2011. http://network.nationalpost.com/np/blogs/posted/archive/2009/12/11/paper-bag-ban.aspx.

Sibun, Jonathan. 2008. "Porsche Goes to Court over Congestion Charge." *Telegraph,* April 3, 5.

Siegle, Lucy. 2008. "It's Just Water, Right? Wrong. Bottled Water Is Set to Be the Latest Battleground in the Eco War." *Observer,* February 10, 30.

Sierra Club of Canada. 2007. *Stopping Global Warming: Towards a Low-Carbon Canada.* Ottawa: Sierra Club of Canada.

– 2011. "Sierra Club Prairie Chapter Statement on Keystone XL Pipeline." Edmonton: Sierra Club of Canada Prairie Chapter. Accessed September 26, 2011. http://www.sierraclub.ca/en/node/4568.

Simms, Andrew. 2005. *Ecological Debt: The Health of the Planet and the Wealth of Nations.* London: Pluto Press.

– 2007. "Beyond the Hype: Get Ecological." *Observer,* November 25, Green Business Guide, 7.

Simms, Andrew, Victoria Johnson, and Peter Chowla. 2010. *Growth Isn't Possible: Why We Need a New Economic Direction.* London: New Economics Foundation.

Simms, Andrew, and Joe Smith. 2008a. *Do Good Lives Have to Cost the Earth?* London: Constable.

– 2008b. "Introduction." In *Do Good Lives Have to Cost the Earth?,* A. Simms and J. Smith, edited by A. Simms and J. Smith, 1–23. London: Constable.

Simon, Julian. 1995. "The State of Humanity: Steadily Improving." *Cato*

Policy Report, September. Accessed January 5, 2004. http://www.cato
.org/pubs/policy_report/pr-so-js.html.

Simpson, Isobel J., Josette E. Marrero, Stuart Batterman, Simone Meinardi,
Barbara Barletta, and Donald R. Blake. 2013. "Air Quality in the Indus-
trial Heartland of Alberta, Canada and Potential Impacts on Human
Health." *Atmospheric Environment* 81:702–9.

Simpson, Jeffrey. 2007. "On the Cusp of a New Industrial Revolution – a
Green One." *Globe and Mail*, October 26, A25.

– 2008. "Alberta remains Canada's square peg on emissions." *Globe and
Mail*, March 22, A21.

Simpson, Jeffrey, Mark Jaccard, and Nic Rivers. 2007. *Hot Air: Meeting Canada's Climate Change Challenge*. Toronto: Douglas Gibson Books.

Smith, Alisa, and J.B. Mackinnon. 2007. *The 100-Mile Diet: A Year of Local
Eating*. Toronto: Random House Canada.

Smith, Cameron. 2008. "Heresy: The Upside of Low Growth." *Toronto Star*,
September 13, 8.

Smith, David. 2007. "Stop Shopping … or the Planet Will Go Pop." *Observer*,
April 8, 8.

Smith, David, and Lauren Thompson. 2005. "Beckham's Feats Too Big
for Good of Environment." *Observer*, June 25. Accessed June 27, 2005.
http://observer.guardian.co.uk/carbontrust/story/0,16099,1511913,00
.html.

Smith, Heather A. 2002. "Dollar Discourse: The Devaluation of Canada's
Natural Capital in Canada's Climate Change Policy." In *Canadian
Environmental Policy*, edited by D.L. VanNijnatten and R. Boardman.,
286–98. Second edition. Toronto: Oxford University Press.

Smith, James. 2007. "Acting Now to Manage Emissions." Remarks to
Guardian Climate Change Summit, June 11, London.

Smith, Lewis. 2008. "Bottled Water Industry Is Bordering on the Immoral,
Says Minister." *Times*, February 16, 33.

Smith, Richard A. 2007. "Ecosocialism or Collapse." *Climate and Capitalism*,
June 11. Accessed December 7, 2008. http://climateandcapitalism
.com/?p=115.

Smitherman, George. 2008. "Notes for Remarks by The Honourable
George Smitherman, Deputy Premier, Minister of Energy and Infrastructure." Speech to Canadian Club, Toronto, October 31. Toronto:
Ontario Ministry of Energy and Infrastructure. Accessed January 10,
2009. http://www.energy.gov.on.ca/index.cfm?fuseaction=about
.speeches&speech=31102008.

SMMT. 2007. "4×4 – the Facts." London: Society of Motor Manufacturers
and Traders. Accessed November 14, 2012. https://www.smmt.co.uk/
2007/01/4x4-the-facts/.

– 2012a. *Motor Industry Facts 2012*. London: Society of Motor Manufacturers and Traders.

– 2012b. *New Car co₂ Report 2012*. London: Society of Motor Manufacturers and Traders.

Snow, Nick. 2011. "IHS CERA: State Department's Keystone XL Delay Creates New Uncertainties." *Oil & Gas Journal*, November 11. Accessed November 22, 2011. http://www.ogj.com/articles/2011/11/ihs-cera-state-departments-keystone-xl-delay-creates-new-uncertainties.html.

Soil Association. 2011. "Royal Recognition for Excellence in Hospital Food across the UK." Bristol: Soil Association. Accessed November 12, 2012. http://www.soilassociation.org/news/newsstory/articleid/2887/royal-recognition-for-excellence-in-hospital-food-across-the-uk.

Sonnenfeld, David A. 1998. "From Brown to Green? Late Industrialization, Social Conflict, and Adoption of Environmental Technologies in Thailand's Pulp Industry." *Organization and Environment* 11(1):59–87.

– 2002. "Social Movements and Ecological Modernization: The Transformation of Pulp and Paper Manufacturing." *Development and Change* 33(1):1–27.

Sonnenfeld, David A., and Arthur P. J. Mol. 2006. "Environmental Reform in Asia: Comparisons, Challenges, Next Steps." *Journal of Environment and Development* 15(2):112–37.

Soron, Dennis. 2004. "The Cultural Politics of Kyoto: Lessons from the Canadian Semi-Periphery." *Capitalism, Nature, Socialism* 15(1):43–66.

Sorrell, Steven. 2010. "Energy, Economic Growth and Environmental Sustainability: Five Propositions." *Sustainability* 2(6):1784–1809.

Spelman, Caroline. 2010. Speech at the Angela Marmont Centre for Biodiversity, 20 May 2010. London: Department for Environment, Food and Rural Affairs. Accessed November 21, 2012. http://www.defra.gov.uk/news/2010/05/20/rt-hon-caroline-spelman-mp-speech-at-the-angela-marmont-centre-for-biodiversity-20-may-2010/.

Speth, James Gustave. 2012. "For Rio+20: A Charter for a New Economy." *Solutions*, June, 24–7.

St. Albert Gazette. 2008. "Premier Has Money Challenges." *St. Albert Gazette*, January 9, 18.

Stanford, Jim. 2002. "Two Roads to Kyoto: More or Less." *Policy Options* (December):53–6.

– 2008. *Economics for Everyone: A Short Guide to the Economics of Capitalism.* London: Pluto Press.

Starkey, Richard. 2012. "Personal Carbon Trading: A Critical Survey." *Ecological Economics* 73:7–28.

Statistics Canada. 2006. "Study: The Alberta Economic Juggernaut." *The Daily*, September 14. Accessed November 2, 2008. http://www.statcan.ca/Daily/English/060914/d060914c.htm.

– 2008. "Current Economic Conditions." *The Daily*, March 20. Accessed November 13, 2008. http://www.statcan.ca/Daily/English/080320/do80320e.htm.

Stehfest, Elke, Lex Bouwman, Detlef van Vuuren, Michel den Elzen, Bas Eickhout, and Pavel Kabat. 2009. "Climate Benefits of Changing Diet." *Climatic Change* 95(1):83–102.

Steinfeld, Henning, Pierre Gerber, Tom Wassenaar, Vincent Castel, Mauricio Rosales, and Cees de Haan. 2006. *Livestock's Long Shadow: Environmental Issues and Options*. Rome: Food and Agricultural Organization.

Stelmach, Ed. 2007a. "Rotary Club of Calgary Valentine's Luncheon Address." Calgary, February 13. Premier's Office. Accessed November 11, 2008. http://www.premier.alberta.ca/speeches/speeches-2007-feb-13-Calgary_Rotary.cfm.

– 2007b. "Speech to Economics Society of Calgary Luncheon Meeting." Calgary, February 22. Premier's Office. Accessed November 17, 2008. http://premier.alberta.ca/speeches/speeches-2007-feb-22-Economics_Society.cfm.

– 2008. "Speech to Canada-UK Chamber of Commerce." London, November 10. Alberta Government. Accessed November 11, 2008. http://premier.alberta.ca/speeches/speeches-2008-Nov-10-UK_Chamber_of_Commerce.cfm.

Stephenson, John. 2010. *Livestock and Climate Policy: Less Meat or Less Carbon?* Paris: Organisation for Economic Co-operation and Development.

Stern, David I. 2004. "The Rise and Fall of the Environmental Kuznets Curve." *World Development* 32(8):1419–39.

Stern, Nicholas. 2006. *Stern Review: The Economics of Climate Change*. London: HM Treasury.

– 2008. "Green Routes to Growth." *Guardian*, October 23.

– 2009. "Time for a Green Industrial Revolution." *New Scientist*, January 21. Accessed February 7, 2009. http://www.newscientist.com/article/mg20126926.600-comment-time-for-a-green-industrial-revolution.html.

– 2011. "The EU Risks Falling behind the Green Century." *Financial Times*, July 4. Accessed July 11, 2011. http://www.ft.com/intl/cms/s/0/9769ab72-a671-11e0-ae9c-00144feabdc0.html#axzz1RoofvDVo.

Stevenson, Betsey, and Justin Wolfers. 2008. "Economic Growth and Subjective Well-Being: Reassessing the Easterlin Paradox." *Brookings Papers on Economic Activity* 39(1):1–102.

Stevenson, Tom. 2007. "Happy Iceland Leaves Britain out in the Cold." *Telegraph*, July 16, 3.

Steward, Gillian. 2008. "Bust Takes Alberta by Surprise." *Toronto Star*, November 23, A21.

Stewart, Heather, and Larry Elliott. 2013. "Nicholas Stern: 'I Got It Wrong on Climate Change – It's Far, Far Worse'." *Observer*, January 26, 3.

Stewart, John. 2009. "Heathrow Campaigners – Heading for a Historic Victory?" *International Journal of Green Economics* 3(3/4):462–8.

– 2010. *Victory Against All The Odds: The Story of How the Campaign to Stop a Third Runway at Heathrow Was Won*. Twickenham, UK: HACAN.

Stocks-Moore, Laurie. 2008. "Villagers Demonstrate Their Energy-Saving Credentials." *Chester Chronicle*, September 26. Accessed March 14, 2009. http://www.chesterchronicle.co.uk/chester-news/local-chester-news/2008/09/26/villagers-demonstrate-their-energy-saving-credentials-59067-21902670/.

Straight Goods. 2011. "Bottled Water Bans Spread across Canada." *Straight Goods*, February 24. Accessed May 27, 2011. http://www.publicvalues.ca/ViewArticle.cfm?Ref=00885.

Strategic Counsel. 2008. "Views Towards Alberta Oil Sands Development." Toronto: Strategic Counsel. Accessed September 26, 2011. http://www.thestrategiccounsel.com/our_news/polls/Alberta%20and%20National%20Jan%2022-23%20Oil%20Sands%20Development.pdf.

Stratton, Allegra. 2010. "Happiness Index to Gauge Britain's National Mood." *Guardian*, November 15, 1.

Stuart, Tristram. 2009. "Perishing Possessions." *Food Ethics* 4(3):8–10.

Stueck, Wendy, and Shawn McCarthy. 2008. "B.C.'s 'Pioneering' Carbon Rules Worry Industry." *Globe and Mail*, April 4, A7.

STWR. 2007. "Open Letter to the G8 Ministers." Appearing in the *Guardian*, June 6, and the *Independent*, June 7. London: Share the World's Resources. Accessed June 10, 2007. http://www.stwr.net/content/view/1964/37/.

Sumburn, Paul. 2007. "Why I'm Sticking It out at Camp Heathrow." *Telegraph*, August 17, 27.

Sunday Times. 2009. "Be Bold, Not Foolhardy, over Heathrow's Runway." *Sunday Times*, December 11, 16.

SustainAbility and Globescan. 2011. *Sustainability Survey 2011: Survey on Sustainable Consumption*. Washington, DC and Toronto: SustainAbility and Globescan.

Sustainable Aviation. 2012. *CO_2 Road-Map*. London: Sustainable Aviation.

Suzuki, David. 2007. "Dialogue on Climate Change." Address to the Canadian Club of Toronto, February 9. Accessed June 25, 2008. http://www.vvc1.ca/client/canclub/02092007/.

Taber, Jane. 2011. "Tory Axe Hits 'Muscle and Bone' of Climate Science, Elizabeth May Says." *Globe and Mail*, June 22. Accessed January 20, 2012. http://www.theglobeandmail.com/news/politics/ottawa-notebook/tory-axe-hits-muscle-and-bone-of-climate-science-elizabeth-may-says/article2070874/.

Tapia Granados, José A., Edward L. Ionides, and Óscar Carpintero. 2012. "Climate Change and the World Economy: Short-Run Determinants of Atmospheric CO_2." *Environmental Science & Policy* 21:50–62.

Tarrow, Sidney. 1998. *Power in Movement: Social Movements and Contentious Politics.* Second edition. Cambridge, UK: Cambridge University Press.

Taylor, Amy. 2005. *The Alberta GPI Summary Report.* Drayton Valley, AB: Pembina Institute.

Telegraph. 2006. "BP to Back Carbon Offset Windfarm Schemes." *Telegraph,* August 26, 3.

– 2013. "Too Much Green Energy Is Bad for Britain." *Sunday Telegraph,* March 24, 33.

Tellus Institute. 2002. "The Bottom Line on Kyoto: Economic Benefits of Canadian Action." Vancouver and Toronto: David Suzuki Foundation and WWF-Canada. Accessed November 28, 2008. http://www.david suzuki.org/files/kyotoreport.pdf.

Tesco. 2008. "Sustainable Consumption Institute." Cheshunt, Hertfordshire: Tesco Plc. Accessed April 2, 2009. http://www.tescoplc.com/ plc/corporate_responsibility/caring_environment/climate_change/ working_with_others/sustainable_consumption_institut/.

– 2012. "New Packaging That Will Keep Fruit and Vegetables Fresher for Days Longer." Cheshunt, Hertfordshire: Tesco PLC. Accessed November 19, 2012. http://www.tescoplc.com/index.asp?pageid=17&newsid=600.

Tetley, Deborah. 2005. "Storm Clouds over Boomtown." *Saskatoon Star-Phoenix,* November 5. Accessed November 17, 2008. http://www .canada.com/saskatoon/starphoenix/news/story.html?id=55f4318f-68f7-4040-b1b2-3c546a58a5a3.

TfL. 2009. "Major Boost for Electric Vehicles." London: Transport for London. Accessed June 27, 2012. http://origin.tfl.gov.uk/corporate/ media/newscentre/metro/13870.aspx.

TGI. 2007. "Green Values: Consumers and Branding." London: TGI.

Thatcher, Margaret. 1988. Speech to the Royal Society. London, September 27. Accessed February 19, 2009. http://www.margaretthatcher .org/speeches/displaydocument.asp?docid=107346.

– 1989. Speech to United Nations General Assembly (Global Environment). New York, November 11. Accessed February 18, 2009. http://www .margaretthatcher.org/speeches/displaydocument.asp?docid=107817.

– 1993. *The Downing Street Years.* First. London: HarperCollins.

Thomas, Jennifer, and Joanne Evans. 2010. "There's More to Life than GDP but How Can We Measure It?" *Economic & Labour Market Review (Office for National Statistics)* 4 (9):29–36.

Thompson, Emma. 2009. "Strike a Blow to the Government's Insane Plans to Expand Heathrow." Letter to Greenpeace Supporters, January 23. Accessed May 2, 2011. http://www.greenpeace.org.uk/blog/climate/

emma-thompson-strike-blow-governments-insane-plans-expand-heathrow
-20090123.

Thompson, Sam, Saamah Abdallah, Nic Marks, Andrew Simms, and Victoria Johnson. 2007. *The European Happy Planet Index: An Index of Carbon Efficiency and Well-Being in the EU*. London: New Economics Foundation.

Thomson, Graham. 2013. "Redford Waving a Tattered Flag in D.C." *Edmonton Journal*, November 11, A17.

Thumim, Joshua, and Vicki White. 2008. "Distributional Impacts of Personal Carbon Trading." London: Department for Environment, Food and Rural Affairs.

Tibbetts, Janice. 2007. "Alta.-Ottawa Clash Inevitable." *Edmonton Journal*, August 15, A3.

Together. 2007. "Keep Your Mobile to Make a Change." London: Climate Group. Accessed March 28, 2009. http://www.together.com/solutions/17.

Tomorrow Today. 2008. *Tomorrow Today: How Canada Can Make a World of Difference*. Canadian Parks and Wilderness Society, David Suzuki Foundation, Ecojustice, Environmental Defence, Equiterre, Greenpeace Canada, Nature Canada, Pembina Institute, Pollution Probe, Sierra Club Canada and WWF-Canada.

Tooze, Adam, and Paul Warde. 2005. "A Long-Run Historical Perspective on the Prospects for Uncoupling Economic Growth and CO_2 Emissions." Submission to *Stern Review on the Economics of Climate Change*. London: HM Treasury. Accessed June 13, 2007. http://www.hm-treasury.gov.uk/media/2/1/climatechange_drjatooze_1.pdf.

Toronto. 2007. *Change Is in the Air: Climate Change, Clean Air and Sustainable Energy Action Plan: Moving From Framework to Action Phase 1*. Toronto: City of Toronto.

– 2012. *Report from the City Manager on Voluntary Contributions of Plastic Bag Fee Proceeds*. Toronto: City of Toronto.

Toronto Vegetarian Society. 2007. "Climate Change: The Inconvenient Truth about What We Eat." Toronto: Toronto Vegetarian Society. Accessed December 30, 2008. http://www.veg.ca/content/view/136/111/.

Torrie, Ralph D. 2006. "History, Hope and the Culture of Conservation in Ontario's Electricity System." Address to Workshop on Developing Sustainable Energy Policy, University of Western Ontario, London, ON, October 23–4. Accessed January 9, 2009. www.ivey.uwo.ca/Lawrence Centre/energy/Supplementary/Torrie.pdf.

Torrie, Ralph D., Tyler Bryant, Mitchell Beer, Blake Anderson, Dale Marshall, Ryan Kadowaki, and Johanne Whitmore. 2013. *An Inventory of Low-Carbon Energy for Canada*. Vancouver / Ottawa: David Suzuki Foundation / Canadian Academy of Engineering.

Tory Radio. 2007. "Supply Side Tax Cutters or Environmental Interventionists?" Accessed March 16, 2008. http://www.toryradio.com/2007/09/12/.

Toynbee, Polly. 2008. "Carbon Credits Tick All the Boxes. What's the Delay?" *Guardian*, August 16, 35.

– 2010. "An Unhappiness Index Is More David Cameron's Style." *Guardian*, November 16, 29.

TUC. 2007. "TUC Comment on Climate Change Bill." Press Release, March 13. London: Trades Union Congress. Accessed April 11, 2009. http://www.tuc.org.uk/economy/tuc-13068-fo.cfm.

– 2009. *Unlocking Green Enterprise: A Low-Carbon Strategy for the UK Economy.* London: Trades Union Congress.

Tuppen, Chris. 2007. "What's BT Doing about Climate Change?" Presentation by BT's Head of Sustainable Development and Corporate Accountability to Corporate Climate Response Conference. London, May 29.

Turner, Adair. 2008. "Dethroning Growth." In *Do Good Lives Have to Cost the Earth?*, edited by A. Simms and J. Smith, 91–7. London: Constable.

– 2012. *Economics After the Crisis: Objectives and Means.* Cambridge, MA: MIT Press.

Turner, Chris. 2013. *The War on Science: Muzzled Scientists and Wilful Blindness in Stephen Harper's Canada.* Vancouver: Greystone.

Turner, Graham M. 2008. "A Comparison of The Limits to Growth with 30 Years of Reality." *Global Environmental Change* 18(3):397–411.

Turner, Janice. 2008. "I'm Sick of Ken and His Offensive Emissions." *Times*, February 16, 21.

UKERC. 2007a. "'Rebound Effects' Threaten Success of UK Climate Policy." Press Release, November 1. Accessed November 4, 2007. http://www.ukerc.ac.uk/MediaCentre/UKERCPressReleases/Releases2007/0710 ReboundEffects.aspx.

– 2007b. *The Rebound Effect: An Assessment of the Evidence for Economy-Wide Energy Savings from Improved Energy Efficiency.* London: UK Energy Research Centre.

UKTI. 2008. *Market Opportunities in Environmental Goods and Services, Renewable Energy, Carbon Finance and CATs: Overview Report.* London: UK Trade & Investment.

Unander, Fridtjof. 2003. *From Oil Crisis to Climate Challenge: Understanding CO_2 Emission Trends in IEA Countries.* Paris: International Energy Agency/Organisation for Economic Co-operation and Development.

UNDP. 2007. *Human Development Report 2007/2008 – Fighting Climate Change: Human Solidarity in a Divided World.* New York: United Nations Development Programme.

UNEP. 2012. *Growing Greenhouse Gas Emissions Due to Meat Production.* Nairobi: United Nations Environment Programme.

Ungoed-Thomas, Jon. 2007. "British Prawns Go to China to Be Shelled."
    Sunday Times, May 20, 4.
– 2008. "Labour's Flying Club Lobbies for BAA." *Sunday Times,* March 16, 10.
Unison, TSSA, et al. 2008. "Scrap the Plans for Heathrow Expansion Now."
    Advertisement. *Times,* October 14. Accessed December 19, 2013.
    http://www.bettertransport.org.uk/system/files/08.10.14.aviation_
    advert.pdf.
Unite. 2007. "Unite's Reaction to the Expansion of Heathrow Consulta-
    tion." News Release, November 23. London: Unite. Accessed May 23,
    2008. http://http://www.unitetheunion.com/default.aspx?page=
    7544.
University of Nottingham. 2011. "University Car Parking Charges Ap-
    proved Scheme for 2011/2012." Nottingham: University of Notting-
    ham. Accessed November 13, 2012. http://www.nottingham.ac.uk/
    estates/documents/approvedcarparkingschemesummary.pdf.
Upham, Paul, and Mercedes Bleda. 2009. *Carbon Labelling: Public Perceptions
    of the Debate.* Manchester: Sustainable Consumption Institute, Univer-
    sity of Manchester.
Usborne, David. 2008. "The Rumble in the Tumble: Fight for the Right to
    Dry." *Independent,* April 23. Accessed January 10, 2009. http://www
    .independent.co.uk/environment/green-living/the-rumble-in-the-
    tumble-fight-for-the-right-to-dry-814069.html.
Van den Bergh, Jeroen C.J.M., and Giorgos Kallis. 2012. "Growth, A-
    Growth or Degrowth to Stay within Planetary Boundaries?" *Journal of
    Economic Issues* XLVI(4):909–19.
Van Loon, Jeremy, and Andrew Mayeda. 2013. "PM Wrong to Fight Carbon
    Tax, Industry Says; Oil Companies See Advantages in Greenhouse-Gas
    Levy." *Edmonton Journal,* February 1, C13.
Vancouver. 2009. *Vancouver 2020 A Bright Green Future: An Action Plan for
    Becoming the World's Greenest City by 2020.* Vancouver: Greenest City Ac-
    tion Team.
Vancouver Humane Society. 2008. "Support VHS's Eat Less Meat Project."
    Vancouver: Vancouver Humane Society. Accessed January 2, 2009.
    http://www.vancouverhumanesociety.bc.ca/eatlessmeat.
Vanderklippe, Nathan and Carrie Tait. 2012. "Third Oil Spill Fuels Calls
    for Alberta Pipeline Review." *Globe and Mail,* June 19, 6.
VanNijnatten, Debora. 2004. "Same Old, Same Old – The Environment As
    Science and Technology Strategy." *Policy Options* April: 38–41.
Vaughan, Scott, Kimberly Leach, and James Reinhart. 2013. "Canada's
    Climate Policy Choices." *Hill Times,* January 21. Accessed January
    31, 2013. http://www.hilltimes.com/policy-briefing/2013/01/21/
    canada%E2%80%99s-climate-policy-choices/33389.

Vegetarian Society. 2007. "Silent But Deadly: New Advertising Campaign
    Launched by The Vegetarian Society." Press Release, September.
    Altrincham, Cheshire: Vegetarian Society of the United Kingdom." Ac-
    cessed April 3, 2008. http://www.vegsoc.org/press/2007/silent.html.
Victor, Peter. 2008. *Managing Without Growth: Slower by Design, Not Disaster.*
    Cheltenham, UK: Edward Elgar.
– 2012. "Growth, Degrowth and Climate Change: A Scenario Analysis."
    Ecological Economics 84:206–12.
Vidal, John. 2007. "Labour's Plan to Abandon Renewable Energy Targets."
    Guardian, October 23,1.
– 2008. "No New Coal – the Calling Card of the 'Green Banksy' Who
    Breached Fortress Kingsnorth." *Guardian*, December 11, 3.
– 2009. "Clean Coal Push Marks Reversal of UK Energy Policy." *Guard-
    ian*, April 23. Accessed April 24, 2009. http://www.guardian.co.uk/
    environment/2009/apr/23/clean-coal-energy-policy.
– 2013. "Margaret Thatcher: An Unlikely Green Hero?" *Guardian*, April 9.
    Accessed April 12, 2013. http://www.guardian.co.uk/environment/
    blog/2013/apr/09/margaret-thatcher-green-hero.
Villiers, Theresa. 2008. "Serious about Going Green." Speech, September
    29. London: Conservative Party." Accessed May 1, 2011. http://www
    .conservatives.com/News/Speeches/2008/09/Theresa_Villiers_
    Serious_about_going_green.aspx.
– 2009. "The Conservative Position on Aviation." Speech, July 12. London:
    Conservative Party. Accessed May 1, 2011. http://www.conservatives
    .com/News/Speeches/2009/12/Theresa_Villiers_The_Conservative_
    position_on_aviation.aspx.
Virgin. 2008. "Virgin Atlantic Becomes World's First Airline to Fly a Plane
    on Biofuel." News Release, February 24. Crawley, West Sussex: Virgin
    Atlantic. Accessed May 24, 2008. http://www.sustainableaviation
    .co.uk/pages/news/virgin-atlantic-becomes-worlds-first-airline-to-fly-a-
    plane-on-biofuel.html.
Viva! 2007. "Viva! HOT! Campaign." Bristol, UK: Viva! Vegetarians Inter-
    national Voice for Animals. Accessed April 4, 2008. http://www.viva
    .org.uk/campaigns/hot/index.php.
Wackernagel, Mathis and William E. Rees. 1996. *Our Ecological Footprint:
    Reducing Human Impact on the Earth.* Gabriola Island, BC: New Society
    Publishers.
Walsh, Luke. 2011. "Biofuels over Claims CCC Chief Executive." *Edie*, June
    10. Accessed July 9, 2011. http://www.edie.net/news/news_story
    .asp?id=20103.
Walton, Dawn. 2007. "Fort McMoney: Can Its Mayor Put the Brakes on the
    Boom?" *Globe and Mail*, February 27, A9.

Warde, Paul. 2007. "Facing the Challenge of Climate Change: Energy Efficiency and Energy Consumption." *History & Policy* (October). Accessed
February 12, 2008. http://www.historyandpolicy.org/papers/policy-
paper-65.html.

Wardell, Jane. 2011. "Recession-Weary Britons Get Happiness Index."
Bloomberg Businessweek, January 10. Accessed July 12, 2012. http://www
.businessweek.com/ap/financialnews/D9KLDQL82.htm.

Warren, Rachel. 2006. "Impacts of Global Climate Change at Different
Annual Mean Global Temperature Increases." In *Avoiding Dangerous
Climate Change,* edited by H.J. Schellnhuber, 93–131. Cambridge, UK:
Cambridge University Press.

Water Monitoring Data Review Committee. 2011. *Evaluation of Four Reports
on Contamination of the Athabasca River System by Oil Sands Operations.*
Edmonton: Water Monitoring Data Review Committee.

Watt, Nicholas. 2012. "Tory MPs Press George Osborne to Build More Runways at Heathrow." *Guardian,* July 9, 20.

Watts, Jonathan. 2009. "Stern: Rich Nations Will Have to Forget about
Growth to Stop Climate Change." *Guardian,* September 11, 35.

Webb, Janette. 2012. "Climate Change and Society: The Chimera of Behaviour Change Technologies." *Sociology* 46(1):109–25.

Webster, Ben. 2009. "Third Heathrow Runway Would Scupper Stansted
and Glasgow Expansion." *Times,* January 28, 3.

Weeks, Carly. 2008. "Cities Ponder Restrictions in Wake of London Bottle
Ban." *Globe and Mail,* August 19, A1.

Weidner, Helmut. 2002. "Capacity Building for Ecological Modernization:
Lessons from Cross-National Research." *American Behavioral Scientist*
45(9):1340–68.

Wente, Margaret. 2007a. "Change a Bulb, Save a Planet." *Globe and Mail,*
April 26, A21.

– 2007b. "That Ol' Beer-Fridge Paradox." *Globe and Mail,* December 4, A23.

While, Aidan, Andrew E G Jonas, and David Gibbs. 2010. "From Sustainable Development to Carbon Control: Eco-State Restructuring and
the Politics of Urban and Regional Development." *Transactions of the
Institute of British Geographers* 35(1):76–93.

White, Michael, and Hugh Muir. 2004. "Livingstone Takes Aim at Four-
Wheel Drive 'Idiots.'" *Guardian,* May 22, 8.

Whittington, Les. 2007. "Liberals Knew Kyoto a Long Shot." *Toronto Star,*
February 23, A6.

Williams, Adrian. 2007. *Comparative Study of Cut Roses for the British Market
Produced in Kenya and the Netherlands.* Précis Report for World Flowers,
February 12.

Williams, Adrian, Emma Pell, J. Webb, E. Tribe, D. Evans, Ed Moore-
house, and P. Watkiss. 2009. *Comparative Life Cycle Assessment of Food*

Commodities Procured for UK Consumption through a Diversity of Supply Chains. London: Department for Environment, Food and Rural Affairs.

Williams, David. 2010. "Car Parking Wars." *Telegraph*, June 4. Accessed November 14, 2012. http://www.telegraph.co.uk/motoring/green-motoring/7733412/Car-parking-wars.html.

– 2011. "Triumph for Motorists as 'Council That Hates Cars' Ditches 'Failed' CO_2 Parking Scheme." *Telegraph*, March 7. Accessed November 14, 2012. http://www.telegraph.co.uk/motoring/news/8366599/Triumph-for-motorists-as-council-that-hates-cars-ditches-failed-co2-parking-scheme.html.

Williams, Jon. 2007. "Banking on Sustainability." Speech to Guardian Climate Change Summit, June 11, London.

Williams, Rowan. 2008. "A New Spiritual Politics of Limits." *Guardian*, July 26. Accessed July 28, 2008. http://www.guardian.co.uk/commentisfree/2008/jul/26/climatechange.religion.

– 2012. *Faith in the Public Square*. London: Bloomsbury Continuum.

Williamson, Mark. 2012. "A Vital Shift in Priorities." *Action for Happiness*. Accessed July 12, 2012. http://www.actionforhappiness.org/news/a-vital-shift-in-priorities.

Wilson, Jeffrey, and Peter Tyedmers. 2013. "Rethinking What Counts: Perspectives on Wellbeing and Genuine Progress Indicator Metrics from a Canadian View Point." *Sustainability* 5(1):187–202.

Winter, Chris. 2007. "We Conserve: Are You in?" Toronto: Conservation Council of Ontario. Accessed December 30, 2008. http://www.weconserve.ca/are_you_in.pdf.

– 2008. "Ontario's Conservation Capacity." In "Ontario's Fourth Conservation Summit – Workbook." Toronto: Conservation Council of Ontario, 6–10. Accessed December 30, 2008. http://weconserve.ca/pdf/Summit4%20workbook.pdf.

Wintour, Patrick. 2006. "Miliband Plans Carbon Trading 'Credit Cards' for Everyone." *Guardian*, December 11, 4.

Woodward, Will, and Nicholas Watt. 2007. "Blair, Monday: I'm Not Offsetting Carbon. Blair, Yesterday: Er, I've Had a Rethink." *Guardian*, January 10, 3.

Woolf, Marie, and Jon Ungoed-Thomas. 2008. "The Great Heathrow Evidence Fit-Up." *Sunday Times*, March 9, 7.

World Bank. 2008. "Rising Food Prices: Policy Options and World Bank Response." Background Note, April 8. Washington DC: World Bank. Accessed April 24, 2008. http://siteresources.worldbank.org/NEWS/Resources/risingfoodprices_backgroundnote_apro8.pdf.

Woudhuysen, James. 2006. Debate with Mayer Hillman on Carbon Rationing. BBC Breakfast. July 20. Accessed December 1, 2007. http://www.youtube.com/watch?v=U7HF-ANJLXk.

Woudhuysen, James. 2007a. "Act Macro: Technological Alternatives to Green Austerity." *Mute Magazine*, May 9. Accessed May 10, 2009. http://www.metamute.org/en/Act-Macro-Technological-Alternatives -to-Green-Austerity.

– 2007b. Remarks at the Debate London Event on "How Can a Boom Town Be Green?" June 24, Tate Modern Gallery, London.

Woynillowicz, Dan, Chris Severson-Baker, and Marlo Raynolds. 2005. *Oil Sands Fever: The Environmental Implications of Canada's Oil Sands Rush.* Drayton Valley, AB: Pembina Institute.

WRAP. 2007a. "Food Waste Is Environmental Sleeping Giant Says WRAP." News Release, November 1. Banbury, Oxon: Waste & Resources Action Programme. Accessed April 2, 2008. http://www.wrap.org.uk/ wrap_corporate/news/food_waste_is.html.

– 2007b. *Understanding Food Waste.* Banbury, Oxon: Waste & Resources Action Programme.

– 2008. "Love Food Hate Waste." Banbury, Oxon: Waste & Resources Action Programme. Accessed April 2, 2008. http://www.lovefoodhate waste.com.

– 2009. "Retailers Exceed Carrier Bag Reduction Target." News Release, February 26. Banbury, Oxon: Waste & Resources Action Programme. Accessed April 29, 2009. http://www.wrap.org.uk/wrap_corporate/ news/retailers_exceed.html.

– 2011. *New Estimates for Household Food and Drink Waste in the UK.* Banbury, Oxon: Waste & Resources Action Programme.

– 2013a. *Household Food and Drink Waste in the United Kingdom 2012.* Banbury, Oxon: Waste & Resources Action Programme.

– 2013b. "WRAP Publishes New Figures on Carrier Bag Use." News Release, July 18. Banbury, Oxon: Waste & Resources Action Programme. Accessed November 22, 2013. http://www.wrap.org.uk/content/ wrap-publishes-new-figures-carrier-bag-use.

WRI. 2012. "CAIT: Indicators: GHG Emissions: Cumulative Emissions." Washington, DC: World Resources Institute. Accessed June 23, 2012. http:// www.wri.org/project/cait/.

Wuppertal Institute. 2008. "Eco-Sufficiency." Wuppertal, Germany: Wuppertal Institute for Climate, Environment, and Energy. Accessed September 5, 2009. http://www.wupperinst.org/en/projects/topics_ online/eco_sufficiency/index.html.

WWF-Canada. 2007. "Next Five Years Key to Cracking Climate Crisis." Press Release, May 11. Accessed May 27, 2008. http://www.wwf.ca/NewsAnd Facts/NewsRoom/default.asp?section=archive&page=display&ID=1537 &lang=EN).

– 2008. "The Good Life." Toronto: WWF-Canada. Accessed December 30, 2008. http://thegoodlife.wwf.ca/Home.cfm.

WWF-International, and Allianz SE. 2008. "G8 Climate Scorecards 2008." Gland, Switzerland: WWF-International. Accessed July 1, 2008. http://assets.panda.org/downloads/2008_g8_climate_scorecards.pdf.

– 2009. "G8 Climate Scorecards 2009." Gland, Switzerland: WWF-International. Accessed August 9, 2009. http://assets.wwf.ca/downloads/wwf_g8scorecards_july2009.pdf.

WWF-UK. 2008. "Travelling Light: Why the UK's Biggest Companies Are Seeking Alternatives to Flying." London: WWF-UK. Accessed May 31, 2008. http://www.wwf.org.uk/filelibrary/pdf/travelling_light.pdf.

WWF-UK, IPPR, and RSPB. 2007. "80% Challenge: Delivering a Low-Carbon UK." London: WWF-UK, Institute for Public Policy Research, and Royal Society for the Protection of Birds. Accessed February 11, 2009. http://www.ippr.org/publicationsandreports/publication.asp?id=573.

Yakabuski, Konrad. 2011. "Selling Oil Sands Coast to Coast." *Globe and Mail*, August 24, A12.

Yeo, Tim. 2010. "The Coalition Should Introduce Personal Carbon Trading." *ConservativeHome*, July 19. Accessed May 30, 2012. http://conservativehome.blogs.com/platform/2010/07/tim-yeo-mp.html#more.

– 2012. "Heathrow Expansion: A Third Runway Must Be Cleared for Take-Off." *Telegraph*, August 27. Accessed December 1, 2012. http://www.telegraph.co.uk/news/aviation/9501875/Heathrow-expansion-A-third-runway-must-be-cleared-for-take-off.html.

York, Richard. 2008. "De-Carbonization in Former Soviet Republics, 1992–2000: The Ecological Consequences of De-Modernization." *Social Problems* 55(3):370–90.

– 2012. "Asymmetric Effects of Economic Growth and Decline on CO_2 Emissions." *Nature Climate Change* 2(11):762–4.

York, Richard, and Eugene A. Rosa. 2003. "Key Challenges to Ecological Modernization Theory: Institutional Efficacy, Case Study Evidence, Units of Analysis, and the Pace of Eco-Efficiency." *Organization Environment* 16(3):273–88.

York, Richard, Eugene A. Rosa, and Thomas Dietz. 2003a. "A Rift in Modernity? Assessing the Anthropogenic Sources of Global Climate Change with the STIRPAT Model." *International Journal of Sociology and Social Policy* 23 (10):31–51.

– 2003b. "Footprints on the Earth: The Environmental Consequences of Modernity." *American Sociological Review* 68(2):279–300.

– 2004. "The Ecological Footprint Intensity of National Economies." *Journal of Industrial Ecology* 8(4):139–54.

– 2011. "Ecological Modernization Theory: Theoretical and Empirical Challenges." In *International Handbook of Environmental Sociology*, edited by M. Redclift and G. Woodgate, 77–90. Second edition. London: Edward Elgar.

Young, Barbara. 2007. Remarks to "On Target? Environment Policy and the Climate Change Bill" Conference Hosted by Trades Union Congress, London, June 4.

Zellen, Barry S. 2008. "We Should Warm to the Idea of Melting Poles." *Globe and Mail*, April 28. Accessed November 1, 2008. http://www.theglobeandmail.com/news/opinions/article682246.ece.

Zenith International. 2012. "Momentum Grows for UK Bottled Water." Bath: Zenith International Ltd. Accessed November 17, 2012. http://www.zenithinternational.com/articles/1037/Momentum+grows+For+UK+bottled+water.

Ziegler, Jean. 2013. "Burning Food Crops to Produce Biofuels Is a Crime against Humanity." *Guardian*, November 26. Accessed December 12, 2013. http://www.theguardian.com/global-development/poverty-matters/2013/nov/26/burning-food-crops-biofuels-crime-humanity.

Index

402–6, 403–6; electoral status, 63; and Keystone XL pipeline, 193; opposition to Kyoto Protocol, 3, 45, 403, 471n13; Promethean views, 10; support for oil/tar sands, 168–9, 177, 179, 183–4, 188–90, 189, 191–2; Turning the Corner plan, 49–52, 56, 404; views on climate science, 55–7. *See also* Canadian Alliance; Progressive Conservative Party

Conservative Party (UK): BAU voices in, 13, 240, 405, 415, 425; *Blueprint for a Green Economy*, 311–15 (*see also* Quality of Life Policy Group); divisions on climate issues, 240–1; Economic Competitiveness Policy Group, 314; greening and renewal of, 203–4, 366–7, 402–6; *The Low Carbon Economy*, 235; under Major, 247, 378; under Thatcher, 13, 201, 237, 240, 241, 247, 471–2n1

– Conservative/Liberal Democrat coalition government (UK, under Cameron): austerity policies and program, 389, 397, 398–9, 483n8; aviation policies, 250, 370–2; climate and green growth policies, 216, 230–1, 240, 243–4, 290, 403–6, 410–11, 412; contradictory environmental policies, 246, 250–2, 277, 296; EM rhetoric, 202, 203–4; and food miles campaign, 336; and Heathrow expansion, 226, 364–71, 368, 373, 375, 405, 408, 424, 429; minimum carbon price, 230, 481n3; modifications to CRC, 254, 255; and Sustainable Communities

Bill, 280; on threat of climate change, 235; well-being/happiness discourse, 305–6, 387–9, 390, 426. *See also* Cameron, David; Liberal Democratic Party

Conservatives for International Travel, 364

conserver society, 469n10

consumption: and advertising, 105, 107, 305, 385; business sector views on, 94–5, 139–43; capitalism sustained by, 287–8; of food, 332–44; The Kinks on, 378; linked with sin, 286; of low-carbon products, 144; mixed messages on, 382–3, 386, 480n3; political aspects of, 140–1; public or mainstream views on, 107–8; selfish capitalism and "affluenza," 306; vs sufficiency, 107–8; and treadmill of production, 26, 108–9, 291, 292, 305, 313, 417, 420, 436; types of, 143, 383–4, 386, 398; well-being decoupled from, 24–5. *See also* growth

consumption-side accounting of GHG emissions, 276–7, 418, 464n5

contraction and convergence, 281, 286, 318, 340, 392, 433, 476n1, 478n1

Co-operative Asset Management (UK), 187

Copenhagen Summit and Accord (2009), 52, 131, 228, 242–3, 269

Copps, Sheila, 48, 76

Corcoran, Terence, 58, 61

Coren, Giles, 329

cornucopian world view, 10, 76, 89, 162

just transition, 46, 62, 110–11, 128, 149, 436

Kahn, Herman, 10, 162, 170
Kairos, 103, 179
Kasawski, Kyle, 60
Kasteren, Joost Van, 331
Kaufman, Stephen, 182
Kelly, Erin N., 167
Kelly, Ruth, 263, 360
Kelly, Tom, 479n8
Kenber, Mark, 218–19, 220, 434
Kennedy, David, 276
Kennedy, Robert F., 386–7
Kent, Peter, 55, 168
Kenya, 246, 336, 337
Kerr, Claire, 270
Kersley, Helen, 367
Kesling, Ben, 168
Keystone XL. *See under* pipelines
Khazzoom-Brookes (K-B) postulate, 267, 474n6
Ki-moon, Ban, 4
King, David, 262, 271, 340
King, Julia, 478–9n5
Kingsnorth power plant, 211, 248–9
Kinks, The, 378
Klaus, Václav, 13
Klein, Naomi, 102
Koch, Charles, 13
Koch, David, 13
Koch Industries, 13
Kolbert, Elizabeth, 182
Kovel, Joel, 25
Kurek, Joshua, 167
Kuznets Curve (Environmental Kuznets Curve, EKC), 30, 463n4
Kyoto Protocol: Canada's difficulties with, 40, 42–3, 48, 124, 145, 164, 183–4, 408–9; Canada's ratification of, 45–6,

73; Canadian targets for, 42–3, 46–7, 145; EU commitment to, 9, 183; Harper's opposition to, 3, 45, 403, 471n13; labour union views of, 46, 65–6, 111; offsets from developing countries, 471n13; UK targets for, 183, 201, 293. *See also* Copenhagen summit and Accord (2009)

labels and labelling: air freight labels, 336, 337; aviation warnings, 352*f*; carbon labels, 213–14, 215*f*, 402; fuel economy labels, 348, 478–9n5
Labour Party and governments (UK): and anti-aviation campaign, 350–64, 479n8; aspirational climate discourse, 19, 414; and bottled water campaign, 329; and campaign against 4×4s, 347–8; carbon budgeting, 224–6, 250, 414; and carbon market, 204–6; coal-fired power plants proposal, 248–9; contradictory environmental policies, 245–52, 277; and CRC, 252–9; EM rhetoric and reforms, 19, 202, 203, 235, 397, 405, 412; food miles policy, 337; fuel tax and road-building policies, 247–8; and Heathrow expansion, 350, 360–4, 366, 424; incandescent light bulbs phase-out, 331; lifestyle/behaviour change, 378–9; and plastic bag reduction, 326; responses to green critique of growth, 288–9, 290; Third Way ideology, 203, 215, 283, 290, 378–9, 380–1; Trident nuclear weapon system, 248; well-being discourse, 306.

Thompson, Sam, 307, 308*f*
Thomson, Graham, 192
Thumim, Joshua, 393, 480n6
Tibbetts, Janice, 179
Tickell, Crispin, 472n1
Tomorrow Today, 63–4, 134,
466n9
Tooke, Wendy, 334
Tooze, Adam, 299
Toronto: bottled water and plastic
bag reduction, 130–1; climate
action plan, 68–9, 93–4, 132;
Environmental Defence, 157;
Global Aware group, 102; lo-
cal food promotion, 132; Our
Changing Atmosphere confer-
ence (1988), 39; Post Carbon
Toronto, 101; Toronto Veg-
etarian Society, 468n2. *See also*
Ontario
Torrie, Ralph, 134, 135
Total, 189, 190, 470n7
Toynbee, Polly, 388, 389, 393
Toyota and Lexus, 211
Trades Union Congress (TUC),
203, 223, 351, 360, 479n9
trade unions. *See* labour unions
trains. *See* railroads
TransAlta, 470n7
TransCanada, 146, 192
Transition Towns, 102, 210, 282,
373; Brixton, 282, 294
Transport 2000, 247
Transport and General Workers
Union, 360
transportation. *See* aviation and air
travel; railroads; vehicles and
road travel
Transport Workers Union, 192
treadmill of production, 26, 108–9,
291, 292, 305, 313, 417, 420,
436
Trudeau, Pierre Elliott, 162

TUC. *See* Trades Union Congress
Tuppen, Chris, 212, 214, 216, 217
Turner, Adair, 308, 310, 321–2,
369, 421, 432
Turner, Chris, 57
Turner, Graham M., 30
Turner, Janice, 346
Tyedmers, Peter, 150, 151, 340
Tyndall Centre for Climate Change
Research, 293–6, 353, 355, 392

UKERC. *See* Energy Research Centre
UKIP. *See* United Kingdom Independence Party
UNFCCC. *See under* United Nations
Ungoed-Thomas, Jon, 360, 479n8
Unison, 369, 479n9
United Church of Canada, 104
United Kingdom (UK): BAU views
and climate scepticism in,
239–45; Canada compared
with, 7–10, 75, 401–30; Climate Change Levy, 204, 253,
402, 407; Climate Change
Programme, 204, 275; consensus on carbon reduction, 239,
424, 425; easy climate action
choices for, 231–5, 412–14;
EM approaches in, 199–278,
296–303, 401–2, 414–19, 423;
energy security concerns, 217,
409; and EU FQD, 189–90; EU
influence on, 9, 233, 409; GHG
emissions, 200–1, 227, 274–9,
278, 416, 418, 463–4n5; Green
Investment Bank, 230, 231,
402, 473n12; international
climate advocacy, 227–30, 366;
leadership in climate reform,
200–4; local climate initiatives,
131, 206–10, 236; manufacturing sector, 232–3; micro-sufficiency in, 325–74; sufficiency